HAMMOND

Explorer World Atlas

Mapmakers for the 21st Century

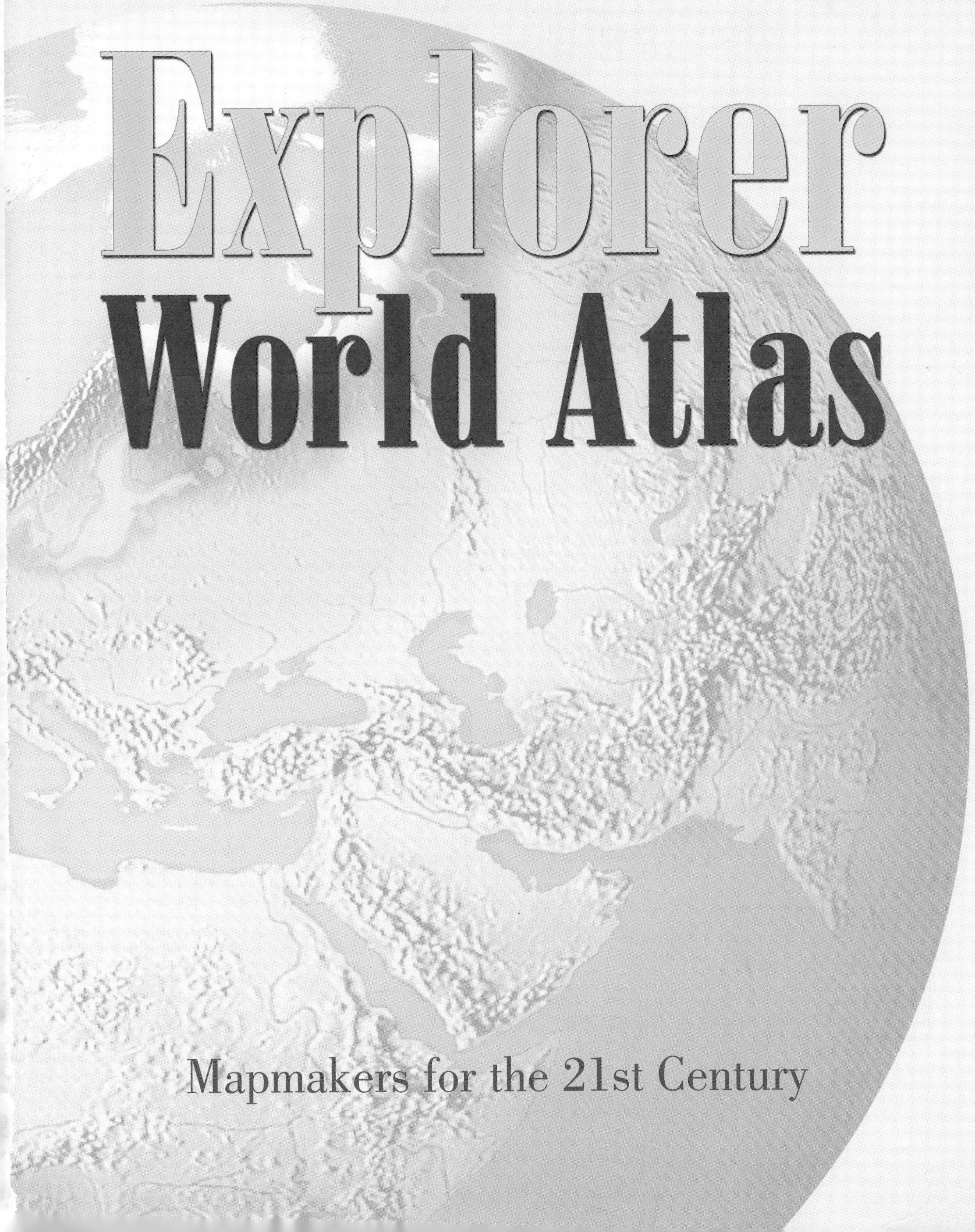

Contents

Interpreting Maps

Designed to enhance your knowledge and enjoyment of the atlas, these pages explain map principles, scales, symbology and how to locate information quickly.

Geographic Comparisons

These eight pages contain flags and important facts about each independent country, plus dimensions of the earth's major mountains, longest rivers and largest lakes and islands.

Maps of the World

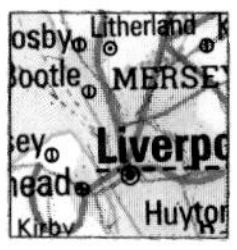

New maps, derived from a computer database, accurately present political detail while proprietary map projections show the most distortion-free views of the continents.

Europe and Northern Asia

Asia

Pacific, Australia

Africa, Antarctica

North America

South America

Index

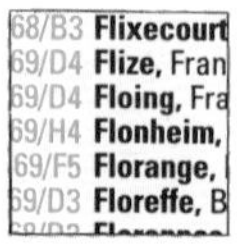

A 13,000-entry A to Z index lists major places and geographic features in the atlas, complete with page numbers and easy-to-use alpha-numeric references.

Revised 2004 Edition

Entire Contents © Copyright 2000 by Hammond World Atlas Corporation
All rights reserved. No part of this book may be reproduced or utilized in any form or by any means, electronic or mechanical, including photocopying, recording or by any information storage and retrieval system, without permission in writing from the Publisher. Printed in The United States of America.

Library of Congress Cataloging-in-Publication Data

Hammond World Atlas Corporation.
Hammond explorer world atlas.
p. cm.
Rev. ed. of: Explorer Atlas of the World/Hammond Incorporated.
Includes index.
ISBN 0-8437-0872-7
1. Atlases.
I Hammond Incorporated. Explorer atlas of the world. II. Title. III. Title: Explorer world atlas.
G1021. H2457 1999 <G&M>
912--DC21 99-28550
CIP
MAPS

Map Projections

Simply stated, the mapmaker's challenge is to project the earth's curved surface onto a flat plane. To achieve this elusive goal, cartographers have developed map projections — equations which govern this conversion of geographic data.

This section explores some of the most widely used projections. It also introduces a new projection, the Hammond Optimal Conformal.

General Principles and Terms

The earth rotates around its axis once a day. Its end points are the North and South poles; the line circling the earth midway between the poles is the equator. The arc from the equator to either pole is divided into 90 degrees of latitude. The equator represents 0° latitude. Circles of equal latitude, called parallels, are traditionally shown at every fifth or tenth degree.

The equator is divided into 360 degrees. Lines circling the globe from pole to pole through the degree points on the equator are called meridians, or great circles. All meridians are equal in length, but by international agreement the meridian passing through the Greenwich Observatory near London has been chosen as the prime meridian or 0° longitude. The distance in degrees from the prime meridian to any point east or west is its longitude.

While meridians are all equal in length, parallels become shorter as they approach the poles. Whereas one degree of latitude represents approximately 69 miles (112 km.) anywhere on the globe, a degree of longitude varies from 69 miles (112 km.) at the equator to zero at the poles. Each degree of latitude and longitude is divided into 60 minutes. One minute of latitude equals one nautical mile (1.15 land miles or 1.85 km.).

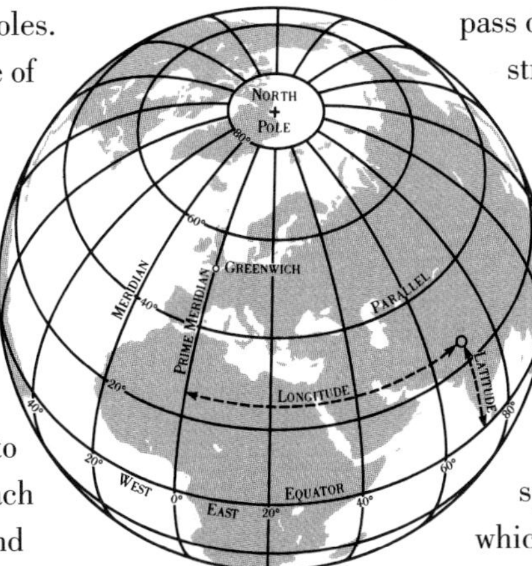

How to Flatten a Sphere: The Art of Controlling Distortion

There is only one way to represent a sphere with absolute precision: on a globe. All attempts to project our planet's surface onto a plane unevenly stretch or tear the sphere as it flattens, inevitably distorting shapes, distances, area (sizes appear larger or smaller than actual size), angles or direction.

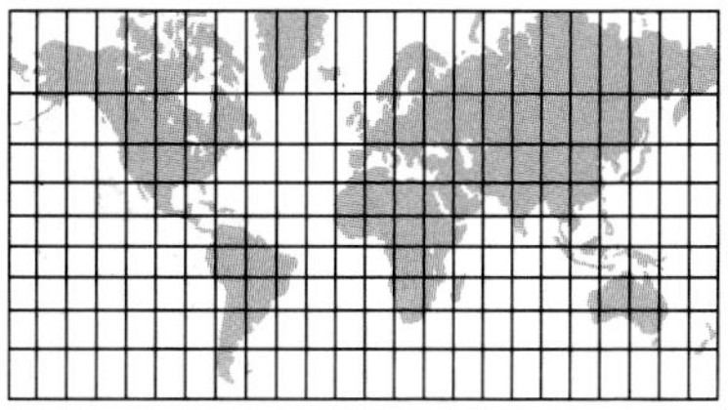

FIGURE 1 **Mercator Projection**

Since representing a sphere on a flat plane always creates distortion, only the parallels or the meridians (or some other set of lines) can maintain the same length as on a globe of corresponding scale. All other lines must be either too long or too short. Accordingly, the scale on a flat map cannot be true everywhere; there will always be different scales in different parts of a map. On world maps or very large areas, variations in scale may be extreme. Most maps seek to preserve either true area relationships (equal area projections) or true angles and shapes (conformal projections); some attempt to achieve overall balance.

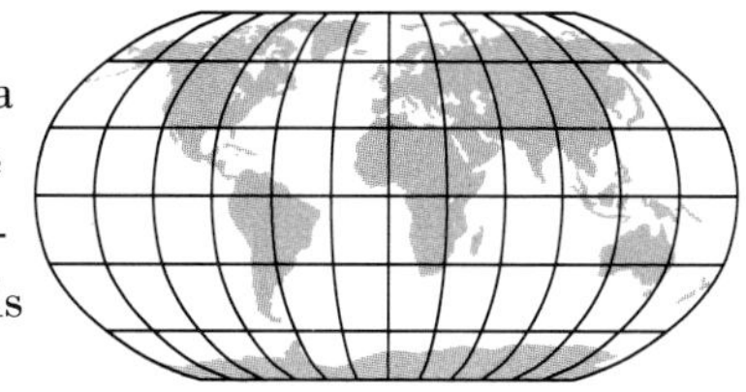

FIGURE 2 **Robinson Projection**

Projections: Selected Examples

Mercator (Fig. 1): This projection is especially useful because all compass directions appear as straight lines, making it a valuable navigational tool. Moreover, every small region conforms to its shape on a globe — hence the name conformal. But because its meridians are evenly-spaced vertical lines which never converge (unlike the globe), the horizontal parallels must be drawn farther and farther apart at higher latitudes to maintain a correct relationship. Only the equator is true to scale, and the size of areas in the higher latitudes is dramatically distorted.

Robinson (Fig. 2): To create the two-page world map in the Maps of the World section, the Robinson projection was used. It combines elements of both conformal and equal area projections to show the whole earth with relatively true shapes and reasonably equal areas.

Conic (Fig. 3): This projection has been used frequently for air navigation charts and to create most of the national and regional maps in this atlas. (See text in margin at right).

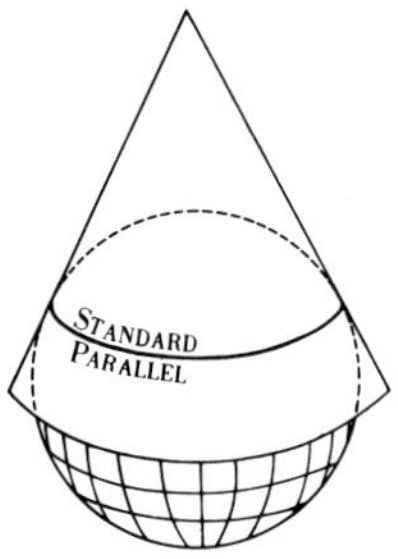

FIGURE 3 **Conic Projection**

Hammond Optimal Conformal

As its name implies, this new conformal projection (Fig. 4) presents the optimal view of an area by reducing shifts in scale over an entire region to the minimum degree possible. While conformal maps generally preserve all small shapes, large shapes can become very distorted because of varying scales, causing considerable inaccuracy in distance measurements. The concept underlying the Optimal Conformal is that for any region on the globe, there is an ideal projection for which scale variation can be made as small as possible. Consequently, unlike other projections, the Optimal Conformal does not use one standard formula to construct a map. Each map is a unique projection — the optimal projection for that particular area.

After a cartographer defines the subject area, a sophisticated computer program evaluates the size and shape of the region, projecting the most distortion-free map possible. All of the continent maps in this atlas, except Antarctica, have been drawn using the Optimal projection.

FIGURE 4 **Hammond Optimal Conformal Projection**

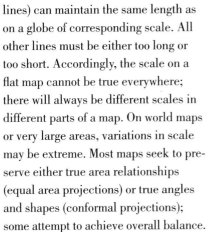

Using This Atlas

How to Locate Information Quickly

Our Maps of the World section is organized by continent. If you're looking for a major region of the world, consult the Contents on page two.

Australia
Page/Location: 70
Area: 2,966,136 sc
7,682,300 s
Population: 17,
Capital: Can

World Reference Guide

This concise guide lists the countries of the world alphabetically. If you're looking for the largest scale map of any country, you'll find a page and alpha-numeric reference at a glance, as well as information about each country, including its flag.

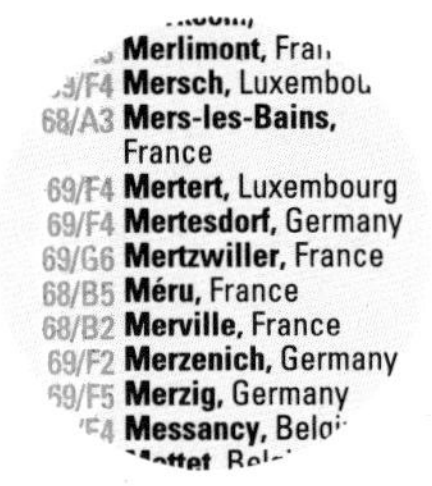

Merlimont, Fra
Mersch, Luxembou
68/A3 Mers-les-Bains, France
69/F4 Mertert, Luxembourg
69/F4 Mertesdorf, Germany
69/G6 Mertzwiller, France
68/B5 Méru, France
68/B2 Merville, France
69/F2 Merzenich, Germany
Merzig, Germany
Messancy, Belg

Master Index

When you're looking for a specific place or physical feature, your quickest route is the Master Index. This 6,000-entry alphabetical index lists both the page number and alpha-numeric reference for major places and features in Maps of the World.

This new atlas is created from a unique digital database, and its computer-generated maps represent a new phase in map-making technology.

How Computer-Generated Maps Are Made

To build a digital database capable of generating this world atlas, the latitude and longitude of every significant town, river, coastline, natural and political border, transportation network and peak elevation was researched and digitized. Hundreds of millions of data points describing every important geographic feature are organized into thousands of different map feature codes.

There are no maps in this unique system. Rather, it consists entirely of coded points, lines and polygons. To create a map, cartographers simply determine what specific information they wish to show, based upon considerations of scale, size, density and importance of different features.

New technology developed by mathematical physicist Mitchell Feigenbaum uses fractal geometry to describe and re-configure coastlines, borders and mountain ranges to fit a variety of map scales and projections. Dr. Feigenbaum has also created a computerized type placement program which allows thousands of map labels to be placed accurately in minutes. After these steps have been completed, the computer then draws the final map.

Each section of this atlas has been designed to be both easy and enjoyable to use. Familiarizing yourself with its organization will help you to benefit fully from its use.

World Flags and Reference Guide

This colorful section portrays each nation of the world, its flag, important geographical data, such as size, population and capital, and its location in the Maps of the World section.

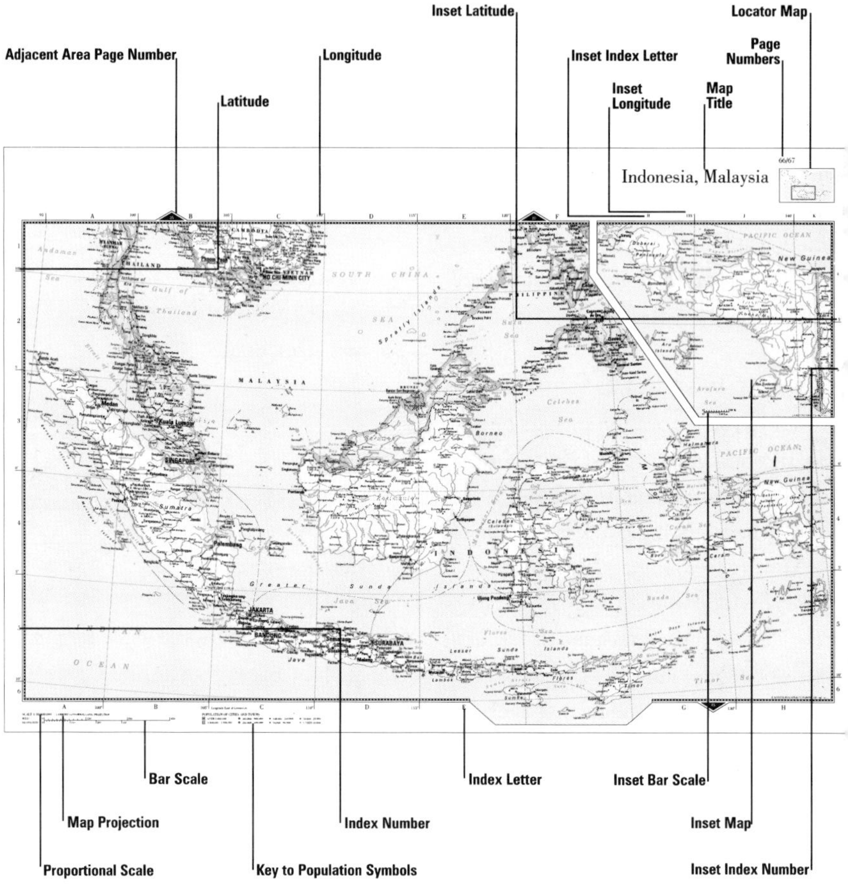

Inset Latitude
Locator Map
Page Numbers
Adjacent Area Page Number
Longitude
Inset Index Letter
Latitude
Inset Longitude
Map Title
Indonesia, Malaysia
Bar Scale
Index Letter
Inset Bar Scale
Map Projection
Index Number
Inset Map
Proportional Scale
Key to Population Symbols
Inset Index Number

Symbols Used on Maps of the World

Symbol		Symbol		Symbol	
—·–·	First Order (National) Boundary		City and Urban Area Limits	Rome	First Order (National) Capital
—·–·	First Order Water Boundary		Demilitarized Zone	Belfast	Second Order (Internal) Capital
— —	First Order Disputed Boundary		National Park/Preserve/Scenic Area	Hull	Third Order (Internal) Capital
—·—·	Second Order (Internal) Boundary		National Forest/Forest Reserve	□	Neighborhood
····	Second Order Water Boundary		National Wilderness/Grassland		Pass
– – – –	Third Order (Internal) Boundary		National Recreation Area/Monument		Ruins
··········	Undefined Boundary		National Seashore/Lakeshore	●	Falls
——	International Date Line		National Wildlife/Wilderness Area	*	Rapids
——	Shoreline, River		Native Reservation/Reserve	●	Dam
– · –	Intermittent River		Military/Government Reservation	▲	Point Elevation
- - - -	Canal/Aqueduct		Lake, Reservoir		Park
········	Continental Divide		Intermittent Lake		Wildlife Area
——	Highways		Dry Lake	■	Point of Interest
——	Roads		Salt Pan	◡	Well
——	Railroads		Desert/Sand Area		International Airport
- - - -	Ferries		Swamp		Other Airport
- - - -	Tunnels (Road, Railroad)		Lava Flow		Air Base
⊓⊓⊓⊓	Ancient Walls		Glacier		Naval Base

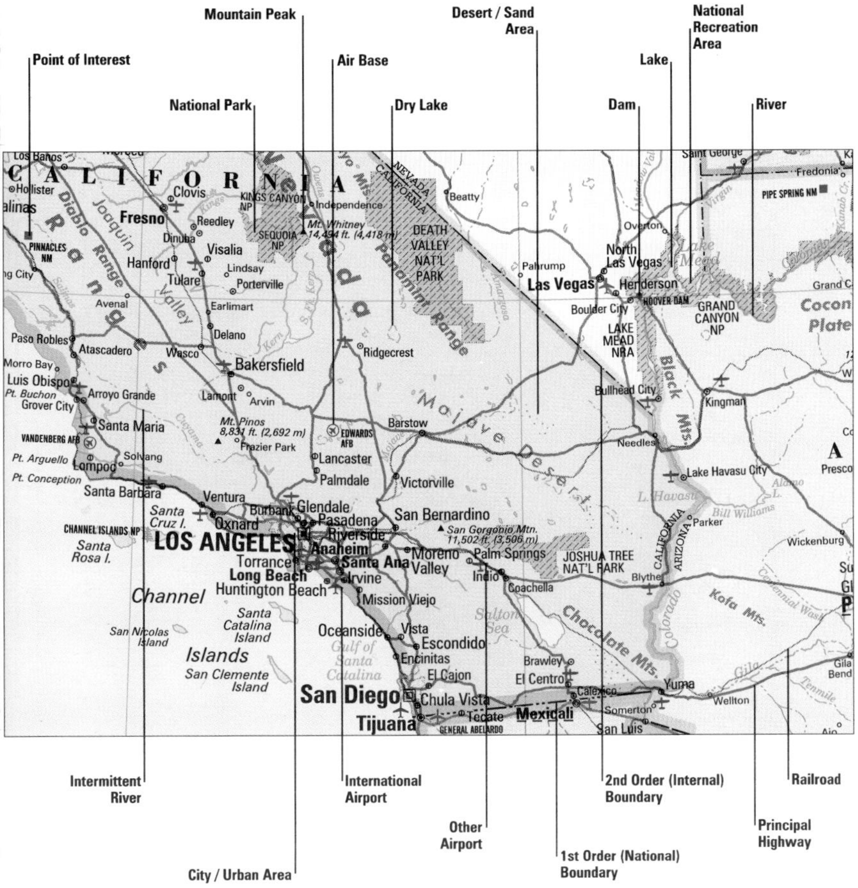

Principal Map Abbreviations

Abor. Rsv.	Aboriginal Reserve	Ind. Res.	Indian Reservation	NWR	National Wildlife
Admin.	Administration	Int'l	International		Reserve
AFB	Air Force Base	IR	Indian Reservation	Obl.	Oblast
Amm. Dep.	Ammunition Depot	Isth.	Isthmus	Occ.	Occupied
Arch.	Archipelago	Jct.	Junction	Okr.	Okrug
Arpt.	Airport	L.	Lake	Par.	Parish
Aut.	Autonomous	Lag.	Lagoon	Passg.	Passage
B.	Bay	Lakesh.	Lakeshore	Pen.	Peninsula
Bfld.	Battlefield	Mem.	Memorial	Pk.	Peak
Bk.	Brook	Mil.	Military	Plat.	Plateau
Bor.	Borough	Miss.	Missile	PN	Park National
Br.	Branch	Mon.	Monument	Pref.	Prefecture
C.	Cape	Mt.	Mount	Prom.	Promontory
Can.	Canal	Mtn.	Mountain	Prov.	Province
Cap.	Capital	Mts.	Mountains	Prsv.	Preserve
C.G.	Coast Guard	Nat.	Natural	Pt.	Point
Chan.	Channel	Nat'l	National	R.	River
Co.	County	Nav.	Naval	RA	Recreation Area
Cr.	Creek	NB	National	Ra.	Range
Ctr.	Center		Battlefield	Rec.	Recreation(al)
Dep.	Depot	NBP	National	Ref.	Refuge
Depr.	Depression		Battlefield Park	Reg.	Region
Dept.	Department	NBS	National	Rep.	Republic
Des.	Desert		Battlefield Site	Res.	Reservoir,
Dist.	District	NHP	National Historical		Reservation
DMZ	Demilitarized Zone		Park	Rvwy.	Riverway
Dpcy.	Dependency	NHPP	National Historical	Sa.	Sierra
Eng.	Engineering		Park and Preserve	Sd.	Sound
Est.	Estuary	NHS	National Historic	Seash.	Seashore
Fd.	Fiord, Fjord		Site	So.	Southern
Fed.	Federal	NL	National Lakeshore	SP	State Park
Fk.	Fork	NM	National Monument	Spr., Sprs.	Spring, Springs
Fld.	Field	NMEMP	National Memorial	St.	State
For.	Forest		Park	Sta.	Station
Ft.	Fort	NMILP	National Military	Stm.	Stream
G.	Gulf		Park	Str.	Strait
Gov.	Governor	No.	Northern	Terr.	Territory
Govt.	Government	NP	National Park	Tun.	Tunnel
Gd.	Grand	NPP	National Park and	Twp.	Township
Gt.	Great		Preserve	Val.	Valley
Har.	Harbor	NPRSV	National Preserve	Vill.	Village
Hd.	Head	NRA	National	Vol.	Volcano
Hist.	Historic(al)		Recreation Area	Wild.	Wildlife,
Hts.	Heights	NRSV	National Reserve		Wilderness
I., Is.	Island(s)	NS	National Seashore	Wtr.	Water

World Statistics

World Statistics lists the dimensions of the earth's principal mountains, islands, rivers and lakes, along with other useful geographic information.

Maps of the World

These detailed regional maps are arranged by continent, and introduced by a political map of that continent. The continent maps, which utilize Hammond's new Optimal Conformal projection, are distinguished by individual colors for each country to highlight political divisions.

On the regional maps, different colors and textures highlight distinctive features such as parks, forests, deserts and urban areas. These maps also provide considerable information concerning geographic features and political divisions.

Master Index

This is an A-Z listing of names found on the political maps. It also has its own abbreviation list which, along with other Index keys, appears on page 110.

Map Scales

A map's scale is the relationship of any length on the map to an identical length on the earth's surface. A scale of 1:3,000,000 means that one inch on the map represents 3,000,000 inches (47 miles, 76 km.) on the earth's surface. Thus, a 1:1,000,000 scale is larger than 1:3,000,000, just as 1/1 is larger than 1/3.

The most densely populated areas are shown at a scale of 1:1,170,000, while selected metropolitan areas are covered at either 1:587,000 or 1:1,170,000. Other populous areas are presented at 1:3,500,000 and 1:7,000,000, allowing you to accurately compare areas and distances of similar regions. Remaining regions are scaled at 1:10,500,000. The continent maps, as well as the United States, Canada, Russia, Pacific and World have smaller scales.

Boundary Policies

This atlas observes the boundary policies of the U.S. Department of State. Boundary disputes are customarily handled with a special symbol treatment, but de facto boundaries are favored if they seem to have any degree of permanence, in the belief that boundaries should reflect current geographic and political realities. The portrayal of independent nations in the atlas follows their recognition by the United Nations and/or the United States government.

Hammond also uses accepted conventional names for certain major foreign places. Usually, space permits the inclusion of the local form in parentheses. To make the maps more readily understandable to English-speaking readers, many foreign physical features are translated into more recognizable English forms.

A Word About Names

Our source for all foreign names and physical names in the United States is the decision lists of the U.S. Board of Geographic Names, which contain hundreds of thousands of place names. If a place is not listed, the Atlas follows the name form appearing on official foreign maps or in official gazetteers of the country concerned. For rendering domestic city, town and village names, this atlas follows the forms and spelling of the U.S. Postal Service.

World Flags and Reference Guide

Afghanistan
Page/Location: 53/H2
Area: 250,775 sq. mi.
649,507 sq. km.
Population: 29,547,078
Capital: Kabul
Largest City: Kabul
Highest Point: Noshaq
Monetary Unit: Afghani

Albania
Page/Location: 39/F2
Area: 11,110 sq. mi.
28,749 sq. km.
Population: 3,544,808
Capital: Tiranë
Largest City: Tiranë
Highest Point: Korab
Monetary Unit: lek

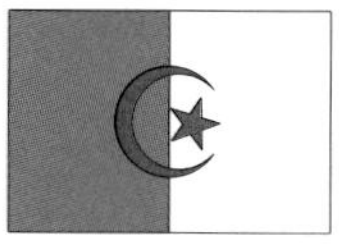

Algeria
Page/Location: 76/F2
Area: 919,519 sq. mi.
2,381,740 sq. km.
Population: 33,357,089
Capital: Algiers
Largest City: Algiers
Highest Point: Tahat
Monetary Unit: Algerian dinar

Andorra
Page/Location: 35/F1
Area: 174 sq. mi.
450 sq. km.
Population: 69,865
Capital: Andorra la Vella
Largest City: Andorra la Vella
Highest Point: Coma Pedrosa
Monetary Unit: euro

Angola
Page/Location: 82/C3
Area: 481,351 sq. mi.
1,246,700 sq. km.
Population: 10,978,552
Capital: Luanda
Largest City: Luanda
Highest Point: Morro de Môco
Monetary Unit: kwanza

Antigua and Barbuda
Page/Location: 104/F3
Area: 171 sq. mi.
443 sq. km.
Population: 68,320
Capital: St. John's
Largest City: St. John's
Highest Point: Boggy Peak
Monetary Unit: East Caribbean dollar

Argentina
Page/Location: 109/C4
Area: 1,068,296 sq. mi.
2,766,890 sq. km.
Population: 39,144,753
Capital: Buenos Aires
Largest City: Buenos Aires
Highest Point: Cerro Aconcagua
Monetary Unit: peso argentino

Armenia
Page/Location: 45/H5
Area: 11,506 sq. mi.
29,800 sq. km.
Population: 3,325,307
Capital: Yerevan
Largest City: Yerevan
Highest Point: Aragats
Monetary Unit: dram

Australia
Page/Location: 70
Area: 2,966,136 sq. mi.
7,682,300 sq. km.
Population: 19,913,144
Capital: Canberra
Largest City: Sydney
Highest Point: Mt. Kosciusko
Monetary Unit: Australian dollar

Austria
Page/Location: 33/L3
Area: 32,375 sq. mi.
83,851 sq. km.
Population: 8,174,762
Capital: Vienna
Largest City: Vienna
Highest Point: Grossglockner
Monetary Unit: euro

Azerbaijan
Page/Location: 45/H4
Area: 33,436 sq. mi.
86,600 sq. km.
Population: 7,868,385
Capital: Baku
Largest City: Baku
Highest Point: Bazardüzü
Monetary Unit: manat

Bahamas
Page/Location: 104/B2
Area: 5,382 sq. mi.
13,939 sq. km.
Population: 299,697
Capital: Nassau
Largest City: Nassau
Highest Point: Mt. Alvernia
Monetary Unit: Bahamian dollar

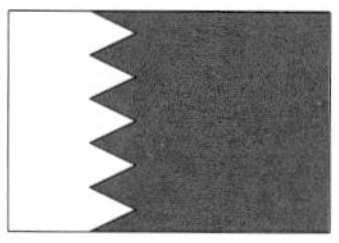

Bahrain
Page/Location: 52/F3
Area: 240 sq. mi.
622 sq. km.
Population: 677,886
Capital: Manama
Largest City: Manama
Highest Point: Jabal Dukhān
Monetary Unit: Bahraini dinar

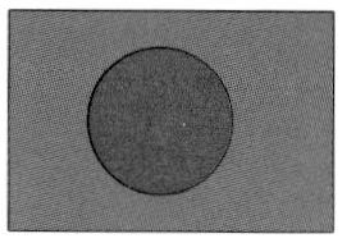

Bangladesh
Page/Location: 60/E3
Area: 55,598 sq. mi.
144,000 sq. km.
Population: 141,340,476
Capital: Dhākā
Largest City: Dhākā
Highest Point: Keokradong
Monetary Unit: taka

Barbados
Page/Location: 104/G4
Area: 186 sq. mi.
430 sq. km.
Population: 278,289
Capital: Bridgetown
Largest City: Bridgetown
Highest Point: Mt. Hillaby
Monetary Unit: Barbadian dollar

Belarus
Page/Location: 18/F3
Area: 80,154 sq. mi.
207,600 sq. km.
Population: 10,310,520
Capital: Minsk
Largest City: Minsk
Highest Point: Dzyarzhynskaya
Monetary Unit: Belarusian ruble

Belgium
Page/Location: 30/C2
Area: 11,781 sq. mi.
30,513 sq. km.
Population: 10,348,276
Capital: Brussels
Largest City: Brussels
Highest Point: Botrange
Monetary Unit: euro

Belize
Page/Location: 102/D2
Area: 8,867 sq. mi.
22,966 sq. km.
Population: 272,945
Capital: Belmopan
Largest City: Belize City
Highest Point: Victoria Peak
Monetary Unit: Belize dollar

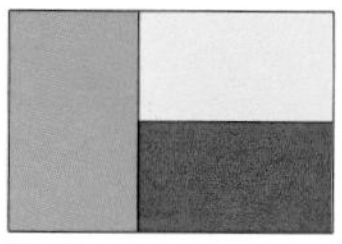

Benin
Page/Location: 79/F4
Area: 43,483 sq. mi.
112,620 sq. km.
Population: 7,250,033
Capital: Porto-Novo
Largest City: Cotonou
Highest Point: Sokbaro
Monetary Unit: CFA franc

Bhutan
Page/Location: 62/E2
Area: 18,147 sq. mi.
47,000 sq. km.
Population: 2,185,569
Capital: Thimphu
Largest City: Thimphu
Highest Point: Kula Kangri
Monetary Unit: ngultrum

Bolivia
Page/Location: 106/F7
Area: 424,163 sq. mi.
1,098,582 sq. km.
Population: 8,724,156
Capital: La Paz; Sucre
Largest City: La Paz
Highest Point: Nevado Sajama
Monetary Unit: boliviano

Bosnia and Herzegovina
Page/Location: 40/C3
Area: 19,940 sq. mi.
51,645 sq. km.
Population: 4,007,608
Capital: Sarajevo
Largest City: Sarajevo
Highest Point: Maglič
Monetary Unit: marka

Botswana
Page/Location: 82/D5
Area: 231,803 sq. mi.
600,370 sq. km.
Population: 1,561,973
Capital: Gaborone
Largest City: Gaborone
Highest Point: Tsodilo Hills
Monetary Unit: pula

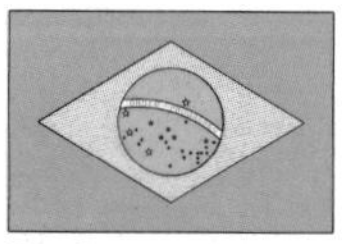

Brazil
Page/Location: 105/D3
Area: 3,286,470 sq. mi.
8,511,965 sq. km.
Population: 184,101,109
Capital: Brasília
Largest City: São Paulo
Highest Point: Pico da Neblina
Monetary Unit: real

Brunei
Page/Location: 66/D2
Area: 2,226 sq. mi.
5,765 sq. km.
Population: 365,251
Capital: Bandar Seri Begawan
Largest City: Bandar Seri Begawan
Highest Point: Bukit Pagon
Monetary Unit: Brunei dollar

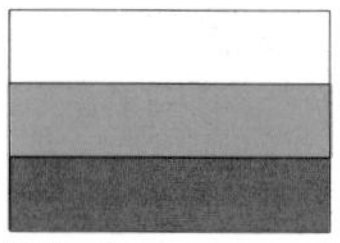

Bulgaria
Page/Location: 41/G4
Area: 42,823 sq. mi.
110,912 sq. km.
Population: 7,517,973
Capital: Sofia
Largest City: Sofia
Highest Point: Musala
Monetary Unit: lev

Burkina Faso
Page/Location: 79/E3
Area: 105,869 sq. mi.
274,200 sq. km.
Population: 13,574,820
Capital: Ouagadougou
Largest City: Ouagadougou
Highest Point: Tena kourou
Monetary Unit: CFA franc

Burundi
Page/Location: 82/E1
Area: 10,747 sq. mi.
27,835 sq. km.
Population: 6,231,221
Capital: Bujumbura
Largest City: Bujumbura
Highest Point: Heha
Monetary Unit: Burundi franc

Cambodia
Page/Location: 65/D3
Area: 69,898 sq. mi.
181,036 sq. km.
Population: 13,363,421
Capital: Phnom Penh
Largest City: Phnom Penh
Highest Point: Phnum Aoral
Monetary Unit: riel

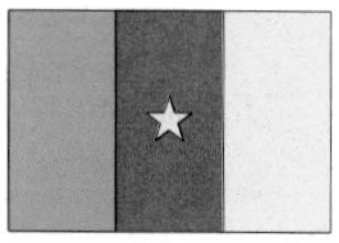

Cameroon
Page/Location: 76/H7
Area: 183,568 sq. mi.
475,441 sq. km.
Population: 16,063,678
Capital: Yaoundé
Largest City: Douala
Highest Point: Mt. Fako
Monetary Unit: CFA franc

anada
age/Location: 86
ea: 3,851,787 sq. mi.
9,976,139 sq. km.
opulation: 32,507,874
apital: Ottawa
argest City: Toronto
ighest Point: Mt. Trudeau
onetary Unit: Canadian dollar

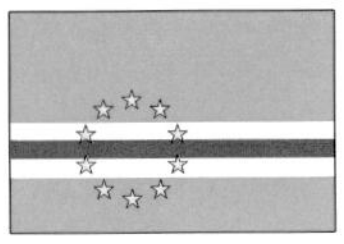

Cape Verde
Page/Location: 74/K9
Area: 1,557 sq. mi.
4,033 sq. km.
Population: 415,294
Capital: Praia
Largest City: Praia
Highest Point: Mt. Fogo
Monetary Unit: Cape Verde escudo

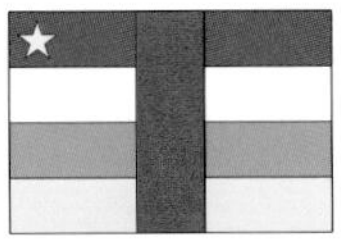

Central African Republic
Page/Location: 77/J6
Area: 240,533 sq. mi.
622,980 sq. km.
Population: 3,742,482
Capital: Bangui
Largest City: Bangui
Highest Point: Mt. Ngaoui
Monetary Unit: CFA franc

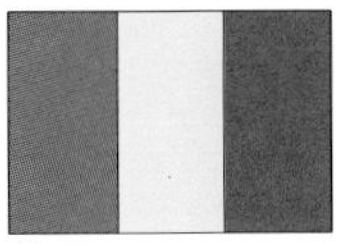

Chad
Page/Location: 77/J4
Area: 495,752 sq. mi.
1,283,998 sq. km.
Population: 9,538,544
Capital: N'Djamena
Largest City: N'Djamena
Highest Point: Emi Koussi
Monetary Unit: CFA franc

Chile
Page/Location: 109/B3
Area: 292,257 sq. mi.
756,946 sq. km.
Population: 15,827,180
Capital: Santiago
Largest City: Santiago
Highest Point: Nevado Ojos del Salado
Monetary Unit: Chilean peso

China
Page/Location: 48/J6
Area: 3,705,386 sq. mi.
9,596,960 sq. km.
Population: 1,294,629,555
Capital: Beijing
Largest City: Shangai
Highest Point: Mt. Everest
Monetary Unit: yuan

olombia
age/Location: 106/D3
rea: 439,513 sq. mi.
1,138,339 sq. km.
opulation: 42,310,775
apital: Bogotá
argest City: Bogotá
ighest Point: Pico Cristóbal Colón
onetary Unit: Colombian peso

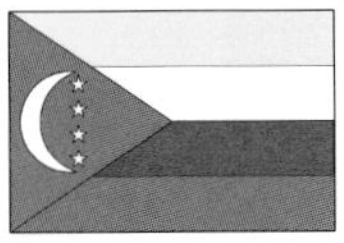

Comoros
Page/Location: 74/G6
Area: 838 sq. mi.
2,170 sq. km.
Population: 651,901
Capital: Moroni
Largest City: Moroni
Highest Point: Karthala
Monetary Unit: Comorian franc

Congo, Dem. Rep. of the
Page/Location: 74/E5
Area: 905,563 sq. mi.
2,345,410 sq. km.
Population: 58,317,930
Capital: Kinshasa
Largest City: Kinshasa
Highest Point: Margherita Peak
Monetary Unit: Congolese franc

Congo, Rep. of the
Page/Location: 74/D5
Area: 132,046 sq. mi.
342,000 sq. km.
Population: 2,998,040
Capital: Brazzaville
Largest City: Brazzaville
Highest Point: Mt. Berongou
Monetary Unit: CFA franc

Costa Rica
Page/Location: 103/F4
Area: 19,730 sq. mi.
51,100 sq. km.
Population: 3,956,507
Capital: San José
Largest City: San José
Highest Point: Cerro Chirripó Grande
Monetary Unit: Costa Rican Colón

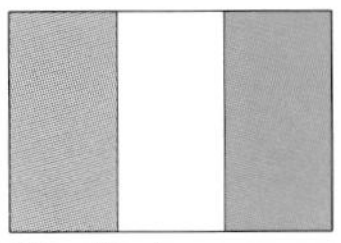

Côte d'Ivoire
Page/Location: 78/D5
Area: 124,504 sq. mi.
322,465 sq. km.
Population: 17,327,724
Capital: Yamoussoukro
Largest City: Abidjan
Highest Point: Mt. Nimba
Monetary Unit: CFA franc

roatia
age/Location: 40/C3
rea: 22,050 sq. mi.
57,110 sq. km.
opulation: 4,435,960
apital: Zagreb
argest City: Zagreb
ighest Point: Dinara
onetary Unit: Croatian kuna

Cuba
Page/Location: 103/F1
Area: 42,803 sq. mi.
110,860 sq. km.
Population: 11,308,764
Capital: Havana
Largest City: Havana
Highest Point: Pico Turquino
Monetary Unit: Cuban peso

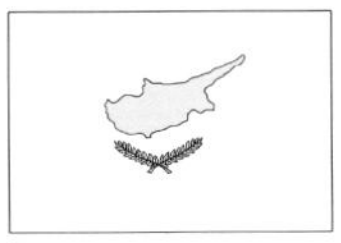

Cyprus
Page/Location: 49/C2
Area: 3,571 sq. mi.
9,250 sq. km.
Population: 775,927
Capital: Nicosia
Largest City: Nicosia
Highest Point: Olympus
Monetary Unit: Cypriot pound

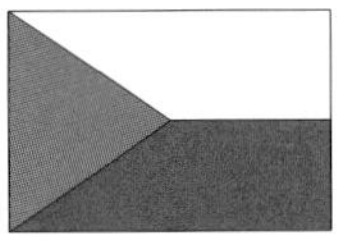

Czech Republic
Page/Location: 27/H4
Area: 30,387 sq. mi.
78,703 sq. km.
Population: 10,246,178
Capital: Prague
Largest City: Prague
Highest Point: Sněžka
Monetary Unit: Czech koruna

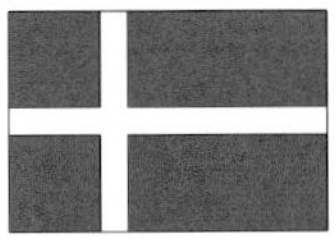

Denmark
Page/Location: 20/C5
Area: 16,629 sq. mi.
43,069 sq. km.
Population: 5,413,392
Capital: Copenhagen
Largest City: Copenhagen
Highest Point: Yding Skovhøj
Monetary Unit: Danish krone

Djibouti
Page/Location: 77/P5
Area: 8,494 sq. mi.
22,000 sq. km.
Population: 466,900
Capital: Djibouti
Largest City: Djibouti
Highest Point: Moussa Ali
Monetary Unit: Djibouti franc

ominica
age/Location: 104/F4
rea: 290 sq. mi.
751 sq. km.
opulation: 69,278
apital: Roseau
argest City: Roseau
ighest Point: Morne Diablotins
onetary Unit: East Caribbean dollar

Dominican Republic
Page/Location: 104/D3
Area: 18,815 sq. mi.
48,730 sq. km.
Population: 8,833,634
Capital: Santo Domingo
Largest City: Santo Domingo
Highest Point: Pico Duarte
Monetary Unit: Dominican peso

East Timor
Page/Location: 67/G5
Area: 5,743 sq. mi.
14,874 sq. km.
Population: 1,019,252
Capital: Dili
Largest City: Dili
Highest Point: Teta Mailau
Monetary Unit: U. S. dollar

Ecuador
Page/Location: 106/C4
Area: 109,483 sq. mi.
283,561 sq. km.
Population: 13,971,798
Capital: Quito
Largest City: Guayaquil
Highest Point: Chimborazo
Monetary Unit: U.S. dollar

Egypt
Page/Location: 77/L2
Area: 386,659 sq. mi.
1,001,447 sq. km.
Population: 76,117,421
Capital: Cairo
Largest City: Cairo
Highest Point: Mt. Catherine
Monetary Unit: Egyptian pound

El Salvador
Page/Location: 102/D3
Area: 8,124 sq. mi.
21,040 sq. km.
Population: 6,587,541
Capital: San Salvador
Largest City: San Salvador
Highest Point: El Pital
Monetary Unit: Salvadoran colón

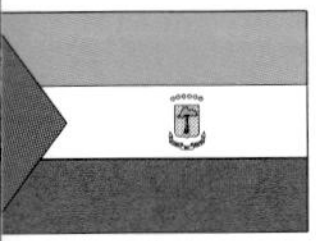

quatorial Guinea
age/Location: 76/G7
rea: 10,831 sq. mi.
28,052 sq. km.
opulation: 523,051
apital: Malabo
argest City: Malabo
ighest Point: Basile
onetary Unit: CFA franc

Eritrea
Page/Location: 52/C5
Area: 46,842 sq. mi.
121,320 sq. km.
Population: 4,447,307
Capital: Asmara
Largest City: Asmara
Highest Point: Soira
Monetary Unit: nafka

Estonia
Page/Location: 42/E4
Area: 17,413 sq. mi.
45,100 sq. km.
Population: 1,401,945
Capital: Tallinn
Largest City: Tallinn
Highest Point: Munamägi
Monetary Unit: kroon

Ethiopia
Page/Location: 77/N6
Area: 435,184 sq. mi.
1,127,127 sq. km.
Population: 67,851,281
Capital: Addis Ababa
Largest City: Addis Ababa
Highest Point: Ras Dejen
Monetary Unit: birr

Fiji
Page/Location: 68/G6
Area: 7,055 sq. mi.
18,272 sq. km.
Population: 880,874
Capital: Suva
Largest City: Suva
Highest Point: Tomaniivi
Monetary Unit: Fijian dollar

Finland
Page/Location: 20/H2
Area: 130,128 sq. mi.
337,032 sq. km.
Population: 5,214,512
Capital: Helsinki
Largest City: Helsinki
Highest Point: Haltia
Monetary Unit: euro

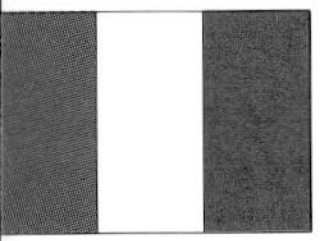

rance
age/Location: 32/D3
rea: 211,208 sq. mi.
547,030 sq. km.
opulation: 60,424,213
apital: Paris
argest City: Paris
ighest Point: Mont Blanc
onetary Unit: euro

Gabon
Page/Location: 76/H7
Area: 103.346 sq. mi.
267,666 sq. km.
Population: 1,355,246
Capital: Libreville
Largest City: Libreville
Highest Point: Mt. Iboundji
Monetary Unit: CFA franc

Gambia, The
Page/Location: 78/B3
Area: 4,363 sq. mi.
11,300 sq. km.
Population: 1,546,848
Capital: Banjul
Largest City: Banjul
Highest Point: 174 ft. (53 m)
Monetary Unit: dalasi

Georgia
Page/Location: 45/G4
Area: 26,911 sq. mi.
69,700 sq. km.
Population: 4,909,633
Capital: T'bilisi
Largest City: T'bilisi
Highest Point: Mt'a Shkhara
Monetary Unit: lari

Germany
Page/Location: 26/E3
Area: 137,803 sq. mi.
356,910 sq. km.
Population: 82,424,609
Capital: Berlin
Largest City: Berlin
Highest Point: Zugspitze
Monetary Unit: euro

Ghana
Page/Location: 79/E4
Area: 92,099 sq. mi.
238,536 sq. km.
Population: 20,757,032
Capital: Accra
Largest City: Accra
Highest Point: Afadjato
Monetary Unit: cedi

World Flags and Reference Guide

Greece
Page/Location: 39/G3
Area: 50,944 sq. mi.
131,945 sq. km.
Population: 10,647,529
Capital: Athens
Largest City: Athens
Highest Point: Mt. Olympus
Monetary Unit: euro

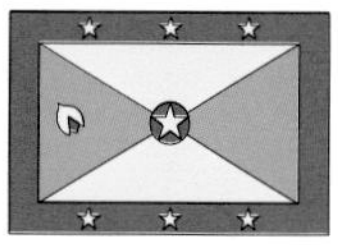

Grenada
Page/Location: 104/F5
Area: 133 sq. mi.
344 sq. km.
Population: 89,357
Capital: St. George's
Largest City: St. George's
Highest Point: Mt. St. Catherine
Monetary Unit: East Caribbean dollar

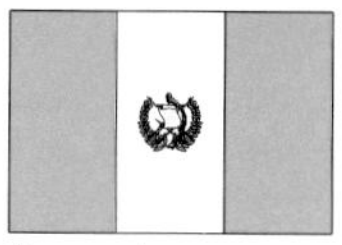

Guatemala
Page/Location: 102/D3
Area: 42,042 sq. mi.
108,899 sq. km.
Population: 14,280,596
Capital: Guatemala
Largest City: Guatemala
Highest Point: Tajumulco
Monetary Unit: quetzal

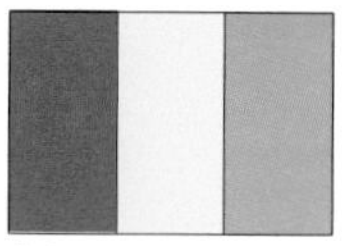

Guinea
Page/Location: 78/C4
Area: 94,925 sq. mi.
245,856 sq. km.
Population: 9,246,462
Capital: Conakry
Largest City: Conakry
Highest Point: Mt. Nimba
Monetary Unit: Guinea franc

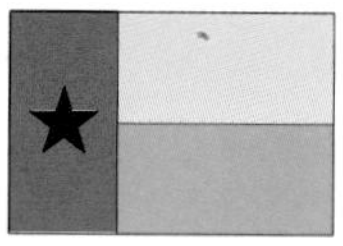

Guinea-Bissau
Page/Location: 78/B3
Area: 13,948 sq. mi.
36,125 sq. km.
Population: 1,388,363
Capital: Bissau
Largest City: Bissau
Highest Point: 984 ft. (300 m)
Monetary Unit: CFA franc

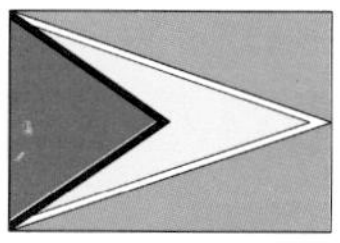

Guyana
Page/Location: 106/G2
Area: 83,000 sq. mi.
214,970 sq. km.
Population: 705,803
Capital: Georgetown
Largest City: Georgetown
Highest Point: Mt. Roraima
Monetary Unit: Guyana dollar

Haiti
Page/Location: 103/H2
Area: 10,694 sq. mi.
27,697 sq. km.
Population: 7,656,166
Capital: Port-au-Prince
Largest City: Port-au-Prince
Highest Point: Pic la Selle
Monetary Unit: gourde

Honduras
Page/Location: 102/E3
Area: 43,277 sq. mi.
112,087 sq. km.
Population: 6,823,568
Capital: Tegucigalpa
Largest City: Tegucigalpa
Highest Point: Cerro de las Minas
Monetary Unit: lempira

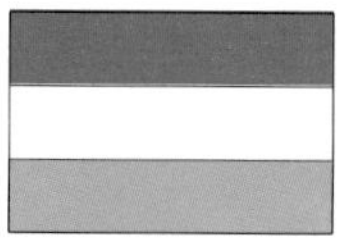

Hungary
Page/Location: 40/D2
Area: 35,919 sq. mi.
93,030 sq. km.
Population: 10,032,375
Capital: Budapest
Largest City: Budapest
Highest Point: Kékes
Monetary Unit: forint

Iceland
Page/Location: 20/N7
Area: 39,768 sq. mi.
103,000 sq. km.
Population: 282,151
Capital: Reykjavík
Largest City: Reykjavík
Highest Point: Hvannadalshnúkur
Monetary Unit: króna

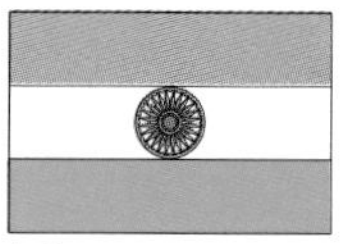

India
Page/Location: 62/C3
Area: 1,269,339 sq. mi.
3,287,588 sq. km.
Population: 1,065,070,607
Capital: New Delhi
Largest City: Mumbai
Highest Point: Kanchenjunga
Monetary Unit: Indian rupee

Indonesia
Page/Location: 67/E4
Area: 741,096 sq. mi.
1,919,440 sq. km.
Population: 238,452,952
Capital: Jakarta
Largest City: Jakarta
Highest Point: Puncak Jaya
Monetary Unit: rupiah

Iran
Page/Location: 51/H3
Area: 636,293 sq. mi.
1,648,000 sq. km.
Population: 69,018,924
Capital: Tehrān
Largest City: Tehrān
Highest Point: Qolleh-ye Damāvand
Monetary Unit: Iranian rial

Iraq
Page/Location: 50/E3
Area: 168,753 sq. mi.
437,072 sq. km.
Population: 25,374,691
Capital: Baghdad
Largest City: Baghdad
Highest Point: Haji Ibrahim
Monetary Unit: Iraqi dinar

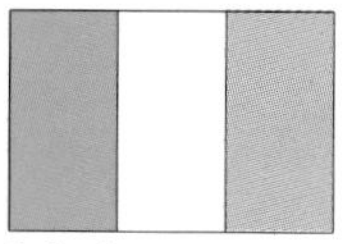

Ireland
Page/Location: 21/A4
Area: 27,136 sq. mi.
70,282 sq. km.
Population: 3,969,558
Capital: Dublin
Largest City: Dublin
Highest Point: Carrauntoohil
Monetary Unit: euro

Israel
Page/Location: 49/D3
Area: 8,019 sq. mi.
20,770 sq. km.
Population: 6,199,008
Capital: Jerusalem
Largest City: Jerusalem
Highest Point: Har Meron
Monetary Unit: new Israeli shekel

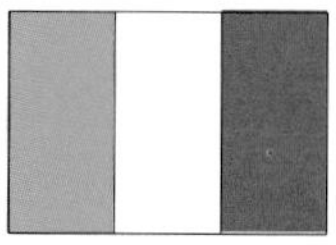

Italy
Page/Location: 18/E4
Area: 116,303 sq. mi.
301,225 sq. km.
Population: 58,057,477
Capital: Rome
Largest City: Rome
Highest Point: Mont Bianco
Monetary Unit: euro

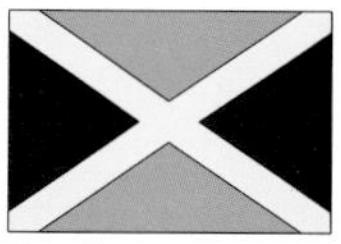

Jamaica
Page/Location: 103/G2
Area: 4,243 sq. mi.
10,990 sq. km.
Population: 2,713,130
Capital: Kingston
Largest City: Kingston
Highest Point: Blue Mountain Pk.
Monetary Unit: Jamaican dollar

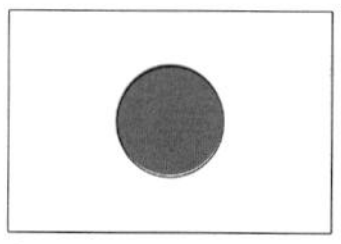

Japan
Page/Location: 55/M4
Area: 145,882 sq. mi.
377,835 sq. km.
Population: 127,333,002
Capital: Tokyo
Largest City: Tokyo
Highest Point: Fujiyama
Monetary Unit: yen

Jordan
Page/Location: 49/E4
Area: 34,445 sq. mi.
89,213 sq. km.
Population: 5,611,202
Capital: Ammān
Largest City: Ammān
Highest Point: Jabal Ramm
Monetary Unit: Jordanian dinar

Kazakhstan
Page/Location: 46/G5
Area: 1,049,150 sq. mi.
2,717,300 sq. km.
Population: 16,798,552
Capital: Astana
Largest City: Almaty
Highest Point: Khan-Tengri
Monetary Unit: Kazakhstani tenge

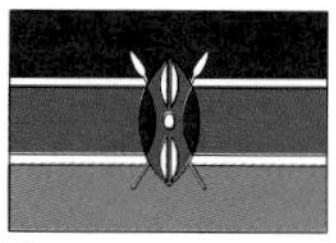

Kenya
Page/Location: 77/M7
Area: 224,960 sq. mi.
582,646 sq. km.
Population: 32,021,856
Capital: Nairobi
Largest City: Nairobi
Highest Point: Mt. Kenya
Monetary Unit: Kenya shilling

Kiribati
Page/Location: 69/H5
Area: 277 sq. mi.
717 sq. km.
Population: 100,798
Capital: Tarawa
Largest City: —
Highest Point: Banaba Island
Monetary Unit: Australian dollar

Korea, North
Page/Location: 58/D2
Area: 46,540 sq. mi.
120,539 sq. km.
Population: 22,697,553
Capital: P'yŏngyang
Largest City: P'yŏngyang
Highest Point: Paektu-san
Monetary Unit: North Korean won

Korea, South
Page/Location: 58/D4
Area: 38,023 sq. mi.
98,480 sq. km.
Population: 48,598,175
Capital: Seoul
Largest City: Seoul
Highest Point: Halla-san
Monetary Unit: South Korean won

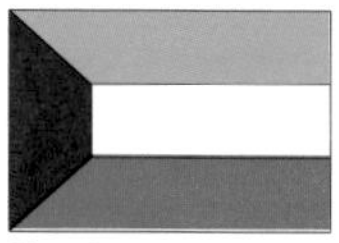

Kuwait
Page/Location: 51/F4
Area: 6,880 sq. mi.
17,820 sq. km.
Population: 2,257,549
Capital: Kuwait
Largest City: As Sālimiyah
Highest Point: 1,003 ft. (306 m)
Monetary Unit: Kuwaiti dinar

Kyrgyzstan
Page/Location: 46/H5
Area: 76,641 sq. mi.
198,500 sq. km.
Population: 4,965,081
Capital: Bishkek
Largest City: Bishkek
Highest Point: Pik Pobedy
Monetary Unit: som

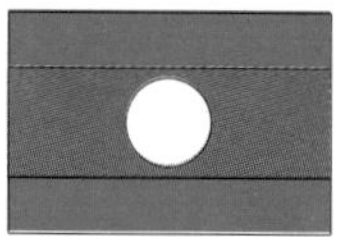

Laos
Page/Location: 65/C2
Area: 91,428 sq. mi.
236,800 sq. km.
Population: 6,068,117
Capital: Vientiane
Largest City: Vientiane
Highest Point: Phou Bia
Monetary Unit: kip

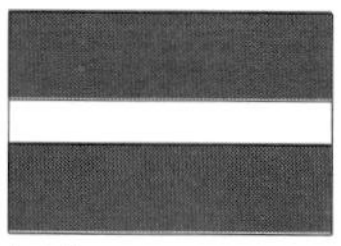

Latvia
Page/Location: 42/E4
Area: 24,749 sq. mi.
64,100 sq. km.
Population: 2,332,078
Capital: Riga
Largest City: Riga
Highest Point: Gaizina Kalns
Monetary Unit: Latvian lat

Lebanon
Page/Location: 49/D3
Area: 4,015 sq. mi.
10,399 sq. km.
Population: 3,777,218
Capital: Beirut
Largest City: Beirut
Highest Point: Qurnat as Sawdā'
Monetary Unit: Lebanese pound

sotho
ge/Location: 80/E3
ea: 11,720 sq. mi.
30,355 sq. km.
pulation: 1,865,040
pital: Maseru
rgest City: Maseru
ghest Point: Thabana-Ntlenyana
onetary Unit: loti

Liberia
Page/Location: 78/C4
Area: 43,000 sq. mi.
111,370 sq. km.
Population: 3,390,635
Capital: Monrovia
Largest City: Monrovia
Highest Point: Mt. Wuteve
Monetary Unit: Liberian dollar

Libya
Page/Location: 77/J2
Area: 679,358 sq. mi.
1,759,537 sq. km.
Population: 5,631,585
Capital: Tripoli
Largest City: Tripoli
Highest Point: Bīkkū Bīttī
Monetary Unit: Libyan dinar

Liechtestein
Page/Location: 37/F3
Area: 61 sq. mi.
158 sq. km.
Population: 33,436
Capital: Vaduz
Largest City: Vaduz
Highest Point: Grauspitz
Monetary Unit: Swiss franc

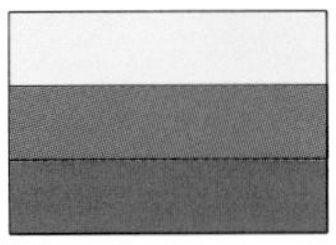

Lithuania
Page/Location: 42/D5
Area: 25,174 sq. mi.
65,200 sq. km.
Population: 3,584,836
Capital: Vilnius
Largest City: Vilnius
Highest Point: Juozapines
Monetary Unit: litas

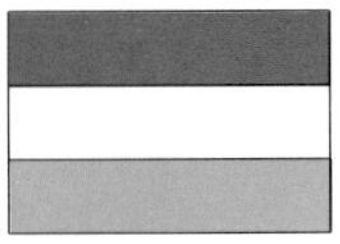

Luxembourg
Page/Location: 31/F4
Area: 999 sq. mi.
2,587 sq. km.
Population: 462,690
Capital: Luxembourg
Largest City: Luxembourg
Highest Point: Buurgplaatz
Monetary Unit: euro

acedonia (F.Y.R.O.M.)
ge/Location: 39/G2
ea: 9,781 sq. mi.
25,333 sq. km.
pulation: 2,071,210
pital: Skopje
rgest City: Skopje
ghest Point: Korab
onetary Unit: denar

Madagascar
Page/Location: 81/H8
Area: 226,657 sq. mi.
587,041 sq. km.
Population: 17,501,871
Capital: Antananarivo
Largest City: Antananarivo
Highest Point: Maromokotro
Monetary Unit: Malagasy franc

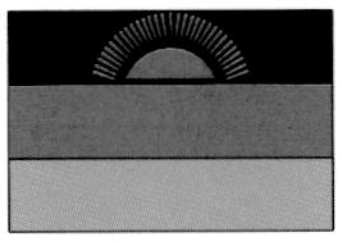

Malawi
Page/Location: 82/F3
Area: 45,747 sq. mi.
118,485 sq. km.
Population: 11,906,855
Capital: Lilongwe
Largest City: Blantyre
Highest Point: Sapitwa
Monetary Unit: Malawi kwacha

Malaysia
Page/Location: 67/C2
Area: 127,316 sq. mi.
329,750 sq. km.
Population: 23,522,482
Capital: Kuala Lumpur
Largest City: Kuala Lumpur
Highest Point: Gunung Kinabalu
Monetary Unit: ringgit

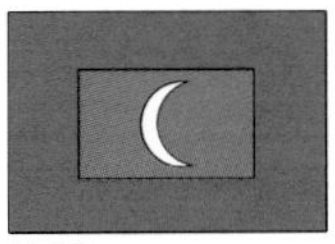

Maldives
Page/Location: 48/G9
Area: 115 sq. mi.
298 sq. km.
Population: 339,330
Capital: Male
Largest City: Male
Highest Point: 8 ft. (2.4 m)
Monetary Unit: rufiyaa

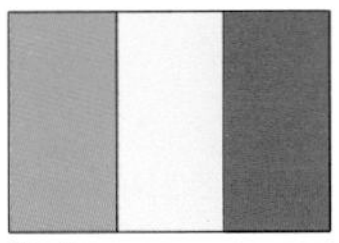

Mali
Page/Location: 76/E4
Area: 478,764 sq. mi.
1,240,000 sq. km.
Population: 11,956,788
Capital: Bamako
Largest City: Bamako
Highest Point: Hombori Tondo
Monetary Unit: CFA franc

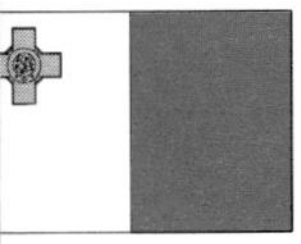

alta
ge/Location: 38/D5
ea: 122 sq. mi.
316 sq. km.
pulation: 403,342
pital: Valletta
rgest City: Valletta
ghest Point: Ta'Dmejrek
onetary Unit: Maltese lira

Marshall Islands
Page/Location: 68/G3
Area: 70 sq. mi.
181 sq. km.
Population: 57,738
Capital: Majuro
Largest City: —
Highest Point: 33 ft. (10 m)
Monetary Unit: U.S. dollar

Mauritania
Page/Location: 76/C4
Area: 397.953 sq. mi.
1,030,700 sq. km.
Population: 2,998,563
Capital: Nouakchott
Largest City: Nouakchott
Highest Point: Kediet Ijill
Monetary Unit: Ouguiya

Mauritius
Page/Location: 81/S15
Area: 718 sq. mi.
1,860 sq. km.
Population: 1,220,481
Capital: Port Louis
Largest City: Port Louis
Highest Point: Mont Piton
Monetary Unit: Mauritian rupee

Mexico
Page/Location: 84/G7
Area: 761,601 sq. mi.
1,972,546 sq. km.
Population: 104,959,594
Capital: Mexico
Largest City: Mexico
Highest Point: Citlaltépetl
Monetary Unit: Mexican peso

Micronesia
Page/Location: 68/D4
Area: 271 sq. mi.
702 sq. km.
Population: 108,155
Capital: Palikir
Largest City: Kolonia
Highest Point: Totolom
Monetary Unit: U.S. dollar

oldova
ge/Location: 41/J2
ea: 13,012 sq. mi.
33,700 sq. km.
pulation: 4,446,455
pital: Chişinău
rgest City: Chişinău
ghest Point: Dealul Balanesti
onetary Unit: leu

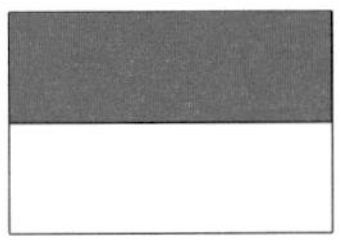

Monaco
Page/Location: 33/G5
Area: 0.7 sq. mi.
1.9 sq. km.
Population: 32,270
Capital: Monaco
Largest City: —
Highest Point: Mont Agel
Monetary Unit: euro

Mongolia
Page/Location: 54/D2
Area: 606,163 sq. mi.
1,569,962 sq. km.
Population: 2,751,314
Capital: Ulaanbaatar
Largest City: Ulaanbaatar
Highest Point: Nayramadlīn Orgil
Monetary Unit: tughrik

Morocco
Page/Location: 76/C1
Area: 172,414 sq. mi.
446,550 sq. km.
Population: 32,209,101
Capital: Rabat
Largest City: Casablanca
Highest Point: Jebal Toubkal
Monetary Unit: Moroccan dirham

Mozambique
Page/Location: 82/G4
Area: 309,494 sq. mi.
801,590 sq. km.
Population: 18,811,731
Capital: Maputo
Largest City: Maputo
Highest Point: Monte Binga
Monetary Unit: metical

Myanmar (Burma)
Page/Location: 63/G3
Area: 261,969 sq. mi.
678,500 sq. km.
Population: 42,720,196
Capital: Yangon (Rangoon)
Largest City: Yangon (Rangoon)
Highest Point: Hkakabo Razi
Monetary Unit: kyat

amibia
ge/Location: 82/C5
ea: 318,694 sq. mi.
825,418 sq. km.
pulation: 1,954,033
pital: Windhoek
rgest City: Windhoek
ghest Point: Königstein
onetary Unit: Namibian dollar

Nauru
Page/Location: 68/F5
Area: 7.7 sq. mi.
20 sq. km.
Population: 12,809
Capital: Yaren (district)
Largest City: —
Highest Point: 200 ft. (61 m)
Monetary Unit: Australian dollar

Nepal
Page/Location: 62/D2
Area: 54,663 sq. mi.
141,577 sq. km.
Population: 27,070,666
Capital: Kāthmāndu
Largest City: Kāthmāndu
Highest Point: Mt. Everest
Monetary Unit: Nepalese rupee

Netherlands
Page/Location: 28/B5
Area: 14,413 sq. mi.
37,330 sq. km.
Population: 16,318,199
Capital: The Hague; Amsterdam
Largest City: Amsterdam
Highest Point: Vaalserberg
Monetary Unit: euro

New Zealand
Page/Location: 71/Q10
Area: 103,736 sq. mi.
268,676 sq. km.
Population: 3,993,817
Capital: Wellington
Largest City: Auckland
Highest Point: Mt. Cook
Monetary Unit: New Zealand dollar

Nicaragua
Page/Location: 103/E3
Area: 49.998 sq. mi.
129,494 sq. km.
Population: 5,232,216
Capital: Managua
Largest City: Managua
Highest Point: Pico Mogotón
Monetary Unit: gold cordoba

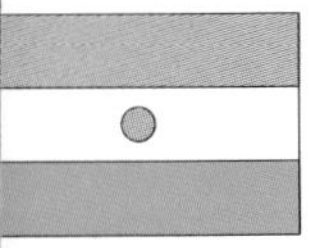

iger
ge/Location: 76/G4
ea: 489,189 sq. mi.
1,267,000 sq. km.
pulation: 11,360,538
pital: Niamey
rgest City: Niamey
ghest Point: Bagzane
onetary Unit: CFA franc

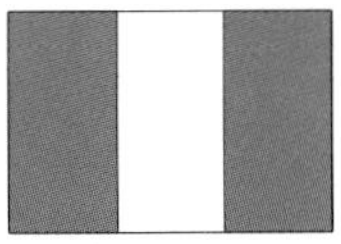

Nigeria
Page/Location: 76/G6
Area: 356,668 sq. mi.
923,770 sq. km.
Population: 137,253,133
Capital: Abuja
Largest City: Lagos
Highest Point: Chappal Waddi
Monetary Unit: naira

Norway
Page/Location: 20/C3
Area: 125,053 sq. mi.
323,887 sq. km.
Population: 4,574,560
Capital: Oslo
Largest City: Oslo
Highest Point: Galdhøppigen
Monetary Unit: Norwegian krone

Oman
Page/Location: 53/G4
Area: 82,031 sq. mi.
212,460 sq. km.
Population: 2,903,165
Capital: Muscat
Largest City: Muscat
Highest Point: Jabal ash Shams
Monetary Unit: Omani rial

Pakistan
Page/Location: 53/H3
Area: 310,403 sq. mi.
803,944 sq. km.
Population: 153,705,278
Capital: Islāmābād
Largest City: Karāchi
Highest Point: K2 (Godwin-Austen)
Monetary Unit: Pakistani rupee

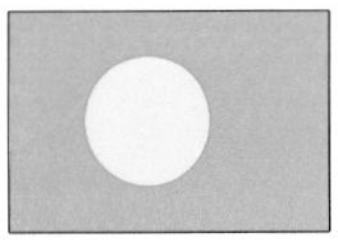

Palau
Page/Location: 68/C4
Area: 177 sq. mi.
458 sq. km.
Population: 20,016
Capital: Koror
Largest City: Koror
Highest Point: Mt. Ngerchelchauus
Monetary Unit: U.S. dollar

World Flags and Reference Guide

Panama
Page/Location: 103/F4
Area: 30,193 sq. mi.
78,200 sq. km.
Population: 3,000,463
Capital: Panamá
Largest City: Panamá
Highest Point: Barú
Monetary Unit: balboa

Papua New Guinea
Page/Location: 68/D5
Area: 178,259 sq. mi.
461,690 sq. km.
Population: 5,420,280
Capital: Port Moresby
Largest City: Port Moresby
Highest Point: Mt. Wilhelm
Monetary Unit: kina

Paraguay
Page/Location: 105/D5
Area: 157,047 sq. mi.
406,752 sq. km.
Population: 6,191,368
Capital: Asunción
Largest City: Asunción
Highest Point: Cerro Pero
Monetary Unit: guaraní

Peru
Page/Location: 106/C5
Area: 496,222 sq. mi.
1,285,215 sq. km.
Population: 28,863,494
Capital: Lima
Largest City: Lima
Highest Point: Nevado Huascarán
Monetary Unit: nuevo sol

Philippines
Page/Location: 48/M8
Area: 115,830 sq. mi.
300,000 sq. km.
Population: 86,241,697
Capital: Manila
Largest City: Manila
Highest Point: Mt. Apo
Monetary Unit: Philippine peso

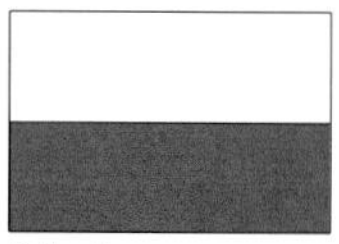

Poland
Page/Location: 27/K2
Area: 120,725 sq. mi.
312,678 sq. km.
Population: 38,626,349
Capital: Warsaw
Largest City: Warsaw
Highest Point: Rysy
Monetary Unit: zloty

Portugal
Page/Location: 34/A3
Area: 35,549 sq. mi.
92,072 sq. km.
Population: 10,119,250
Capital: Lisbon
Largest City: Lisbon
Highest Point: Serra da Estrela
Monetary Unit: euro

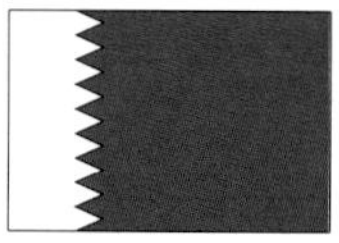

Qatar
Page/Location: 52/F3
Area: 4,247 sq. mi.
11,000 sq. km.
Population: 840,290
Capital: Doha
Largest City: Doha
Highest Point: Ţuwayyir al Ḩamīr
Monetary Unit: Qatari riyal

Romania
Page/Location: 41/F3
Area: 91,699 sq. mi.
237,500 sq. km.
Population: 22,355,551
Capital: Bucharest
Largest City: Bucharest
Highest Point: Moldoveanu
Monetary Unit: lei

Russia
Page/Location: 46/H3
Area: 6,592,812 sq. mi.
17,075,400 sq. km.
Population: 144,112,353
Capital: Moscow
Largest City: Moscow
Highest Point: El'brus
Monetary Unit: Russian ruble

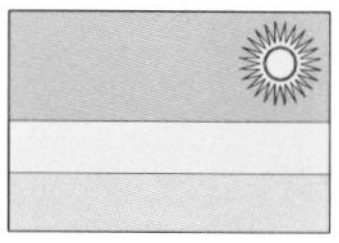

Rwanda
Page/Location: 82/E1
Area: 10,169 sq. mi.
26,337 sq. km.
Population: 7,954,013
Capital: Kigali
Largest City: Kigali
Highest Point: Karisimbi
Monetary Unit: Rwanda franc

Saint Kitts and Nevis
Page/Location: 104/F3
Area: 104 sq. mi.
269 sq. km.
Population: 38,836
Capital: Basseterre
Largest City: Basseterre
Highest Point: Mt. Liamuiga
Monetary Unit: East Caribbean dollar

Saint Lucia
Page/Location: 104/F4
Area: 238 sq. mi.
616 sq. km.
Population: 164,213
Capital: Castries
Largest City: Castries
Highest Point: Mt. Gimie
Monetary Unit: East Caribbean dollar

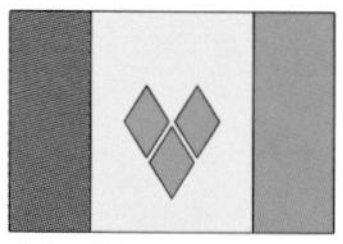

Saint Vincent and the Granadines
Page/Location: 104/F4
Area: 131 sq. mi.
340 sq. km.
Population: 117,193
Capital: Kingstown
Largest City: Kingstown
Highest Point: Soufière
Monetary Unit: East Caribbean dollar

Samoa
Page/Location: 69/H6
Area: 1,104 sq. mi.
2,860 sq. km.
Population: 177,714
Capital: Apia
Largest City: Apia
Highest Point: Mt. Silisili
Monetary Unit: tala

San Marino
Page/Location: 33/K5
Area: 23.4 sq. mi.
60.6 sq. km.
Population: 28,503
Capital: San Marino
Largest City: San Marino
Highest Point: Monte Titano
Monetary Unit: euro

São Tomé and Príncipe
Page/Location: 76/G7
Area: 371 sq. mi.
960 sq. km.
Population: 181,565
Capital: São Tomé
Largest City: São Tomé
Highest Point: Pico de São Tomé
Monetary Unit: dobra

Saudi Arabia
Page/Location: 104/F3
Area: 756,981 sq. mi.
1,960,582 sq. km.
Population: 25,100,425
Capital: Riyadh
Largest City: Riyadh
Highest Point: Jabal Sawdā'
Monetary Unit: Saudi riyal

Senegal
Page/Location: 78/B3
Area: 75,954 sq. mi.
196,720 sq. km.
Population: 10,852,147
Capital: Dakar
Largest City: Dakar
Highest Point: 1,906 ft, (581 m)
Monetary Unit: CFA franc

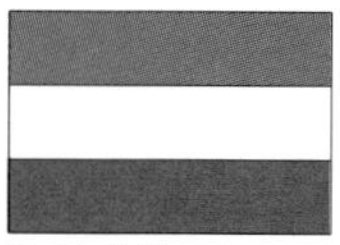

Serbia & Montenegro
Page/Location: 40/E3
Area: 39,517 sq. mi.
102,350 sq. km.
Population: 10,663,022
Capital: Belgrade
Largest City: Belgrade
Highest Point: Đaravica
Monetary Unit: Yugoslav new dinar

Seychelles
Page/Location: 74/H5
Area: 176 sq. mi.
455 sq. km.
Population: 80,832
Capital: Victoria
Largest City: Victoria
Highest Point: Morne Seychellois
Monetary Unit: Seychelles rupee

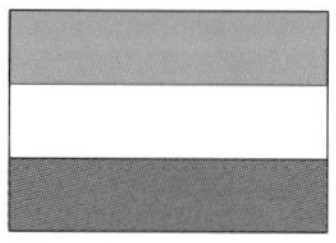

Sierra Leone
Page/Location: 78/B4
Area: 27,699 sq. mi.
71,740 sq. km.
Population: 5,883,889
Capital: Freetown
Largest City: Freetown
Highest Point: Loma Mansa
Monetary Unit: leone

Singapore
Page/Location: 66/B3
Area: 244 sq. mi.
632.6 sq. km.
Population: 4,767,974
Capital: Singapore
Largest City: Singapore
Highest Point: Bukit Timah
Monetary Unit: Singapore dollar

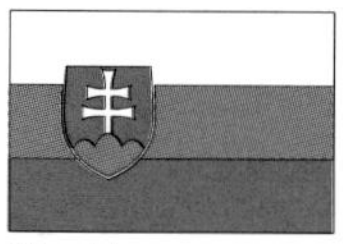

Slovakia
Page/Location: 27/K4
Area: 18,924 sq. mi.
49,013 sq. km.
Population: 5,423,567
Capital: Bratislava
Largest City: Bratislava
Highest Point: Gerlachovský Štít
Monetary Unit: Slovak koruna

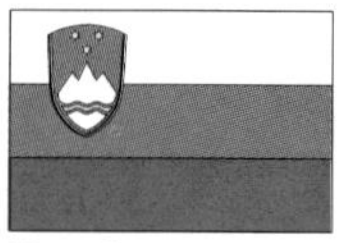

Slovenia
Page/Location: 40/B3
Area: 7,898 sq. mi.
20,456 sq. km.
Population: 1,938,282
Capital: Ljubljana
Largest City: Ljubljana
Highest Point: Triglav
Monetary Unit: tolar

Solomon Islands
Page/Location: 68/E6
Area: 11,500 sq. mi.
29,785 sq. km.
Population: 523,617
Capital: Honiara
Largest City: Honiara
Highest Point: Mt. Makarakomburu
Monetary Unit: Solomon Islands dolar

Somalia
Page/Location: 77/Q6
Area: 246,200 sq. mi.
637,658 sq. km.
Population: 8,304,601
Capital: Mogadishu
Largest City: Mogadishu
Highest Point: Shimbiris
Monetary Unit: Somali shilling

South Africa
Page/Location: 80/C3
Area: 471,008 sq. mi.
1,219,912 sq. km.
Population: 42,718,530
Capital: Cape Town; Pretoria
Largest City: Johannesburg
Highest Point: Njesuti
Monetary Unit: rand

Spain
Page/Location: 34/C2
Area: 194,881 sq. mi.
504,742 sq. km.
Population: 40,280,780
Capital: Madrid
Largest City: Madrid
Highest Point: Pico de Teide
Monetary Unit: euro

Sri Lanka
Page/Location: 62/D6
Area: 25,332 sq. mi.
65,610 sq. km.
Population: 19,905,165
Capital: Colombo
Largest City: Colombo
Highest Point: Pidurutalagala
Monetary Unit: Sri Lanka rupee

udan
age/Location: 77/L5
rea: 967,494 sq. mi.
2,505,809 sq. km.
opulation: 39,148,162
apital: Khartoum
rgest City: Omdurman
ighest Point: Kinyeti
onetary Unit: Sudanese dinar

Suriname
Page/Location: 107/G3
Area: 63,039 sq. mi.
163,270 sq. km.
Population: 436,935
Capital: Paramaribo
Largest City: Paramaribo
Highest Point: Juliana Top
Monetary Unit: Surimane guilder

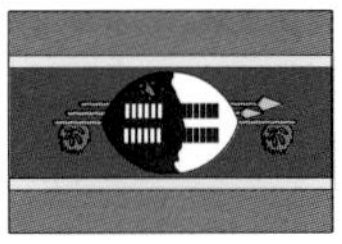

Swaziland
Page/Location: 81/E2
Area: 6,705 sq. mi.
17,366 sq. km.
Population: 1,169,241
Capital: Mbabane: Lobamba
Largest City: Mbabane
Highest Point: Emlembe
Monetary Unit: lilangeni

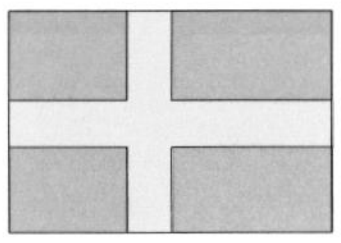

Sweden
Page/Location: 20/E3
Area: 173,665 sq. mi.
449,792 sq. km.
Population: 8,986,400
Capital: Stockholm
Largest City: Stockholm
Highest Point: Kebnekaise
Monetary Unit: krona

Switzerland
Page/Location: 36/D4
Area: 15,943 sq. mi.
41,292 sq. km.
Population: 7,450,867
Capital: Bern
Largest City: Zürich
Highest Point: Dufourspitze
Monetary Unit: Swiss franc

Syria
Page/Location: 50/D3
Area: 71,498 sq. mi.
185,180 sq. km.
Population: 18,016,874
Capital: Damascus
Largest City: Damascus
Highest Point: Jabal ash Shaykh
Monetary Unit: Syrian pound

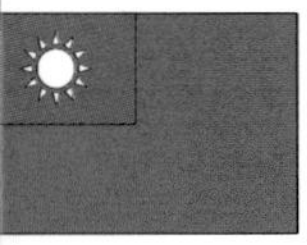

aiwan
age/Location: 61/J3
rea: 13,971 sq. mi.
26,185 sq. km.
opulation: 22,749,838
apital: T'aipei
argest City: T'aipei
ighest Point: Yü Shan
onetary Unit: new Taiwan dollar

Tajikistan
Page/Location: 46/H6
Area: 55,251 sq. mi.
143,100 sq. km.
Population: 7,011,556
Capital: Dushanbe
Largest City: Dushanbe
Highest Point: Pik Imeni Ismail Samani
Monetary Unit: somoni

Tanzania
Page/Location: 82/F2
Area: 364,699 sq. mi.
945,090 sq. km.
Population: 36,588,225
Capital: Dar es Salaam
Largest City: Dar es Salaam
Highest Point: Kilimanjaro
Monetary Unit: Tanzanian shilling

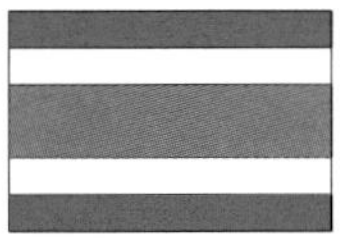

Thailand
Page/Location: 65/C3
Area: 198,455 sq. mi.
513,998 sq. km.
Population: 64,865,523
Capital: Bangkok
Largest City: Bangkok
Highest Point: Doi Inthanon
Monetary Unit: baht

Togo
Page/Location: 79/F4
Area: 21,927 sq. mi.
56,790 sq. km.
Population: 5,556,812
Capital: Lomé
Largest City: Lomé
Highest Point: Mt. Agou
Monetary Unit: CFA franc

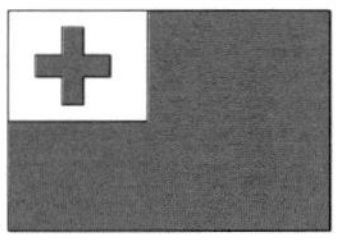

Tonga
Page/Location: 69/H7
Area: 289 sq. mi.
748 sq. km.
Population: 110,237
Capital: Nuku'alofa
Largest City: Nuku'alofa
Highest Point: Kao Island
Monetary Unit: pa'anga

rinidad and Tobago
age/Location: 104/F5
rea: 1,980 sq. mi.
5,128 sq. km.
opulation: 1,096,585
apital: Port-of-Spain
argest City: Port-of-Spain
ighest Point: El Cerro del Aripo
onetary Unit: Trin. and Tob. dollar

Tunisia
Page/Location: 76/G1
Area: 63,170 sq. mi.
163,610 sq. km.
Population: 10,032,050
Capital: Tūnis
Largest City: Tūnis
Highest Point: Jebel ech Chambi
Monetary Unit: Tunisian dinar

Turkey
Page/Location: 50/C2
Area: 301,382 sq. mi.
780,580 sq. km.
Population: 68,893,918
Capital: Ankara
Largest City: Istanbul
Highest Point: Mt. Ararat
Monetary Unit: Turkish lira

Turkmenistan
Page/Location: 46/F6
Area: 188,455 sq. mi.
488,100 sq. km.
Population: 4,863,169
Capital: Ashgabat
Largest City: Ashgabat
Highest Point: Ayrybaba
Monetary Unit: manat

Tuvalu
Page/Location: 68/G5
Area: 9.78 sq. mi.
25.33 sq. km.
Population: 11,468
Capital: Funafuti
Largest City: —
Highest Point: 16 ft. (5 m)
Monetary Unit: Australian dollar

Uganda
Page/Location: 77/M7
Area: 91,076 sq. mi.
235,887 sq. km.
Population: 26,404,543
Capital: Kampala
Largest City: Kampala
Highest Point: Margherita Peak
Monetary Unit: Ugandan shilling

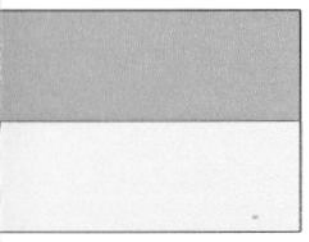

kraine
age/Location: 44/D2
rea: 233,089 sq. mi.
603,700 sq. km.
opulation: 47,732,079
apital: Kiev
argest City: Kiev
ighest Point: Hoverla
onetary Unit: hryvnia

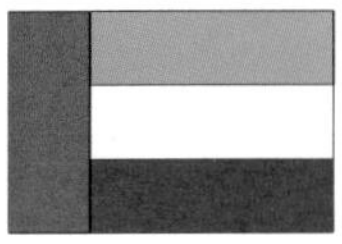

United Arab Emirates
Page/Location: 52/F4
Area: 29,182 sq. mi.
75,581 sq. km.
Population: 2,523,915
Capital: Abu Dhabi
Largest City: Dubayy
Highest Point: Jabal Yibir
Monetary Unit: Emirian dirham

United Kingdom
Page/Location: 21
Area: 94,399 sq. mi.
244,493 sq. km.
Population: 60,270,708
Capital: London
Largest City: London
Highest Point: Ben Nevis
Monetary Unit: pound sterling

United States
Page/Location: 88
Area: 3,618,765 sq. mi.
9,372,610 sq. km.
Population: 293,027,571
Capital: Washington, D.C.
Largest City: New York
Highest Point: Mt. McKinley
Monetary Unit: U.S. dollar

Uruguay
Page/Location: 109/E3
Area: 68,039 sq. mi.
176,220 sq. km.
Population: 3,440,205
Capital: Montevideo
Largest City: Montevideo
Highest Point: Cerro Catedral
Monetary Unit: Uruguayan peso

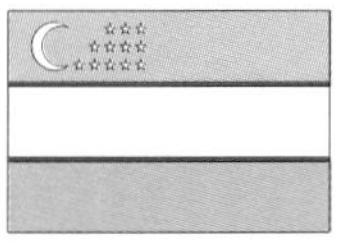

Uzbekistan
Page/Location: 46/G5
Area: 172,741 sq. mi.
447,400 sq. km.
Population: 26,410,416
Capital: Tashkent
Largest City: Tashkent
Highest Point: Adelunga Toghi
Monetary Unit: sum

anuatu
age/Location: 68/F6
rea: 5,700 sq. mi.
14,763 sq. km.
opulation: 202,609
apital: Port-Vila
argest City: Port-Vila
ighest Point: Tabwemasana
onetary Unit: vatu

Vatican City
Page/Location: 38/C2
Area: 0.17 sq. mi.
0.44 sq. km.
Population: 911
Capital: —
Largest City: —
Highest Point: 246 ft. (75 m)
Monetary Unit: euro

Venezuela
Page/Location: 106/E2
Area: 352,143 sq. mi.
912,050 sq. km.
Population: 25,017,387
Capital: Caracas
Largest City: Caracas
Highest Point: Pico Bolívar
Monetary Unit: bolívar

Vietnam
Page/Location: 65/D2
Area: 127,243 sq. mi.
329,560 sq. km.
Population: 82,689,518
Capital: Hanoi
Largest City: Ho Chi Minh City
Highest Point: Fan Si Pan
Monetary Unit: dong

Yemen
Page/Location: 52/E5
Area: 203,849 sq. mi.
527,970 sq. km.
Population: 20,024,867
Capital: Sanaa
Largest City: Aden
Highest Point: Nabī Shu'ayb
Monetary Unit: Yemeni rial

Zambia
Page/Location: 82/E3
Area: 290,568 sq. mi.
752,618 sq. km.
Population: 10,462,436
Capital: Lusaka
Largest City: Lusaka
Highest Point: Mafinga Hills
Monetary Unit: Zambian kwacha

imbabwe
age/Location: 82/E4
rea: 150,803 sq. mi.
390,580 sq. km.
opulation: 12,671,860
apital: Harare
argest City: Harare
ighest Point: Inyangani
onetary Unit: Zimbabwe dollar

World Statistics

Elements of the Solar System

	Mean Distance from Sun: in Miles	in Kilometers	Period of Revolution around Sun	Period of Rotation on Axis	Equatorial Diameter in Miles	in Kilometers	Surface Gravity (Earth = 1)	Mass (Earth = 1)	Mean Density (Water = 1)	Number of Satellites
Mercury	35,990,000	57,900,000	87.97 days	58.7 days	3,032	4,880	0.38	0.055	5.4	0
Venus	67,240,000	108,200,000	224.70 days	243.7 days†	7,521	12,104	0.91	0.815	5.2	0
Earth	93,000,000	149,700,000	365.26 days	23h 56m	7,926	12,755	1.00	1.00	5.5	1
Mars	141,610,000	227,900,000	686.98 days	24h 37m	4,221	6,794	0.38	0.107	3.9	2
Jupiter	483,675,000	778,400,000	11.86 years	9h 55m	88,846	142,984	2.36	317.8	1.3	39
Saturn	886,572,000	1,426,800,000	29.46 years	10h 30m	74,898	120,536	0.92	95.2	0.7	30
Uranus	1,783,957,000	2,871,000,000	84.01 years	17h 14m†	31,763	51,118	0.89	14.5	1.3	21
Neptune	2,795,114,000	4,498,300,000	164.79 years	16h 6m	30,778	49,532	1.13	17.1	1.6	8
Pluto	3,670,000,000	5,906,400,000	247.70 years	6.4 days†	1,413	2,274	0.07	0.002	2.1	1

† Retrograde motion

Source: NASA, National Space Science Data Center

Dimensions of the Earth

	Area in: Sq. Miles	Sq. Kilometers
Superficial area	196,939,000	510,072,000
Land surface	57,506,000	148,940,000
Water surface	139,433,000	361,132,000
	Distance in: Miles	**Kilometers**
Equatorial circumference	24,902	40,075
Polar circumference	24,860	40,007
Equatorial diameter	7,926.4	12,756.4
Polar diameter	7,899.8	12,713.6
Equatorial radius	3,963.2	6,378.2
Polar radius	3,949.9	6,356.8
Volume of the Earth	2.6×10^{11} cubic miles	10.84×10^{11} cubic kilometers
Mass or weight	6.6×10^{21} short tons	6.0×10^{21} metric tons
Maximum distance from Sun	94,600,000 miles	152,000,000 kilometers
Minimum distance from Sun	91,300,000 miles	147,000,000 kilometers

Oceans and Major Seas

	Area in: Sq. Miles	Sq. Kms.	Greatest Depth in: Feet	Meters
Pacific Ocean	63,855,000	166,241,000	36,198	11,033
Atlantic Ocean	31,744,000	82,217,000	28,374	8,648
Indian Ocean	28,417,000	73,600,000	25,344	7,725
Arctic Ocean	5,427,000	14,056,000	17,880	5,450
Caribbean Sea	970,000	2,512,300	24,720	7,535
Mediterranean Sea	969,000	2,509,700	16,896	5,150
South China Sea	895,000	2,318,000	15,000	4,600
Bering Sea	875,000	2,266,250	15,800	4,800
Gulf of Mexico	600,000	1,554,000	12,300	3,750
Sea of Okhotsk	590,000	1,528,100	11,070	3,370
East China Sea	482,000	1,248,400	9,500	2,900
Yellow Sea	480,000	1,243,200	350	107
Sea of Japan	389,000	1,007,500	12,280	3,740
Hudson Bay	317,500	822,300	846	258
North Sea	222,000	575,000	2,200	670
Black Sea	185,000	479,150	7,365	2,245
Red Sea	169,000	437,700	7,200	2,195
Baltic Sea	163,000	422,170	1,506	459

The Continents

	Area in: Sq. Miles	Sq. Kms.	Percent of World's Land
Asia	17,159,867	44,444,100	29.8
Africa	11,701,147	30,306,000	20.2
North America	9,355,975	24,232,000	16.3
South America	6,879,916	17,819,000	12.0
Antarctica	5,405,000	14,000,000	9.4
Europe	4,066,019	10,531,000	7.1
Australia	2,966,136	7,682,300	5.1

Major Ship Canals

	Length in: Miles	Kms.	Minimum Depth in: Feet	Meters
Volga-Baltic, Russia	225	362	–	–
Baltic-White Sea, Russia	140	225	16	5
Suez, Egypt	100.76	162	42	13
Albert, Belgium	80	129	16.5	5
Moscow-Volga, Russia	80	129	18	6
Volga-Don, Russia	62	100	–	–
Göta, Sweden	54	87	10	3
Kiel (Nord-Ostsee), Germany	53.2	86	38	12
Panama Canal, Panama	50.72	82	41.6	13
Houston Ship, U.S.A.	50	81	36	11

Largest Islands

	Area in: Sq. Miles	Sq. Kms.
Greenland	840,000	2,175,600
New Guinea	305,000	789,950
Borneo	286,000	740,740
Madagascar	226,657	587,041
Baffin, Canada	195,928	507,454
Sumatra, Indonesia	164,000	424,760
Honshu, Japan	88,000	227,920
Great Britain	84,400	218,896
Victoria, Canada	83,896	217,290
Ellesmere, Canada	75,767	196,236
Celebes, Indonesia	72,986	189,034
South I., New Zealand	58,393	151,238
Java, Indonesia	48,842	126,501
North I., New Zealand	44,187	114,444
Cuba	42,803	110,860
Newfoundland, Canada	42,031	108,860
Luzon, Philippines	40,420	104,688
Iceland	39,768	103,000
Mindanao, Philippines	36,537	94,631
Hokkaidō, Japan	30,436	78,829
Sakhalin, Russia	29,500	76,405
Hispaniola, Haiti & Dom. Rep.	29,399	76,143

	Area in: Sq. Miles	Sq. Kms.
Ireland	27,136	70,282
Banks, Canada	27,038	70,028
Tasmania, Australia	26,410	68,402
Ceylon,Sri Lanka	25,332	65,610
Svalbard, Norway	23,957	62,049
Devon, Canada	21,331	55,247
Novaya Zemlya (north isl.), Russia	18,600	48,200
Tierra del Fuego, Chile & Argentina	18,301	47,400
Marajó, Brazil	17,991	46,597
Alexander, Antarctica	16,700	43,250
Axel Heiberg, Canada	16,671	43,178
Melville, Canada	16,274	42,150
Southhampton, Canada	15,913	41,215
New Britain, Papua New Guinea	14,100	36,519
Taiwan, China	13,971	36,185
Kyushu, Japan	13,770	35,664
Hainan, China	13,127	33,999
Prince of Wales, Canada	12,872	33,338
Spitsbergen, Norway	12,355	31,999
Vancouver, Canada	12,079	31,285
Timor, Indonesia	11,527	29,855
Sicily, Italy	9,926	25,708

	Area in: Sq. Miles	Sq. Kms.
Somerset, Canada	9,570	24,786
Sardinia, Italy	9,301	24,090
Shikoku, Japan	6,860	17,767
New Caledonia, France	6,530	16,913
Nordaustlandet, Norway	6,409	16,599
Samar, Philippines	5,050	13,080
Negros, Philippines	4,906	12,707
Palawan, Philippines	4,550	11,785
Panay, Philippines	4,446	11,515
Jamaica	4,232	10,961
Hawaii, Hawaii, U.S.A.	4,038	10,458
Viti Levu, Fiji	4,010	10,386
Cape Breton, Canada	3,981	10,311
Mindoro, Philippines	3,759	9,736
Kodiak, Alaska, U.S.A.	3,670	9,505
Cyprus	3,572	9,251
Puerto Rico, U.S.A.	3,435	8,897
Corsica, France	3,352	8,682
New Ireland, Papua New Guinea	3,340	8,651
Crete, Greece	3,218	8,335
Anticosti, Canada	3,066	7,941
Wrangel, Russia	2,819	7,301

PRINCIPAL MOUNTAINS

	Height in: Feet	Meters
Everest, Nepal-China	29,028	8,848
K2 (Godwin Austen), Pakistan-China	28,250	8,611
Kanchenjunga, Nepal-India	28,208	8,598
Lhotse, Nepal-China	27,923	8,511
Makalu, Nepal-China	27,789	8,470
Dhaulagiri, Nepal	26,810	8,172
Nanga Parbat, Pakistan	26,660	8,126
Annapurna, Nepal	26,504	8,078
Nanda Devi, India	25,645	7,817
Rakaposhi, Pakistan	25,550	7,788
Kongur Shan, China	25,325	7,719
Tirich Mir, Pakistan	25,230	7,690
Gongga Shan, China	24,790	7,556
Ismail Samani Peak, Tajikistan	24,590	7,495
Pobedy Peak, Kyrgyzstan	24,406	7,439
Chomo Lhari, Bhutan-China	23,997	7,314
Muztag, China	23,891	7,282
Cerro Aconcagua, Argentina	22,831	6,959
Ojos del Salado, Chile-Argentina	22,572	6,880
Bonete, Chile-Argentina	22,546	6,872
Tupungato, Chile-Argentina	22,310	6,800

	Height in: Feet	Meters
Pissis, Argentina	22,241	6,779
Mercedario, Argentina	22,211	6,770
Huascarán, Peru	22,205	6,768
Llullaillaco, Chile-Argentina	22,057	6,723
Nevada Ancohuma, Bolivia	21,489	6,550
Chimborazo, Ecuador	20,561	6,267
McKinley, Alaska	20,320	6,194
Trudeau, Yukon, Canada	19,524	5,951
Cotopaxi, Ecuador	19,347	5,897
Kilimanjaro, Tanzania	19,340	5,895
El Misti, Peru	19,101	5,822
Pico Cristóbal Colón, Colombia	18,947	5,775
Huila, Colombia	18,865	5,750
Citlaltépetl (Orizaba), Mexico	18,700	5,700
Damavand, Iran	18,605	5,671
El'brus, Russia	18,510	5,642
St. Elias, Alaska, U.S.A.-Yukon, Canada	18,008	5,489
Dykh-tau, Russia	17,070	5,203
Batian (Kenya), Kenya	17,058	5,199
Ararat, Turkey	16,946	5,165
Vinson Massif, Antarctica	16,864	5,140

	Height in: Feet	Meters
Margherita (Ruwenzori), Africa	16,795	5,119
Kazbek, Georgia-Russia	16,558	5,047
Puncak Jaya, Indonesia	16,503	5,030
Blanc, France	15,771	4,807
Klyuchevskaya Sopka, Russia	15,584	4,750
Fairweather, Br. Col., Canada	15,300	4,663
Dufourspitze (Mte. Rosa), Italy-Switzerland	15,203	4,634
Ras Dashen, Ethiopia	15,157	4,620
Matterhorn, Switzerland	14,691	4,478
Whitney, California, U.S.A.	14,494	4,418
Elbert, Colorado, U.S.A.	14,433	4,399
Rainier, Washington, U.S.A.	14,410	4,392
Shasta, California, U.S.A.	14,162	4,317
Pikes Peak, Colorado, U.S.A.	14,110	4,301
Finsteraarhorn, Switzerland	14,022	4,274
Mauna Kea, Hawaii, U.S.A.	13,796	4,205
Mauna Loa, Hawaii, U.S.A.	13,677	4,169
Jungfrau, Switzerland	13,642	4,158
Grossglockner, Austria	12,457	3,797
Fujiyama, Japan	12,389	3,776
Cook, New Zealand	12,349	3,764

LONGEST RIVERS

	Length in: Miles	Kms.
Nile, Africa	4,145	6,671
Amazon, S. America	4,007	6,448
Mississippi-Missouri-Red Rock, U.S.A.	3,710	5,971
Chang Jiang (Yangtze), China	3,500	5,633
Ob'-Irtysh, Russia-Kazakhstan	3,362	5,411
Yenisey-Angara, Russia	3,100	4,989
Huang He (Yellow), China	2,950	4,747
Congo (Zaire), Africa	2,780	4,474
Amur-Shilka-Onon, Asia	2,744	4,416
Lena, Russia	2,734	4,400
Mackenzie-Peace-Finlay,Canada	2,635	4,241
Paraná-La Plata, S. America	2,630	4,232
Mekong, Asia	2,610	4,200
Niger, Africa	2,580	4,152
Missouri-Red Rock, U.S.A.	2,564	4,125
Yenisey, Russia	2,500	4,028
Mississippi, U.S.A.	2,348	3,778
Murray-Darling, Australia	2,310	3,718
Volga, Russia	2,290	3,685
Madeira, S. America	2,013	3,240
Purus, S. America	1,995	3,211
Yukon, Alaska-Canada	1,979	3,185
Zambezi, Africa	1,950	3,138
St. Lawrence, Canada-U.S.A.	1,900	3,058
Rio Grande, Mexico-U.S.A.	1,885	3,034

	Length in: Miles	Kms.
Syrdar'ya-Naryn, Asia	1,859	2,992
São Francisco, Brazil	1,811	2,914
Indus, Asia	1,800	2,897
Danube, Europe	1,775	2,857
Brahmaputra, Asia	1,760	2,832
Tocantins, Brazil	1,677	2,699
Salween, Asia	1,675	2,696
Euphrates, Asia	1,650	2,655
Xi (Si), China	1,650	2,655
Amu Darya, Asia	1,616	2,601
Nelson-Saskatchewan, Canada	1,600	2,575
Orinoco, S. America	1,600	2,575
Paraguay, S. America	1,584	2,549
Kolyma, Russia	1,562	2,514
Ganges, Asia	1,550	2,494
Ural, Russia-Kazakhstan	1,509	2,428
Japurá, S. America	1,500	2,414
Arkansas, U.S.A.	1,450	2,334
Colorado, U.S.A.-Mexico	1.450	2,334
Negro, S. America	1,400	2,253
Dnepr, Russia-Belarus-Ukraine	1,368	2,202
Orange, Africa	1,350	2,173
Irrawaddy, Myanmar	1,325	2,132
Brazos, U.S.A.	1,309	2,107
Ohio-Allegheny, U.S.A.	1,306	2,102

	Length in: Miles	Kms.
Kama, Russia	1,252	2,031
Don, Russia	1,222	1,967
Red, U.S.A.	1,222	1,966
Columbia, U.S.A.-Canada	1,214	1,953
Tigris, Asia	1,181	1,901
Darling, Australia	1,160	1,867
Angara, Russia	1,135	1,827
Sungari, Asia	1,130	1,819
Pechora, Russia	1,124	1,809
Snake, U.S.A.	1,038	1,670
Churchill, Canada	1,000	1,609
Pilcomayo, S. America	1,000	1,609
Uruguay, S. America	994	1.600
Platte-N. Platte, U.S.A.	990	1,593
Ohio, U.S.A.	981	1,578
Magdalena, Colombia	956	1,538
Pecos, U.S.A.	926	1,490
Oka, Russia	918	1,477
Canadian, U.S.A.	906	1,458
Colorado, Texas, U.S.A.	894	1,439
Dniester, Ukraine-Moldova	876	1,410
Fraser, Canada	850	1,369
Rhine, Europe	820	1,319
Northern Dvina, Russia	809	1,302
Ottawa, Canada	790	1,271

PRINCIPAL NATURAL LAKES

	Area in:		Max. Depth in:	
	Sq. Miles	Sq. Kms.	Feet	Meters
Caspian Sea, Asia	143,243	370,999	3,264	995
Lake Superior, U.S.A.-Canada	31,820	82,414	1,329	405
Lake Victoria, Africa	26,828	69,485	270	82
Lake Huron, U.S.A.-Canada	23,010	59,596	748	228
Lake Michigan, U.S.A.	22,400	58,016	923	281
Aral Sea, Kazakhstan-Uzbekistan	15,830	41,000	213	65
Lake Tanganyika, Africa	12,650	32,764	4,700	1,433
Lake Baykal, Russia	12,162	31,500	5,316	1,620
Great Bear Lake, Canada	12,096	31,328	1,356	413
Lake Nyasa (Malawi), Africa	11,555	29,928	2,320	707
Great Slave Lake, Canada	11,031	28,570	2,015	614
Lake Erie, U.S.A.-Canada	9,940	25,745	210	64
Lake Winnipeg, Canada	9,417	24,390	60	18
Lake Ontario, U.S.A.-Canada	7,540	19,529	775	244
Lake Balkhash, Kazakhstan	7,081	18,340	87	27
Lake Chad, Africa*	7,000	18,130	25	8
Lake Ladoga, Russia	6,900	17,871	738	225
Lake Maracaibo, Venezuela	5,120	13,261	100	31
Lake Onega, Russia	3,761	9,741	377	115

* Area and depth figures subject to great seasonal variations.

	Area in:		Max. Depth in:	
	Sq. Miles	Sq. Kms.	Feet	Meters
Lake Eyre, Australia*	3,500-0	9,000-0	–	–
Lake Titicaca, Peru-Bolivia	3,200	8,288	1,000	305
Lake Nicaragua, Nicaragua	3,100	8,029	230	70
Lake Athabasca, Canada	3,064	7,936	400	122
Reindeer Lake, Canada*	2,568	6,651	–	–
Lake Turkana (Rudolf), Africa	2,463	6,379	240	73
Ysyk-Köl, Kyrgyzstan	2,425	6,281	2,303	702
Lake Torrens, Australia*	2,230	5,776	–	–
Vänern, Sweden	2,156	5,584	328	100
Nettilling Lake, Canada*	2,140	5,543	–	–
Lake Winnipegosis, Canada	2,075	5,374	38	12
Lake Albert, Africa	2,075	5,374	160	49
Kariba Lake, Zambia-Zimbabwe	2,050	5,310	295	90
Lake Nipigon, Canada	1,872	4,848	540	165
Lake Mweru, Dem. Rep. of the Congo-Zambia	1,800	4,662	60	18
Lake Manitoba, Canada	1,799	4,659	12	4
Lake Taymyr, Russia	1,737	4,499	85	26
Lake Khanka, China-Russia	1,700	4,403	33	10
Lake Kioga, Uganda	1,700	4,403	25	8
Lake of the Woods, U.S.A.-Canada	1,679	4,349	70	21

ARCTIC OCEAN
CANADA BASIN
Beaufort Sea
QUEEN ELIZABETH ISLANDS
Ellesmere I.
Devon I.
GREENLAND
Baffin Bay
Baffin Island
Wrangel I.
Pt. Barrow
Banks I.
Victoria I.
Chukchi Sea
Yukon
Mt. McKinley
MacKenzie
Great Bear L.
Great Slave L.
Peace
Hudson Bay
LABRADOR BASIN
Denmark Str.
Arctic Circle
Iceland
IRMINGER BASIN
ICELAND BASIN
Great Britain
Ireland
CHARLIE-GIBBS FRACTURE ZONE
Bering Sea
ALEUTIAN BASIN
ALEUTIAN ISLANDS
Gulf of Alaska
ALEUTIAN TRENCH
ROCKY Mountains
Great Plains
NORTH AMERICA
Great Lakes
Newfoundland
C. Race
Appalachian Mts.
MENDOCINO FRACTURE ZONE
C. Mendocino
Colorado
Missouri
Ohio
Mississippi
C. Hatteras
Rio Grande
ATLANTIC
MID-ATLANTIC RIDGE
HAWAIIAN ISLANDS
HAWAIIAN RIDGE
MOLOKAI FRACTURE ZONE
Lower California
Tropic of Cancer
Gulf of Mexico
Cuba
WEST INDIES
−28,232 ft. (−8605 m)
Caribbean Sea
C. Verde
CENTRAL PACIFIC BASIN
CLIPPERTON FRACTURE ZONE
PACIFIC
GUATEMALA BASIN
Orinoco
Negro
Amazon
Equator
ROMANCHE FRACTURE ZONE
C. de São Roque
Madeira
São Francisco
PERU-CHILE TRENCH
EAST PACIFIC RISE
PERU BASIN
SOUTH AMERICA
BRAZIL BASIN
OCEAN
TONGA TRENCH
Tropic of Capricorn
NAZCA RIDGE
−26,457 ft. (−8064 m)
CHILE BASIN
Paraná
Cerro Aconcagua
KERMADEC TRENCH
SOUTHWEST PACIFIC BASIN
ARGENTINE BASIN
Falkland Is.
Tierra del Fuego
−27,313 ft. (−8325 m)
C. Horn
SOUTH SANDWICH TRENCH
Drake Passage
PACIFIC-ANTARCTIC RIDGE
Antarctic Circle
AMUNDSEN ABYSSAL PLAIN
Antarctic Peninsula
WEDDELL ABYSSAL PLAIN
Bellingshausen Sea
Weddell Sea
Ross Sea
ANTARCTICA

World

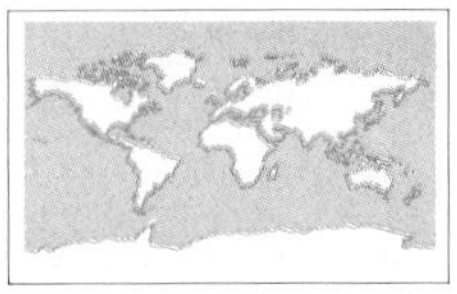

−17,881 ft.
(−5450 m)
ARCTIC
OCEAN
FRANZ JOSEF LAND
SEVERNAYA
ZEMLYA
SVALBARD
NOVAYA
ZEMLYA
NEW SIBERIAN IS.
Laptev
Sea
Kara
Sea
Barents
Sea
Nordkapp
Kjølen
Wrangel I.
Siberia
Ural Mountains
Ob'
Yenisey
Lena
Aldan
Angara
L. Ladoga
Baltic Sea
Volga
Irtysh
Ob'
Lena
L. Baykal
Bering
Sea
ALEUTIAN
BASIN
ALEUTIAN ISLANDS
ALEUTIAN TRENCH
Kamchatka
Pen.
Sea
of
Okhotsk
Sakhalin
KURIL-KAMCHATKA TRENCH
EUROPE
Dnieper
ASIA
Amur
Danube
Black Sea
Caspian Sea
Aral
Sea
L. Balkhash
Gobi
Sea of
Japan
Honshu
NORTHWEST
PACIFIC
BASIN
JAPAN
TRENCH
Mediterranean Sea
Euphrates
Kunlun
Himalaya
Mt. Everest
Huang
East
China
Sea
Indus
Ganges
Chang
PACIFIC
Nile
Red Sea
Arabian
Sea
ARABIAN
BASIN
Bay
of
Bengal
Salween
Mekong
South
China
Sea
Taiwan
PHILIPPINE
BASIN
Luzon
MARIANA IS.
MARIANA
TRENCH
Challenger Deep
−36,198 ft.
(−11,033 m)
Tropic of Cancer
MARSHALL IS.
CENTRAL
PACIFIC
BASIN
AFRICA
CARLSBERG
RIDGE
C. Comorin
Ceylon
CEYLON
PLAIN
NINETYEAST RIDGE
Borneo
Mindanao
CAROLINE IS.
MELANESIAN
BASIN
Equator
L.
Victoria
Kilimanjaro
SOMALI
BASIN
CENTRAL
INDIAN
RIDGE
Sumatra
Java
Celebes
New Guinea
OCEAN
Congo
JAVA TRENCH
24,443 ft.
(−7450 m)
INDIAN
Zambezi
Madagascar
Coral
Sea
Great Barrier Reef
Fiji Is.
OCEAN
BROKEN
PLATEAU
AUSTRALIA
Tropic of Capricorn
Orange
CAPE
Good Hope
BASIN
C. Leeuwin
S. AUSTRALIA BASIN
Tasman
Sea
North Cape
North I.
South I.
Tasmania
SOUTHWEST INDIAN RIDGE
SOUTHEAST INDIAN RIDGE
KERGUELEN
PLATEAU
ENDERBY ABYSSAL PLAIN
AUSTRALIAN-ANTARCTIC BASIN
Antarctic Circle
C. Adare
Amery
Ice Shelf
ANTARCTICA
Ross Sea

180°
A 160°
B 140°
C 120°
D 100°
E 80°
F 60°
G 40°
H 20°
1
2
3
4
5
6
7
8
9
10
80°
60°
40°
20°
0°
ARCTIC OCEAN
Beaufort Sea
CHUKCHI SEA
ASIA
Barrow
Pt. Barrow
ALASKA (U.S.)
Yukon
Nome
Mt. McKinley 20,320 ft. (6,194 m)
Fairbanks
Anchorage
Bethel
Whitehorse
Juneau
BERING SEA
Gulf of Alaska
ALEUTIAN IS.
Inuvik
Victoria I.
Arctic Circle
Great Bear L.
Yellowknife
Great Slave L.
Ellesmere I.
Baffin I.
Baffin Bay
GREENLAND (KALAALLIT NUNAAT) (DEN.)
Upernavik
Sisimiut
Iqaluit
Nuuk
Qaqortoq
Ammassalik
Kap Farvel
Reykjavík
ICELAND
Faroe I. (DEN.)
Rankin Inlet
Churchill
Hudson Bay
Nelson
C. Chidley
LABRADOR SEA
Prince Rupert
Edmonton
Saskatoon
CANADA
L. Winnipeg
Calgary
Regina
Winnipeg
Rocky Mountains
Great Plains
Happy Valley - Goose Bay
Newfoundland
Moosonee
Vancouver
Seattle
Spokane
Great Falls
C. Flattery
Portland
Missouri
Fargo
Minneapolis
Duluth
Great Lakes
Québec
Ottawa
Montréal
St. John's
C. Race
ST. PIERRE & MIQUELON (FR.)
Halifax
Boise
UNITED STATES
Cascade Ra.
Toronto
Detroit
Cleveland
Boston
Chicago
New York
Philadelphia
Washington
Norfolk
C. Hatteras
C. Mendocino
Salt Lake City
Cheyenne
Denver
Sacramento
Reno
San Francisco
Las Vegas
Kansas City
Indianapolis
Cincinnati
St. Louis
Nashville
Appalachian Mts.
Los Angeles
San Diego
Tijuana
Albuquerque
Phoenix
Dallas
Memphis
Atlanta
Savannah
Sierra Nevada
Colorado
Arkansas
Mississippi
NORTH AMERICA
NORTH ATLANTIC OCEAN
AZORES (PORT.)
Bermuda (U.K.)
EUROPE
C. Fisterra
Porto
PORTUGAL
Lisbon
Seville
Casablanca
MOROCCO
Madeira (PORT.)
Marrakech
CANARY IS. (SP.)
WESTERN SAHARA (Occ. by Morocco)
MAURITANIA
Nouakchott
Tombouctou
CAPE VERDE
Saint-Louis
C. Verde
Dakar
GAMBIA
GUINEA-BISSAU
GUINEA
Conakry
Freetown
SIERRA LEONE
Monrovia
LIBERIA
Bamako
Glasgow
Dublin
IRELAND
C. Clear
El Paso
Houston
San Antonio
New Orleans
Tampa
C. Canaveral
Miami
Chihuahua
Torreón
MEXICO
Monterrey
Gulf of Mexico
I. Guadalupe (MEX.)
NORTH PACIFIC OCEAN
Midway Is.
French Frigate Shoals
HAWAIIAN ISLANDS (U.S.)
Honolulu
Hawaii
Johnston Atoll (U.S.)
C. Falso
Is. Revillagigedo (MEX.)
I. Clarion
Guadalajara
León
Tampico
Mexico
Veracruz
Havana
CUBA
BAHAMAS
Tropic of Cancer
Mérida
West Indies
Greater Antilles
HAITI
DOMINICAN REP.
Puerto Rico (U.S.)
ANTIGUA AND BARBUDA
BELIZE
HONDURAS
JAMAICA
GUATEMALA
Guatemala
Tegucigalpa
EL SALVADOR
NICARAGUA
Managua
San José
COSTA RICA
PANAMA
Panama
CARIBBEAN SEA
Lesser Antilles
DOMINICA
BARBADOS
GRENADA
TRINIDAD AND TOBAGO
Barranquilla
Caracas
Maracaibo
VENEZUELA
GUYANA
Georgetown
SURINAME
Paramaribo
Cayenne
FRENCH GUIANA
Clipperton I. (FR.)
Medellín
COLOMBIA
Cali
Bogotá
Boa Vista
Quito
ECUADOR
Guayaquil
Equator
Galápagos Is. (ECU.)
Punta Aguja
Iquitos
Amazon
Belém
São Luís
Fortaleza
Fernando de Noronha (BRAZ.)
C. de São Roque
Natal
St. Peter & St. Paul Rocks (BRAZ.)
Manaus
Selvas
Recife
Ascension (ST. H.)
Trujillo
Rio Branco
Porto Velho
BRAZIL
PERU
Lima
Cusco
BOLIVIA
La Paz
Cuiabá
Brasília
Salvador
SOUTH AMERICA
Arequipa
Santa Cruz
Goiânia
Sucre
Belo Horizonte
Iquique
Gran Chaco
PARAGUAY
São Paulo
C. Frio
Rio de Janeiro
Santos
Asunción
Antofagasta
Curitiba
St. Helena (U.K.)
Is. Martin Vaz (BRAZ.)
Tropic of Capricorn
CHILE
San Miguel de Tucumán
Córdoba
Porto Alegre
La Serena
Cerro Aconcagua 6,959 m
Valparaíso
Santiago
Mendoza
Rosario
URUGUAY
Montevideo
Buenos Aires
La Plata
Pampas
R. de la Plata
ARGENTINA
Andes
Concepción
Valdivia
Bahía Blanca
Viedma
Comodoro Rivadavia
C. Tres Puntas
Stanley
Falkland Is. (U.K.)
Punta Arenas
Tierra del Fuego
Cape Horn
Drake Passage
S. Georgia (U.K.)
S. Sandwich Is. (U.K.)
S. Shetland Is. (U.K.)
South Orkney Is. (U.K.)
SOUTH ATLANTIC OCEAN
Tristan da Cunha (ST. H.)
Gough I. (ST. H.)
Antarctic Circle
Peter I Island (NOR.)
Antarctic Pen.
WEDDELL SEA
C. Norvegia
ROSS SEA
Is. Juan Fernández (CHILE)
Easter I. (CHILE)
Sala y Gomez (CHILE)
SOUTH PACIFIC OCEAN
Palmyra (U.S.)
Teraina (Washington I.)
Tabuaeran (Fanning I.)
Kiritimati (Christmas I.)
LINE ISLANDS
International Date Line
Howland I. (U.S.)
Baker I. (U.S.)
Jarvis I. (U.S.)
PHOENIX IS.
KIRIBATI
Malden I.
Starbuck I.
TOKELAU IS. (N.Z.)
Atafu
Fakaofo
Tongareva
Vostok I.
Caroline I.
Nuku Hiva
MARQUESAS IS.
Hiva Oa
Atuona
Manihiki
Nassau
Flint I.
Mata Utu
Wallis Is. (FR.)
Futuna
Apia
SAMOA
Pago Pago
AMER. SAMOA (U.S.)
Suwarrow
COOK ISLANDS (N.Z.)
Rangiroa
Manihi
FRENCH POLYNESIA
Disappointment Is.
Puka Puka
Palmerston Atoll
Uturoa
SOCIETY IS.
Papeete
Tahiti
TUAMOTU ARCH.
Takatoko
Reao
Hikueru
Hao
TONGA
Niue (N.Z.)
Atiu
Nuku'alofa
Tongatapu
Rarotonga
Mangaia
Tubuai
Mururoa
Marutea
Rikitea
Gambier Is. (FR.)
Henderson I. (U.K.)
Oeno I. (U.K.)
Ducie I. (U.K.)
TUBUAI IS. (FR.)
Rapa I.
Bass Is.
Pitcairn I. (U.K.)
PITCAIRN IS. (U.K.)
Kermadec Is. (N.Z.)
Chatham Is. (N.Z.)
Fontur

L 40° M 60° N 80° P 100° Q 120° R 140° S 160° T 180°
ARCTIC OCEAN
FRANZ JOSEF LAND (RUS.)
Severnaya Zemlya
New Siberian Is.
BARENTS SEA
Kara Sea
Novaya Zemlya
Hammerfest
North Cape
Tromsø
Murmansk
Khatanga
Noril'sk
Verkhoyansk
Arctic Circle
Anadyr'
Vorkuta
Nar'yan-Mar
Archangel'sk
Salekhard
RUSSIA
Tura
Siberia
Lensk
Yakutsk
Magadan
Okhotsk
Surgut
Nizhnevartovsk
Syktyvkar
FINLAND
Helsinki
Oulu
Kiruna
Umeå
Tampere
SWEDEN
ESTONIA
Stockholm
Göteborg
LATVIA
LITH.
St. Petersburg
Yaroslavl'
Moscow
Nizhniy Novgorod
Perm'
Nizhniy Tagil
Yekaterinburg
Chelyabinsk
Magnitogorsk
Izhevsk
Kazan'
Ufa
Samara
Orenburg
Tomsk
Novosibirsk
Omsk
Krasnoyarsk
Novokuznetsk
Bratsk
Bodaybo
Barnaul
Irkutsk
L. Baykal
Chita
Ulan-Ude
Blagoveshchensk
Komsomol'sk-na-Amure
SEA OF OKHOTSK
Kamchatka Pen.
Petropavlovsk-Kamchatskiy
Mys Lopatka
BERING SEA
Int'l Date Line
Sakhalin
Khabarovsk
Minsk
BELARUS
Warsaw
POLAND
Berlin
Prague
Kiev
UKRAINE
Kharkiv
Tula
Ryazan'
Voronezh
Saratov
Volgograd
Donets'k
Odesa
Rostov
Vienna
Budapest
Milan
Belgrade
ROMANIA
Bucharest
MOL.
Sofia
BUL.
Istanbul
Ankara
Rome
Naples
ALB.
GREECE
Athens
Crete
Izmir
TURKEY
Adana
CYPRUS
SYRIA
LEBANON
ISRAEL
Damascus
Amman
JORDAN
Baghdad
IRAQ
Al Basrah
KUWAIT
Tehrān
IRAN
Eşfahān
Shīrāz
Mashhad
Tabriz
GEORGIA
ARMENIA
AZER.
Baku
Atyraū
Astrakhan'
Aral Sea
El'brus 5,642 m
Black Sea
Caspian Sea
Qaraghandy
KAZAKHSTAN
Astana
Semey
L. Balkhash
Almaty
Bishkek
KYRGYZSTAN
UZBEKISTAN
Nukus
Tashkent
TURKMENISTAN
Ashgabat
Dushanbe
TAJIKISTAN
AFGHANISTAN
Kabul
Islāmābād
Lahore
PAKISTAN
Karāchi
Hyderābād
Delhi
New Delhi
Kānpur
NEPAL
Kāthmāndu
Mt. Everest 8,848 m
BHUTAN
BANGLADESH
Dhaka
Kolkata
Ahmadābād
INDIA
Mumbai
Pune
Hyderābād
Bangalore
Chennai
Coimbatore
Lakshadweep Is. (INDIA)
SRI LANKA
Colombo
C. Comorin
Dondra Head
MALDIVES
Male
ARABIAN SEA
BAY OF BENGAL
Andaman Is. (INDIA)
Nicobar Is. (INDIA)
ASIA
MONGOLIA
Gobi
Ulaanbaatar
Choybalsan
Yining
Ürümqi
Takla Makan
Yumen
Tibet
Lhasa
CHINA
Lanzhou
Yinchuan
Baotou
Beijing
Tianjin
Taiyuan
Xi'an
Jinan
Chengdu
Chongqing
Wuhan
Nanjing
Shanghai
Changsha
Guiyang
Fuzhou
Kunming
Nanning
Guangzhou
HONG KONG
Hainan
T'aipei
TAIWAN
Qiqihar
Harbin
Changchun
Jilin
Shenyang
Dalian
Vladivostok
N. KOREA
P'yŏngyang
Seoul
S. KOREA
Pusan
Fukuoka
Yellow Sea
Sea of Japan
JAPAN
Hokkaido
Sapporo
Hakodate
Honshu
Sendai
Tōkyō
Yokohama
Kyōto
Ōsaka
Kyūshū
EAST CHINA SEA
Okinawa
RYUKYU IS.
KURIL IS.
VOLCANO IS. (JAP.)
BONIN IS. (JAP.)
Iwo Jima
Daito Is. (JAP.)
Okino-Tori-Shima (JAP.)
MYANMAR
Mandalay
Yangon
THAILAND
Bangkok
LAOS
Vientiane
Hanoi
VIETNAM
CAMBODIA
Phnom Penh
Ho Chi Minh City
SOUTH CHINA SEA
PHILIPPINE SEA
PHILIPPINES
Luzon
Manila
C. Engaño
Samar
Palawan
Mindanao
Davao
Sulu Sea
Celebes Sea
MALAYSIA
Kuala Lumpur
Medan
SINGAPORE
BRUNEI
Borneo
Sumatra
Palembang
INDONESIA
Banjarmasin
Celebes
Jakarta
Bandung
Surabaya
Java
Java Sea
Bali
Sumba
Ujung Pandang
Banda Sea
EAST TIMOR
Timor
Timor Sea
Arafura Sea
Halmahera
Jayapura
New Guinea
PAPUA NEW GUINEA
Port Moresby
Bismarck Arch.
New Britain
New Ireland
Admiralty Is.
Bougainville
SOLOMON IS.
Honiara
Guadalcanal
Malaita
Sta. Isabel
San Cristobal
Rennell I.
Torres Is.
Espiritu Santo
VANUATU
Port-Vila
Rotuma I. (FIJI)
FIJI
Suva
New Caledonia (FR.)
Nouméa
Loyalty Is.
CORAL SEA
NORTH PACIFIC OCEAN
Tropic of Cancer
Minami-Tori-Shima (JAP.)
Farrallon de Pajaros
Maug Is.
Pagan
Alamagan
Anathan
Saipan
NORTHERN MARIANAS (U.S.)
Hagåtña
Guam (U.S.)
Wake I. (U.S.)
Yap Is.
Ulithi
Ngulu
PALAU
Koror
Babelthuap
Sonsoral Is.
Elato
Lamotrek
Namonuito
Chuuk Is.
Satawan
CAROLINE IS.
FED. STATES OF MICRONESIA
Equator
Ujelang
Hall Is.
Senyavin Is.
Palikir
Kosrae
Enewetak
Bikini
Rongelap
RALIK CHAIN
MARSHALL IS.
Maloelap
Kwajalein
Majuro
Mili
Butaritari
GILBERT
Tarawa
KIRIBATI
Banaba
NAURU
Tabiteuea
Arorae
Nanumea
TUVALU
Funafuti
Ontong Java
Sta. Cruz Is. (S.I.)
SAUDI ARABIA
Medina
Riyadh
Mecca
BAHRAIN
QATAR
U.A.E.
Muscat
OMAN
Rub al Khali
YEMEN
Sanaa
Aden
Gulf of Aden
Socotra (YEMEN)
Persian Gulf
Red Sea
EGYPT
Cairo
Alexandria
Asyūţ
Aswān
LIBYA
Tripoli
Benghāzi
Surt
Sabhā
TUNISIA
MEDITERRANEAN SEA
Port Sudan
SUDAN
Khartoum
Omdurman
ERITREA
Asmara
DJIBOUTI
ETHIOPIA
Addis Ababa
SOMALIA
Mogadishu
CHAD
N'Djamena
L. Chad
NIGER
Zinder
Kano
NIGERIA
Abuja
CAMEROON
Yaoundé
Libreville
GABON
CONGO
Brazzaville
Kinshasa
DEM. REP. OF THE CONGO
Kisangani
Kananga
Lubumbashi
Malakal
Juba
Bangui
CENTRAL AFRICAN REP.
Sarh
UGANDA
Kampala
KENYA
Nairobi
RWANDA
BURUNDI
L. Victoria
Kilimanjaro 5,895 m
Mombasa
TANZANIA
Dar es Salaam
L. Tanganyika
Mbeya
L. Nyasa
MALAWI
Lilongwe
ZAMBIA
Lusaka
ANGOLA
Luanda
Benguela
Huambo
NAMIBIA
Windhoek
BOTSWANA
Gaborone
Kalahari
ZIMBABWE
Harare
Beira
MOZAMBIQUE
Mozambique Chan.
Maputo
SWAZILAND
Pretoria
Johannesburg
LESOTHO
Bloemfontein
Durban
SOUTH AFRICA
Cape Town
Cape of Good Hope
C. Agulhas
Port Elizabeth
C. Fria
Orange
MADAGASCAR
Antananarivo
Toamasina
Toliara
Tanjona Vohimena
Tanjon'i Bobaomby
Antsiranana
COMOROS
Mayotte (FR.)
Aldabra Is. (SEY.)
Farquhar Group
Agalega Is. (MRTS.)
Amirante Is.
SEYCHELLES
Victoria
Mahé
Coëtivy I.
Tromelin I. (FR.)
Port Louis
MAURITIUS
Réunion (FR.)
Rodrigues (MRTS.)
INDIAN OCEAN
BRITISH INDIAN OCEAN TERR.
Chagos Arch.
Diego Garcia
Cocos Is. (AUSTL.)
Christmas I. (AUSTL.)
Tropic of Capricorn
Amsterdam I. (FR.)
St. Paul I. (FR.)
Prince Edward Is. (S. AFR.)
Crozet Is. (FR.)
Kerguélen (FR.)
McDonald Is. (AUSTL.)
AUSTRALIA
Darwin
Gulf of Carpentaria
Cape York Pen.
Cairns
Townsville
Port Hedland
Great Sandy Desert
North West C.
Alice Springs
Rockhampton
Great Dividing Ra.
Brisbane
Geraldton
Perth
Kalgoorlie
Great Victoria Desert
Broken Hill
Whyalla
Darling
Newcastle
Sydney
Canberra
C. Leeuwin
Albany
Great Australian Bight
Adelaide
Murray
Mt. Kosciusko 2,228 m
Melbourne
Tasmania
Hobart
South East C.
TASMAN SEA
Lord Howe I. (AUSTL.)
Norfolk I. (AUSTL.)
NEW ZEALAND
North I.
North C.
Auckland
Wellington
Christchurch
South I.
Dunedin
South C.
Bounty Is. (N.Z.)
Antipodes Is. (N.Z.)
Auckland Is. (N.Z.)
Campbell I. (N.Z.)
Macquarie I. (AUSTL.)
C. Batterbee
Antarctic Circle
C. Adare
ROSS SEA
ANTARCTICA
1 2 3 4 5 6 7 8 9 10
80° 60° 40° 20° 0° 20° 40° 60° 80°
© HAMMOND WORLD ATLAS CORPORATION CI - 1001 - A

POPULATION OF CITIES AND TOWNS

- ◉ OVER 5,000,000
- ⊕ 2,000,000 - 4,999,999
- ⊙ 500,000 - 1,999,999
- ○ UNDER 500,000

SCALE 1:81,700,000 ROBINSON PROJECTION STANDARD PARALLELS 38°N AND 38°S

MILES 0 | 1000 | 2000 | 3000 | 4000

KILOMETERS 0 | 1000 | 2000 | 3000 | 4000

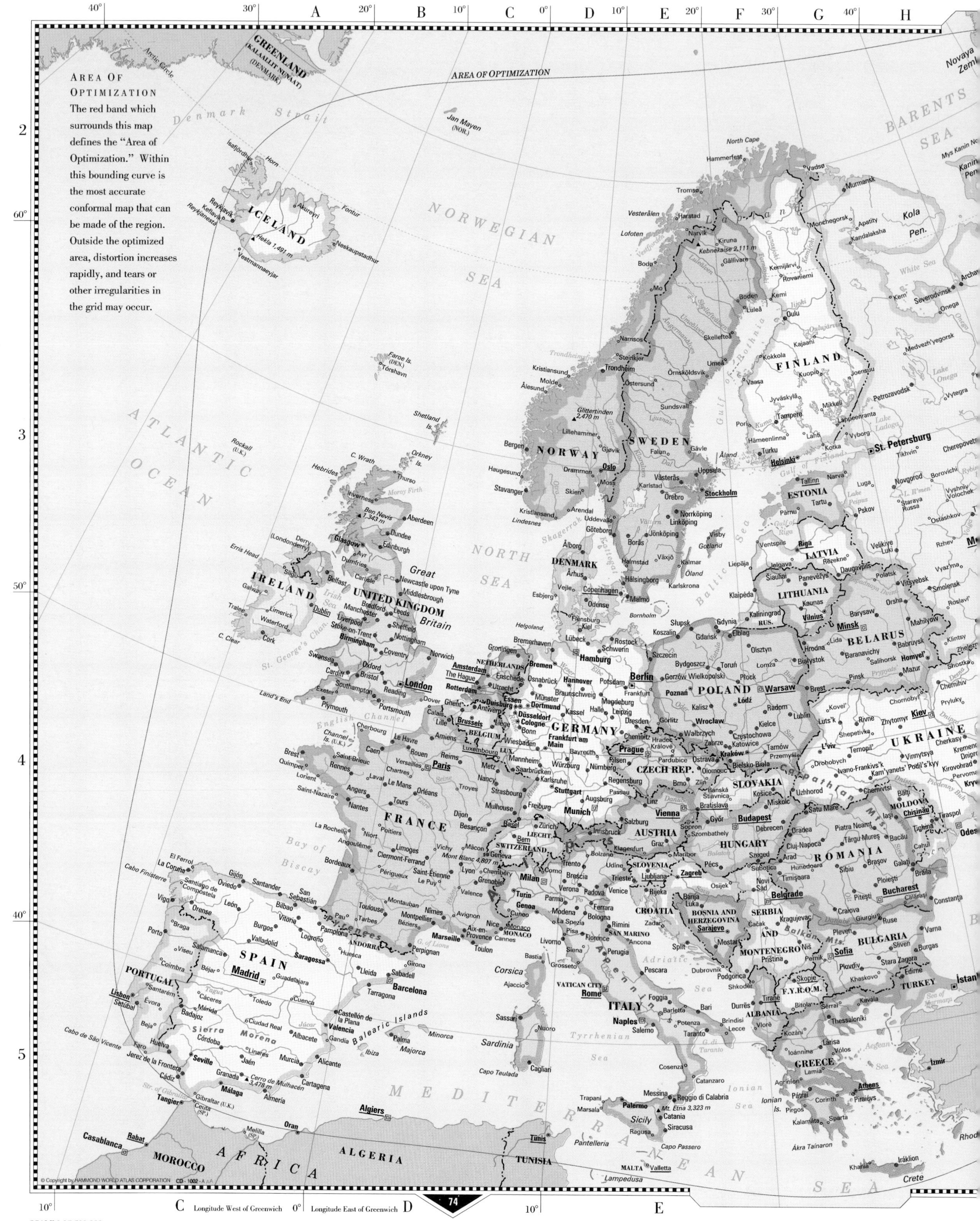

SCALE 1:17,500,000 OPTIMAL CONFORMAL PROJECTION

MILES 0 250 500 750

KILOMETERS 0 250 500 750

POPULATION OF CITIES AND TOWNS

- OVER 3,000,000
- 1,000,000 - 2,999,999
- 500,000 - 999,999
- 100,000 - 499,999
- UNDER 100,000

Europe

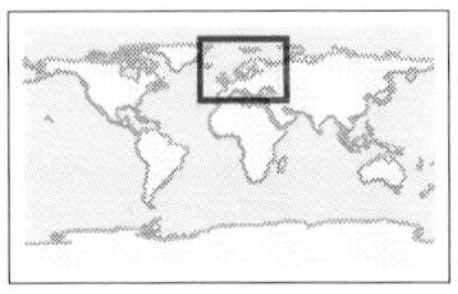

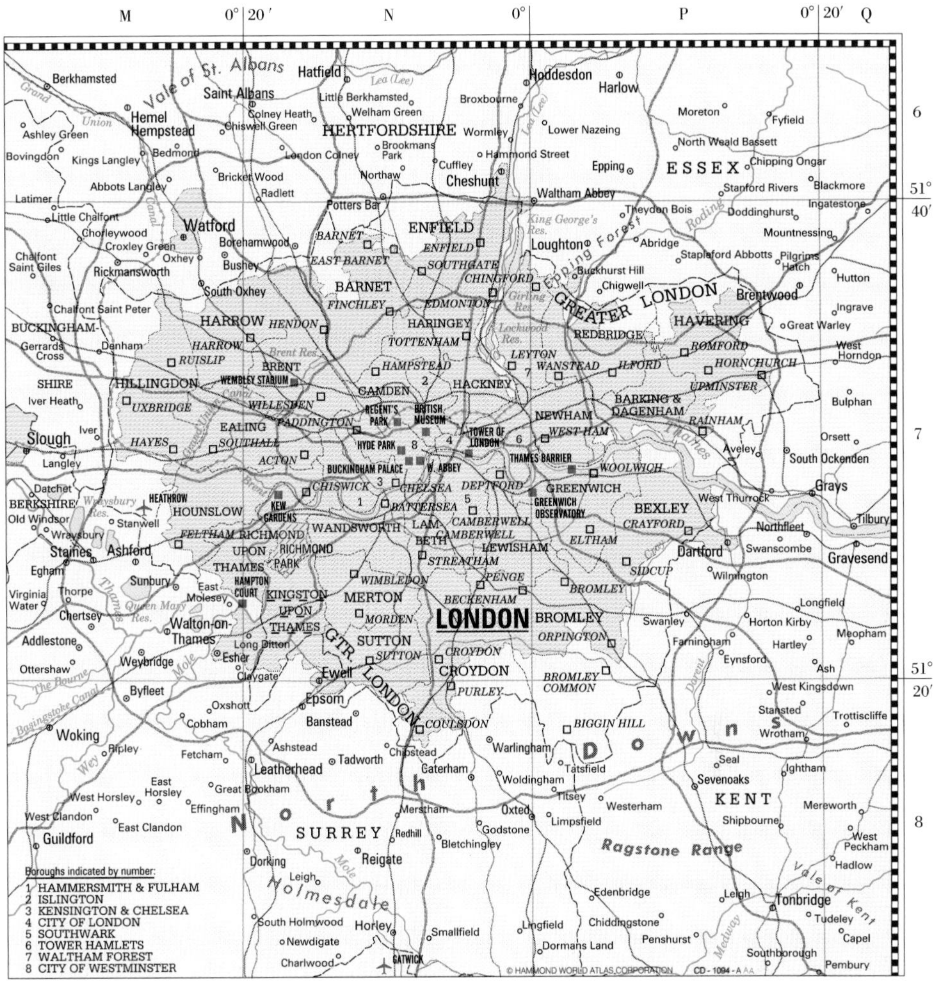

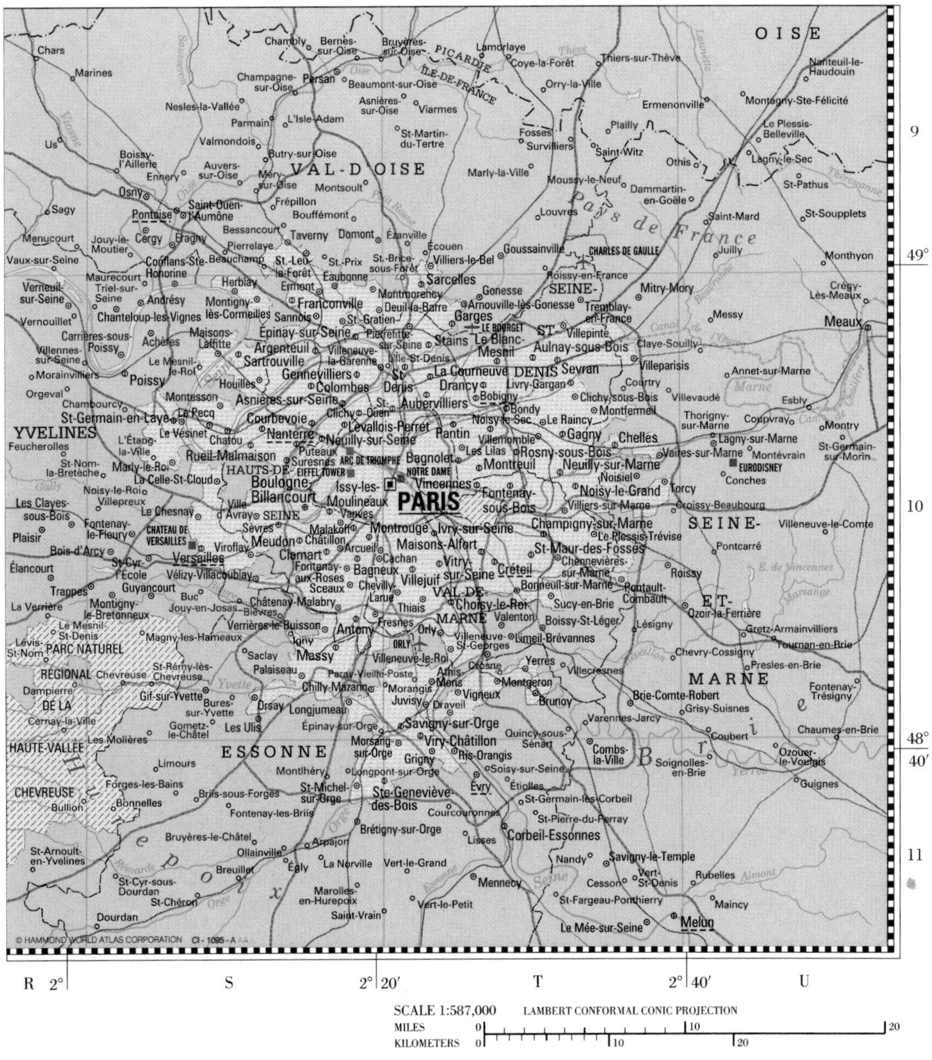

SCALE 1:587,000 LAMBERT CONFORMAL CONIC PROJECTION

MILES 0 10 20

KILOMETERS 0 10 20

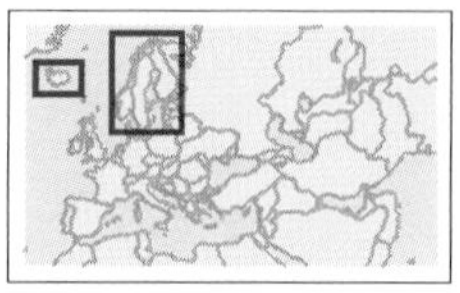

Scandinavia and Finland, Iceland

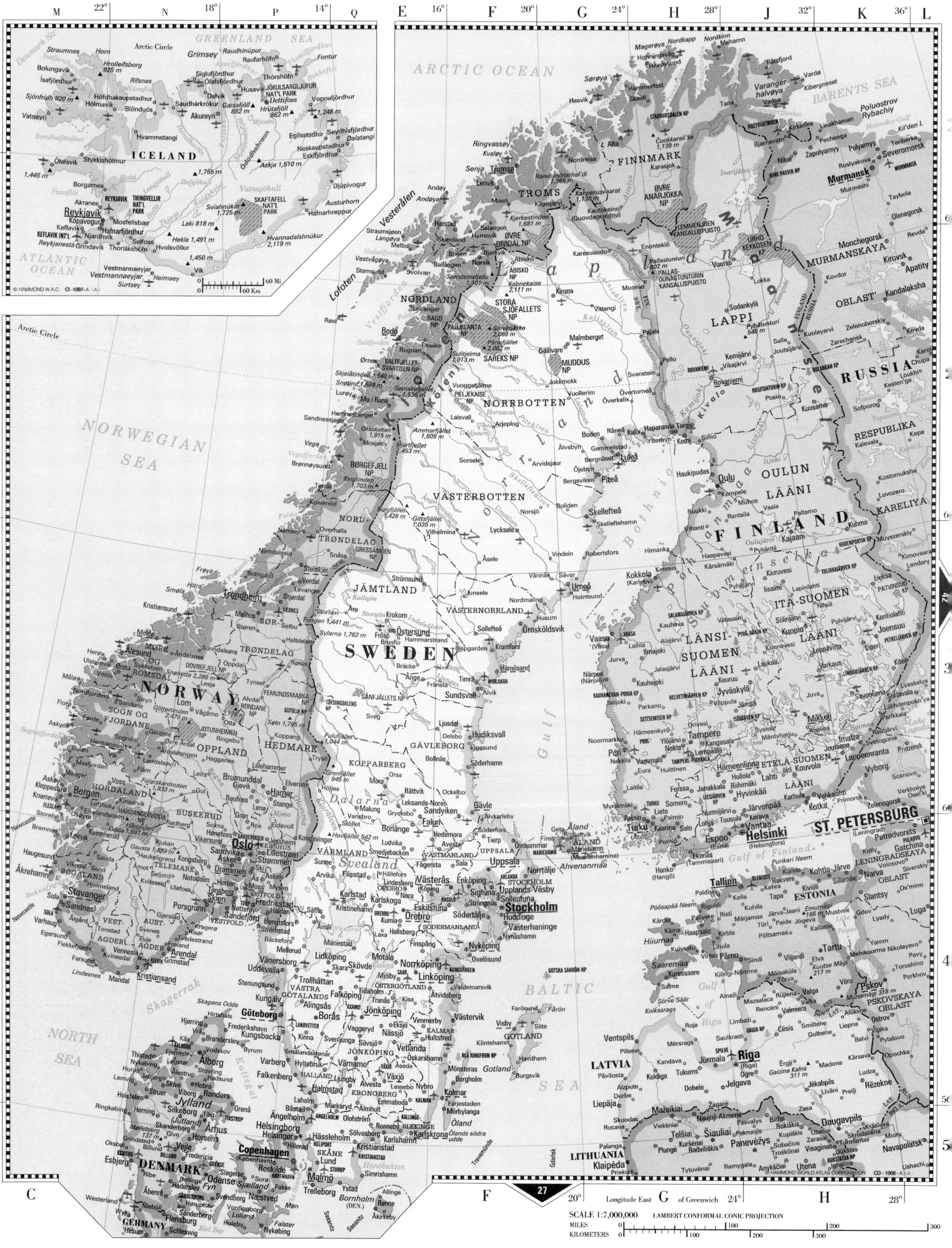

United Kingdom, Ireland

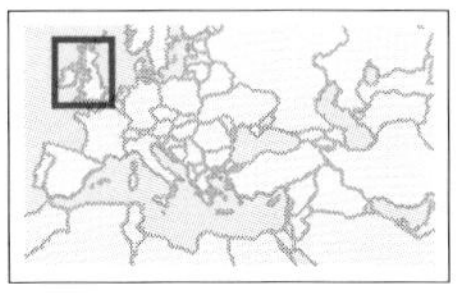

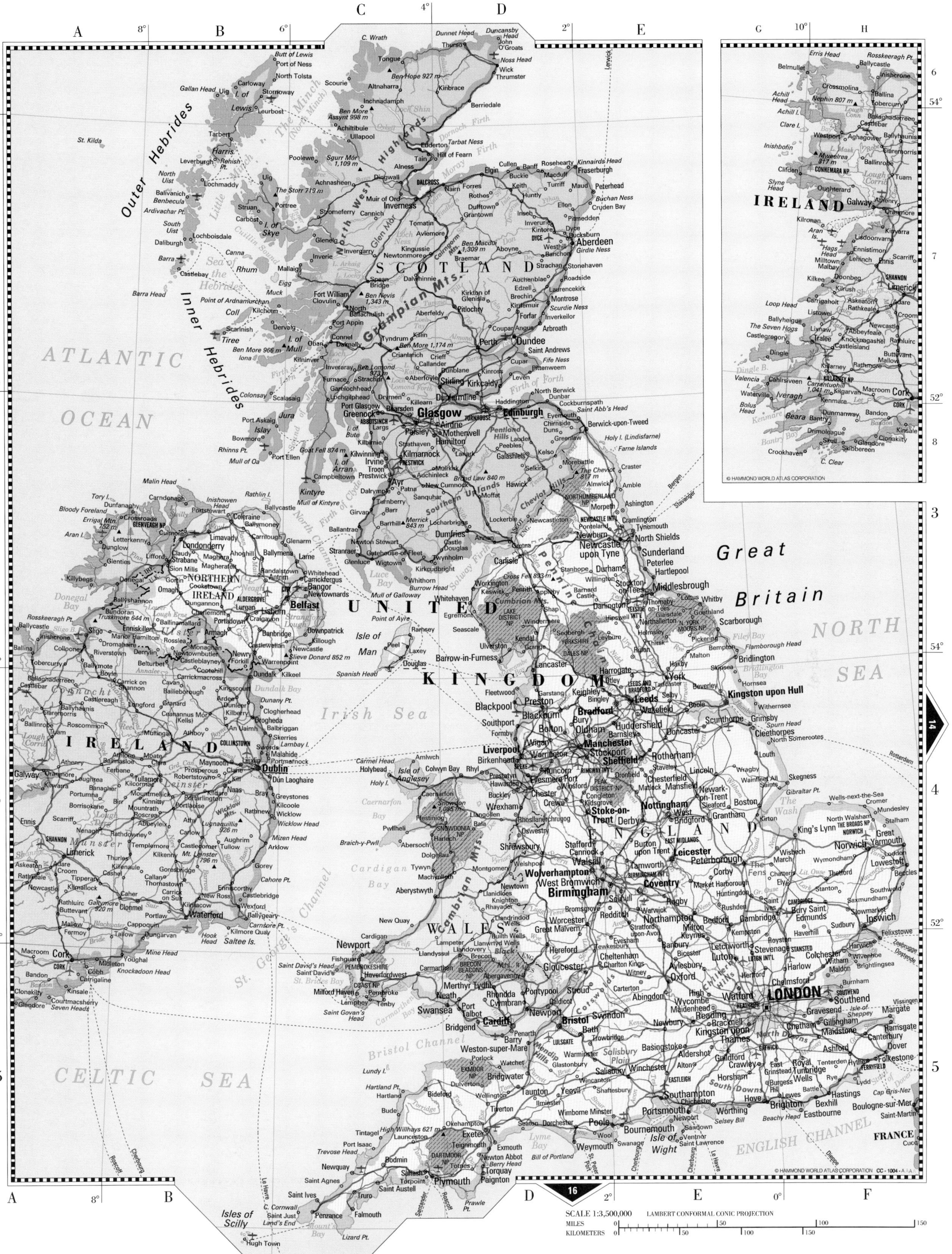

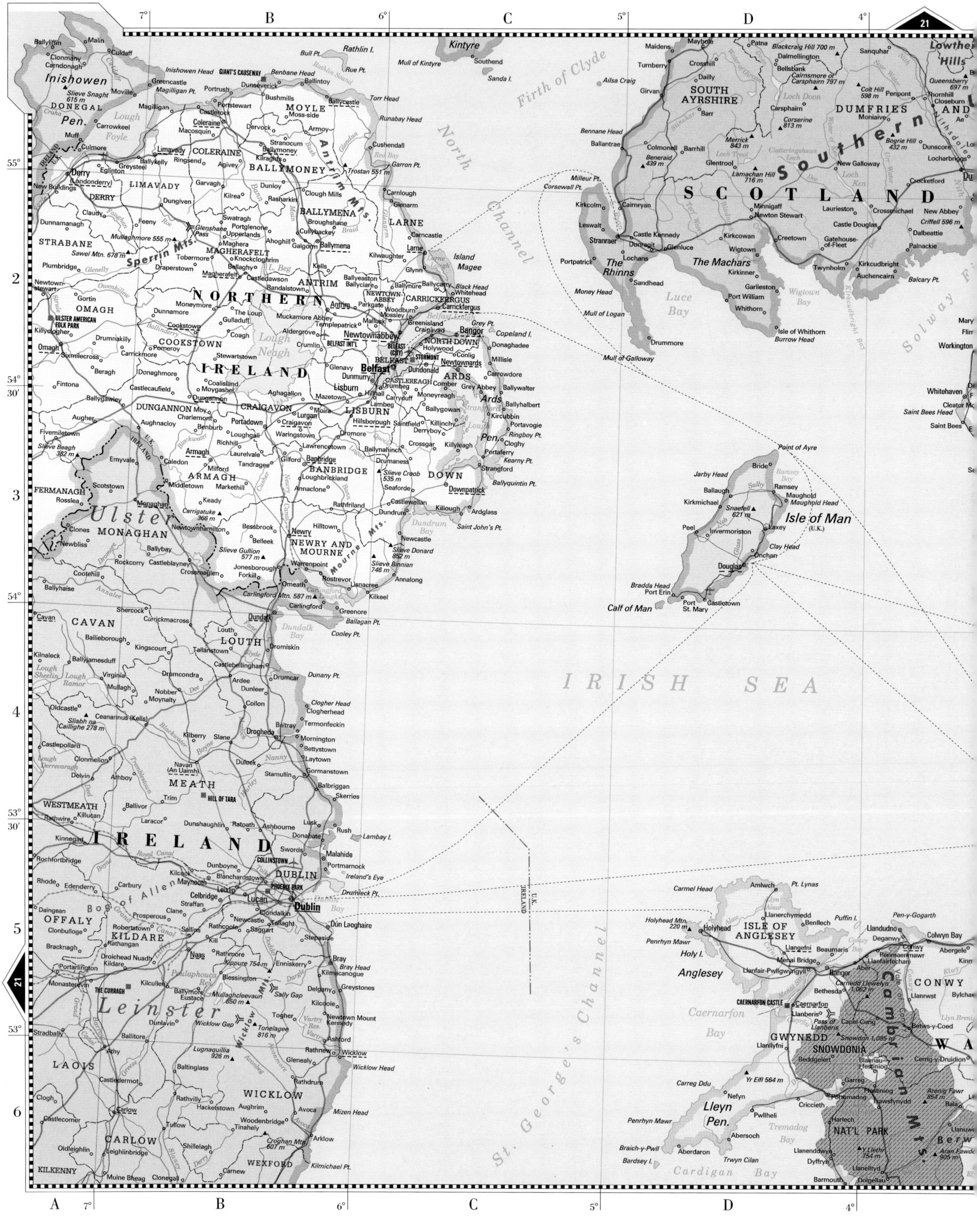

21
7°
B
6°
C
5°
D
4°
Inishowen
DONEGAL
Malin
Culdaff
Ballyliffin
Clonmany
Carndonagh
Slieve Snaght 615 m
Moville
Greencastle
Magilligan Pt.
Inishowen Head
GIANT'S CAUSEWAY
Benbane Head
Rathlin I.
Bull Pt.
Rue Pt.
Mull of Kintyre
Kintyre
Southend
Sanda I.
Firth of Clyde
Ailsa Craig
Portrush
Dunseverick
Ballintoy
Bushmills
Portstewart
Castlerock
Coleraine
MOYLE
Ballycastle
Torr Head
Runabay Head
Moss-side
Armoy
Cushendall
Red Bay
Garron Pt.
Trostan 551 m
Antrim Mts.
Lough Foyle
Pen.
Carrowkeel
Muff
Culmore
Derry (Londonderry)
Eglinton
Greysteel
Limavady
Ballykelly
COLERAINE
Ringsend
Aghadowey
Macosquin
Dervock
Stranocum
Ballymoney
Kilraghts
BALLYMONEY
LIMAVADY
DERRY
New Buildings
Garvagh
Kilrea
Dunloy
Rasharkin
Clough Mills
BALLYMENA
Carnlough
Glenarm
LARNE
Dungiven
Claudy
Feeny
Glenshane Pass
Swatragh
Portglenone
Upperlands
Broughshane
Cullybackey
Ballymena
Ahoghill
Galgorm
Dunnamanagh
STRABANE
Mullaghmore 555 m
Sawel Mtn. 678 m
Sperrin Mts.
Maghera
MAGHERAFELT
Tobermore
Knockcloghrim
Carncastle
Larne
Island Magee
Larne Lough
Kilwaughter
Plumbridge
Draperstown
Magherafelt
Bellaghy
Castledawson
Randalstown
Kells
ANTRIM
Ballyeaston
Ballyclare
Glynn
Ballycarry
Black Head
Whitehead
Newtownstewart
Gortin
OMAGH
ULSTER AMERICAN FOLK PARK
Killyclogher
Omagh
NORTHERN
Moneymore
The Loup
Dunnamore
Gulladuff
Antrim
Muckamore Abbey
Templepatrick
NEWTOWNABBEY
Parkgate
CARRICKFERGUS
Carrickfergus
Woodburn
Mossley
Belfast Lough
Greenisland
Newtownabbey
Cookstown
COOKSTOWN
Drumnakilly
Pomeroy
Coagh
Lough Neagh
Aldergrove
Crumlin
Mallusk
BELFAST INT'L
BELFAST (CITY)
Craigavad
Bangor
Holywood
NORTH DOWN
STORMONT
Grey Pt.
Copeland I.
Donaghadee
Sixmilecross
Carrickmore
Beragh
IRELAND
Stewartstown
Glenavy
Dunmurry
Belfast
BELFAST
Dundonald
Conlig
Newtownards
Millisle
Fintona
Castlecaufield
Coalisland
Moygashel
Dungannon
Aghagallon
Lisburn
CASTLEREAGH
Comber
ARDS
Carrowdore
Ballywalter
Ballygawley
DUNGANNON
Moy
Charlemont
CRAIGAVON
Mazetown
Hillhall
Drumbeg
Carryduff
Moneyreagh
Grey Abbey
Ards
Ballyhalbert
Augher
Aughnacloy
Benburb
Portadown
Lurgan
Moira
Lambeg
LISBURN
Hillsborough
Ballygowan
Strangford Lough
Kircubbin
Portavogie
Fivemiletown
Loughgall
Craigavon
Waringstown
Saintfield
Killinchy
Derryboy
Ringboy Pt.
Pen.
Slieve Beagh 382 m
Richhill
Dromore
Crossgar
Killyleagh
Cloghy
Armagh
Laurelvale
Lawrencetown
Ballynahinch
Portaferry
Emyvale
Caledon
Tandragee
Gilford
Banbridge
Drumaness
Kearney Pt.
Milford
ARMAGH
Loughbrickland
BANBRIDGE
Slieve Croob 535 m
Strangford
Ballyquintin Pt.
FERMANAGH
Scotstown
Middletown
Markethill
Annaclone
Seaforde
DOWN
Downpatrick
Rosslea
Monaghan
Keady
Rathfriland
Castlewellan
Killough
Ulster
Carrigatuke 366 m
Dundrum
Ardglass
MONAGHAN
Clones
Newtownhamilton
Bessbrook
Hilltown
Dundrum Bay
St. John's Pt.
Newbliss
Ballybay
Belleek
Newry
Mourne Mts.
Newcastle
Rockcorry
Castleblayney
Slieve Gullion 577 m
NEWRY AND MOURNE
Slieve Donard 852 m
Cootehill
Crossmaglen
Jonesborough
Warrenpoint
Slieve Binnian 746 m
Ballyhaise
Forkill
Rostrevor
Annalong
Omeath
Lisnacree
Carlingford Mtn. 587 m
Carlingford Lough
Kilkeel
Carlingford
Greenore
Shercock
Cavan
CAVAN
Carrickmacross
Dundalk
Ballagan Pt.
Cooley Pt.
Dundalk Bay
Bailieborough
Kingscourt
Louth
LOUTH
Kilnaleck
Ballyjamesduff
Tallanstown
Dromiskin
Lough Sheelin
Lough Ramor
Virginia
Castlebellingham
Mullagh
Drumcondra
Drumcar
Dunany Pt.
Nobber
Ardee
Moynalty
Dunleer
Collon
Clogher Head
Clogherhead
Oldcastle
Ceanannus (Kells)
Sliabh na Cailliqhe 278 m
Kilberry
Slane
Drogheda
Baltray
Termonfeckin
Castlepollard
Mornington
Bettystown
Lough Derravaragh
Clonmellon
Navan (An Uaimh)
Duleek
Laytown
Delvin
Athboy
MEATH
Stamullin
Gormanstown
HILL OF TARA
Balbriggan
Trim
Skerries
WESTMEATH
Ballivor
Rathwire
Killucan
Laracor
Dunshaughlin
Ratoath
Ashbourne
Lusk
Rush
Lambay I.
Donabate
Kinnegad
IRELAND
Swords
Malahide
Rochfortbridge
Royal Canal
COLLINSTOWN
Portmarnock
Dunboyne
Kilcock
Blanchardstown
DUBLIN
Ireland's Eye
Rhode
Edenderry
Carbury
Maynooth
PHOENIX PARK
Bog of Allen
Celbridge
Leixlip
Lucan
Drumleck Pt.
Straffan
Dublin Bay
Daingean
OFFALY
Prosperous
Clane
Newcastle
Clondalkin
Dublin
Clonbullogue
Robertstown
KILDARE
Sallins
Rathcoole
Tallaght
Saggart
Dún Laoghaire
Rathangan
Grand Canal
Stepaside
Bracknagh
Droichead Nuadh
Naas
Rathmore
Kippure 754 m
Enniskerry
Bray
Bray Head
Portarlington
Kildare
Pollaphouca Res.
Blessington
Kilmacanogue
Monasterevin
THE CURRAGH
Kilcullen
Ballymore Eustace
Delgany
Greystones
Leinster
Mullaghcleevaun 850 m
Sally Gap
Kilcoole
Wicklow Mts.
Dunlavin
Wicklow Gap
Togher
Vartry Res.
Newtown Mount Kennedy
Stradbally
Ballitore
Tonelagee 816 m
Ashford
Athy
Lugnaquillia 926 m
Rathnew
Wicklow
Wicklow Head
LAOIS
Baltinglass
Glenealy
Castledermot
Rathdrum
Rathvilly
Hacketstown
Aughrim
WICKLOW
Avoca
Mizen Head
Clogh
Carlow
Castlecomer
Tullow
Woodenbridge
Tinahely
CARLOW
Croghan Mtn 607 m
Arklow
Oldleighlin
Leighlinbridge
Shillelagh
KILKENNY
Muine Bheag
Clonegall
Carnew
WEXFORD
Kilmichael Pt.
North Channel
IRISH SEA
St. George's Channel
U.K.
IRELAND
Maidens
Maybole
Patna
Blackcraig Hill 700 m
Dalmellington
Sanquhar
Lowther Hills
Turnberry
Crosshill
Bellsbank
Dailly
Cairnsmore of Carsphairn 797 m
Queensberry 697 m
Girvan
SOUTH AYRSHIRE
Loch Doon
Carsphairn
Colt Hill 598 m
Penpont
Thornhill
Closeburn
DUMFRIES
Barr
Moniaive
Corserine 813 m
Bennane Head
Ballantrae
Colmonell
Barrhill
Merrick 843 m
Southern
Bogrie Hill 432 m
Dunscore
Locharbriggs
Beneraid 439 m
Glentrool
Lamachan Hill 716 m
New Galloway
Milleur Pt.
Corsewall Pt.
SCOTLAND
Crocketford
Kirkcolm
Cairnryan
Minnigaff
Newton Stewart
Laurieston
Crossmichael
New Abbey
Leswalt
Castle Kennedy
Castle Douglas
Criffell 596 m
Stranraer
Dunragit
Glenluce
Kirkcowan
Creetown
Gatehouse-of-Fleet
Dalbeattie
Portpatrick
The Rhinns
Lochans
Wigtown
The Machars
Palnackie
Sandhead
Kirkinner
Twynholm
Kirkcudbright
Auchencairn
Balcary Pt.
Money Head
Luce Bay
Garlieston
Wigtown Bay
Mull of Logan
Port William
Whithorn
Isle of Whithorn
Burrow Head
Drummore
Mull of Galloway
Solway
Workington
Whitehaven
Saint Bees Head
Saint Bees
Point of Ayre
Jarby Head
Bride
Ramsey Bay
Ballaugh
Ramsey
Kirkmichael
Maughold
Maughold Head
Snaefell 621 m
Isle of Man (U.K.)
Peel
Invermoriston
Laxey
Clay Head
Onchan
Douglas
Bradda Head
Port Erin
Calf of Man
Port St. Mary
Castletown
Carmel Head
Amlwch
Pt. Lynas
Holyhead Mtn. 220 m
Holyhead
Llanerchymedd
Benllech
Puffin I.
Pen-y-Gogarth
Llandudno
Colwyn Bay
ISLE OF ANGLESEY
Penrhyn Mawr
Holy I.
Llangefni
Beaumaris
Deganwy
Conwy
Penmaenmawr
Llanfairfechan
Abergele
Menai Bridge
Anglesey
Llanfair-Pwllgwyngyll
Bangor
Aber
Bethesda
Carnedd Llewelyn 1,062 m
CONWY
Llanrwst
CAERNARFON CASTLE
Caernarfon
Llanberis
Pass of Llanberis
Capel-Curig
Betws-y-Coed
Cambrian Mts.
Caernarfon Bay
GWYNEDD
Snowdon 1,085 m
SNOWDONIA
Llanllyfni
Beddgelert
Blaenau-Ffestiniog
Cerrig-y-Druidion
Yr Eifl 564 m
Carreg Ddu
Garreg
Nefyn
Ffestiniog
Porthmadog
Trawsfynydd
Arenig Fawr 854 m
Bala
Lleyn Pen.
Pwllheli
Criccieth
Penrhyn Mawr
Tremadog Bay
Harlech
NAT'L PARK
Abersoch
Braich-y-Pwll
Aberdaron
Trwyn Cilan
Llanenddwyn
Dyffryn
Y Llethr 754 m
Aran Fawddwy 905 m
Bardsey I.
Cardigan Bay
Llanelltyd
Barmouth
Dolgellau
A
7°
B
6°
C
5°
D
4°

Northeastern Ireland, Northern England and Wales

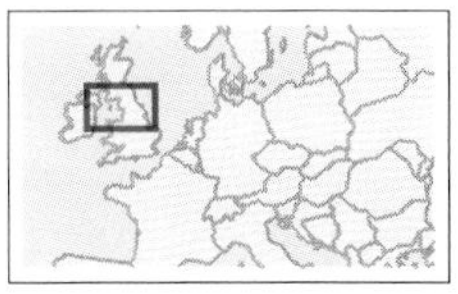

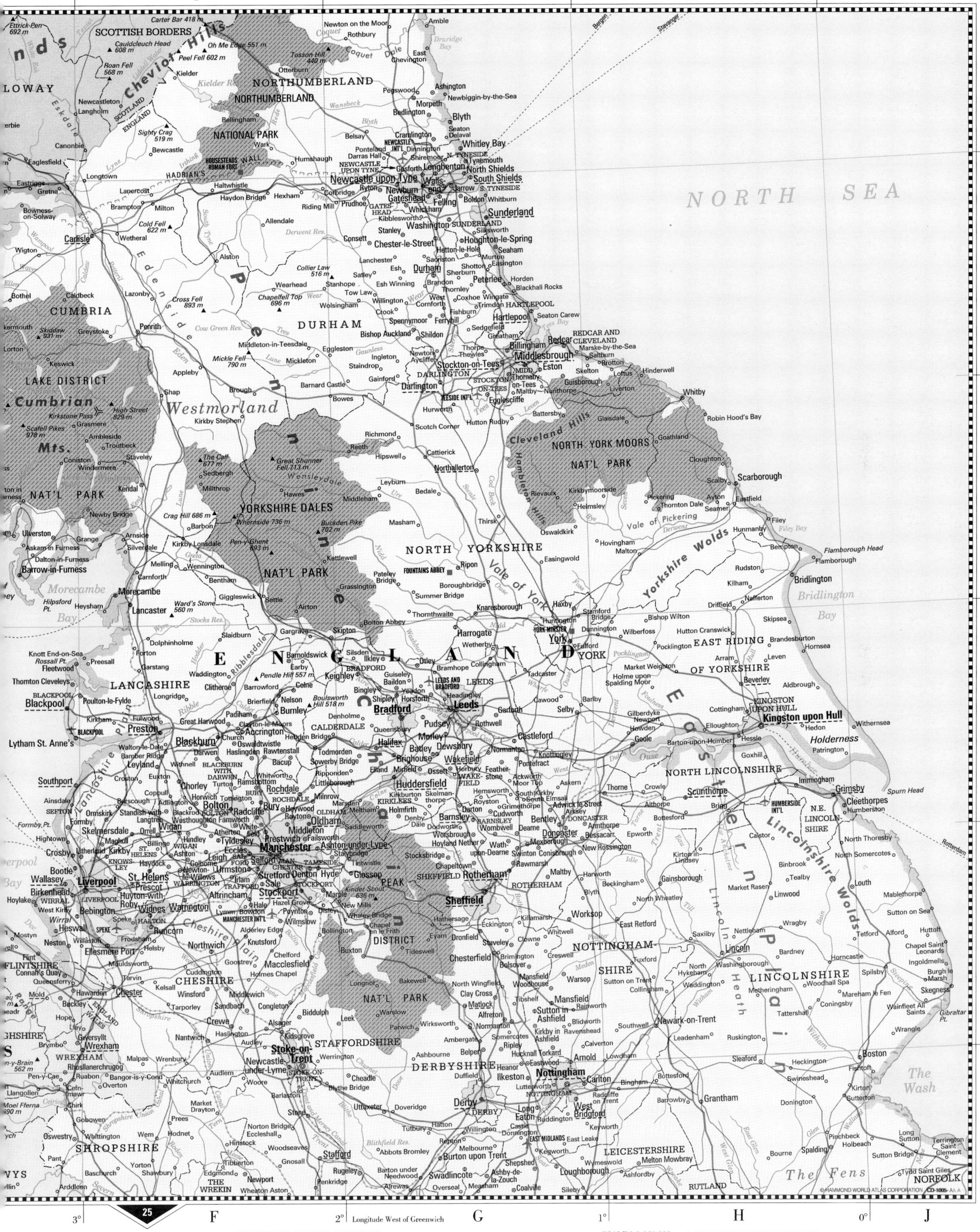

25

POPULATION OF CITIES AND TOWNS

■ OVER 2,000,000 ◉ 500,000 - 999,999 ● 100,000 - 249,999 ⊙ 10,000 - 29,999

□ 1,000,000 - 1,999,999 ◎ 250,000 - 499,999 ⊕ 30,000 - 99,999 ○ UNDER 10,000

SCALE 1:1,170,000 LAMBERT CONFORMAL CONIC PROJECTION

MILES 0 10 20 30 40 50

KILOMETERS 0 10 20 30 40 50

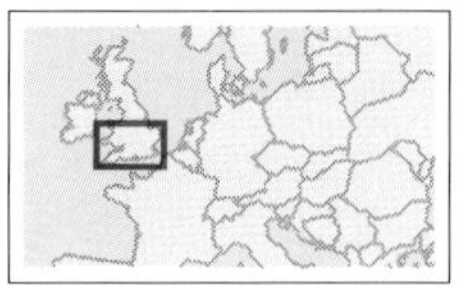

Southern England and Wales

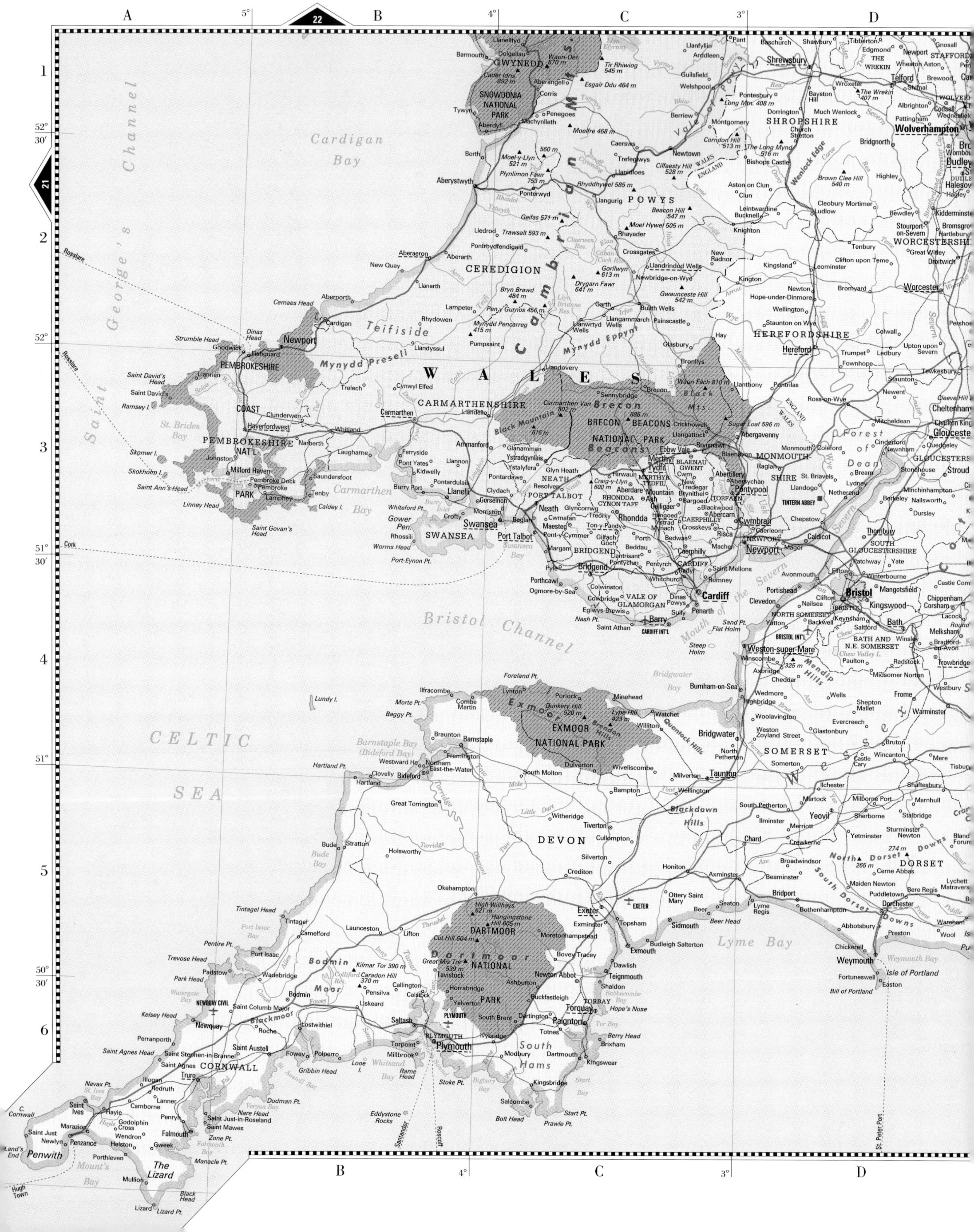

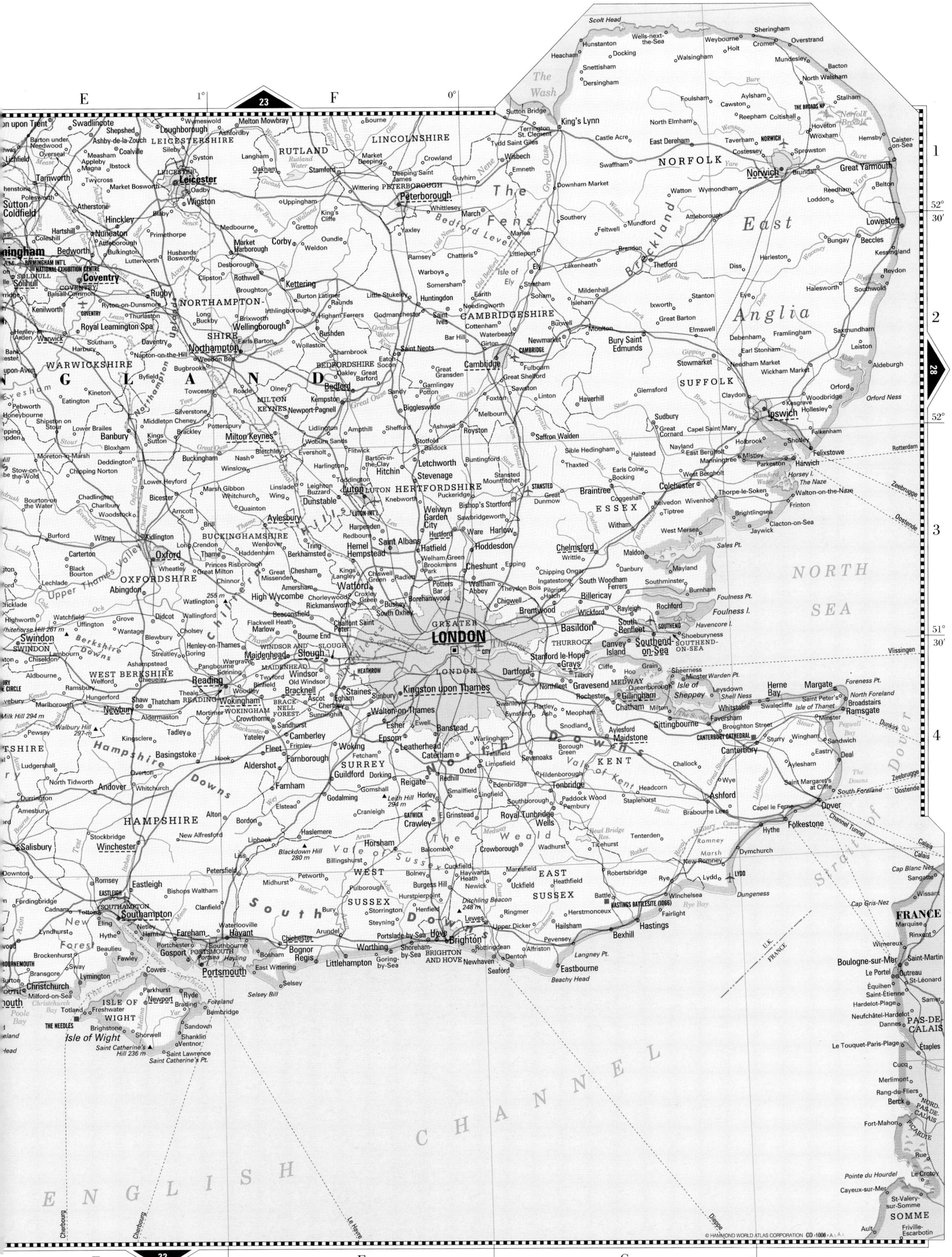

E F 0° G 1°

1° Longitude West of Greenwich

POPULATION OF CITIES AND TOWNS

- ■ OVER 2,000,000
- □ 1,000,000 - 1,999,999
- ⦿ 500,000 - 999,999
- ◎ 250,000 - 499,999
- ⊕ 100,000 - 249,999
- ⊕ 30,000 - 99,999
- ⊙ 10,000 - 29,999
- ○ UNDER 10,000

SCALE 1:1,170,000 LAMBERT CONFORMAL CONIC PROJECTION

MILES 0 10 20 30 40 50

KILOMETERS 0 10 20 30 40 50

BRANDENBURG
BERLIN
Potsdam
Köpenick
TEGEL
SCHÖNEFELD
SCHLOSS SANSSOUCI
© HAMMOND W.A.C.
NORTH SEA
North Frisian Islands
East Frisian Islands
West Frisian Islands
Helgoländer Bucht
DENMARK
Copenhagen
Great Britain
U.K.
NETHERLANDS
Amsterdam
The Hague
Rotterdam
BELGIUM
Brussels
LUXEMBOURG
PARIS
FRANCE
GERMANY
Hamburg
Bremen
Hannover
Düsseldorf
Cologne
Frankfurt am Main
Stuttgart
Munich
NIEDERSACHSEN
NORDRHEIN-WESTFALEN
HESSEN
RHEINLAND-PFALZ
SAARLAND
BADEN-WÜRTTEMBERG
BAYERN
THÜRINGEN
SACHSEN-ANHALT
SCHLESWIG-HOLSTEIN
MECKLENBURG-VORPOMMERN
PICARDIE
CHAMPAGNE-ARDENNE
LORRAINE
ALSACE
BOURGOGNE
FRANCHE-COMTÉ
CENTRE
ILE-DE-FRANCE
NORD-PAS-DE-CALAIS
SWITZERLAND
AUSTRIA
Longitude East of Greenwich

20
25
32
33

North Central Europe

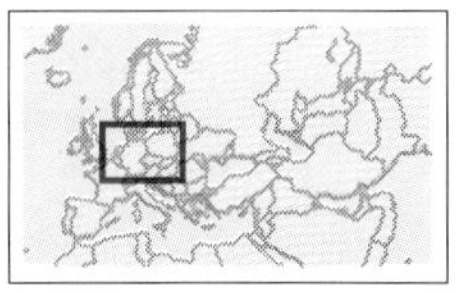

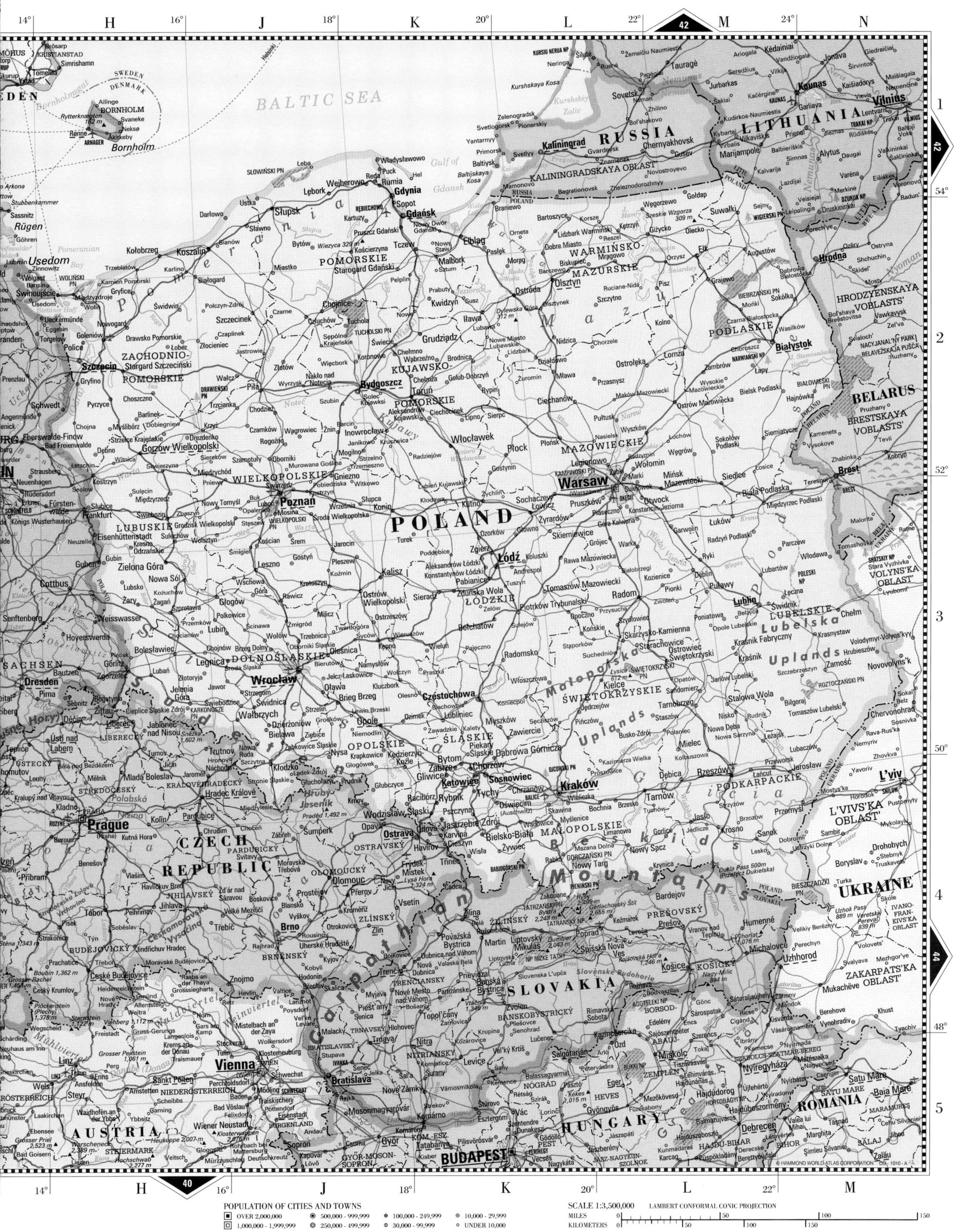

POPULATION OF CITIES AND TOWNS

OVER 2,000,000	1,000,000 - 1,999,999
500,000 - 999,999	250,000 - 499,999
100,000 - 249,999	30,000 - 99,999
10,000 - 29,999	UNDER 10,000

SCALE 1:3,500,000 LAMBERT CONFORMAL CONIC PROJECTION

MILES 0 50 100 150

KILOMETERS 0 50 100 150

Netherlands, Northwestern Germany

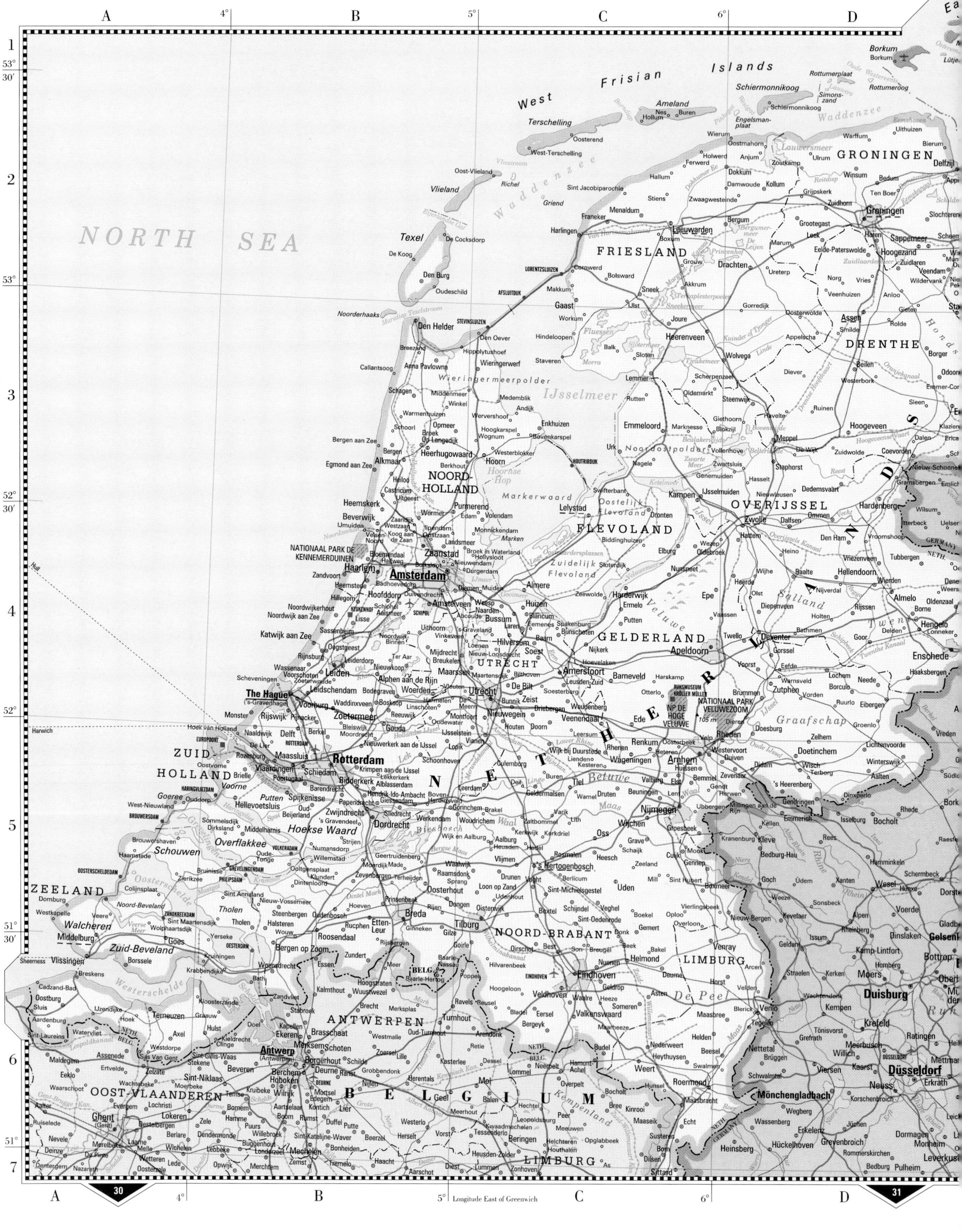

30
31

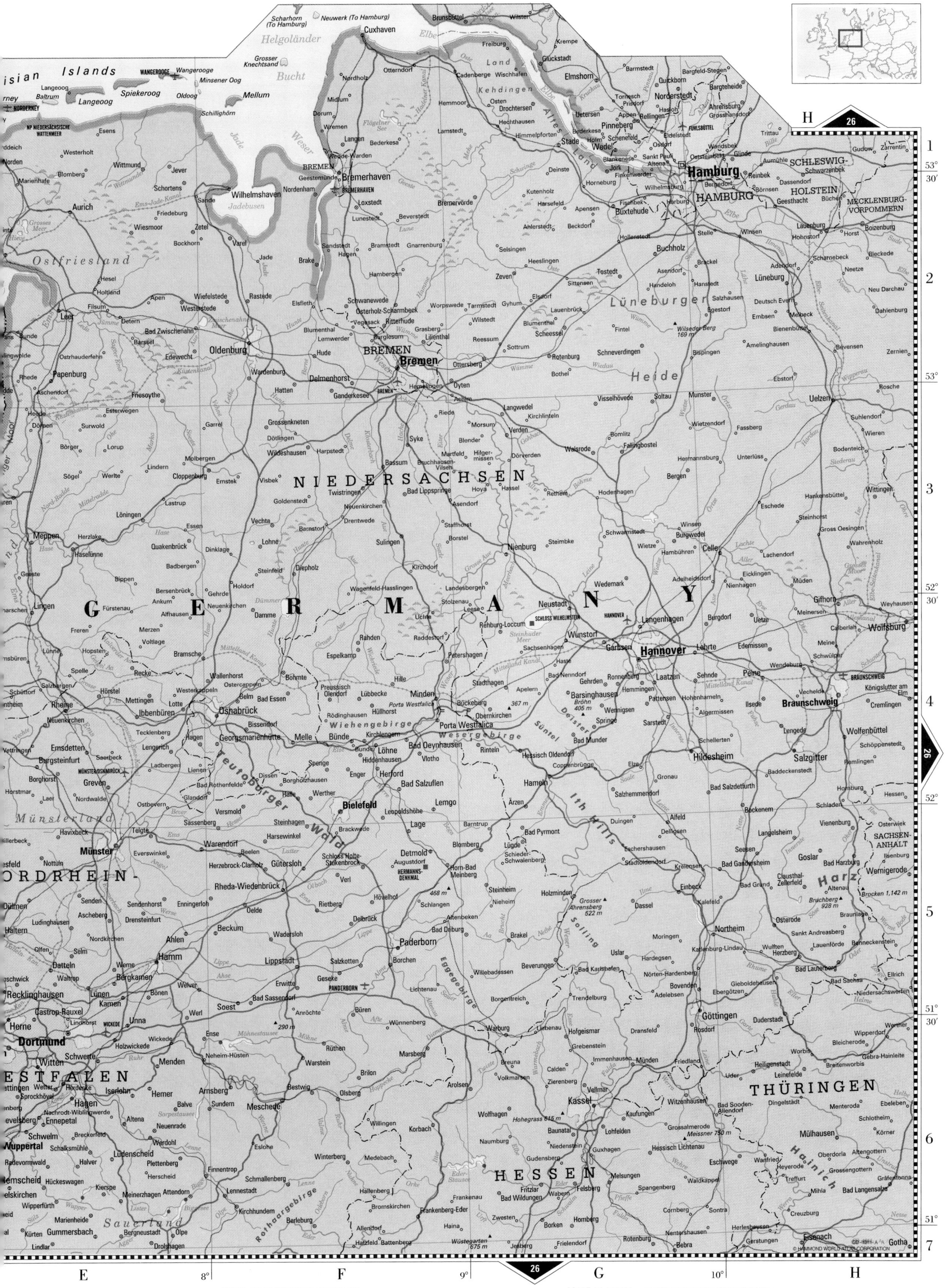

POPULATION OF CITIES AND TOWNS

- OVER 2,000,000
- 1,000,000 - 1,999,999
- 500,000 - 999,999
- 250,000 - 499,999
- 100,000 - 249,999
- 30,000 - 99,999
- 10,000 - 29,999
- UNDER 10,000

SCALE 1:1,170,000 LAMBERT CONFORMAL CONIC PROJECTION

MILES 0 10 20 30 40 50

KILOMETERS 0 10 20 30 40 50

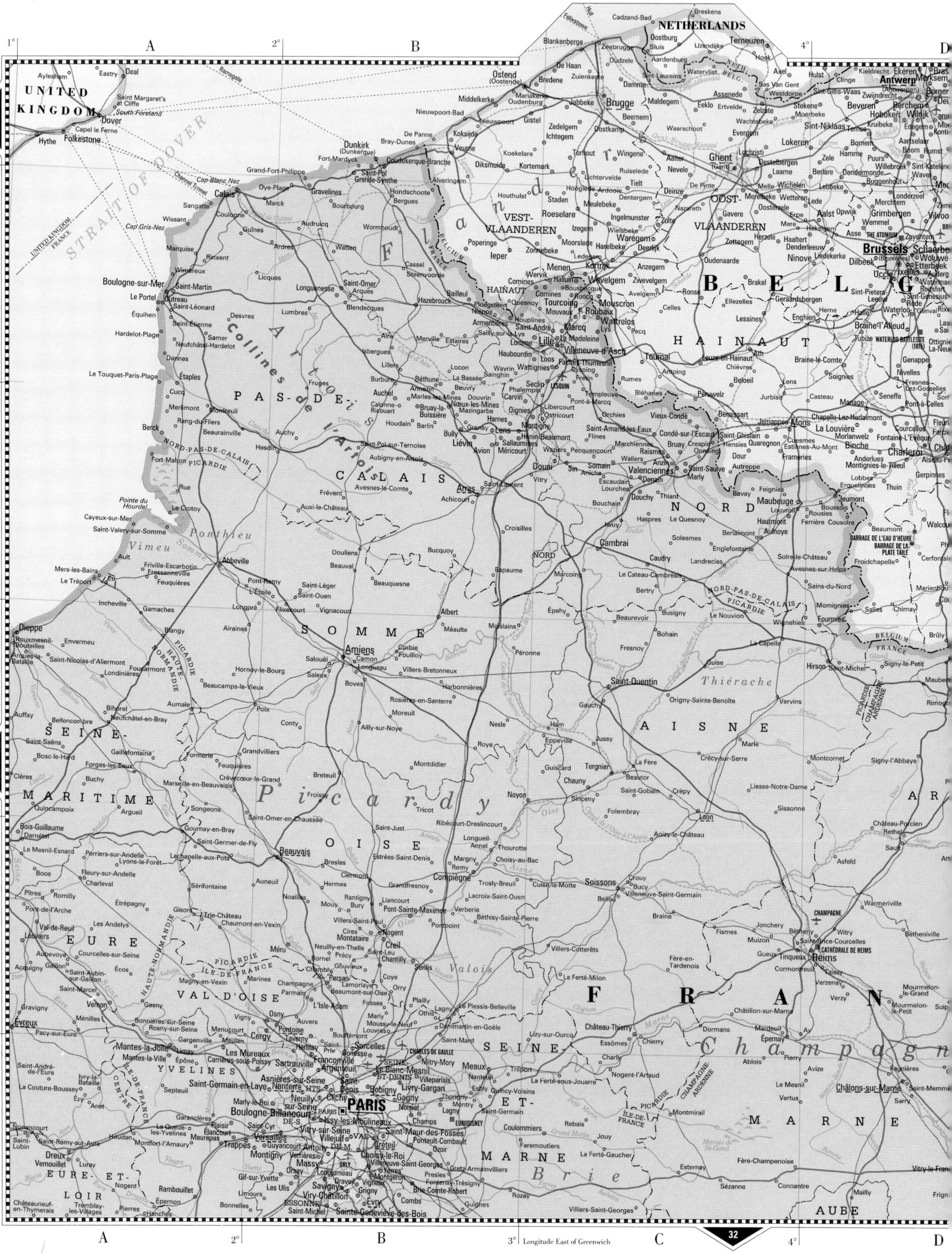
NETHERLANDS
UNITED KINGDOM
STRAIT OF DOVER
BELGIUM
B E L G
FRANCE
F R A N
Flandre
VEST-VLAANDEREN
OOST-VLAANDEREN
HAINAUT
NORD
PAS-DE-CALAIS
Artois
Collines de l'Artois
SOMME
Picardy
AISNE
OISE
SEINE-MARITIME
EURE
VAL-D'OISE
YVELINES
SEINE-ET-MARNE
EURE-ET-LOIR
ESSONNE
MARNE
AUBE
Champagne
Brie
Valois
Thiérache
Ponthieu
Vimeu
NORD-PAS-DE-CALAIS
PICARDIE
HAUTE-NORMANDIE
ÎLE-DE-FRANCE
CENTRE
CHAMPAGNE-ARDENNE
Dover
Folkestone
Hythe
Deal
Calais
Boulogne-sur-Mer
Dunkirk (Dunkerque)
Ostend (Oostende)
Brugge
Ghent (Gent)
Antwerp
Brussels (Bruxelles)
Lille
Roubaix
Tourcoing
Tournai
Mons
Charleroi
Valenciennes
Douai
Arras
Lens
Cambrai
Saint-Quentin
Abbeville
Amiens
Beauvais
Compiègne
Soissons
Laon
Reims
Châlons-sur-Marne
Épernay
Château-Thierry
Meaux
Dieppe
Le Tréport
Le Touquet-Paris-Plage
Étaples
Berck
Montreuil
Saint-Omer
Hazebrouck
Béthune
Maubeuge
Noyon
Senlis
Creil
Pontoise
Versailles
Saint-Denis
PARIS
Évreux
Dreux
Mantes-la-Jolie
Rambouillet
Évry
Melun
Sézanne
Longitude East of Greenwich
1° 2° 3° 4°
51° 50° 30′ 50° 49° 30′ 49°
A B C D
1 2 3 4 5 6
25
32
32

Belgium, Northern France, Western Germany

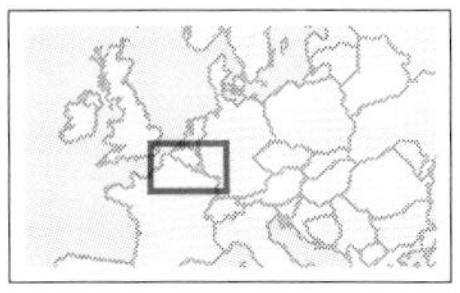

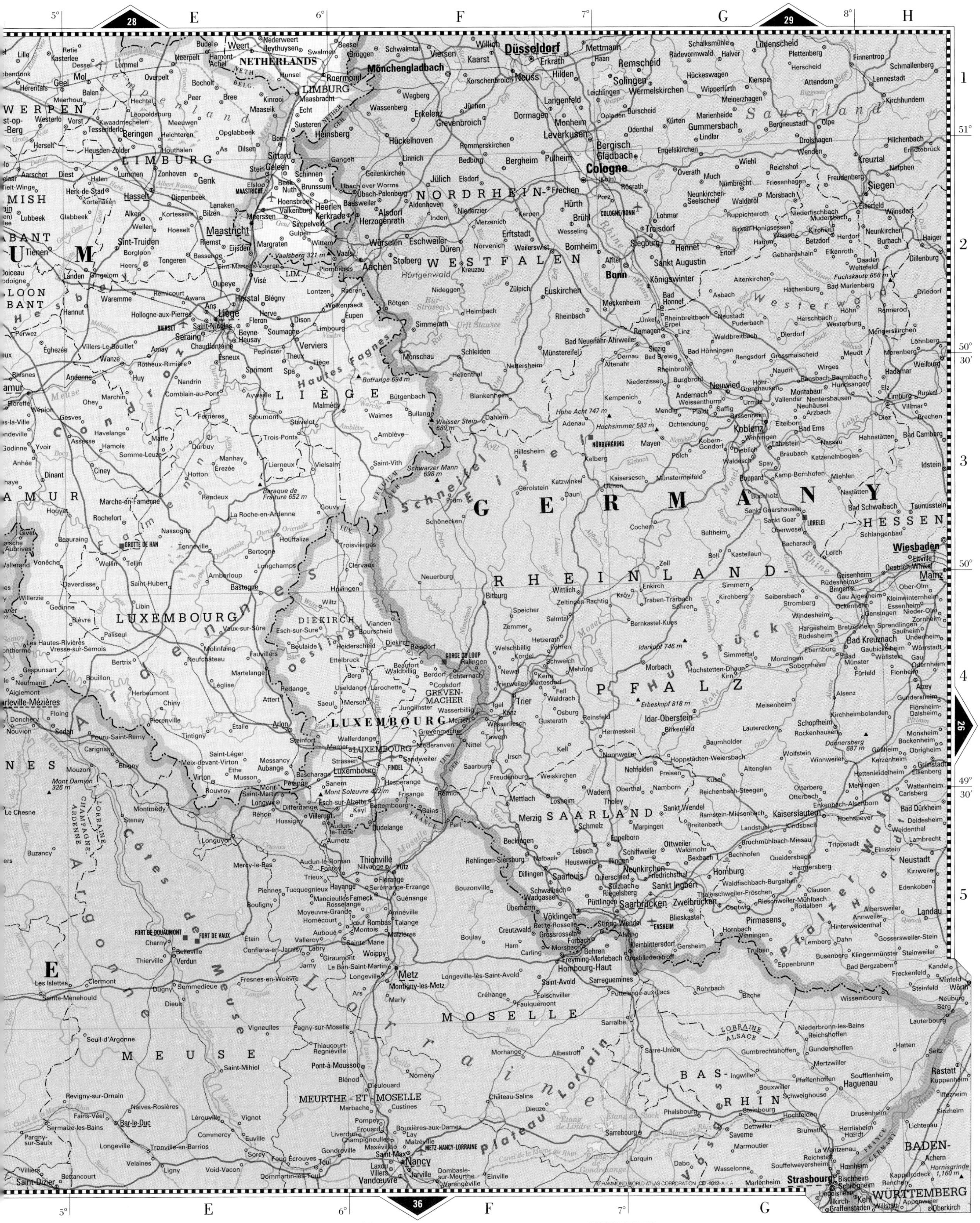

POPULATION OF CITIES AND TOWNS
- OVER 2,000,000
- 1,000,000 - 1,999,999
- 500,000 - 999,999
- 250,000 - 499,999
- 100,000 - 249,999
- 30,000 - 99,999
- 10,000 - 29,999
- UNDER 10,000

SCALE 1:1,170,000 LAMBERT CONFORMAL CONIC PROJECTION

MILES 0 10 20 30 40 50

KILOMETERS 0 10 20 30 40 50

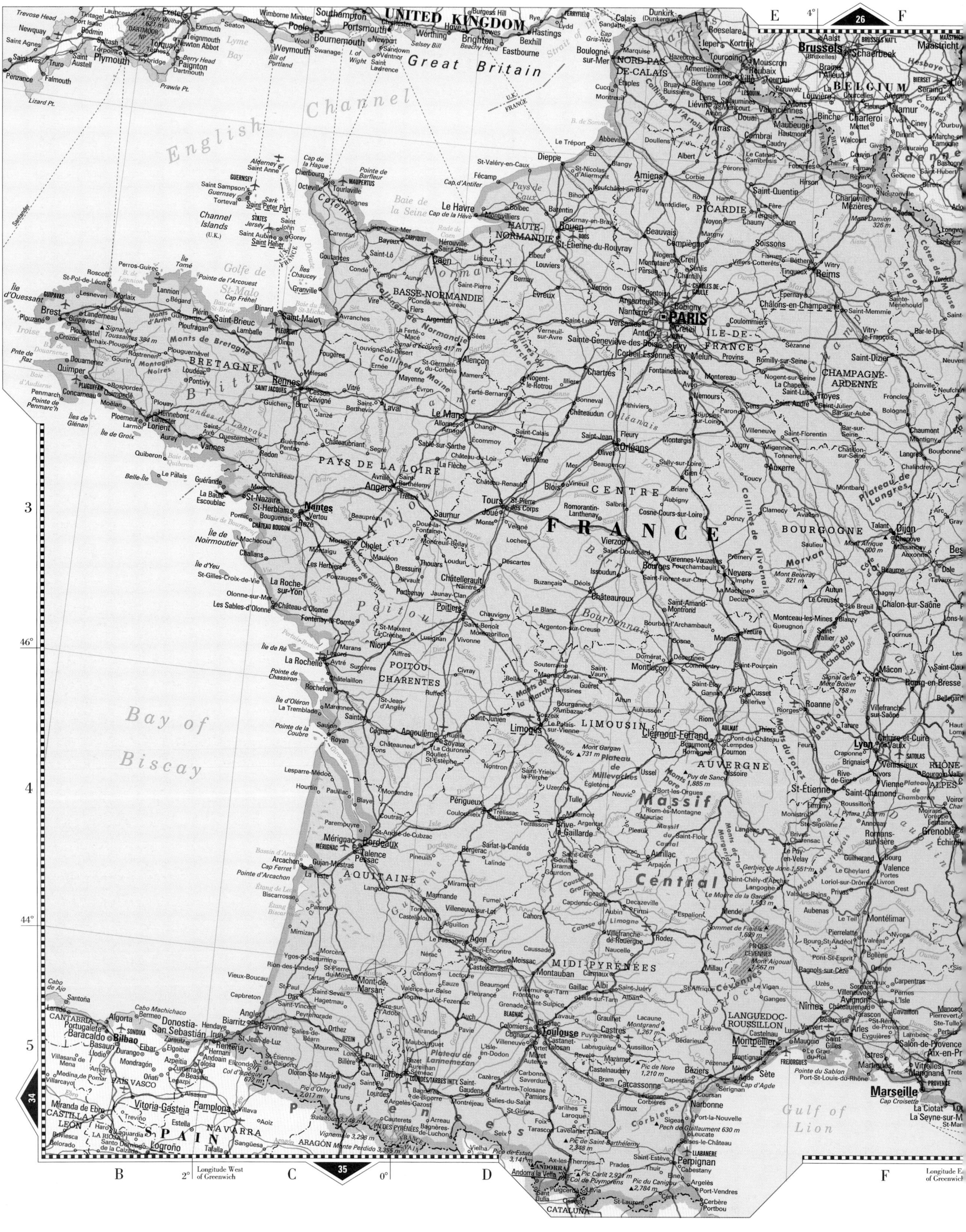
UNITED KINGDOM
Great Britain
English Channel
Channel Islands (U.K.)
Golfe de St-Malo
Bay of Biscay
Gulf of Lion
FRANCE
BELGIUM
SPAIN
Brussels
PARIS
Lyon
Marseille
Toulouse
Bordeaux
Nantes
Rennes
Lille
Orléans
Tours
Poitiers
Limoges
Clermont-Ferrand
Montpellier
Nîmes
Dijon
Reims
Amiens
Rouen
Le Havre
Caen
Cherbourg
Brest
Quimper
Lorient
Vannes
Saint-Nazaire
Angers
Le Mans
Chartres
La Rochelle
Rochefort
Angoulême
Périgueux
Bayonne
Biarritz
Pau
Tarbes
Lourdes
Perpignan
Narbonne
Carcassonne
Béziers
Sète
Arles
Avignon
Valence
Grenoble
Saint-Étienne
Vichy
Nevers
Bourges
Auxerre
Troyes
Chaumont
Calais
Dunkirk
Boulogne-sur-Mer
Dieppe
Plymouth
Portsmouth
Southampton
Brighton
Bilbao
Donostia-San Sebastián
Pamplona
Vitoria-Gasteiz
Logroño
Andorra la Vella
NORD-PAS-DE-CALAIS
PICARDIE
HAUTE-NORMANDIE
BASSE-NORMANDIE
BRETAGNE
PAYS DE LA LOIRE
CENTRE
ILE-DE-FRANCE
CHAMPAGNE-ARDENNE
BOURGOGNE
POITOU-CHARENTES
LIMOUSIN
AUVERGNE
AQUITAINE
MIDI-PYRÉNÉES
LANGUEDOC-ROUSSILLON
RHÔNE-ALPES
PROVENCE
Massif Central
Pyrenees
Cévennes
E
F
B
C
D
4°
2°
0°
Longitude West of Greenwich
Longitude East of Greenwich
46°
44°
3
4
5
26
34
35

West Central Europe

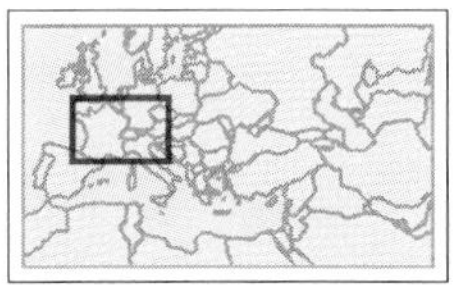

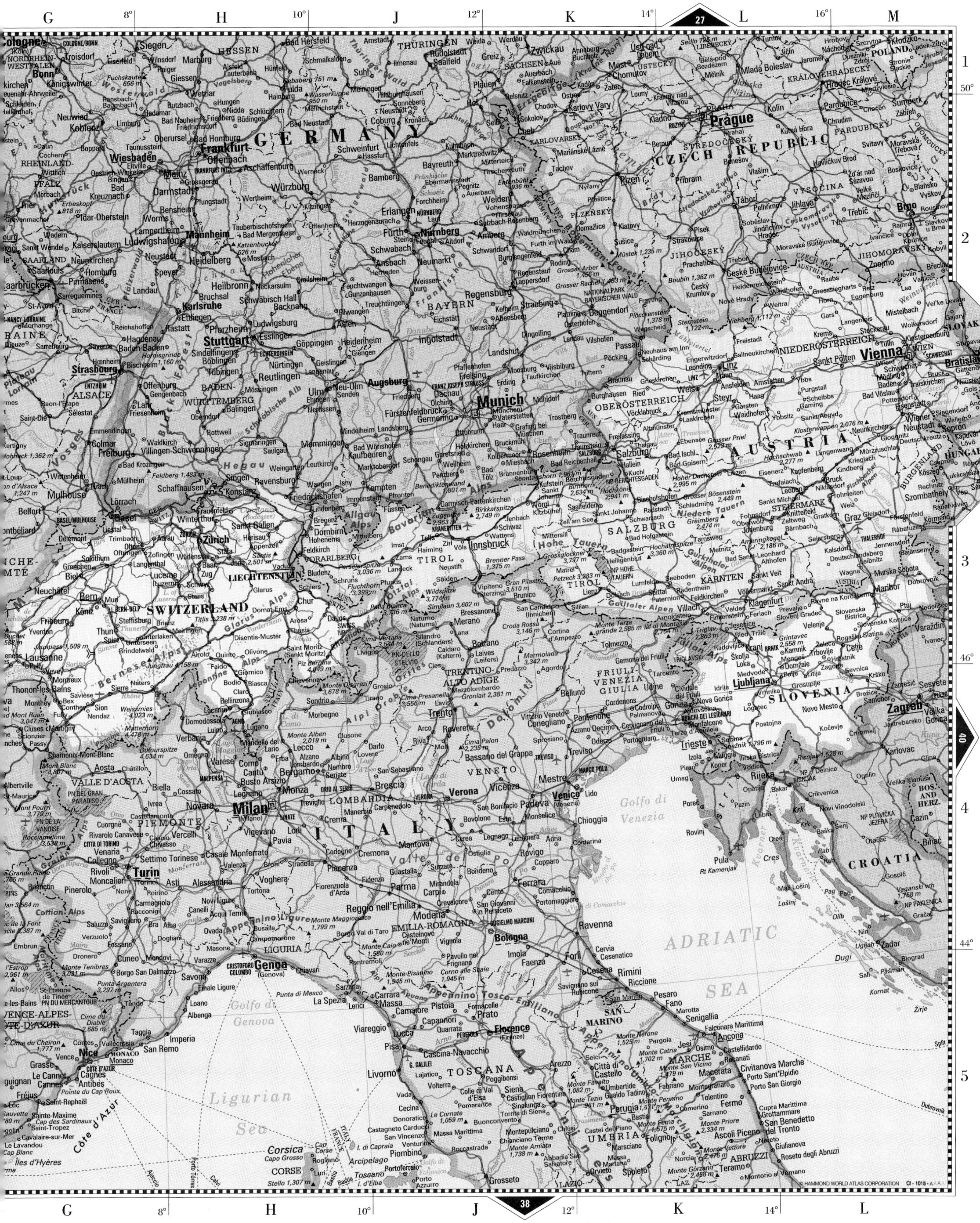

POPULATION OF CITIES AND TOWNS

- OVER 2,000,000
- 1,000,000 - 1,999,999
- 500,000 - 999,999
- 250,000 - 499,999
- 100,000 - 249,999
- 30,000 - 99,999
- 10,000 - 29,999
- UNDER 10,000

SCALE 1:3,500,000 LAMBERT CONFORMAL CONIC PROJECTION

MILES 0 50 100 150

KILOMETERS 0 50 100 150

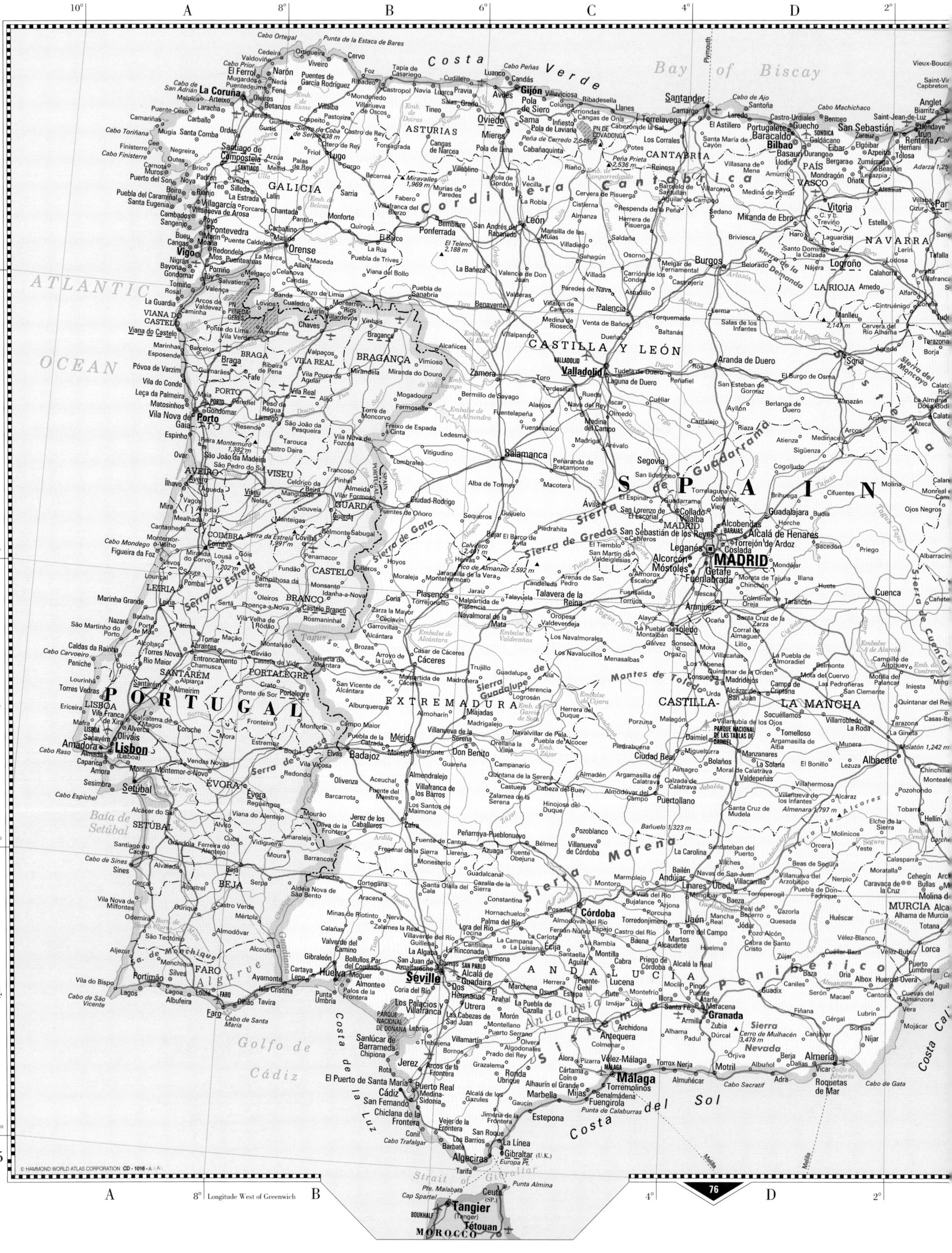
Bay of Biscay
ATLANTIC OCEAN
Costa Verde
Cordillera Cantábrica
PORTUGAL
SPAIN
GALICIA
ASTURIAS
CANTABRIA
PAÍS VASCO
NAVARRA
LA RIOJA
CASTILLA Y LEÓN
EXTREMADURA
CASTILLA-LA MANCHA
ANDALUCIA
MURCIA
MADRID
Lisbon
Porto
Seville
Córdoba
Granada
Málaga
Valladolid
Salamanca
Toledo
Badajoz
Cáceres
Bilbao
Santander
Oviedo
Gijón
León
Burgos
La Coruña
Vigo
Orense
Lugo
Santiago de Compostela
Braga
Coimbra
Évora
Setúbal
Faro
Huelva
Cádiz
Jerez
Algeciras
Gibraltar (U.K.)
Tangier (Tanger)
Tétouan
Ceuta (SP.)
MOROCCO
Strait of Gibraltar
Golfo de Cádiz
Costa de la Luz
Costa del Sol
Sierra Nevada
Sierra Morena
Sierra de Gredos
Sierra de Guadarrama
Serra da Estrela
Montes de Toledo
Sistema Ibérico
Algarve
Tagus
Douro
Cabo Finisterre
Cabo de São Vicente
Cabo Trafalgar
Cabo de Gata
Baía de Setúbal
Longitude West of Greenwich
10°
8°
6°
4°
2°
42°
40°
38°
36°
A
B
C
D
1
2
3
4
5

Spain, Portugal

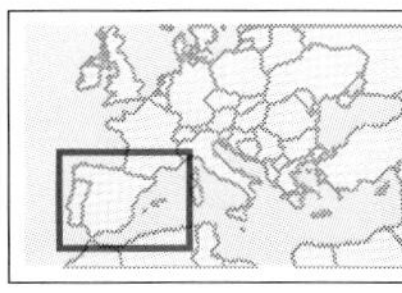

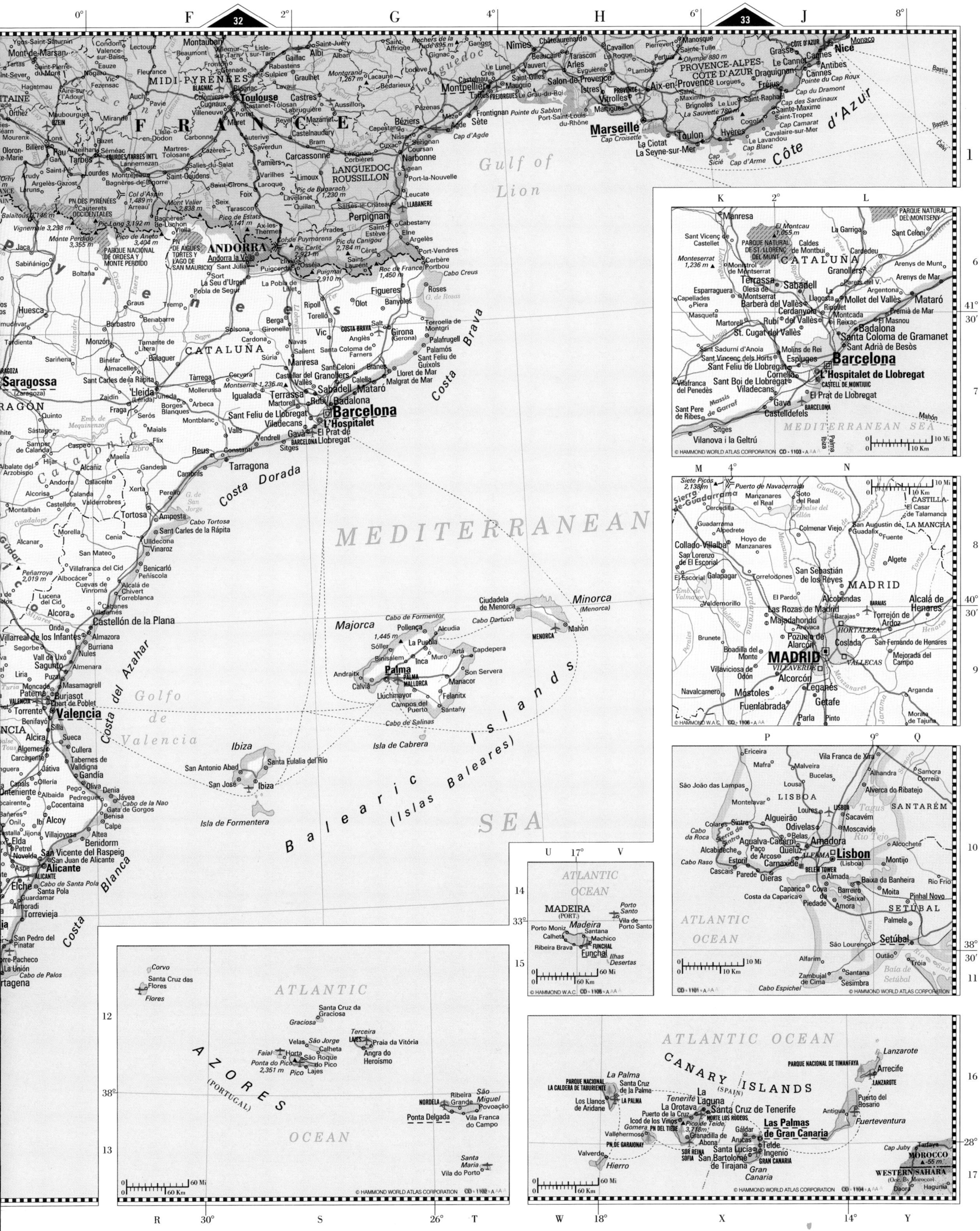

POPULATION OF CITIES AND TOWNS

- ■ OVER 2,000,000
- ◻ 1,000,000 - 1,999,999
- ◉ 500,000 - 999,999
- ◎ 250,000 - 499,999
- ● 100,000 - 249,999
- ◉ 30,000 - 99,999
- ◎ 10,000 - 29,999
- ○ UNDER 10,000

SCALE 1:3,500,000 LAMBERT CONFORMAL CONIC PROJECTION

MILES 0 50 100 150

KILOMETERS 0 50 100 150

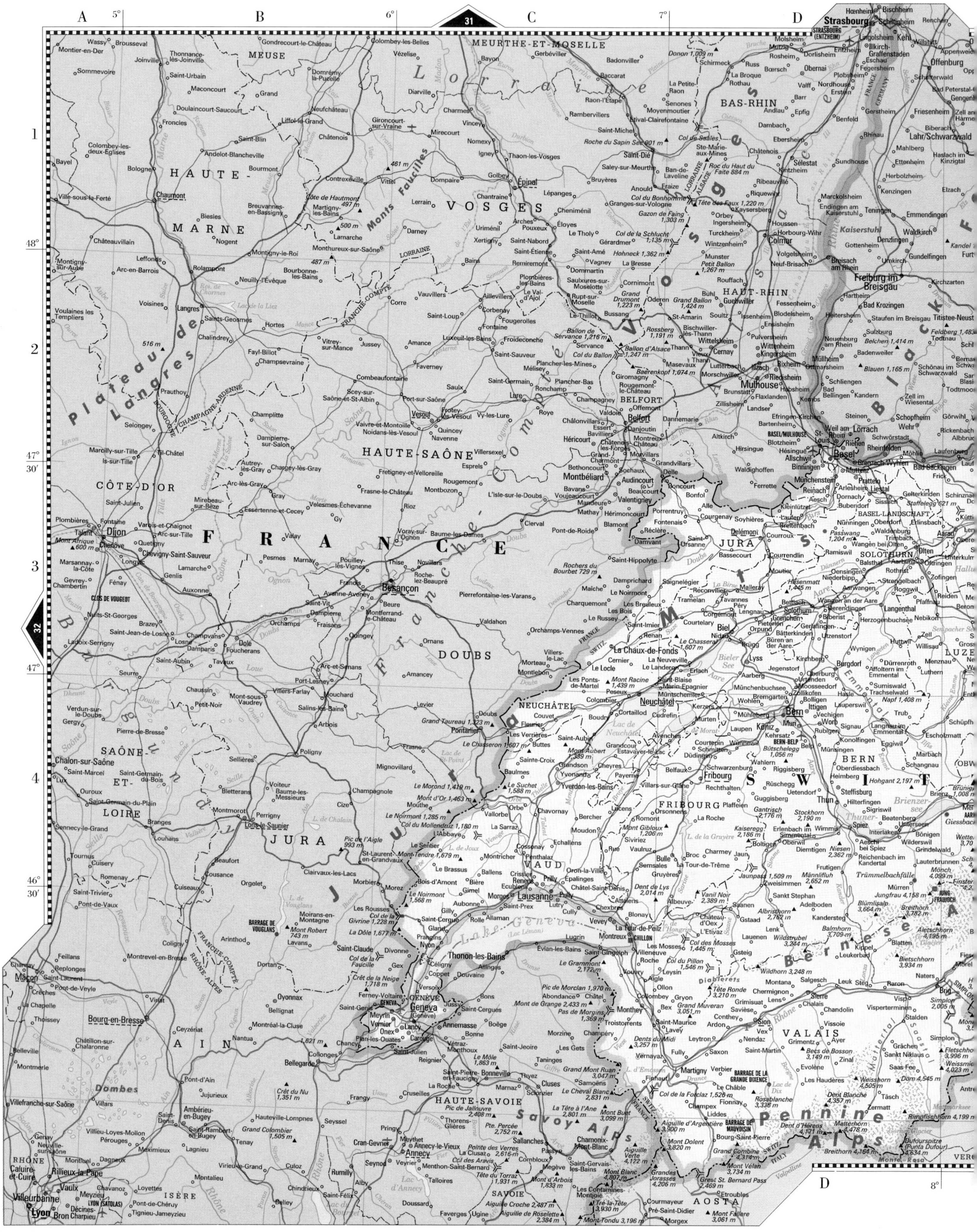
31
32
A
B
C
D
1
2
3
4
5°
6°
7°
8°
48°
47° 30′
47°
46° 30′
FRANCE
SWITZERLAND
Lorraine
Vosges
Plateau de Langres
Bourgogne
Franche-Comté
Jura Mts
Jura
Bernese Alps
Pennine Alps
Savoy Alps
Black Forest
MEURTHE-ET-MOSELLE
MEUSE
HAUTE-MARNE
VOSGES
BAS-RHIN
HAUT-RHIN
HAUTE-SAÔNE
CÔTE-D'OR
DOUBS
JURA
SAÔNE-ET-LOIRE
AIN
HAUTE-SAVOIE
SAVOIE
ISÈRE
RHÔNE
BELFORT
NEUCHÂTEL
VAUD
FRIBOURG
BERN
SOLOTHURN
BASEL-LANDSCHAFT
VALAIS
AOSTA
ITALY
LORRAINE
ALSACE
CHAMPAGNE-ARDENNE
RHÔNE-ALPES
Strasbourg
Colmar
Mulhouse
Freiburg im Breisgau
Basel
Belfort
Montbéliard
Épinal
Chaumont
Langres
Dijon
Vesoul
Besançon
Dole
Lons-le-Saunier
Mâcon
Bourg-en-Bresse
Lyon
Villeurbanne
Geneva (Genève)
Lausanne
Neuchâtel
Biel
Bern
Fribourg
Thun
Sion
Annecy
Chambéry
Chamonix-Mont-Blanc
Lake Geneva (Lac Léman)
Lac de Neuchâtel
Bieler See
Mont Blanc 4,807 m
Grandes Jorasses 4,206 m
Dent Blanche 4,357 m
Weisshorn 4,505 m
Dom 4,545 m
Jungfrau 4,158 m
Mönch 4,099 m
Finsteraarhorn
Aletschhorn 4,195 m
Le Grand Ballon 1,424 m
Hohneck 1,362 m
Ballon d'Alsace 1,247 m
Feldberg 1,493 m
Le Crêt de la Neige 1,718 m
La Dôle 1,677 m
Le Chasseral 1,607 m
Mont Tendre 1,679 m
Mont d'Or 1,463 m
Rhône
Saône
Doubs
Rhin
Aare
Moselle

Central Alps Region

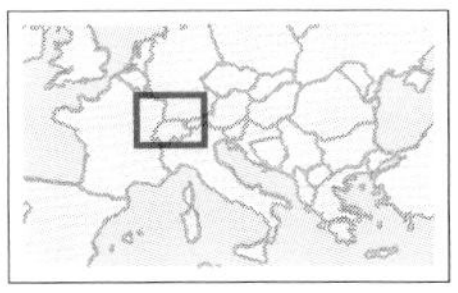

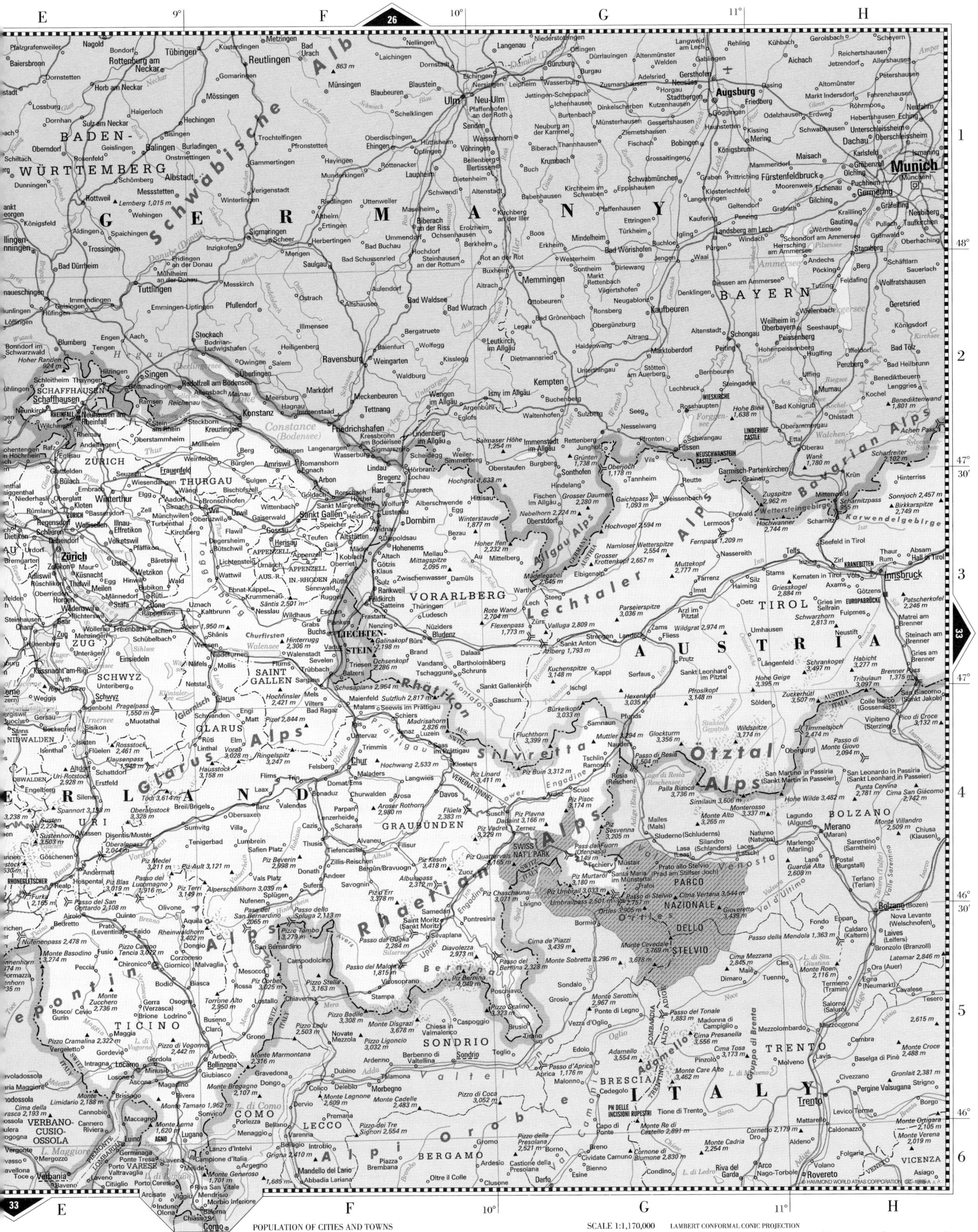

POPULATION OF CITIES AND TOWNS
- OVER 2,000,000
- 1,000,000 - 1,999,999
- 500,000 - 999,999
- 250,000 - 499,999
- 100,000 - 249,999
- 30,000 - 99,999
- 10,000 - 29,999
- UNDER 10,000

SCALE 1:1,170,000 LAMBERT CONFORMAL CONIC PROJECTION

MILES 0 10 20 30 40 50

KILOMETERS 0 10 20 30 40 50

SCALE 1:3,500,000 LAMBERT CONFORMAL CONIC PROJECTION

MILES 0 50 100 150
KILOMETERS 0 50 100 150

Longitude East of Greenwich

POPULATION OF CITIES AND TOWNS

- OVER 2,000,000
- 1,000,000 - 1,999,999
- 500,000 - 999,999
- 250,000 - 499,999
- 100,000 - 249,999
- 30,000 - 99,999
- 10,000 - 29,999
- UNDER 10,000

Southern Italy, Albania, Greece

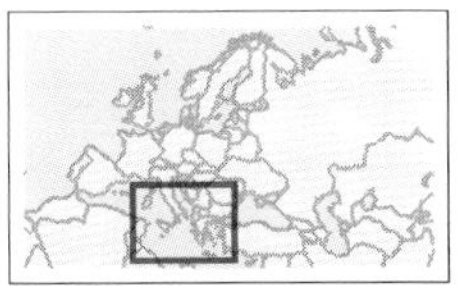

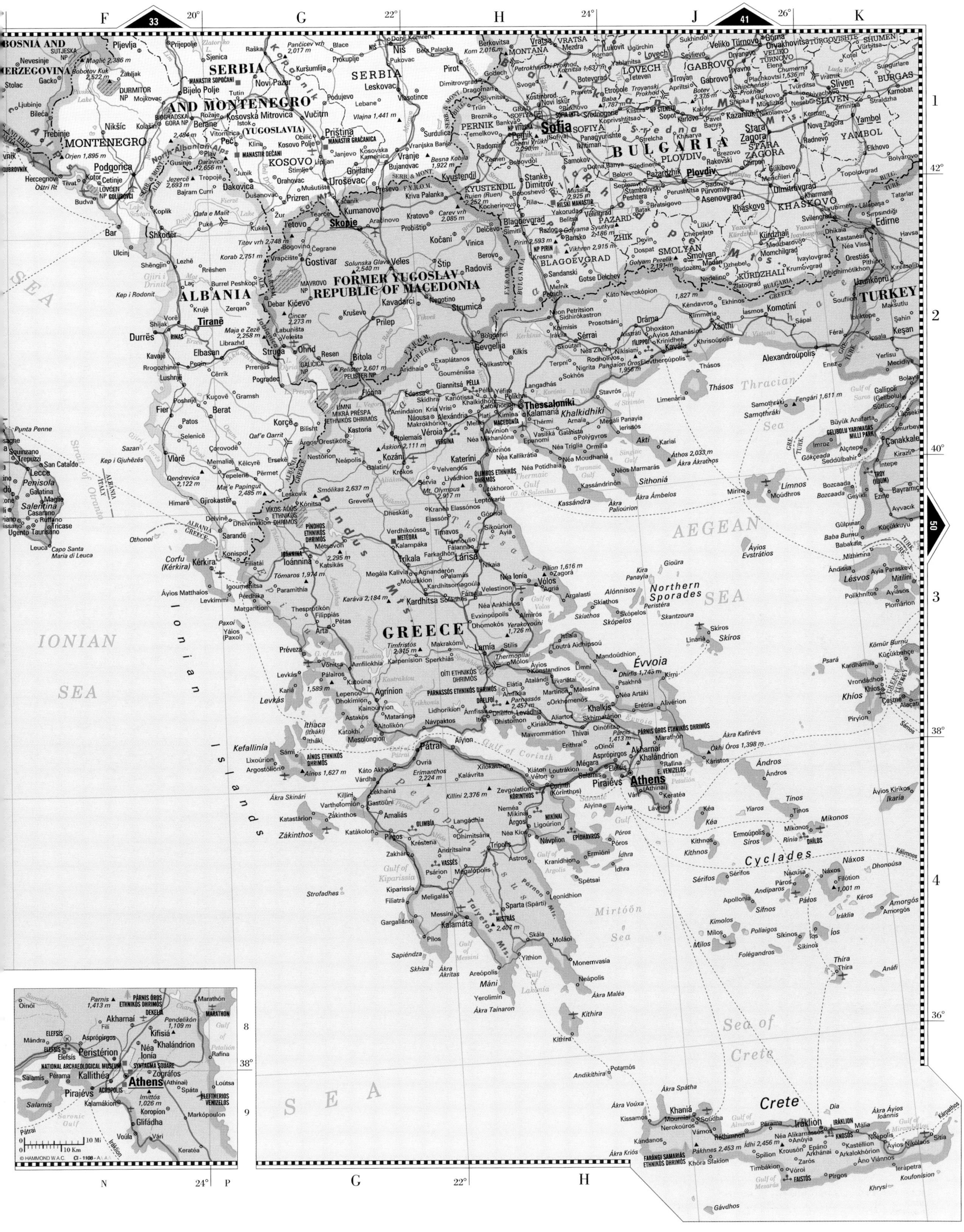

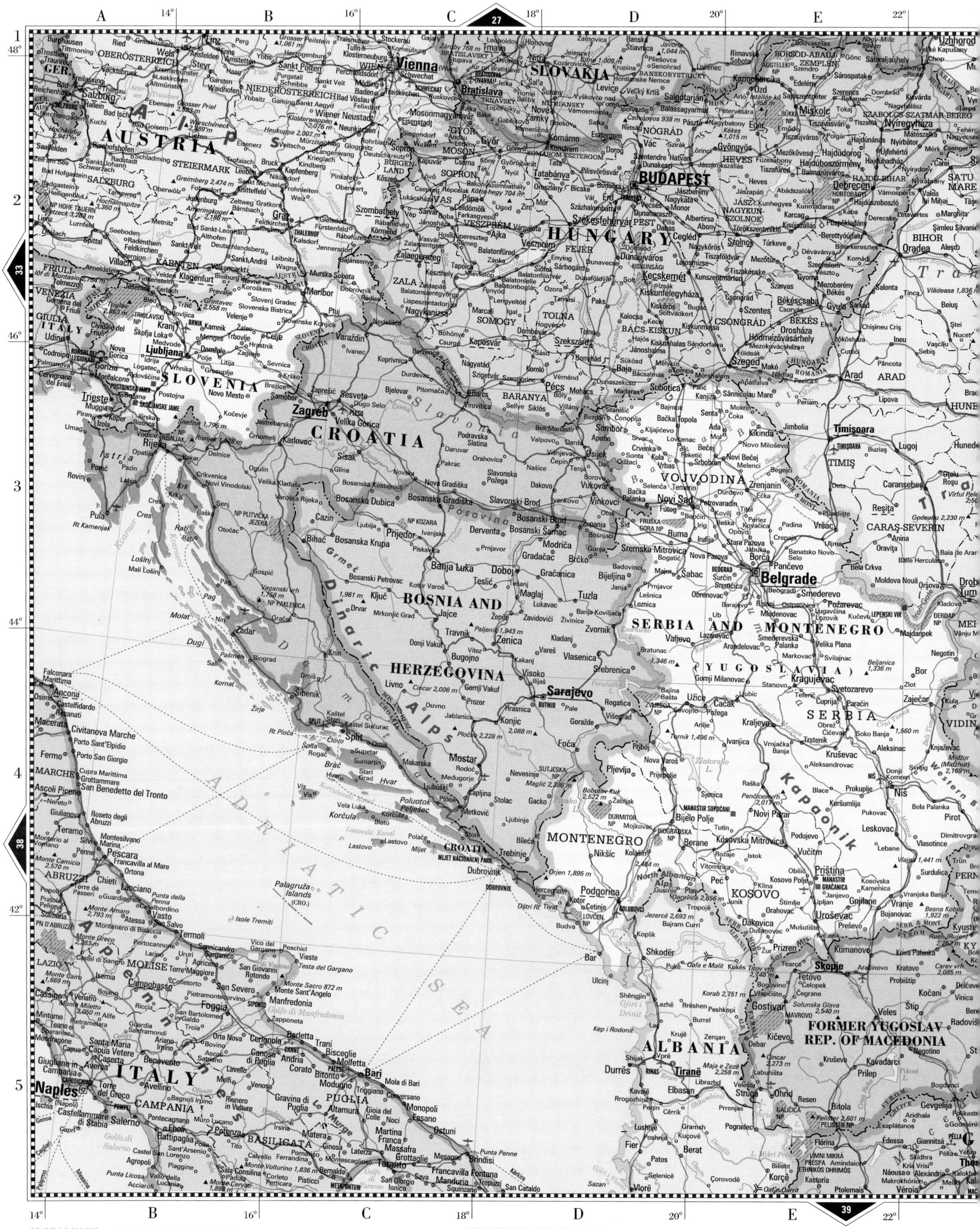

SCALE 1:3,500,000 LAMBERT CONFORMAL CONIC PROJECTION

MILES 0 50 100 150

KILOMETERS 0 50 100 150

POPULATION OF CITIES AND TOWNS

OVER 2,000,000	500,000 - 999,999	100,000 - 249,999	10,000 - 29,999
1,000,000 - 1,999,999	250,000 - 499,999	30,000 - 99,999	UNDER 10,000

Hungary and Northern Balkan States

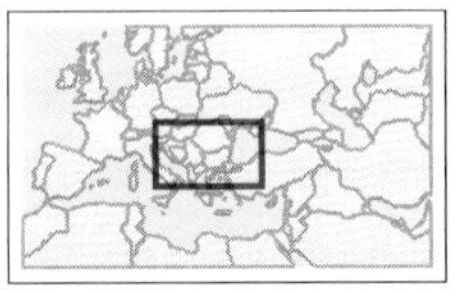

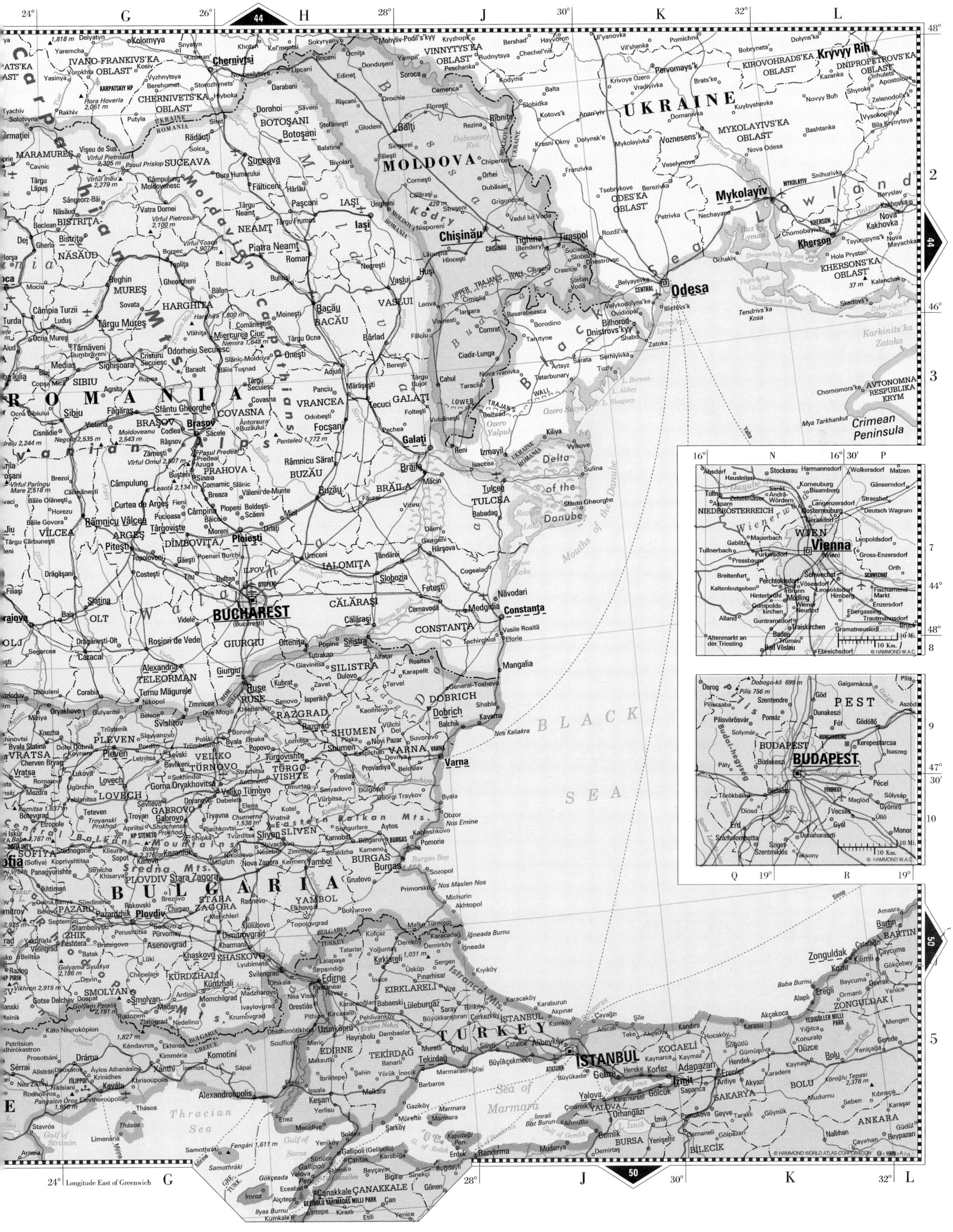

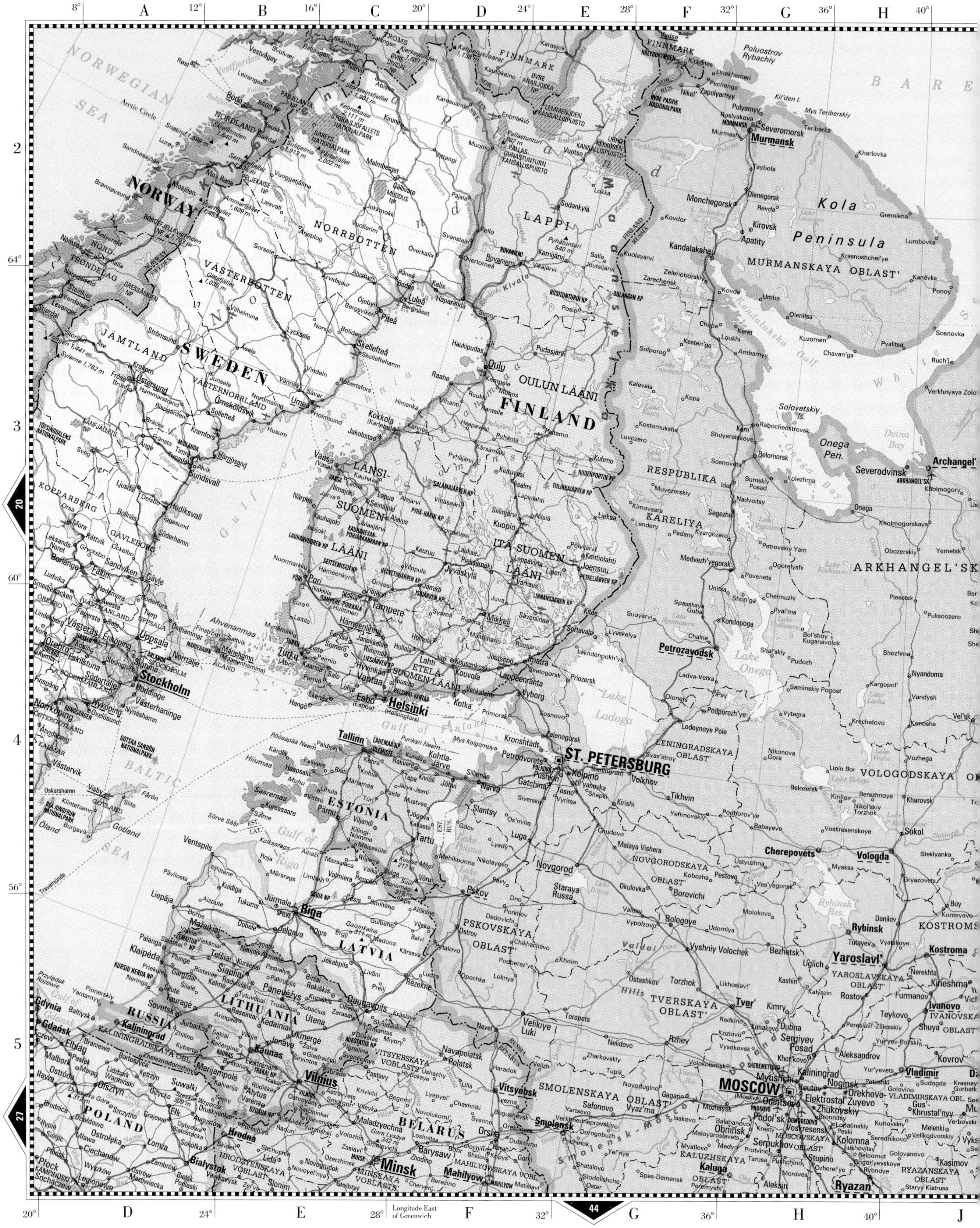

8° A 12° B 16° C 20° D 24° E 28° F 32° G 36° H 40°
20° D 24° E 28° F 32° G 36° H 40° J
Longitude East of Greenwich
2
3
4
5
64°
60°
56°
20
27
44
NORWEGIAN SEA
Arctic Circle
Vestfjorden
Lofoten
NORWAY
SWEDEN
FINLAND
ESTONIA
LATVIA
LITHUANIA
RUSSIA
BELARUS
POLAND
Gulf of Bothnia
Gulf of Finland
Gulf of Riga
BALTIC SEA
Kola Peninsula
Poluostrov Rybachiy
BARENTS
White Sea
Kandalaksha Gulf
Onega Bay
Onega Pen.
Dvina Bay
Lake Onega
Lake Ladoga
Lake Peipus
Rybinsk Res.
Lake Beloye
Lapland
FINNMARK
NORDLAND
TRØNDELAG
NORRBOTTEN
VÄSTERBOTTEN
JÄMTLAND
VÄSTERNORRLAND
GÄVLEBORG
KOPPARBERG
UPPSALA
STOCKHOLM
SÖDERMANLAND
VÄSTMANLAND
ÖSTERGÖTLAND
KALMAR
GOTLAND
ÖREBRO
LAPPI
OULUN LÄÄNI
LÄNSI-SUOMEN LÄÄNI
ITÄ-SUOMEN LÄÄNI
ETELÄ-SUOMEN LÄÄNI
ÅLAND
MURMANSKAYA OBLAST'
RESPUBLIKA KARELIYA
ARKHANGEL'SKAYA
LENINGRADSKAYA OBLAST'
VOLOGODSKAYA
NOVGORODSKAYA OBLAST'
PSKOVSKAYA OBLAST'
TVERSKAYA OBLAST'
YAROSLAVSKAYA OBLAST'
KOSTROMS
IVANOVSKAYA OBLAST'
VLADIMIRSKAYA OBL.
SMOLENSKAYA OBLAST'
MOSCOVSKAYA OBLAST'
KALUZHSKAYA OBLAST'
RYAZANSKAYA OBLAST'
VITSYEBSKAYA VOBLASTS'
MINSKAYA VOBLASTS'
HRODZYENSKAYA VOBLASTS'
MAHILYOWSKAYA VOBLASTS'
KALININGRADSKAYA OBL.
Valdai Hills
Smolensk-Moscow Upland
Murmansk
Severomorsk
Monchegorsk
Kirovsk
Apatity
Kandalaksha
Kem'
Belomorsk
Severodvinsk
Archangel'
Onega
Petrozavodsk
Kondopoga
Segezha
Medvezh'yegorsk
Olonets
Lodeynoye Pole
Tikhvin
Volkhov
ST. PETERSBURG
Kolpino
Pushkin
Gatchina
Kronshtadt
Vyborg
Narva
Pskov
Novgorod
Staraya Russa
Velikiye Luki
Tver'
Rybinsk
Yaroslavl'
Kostroma
Ivanovo
Vladimir
Vologda
Cherepovets
Sokol
MOSCOW
(Moskva)
Odintsovo
Podol'sk
Serpukhov
Kolomna
Kaluga
Ryazan'
Smolensk
Vitsyebsk
Orsha
Mahilyow
Minsk
Barysaw
Hrodna
Vilnius
Kaunas
Klaipėda
Šiauliai
Panevėžys
Daugavpils
Riga
Jūrmala
Liepāja
Ventspils
Tartu
Pärnu
Tallinn
Helsinki
(Helsingfors)
Espoo
Vantaa
Lahti
Kotka
Lappeenranta
Imatra
Turku
(Åbo)
Tampere
Pori
Vaasa
Jyväskylä
Kuopio
Joensuu
Mikkeli
Savonlinna
Oulu
Kajaani
Kokkola
Rovaniemi
Kemi
Tornio
Stockholm
Uppsala
Västerås
Örebro
Norrköping
Nyköping
Södertälje
Gävle
Sandviken
Falun
Mora
Hudiksvall
Sundsvall
Härnösand
Örnsköldsvik
Umeå
Skellefteå
Piteå
Luleå
Boden
Kiruna
Gällivare
Östersund
Bodø
Narvik
Tromsø
Kirkenes
Vardø
Gdańsk
Gdynia
Elbląg
Olsztyn
Białystok
Kaliningrad
Sovetsk

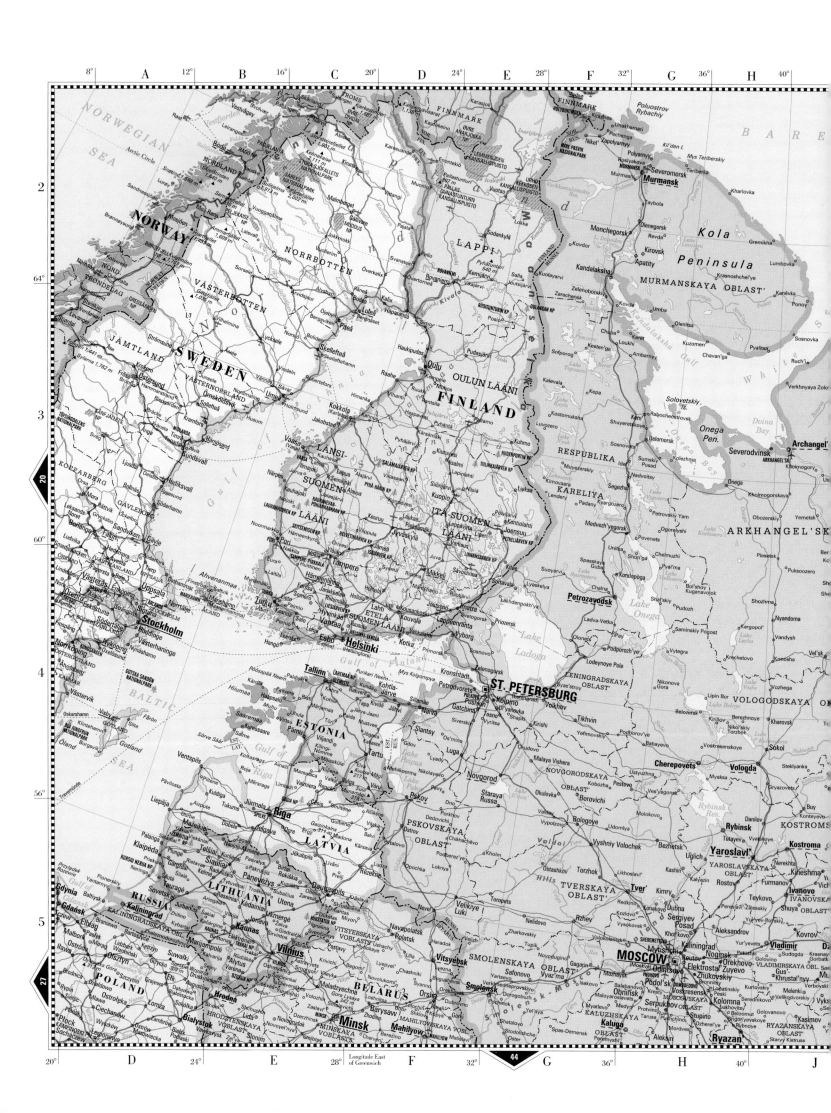

Northeastern Europe

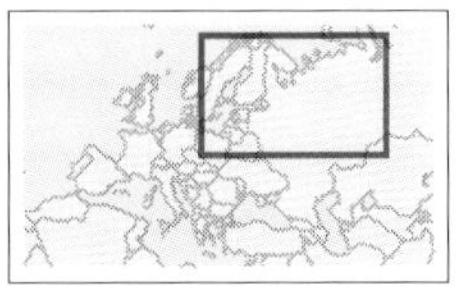

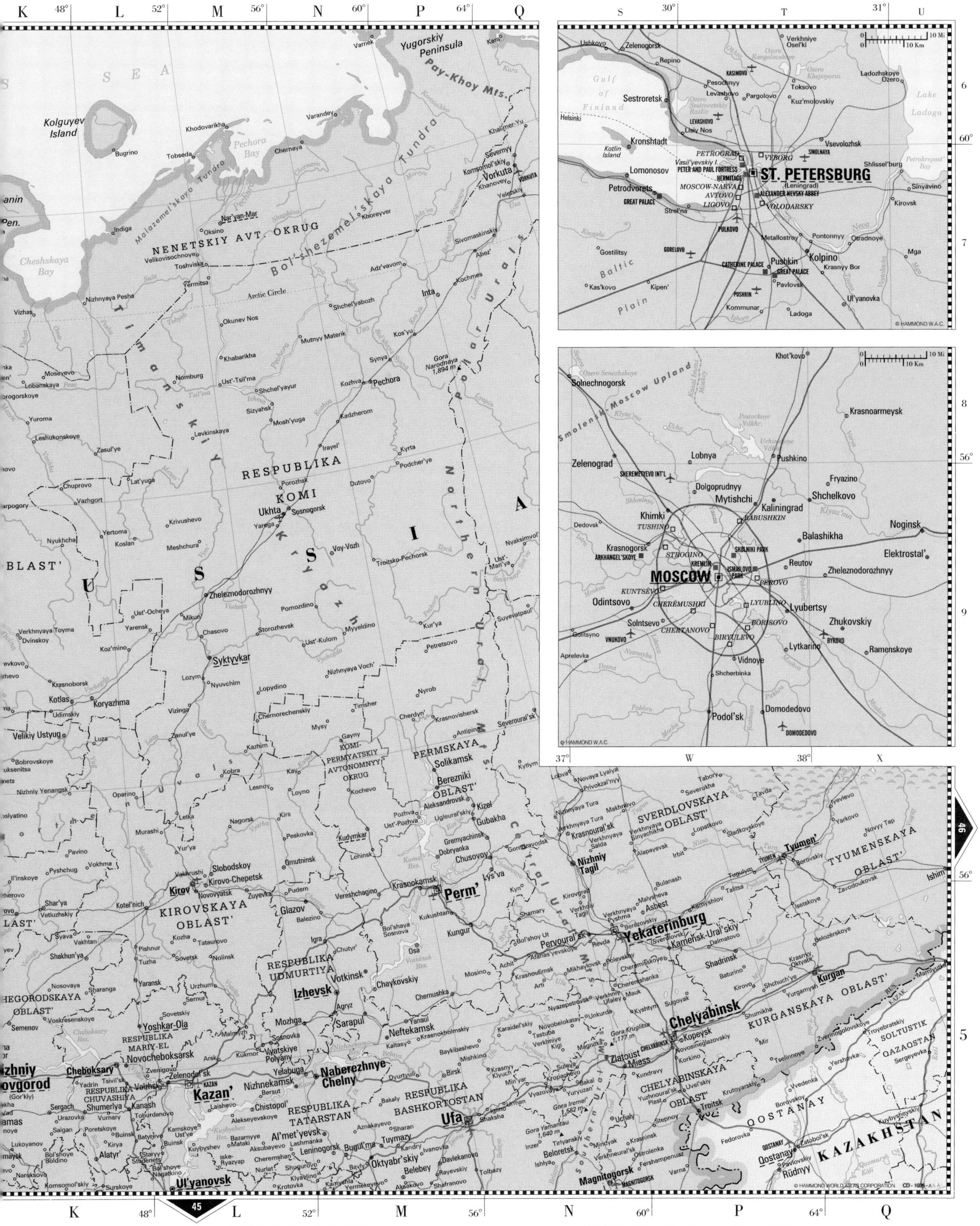

46
45

POPULATION OF CITIES AND TOWNS

■ OVER 2,000,000	◉ 500,000 - 999,999	⊕ 100,000 - 249,999	⊙ 10,000 - 29,999
◻ 1,000,000 - 1,999,999	◎ 250,000 - 499,999	⊕ 30,000 - 99,999	○ UNDER 10,000

SCALE 1:7,000,000 LAMBERT CONFORMAL CONIC PROJECTION

MILES 0 100 200 300

KILOMETERS 0 100 200 300

SCALE 1:7,000,000 LAMBERT CONFORMAL CONIC PROJECTION

MILES 0 100 200 300

KILOMETERS 0 100 200 300

POPULATION OF CITIES AND TOWNS

- OVER 2,000,000
- 1,000,000 - 1,999,999
- 500,000 - 999,999
- 250,000 - 499,999
- 100,000 - 249,999
- 30,000 - 99,999
- 10,000 - 29,999
- UNDER 10,000

Southeastern Europe

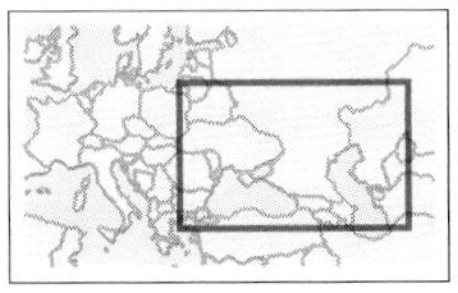

43
46
51
RUSSIA
KAZAKHSTAN
UZBEKISTAN
TURKMENISTAN
AZERBAIJAN
ARMENIA
GEORGIA
IRAN
CASPIAN SEA
Aral Sea
BATYS QAZAQSTAN
ATYRAŪ
AQTÖBE
MANGGHYSTAŪ
QOSTANAY
QYZYLORDA
QORAQALPOG'ISTON RESPUBLIKASI
DAŞOGUZ
BALKAN
AHAL
RESPUBLIKA BASHKORTOSTAN
ORENBURGSKAYA OBLAST'
SAMARSKAYA OBLAST'
SARATOVSKAYA OBLAST'
VOLGOGRADSKAYA OBLAST'
ASTRAKHANSKAYA OBLAST'
RESPUBLIKA KALMYKIYA
STAVROPOL' SKIY KRAY
RESPUBLIKA MORDOVIYA
PENZENSKAYA OBLAST'
UL'YANOVSKAYA OBLAST'
RESPUBLIKA TATARSTAN
CHELYABINSKAYA OBLAST'
RESPUBLIKA DAGESTAN
RESPUBLIKA CHECHNYA
Caspian Plain
Ustyurt Plateau
Mugalzhar Taūy
Ülken Borsyq Qumy
Naryn Qum
Karakumy
Caucasus
Kulandag
Orenburg
Samara
Tol'yatti
Ul'yanovsk
Saratov
Engel's
Penza
Saransk
Volgograd
Volzhskiy
Astrakhan'
Elista
Stavropol'
Groznyy
Makhachkala
Vladikavkaz
Nal'chik
T'bilisi
Yerevan
Baku
Sumqayıt
Gäncä
Oral
Aqtöbe
Atyraū
Aqtau
Orsk
Novotroitsk
Magnitogorsk
Sterlitamak
Türkmenbashy (Krasnovodsk)
Nebitdag
Beyneū
Garabogazköl Aylagy
Zhiloy I.
Mys Peschanyy
Bozashchy Tübegi
© HAMMOND WORLD ATLAS CORPORATION

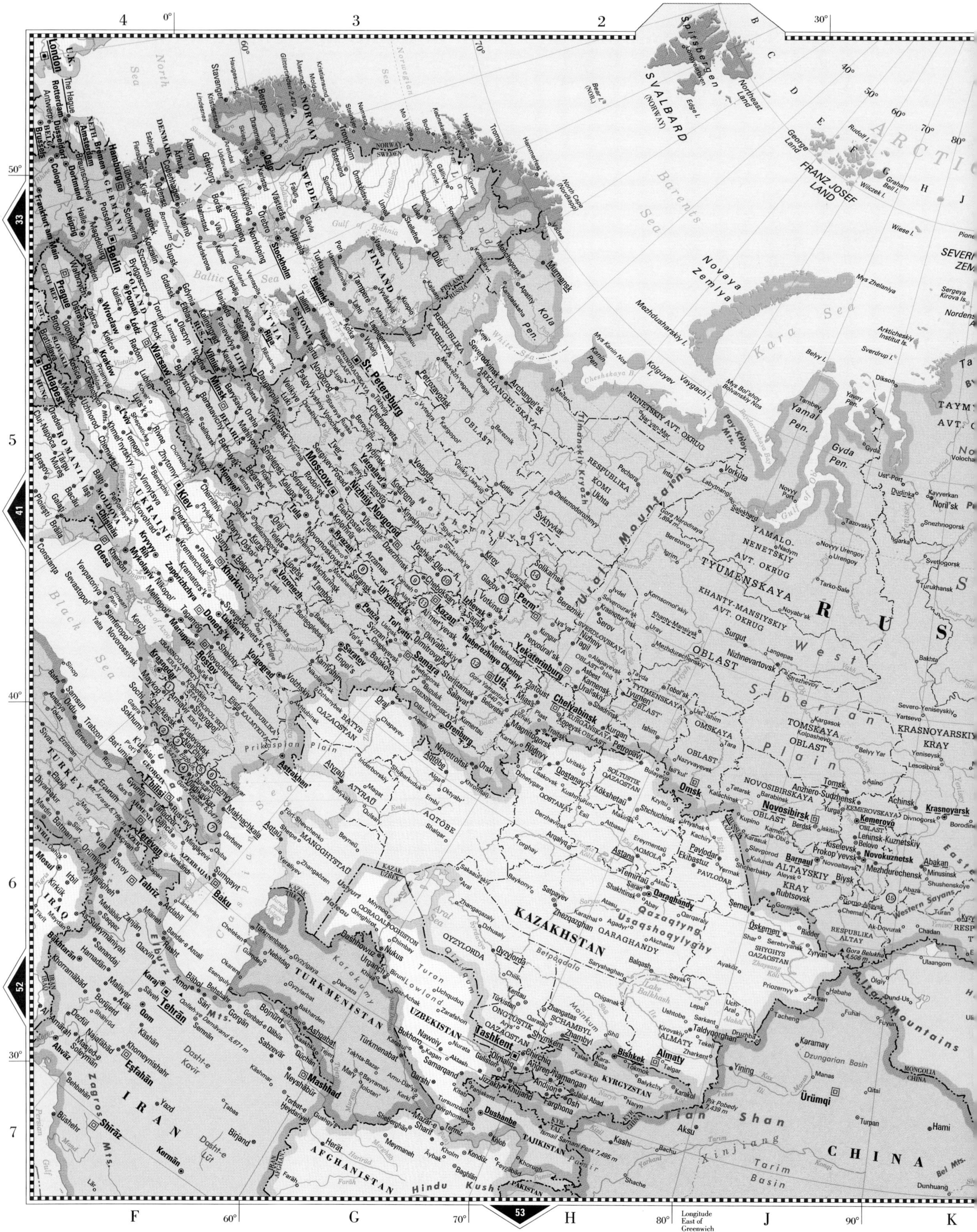
4
0°
3
2
30°
F
60°
G
70°
53
H
80°
Longitude
East of
Greenwich
J
90°
K
33
41
52
5
6
7
50°
40°
30°
ARCTIC
Spitsbergen
SVALBARD
(NORWAY)
Bear I.
(NOR.)
Northeast Land
Edge I.
FRANZ JOSEF LAND
George Land
Graham Bell I.
Wilczek I.
Rudolf I.
Wiese I.
SEVERNAYA ZEMLYA
Barents Sea
Novaya Zemlya
Kara Sea
Mys Zhelaniya
North Sea
Norwegian Sea
Baltic Sea
Gulf of Bothnia
White Sea
Black Sea
Sea of Azov
Caspian Sea
Aral Sea
Lake Balkhash
U.K.
London
The Hague
Rotterdam
Amsterdam
Düsseldorf
Brussels
Antwerp
Cologne
Frankfurt am Main
Hamburg
Bremen
Berlin
Leipzig
Dresden
Prague
GERMANY
DENMARK
Copenhagen
NORWAY
Oslo
Bergen
Stavanger
Trondheim
SWEDEN
Stockholm
Göteborg
Malmö
FINLAND
Helsinki
Tampere
Oulu
Tallinn
ESTONIA
LATVIA
Riga
LITH.
Vilnius
Kaunas
POLAND
Warsaw
Poznań
Łódź
Wrocław
Kraków
Gdańsk
Minsk
BELARUS
Budapest
ROMANIA
Kiev
UKRAINE
Odesa
Kharkiv
Dnipropetrovs'k
Donets'k
Zaporizhzhya
Kryvyy Rih
Mykolayiv
Chişinău
Sevastopol'
Simferopol'
St. Petersburg
Moscow
Nizhniy Novgorod
Yaroslavl'
Tula
Voronezh
Saratov
Samara
Kazan'
Ul'yanovsk
Tol'yatti
Penza
Volgograd
Rostov
Krasnodar
Astrakhan'
Perm'
Izhevsk
Ufa
Yekaterinburg
Chelyabinsk
Orenburg
Arkhangel'sk
Murmansk
Kola Pen.
Kanin Pen.
Kolguyev I.
Vaygach I.
Yamal Pen.
Gyda Pen.
Vorkuta
Salekhard
Noril'sk
Dudinka
Ural Mountains
Timanskiy Kryazh
REPUBLIKA KOMI
Syktyvkar
Ukhta
NENETSKIY AVT. OKRUG
YAMALO-NENETSKIY AVT. OKRUG
KHANTY-MANSIYSKIY AVT. OKRUG
TYUMENSKAYA OBLAST
West Siberian Plain
Tyumen'
Omsk
Novosibirsk
Barnaul
Kemerovo
Novokuznetsk
Krasnoyarsk
Tomsk
KRASNOYARSKIY KRAY
ALTAYSKIY KRAY
RUSSIA
KAZAKHSTAN
Astana
Qaraghandy
Pavlodar
Semey
Öskemen
Almaty
Aqtöbe
Atyraū
Oral
Qostanay
Petropavl
KYRGYZSTAN
Bishkek
UZBEKISTAN
Tashkent
Samarqand
Bukhoro
TURKMENISTAN
Ashgabat
TAJIKISTAN
Dushanbe
AFGHANISTAN
Hindu Kush
Pamirs
IRAN
Tehrān
Mashhad
Eşfahān
Shīrāz
Kermān
Tabrīz
Elburz Mts.
Zagros Mts.
Dasht-e Kavīr
Dasht-e Lūt
IRAQ
Mosul
TURKEY
Trabzon
Sinop
Samsun
GEORGIA
Tbilisi
ARMENIA
Yerevan
AZERBAIJAN
Baku
Makhachkala
Caucasus
Groznyy
CHINA
Ürümqi
Tian Shan
Tarim Basin
Xinjiang
Kashi
Altai Mountains
Dzungarian Basin
MONGOLIA
Turan Lowland
Kyzylkum
Karakum
Ustyurt Plateau
Caspian Plain
Pik Pobedy 7,439 m
Gora Belukha 4,506 m
Gora Narodnaya 1,894 m

Russia and Neighboring Countries

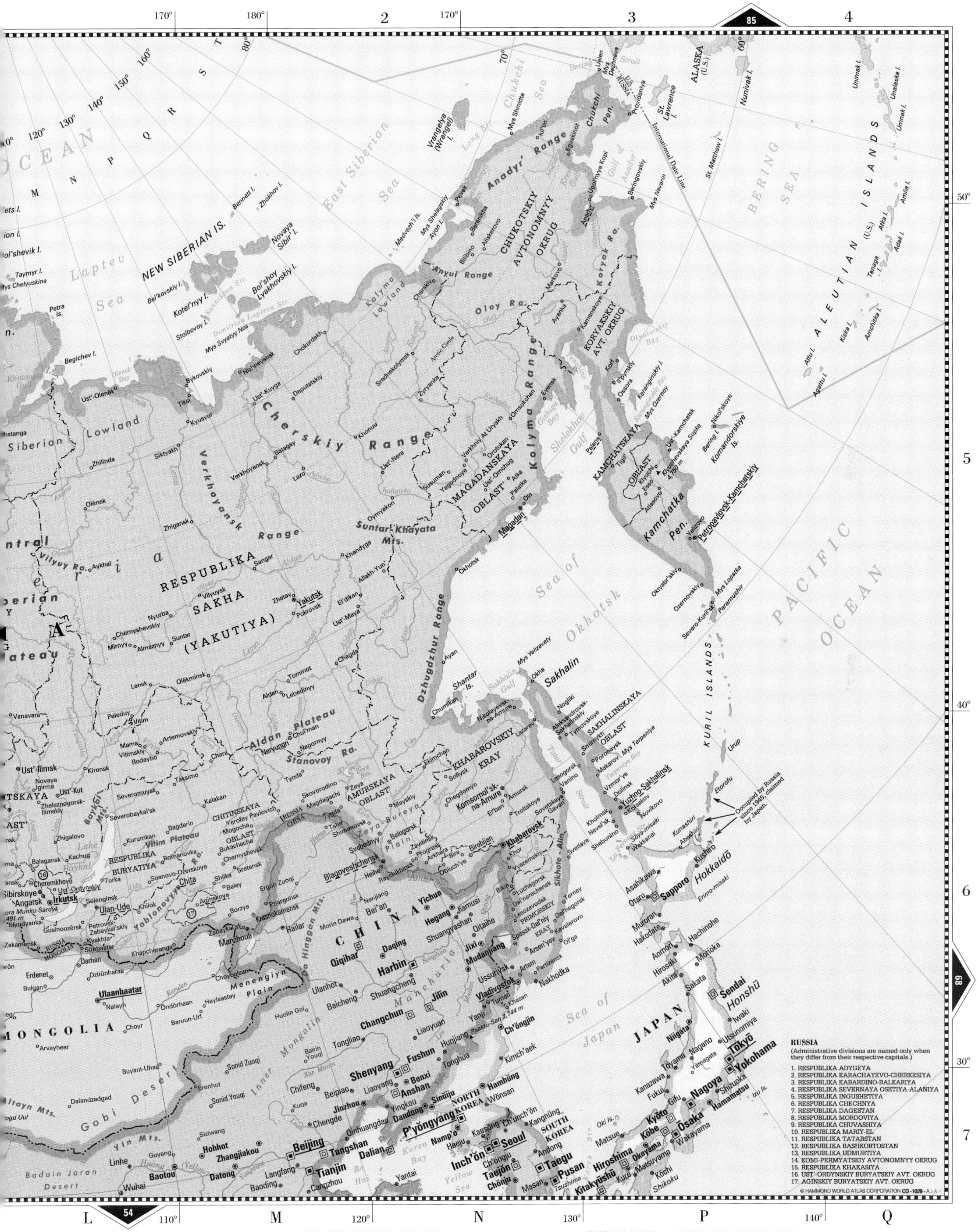

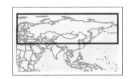

POPULATION OF CITIES AND TOWNS

■ OVER 2,000,000	◉ 500,000 - 999,999	○ 50,000 - 99,999
▣ 1,000,000 - 1,999,999	● 100,000 - 499,999	∘ UNDER 50,000

SCALE 1:21,000,000 LAMBERT CONFORMAL CONIC PROJECTION

MILES 0 300 600 900

KILOMETERS 0 300 600 900

Asia

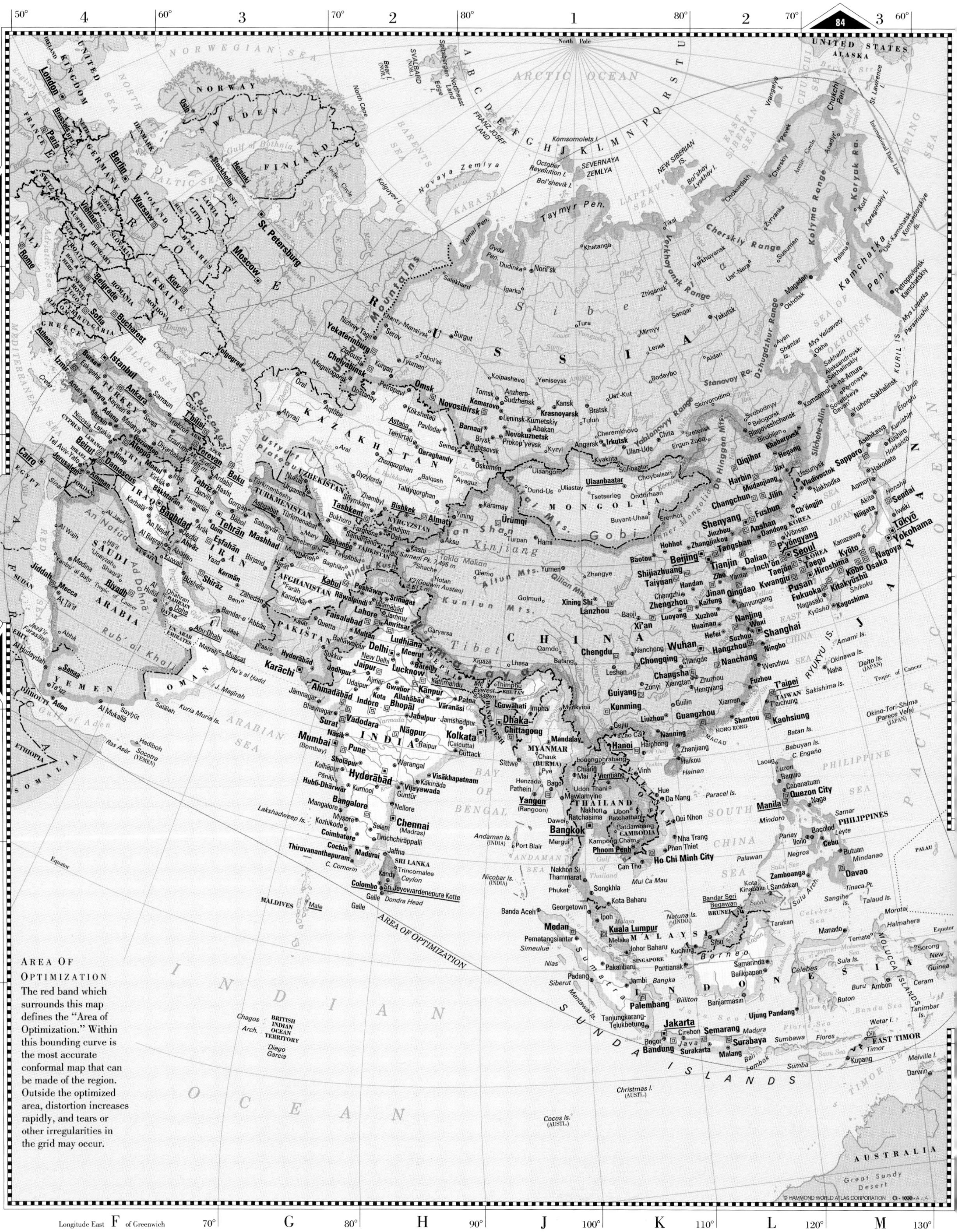

Area of Optimization

The red band which surrounds this map defines the "Area of Optimization." Within this bounding curve is the most accurate conformal map that can be made of the region. Outside the optimized area, distortion increases rapidly, and tears or other irregularities in the grid may occur.

SCALE 1:49,000,000 OPTIMAL CONFORMAL PROJECTION

MILES 0 700 1400 2100

KILOMETERS 0 700 1400 2100

POPULATION OF CITIES AND TOWNS

- ■ OVER 3,000,000
- ⊡ 1,000,000 - 2,999,999
- ⊛ 500,000 - 999,999
- ⊕ 100,000 - 499,999
- ○ UNDER 100,000

Eastern Mediterranean Region

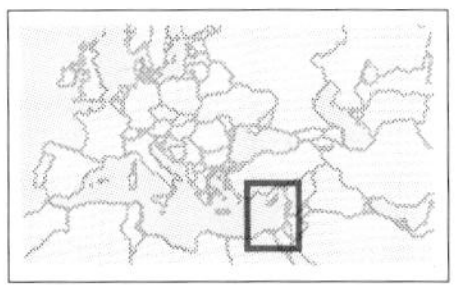

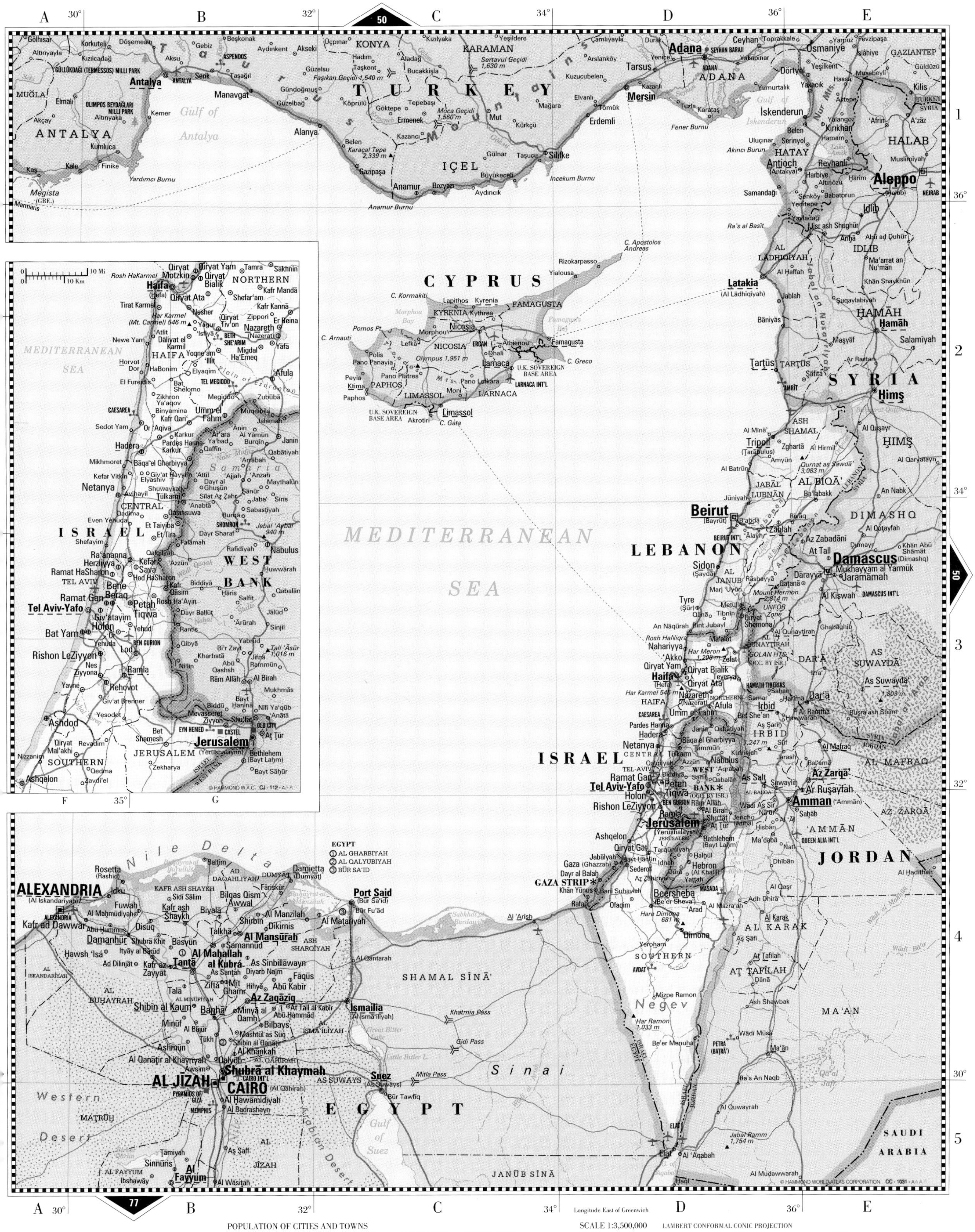

POPULATION OF CITIES AND TOWNS

- OVER 2,000,000
- 1,000,000 - 1,999,999
- 500,000 - 999,999
- 250,000 - 499,999
- 100,000 - 249,999
- 30,000 - 99,999
- 10,000 - 29,999
- UNDER 10,000

SCALE 1:3,500,000 LAMBERT CONFORMAL CONIC PROJECTION

MILES 0 50 100 150

KILOMETERS 0 50 100 150

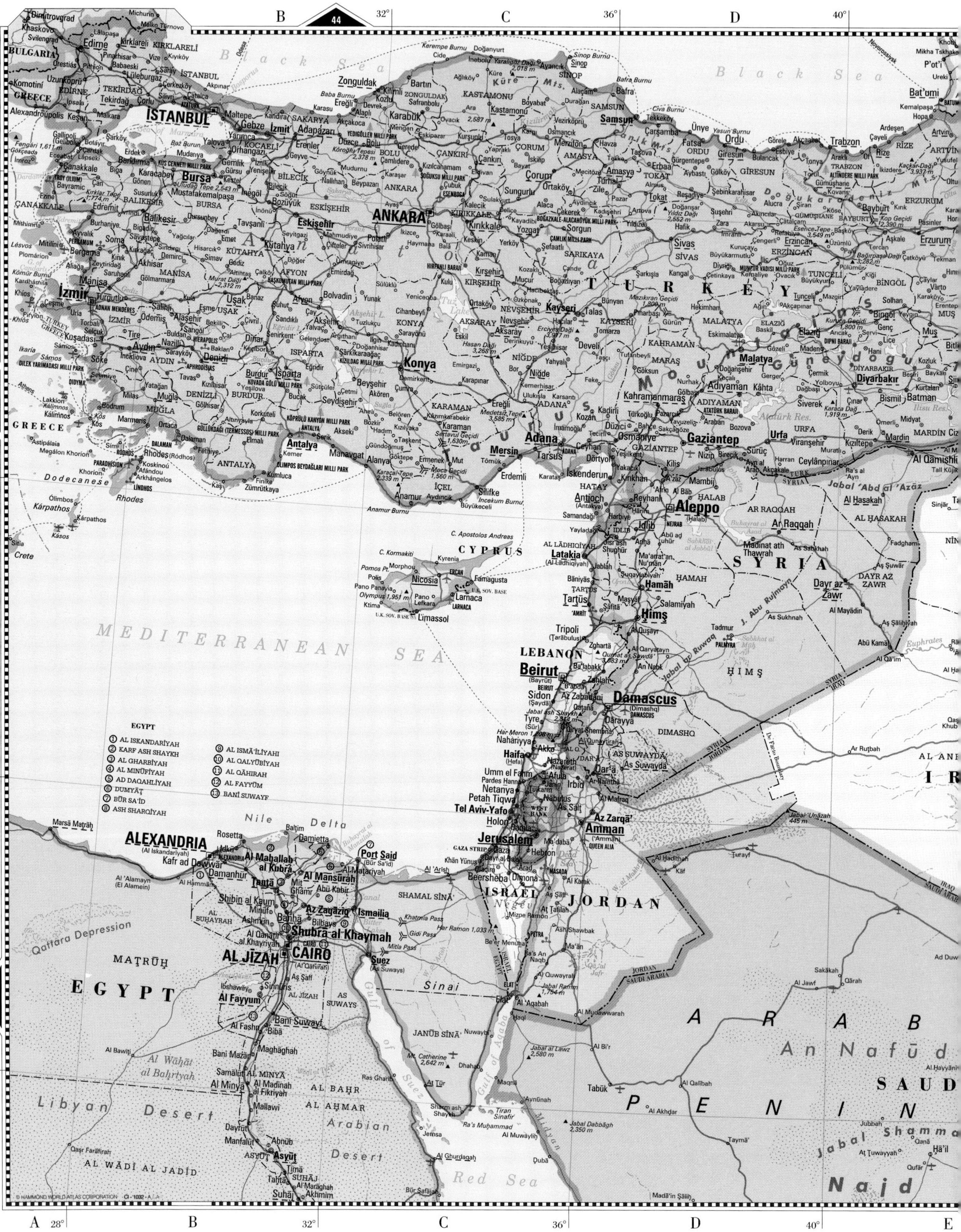

SCALE 1:7,000,000 LAMBERT CONFORMAL CONIC PROJECTION

MILES 0 100 200 300

KILOMETERS 0 100 200 300

POPULATION OF CITIES AND TOWNS

■ OVER 2,000,000	◉ 500,000 - 999,999	⊕ 100,000 - 249,999
▣ 1,000,000 - 1,999,999	◎ 250,000 - 499,999	⊕ 30,000 - 99,999
⊙ 10,000 - 29,999	○ UNDER 10,000	

Northern Middle East

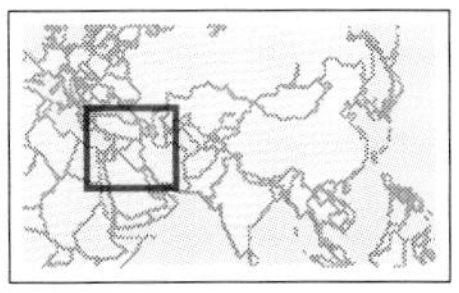

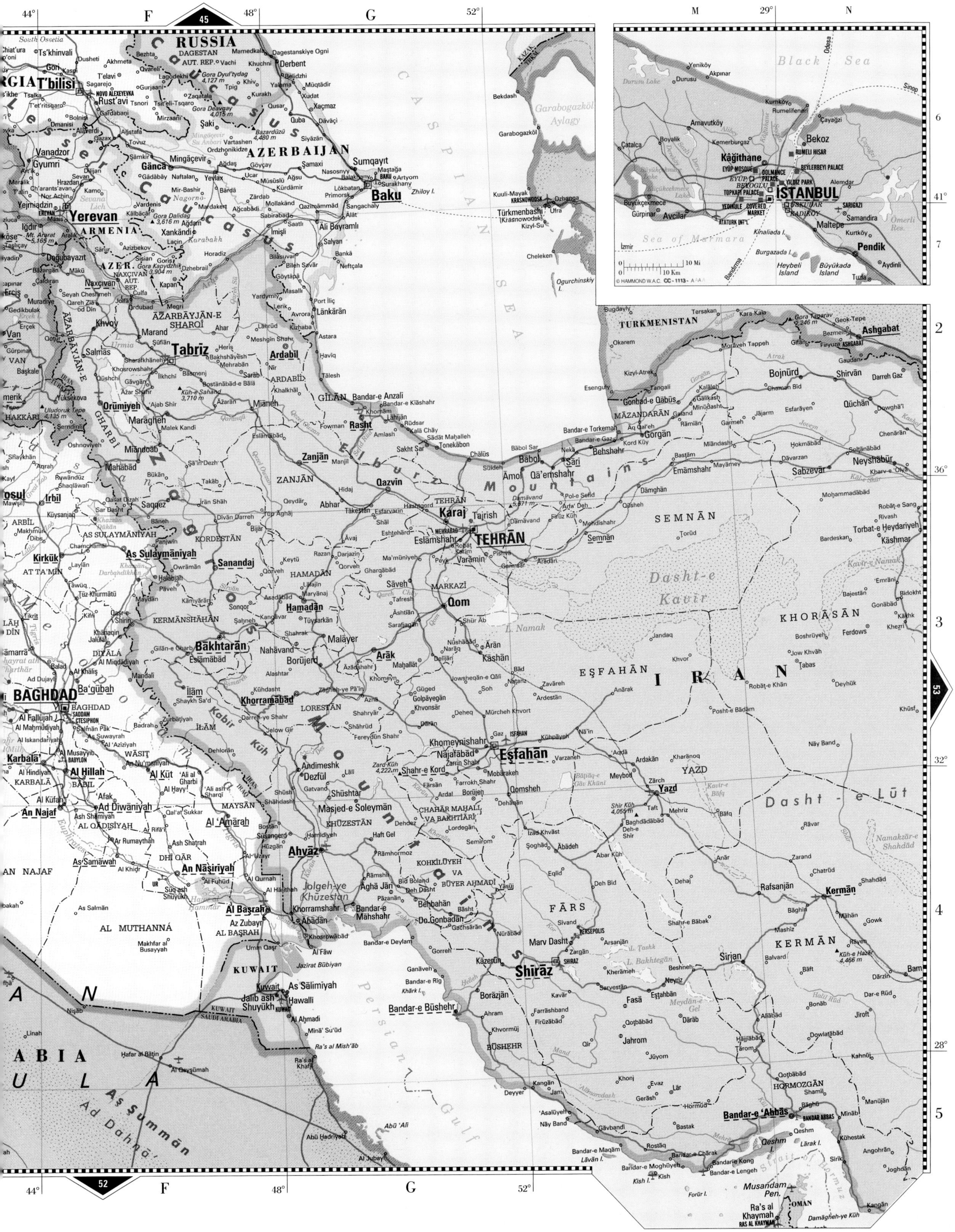

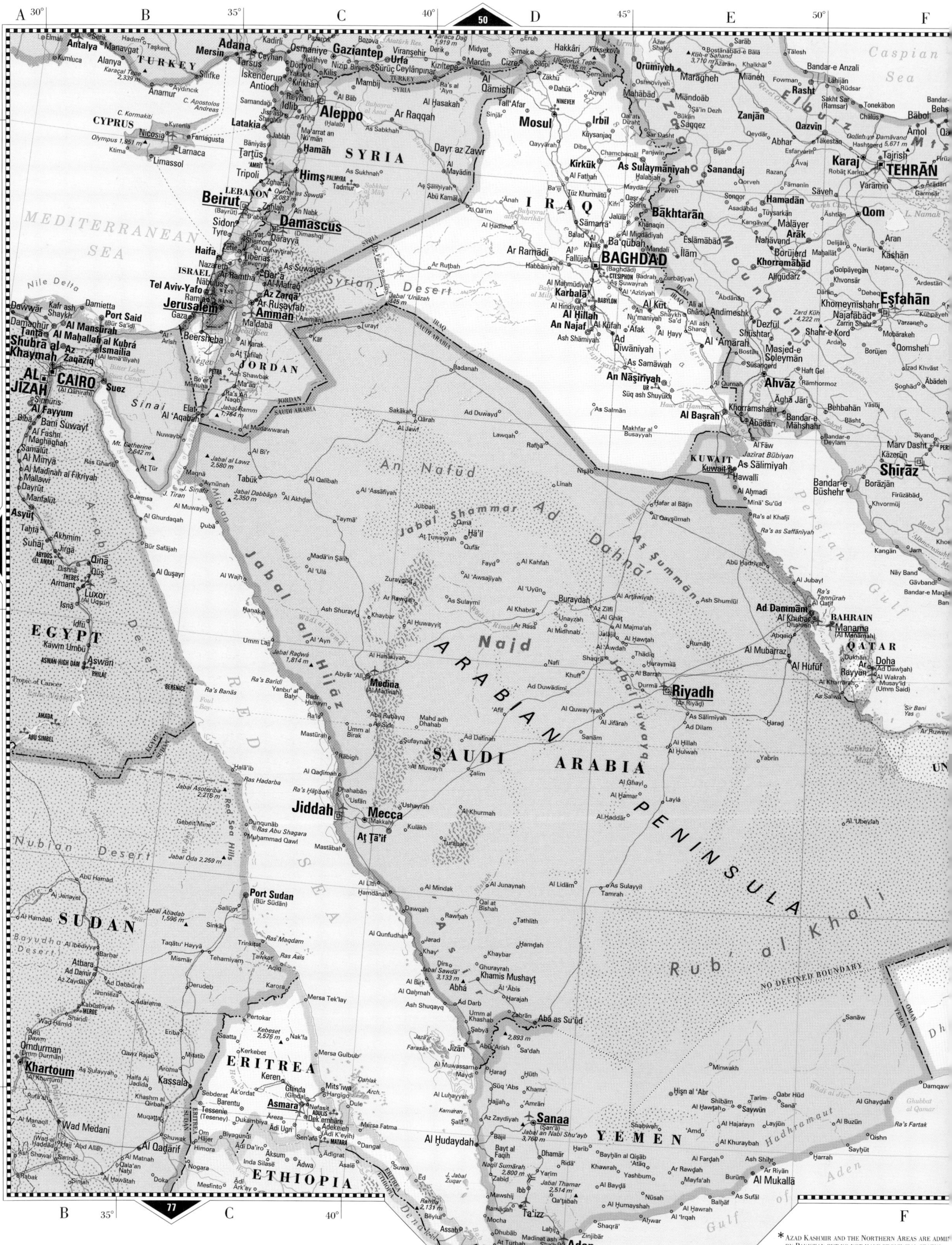

* Azad Kashmir and the Northern Areas are administered by Pakistan but do not have provincial status.

Southwestern Asia

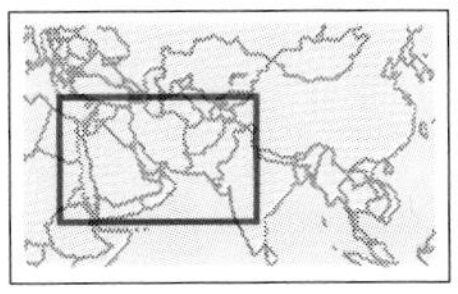

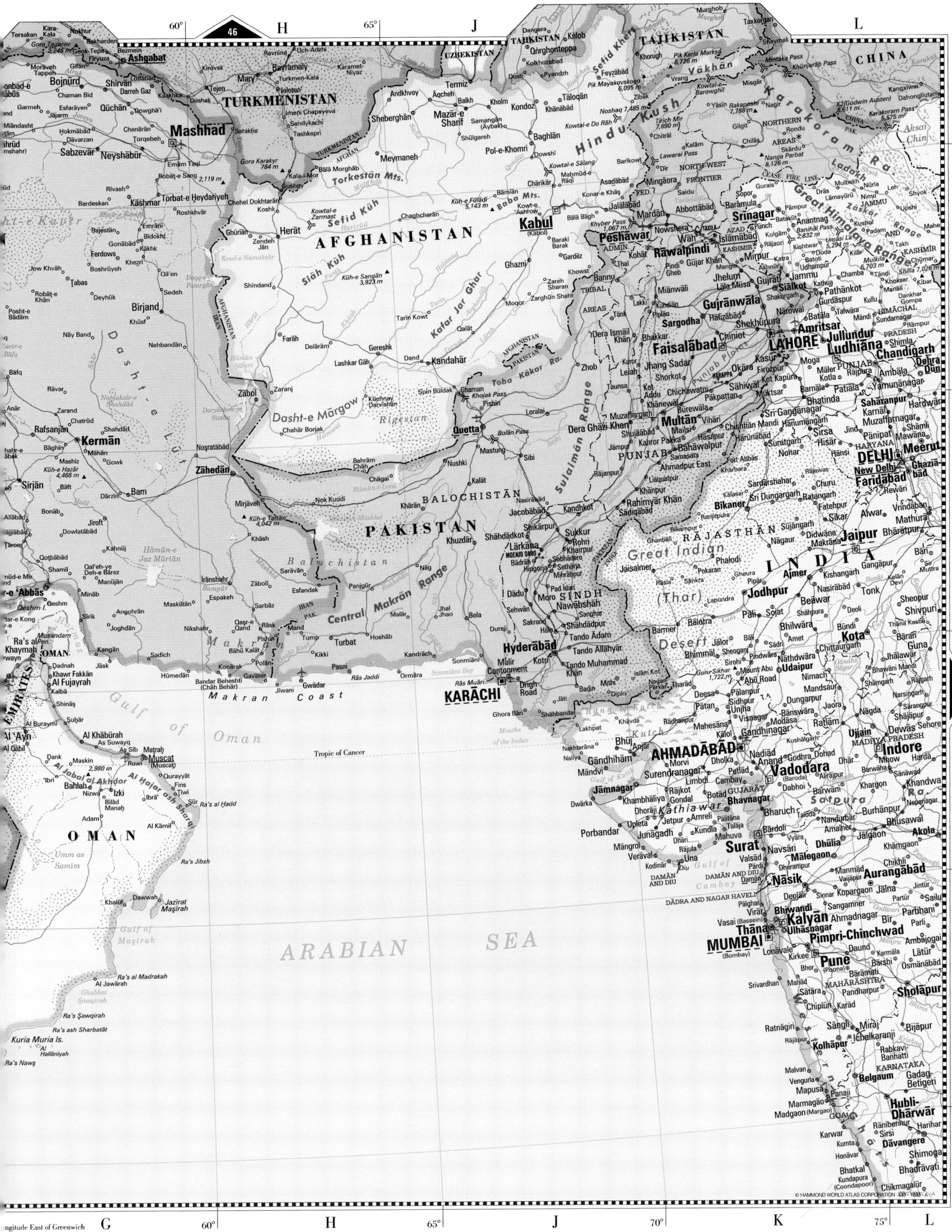

60°
65°
70°
75°
G
H
J
K
L
46
62
1
2
3
4
5
6
35°
30°
25°
20°
15°
TURKMENISTAN
UZBEKISTAN
TAJIKISTAN
CHINA
AFGHANISTAN
PAKISTAN
INDIA
OMAN
IRAN
NORTHERN AREAS
NORTH-WEST FRONTIER
FED. ADMIN. TRIBAL AREAS
AZAD KASHMIR
JAMMU AND KASHMIR
PUNJAB
BALOCHISTĀN
SINDH
RAJASTHAN
GUJARAT
MAHĀRĀSHTRA
MADHYA PRADESH
HARYANA
HIMACHAL PRADESH
KARNATAKA
GOA
DAMĀN AND DIU
DĀDRA AND NAGAR HAVELI
Ashgabat
Mashhad
Mary
Kabul
(Kābol)
Herāt
Kandahār
Quetta
Peshāwar
Islāmābād
Rāwalpindi
Lahore
Faisalābād
Multān
Hyderābād
KARĀCHI
Srīnagar
Amritsar
Ludhiāna
Chandīgarh
DELHI
New Delhi
Jaipur
Jodhpur
AHMADĀBĀD
Vadodara
Surat
MUMBAI
(Bombay)
Pune
Nāsik
Kalyān
Thāna
Indore
Kermān
Zāhedān
Muscat
Hindu Kush
Karakoram Ra.
Great Himalaya Range
Sulaimān Range
Central Makrān Range
Toba Kākar Ra.
Dasht-e Lūt
Dasht-e Mārgow
Great Indian Desert (Thar)
Rann of Kutch
Kathiawar
Makran Coast
Gulf of Oman
Gulf of Kutch
Gulf of Cambay
Gulf of Maşīrah
ARABIAN SEA
Tropic of Cancer
Mouths of the Indus
Sātpura Ra.
Western Ghats
Kuria Muria Is.
Jazīrat Maşīrah
Pik Kommunizma
K2 (Godwin Austen) 8,611 m
Nanga Parbat 8,126 m
Tirich Mir 7,690 m
© HAMMOND WORLD ATLAS CORPORATION

Longitude East of Greenwich

POPULATION OF CITIES AND TOWNS
- ■ OVER 2,000,000
- □ 1,000,000 - 1,999,999
- ◉ 500,000 - 999,999
- ◎ 250,000 - 499,999
- ⊕ 100,000 - 249,999
- ⊙ 30,000 - 99,999
- ⊙ 10,000 - 29,999
- ○ UNDER 10,000

SCALE 1:10,500,000 LAMBERT CONFORMAL CONIC PROJECTION

MILES 0 150 300 450

KILOMETERS 0 150 300 450

A
85°
46
B
90°
C
95°
D
100°
E
105°
F
110°
G
115°
50°
45°
40°
35°
30°
2
3
4
5
6
Western Sayans
Eastern Sayans
Akademik Obruchev Mts.
RESPUBLIKA ALTAY
RESPUBLIKA TYVA
Tannu-Ola Mts.
IRKUTSKAYA OBLAST'
UST'-ORDYNSKIY BURYATSKIY AVT. OKRUG
R U S S I A
Lake Baykal
Irkutsk
Angarsk
Usol'ye-Sibirskoye
Ulan-Burgasy Mts.
RESPUBLIKA BURYATIYA
Ulan-Ude
Vitim Plateau
Chita
Yablonovyy Range
AGINSKIY BURYATSKIY AVT. OKRUG
Khamar-Daban Mts.
KAZAKHSTAN
Zaysan
BAYAN-ÖLGIY
Ölgiy
UVS
Ulaangom
HÖVSGÖL
Mörön
HOVD
Dund-Us
ZAVHAN
Uliastay
Bulnayn Mts.
Tarvagatay Mts.
Hangayn Mts.
ARHANGAY
Tsetserleg
BULGAN
SELENGE
Darhan
Sühbaatar
Büteeliyn Mts.
Bürengiyn Mts.
Ulaanbaatar
TÖV
HENTIY
Hentiyn Mts.
DORNOD
Choybalsan
Kerulen (Herlen)
SÜHBAATAR
Baruun-Urt
M O N G O L I A
Altai Mountains
GOVĬ-ALTAY
Altay
BAYANHONGOR
Bayanhongor
ÖVÖRHANGAY
Arvayheer
DUNDGOVĬ
Mandalgovĭ
DORNOGOVĬ
Sayanshand
ÖMNÖGOVĬ
Dalandzadgad
Govĭ Altayn Mts.
Gobi Desert
Karakorum
Dzungarian Basin
Ürümqi
Bogda Mts.
Bogda Feng 5,445 m
Turpan
Turpan Depression -154 m
Hami
XINJIANG UYGUR AUT. REG.
Kuruktag
Tarim Basin
Lop Lake
Bei Mts.
Bor Ul Mts.
NEI MONGOL AUT. REG.
Badain Jaran Desert
Yin Mountains
Baotou
Hohhot
Zhangjiakou
Datong
BEIJING
Altun Mountains
Serteng Mts.
Qaidam Basin
Tergun Daba Mts.
Qilian Mts.
Qilian Shan 5,547 m
Longshou Mts.
Datong Mts.
GANSU
Jiayuguan
Yumen
Zhangye
Jinchang
Wuwei
Tengger Desert
Helan Mts.
Wuhai
Ordos
Yinchuan
NINGXIA HUIZU AUT. REG.
Qinghai Lake
Xining
Lanzhou
Kunlun Mts.
Golmud
Burhan Budai Mts.
Qinghai Mts.
QINGHAI
A'nyêmaqên Mts.
Bayan Har Mountains
C H I N A
Xiqing Mts.
Tianshui
Baoji
Xianyang
Xi'an
SHAANXI
Taiyuan
SHANXI
Shijiazhuang
HEBEI
Zhengzhou
Luoyang
Kaifeng
HENAN
Xizang (Tibet) AUT. REG.
Chola Mts.
Daxue Mts.
Shaluli Mts.
Qionglai Mts.
SICHUAN
Chengdu
Mianyang
Nanchong
Daba Mts.
HUBEI
Xiangfan
Yichang
WUHAN
Brahmaputra
Namjagbarwa Feng 7,772 m
INDIA
Gongga Shan 7,556 m
C 95°
D
100° Longitude East of Greenwich
E
105°
63
F
110°
G
115°

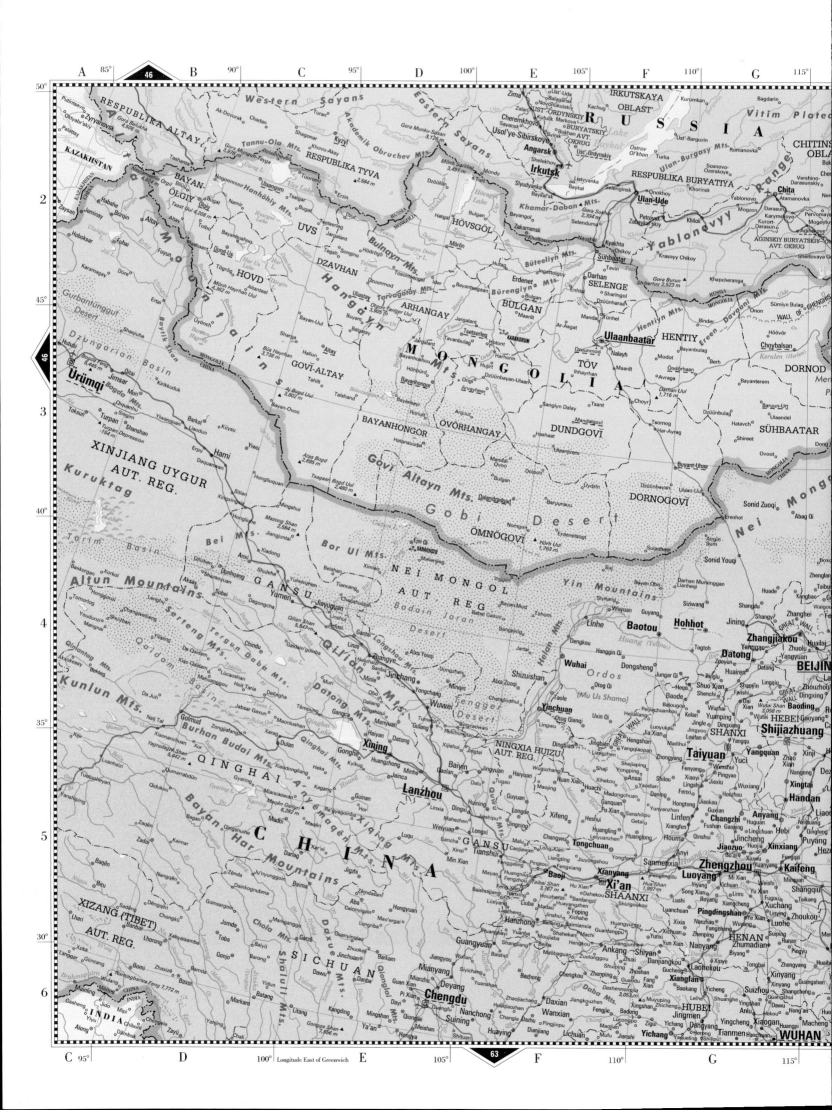

Eastern Asia

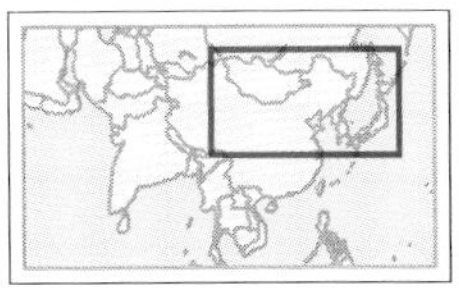

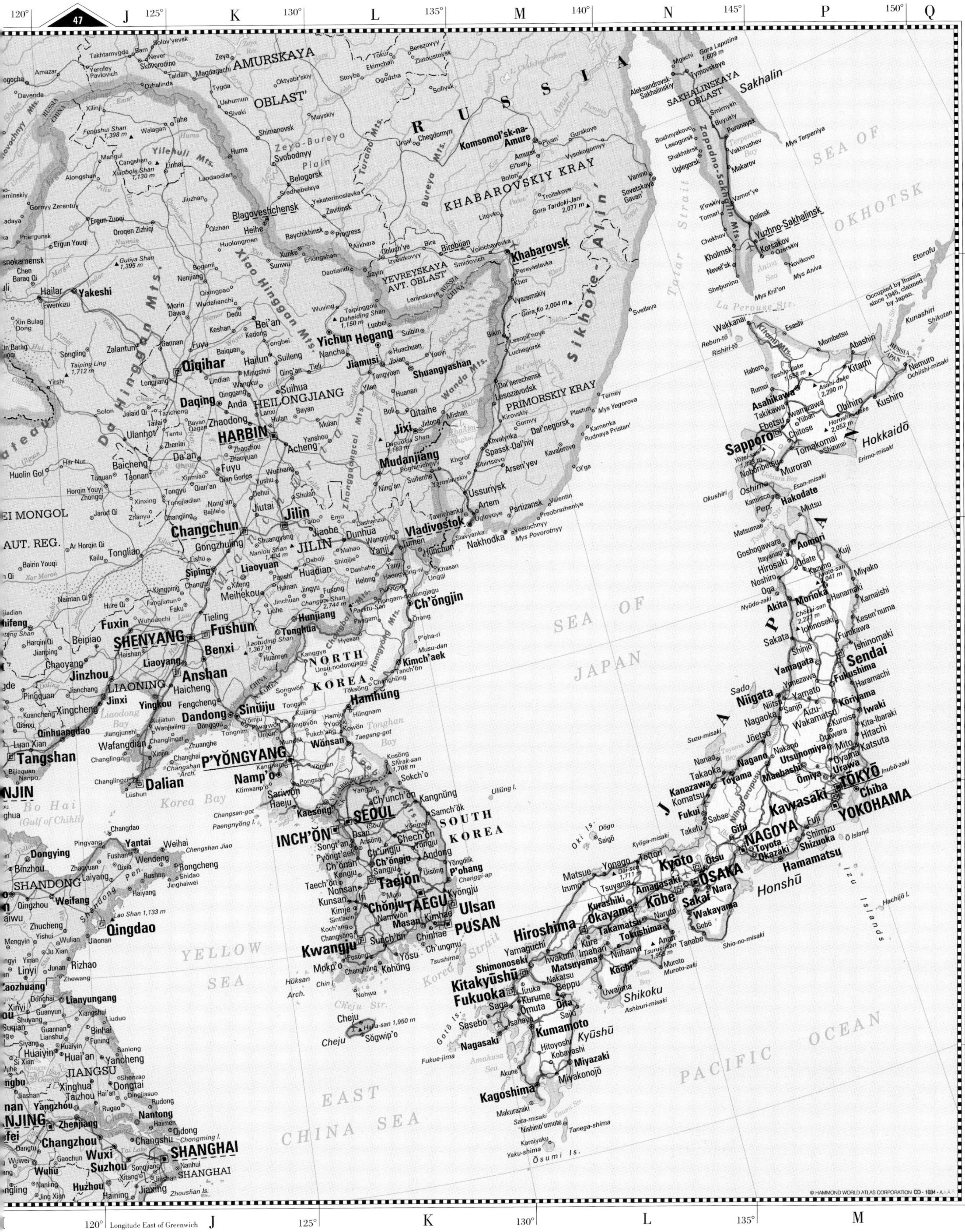

POPULATION OF CITIES AND TOWNS

- OVER 2,000,000
- 1,000,000 - 1,999,999
- 500,000 - 999,999
- 250,000 - 499,999
- 100,000 - 249,999
- 30,000 - 99,999
- 10,000 - 29,999
- UNDER 10,000

SCALE 1:10,500,000 LAMBERT CONFORMAL CONIC PROJECTION

MILES 0 150 300 450

KILOMETERS 0 150 300 450

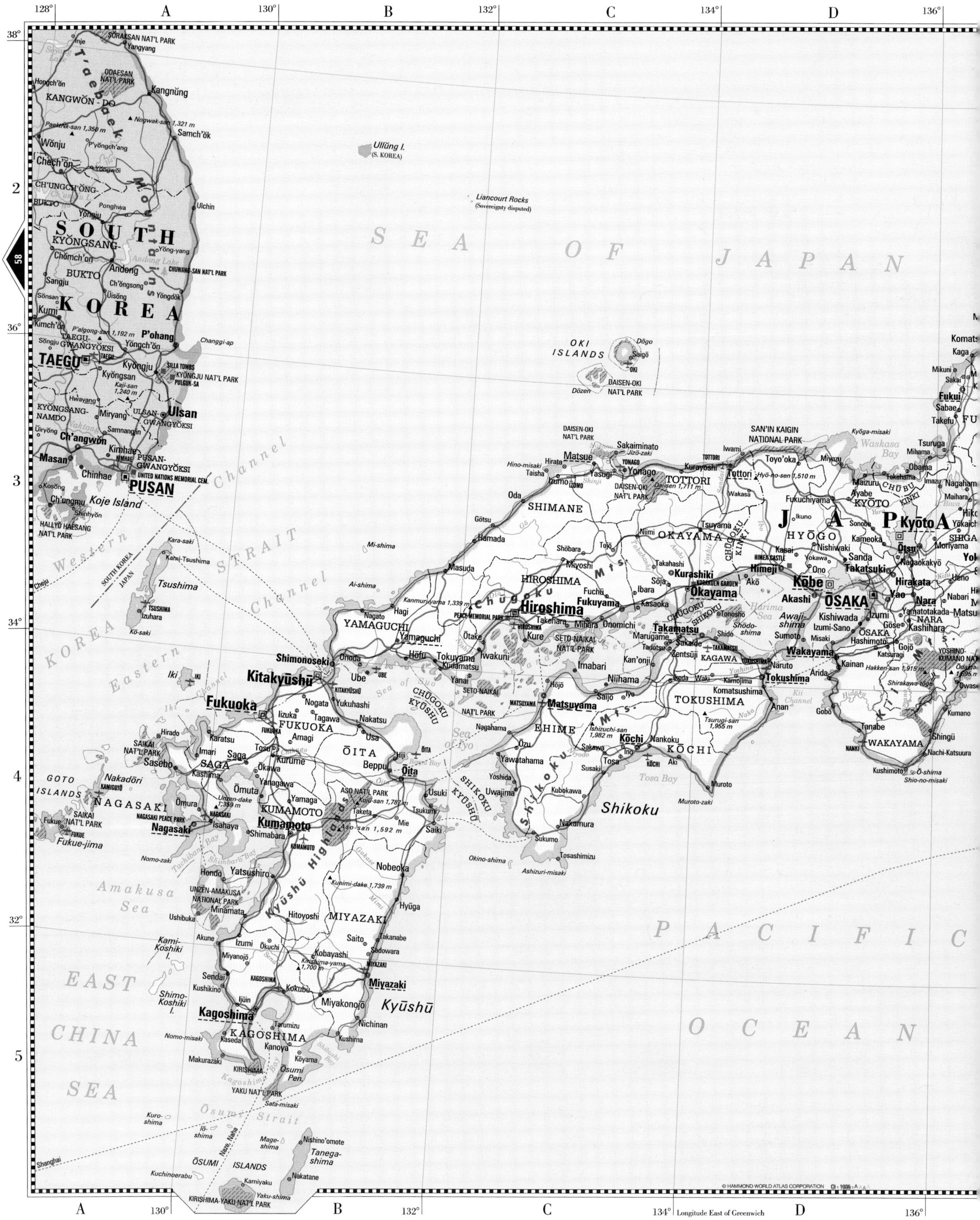
128°
A
130°
B
132°
C
134°
D
136°
38°
2
3
36°
34°
4
32°
5
58
SEA OF JAPAN
PACIFIC OCEAN
EAST CHINA SEA
KOREA STRAIT
Western Channel
Eastern Channel
Amakusa Sea
Ōsumi Strait
SOUTH KOREA
JAPAN
Ullŭng I.
(S. KOREA)
Liancourt Rocks
(Sovereignty disputed)
OKI ISLANDS
Dōgo
Saigō
Dōzen
DAISEN-OKI NAT'L PARK
SORAKSAN NAT'L PARK
Inje
Yangyang
T'aebaek Mts.
ODAESAN NAT'L PARK
Hongch'ŏn
Kangnŭng
KANGWŎN-DO
Noriwak-san 1,321 m
Paeknk-san 1,350 m
Samch'ŏk
Wŏnju
P'yŏngch'ang
Chech'ŏn
Yŏngwŏl
CH'UNGCH'ŎNG-BUKTO
Ponghwa
Ulchin
Yŏngju
KYŎNGSANG-BUKTO
Chŏmch'on
Yŏng-yang
Andong Lake
CHUWANG-SAN NAT'L PARK
Andong
Sangju
Ch'ŏngsong
Ŭisŏng
Yŏngdŏk
Sŏnsan
Kumi
Kimch'ŏn
P'algong-san 1,192 m
P'ohang
Sŏngju
TAEGU-GWANGYŎKSI
Yŏngch'ŏn
Changgi-ap
TAEGU
Kyŏngju
SILLA TOMBS
KYŎNGJU NAT'L PARK
PULGUK-SA
Kyŏngsan
Kaji-san 1,240 m
Hwayang
KYŎNGSANG-NAMDO
Miryang
ULSAN-GWANGYŎKSI
Ulsan
Ŭiryŏng
Naktong
Samnangjin
Ch'angwŏn
Kimhae
Masan
PUSAN-GWANGYŎKSI
Chinhae
PUSAN
UNITED NATIONS MEMORIAL CEM.
Kosŏng
Ch'ungmu
Koje Island
Shinhyŏn
HALLYŎ HAESANG NAT'L PARK
Cheju
Kami-Tsushima
Tsushima
TSUSHIMA
Izuhara
Kō-saki
Iki
IKI
Mi-shima
Ai-shima
Hirado
SAIKAI NAT'L PARK
Imari
Karatsu
Sasebo
SAGA
Saga
Tosu
Kurume
GOTO ISLANDS
Nakadōri
KAMIGOTO
NAGASAKI
Ōmura
Kashima
Unzen-dake 1,359 m
NAGASAKI PEACE PARK
Nagasaki
Isahaya
Fukue
SAIKAI NAT'L PARK
Fukue-jima
Nomo-zaki
Shimabara
Tachibana Bay
Hondo
Yatsushiro
UNZEN-AMAKUSA NATIONAL PARK
Minamata
Ushibuka
Kami-Koshiki I.
Akune
Izumi
Ōkuchi
Miyanojō
Sendai
Kushikino
Shimo-Koshiki I.
Kagoshima
KAGOSHIMA
Nomo-misaki
Kaseda
Makurazaki
Kagoshima Bay
KIRISHIMA-YAKU NAT'L PARK
Sata-misaki
Kuro-shima
Iō-shima
Mage-shima
Nishino'omote
Tanega-shima
ŌSUMI ISLANDS
Kuchinoerabu
Kamiyaku
Yaku-shima
Nakatane
Shanghai
Naze, Naha
Shimonoseki
Kitakyūshū
KITAKYŪSHŪ
Fukuoka
FUKUOKA
Iizuka
Nogata
Yukuhashi
Tagawa
Amagi
Nakatsu
Usa
Ōkawa
Yanagawa
Ōmuta
Yamaga
KUMAMOTO
Kumamoto
ASO NAT'L PARK
Kujū-san 1,787 m
Aso-san 1,592 m
Kyūshū Highlands
Taketa
ŌITA
Ōita
Beppu
Hiji
Usuki
Tsukumi
Saiki
Mie
Nobeoka
Kunimi-dake 1,739 m
Hyūga
Hitoyoshi
MIYAZAKI
Saito
Takanabe
Sadowara
Kobayashi
Kirishima-yama 1,700 m
Miyazaki
Kokubu
Miyakonojō
Kyūshū
Nichinan
Tarumizu
Kanoya
Kushima
Kōyama
Ōsumi Pen.
Shibushi Bay
Nagato
Hagi
YAMAGUCHI
Yamaguchi
Onoda
Ube
Hōfu
Tokuyama
Kudamatsu
Iwakuni
Ōtake
Yanai
Sea of Suo
CHŪGOKU KYŪSHŪ
Sea of Iyo
SETO-NAIKAI NAT'L PARK
Nagahama
Ōzu
Yawatahama
Yoshida
Uwajima
SHIKOKU KYŪSHŪ
Shikoku Mts.
Sukumo
Nakamura
Tosashimizu
Ashizuri-misaki
Okino-shima
Shikoku
Kanmuri-yama 1,339 m
Chūgoku Mts.
Masuda
Hamada
Gōtsu
Oda
SHIMANE
Hino-misaki
Taisha
Hirata
Matsue
Izumo
Yasugi
Sakaiminato
Jizō-zaki
Yonago
DAISEN-OKI NAT'L PARK
TOTTORI
Daisen 1,711 m
Kurayoshi
Tottori
Iwami
SAN'IN KAIGIN NATIONAL PARK
Hyō-no-sen 1,510 m
Wakasa
Niimi
OKAYAMA
Shōbara
Tojō
Miyoshi
HIROSHIMA
Fuchū
Fukuyama
Hiroshima
PEACE MEMORIAL PARK
Kure
Takehara
Mihara
Onomichi
SETO-NAIKAI NAT'L PARK
Takahashi
Sōja
Kurashiki
Ibara
Kasaoka
Okayama
KŌRAKUEN GARDEN
CHŪGOKU SHIKOKU
Takamatsu
Marugame
Sakaide
Tadotsu
Zentsūji
KAGAWA
Kan'onji
Imabari
Niihama
Saijo
Iyo
Matsuyama
EHIME
Ishizuchi-san 1,982 m
Kōchi
Nankoku
KŌCHI
Aki
Sakawa
Ino
Tosa
Susaki
Kubokawa
Tosa Bay
Muroto
Muroto-zaki
Ikeda
Waki
Kamojima
Tokushima
Komatsushima
TOKUSHIMA
Anan
Tsurugi-san 1,955 m
Naruto
Kii Channel
Tonoshō
Shōdo-shima
Awaji-shima
Harima Sea
JAPAN
HYŌGO
Tsuyama
Ikuno
Nishiwaki
Kasai
HIMEJI CASTLE
Himeji
Akō
Akashi
Kōbe
Yokawa
Ono
Sanda
Sumoto
Fukuchiyama
Ayabe
Maizuru
Kyōga-misaki
Toyo'oka
Miyazu
Wakasa Bay
Tsuruga
Mihama
Obama
Takahama
CHŪBU KINKI
KYŌTO
Sonobe
Kameoka
Kyōto
Takatsuki
Ōsaka
ŌSAKA
Hirakata
Yao
Kishiwada
Izumi-Sano
Izumi
Misaki
Wakayama
Arida
Kainan
Gobo
Tanabe
WAKAYAMA
Kushimoto
Shio-no-misaki
Ō-shima
Nachi-Katsuura
Shingū
Kumano
Hashimoto
Katsuragi
Gojō
Gose
NARA
Nara
Kashihara
Yamatotakada
Hakken-san 1,915 m
Shirakawa-tōge
YOSHINO-KUMANO NAT'L PARK
Ōtsu
Moriyama
SHIGA
Nagaokakyō
Nabari
Imazu
Nagahama
Maihara
Fukui
Sabae
Takefu
Kaga
Komatsu
Mikuni
Sakai
© HAMMOND WORLD ATLAS CORPORATION
Longitude East of Greenwich

Central and Southern Japan

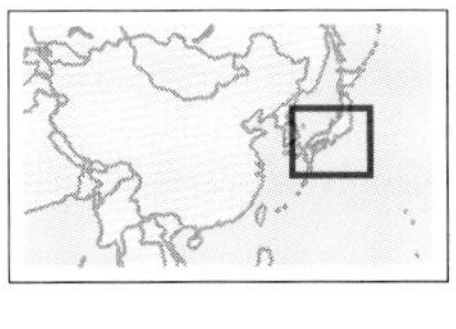

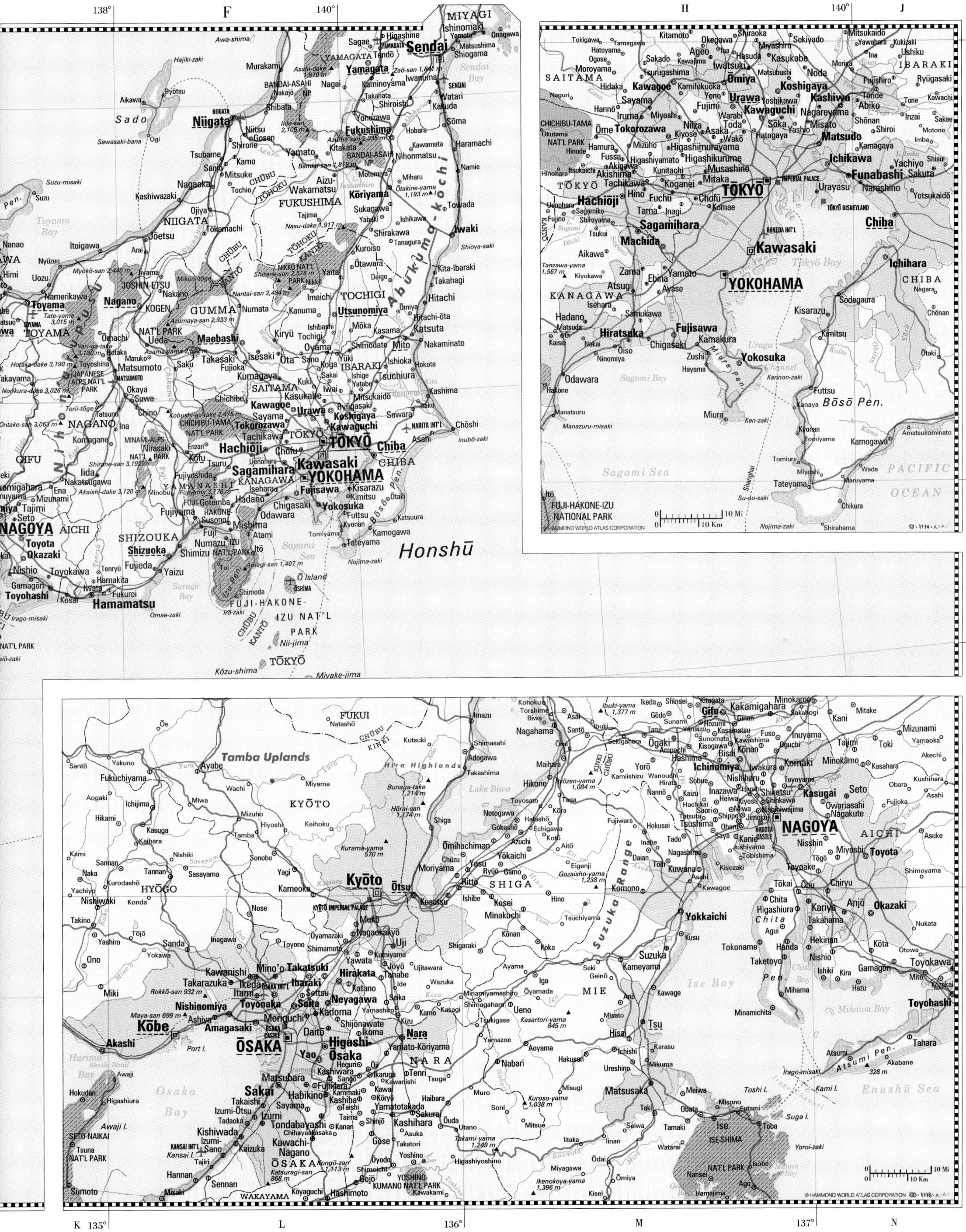

POPULATION OF CITIES AND TOWNS

■ OVER 2,000,000	◉ 500,000 - 999,999	⊕ 100,000 - 249,999	⊙ 10,000 - 29,999
▣ 1,000,000 - 1,999,999	◎ 250,000 - 499,999	⊕ 30,000 - 99,999	○ UNDER 10,000

SCALE 1:3,500,000 LAMBERT CONFORMAL CONIC PROJECTION

MILES 0 50 100 150

KILOMETERS 0 50 100 150

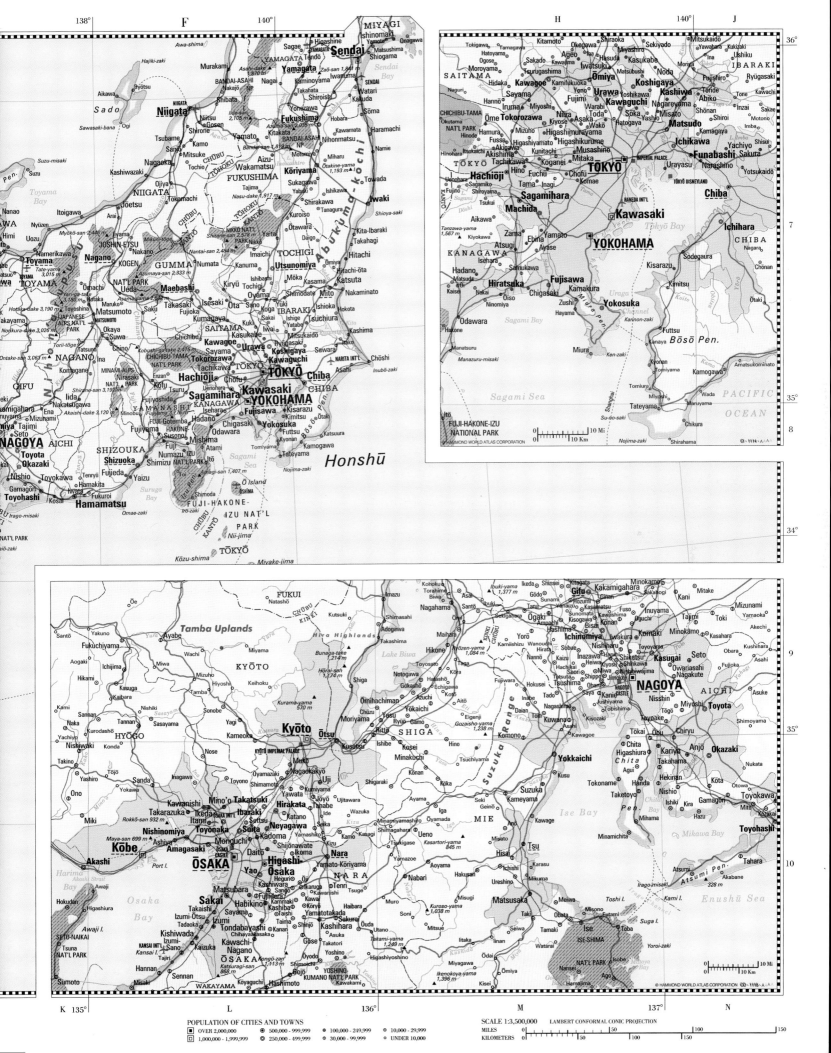

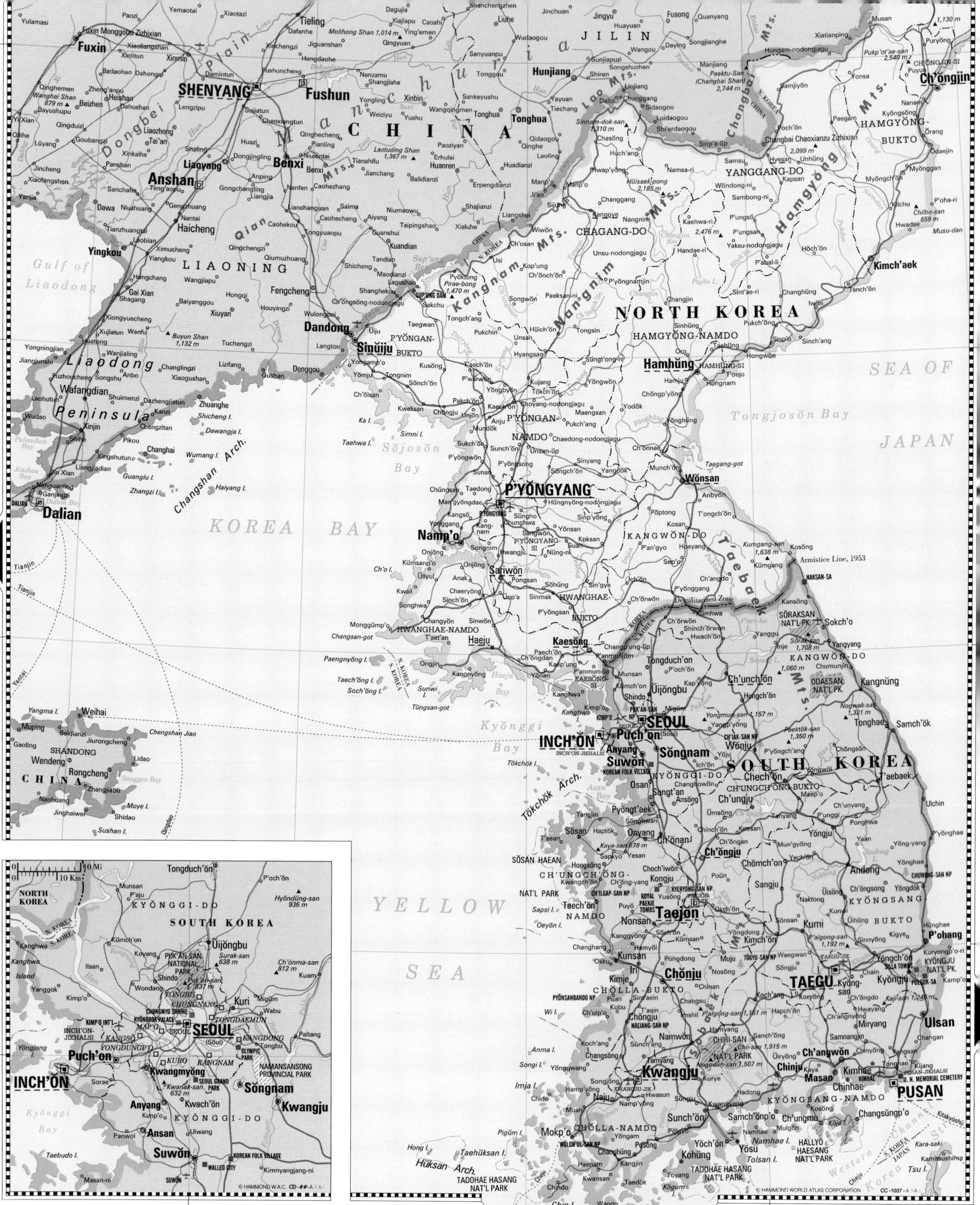

F 127° G Longitude East of Greenwich C 128° E

SCALE 1:3,500,000 LAMBERT CONFORMAL CONIC PROJECTION

MILES 0 50 100 150

KILOMETERS 0 50 100 150

POPULATION OF CITIES AND TOWNS

- OVER 2,000,000
- 1,000,000 - 1,999,999
- 500,000 - 999,999
- 250,000 - 499,999
- 100,000 - 249,999
- 30,000 - 99,999
- 10,000 - 29,999
- UNDER 10,000

Northeastern China

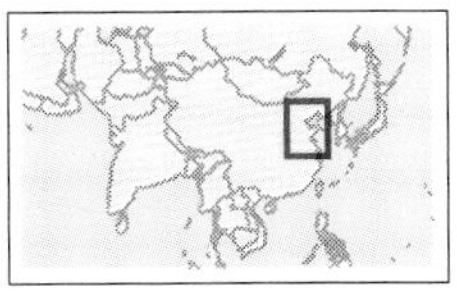

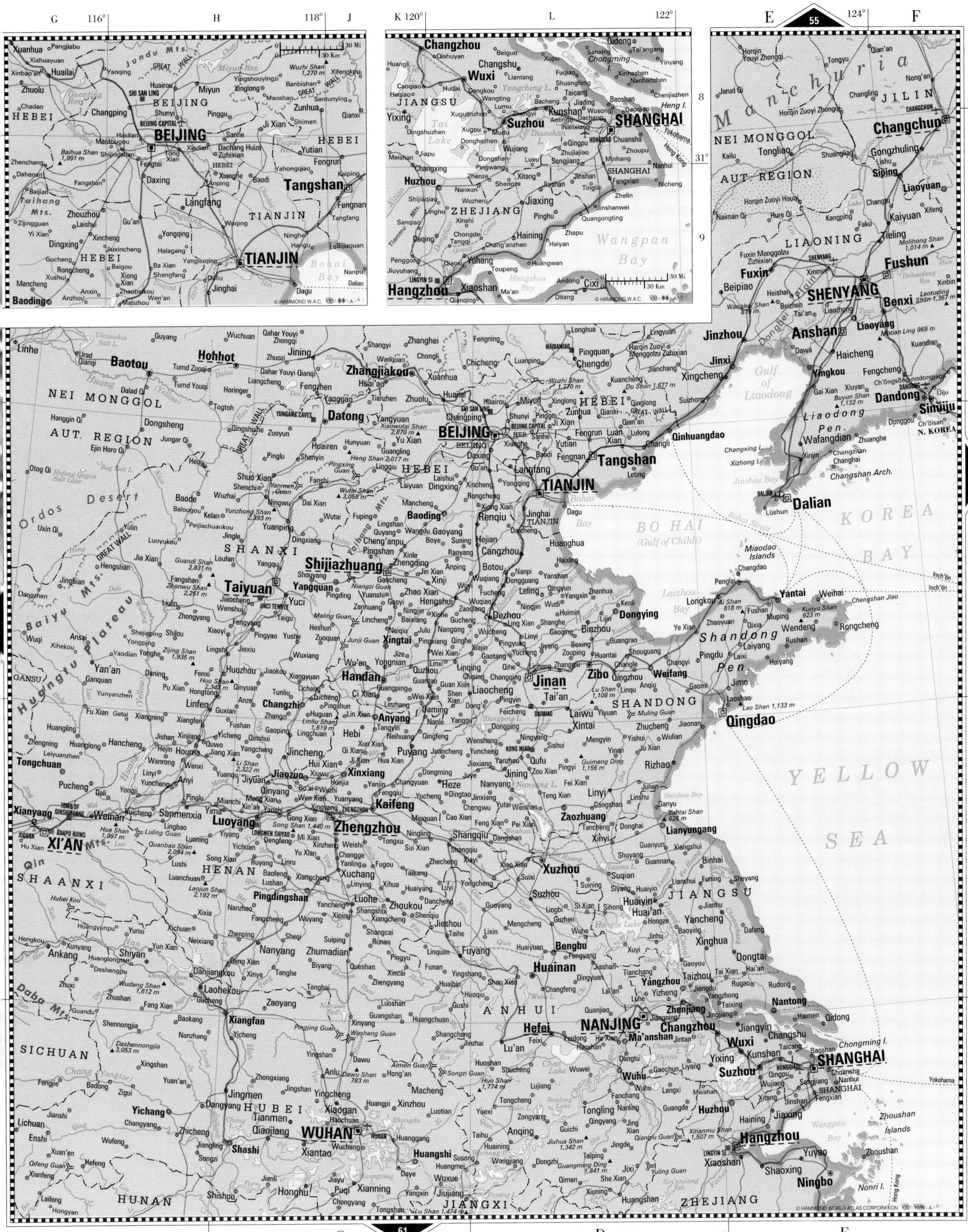

POPULATION OF CITIES AND TOWNS

- OVER 2,000,000
- 1,000,000 - 1,999,999
- 500,000 - 999,999
- 250,000 - 499,999
- 100,000 - 249,999
- 30,000 - 99,999
- 10,000 - 29,999
- UNDER 10,000

SCALE 1:7,000,000 LAMBERT CONFORMAL CONIC PROJECTION

MILES 0 100 200

KILOMETERS 0 100 200 300

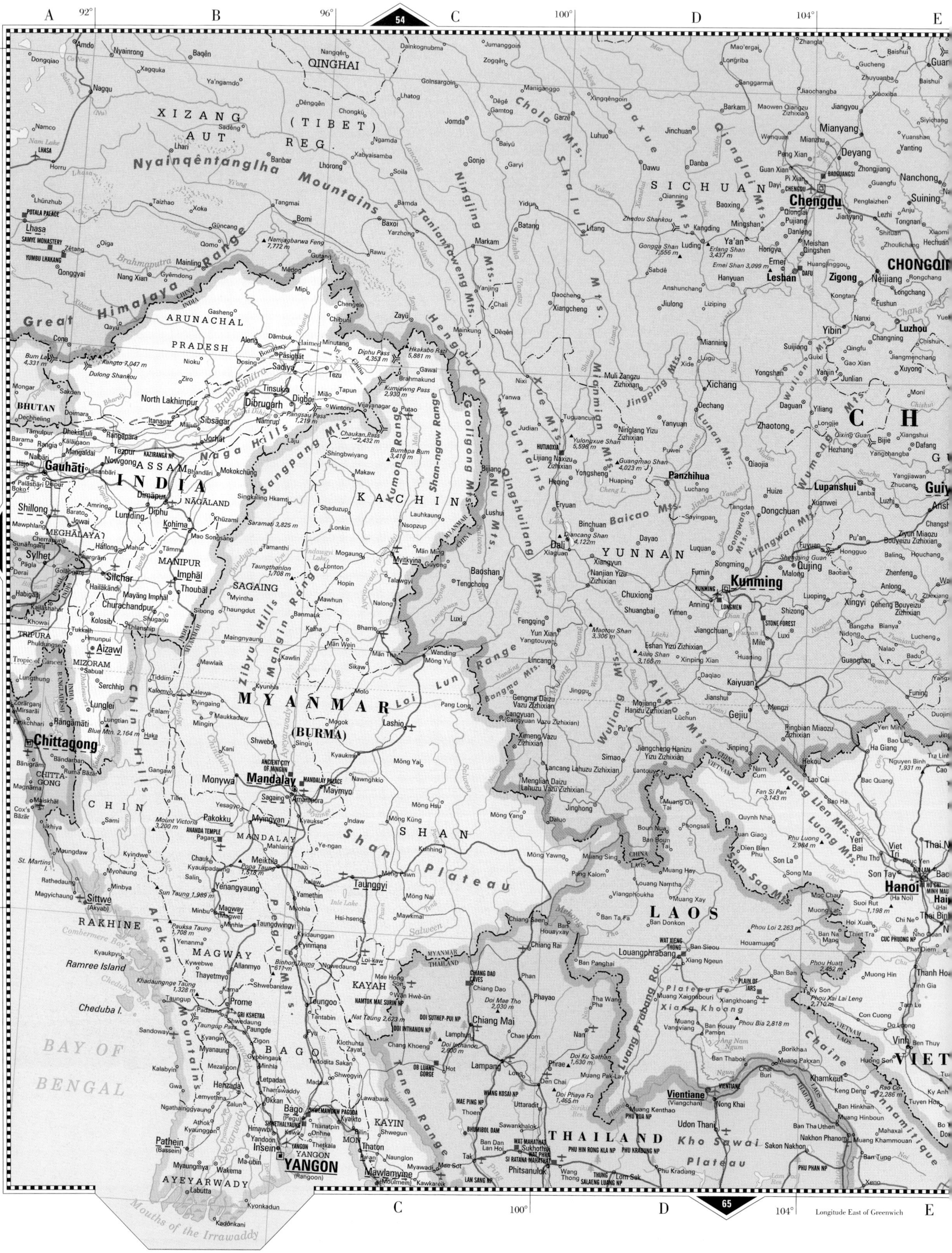

A
B
C
D
E
92°
96°
100°
104°
32°
28°
24°
20°
54
62
65
XIZANG AUT. REG. (TIBET)
QINGHAI
SICHUAN
YUNNAN
INDIA
ARUNACHAL PRADESH
ASSAM
NAGALAND
MANIPUR
MEGHALAYA
TRIPURA
MIZORAM
BHUTAN
BANGLADESH
MYANMAR (BURMA)
KACHIN
SAGAING
CHIN
MANDALAY
MAGWAY
RAKHINE
SHAN
KAYAH
BAGO
KAYIN
MON
AYEYARWADY
YANGON
LAOS
THAILAND
VIET
CH
CHONGQI
Nyainqêntanglha Mountains
Great Himalaya Range
Hengduan Mts.
Ningjing Mts.
Taniantaweng Mts.
Chola Mts.
Shaluli Mts.
Daxue Mts.
Qionglai Mts.
Xue Mts.
Nu Mts.
Gaoligong Mts.
Yun Ling Mountains
Qingshuilang Mts.
Mianmian Mts.
Jingping Mts.
Lunan Mts.
Baicao Mts.
Wumeng Mts.
Wulian Mts.
Gongwang Mts.
Liangwan Mts.
Ailao Mts.
Wuliang Mts.
Bangma Mts.
Lun Range
Loi Lun Range
Hoang Lien Mts.
Phu Luong Mts.
Sam Sao Mts.
Chaîne Annamitique
Luang Prabang Ra.
Tanen Range
Dawna Range
Naga Hills
Sangpang Mts.
Kumon Range
Shan-ngaw Range
Zibyu Hills
Mangin Range
Chin Hills
Arakan Mountains
Pegu Mts.
Shan Plateau
Plateau de Xiang Khoang
Kho Sawai Plateau
Tropic of Cancer
BAY OF BENGAL
Mouths of the Irrawaddy
Lhasa
POTALA PALACE
SAMYE MONASTERY
YUMBU LHAKANG
Nagqu
Namco
Nam Lake
Qonggyai
Nang Xian
Mainling
Gyêmdong
Namjagbarwa Feng 7,772 m
Chamdo
Qamdo
Jomda
Baxoi
Markam
Batang
Litang
Kangding
Ya'an
Chengdu
Dujiangyan
Leshan
Emei
Emei Shan 3,099 m
Gongga Shan 7,556 m
Luding
Erlang Shan 3,437 m
Mianyang
Deyang
Nanchong
Suining
Neijiang
Zigong
Yibin
Luzhou
Xichang
Panzhihua
Dali
Lijiang
Kunming
STONE FOREST
Qujing
Lupanshui
Guiyang
Dongchuan
Zhaotong
Gejiu
Kaiyuan
Mengzi
Hekou
Simao
Jinghong
Baoshan
Tengchong
Mangshi
Lincang
Diancang Shan 4,122 m
Yulongxue Shan 5,596 m
Guangmao Shan 4,023 m
Maotou Shan 3,306 m
Ailao Shan 3,166 m
Gauhati
Shillong
Dibrugarh
Tinsukia
Jorhat
Dimapur
Kohima
Imphal
Silchar
Aizawl
Agartala
Sylhet
Chittagong
Cox's Bazar
Kangto 7,047 m
Hkakabo Razi 5,881 m
Diphu Pass 4,353 m
Pangsau Pass 1,219 m
Chaukan Pass 2,432 m
Saramati 3,825 m
Myitkyina
Bhamo
Lashio
Mandalay
MANDALAY PALACE
ANCIENT CITY OF MINGUN
Sagaing
Amarapura
Maymyo
Monywa
Pakokku
Myingyan
Meiktila
Pagan
ANANDA TEMPLE
Mount Victoria 3,200 m
Popa Taung 1,518 m
Taunggyi
Inle Lake
Magway
Minbu
Sittwe
Prome
Pyinmana
Toungoo
Bago
SHWEMAWDAW PAGODA
Pathein
Yangon
SHWEDAGON PAGODA
Mawlamyine
Ramree Island
Cheduba I.
Chiang Mai
Chiang Rai
Lampang
Phitsanulok
Sukhothai
Doi Inthanon 2,590 m
Louangphrabang
WAT XIENG THONG
PLAIN OF JARS
Phou Bia 2,818 m
Vientiane
Nong Khai
Udon Thani
Hanoi
Lao Cai
Fan Si Pan 3,143 m
Mekong
Salween
Irrawaddy
Chindwin
Brahmaputra
Longitude East of Greenwich

Southeastern China, Northern Indochina

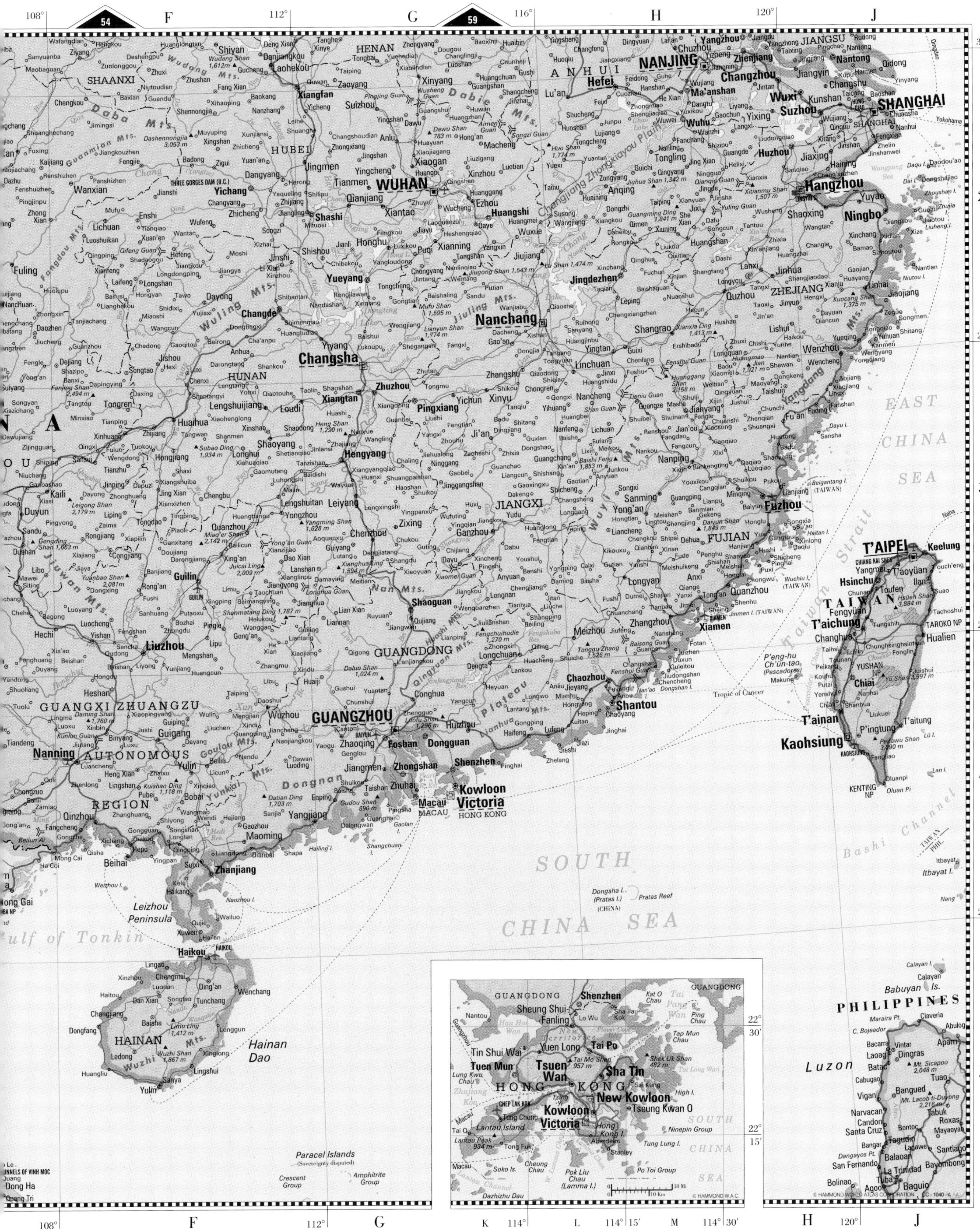

POPULATION OF CITIES AND TOWNS

- OVER 2,000,000
- 1,000,000 - 1,999,999
- 500,000 - 999,999
- 250,000 - 499,999
- 100,000 - 249,999
- 30,000 - 99,999
- 10,000 - 29,999
- UNDER 10,000

SCALE 1:7,000,000 LAMBERT CONFORMAL CONIC PROJECTION

MILES 0 100 200 300

KILOMETERS 0 100 200 300

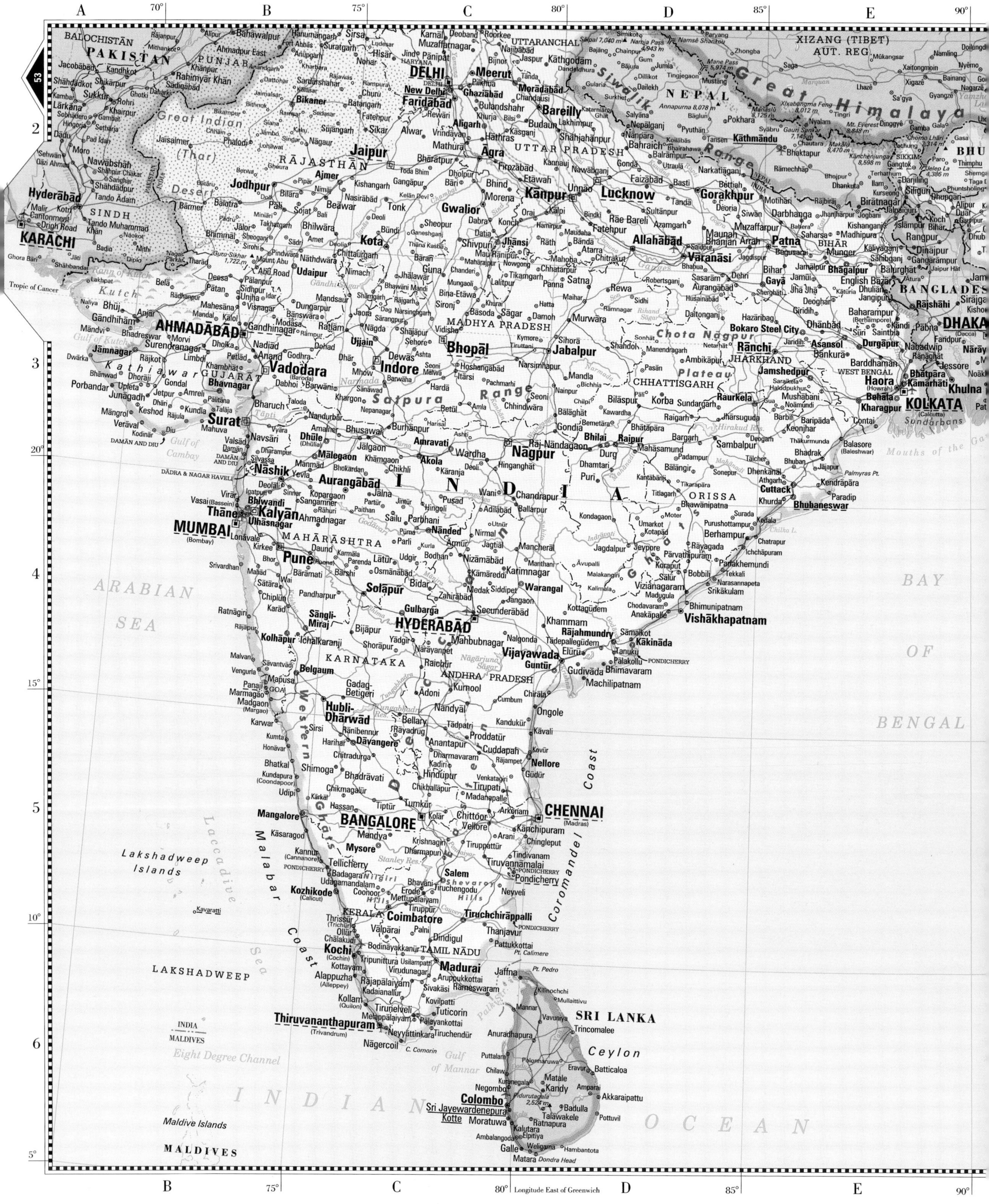

53
A
B
C
D
E
70°
75°
80°
85°
90°
2
3
4
5
6
20°
15°
10°
5°
Longitude East of Greenwich
BALOCHISTĀN
PAKISTAN
PUNJAB
SINDH
Jacobābād
Shikārpur
Sukkur
Lārkāna
Dadu
Moro
Nawābshāh
Hyderābād
Tando Ādam
Malir Cantonment
Drigh Road
Tando Muhammad Khān
KARĀCHI
Badin
Bahāwalpur
Rahimyār Khān
Sādiqābād
Khānpur
Fort Abbās
Great Indian
(Thar)
Desert
Jaisalmer
Phalodi
Bikaner
Jodhpur
Bārmer
Bālotra
Pāli
Sojat
Jālor
Sirohi
Mount Abu
Guru Sikhar 1,722 m
Abu Road
RĀJASTHĀN
Jaipur
Ajmer
Beāwar
Tonk
Kishangarh
Bhīlwāra
Udaipur
Chittaurgarh
Kota
Būndi
Nāthdwāra
Nimach
Alwar
Sīkar
Churu
Hisār
Sirsa
Nohar
HARYANA
Jind
Pānipat
Karnāl
Muzaffarnagar
Deoband
Roorkee
DELHI
New Delhi
Farīdābād
Rewāri
Meerut
Ghāziābād
Pilkhua
Bulandshahr
Aligarh
Hāthras
Mathura
Āgra
Firozābād
Etāwah
Bharatpur
Dholpur
Gwalior
Morena
Bhind
Datia
Jhānsi
Shivpuri
Lalitpur
Guna
UTTARANCHAL
Najibābād
Bijnor
Morādābād
Chandausi
Bareilly
Budaun
Shāhjahānpur
Kāthgodām
Rāmpur
UTTAR PRADESH
Kannauj
Kānpur
Unnāo
Lucknow
Rāe Bareli
Fatehpur
Allahābād
Vārānasi
Jaunpur
Azamgarh
Sultānpur
Faizābād
Gonda
Bahraich
Gorakhpur
Deoria
Basti
Tānda
Nawābganj
Bānda
Kālpi
NEPAL
Siwalik
Range
Great Himalaya
Kāthmāndu
Pokhara
Bhaktapur
Nepalganj
Annapurna 8,078 m
Manaslu 8,125 m
Mt. Everest 8,848 m
Makālu 8,470 m
Kānchenjunga 8,598 m
XIZANG (TIBET) AUT. REG.
Zhongba
Saga
Xigazê
Gyangzê
Lhazê
SIKKIM
Gangtok
Dārjiling
Siliguri
Jalpāiguri
BHU
Thimphu
Biratnagar
Kishanganj
Purnia
Rangpur
Dinājpur
Motihāri
Bettiah
Muzaffarpur
Darbhanga
Patna
Ārrah
BIHĀR
Bihar
Gayā
Munger
Bhāgalpur
Jamālpur
Sasarām
Dehri
Aurangābād
Chota Nāgpur Plateau
Daltonganj
Hazāribāg
Bokāro Steel City
Dhanbād
Āsansol
Rānchi
JHĀRKHAND
Jamshedpur
Durgāpur
WEST BENGAL
Barddhamān
Haora
KOLKATA (Calcutta)
Sundarbans
Kharagpur
Khulna
Jessore
BANGLADESH
Rājshāhi
DHAKA
Baharampur
English Bāzār
Mouths of the Ganges
Balasore
Bhadrak
Cuttack
Bhubaneswar
Puri
Khurda
Kendrāpāra
Paradip
Palmyras Pt.
ORISSA
Sambalpur
Jhārsuguda
Raurkela
Hirakud Res.
Berhampur
Chilka L.
Gopālpur
Rāyagada
Koraput
Jeypore
Vizianagaram
Srikākulam
Vishākhapatnam
Anakāpalle
Kākināda
Rājahmundry
Eluru
Vijayawāda
Guntūr
Machilīpatnam
Gudivāda
Bhīmavaram
Tenāli
Chīrāla
Ongole
Nellore
Kāvali
Gūdūr
ANDHRA PRADESH
Nāgārjuna Sāgar
Khammam
Warangal
HYDERĀBĀD
Secunderābād
Mahbubnagar
Kurnool
Nizāmābād
Karimnagar
Ādilābād
Nirmal
Mancherāl
Nānded
Jagdalpur
CHHATTISGARH
Raipur
Durg
Bhilai
Rāj-Nāndgaon
Bilāspur
Korba
Rāigarh
Dhamtari
Kānker
Gondia
Bālāghāt
Nāgpur
Wardha
Chandrapur
Wāni
Amrāvati
Akola
Jalgaon
Bhusāwal
Dhūle
Mālegaon
Nāshik
Aurangābād
Jālna
Parbhani
Lātūr
Solāpur
Pune
Ahmadnagar
Kalyān
Thāne
Bhiwandi
Ulhāsnagar
MUMBAI (Bombay)
Vasai (Bassein)
MAHĀRĀSHTRA
Sātāra
Sāngli
Miraj
Kolhāpur
Ichalkaranji
Ratnāgiri
Gulbarga
Bijāpur
Bīdar
Belgaum
Hubli-Dhārwād
Gadag-Betigeri
Bellary
Hospet
Raichūr
KARNATAKA
Dāvangere
Shimoga
Chitradurga
Tumkūr
BANGALORE
Mysore
Hassan
Mangalore
Udupi
Kāsaragod
Kannur (Cannanore)
Tellicherry
Kozhikode (Calicut)
Nīlgiri Hills
Palakkad
Coimbatore
Erode
Tiruppur
Salem
Shevaroy Hills
KERALA
Thrissur (Trichur)
Kochi (Cochin)
Alappuzha (Alleppey)
Kollam (Quilon)
Thiruvananthapuram (Trivandrum)
Nāgercoil
C. Comorin
TAMIL NĀDU
Madurai
Dindigul
Tiruchchirāppalli
Thanjāvūr
Pattukkottai
Pt. Calimere
Rāmeswaram
Tuticorin
Tirunelveli
Virudunagar
Rājapālaiyam
Sivakāsi
Cuddalore
Pondicherry
PONDICHERRY
Tiruvannāmalai
Vellore
Kānchipuram
CHENNAI (Madras)
Arkonam
Tirupati
Chittoor
Anantapur
Cuddapah
Proddatūr
Nandyāl
Ādoni
Kurnool
Coromandel Coast
Malabar Coast
Western Ghāts
Eastern Ghāts
Deccan
Satpura Range
Narmada
Tāpti
Godāvari
Krishna
Kāveri
MADHYA PRADESH
Bhopāl
Indore
Ujjain
Dewās
Jabalpur
Sāgar
Vidisha
Satna
Rewa
Katni
Murwāra
Damoh
Chhindwāra
Betūl
Hoshangābād
Khandwa
Burhānpur
Mhow
Ratlām
Mandsaur
Shājāpur
Sehore
Itārsi
Seoni
Mandla
Tikamgarh
Chhatarpur
Panna
GUJARĀT
AHMADĀBĀD
Gāndhīnagar
Mahesāna
Pālanpur
Deesa
Pātan
Sidhpur
Vadodara (Baroda)
Ānand
Nadiād
Bharuch
Surat
Navsāri
Valsād
Bhāvnagar
Rājkot
Jāmnagar
Morvi
Surendranagar
Gondal
Jūnāgadh
Porbandar
Dwārka
Verāval
Bhuj
Kutch
Rann of Kutch
Gulf of Kutch
Kāthiāwār
Gulf of Cambay
DAMĀN AND DIU
DĀDRA & NAGAR HAVELI
Silvassa
Damān
Diu
Panaji
Mormugao
Madgaon (Margao)
GOA
Kārwar
Bhatkal
Tropic of Cancer
ARABIAN SEA
BAY OF BENGAL
INDIAN OCEAN
LAKSHADWEEP
Lakshadweep Islands
Laccadive Sea
Kavaratti
INDIA
MALDIVES
Eight Degree Channel
Maldive Islands
SRI LANKA
Ceylon
Jaffna
Pt. Pedro
Mannar
Vavuniya
Trincomalee
Anuradhapura
Puttalam
Chilaw
Batticaloa
Kurunegala
Matale
Kandy
Negombo
Colombo
Sri Jayewardenepura Kotte
Pidurutalagala 2,524 m
Badulla
Akkaraipattu
Ratnapura
Moratuwa
Kalutara
Galle
Matara
Dondra Head
Hambantota
Gulf of Mannar
Palk Strait

Southern Asia

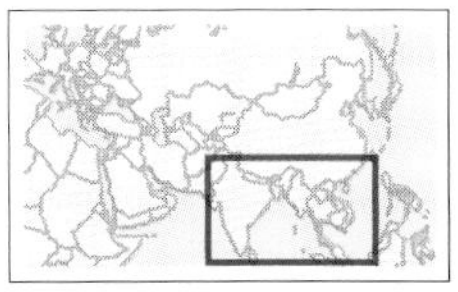

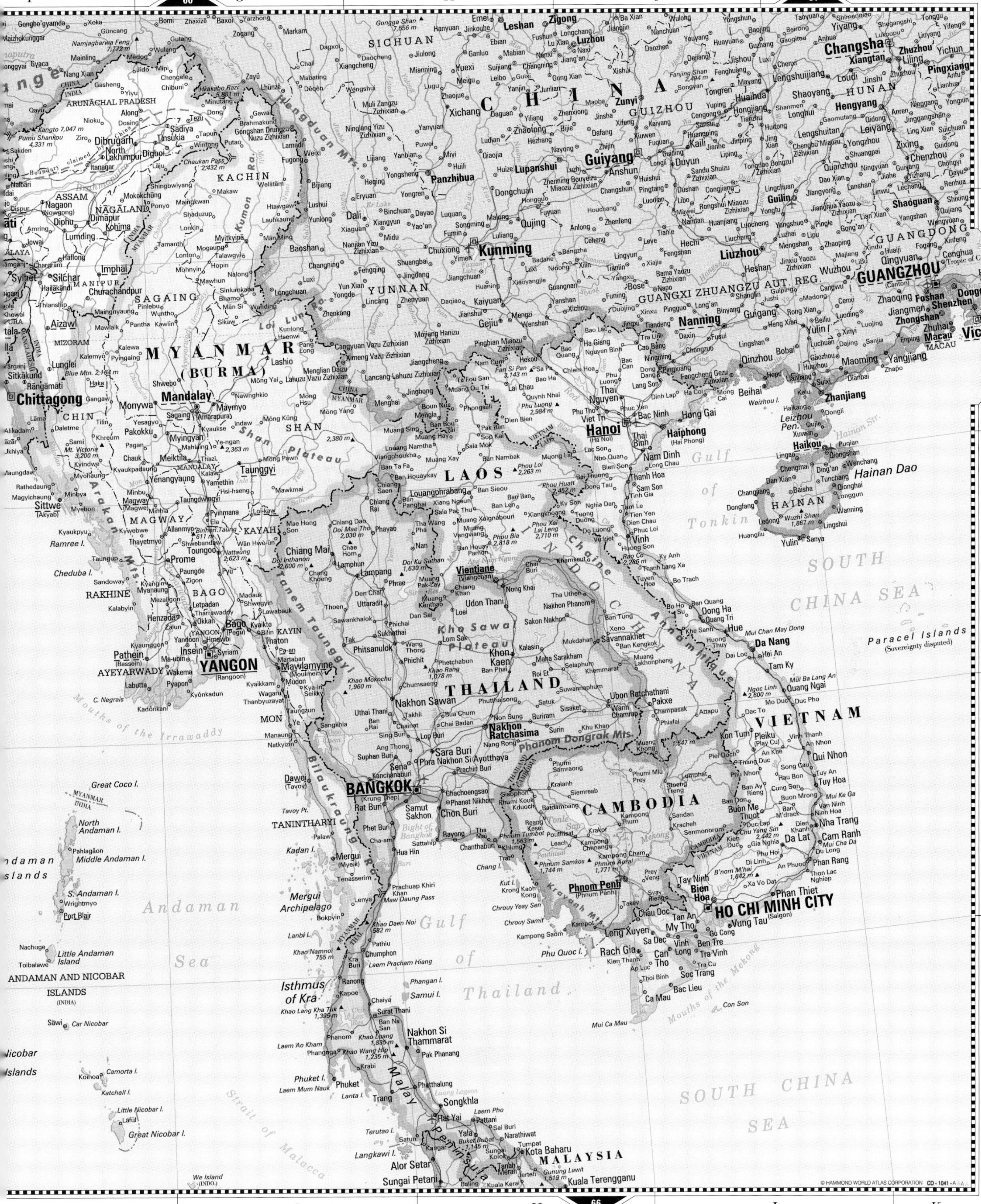

Longitude East of Greenwich

POPULATION OF CITIES AND TOWNS

- ■ OVER 2,000,000
- □ 1,000,000 - 1,999,999
- ◉ 500,000 - 999,999
- ◎ 250,000 - 499,999
- ⊙ 100,000 - 249,999
- ⊙ 30,000 - 99,999
- ○ 10,000 - 29,999
- ○ UNDER 10,000

SCALE 1:10,500,000 LAMBERT CONFORMAL CONIC PROJECTION

MILES 0 150 300 450

KILOMETERS 0 150 300 450

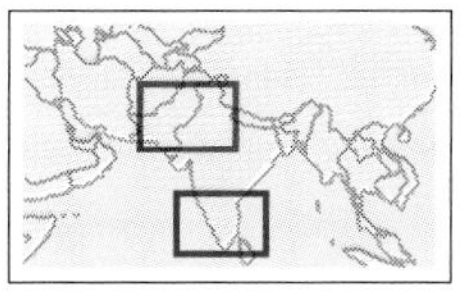

Punjab Plain, Southern India

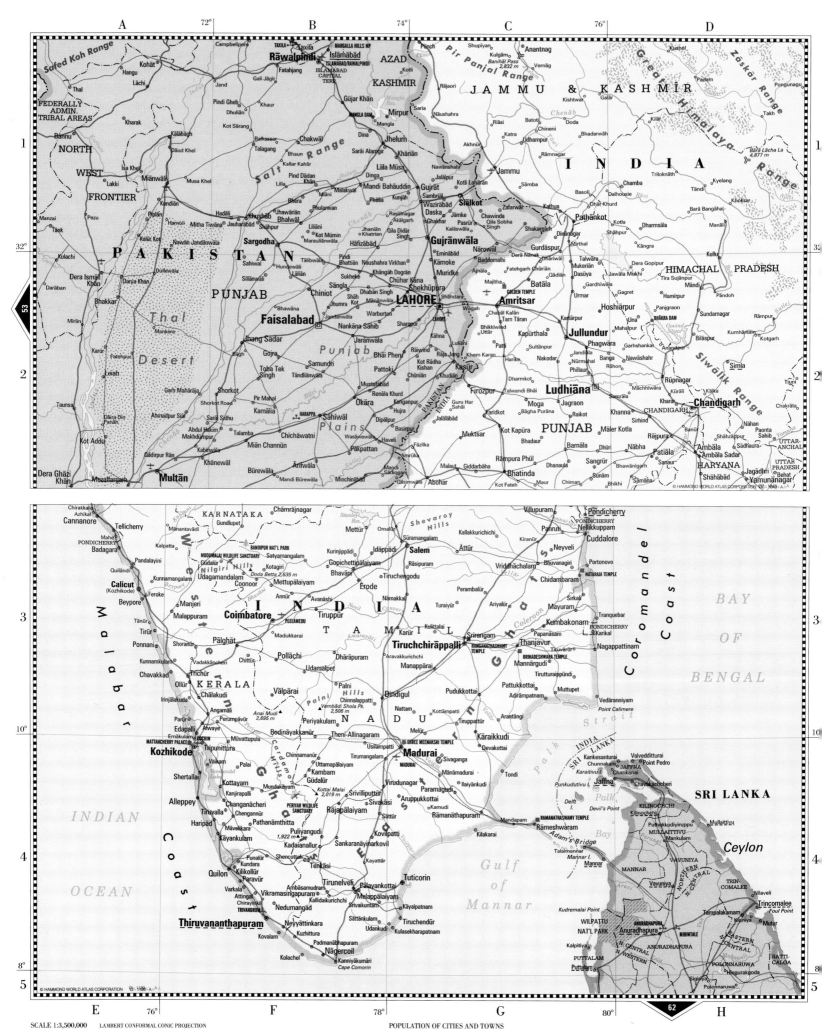

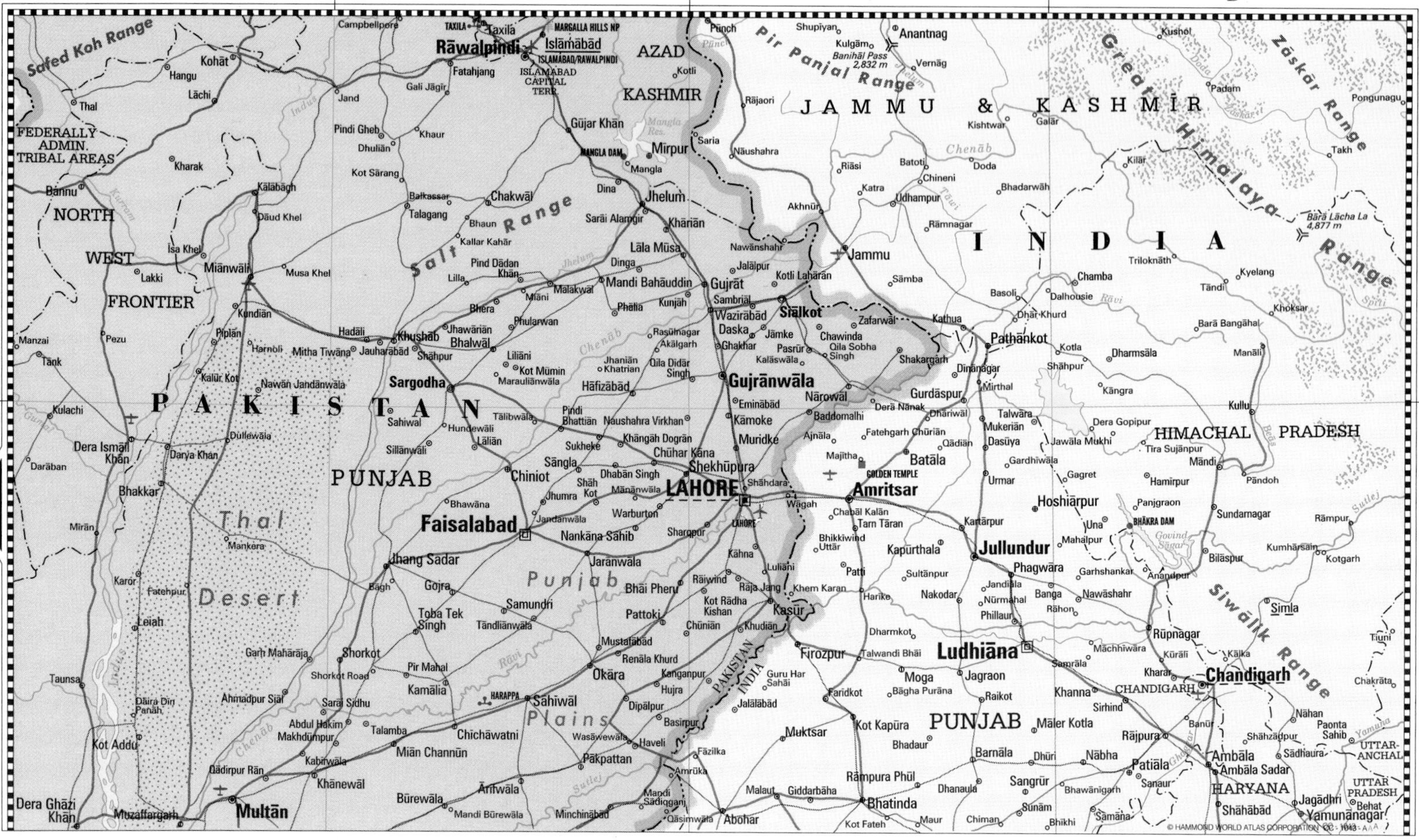

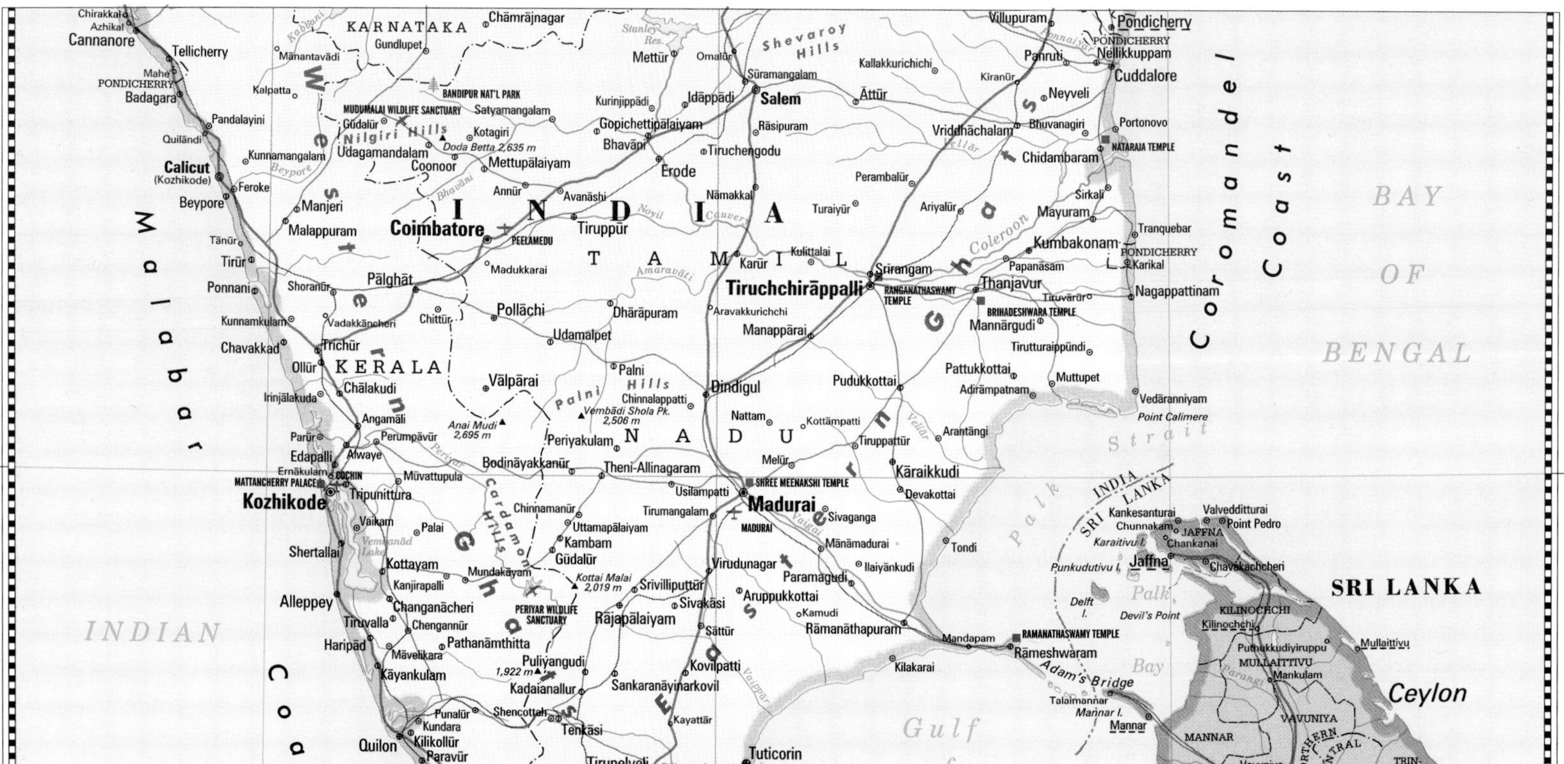

SCALE 1:3,500,000 LAMBERT CONFORMAL CONIC PROJECTION

MILES 0 50 100 150

KILOMETERS 0 50 100 150

POPULATION OF CITIES AND TOWNS

- OVER 2,000,000
- 1,000,000 - 1,999,999
- 500,000 - 999,999
- 250,000 - 499,999
- 100,000 - 249,999
- 30,000 - 99,999
- 10,000 - 29,999
- UNDER 10,000

Indochina

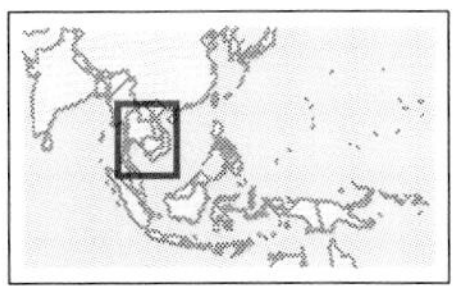

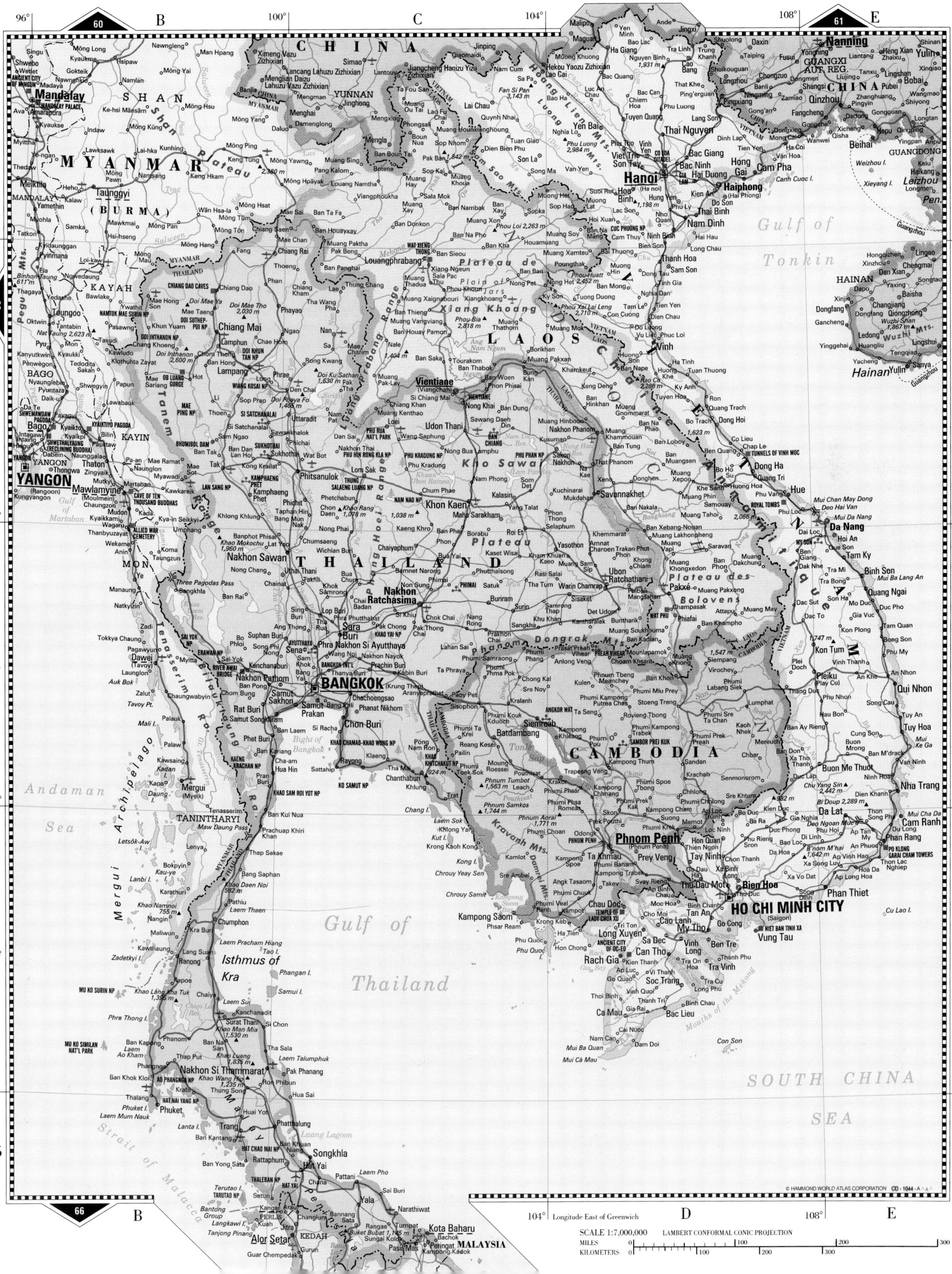

CHINA
MYANMAR
(BURMA)
THAILAND
LAOS
CAMBODIA
VIETNAM
MALAYSIA
HAINAN
Nanning
Hanoi
Haiphong
Mandalay
YANGON
(Rangoon)
BANGKOK
(Krung Thep)
Vientiane
(Viangchan)
Phnom Penh
HO CHI MINH CITY
(Saigon)
Da Nang
Hue
Chiang Mai
Khon Kaen
Nakhon Ratchasima
Luang Prabang
Savannakhet
Pakxé
Siemreab
Batdambang
Kampong Saom
Nha Trang
Qui Nhon
Da Lat
Vung Tau
Can Tho
Songkhla
Hat Yai
Phuket
Surat Thani
Nakhon Si Thammarat
Mawlamyine
(Moulmein)
Dawei
(Tavoy)
Mergui
(Myeik)
Kota Baharu
Alor Setar
Gulf of Tonkin
Gulf of Thailand
Gulf of Martaban
Andaman Sea
Mergui Archipelago
SOUTH CHINA SEA
Strait of Malacca
Isthmus of Kra
Plateau de Xiang Khoang
Khorat Plateau
Plateau des Bolovens
Annamitique
Dongrak Mts.
Kravanh Mts.
Tenasserim Ra.
Shan Plateau
Mouths of the Mekong
Longitude East of Greenwich
SCALE 1:7,000,000
LAMBERT CONFORMAL CONIC PROJECTION
MILES
KILOMETERS
0
100
200
300
© HAMMOND WORLD ATLAS CORPORATION
96°
100°
104°
108°
20°
16°
12°
8°
B
C
D
E
1
2
3
4
5
60
61
66

SCALE 1:10,500,000 LAMBERT CONFORMAL CONIC PROJECTION

MILES 0 50 100 150

KILOMETERS 0 50 100 150 200 250

POPULATION OF CITIES AND TOWNS

- OVER 2,000,000
- 1,000,000 - 1,999,999
- 500,000 - 999,999
- 250,000 - 499,999
- 100,000 - 249,999
- 30,000 - 99,999
- 10,000 - 29,999
- UNDER 10,000

Indonesia, Malaysia

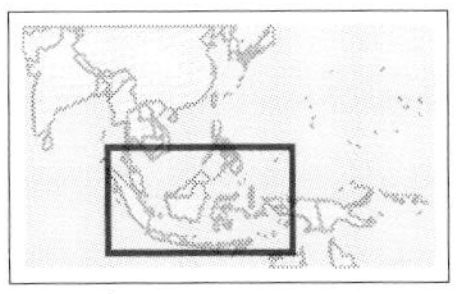

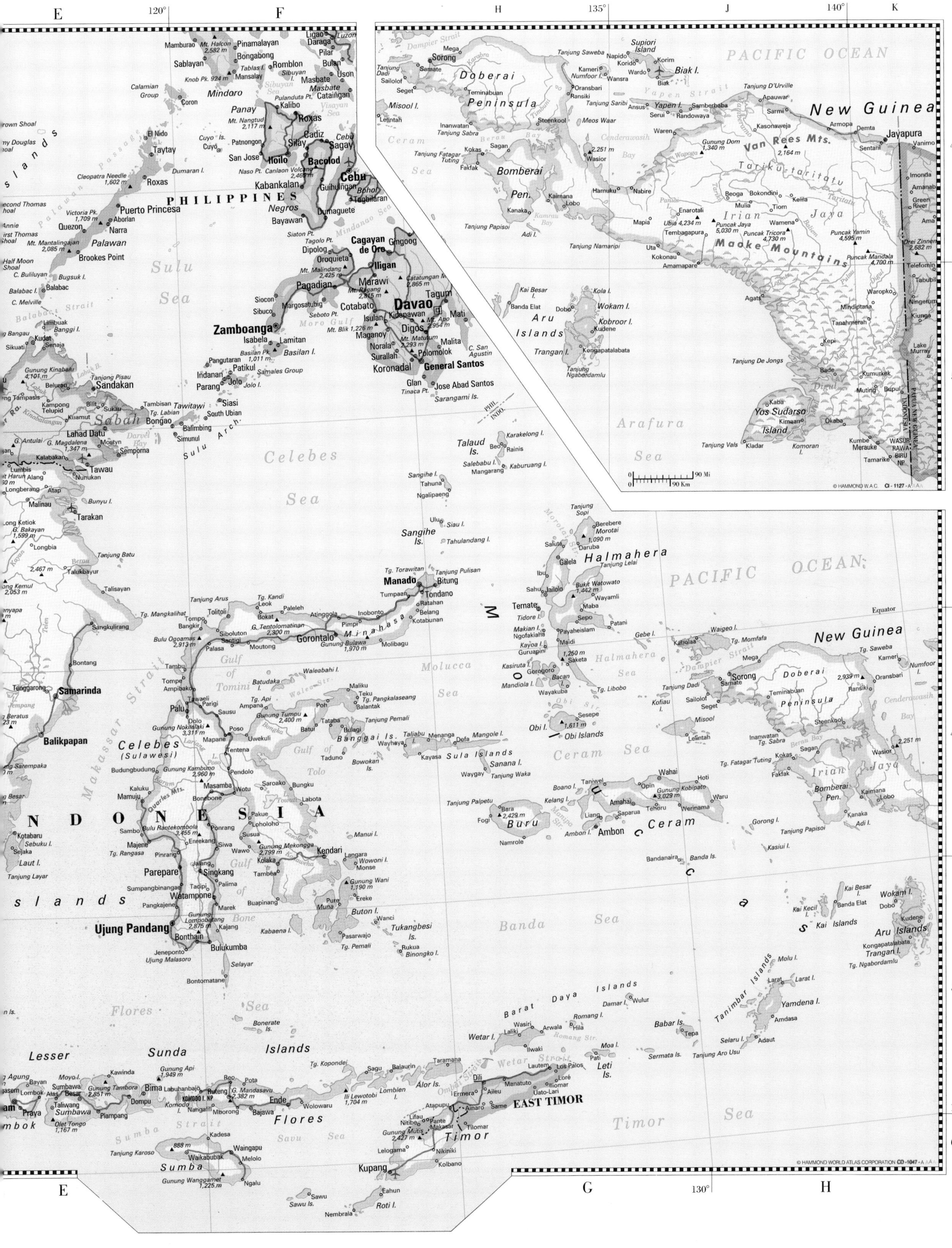

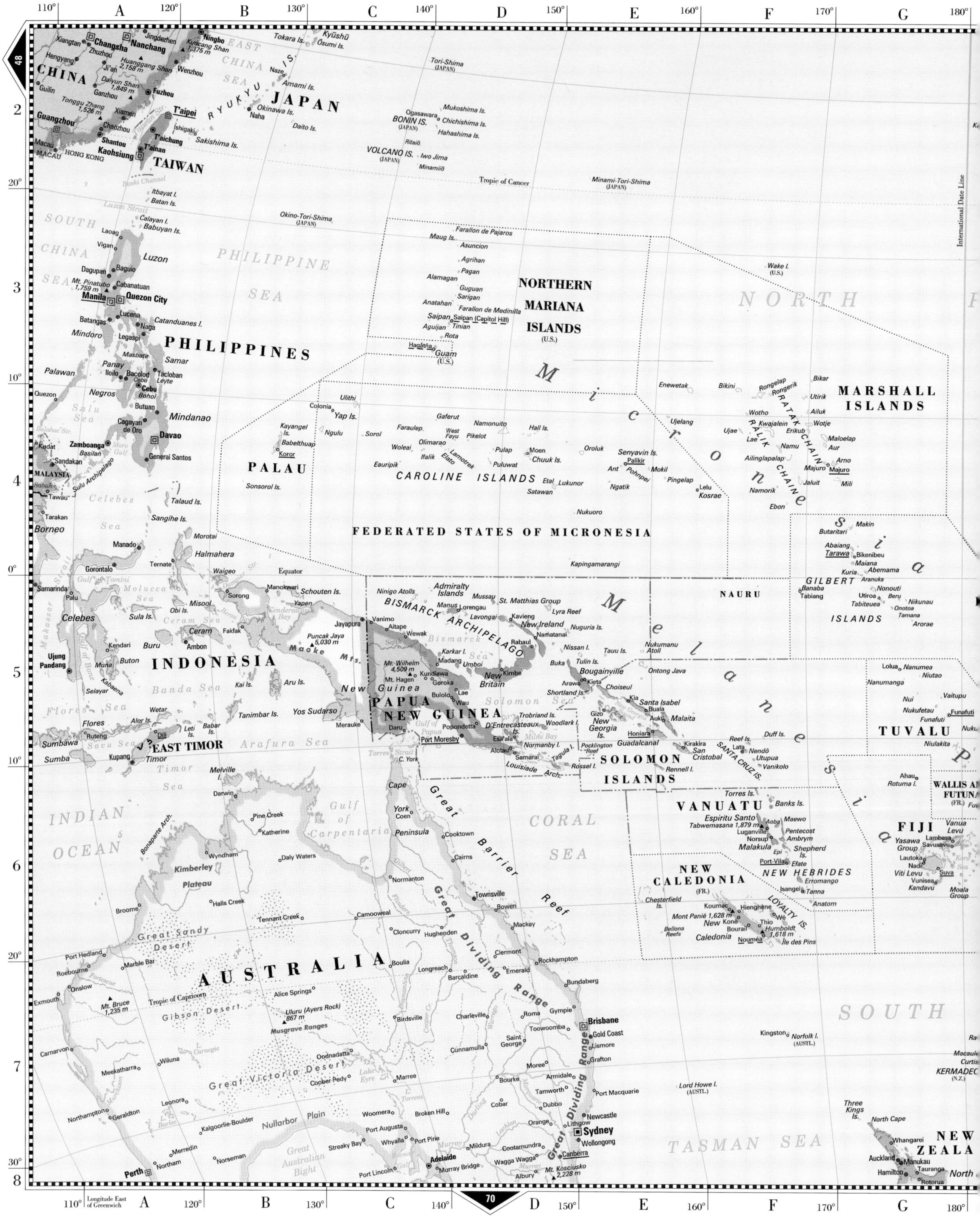

110° A 120° B 130° C 140° D 150° E 160° F 170° G 180°
48
CHINA
Changsha
Nanchang
Ningbo
Jingdezhen
Xiangtan
Zhuzhou
Hengyang
Ji'an
Huanggang Shan 2,158 m
Kuocang Shan 1,375 m
Wenzhou
Daiyun Shan 1,849 m
Ganzhou
Guilin
Fuzhou
Tonggu Zhang 1,526 m
Xiamen
Guangzhou
Chaozhou
Shantou
Macau
MACAU
HONG KONG
T'aipei
T'aichung
T'ainan
Kaohsiung
TAIWAN
Ishigaki
Sakishima Is.
EAST CHINA SEA
Kyūshū
Tokara Is.
Ōsumi Is.
RYUKYU IS.
Naze
Amami Is.
JAPAN
Okinawa Is.
Naha
Daito Is.
Tori-Shima (JAPAN)
Ogasawara
BONIN IS. (JAPAN)
Mukoshima Is.
Chichishima Is.
Hahashima Is.
Ritaiō
VOLCANO IS. (JAPAN)
Iwo Jima
Minamiiō
Tropic of Cancer
Minami-Tori-Shima (JAPAN)
Bashi Channel
Itbayat I.
Batan Is.
Luzon Strait
Calayan I.
Babuyan Is.
Okino-Tori-Shima (JAPAN)
SOUTH CHINA SEA
Laoag
Vigan
Luzon
PHILIPPINE SEA
Dagupan
Baguio
Mt. Pinatubo 1,759 m
Cabanatuan
Manila
Quezon City
Lucena
Batangas
Naga
Catanduanes I.
Mindoro
Legaspi
PHILIPPINES
Masbate
Samar
Panay
Palawan
Iloilo
Bacolod
Tacloban
Leyte
Cebu
Bohol
Negros
Quezon
Butuan
Sulu Sea
Mindanao
Cagayan de Oro
Balabac Str.
Kudat
Zamboanga
Davao
Moro Gulf
Basilan
General Santos
Sandakan
MALAYSIA
Sulu Archipelago
Sabah
Tawau
Celebes Sea
Talaud Is.
Tarakan
Sangihe Is.
Borneo
Morotai
Manado
Halmahera
Ternate
Waigeo
Equator
Gorontalo
Gulf of Tomini
Samarinda
Palu
Molucca Sea
Sorong
Manokwari
Schouten Is.
Yapen
Cenderawasih Bay
Makassar Strait
Celebes
Obi Is.
Misool
Sula Is.
Ceram Sea
Ceram
Fakfak
Jayapura
Vanimo
Kendari
Buru
Ambon
Puncak Jaya 5,030 m
Maoke Mts.
Ujung Pandang
Gulf of Bone
Muna
Buton
INDONESIA
Kabaena
Banda Sea
Kai Is.
Aru Is.
Selayar
Flores Sea
Wetar
Flores
Alor Is.
Leti Is.
Babar Is.
Tanimbar Is.
Yos Sudarso
Merauke
Sumbawa
Ruteng
Savu Sea
Dili
EAST TIMOR
Sumba
Kupang
Timor
Arafura Sea
Timor Sea
Tori-Shima
Farallon de Pajaros
Maug Is.
Asuncion
Agrihan
Pagan
Alamagan
Guguan
Sarigan
Anatahan
Farallon de Medinilla
Saipan
Saipan (Capitol Hill)
Tinian
Aguijan
Rota
NORTHERN MARIANA ISLANDS (U.S.)
Hagåtña
Guam (U.S.)
Wake I. (U.S.)
NORTH PACIFIC
Micronesia
Ulithi
Colonia
Yap Is.
Ngulu
Sorol
Faraulep
Gaferut
West Fayu
Namonuito
Pikelot
Hall Is.
Kayangel Is.
Babelthuap
Koror
PALAU
Sonsorol Is.
Woleai
Olimarao
Ifalik
Eauripik
Elato
Lamotrek
Pulap
Puluwat
Moen
Chuuk Is.
Oroluk
Senyavin Is.
Palikir
Pohnpei
Mokil
Ant
Pingelap
Ngatik
CAROLINE ISLANDS
Etal
Lukunor
Satawan
Lelu
Kosrae
Nukuoro
FEDERATED STATES OF MICRONESIA
Kapingamarangi
Enewetak
Bikini
Rongelap
Rongerik
Bikar
Utirik
MARSHALL ISLANDS
Ailuk
Wotho
Ujelang
Kwajalein
Erikub
Wotje
Ujae
RATAK CHAIN
RALIK CHAIN
Lae
Maloelap
Aur
Namu
Ailinglapalap
Arno
Majuro
Majuro
Jaluit
Mili
Namorik
Ebon
Makin
Butaritari
Abaiang
Tarawa
Bikenibeu
Maiana
Abemama
Kuria
Aranuka
GILBERT ISLANDS
Banaba
Tabiang
Nonouti
Utiroa
Beru
Tabiteuea
Nikunau
Onotoa
Tamana
Arorae
NAURU
Ninigo Atolls
Admiralty Islands
Manus
Lorengau
Mussau
St. Matthias Group
BISMARCK ARCHIPELAGO
Lavongai
Kavieng
Lyra Reef
New Ireland
Namatanai
Nuguria Is.
Aitape
Wewak
Bismarck Sea
Sepik
Karkar I.
Rabaul
Nissan I.
Tauu Is.
Nukumanu Atoll
Madang
Umboi
Mt. Wilhelm 4,509 m
Mt. Hagen
Kundiawa
Goroka
Kimbe
New Britain
Buka
Bougainville
Ontong Java
Lae
Bulolo
Wau
Kieta
Arawa
Choiseul
New Guinea
PAPUA NEW GUINEA
Solomon Sea
Shortland Is.
Kia
Santa Isabel
Buala
Gizo
New Georgia Is.
Auki
Malaita
Trobriand Is.
Woodlark I.
D'Entrecasteaux Is.
Popondetta
Gulf of Papua
Daru
Port Moresby
Milne Bay
Normanby I.
Esa'ala
Alotau
Samarai
Tagula I.
Louisiade Arch.
Rossel I.
Pocklington Reef
Honiara
Guadalcanal
Kirakira
San Cristobal
SOLOMON ISLANDS
Rennell I.
Reef Is.
Lata
Nendō
Utupua
Vanikolo
SANTA CRUZ IS.
Duff Is.
Melanesia
Torres Strait
C. York
Lolua
Nanumea
Niutao
Nanumanga
Vaitupu
Nui
Nukufetau
Funafuti
Funafuti
TUVALU
Niulakita
Ahau
Rotuma I.
WALLIS AND FUTUNA (FR.)
Polynesia
Melville I.
Darwin
Cape York Peninsula
Coen
Great Barrier Reef
Gulf of Carpentaria
CORAL SEA
INDIAN OCEAN
Pine Creek
Katherine
Bonaparte Arch.
Wyndham
Daly Waters
Cooktown
Cairns
Kimberley Plateau
Normanton
Gilbert
Halls Creek
Townsville
Bowen
Mackay
Tennant Creek
Camooweal
Cloncurry
Hughenden
Great Dividing Range
Flinders
Broome
Great Sandy Desert
Port Hedland
Marble Bar
Roebourne
Fortescue
AUSTRALIA
Boulia
Clermont
Rockhampton
Emerald
Longreach
Barcaldine
Bundaberg
Onslow
Exmouth
Mt. Bruce 1,235 m
Tropic of Capricorn
Alice Springs
Gibson Desert
Uluru (Ayers Rock) 867 m
Musgrave Ranges
Birdsville
Charleville
Roma
Gympie
Brisbane
Gold Coast
Toowoomba
Lismore
Saint George
Cunnamulla
Carnarvon
Wiluna
Meekatharra
Oodnadatta
Great Victoria Desert
Coober Pedy
Lake Eyre
Marree
Moree
Armidale
Grafton
Bourke
Tamworth
Port Macquarie
Northampton
Geraldton
Leonora
Lake Barlee
Kalgoorlie-Boulder
Nullarbor Plain
Woomera
Broken Hill
Cobar
Dubbo
Orange
Newcastle
Lithgow
Sydney
Wollongong
Port Augusta
Whyalla
Port Pirie
Streaky Bay
Mildura
Cootamundra
Wagga Wagga
Canberra
Great Australian Bight
Merredin
Norseman
Perth
Northam
Adelaide
Murray Bridge
Port Lincoln
Albury
Mt. Kosciusko 2,228 m
Murray
Darling
Lachlan
TASMAN SEA
Lord Howe I. (AUSTL.)
Kingston
Norfolk I. (AUSTL.)
SOUTH PACIFIC
VANUATU
Torres Is.
Banks Is.
Espiritu Santo
Tabwemasana 1,879 m
Aoba
Maewo
Luganville
Pentecost
Norsup
Ambrym
Malakula
Epi
Shepherd Is.
Port-Vila
Efate
NEW HEBRIDES
Erromango
Isangel
Tanna
Aneityum
NEW CALEDONIA (FR.)
Chesterfield Is.
LOYALTY IS.
Koumac
Hienghène
Mont Panié 1,628 m
Thio
Wé
New Caledonia
Koné
Bourail
Humboldt 1,618 m
Nouméa
Île des Pins
Bellona Reefs
FIJI
Vanua Levu
Lambasa
Yasawa Group
Savusavu
Lautoka
Nadi
Viti Levu
Vunisea
Suva
Kandavu
Moala Group
International Date Line
Macauley
Curtis
KERMADEC (N.Z.)
Three Kings Is.
North Cape
Whangarei
NEW ZEALAND
Auckland
Manukau
Hamilton
Tauranga
Rotorua
North
Longitude East of Greenwich
2 3 4 5 6 7 8
20° 10° 0° 10° 20° 30°
70

Central Pacific Ocean

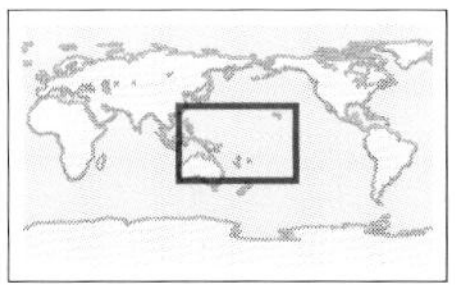

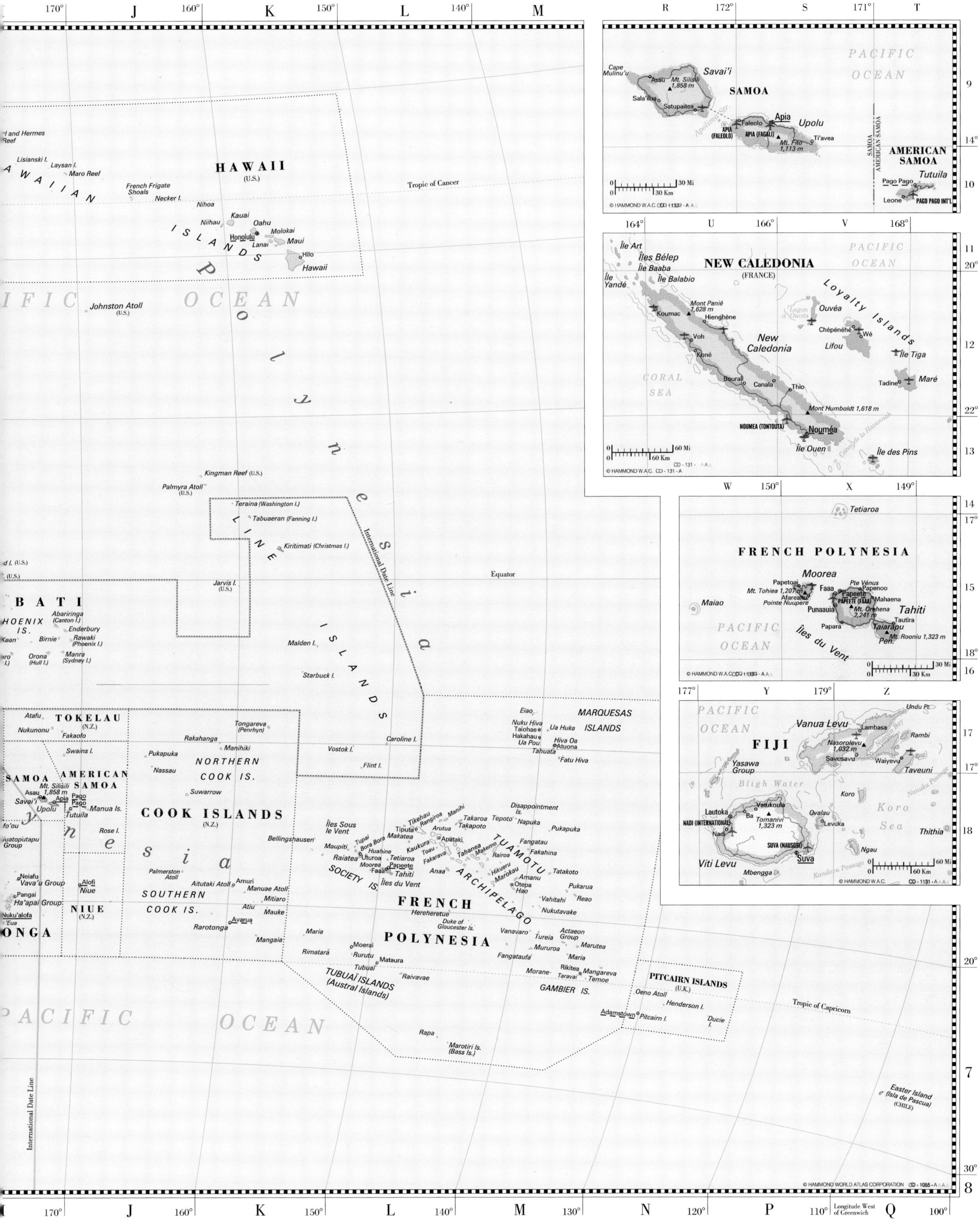

POPULATION OF CITIES AND TOWNS
- OVER 3,000,000
- 1,000,000 - 2,999,999
- 500,000 - 999,999
- 100,000 - 499,999
- UNDER 100,000

SCALE 1:31,500,000 LAMBERT AZIMUTHAL EQUAL-AREA PROJECTION

MILES 0 400 800 1200

KILOMETERS 0 400 800 1200

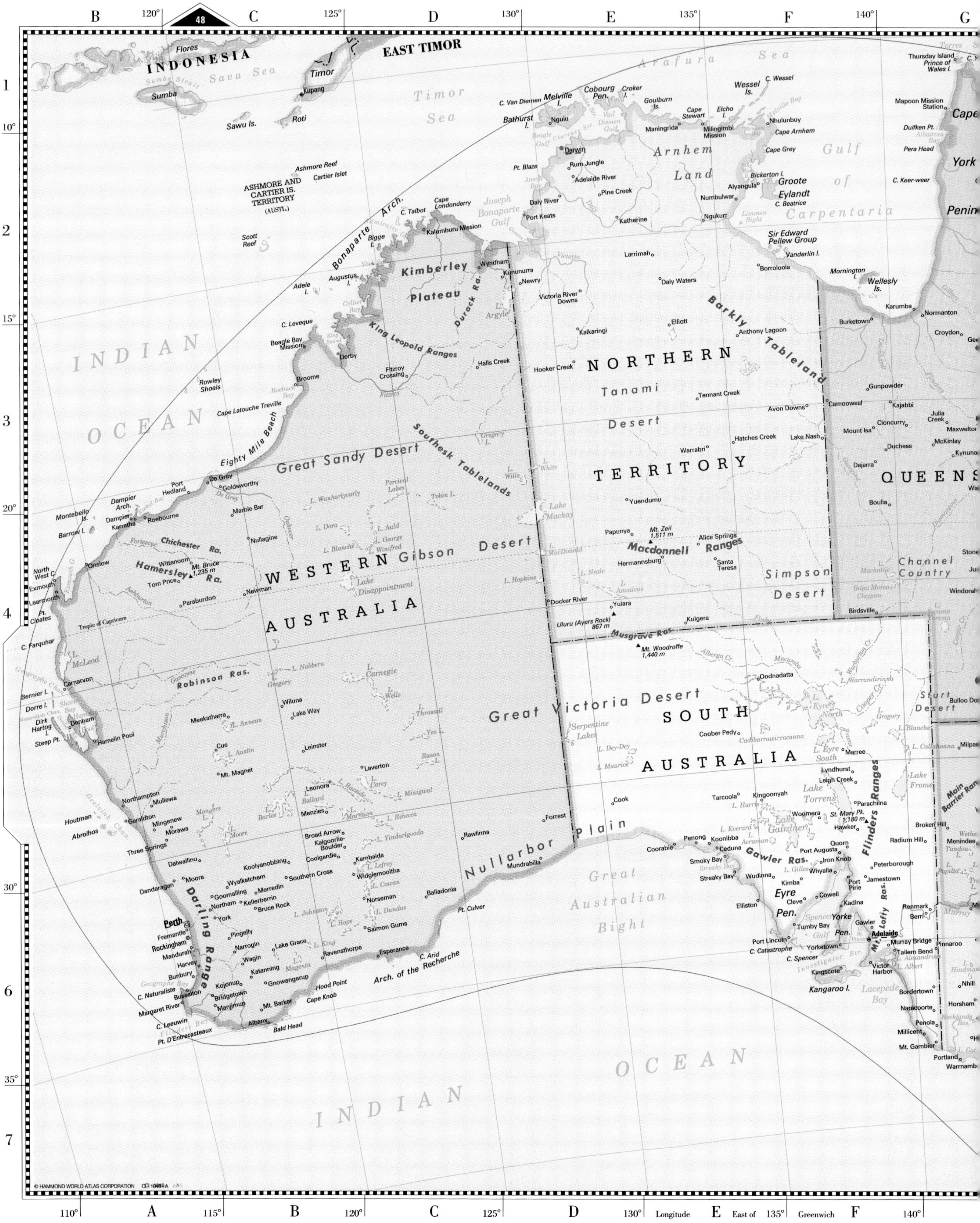
48
INDONESIA
EAST TIMOR
Flores
Sumba
Sumba Strait
Savu Sea
Timor
Kupang
Sawu Is.
Roti
Timor Sea
Arafura Sea
Ashmore Reef
Cartier Islet
ASHMORE AND CARTIER IS. TERRITORY (AUSTL.)
Scott Reef
Bonaparte Arch.
C. Talbot
Cape Londonderry
Kalumburu Mission
Joseph Bonaparte Gulf
Bigge I.
Augustus I.
Adele I.
Kimberley Plateau
Durack Ra.
Wyndham
Kununurra
Newry
L. Argyle
Collier Bay
King Sound
C. Leveque
Beagle Bay Mission
Derby
King Leopold Ranges
Fitzroy Crossing
Halls Creek
Broome
Roebuck Bay
Rowley Shoals
Cape Latouche Treville
Eighty Mile Beach
INDIAN OCEAN
Great Sandy Desert
Southesk Tablelands
Port Hedland
De Grey
Goldsworthy
Dampier Arch.
Dampier
Karratha
Roebourne
Montebello Is.
Barrow I.
Marble Bar
Nullagine
Chichester Ra.
Hamersley Ra.
Wittenoom
Mt. Bruce 1,235 m
Tom Price
Paraburdoo
Newman
Onslow
North West C.
Exmouth
Learmonth
Pt. Cloates
Tropic of Capricorn
C. Farquhar
L. McLeod
Carnarvon
Bernier I.
Dorre I.
Dirk Hartog I.
Steep Pt.
Denham
Hamelin Pool
Robinson Ras.
Gascoyne
Wiluna
Lake Way
Meekatharra
L. Annean
Cue
L. Austin
Mt. Magnet
Leinster
Laverton
Leonora
Menzies
L. Nabberu
L. Carnegie
L. Wells
L. Throssell
Yeo L.
Rason L.
L. Carey
L. Minigwal
L. Rebecca
L. Ballard
L. Barlee
L. Moore
L. Waukarlycarly
Percival Lakes
Tobin L.
L. Dora
L. Auld
L. George
L. Blanche
L. Winifred
Gibson Desert
WESTERN AUSTRALIA
L. Disappointment
L. Mackay
L. Hopkins
L. Wills
L. White
Gregory L.
Northampton
Mullewa
Geraldton
Mingenew
Morawa
Houtman Abrolhos
Three Springs
Dalwallinu
Moora
Dandaragan
Wyalkatchem
Goomalling
Northam
Kellerberrin
Merredin
Bruce Rock
Koolyanobbing
Southern Cross
Broad Arrow
Kalgoorlie-Boulder
Coolgardie
Kambalda
Widgiemooltha
L. Lefroy
L. Cowan
Norseman
L. Dundas
L. Johnston
L. Hope
Salmon Gums
Balladonia
Rawlinna
Forrest
Mundrabilla
Nullarbor Plain
Pt. Culver
Perth
Fremantle
Rockingham
Mandurah
Harvey
Bunbury
Busselton
C. Naturaliste
Margaret River
C. Leeuwin
Pt. D'Entrecasteaux
Darling Range
York
Pingelly
Narrogin
Wagin
Katanning
Lake Grace
L. King
Ravensthorpe
Esperance
Kojonup
Bridgetown
Manjimup
Gnowangerup
Mt. Barker
Albany
Bald Head
Cape Knob
Hood Point
C. Arid
Arch. of the Recherche
C. Van Diemen
Melville I.
Bathurst I.
Nguiu
Cobourg Pen.
Croker I.
Van Diemen Gulf
Clarence Str.
Beagle Gulf
Darwin
Rum Jungle
Adelaide River
Pine Creek
Pt. Blaze
Anson Bay
Daly River
Port Keats
Katherine
Goulburn Is.
Maningrida
Cape Stewart
Elcho I.
Milingimbi Mission
Wessel Is.
C. Wessel
Nhulunbuy
Cape Arnhem
Cape Grey
Arnhem Land
Bickerton I.
Groote Eylandt
Alyangula
C. Beatrice
Numbulwar
Ngukurr
Limmen Bight
Gulf of Carpentaria
Sir Edward Pellew Group
Vanderlin I.
Borroloola
Mornington I.
Wellesly Is.
Larrimah
Daly Waters
Victoria River Downs
Elliott
Barkly Tableland
Anthony Lagoon
Kalkaringi
Hooker Creek
NORTHERN TERRITORY
Tanami Desert
Tennant Creek
Avon Downs
Hatches Creek
Lake Nash
Warrabri
Yuendumu
Papunya
Mt. Zeil 1,511 m
Macdonnell Ranges
Alice Springs
Santa Teresa
Hermannsburg
L. Neale
L. Amadeus
Simpson Desert
Docker River
Yulara
Uluru (Ayers Rock) 867 m
Kulgera
Musgrave Ras.
Mt. Woodroffe 1,440 m
Alberga Cr.
Macumba
Oodnadatta
L. Warrandirinna
Great Victoria Desert
SOUTH AUSTRALIA
Serpentine Lakes
L. Dey-Dey
L. Maurice
Coober Pedy
Cadibarrawirracanna
L. Eyre North
L. Eyre South
Marree
Lyndhurst
Leigh Creek
Lake Torrens
Flinders Ranges
Parachilna
Tarcoola
Kingoonyah
L. Harris
Cook
Lake Gairdner
L. Everard
Woomera
St. Mary Pk. 1,180 m
Hawker
Quorn
Port Augusta
Iron Knob
Whyalla
Penong
Koonibba
Ceduna
Coorabie
Gawler Ras.
Smoky Bay
Streaky Bay
Wudinna
L. Gilles
Kimba
Great Australian Bight
Eyre Pen.
Cleve
Cowell
Elliston
Port Pirie
Jamestown
Peterborough
Kadina
Mt. Lofty Ras.
Yorke Pen.
Spencer Gulf
Tumby Bay
Port Lincoln
C. Catastrophe
C. Spencer
Yorketown
Investigator Str.
Gawler
Adelaide
Kingscote
Kangaroo I.
Murray Bridge
Tailem Bend
L. Alexandrina
L. Albert
Victor Harbor
Lacepede Bay
Bordertown
Naracoorte
Penola
Millicent
Mt. Gambier
Renmark
Berri
Pinnaroo
Lake Frome
Radium Hill
Broken Hill
Menindee
Main Barrier Ran.
Sturt Desert
L. Gregory
L. Blanche
L. Callabonna
Cooper Cr.
Birdsville
Bilpa Morea Claypan
Channel Country
Windorah
Boulia
QUEENS
Mount Isa
Cloncurry
Duchess
McKinlay
Dajarra
Camooweal
Gunpowder
Kajabbi
Julia Creek
Maxwelton
Kynuna
Burketown
Normanton
Karumba
Croydon
Thursday Island
Prince of Wales I.
Torres
Mapoon Mission Station
Cape York Penin.
Duifken Pt.
Albatross Bay
Pera Head
C. Keer-weer
Gulf
Portland
Horsham
Nhill
Warrnamb
INDIAN OCEAN
1
2
3
4
5
6
7
10°
15°
20°
30°
35°
B 120° C 125° D 130° E 135° F 140° G
110° A 115° B 120° C 125° D 130° Longitude E East of 135° Greenwich F 140°
© HAMMOND WORLD ATLAS CORPORATION

Australia; New Zealand

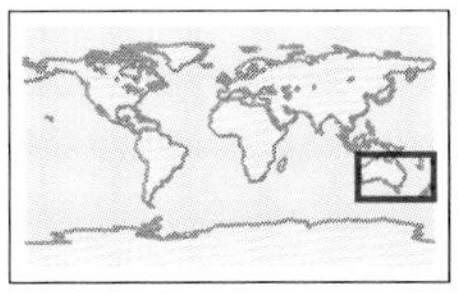

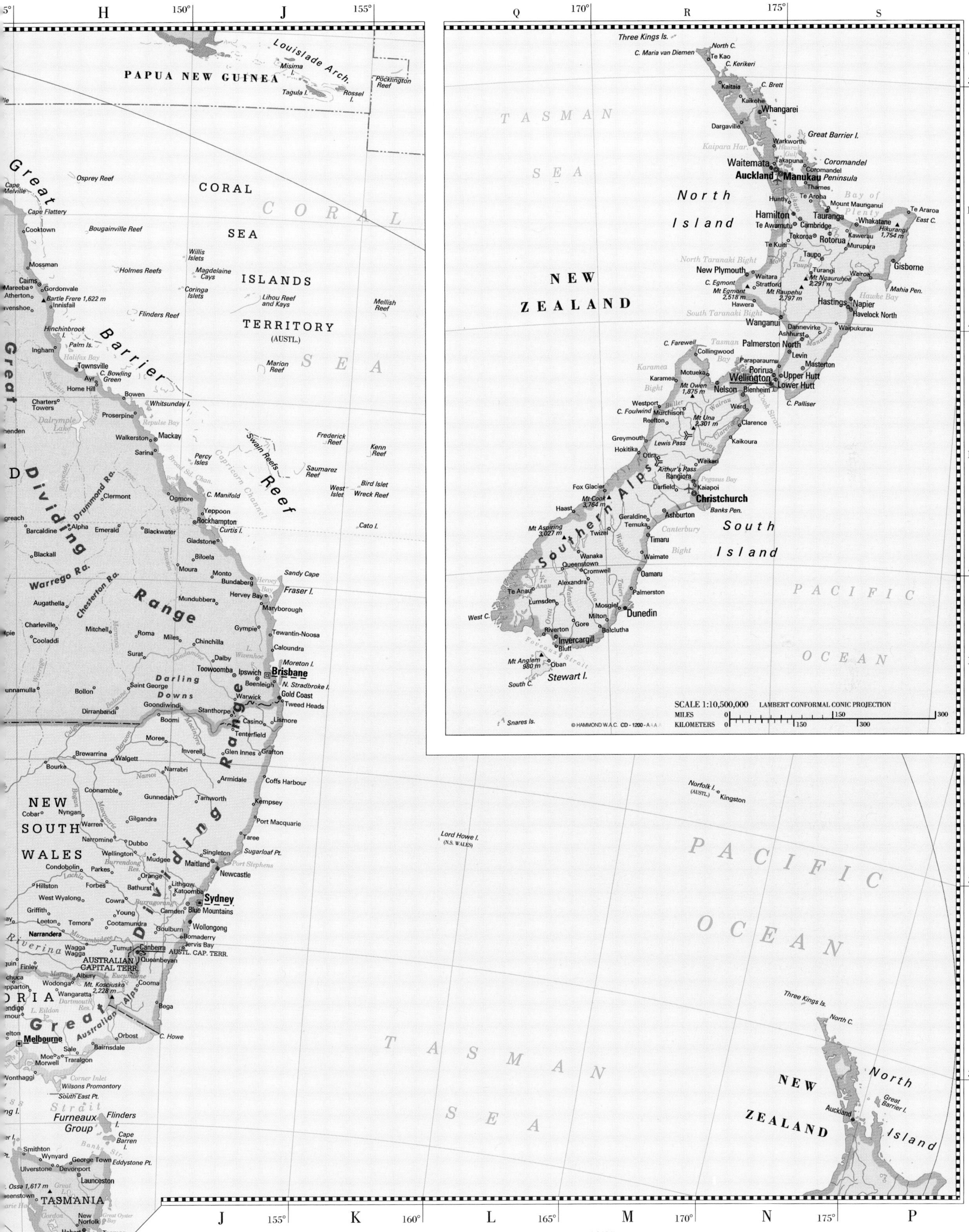

POPULATION OF CITIES AND TOWNS

- ■ OVER 2,000,000
- ▣ 1,000,000 - 1,999,999
- ⊛ 500,000 - 999,999
- ⊕ 100,000 - 499,999
- ⊙ 50,000 - 99,999
- ○ UNDER 50,000

SCALE 1:14,000,000 OPTIMAL CONFORMAL PROJECTION

MILES 0 200 400 600

KILOMETERS 0 200 400 600

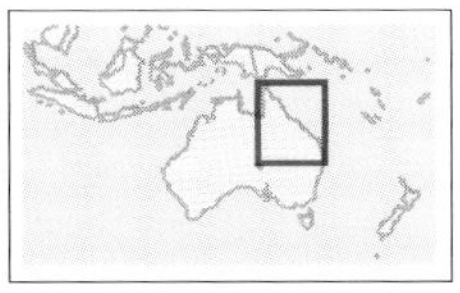

Northeastern Australia

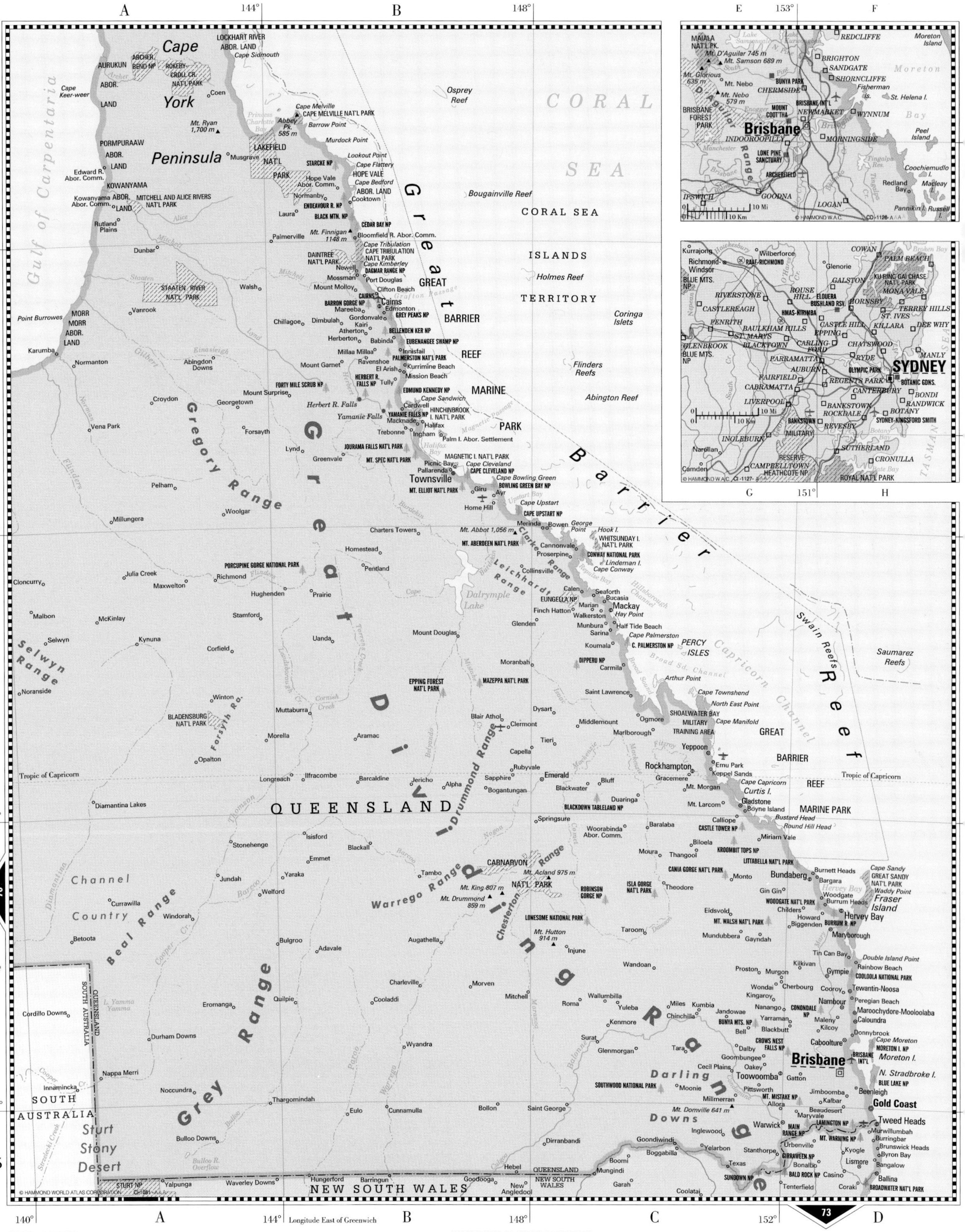

SCALE 1:7,000,000 LAMBERT CONFORMAL CONIC PROJECTION

MILES 0 100 200 300

KILOMETERS 0 100 200 300

POPULATION OF CITIES AND TOWNS

- OVER 2,000,000
- 1,000,000 - 1,999,999
- 500,000 - 999,999
- 250,000 - 499,999
- 100,000 - 249,999
- 30,000 - 99,999
- 10,000 - 29,999
- UNDER 10,000

Southeastern Australia

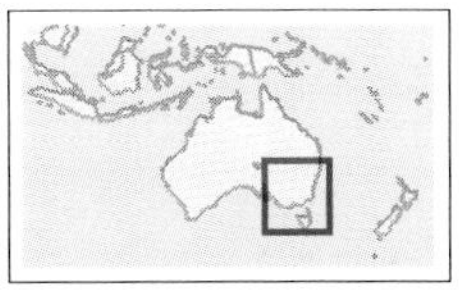

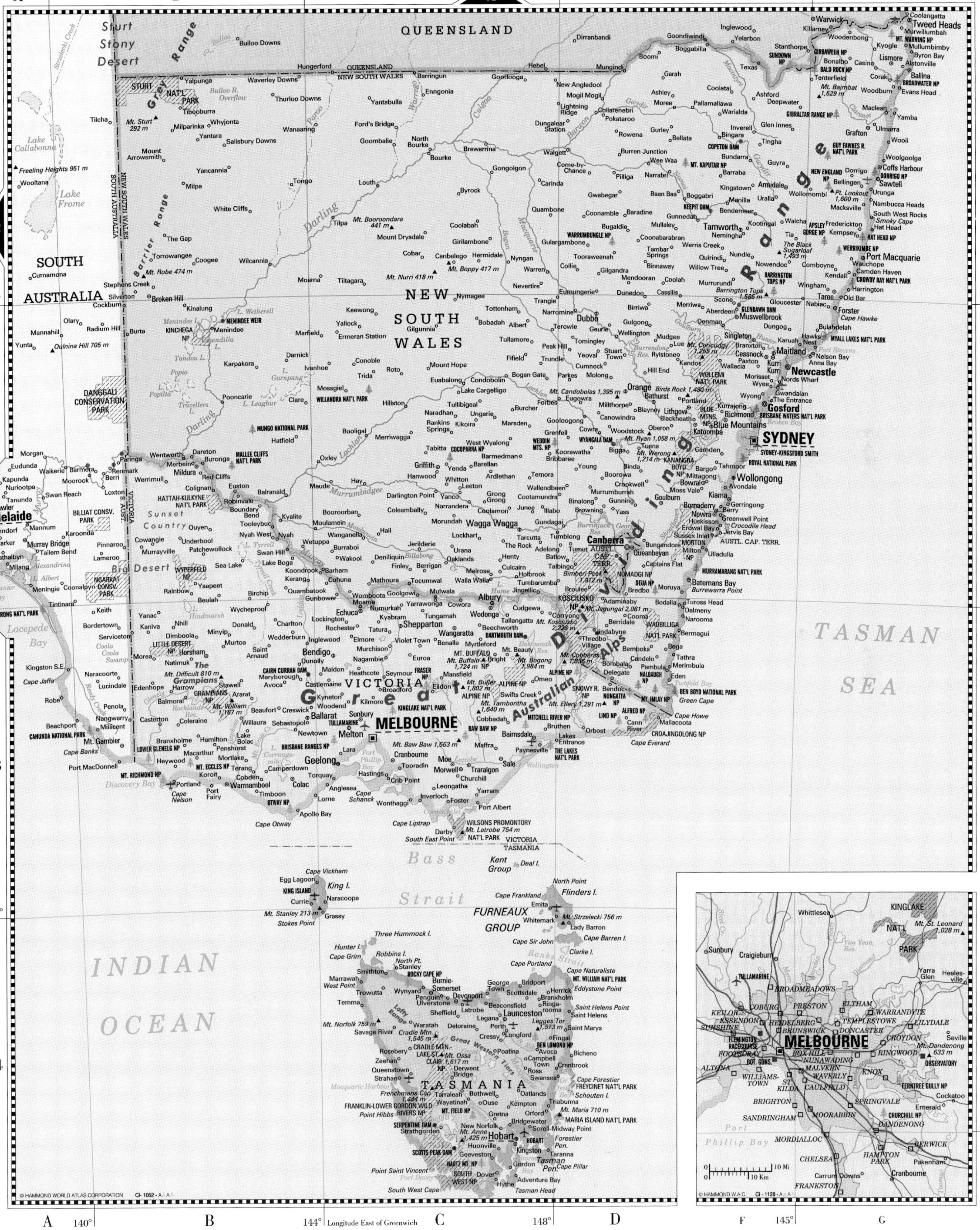

POPULATION OF CITIES AND TOWNS

- OVER 2,000,000
- 1,000,000 - 1,999,999
- 500,000 - 999,999
- 250,000 - 499,999
- 100,000 - 249,999
- 30,000 - 99,999
- 10,000 - 29,999
- UNDER 10,000

SCALE 1:7,000,000 LAMBERT CONFORMAL CONIC PROJECTION

MILES 0 100 200 300

KILOMETERS 0 100 200 300

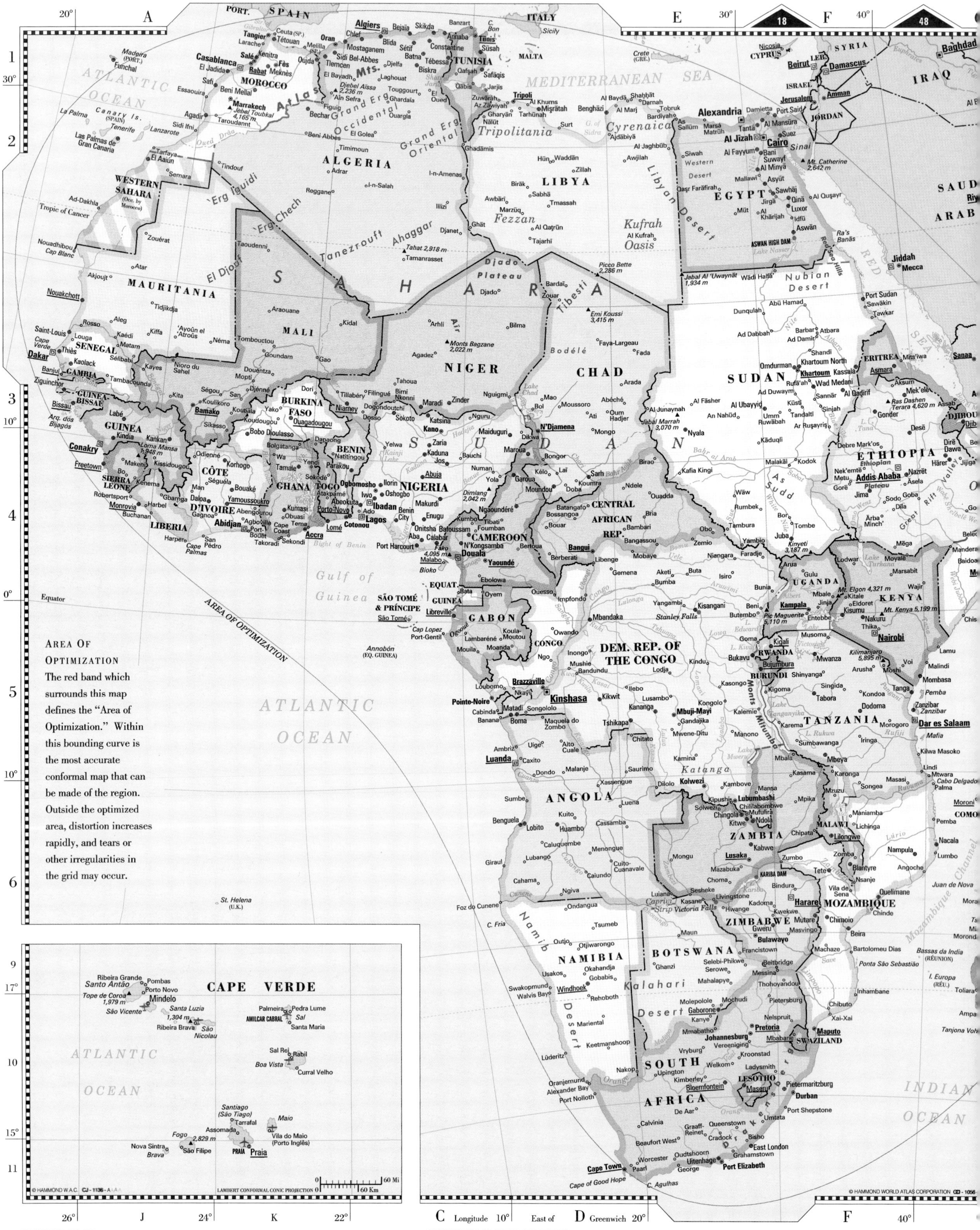

AREA OF OPTIMIZATION

The red band which surrounds this map defines the "Area of Optimization." Within this bounding curve is the most accurate conformal map that can be made of the region. Outside the optimized area, distortion increases rapidly, and tears or other irregularities in the grid may occur.

C Longitude 10° East of D Greenwich 20°

SCALE 1:31,500,000 OPTIMAL CONFORMAL PROJECTION

MILES 0 400 800 1200

KILOMETERS 0 400 800 1200

POPULATION OF CITIES AND TOWNS

- OVER 3,000,000
- 1,000,000 - 2,999,999
- 500,000 - 999,999
- 100,000 - 499,999
- UNDER 100,000

Africa

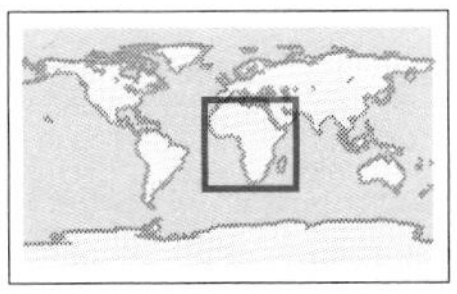

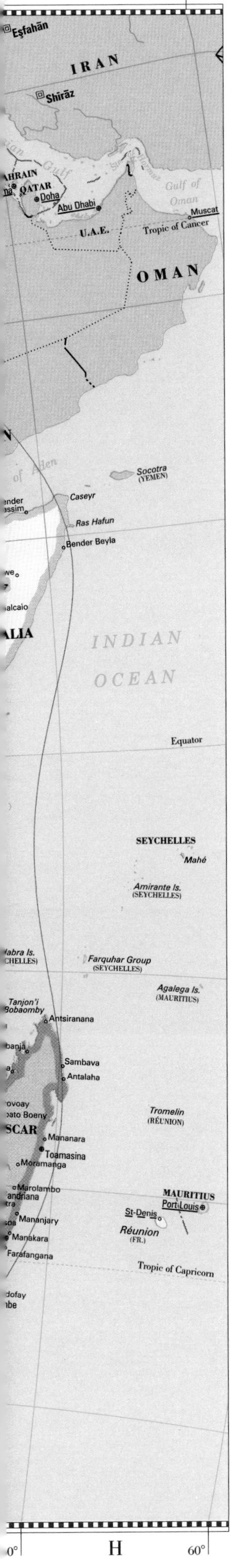

H
60°
Eşfahān
IRAN
Shīrāz
BAHRAIN
QATAR
Doha
Abu Dhabi
Muscat
U.A.E.
Tropic of Cancer
Gulf of Oman
OMAN
Socotra (YEMEN)
Caseyr
Ras Hafun
Bender Beyla
INDIAN
OCEAN
Equator
SEYCHELLES
Mahé
Amirante Is. (SEYCHELLES)
Farquhar Group (SEYCHELLES)
Agalega Is. (MAURITIUS)
Antsiranana
Sambava
Antalaha
Tromelin (RÉUNION)
Mananara
Toamasina
Moramanga
Marolambo
Mananjary
Manakara
Farafangana
MAURITIUS
Port Louis
St-Denis
Réunion (FR.)
Tropic of Capricorn
H
60°

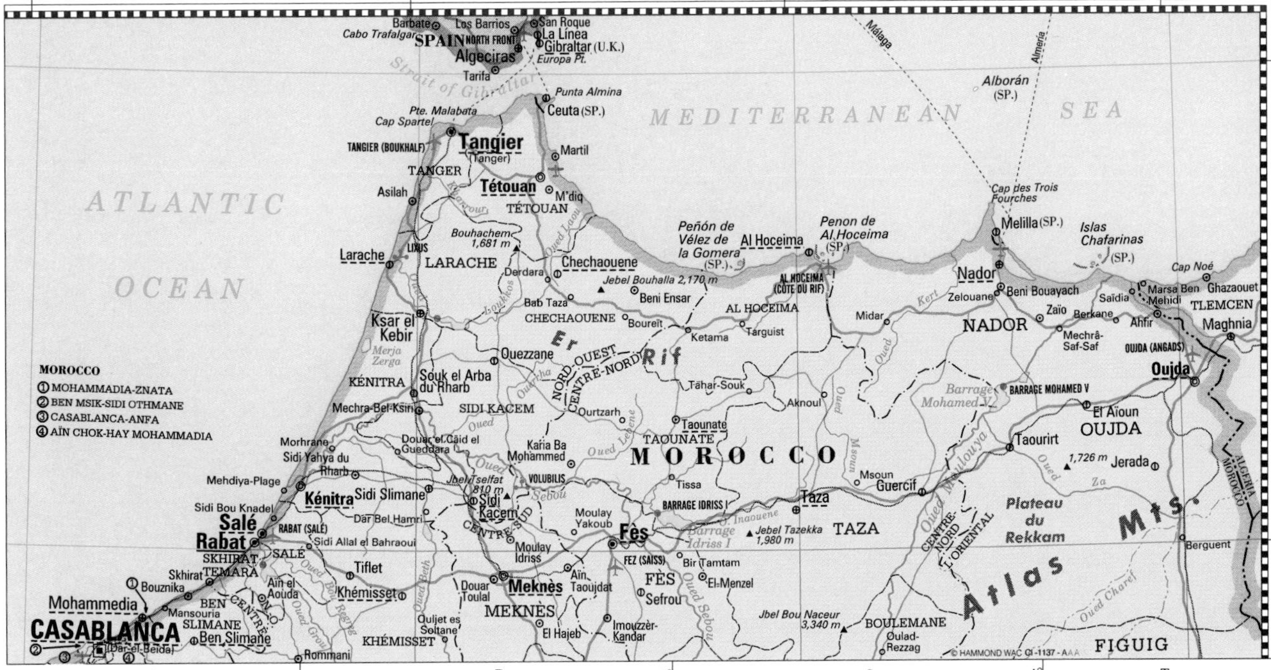

8°
L
6°
M
4°
N
2°
P
12
36°
13
34°
14
Barbate
Los Barrios
San Roque
La Línea
Gibraltar (U.K.)
Europa Pt.
Cabo Trafalgar
SPAIN
Algeciras
Tarifa
Strait of Gibraltar
Punta Almina
Ceuta (SP.)
Pte. Malabata
Cap Spartel
Tangier
Martil
TANGER
Tétouan
M'diq
TÉTOUAN
Asilah
Larache
LARACHE
Chechaouene
CHECHAOUENE
Jebel Bouhalla 2,170 m
Beni Ensar
Ksar el Kebir
Ouezzane
KÉNITRA
Souk el Arba du Rharb
Mechra-Bel-Ksiri
SIDI KACEM
Kénitra
Sidi Slimane
Salé
Rabat
SKHIRAT-TEMARA
Tiflet
Khémisset
Mohammedia
CASABLANCA
BEN SLIMANE
Ben Slimane
KHÉMISSET
Meknès
MEKNÈS
Fès
FÈS
Sefrou
Moulay Yakoub
El Hajeb
Imouzzèr-Kandar
MOROCCO
Taounate
TAOUNATE
Taza
TAZA
Al Hoceima
AL HOCEIMA
Peñón de Vélez de la Gomera (SP.)
Penon de Al Hoceima (SP.)
Rif
Jebel Tazekka 1,980 m
Jbel Bou Naceur 3,340 m
BOULEMANE
Oulad-Rezzag
Melilla (SP.)
Nador
NADOR
Islas Chafarinas (SP.)
Cap des Trois Fourches
Alborán (SP.)
Oujda
OUJDA
Taourirt
Jerada
Berkane
Saïdia
Plateau du Rekkam
Atlas Mts.
FIGUIG
Berguent
TLEMCEN
Maghnia
ATLANTIC
OCEAN
MEDITERRANEAN SEA
MOROCCO
① MOHAMMEDIA-ZNATA
② BEN MSIK-SIDI OTHMANE
③ CASABLANCA-ANFA
④ AÏN CHOK-HAY MOHAMMADIA
© HAMMOND WAC CI - 1137 - AAA

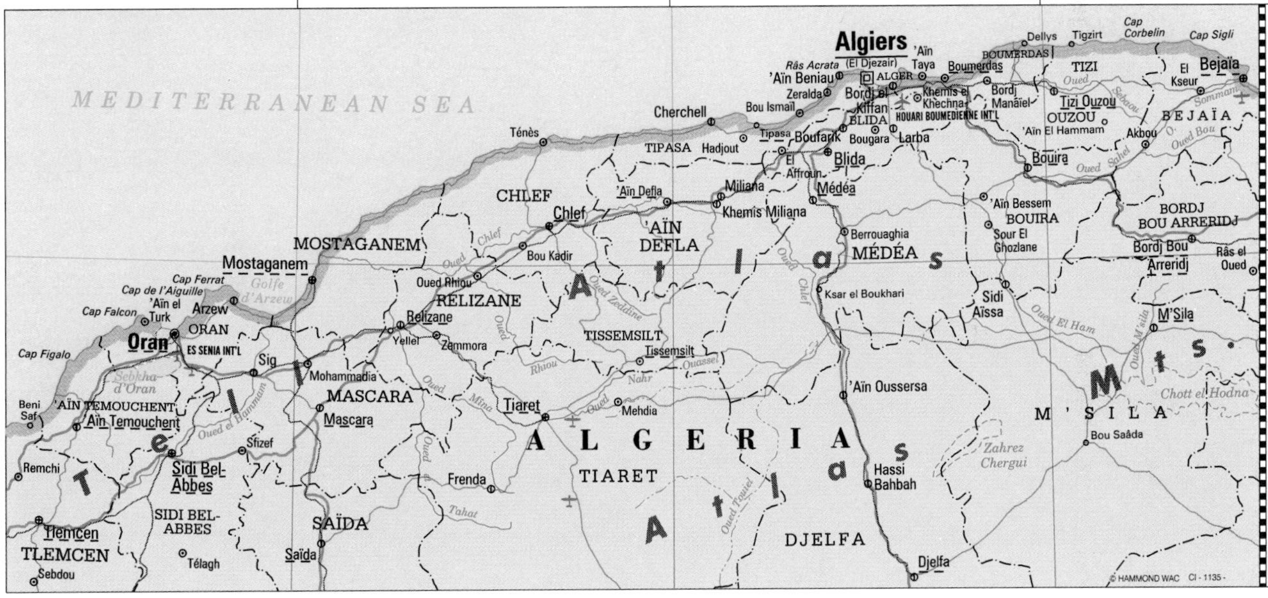

Q
0°
R
2°
S
4°
T
15
36°
16
MEDITERRANEAN SEA
Algiers
ALGER
Dellys
Tigzirt
Cap Corbelin
Cap Sigli
Bejaïa
BEJAÏA
Tizi Ouzou
TIZI OUZOU
BOUMERDAS
Boumerdas
Blida
BLIDA
Cherchell
TIPASA
Ténès
CHLEF
Chlef
Médéa
MÉDÉA
AÏN DEFLA
Miliana
Khemis Miliana
Bouira
BOUIRA
BORDJ BOU ARRERIDJ
Bordj Bou Arreridj
MOSTAGANEM
Mostaganem
Oran
ORAN
Arzew
Cap Falcon
Cap Figalo
Cap Ferrat
RELIZANE
Relizane
MASCARA
Mascara
Tissemsilt
TISSEMSILT
Tiaret
TIARET
ALGERIA
Tell Atlas
Atlas
Sidi Bel-Abbes
SIDI BEL-ABBES
Aïn Temouchent
AÏN TEMOUCHENT
Tlemcen
TLEMCEN
SAÏDA
Saïda
Frenda
Ksar el Boukhari
'Aïn Oussersa
Sidi Aïssa
M'Sila
M'SILA
Chott el Hodna
Bou Saâda
Hassi Bahbah
DJELFA
Djelfa
Mts.
© HAMMOND WAC CI - 1135 -

U
6°
V
8°
W
10°
X
17
36°
18
MEDITERRANEAN SEA
Cap Bougar'oûn
Cap de Fer
Collo
Jijel
JIJEL
Skikda
SKIKDA
ANNABA
Annaba
EL TARF
El Tarf
Constantine
CONSTANTINE
MILA
Mila
SÉTIF
Sétif
GUELMA
Guelma
Souk Ahras
SOUK AHRAS
OUM EL BOUAGHI
Oum El Bouaghi
BATNA
Batna
Barika
KHENCHELA
Khenchela
Tébessa
TÉBESSA
Aures
Mts. de Tébessa
ALGERIA
Cap Serrat
Bizerte (Banzart)
BANZART
Ra's Al Jabal
Tunis
TUNIS
Aryānah
Al Marsā
Ettadhamen-Douar Hicher
NĀBUL
Nābul
Al Hammāmāt
Zaghwān
ZAGHWĀN
JENDOUBA
Jendouba
BĀJAH
Bājah
SILYĀNAH
Silyānah
AL KĀF
Al Kāf
TUNISIA
Dorsale
SŪSAH
Sūsah
Al Munastīr
AL MUNASTĪR
Al Qayrawān
AL QAYRAWĀN
AL QAŞRAYN
Al Qaşrayn
SIDI BŪ ZAYD
Sidi Bū Zayd
AL MAHDĪYAH
Al Mahdīyah
SAFĀQIS
Gulf of Tunis
Gulf of Hammāmāt
Pantelleria (IT.)
Jabal ash Sha'nabī 1,544 m
Jabal Maghila 1,378 m
Djebel Mahmel 2,321 m
© HAMMOND WAC CI - 1138 -

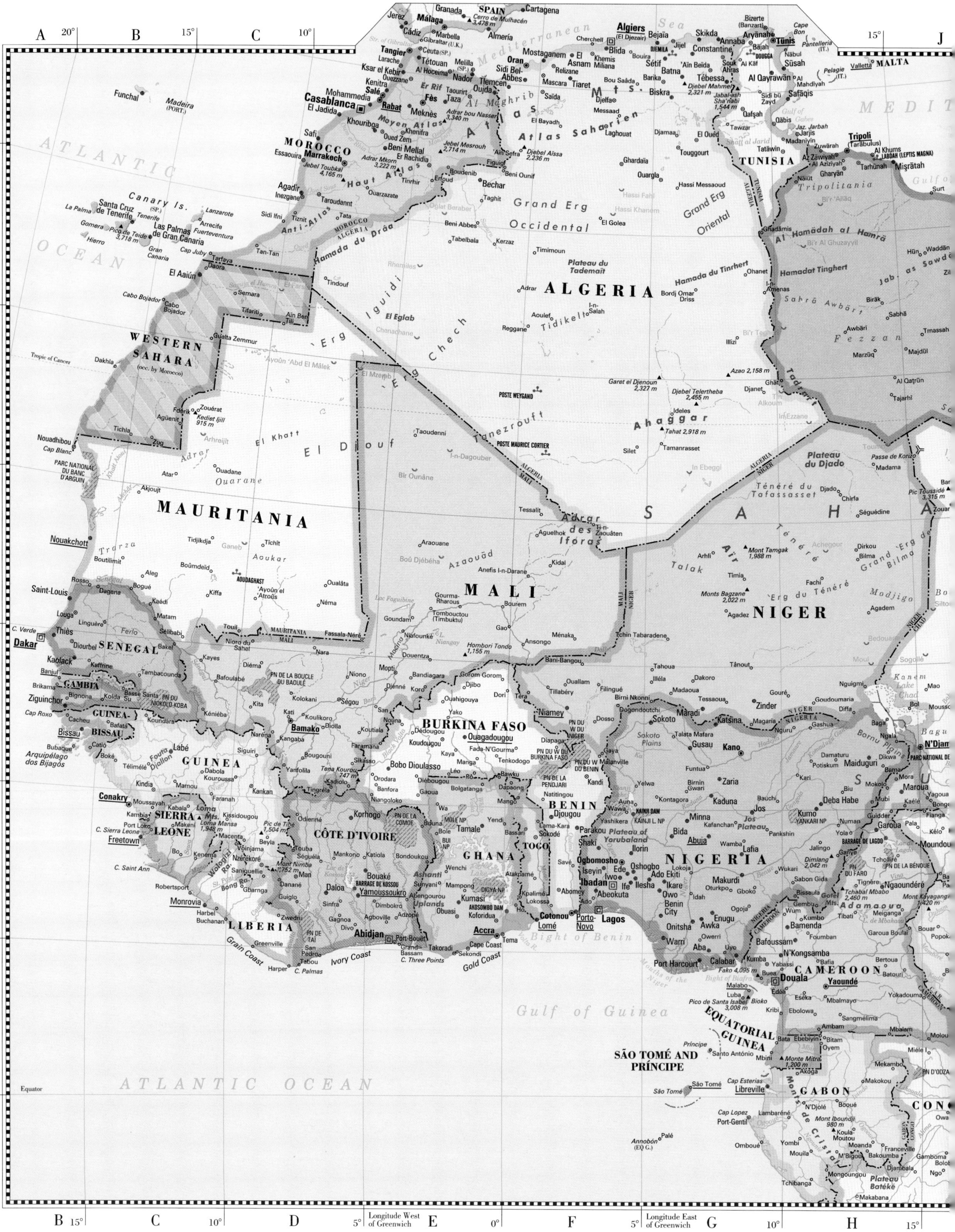

ATLANTIC OCEAN
Mediterranean Sea
Gulf of Guinea
Bight of Benin
Gulf of Gabes
Tropic of Cancer
Equator
Longitude West of Greenwich
Longitude East of Greenwich
SPAIN
MALTA
MOROCCO
ALGERIA
TUNISIA
WESTERN SAHARA (occ. by Morocco)
MAURITANIA
MALI
NIGER
SENEGAL
GAMBIA
GUINEA-BISSAU
GUINEA
SIERRA LEONE
LIBERIA
CÔTE D'IVOIRE
BURKINA FASO
GHANA
TOGO
BENIN
NIGERIA
CAMEROON
EQUATORIAL GUINEA
SÃO TOMÉ AND PRÍNCIPE
GABON
Madeira (PORT.)
Canary Is. (SP.)
Atlas Mts.
Haut Atlas
Moyen Atlas
Anti-Atlas
Atlas Saharien
Grand Erg Occidental
Grand Erg Oriental
Hamada du Drâa
Plateau du Tademaït
Hamada du Tinrhert
Tidikelt
Erg Iguidi
Erg Chech
Tanezrouft
Ahaggar
El Djouf
Adrar des Iforas
Aïr
Ténéré
Grand Erg de Bilma
SAHARA
Fezzan
Tripolitania
Al Hamādah al Hamrā
Plateau du Djado
Jos Plateau
Adamaoua
Grain Coast
Ivory Coast
Gold Coast
Rabat
Casablanca
Marrakech
Algiers (El Djezair)
Tunis
Tripoli (Tarābulus)
Nouakchott
Dakar
Banjul
Bissau
Conakry
Freetown
Monrovia
Yamoussoukro
Abidjan
Bamako
Ouagadougou
Niamey
Accra
Lomé
Porto-Novo
Cotonou
Lagos
Abuja
Malabo
Yaoundé
Douala
Libreville
São Tomé
N'Djamena
Timbuktu (Tombouctou)
Kano
Zaria
Ibadan
Kumasi
Saint-Louis
Agadez
Tamanrasset

Northern Africa

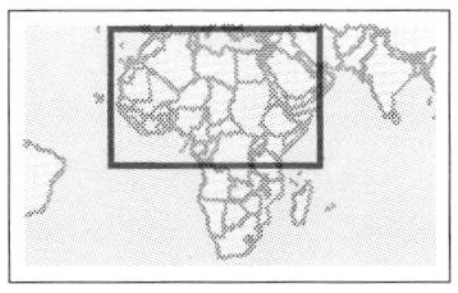

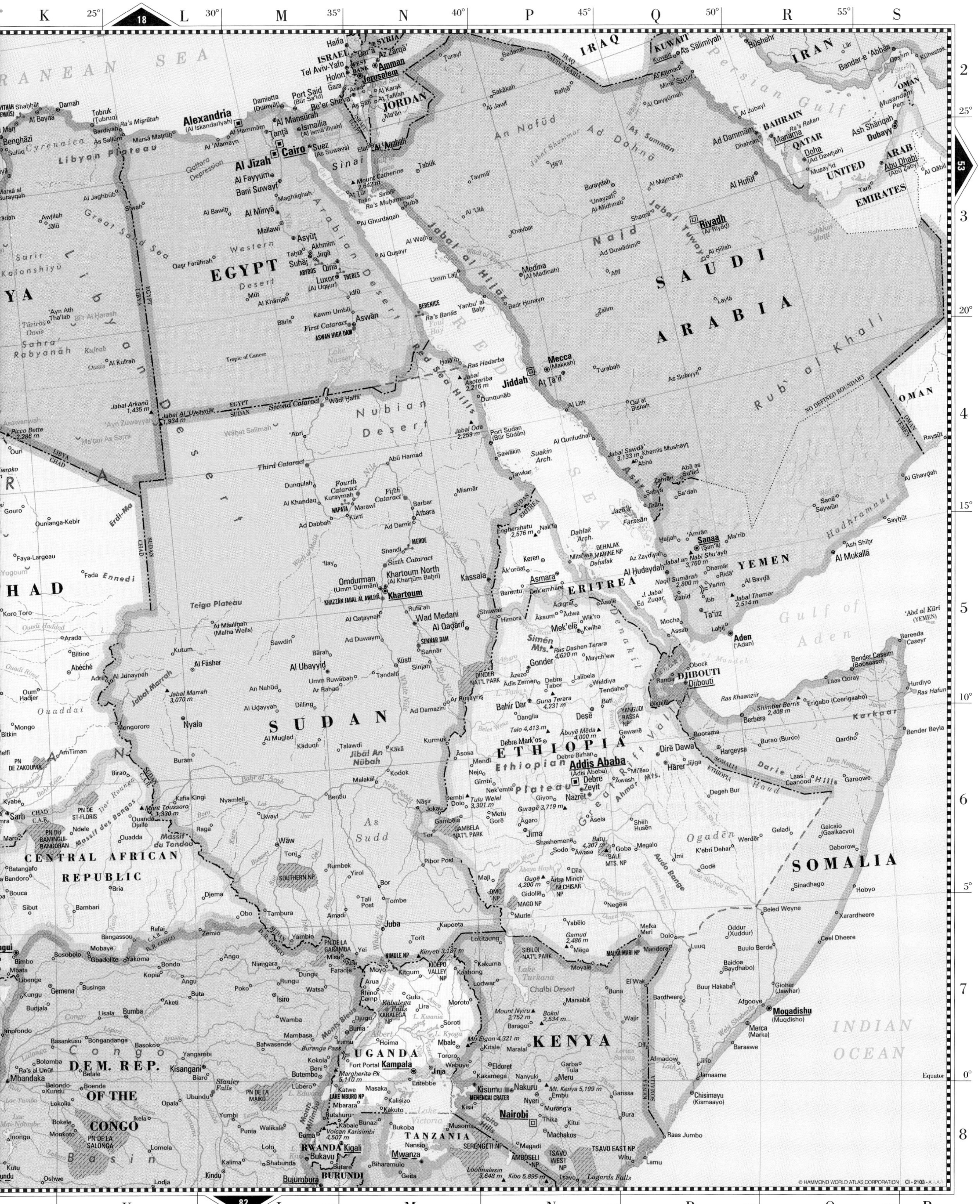

POPULATION OF CITIES AND TOWNS

■ OVER 2,000,000	◉ 500,000 - 999,999
▣ 1,000,000 - 1,999,999	⊕ 100,000 - 499,999
⊙ 50,000 - 99,999	○ UNDER 50,000

SCALE 1:17,500,000 POLYCONIC PROJECTION

MILES 0 250 500 750

KILOMETERS 0 250 500 750

SCALE 1:7,000,000 POLYCONIC PROJECTION

MILES 0 100 200 300

KILOMETERS 0 100 200 300

Southern West Africa

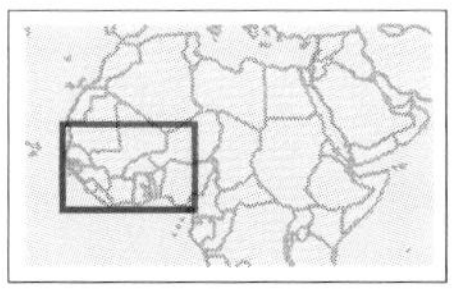

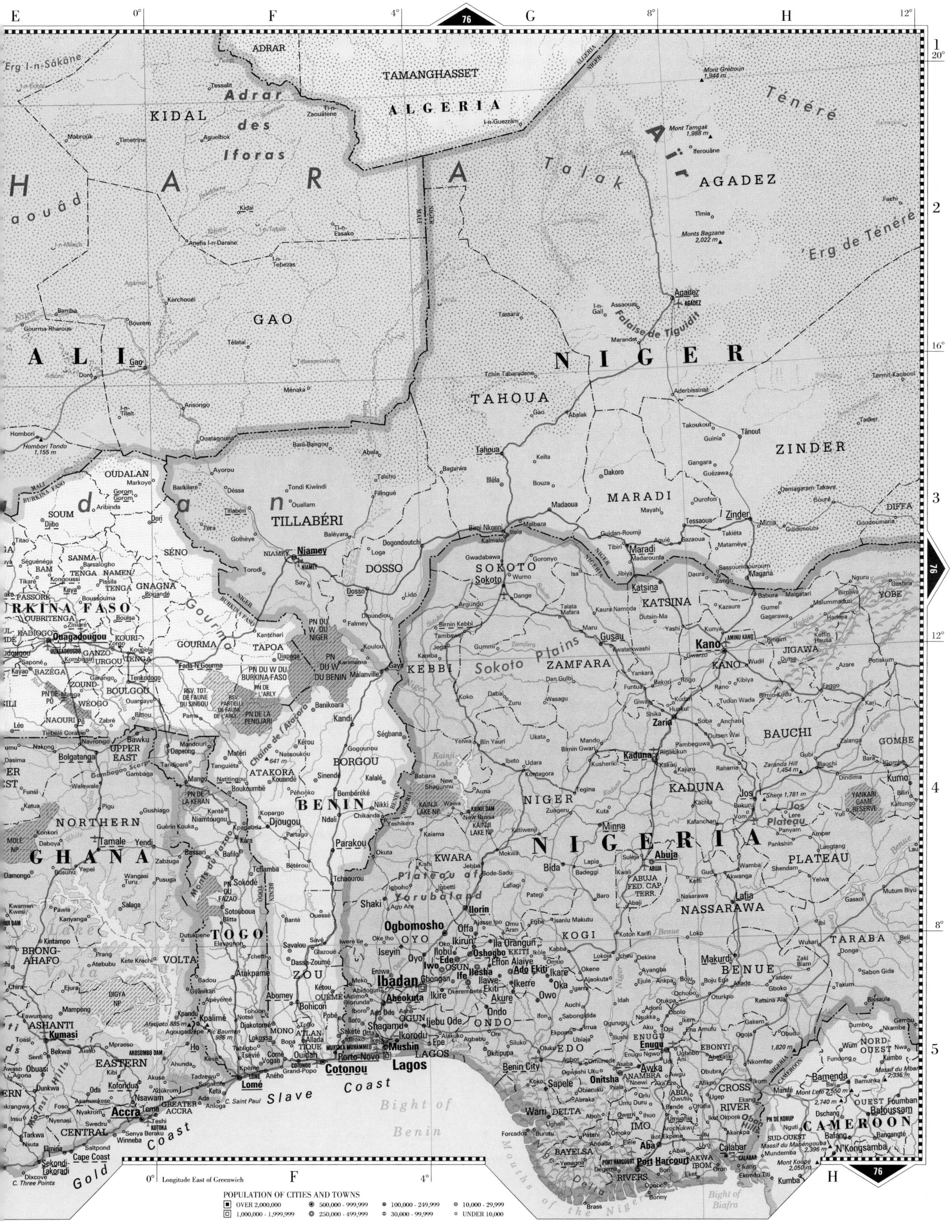

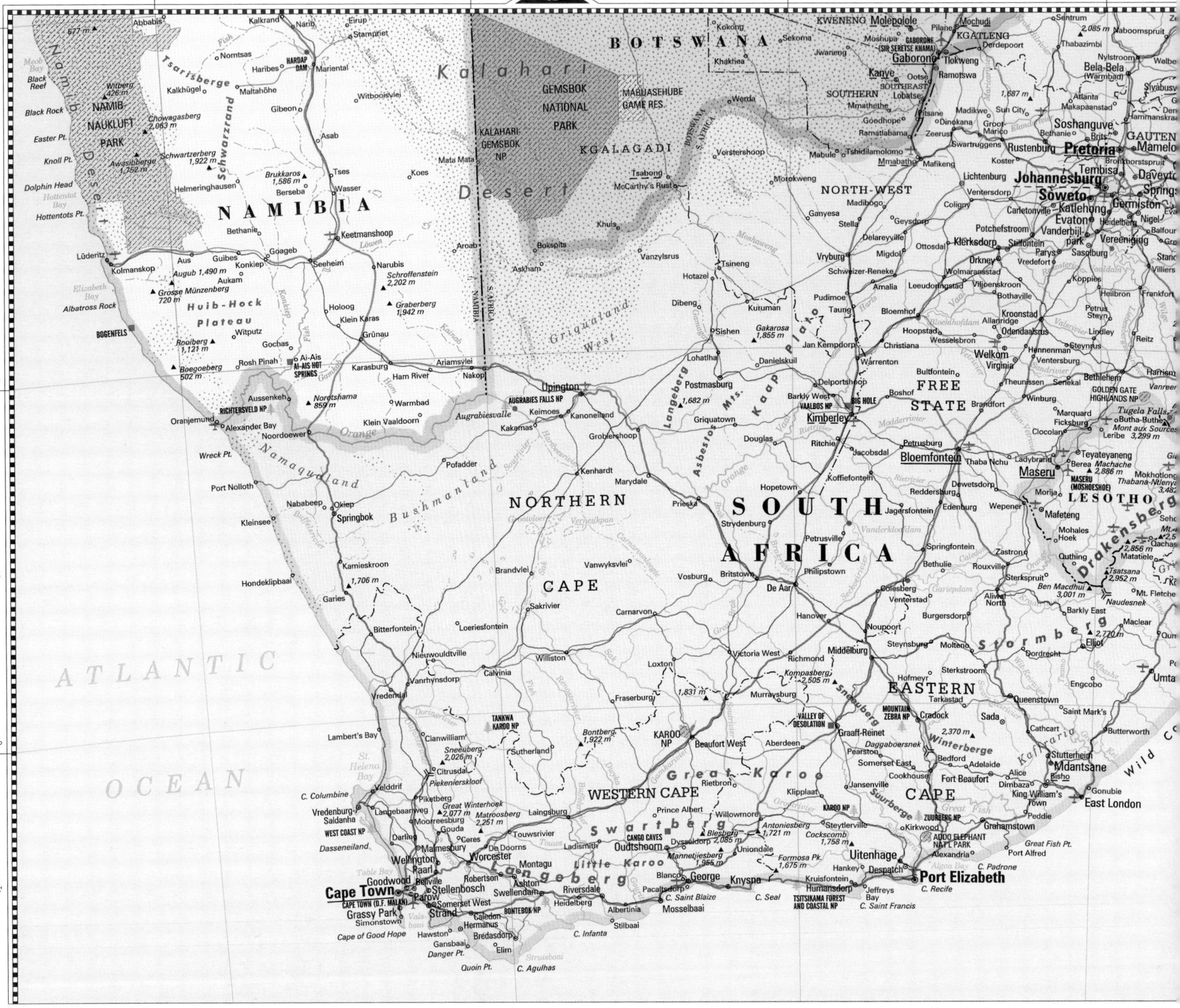

A
16°
B
20°
C
24°
D
28°
24°
28°
32°
2
3
4
NAMIBIA
BOTSWANA
SOUTH AFRICA
LESOTHO
NORTHERN CAPE
WESTERN CAPE
EASTERN CAPE
FREE STATE
NORTH-WEST
KGALAGADI
SOUTHERN
SOUTHEAST
KGATLENG
KWENENG
GAUTENG
ATLANTIC OCEAN
Namib Desert
Kalahari Desert
NAMIB-NAUKLUFT PARK
KALAHARI-GEMSBOK NP
GEMSBOK NATIONAL PARK
MABUASEHUBE GAME RES.
Huib-Hock Plateau
Schwarzrand
Tsarisberge
Namaqualand
Bushmanland
Griqualand West
Kaap Plato
Asbestos Mts.
Langeberg
Great Karoo
Little Karoo
Swartberg
Sneeuberg
Winterberge
Stormberg
Drakensberg
Suurberge
Orange
Lüderitz
Keetmanshoop
Mariental
Gibeon
Bethanie
Aus
Goageb
Seeheim
Karasburg
Noordoewer
Oranjemund
Alexander Bay
Port Nolloth
Springbok
Okiep
Upington
Kakamas
Keimoes
Groblershoop
Kenhardt
Prieska
Kimberley
Postmasburg
Sishen
Kuruman
Vryburg
Mafikeng
Mmabatho
Lobatse
Kanye
Gaborone
Molepolole
Tsabong
Bloemfontein
Maseru
Kroonstad
Welkom
Klerksdorp
Potchefstroom
Johannesburg
Soweto
Pretoria
Rustenburg
Vereeniging
Germiston
Springs
Benoni
De Aar
Colesberg
Middelburg
Graaff-Reinet
Beaufort West
Calvinia
Vanrhynsdorp
Vredendal
Clanwilliam
Lambert's Bay
Vredenburg-Saldanha
Malmesbury
Paarl
Wellington
Worcester
Stellenbosch
Cape Town
Goodwood
Bellville
Parow
Strand
Somerset West
Simonstown
Hermanus
Caledon
Swellendam
Riversdale
Mosselbaai
George
Knysna
Oudtshoorn
Uitenhage
Port Elizabeth
Grahamstown
East London
King William's Town
Queenstown
Cradock
Aliwal North
Cape of Good Hope
C. Agulhas
Port Alfred
Bisho
Mdantsane
Tugela Falls
Thabana-Ntlenyana 3,482 m
Mont aux Sources

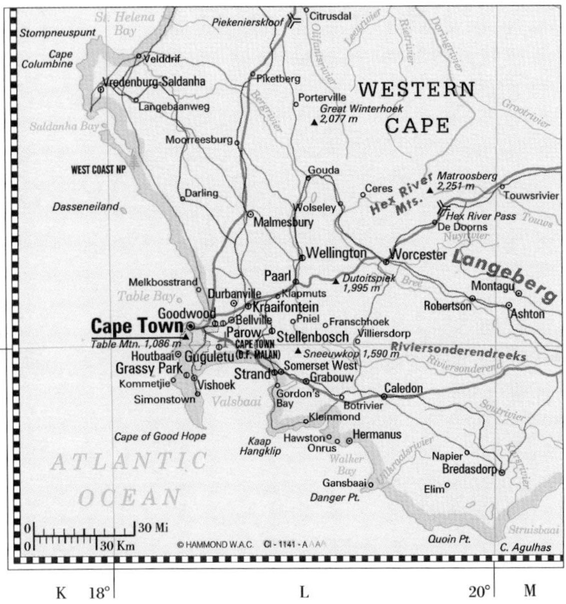

WESTERN CAPE
ATLANTIC OCEAN
Cape Town
Table Mtn. 1,086 m
Stompneuspunt
Cape Columbine
Vredenburg-Saldanha
Langebaanweg
Saldanha Bay
WEST COAST NP
Dasseneiland
Moorreesburg
Darling
Malmesbury
Piketberg
Porterville
Citrusdal
Piekenierskloof
Great Winterhoek 2,077 m
Gouda
Wellington
Paarl
Worcester
Hex River Mts.
Hex River Pass
De Doorns
Touwsrivier
Matroosberg 2,251 m
Langeberg
Montagu
Robertson
Ashton
Stellenbosch
Kraaifontein
Durbanville
Melkbosstrand
Table Bay
Goodwood
Bellville
Parow
Guguletu
Houtbaai
Grassy Park
Kommetjie
Vishoek
Simonstown
Strand
Somerset West
Gordon's Bay
Grabouw
Villiersdorp
Sneeuwkop 1,590 m
Riviersonderendreeks
Caledon
Botrivier
Kleinmond
Hawston
Onrus
Hermanus
Kaap Hangklip
Cape of Good Hope
Walker Bay
Gansbaai
Danger Pt.
Napier
Bredasdorp
Elim
Quoin Pt.
C. Agulhas
Struisbaai
Valsbaai
10
11
34°
18°
20°
K
L
M
30 Mi
30 Km
© HAMMOND W.A.C.
CI - 1141 - A

SOUTH AFRICA
NORTH-WEST
GAUTENG
MPUMALANGA
FREE STATE
LIMPOPO
BOTS.
Lobatse
Pitsane
Dinokana
Zeerust
Mmabatho
Mafikeng
Lichtenburg
Coligny
Ventersdorp
SCHOONSPRUIT NATUURRESERVAAT
Potchefstroom
Klerksdorp
Stilfontein
Orkney
Ottosdal
Wolmaransstad
Leeudoringstad
Viljoenskroon
Koppies
Heilbron
Parys
Vredefort
Sasolburg
Vanderbijlpark
Vereeniging
Meyerton
Evaton
Carletonville
Fochville
Westonaria
Randburg
Roodepoort
Krugersdorp
Johannesburg
Soweto
Germiston
Boksburg
Benoni
Katlehong
Tembisa
Kempton Park
Daveyton
Springs
Nigel
Heidelberg
Delmas
JOHANNESBURG (JAN SMUTS)
SUIKERBOSRAND NATUURRESERVAAT
Balfour
Greylingstad
Vaal
Vaaldam
Villiers
Standerton
Secunda
Bethal
Evander
Kriel
Ogies
Hendrina
Davel
Ermelo
Morgenzon
Amersfoort
Perdekop
Witbank
Middelburg
Belfast
Machadodorp
Bronkhorstspruit
Pretoria
Mamelodi
Atteridgeville
Verwoerdburg
Magaliesberg
MAGALIESBERG NATURE AREA
Rustenburg
Koster
Brits
Ga-Rankuwa
Soshanguve
Mabopane
Bethanie
Swartruggens
Groot-Marico
Madikwe
Sun City
PILANESBERG NP
Pilanesberg
Saulspoort
Atlanta
Makapaanstad
Swartbooistad
Marokolong
Hammanskraal
RUST DE WINTERDAM NATUURRESERVAAT
Siyabuswa
Groblersdal
Dennilton
LOSKOPDAM NATUURRESERVAAT
Stoffberg
Dullstroom
Cullinan
BORAKALALO NP
1,687 m
26°
28°
30°
N
P
Q
30 Km
© HAMMOND W.A.C.
CI - 1142 - A

Southern Africa

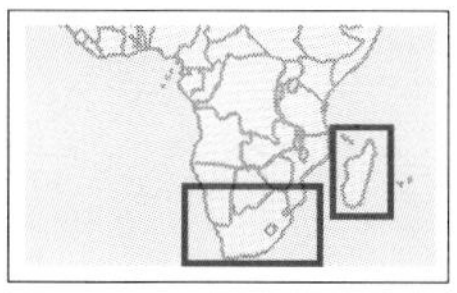

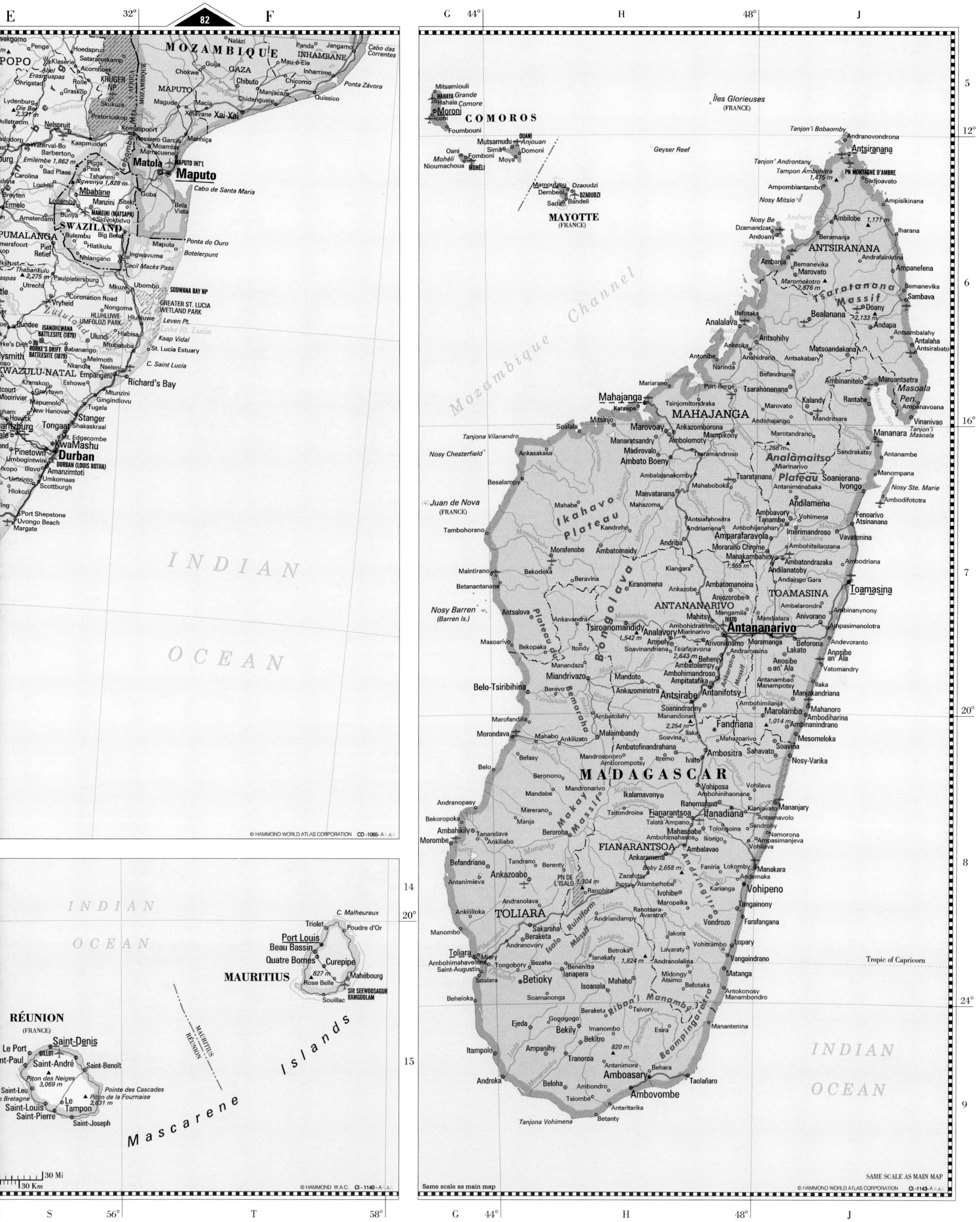

POPULATION OF CITIES AND TOWNS

- ■ OVER 2,000,000
- □ 1,000,000 - 1,999,999
- ◉ 500,000 - 999,999
- ◎ 250,000 - 499,999
- ⊕ 100,000 - 249,999
- ⊕ 50,000 - 99,999
- ⊙ 10,000 - 29,999
- ○ UNDER 10,000

SCALE 1:7,000,000 POLYCONIC PROJECTION

MILES 0 100 200 300

KILOMETERS 0 100 200 300

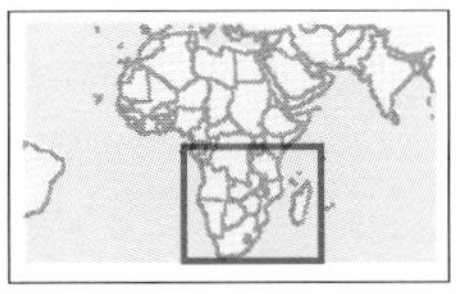

Southern Africa

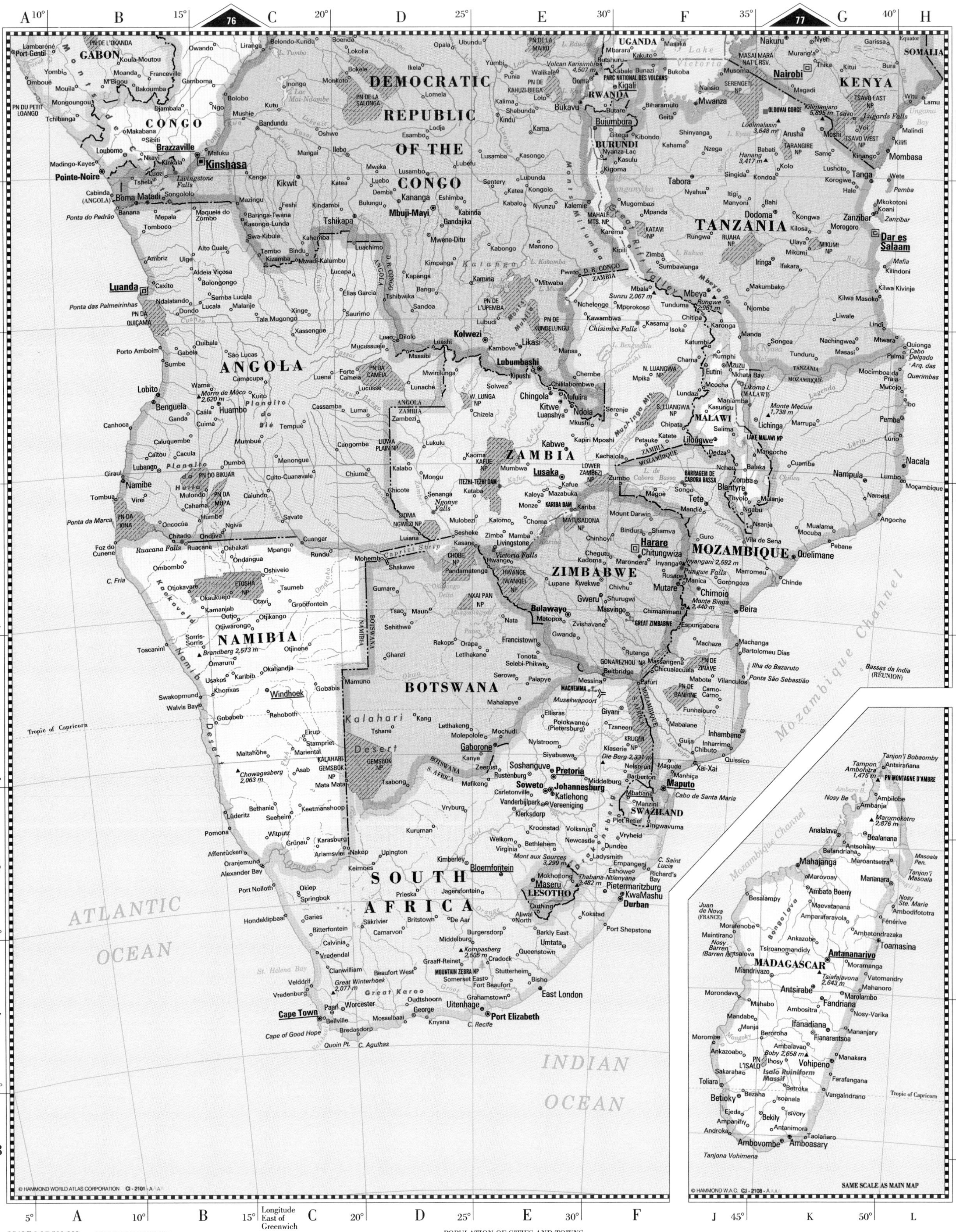

SCALE 1:17,500,000 POLYCONIC PROJECTION

MILES 0 250 500 750

KILOMETERS 0 250 500 750

POPULATION OF CITIES AND TOWNS

■ OVER 2,000,000 ◉ 500,000 - 999,999 ⊙ 50,000 - 99,999

□ 1,000,000 - 1,999,999 ● 100,000 - 499,999 ○ UNDER 50,000

Arctic Regions, Antarctica

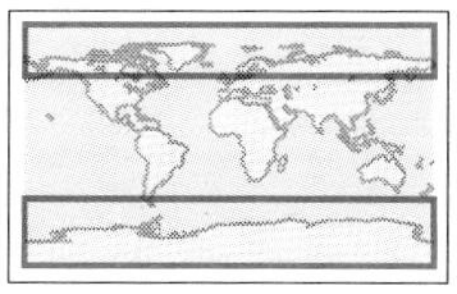

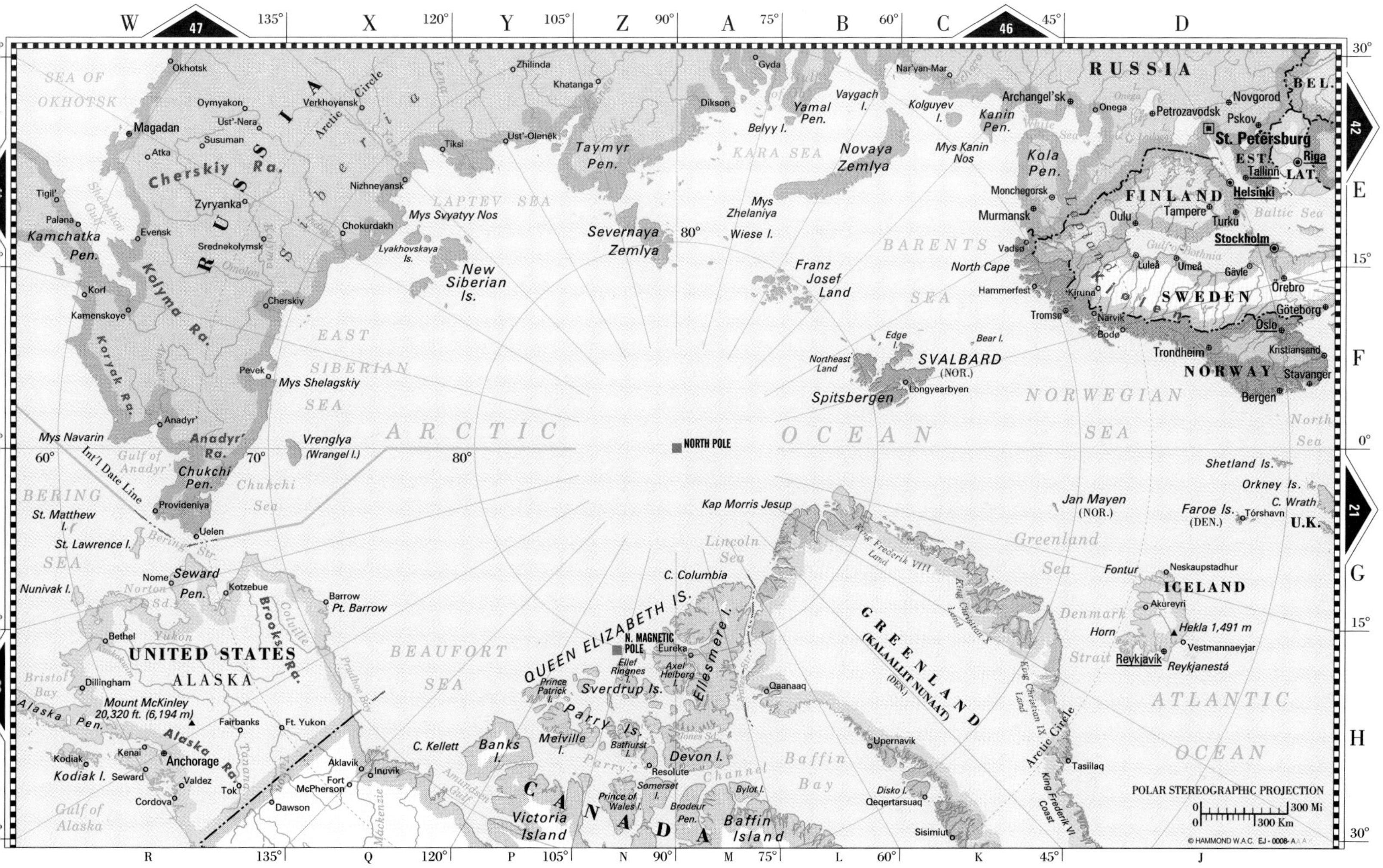

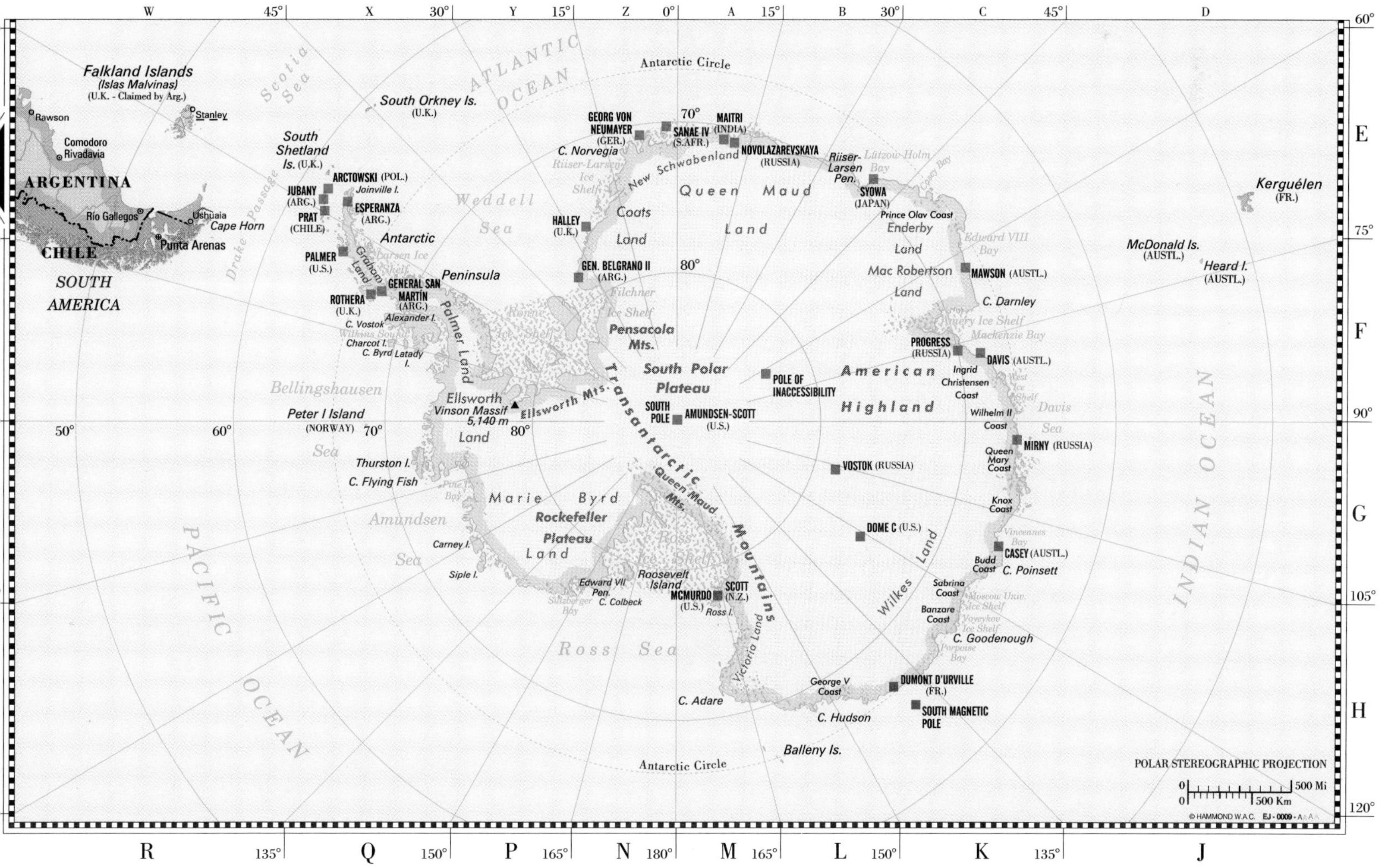

POPULATION OF CITIES AND TOWNS

- OVER 2,000,000
- 1,000,000 - 1,999,999
- 500,000 - 999,999
- 100,000 - 499,999
- 50,000 - 99,999
- UNDER 50,000

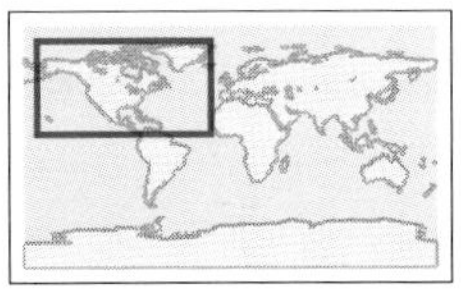

North America

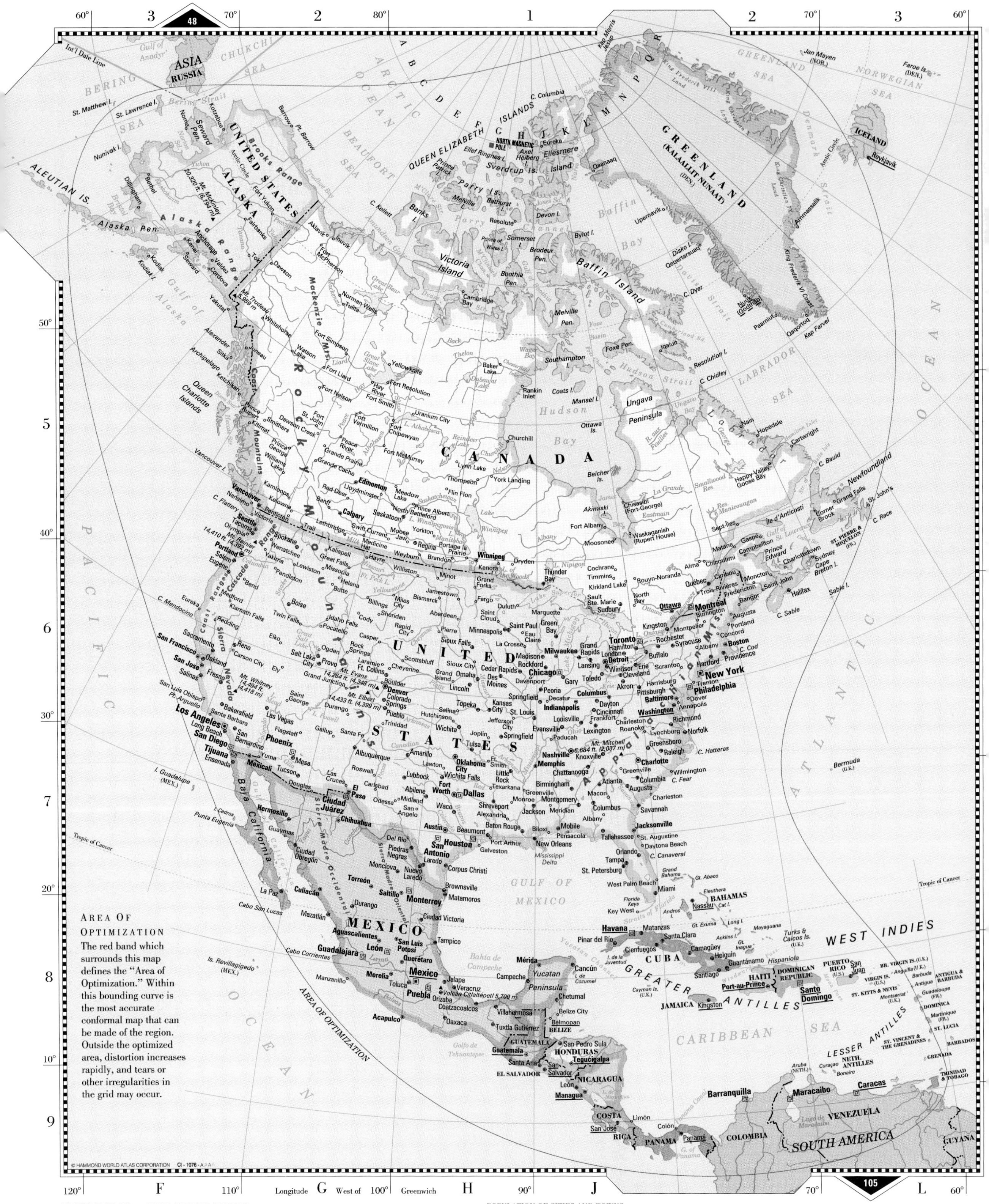

AREA OF OPTIMIZATION

The red band which surrounds this map defines the "Area of Optimization." Within this bounding curve is the most accurate conformal map that can be made of the region. Outside the optimized area, distortion increases rapidly, and tears or other irregularities in the grid may occur.

SCALE 1:35,000,000 OPTIMAL CONFORMAL PROJECTION

MILES 0 500 1000 1500

KILOMETERS 0 500 1000 1500

POPULATION OF CITIES AND TOWNS

- OVER 3,000,000
- 1,000,000 - 2,999,999
- 500,000 - 999,999
- 100,000 - 499,999
- UNDER 100,000

Alaska

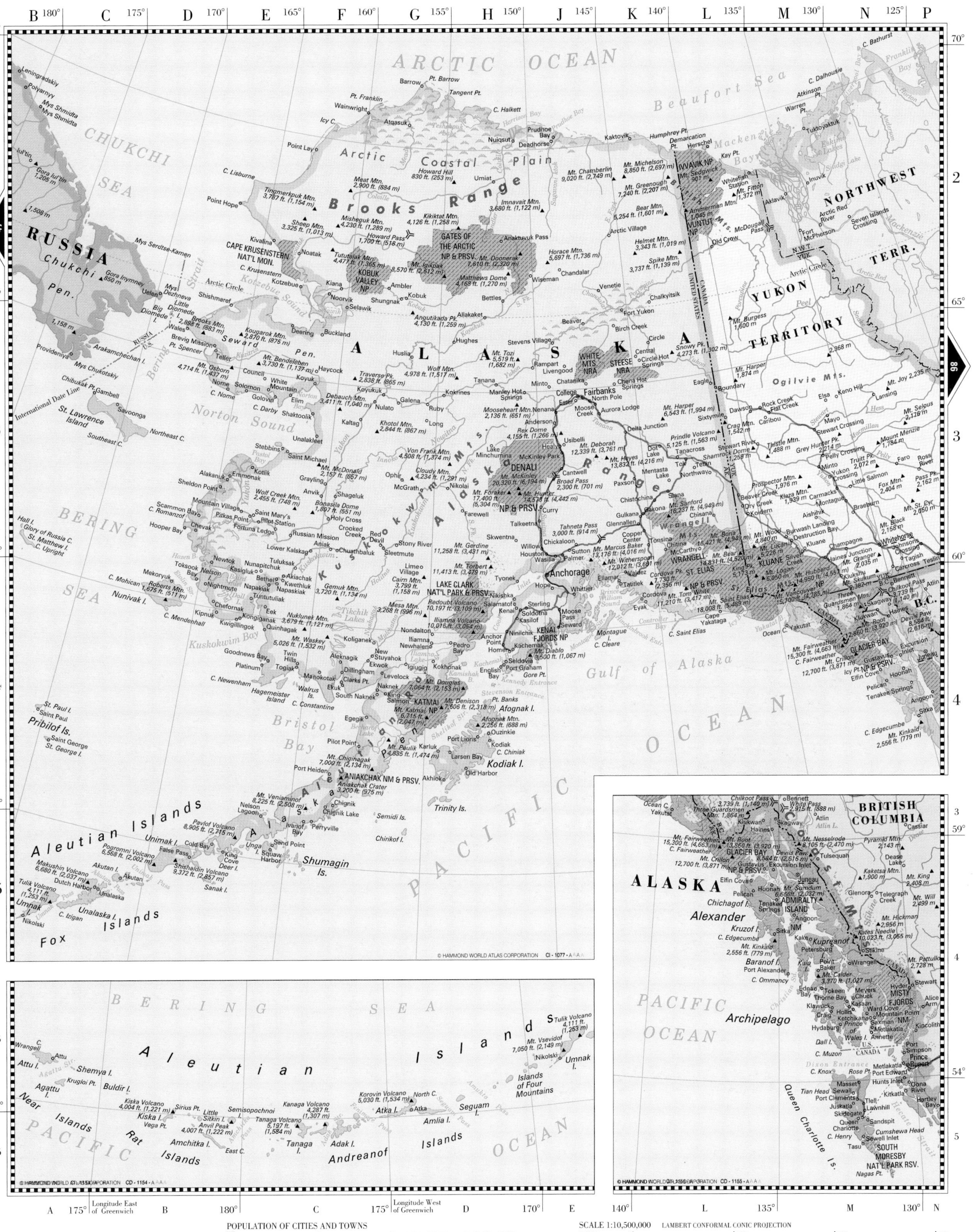

Longitude East of Greenwich | Longitude West of Greenwich

POPULATION OF CITIES AND TOWNS
■ OVER 2,000,000 | ◉ 500,000 - 999,999 | ● 100,000 - 249,999 | ⊙ 10,000 - 29,999
□ 1,000,000 - 1,999,999 | ◎ 250,000 - 499,999 | ⊕ 30,000 - 99,999 | ○ UNDER 10,000

SCALE 1:10,500,000 LAMBERT CONFORMAL CONIC PROJECTION
MILES 0 150 300 450
KILOMETERS 0 150 300 450

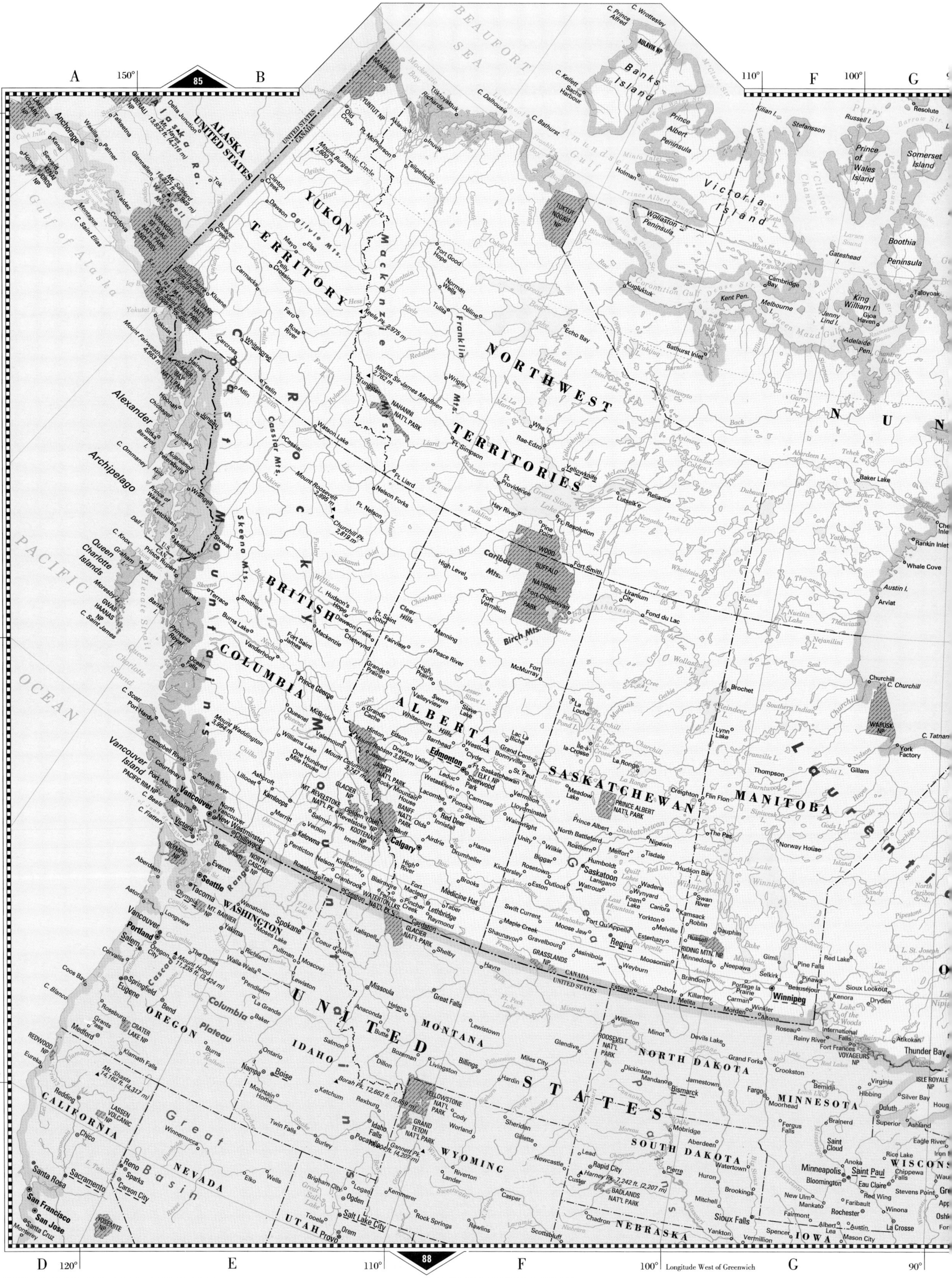

SCALE 1:14,000,000 LAMBERT CONFORMAL CONIC PROJECTION

MILES 0 200 400 600

KILOMETERS 0 200 400 600

POPULATION OF CITIES AND TOWNS

■ OVER 2,000,000	⊙ 500,000 - 999,999	⊙ 50,000 - 99,999
◻ 1,000,000 - 1,999,999	⊕ 100,000 - 499,999	○ UNDER 50,000

Canada

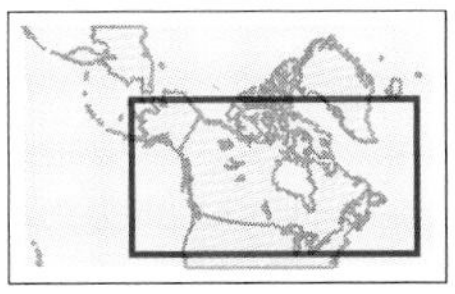

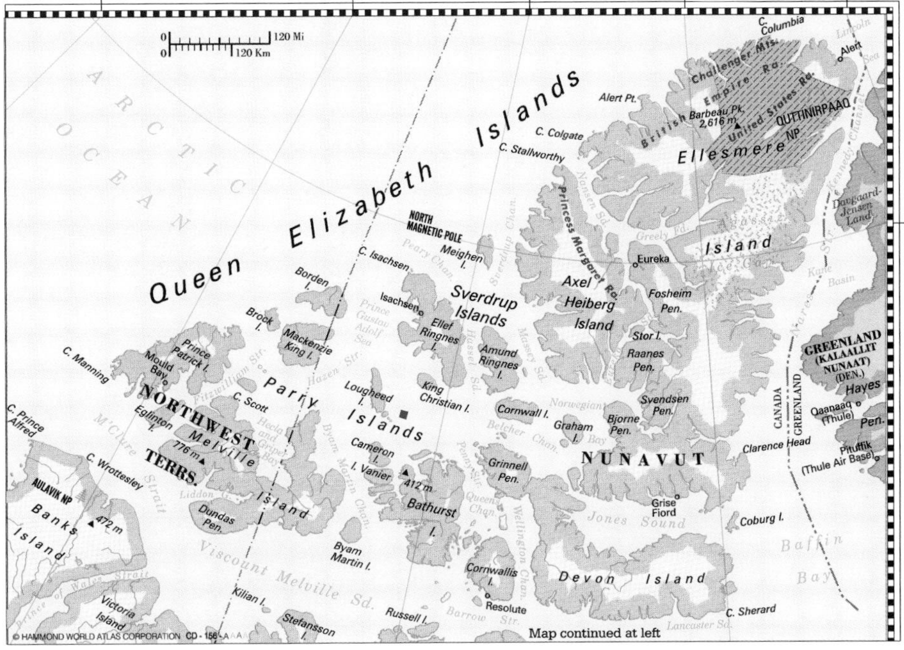

140°
Q
120°
R
100°
S
80°
T
60°
120 Mi
120 Km
ARCTIC OCEAN
Queen Elizabeth Islands
Ellesmere Island
C. Columbia
Alert
Alert Pt.
Challenger Mts.
British Empire Ra.
United States Ra.
Barbeau Pk. 2,616 m
QUTTINIRPAAQ NP
C. Colgate
C. Stallworthy
NORTH MAGNETIC POLE
Meighen I.
Peary Chan.
C. Isachsen
Sverdrup Chan.
Princess Margaret Ra.
Nansen Sd.
Eureka
Greely Fd.
Axel Heiberg Island
Fosheim Pen.
Stor I.
Raanes Pen.
Svendsen Pen.
Bjorne Pen.
Graham I.
Norwegian Bay
Dangaard-Jensen Land
Kennedy Chan.
Basin
GREENLAND (KALAALLIT NUNAAT) (DEN.)
CANADA
GREENLAND
Qaanaaq (Thule)
Hayes Pen.
Pituffik (Thule Air Base)
Clarence Head
Borden I.
Isachsen
Ellef Ringnes I.
Amund Ringnes I.
Sverdrup Islands
Brock I.
Mackenzie King I.
Prince Patrick I.
Mould Bay
C. Manning
Prince Gustav Adolf Sea
Hazen Str.
Lougheed I.
King Christian I.
Parry Islands
C. Scott
NORTHWEST TERRS.
Eglinton I.
Melville Island
776 m
Hecla and Griper Bay
C. Prince Alfred
M'Clure Strait
Cameron I.
I. Vanier
412 m
Bathurst I.
Byam Martin Chan.
Cornwall I.
Belcher Chan.
Grinnell Pen.
NUNAVUT
Grise Fiord
Jones Sound
Coburg I.
AULAVIK NP
C. Wrottesley
Banks Island
472 m
Liddon G.
Dundas Pen.
Viscount Melville Sd.
Byam Martin I.
Queens Chan.
Wellington Chan.
Cornwallis I.
Resolute
Devon Island
Baffin Bay
Victoria Island
Kilian I.
Stefansson I.
Russell I.
Barrow Str.
Lancaster Sd.
C. Sherard
Prince of Wales Strait
6
80°
7
© HAMMOND WORLD ATLAS CORPORATION
Map continued at left

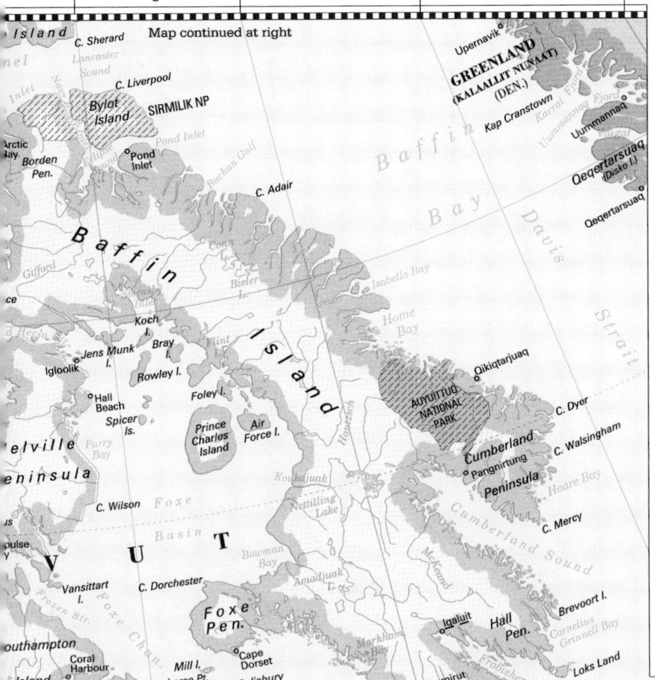

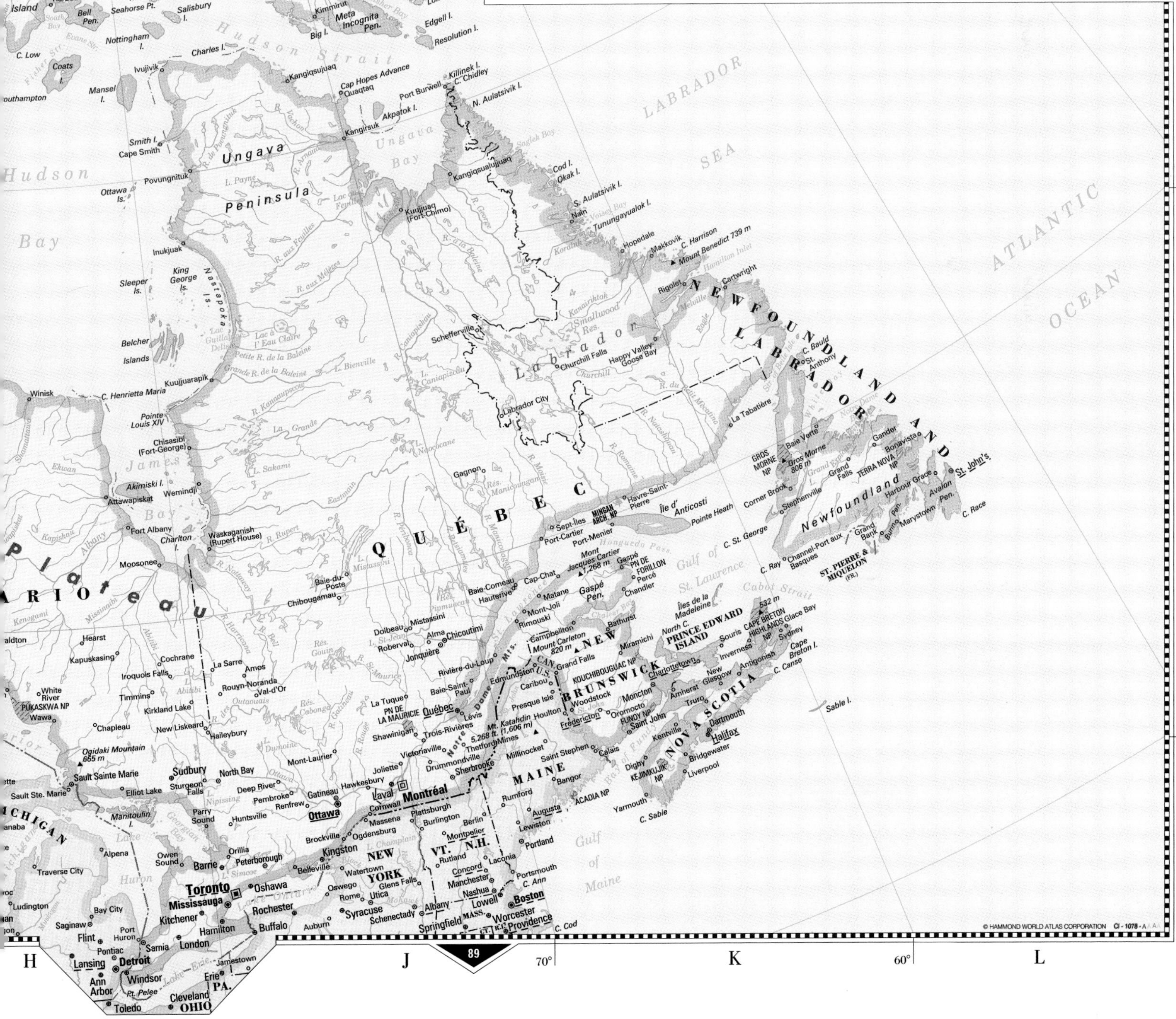

80°
J
70°
K
60°
L
50°
Map continued at right
C. Sherard
Lancaster Sound
C. Liverpool
Bylot Island
SIRMILIK NP
Pond Inlet
Arctic Bay
Borden Pen.
Baffin Bay
Davis Strait
GREENLAND (KALAALLIT NUNAAT) (DEN.)
Upernavik
Kap Cranstown
Uummannaq
Qeqertarsuaq (Disko I.)
Qeqertarsuaq
C. Adair
Baffin Island
Home Bay
Igloolik
Jens Munk I.
Koch I.
Bray I.
Rowley I.
Hall Beach
Foley I.
Spicer Is.
Prince Charles Island
Air Force I.
Qikiqtarjuaq
AUYUITTUQ NATIONAL PARK
C. Dyer
Cumberland Peninsula
Pangnirtung
C. Walsingham
Cumberland Sound
C. Mercy
Hoare Bay
Foxe Basin
C. Wilson
Melville Peninsula
NUNAVUT
Nettilling Lake
Amadjuak L.
Bowman Bay
Vansittart I.
C. Dorchester
Foxe Pen.
Iqaluit
Hall Pen.
Brevoort I.
Southampton Island
Coral Harbour
Cape Dorset
Mill I.
Seahorse Pt.
Salisbury I.
Kimmirut
Frobisher Bay
Meta Incognita Pen.
Loks Land
Edgell I.
Resolution I.
Big I.
Bell Pen.
Nottingham I.
Hudson Strait
Charles I.
C. Low
Coats I.
Mansel I.
Ivujivik
Kangiqsujuaq
Cap Hopes Advance
Quaqtaq
Killinek I.
C. Chidley
Port Burwell
N. Aulatsivik I.
Akpatok I.
Kangirsuk
Ungava Bay
LABRADOR SEA
Smith I.
Cape Smith
Ungava Peninsula
Povungnituk
Hudson Bay
Ottawa Is.
Kangiqsualujjuaq
Cod I.
Okak I.
S. Aulatsivik I.
Nain
Tunungayualok I.
Kuujjuaq (Fort-Chimo)
Hopedale
Makkovik
C. Harrison
Mount Benedict 739 m
Hamilton Inlet
Inukjuak
King George Is.
Nastapoka Is.
Sleeper Is.
Rigolet
Cartwright
Schefferville
Smallwood Res.
Labrador
Happy Valley-Goose Bay
Churchill Falls
Lac à l'Eau Claire
Guillaume-Delisle
Belcher Islands
Petite R. de la Baleine
Grande R. de la Baleine
L. Bienville
L. Caniapiscau
NEWFOUNDLAND AND LABRADOR
C. Bauld
St. Anthony
ATLANTIC OCEAN
Kuujjuarapik
Winisk
C. Henrietta Maria
Labrador City
Pointe Louis XIV
La Grande
Chisasibi (Fort-George)
La Tabatière
Baie Verte
Gander
Bonavista
GROS MORNE NP
Gros Morne 806 m
TERRA NOVA NP
Grand Falls
Harbour Grace
St. John's
Akimiski I.
Attawapiskat
Wemindji
James Bay
Gagnon
Rés. Manicouagan
Havre-Saint-Pierre
Île d'Anticosti
Pointe Heath
Corner Brook
Stephenville
Newfoundland
Marystown
Avalon Pen.
C. Race
Fort Albany
Charlton I.
Waskaganish (Rupert House)
QUÉBEC
Sept-Îles
MINGAN ARCH. NP
Port-Cartier
Port-Menier
Honguedo Pass.
C. St. George
Channel-Port aux Basques
Grand Bank
Burin Pen.
C. Ray
Cabot Strait
ST. PIERRE & MIQUELON (FR.)
Moosonee
L. Mistassini
Baie-du-Poste
Baie-Comeau
Hauterive
Cap-Chat
Matane
Mont Jacques Cartier 1,268 m
Gaspé
PN DE FORILLON
Percé
Gaspé Pen.
Chandler
Gulf of St. Lawrence
Îles de la Madeleine
532 m
ARIO Plateau
Chibougamau
Mont-Joli
Rimouski
Campbellton
Mont Carleton 820 m
Bathurst
NEW BRUNSWICK
Miramichi
North C.
PRINCE EDWARD ISLAND
Souris
CAPE BRETON HIGHLANDS NP
Glace Bay
Sydney
Cape Breton I.
C. Canso
Dolbeau
Mistassini
Roberval
Alma
Chicoutimi
Jonquière
Hearst
Kapuskasing
Cochrane
Iroquois Falls
La Sarre
Amos
Rouyn-Noranda
Val-d'Or
Rés. Gouin
Rivière-du-Loup
Edmundston
Grand Falls
KOUCHIBOUGUAC NP
Charlottetown
Inverness
Antigonish
New Glasgow
Amherst
Truro
Moncton
Fundy NP
Oromocto
Fredericton
Saint John
NOVA SCOTIA
Dartmouth
Halifax
Kentville
Bridgewater
Liverpool
Sable I.
White River
Timmins
Kirkland Lake
La Tuque
PN DE LA MAURICIE
Baie-Saint-Paul
Québec
Caribou
Presque Isle
Houlton
Woodstock
PUKASKWA NP
Wawa
Chapleau
New Liskeard
Haileybury
Shawinigan
Trois-Rivières
Mt. Katahdin 5,268 ft. (1,606 m)
Millinocket
Ogidaki Mountain 665 m
Victoriaville
Thetford Mines
Drummondville
Sherbrooke
Saint Stephen
Calais
Digby
KEJIMKUJIK NP
Sault Sainte Marie
Sault Ste. Marie
Sudbury
North Bay
Sturgeon Falls
L. Nipissing
Mont-Laurier
Deep River
Pembroke
Renfrew
Gatineau
Hawkesbury
Joliette
Laval
Montréal
MAINE
Bangor
ACADIA NP
Yarmouth
C. Sable
Elliot Lake
Manitoulin I.
Parry Sound
Huntsville
Ottawa
Cornwall
Massena
Plattsburgh
Burlington
Berlin
Rumford
Augusta
Lewiston
Portland
Gulf of Maine
MICHIGAN
Escanaba
Alpena
Owen Sound
Barrie
Orillia
Peterborough
Brockville
Ogdensburg
Kingston
Belleville
Watertown
NEW YORK
VT.
N.H.
Montpelier
Rutland
Laconia
Concord
Manchester
Nashua
Lowell
Boston
Portsmouth
C. Ann
Traverse City
Lake Huron
Toronto
Oshawa
Mississauga
Rochester
Oswego
Rome
Utica
Syracuse
Glens Falls
Schenectady
Albany
Springfield
MASS.
Worcester
Providence
R.I.
C. Cod
Ludington
Bay City
Saginaw
Flint
Port Huron
Pontiac
Sarnia
Kitchener
Hamilton
London
Buffalo
Auburn
Lansing
Detroit
Windsor
Ann Arbor
Pt. Pelee
Lake Erie
Jamestown
Erie
PA.
Cleveland
OHIO
Toledo
Muskegon
H
J
70°
K
60°
L
4
50°
40°
5
© HAMMOND WORLD ATLAS CORPORATION

89

86
100
A
B
C
E
F
BRITISH COLUMBIA
ALBERTA
SASKATCHEWAN
WASHINGTON
MONTANA
OREGON
IDAHO
WYOMING
NEVADA
UTAH
COLORADO
CALIFORNIA
ARIZONA
NEW MEXICO
SOUTH DAK
NEBRA
NORTH DAKO
PACIFIC OCEAN
Vancouver Island
Vancouver
Victoria
Calgary
Seattle
Tacoma
Olympia
Portland
Salem
Eugene
Spokane
Boise
Missoula
Helena
Great Falls
Billings
Regina
Salt Lake City
Reno
Carson City
Sacramento
San Francisco
Oakland
San Jose
Fresno
Las Vegas
Los Angeles
Long Beach
San Diego
Tijuana
Mexicali
Phoenix
Tucson
Albuquerque
Santa Fe
Denver
Colorado Springs
Pueblo
Cheyenne
El Paso
Ciudad Juárez
Lubbock
Amarillo
Great Basin
Mt. Rainier 14,410 ft. (4,392 m)
Mt. Hood 11,235 ft. (3,424 m)
Mt. Shasta 14,162 ft. (4,317 m)
Mt. Whitney 14,494 ft. (4,418 m)
Kings Pk. 13,528 ft. (4,123 m)
Mt. Elbert 14,433 ft. (4,399 m)
Pikes Pk. 14,110 ft. (4,301 m)
Humphreys Pk. 12,633 ft. (3,851 m)
Granite Pk. 12,799 ft. (3,901 m)
Gannett Pk. 13,804 ft. (4,207 m)
Borah Pk. 12,662 ft. (3,859 m)
Guadalupe Pk. 8,749 ft. (2,667 m)
YELLOWSTONE NAT'L PARK
GRAND CANYON NAT'L PARK
YOSEMITE NAT'L PARK
DEATH VALLEY NP
CANADA
UNITED STATES
MEXICO
BAJA CALIFORNIA
SONORA
CHIHUAHUA
COAHUILA DE ZARAGOZA
NUEVO LEÓN
ZACATECAS
SAN LUIS POTOSÍ
AGUASCALIENTES
JALISCO
GUANAJUATO
Guadalajara
León
Querétaro
Monterrey
Torreón
Saltillo
HAWAII
Kauai
Niihau
Oahu
Honolulu
Molokai
Lanai
Maui
Kahoolawe
Hawaii
Hilo
Kauai Channel
Kaiwi Channel
Alenuihaha Channel
Mauna Kea 13,796 ft. (4,205 m)
Mauna Loa 13,677 ft. (4,169 m)
Haleakala
HONOLULU
Pearl City
Kaneohe
Kailua
Waipahu
Ewa Beach
© HAMMOND W.A.C.

United States

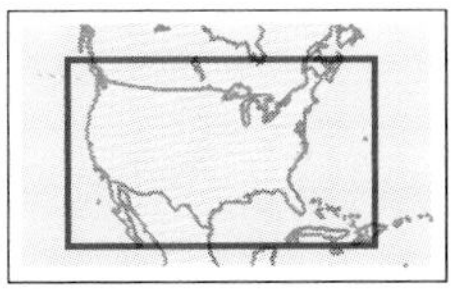

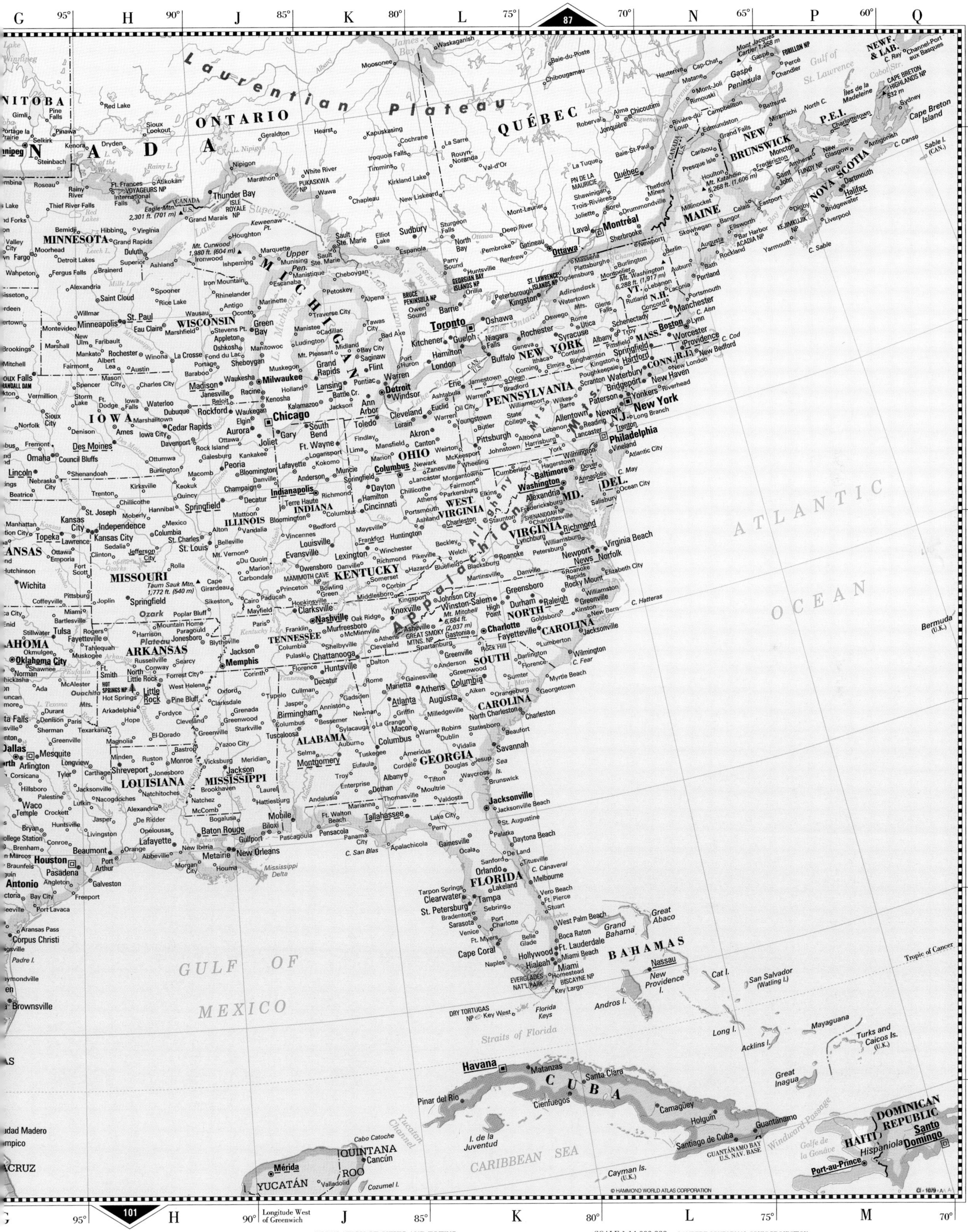

POPULATION OF CITIES AND TOWNS

▣ OVER 2,000,000	◉ 500,000 - 999,999	⊙ 50,000 - 99,999
▣ 1,000,000 - 1,999,999	⊕ 100,000 - 499,999	○ UNDER 50,000

SCALE 1:14,000,000 LAMBERT CONFORMAL CONIC PROJECTION

MILES 0 200 400 600

KILOMETERS 0 200 400 600

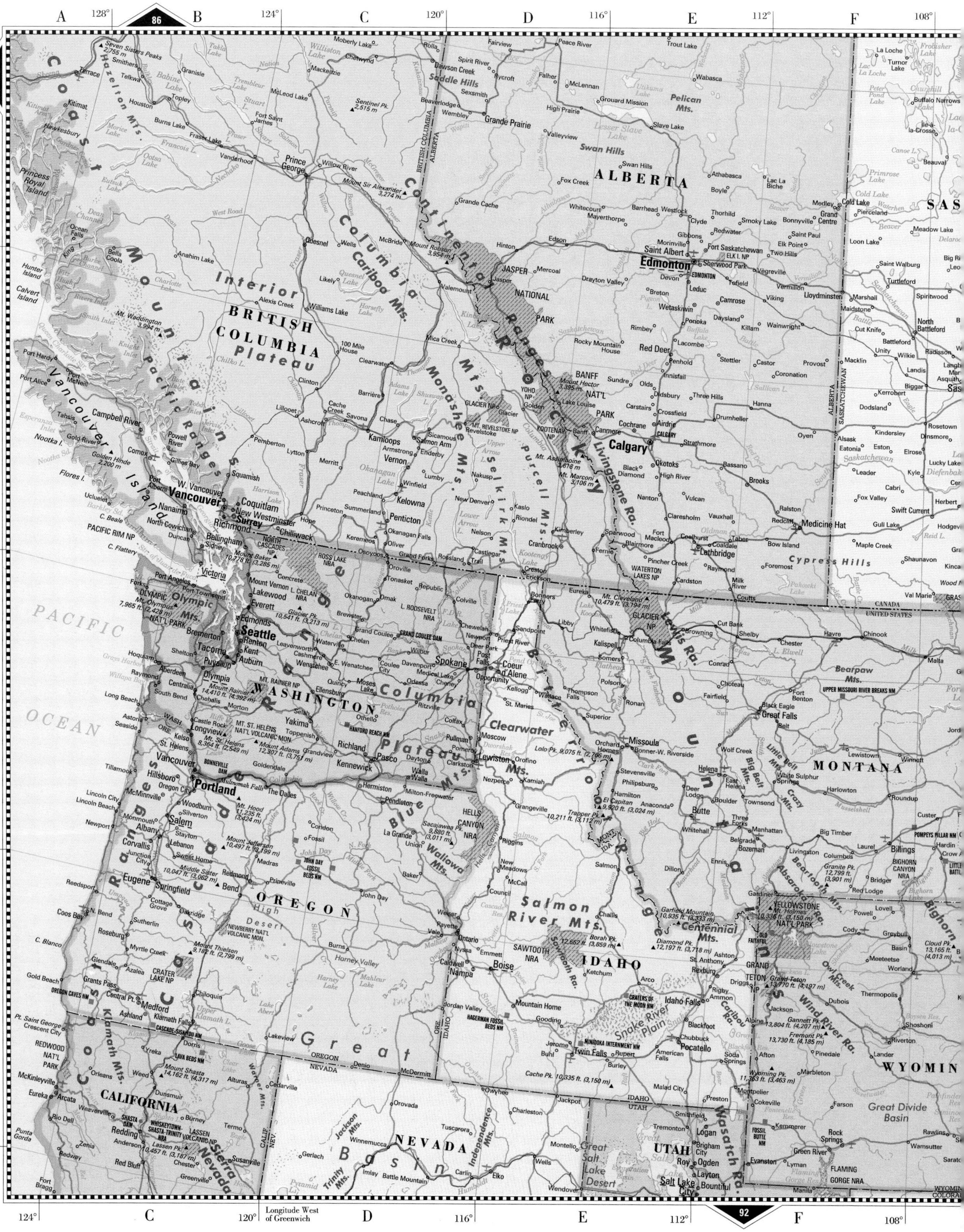

A
128°
86
B
124°
C
120°
D
116°
E
112°
F
108°
85
2
52°
3
48°
4
44°
5
40°
6
124°
C
120°
Longitude West of Greenwich
D
116°
E
112°
92
F
108°
BRITISH COLUMBIA
Interior
COLUMBIA Plateau
ALBERTA
SAS
WASHINGTON
OREGON
IDAHO
MONTANA
WYOMIN
NEVADA
UTAH
CALIFORNIA
PACIFIC
OCEAN
Coast Mountains
Vancouver Island
Pacific Ranges
Continental Ranges
Columbia Mts.
Cariboo Mts.
Monashee Mts.
Selkirk Mts.
Purcell Mts.
Rocky Mountains
Livingstone Ra.
Lewis Ra.
Cascade Range
Coast Ranges
Olympic Mts.
Columbia Plateau
Blue Mts.
Wallowa Mts.
Clearwater Mts.
Salmon River Mts.
Bitterroot Range
Centennial Mts.
Snake River Plain
Wasatch Ra.
Wind River Ra.
Bighorn Mts.
Absaroka Ra.
Beartooth Mts.
Bearpaw Mts.
Cypress Hills
Swan Hills
Pelican Mts.
Saddle Hills
Great Basin
High Desert
Great Divide Basin
Great Salt Lake Desert
Klamath Mts.
Sierra Nevada
JASPER NATIONAL PARK
BANFF NAT'L PARK
GLACIER NP
YELLOWSTONE NAT'L PARK
OLYMPIC NAT'L PARK
NORTH CASCADES NP
MT. RAINIER NP
CRATER LAKE NP
REDWOOD NAT'L PARK
LASSEN VOLCANIC NP
GRAND TETON NP
Mount Robson 3,954 m
Mount Rainier 14,410 ft. (4,392 m)
Mount Hood 11,235 ft. (3,424 m)
Mount Shasta 14,162 ft. (4,317 m)
Mount Baker 10,778 ft. (3,285 m)
Mount Adams 12,307 ft. (3,751 m)
Borah Pk. 12,662 ft. (3,859 m)
Grand Teton 13,770 ft. (4,197 m)
Gannett Pk. 13,804 ft. (4,207 m)
Vancouver
Victoria
Seattle
Tacoma
Spokane
Portland
Salem
Eugene
Boise
Calgary
Edmonton
Red Deer
Lethbridge
Medicine Hat
Kamloops
Kelowna
Prince George
Missoula
Helena
Butte
Great Falls
Billings
Bozeman
Idaho Falls
Pocatello
Twin Falls
Ogden
Salt Lake City
Logan
Medford
Redding
Eureka
Yakima
Walla Walla
Lewiston
Pendleton
Bend
CANADA
UNITED STATES

Southwestern Canada, Northwestern United States

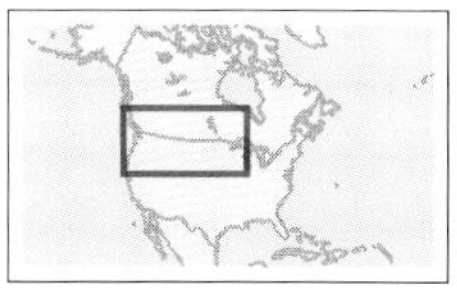

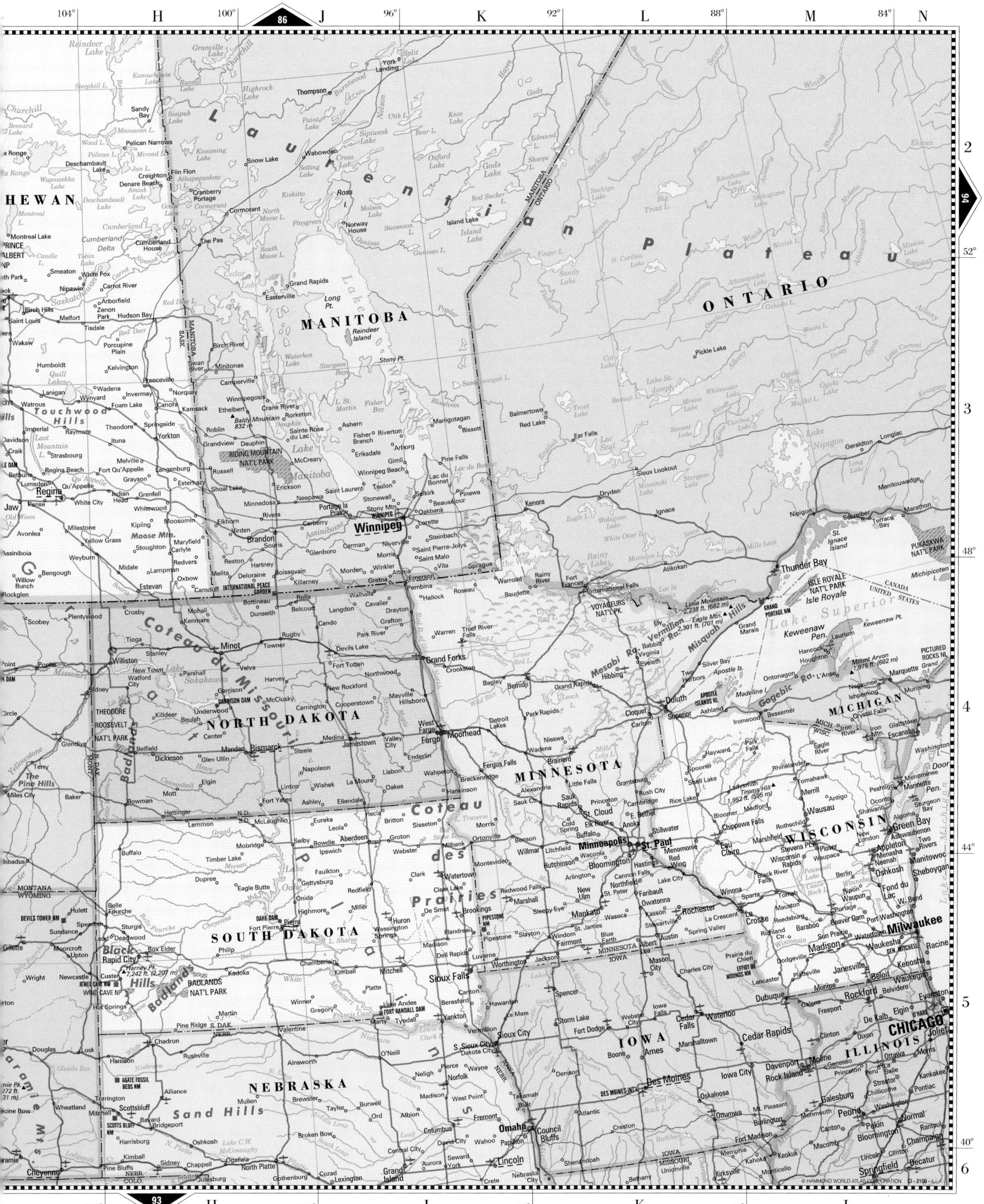

POPULATION OF CITIES AND TOWNS

- OVER 2,000,000
- 1,000,000 - 1,999,999
- 500,000 - 999,999
- 250,000 - 499,999
- 100,000 - 249,999
- 30,000 - 99,999
- 10,000 - 29,999
- UNDER 10,000

SCALE 1:7,000,000 LAMBERT CONFORMAL CONIC PROJECTION

MILES 0 100 200 300

KILOMETERS 0 100 200 300

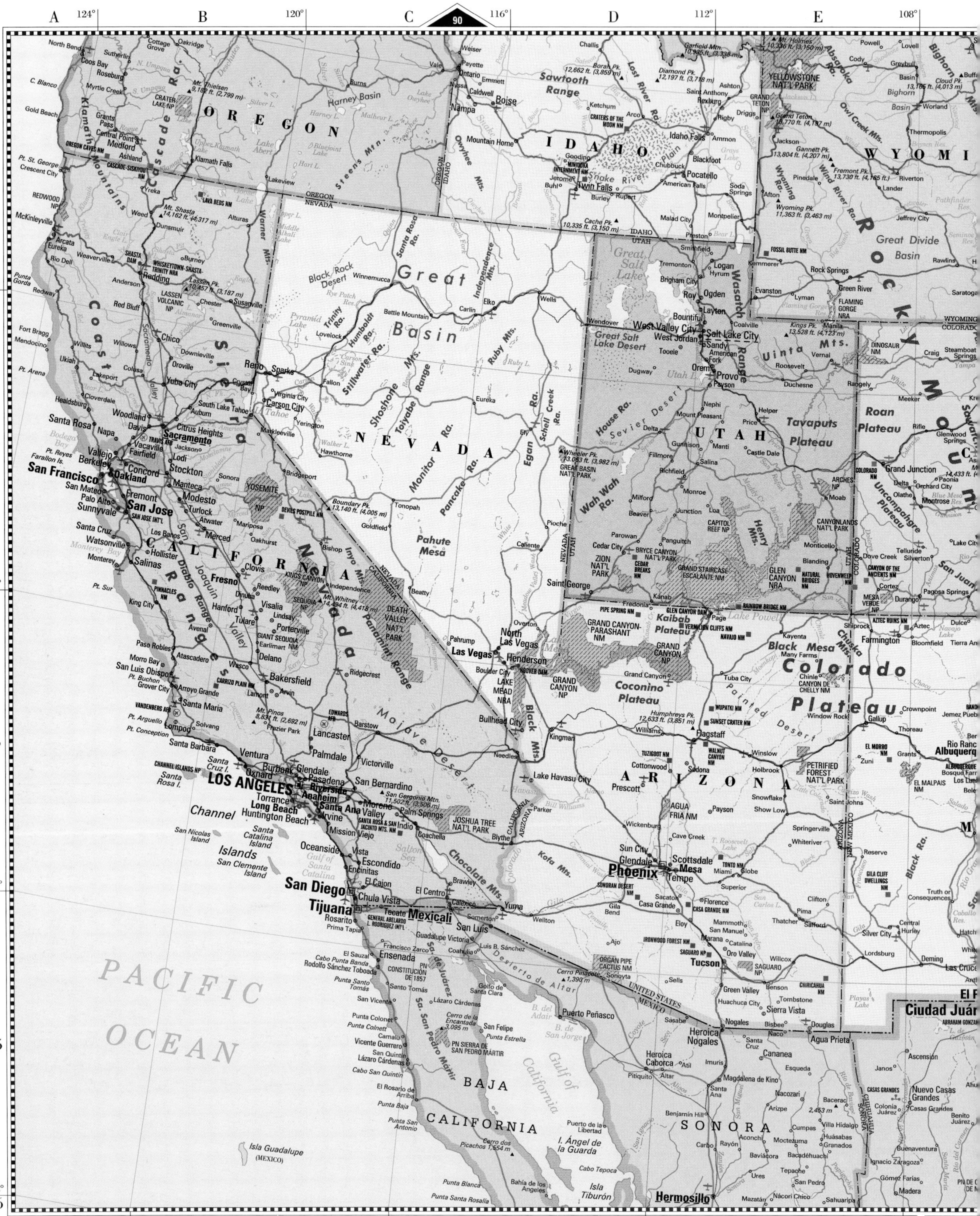

A
B
C
D
E
124°
120°
116°
112°
108°
90
100
2
3
4
5
6
40°
36°
32°
28°
Longitude West of Greenwich
OREGON
IDAHO
WYOMING
NEVADA
UTAH
ARIZONA
CALIFORNIA
Colorado Plateau
Great Basin
Coast Ranges
Sierra Nevada
Cascade Range
Klamath Mountains
Sawtooth Range
Lost River Range
Snake River Plain
Wasatch Range
Uinta Mts.
Great Salt Lake
Great Salt Lake Desert
Great Divide Basin
Rocky Mountains
Tavaputs Plateau
Roan Plateau
Uncompahgre Plateau
Coconino Plateau
Kaibab Plateau
Painted Desert
Mojave Desert
Pahute Mesa
Panamint Range
Black Mts.
Chocolate Mts.
Kofa Mts.
Harney Basin
Steens Mtn.
Owyhee Mts.
Santa Rosa Ra.
Independence Mts.
Ruby Mts.
Schell Creek Ra.
Egan Ra.
Toiyabe Range
Shoshone Mts.
Stillwater Ra.
Humboldt Ra.
Trinity Ra.
Monitor Ra.
Pancake Ra.
House Ra.
Wah Wah Ra.
Henry Mts.
Sevier Desert
Diablo Range
Joaquin Valley
Black Rock Desert
Desierto de Altar
Gulf of California
PACIFIC OCEAN
Channel Islands
Gulf of Santa Catalina
Salton Sea
Lake Powell
Lake Mead
BAJA CALIFORNIA
SONORA
UNITED STATES
MEXICO
Isla Guadalupe (MEXICO)
Isla Tiburón
San Francisco
Oakland
San Jose
Sacramento
Stockton
Fresno
Bakersfield
LOS ANGELES
Long Beach
Anaheim
Riverside
San Bernardino
San Diego
Tijuana
Mexicali
Ensenada
Las Vegas
Reno
Carson City
Boise
Salt Lake City
Ogden
Provo
Phoenix
Mesa
Tucson
Flagstaff
Yuma
Hermosillo
Heroica Nogales
Ciudad Juárez
Albuquerque
Medford
Redding
Eureka
Santa Rosa
Santa Barbara
Ventura
Oxnard
Lancaster
Palmdale
Palm Springs
Idaho Falls
Pocatello
Twin Falls
Elko
Winnemucca
Ely
Tonopah
Kingman
Prescott
Sedona
Gallup
Farmington
Grand Junction
Moab
Saint George
Cedar City
Rock Springs
Mt. Shasta 14,162 ft. (4,317 m)
Mt. Whitney 14,494 ft. (4,418 m)
Lassen Pk. 10,457 ft. (3,187 m)
Mt. Thielsen 9,182 ft. (2,799 m)
Boundary Pk. 13,140 ft. (4,005 m)
Wheeler Pk. 13,063 ft. (3,982 m)
Kings Pk. 13,528 ft. (4,123 m)
Humphreys Pk. 12,633 ft. (3,851 m)
San Gorgonio Mtn. 11,502 ft. (3,506 m)
Mt. Pinos 8,831 ft. (2,692 m)
Borah Pk. 12,662 ft. (3,859 m)
Diamond Pk. 12,197 ft. (3,718 m)
Grand Teton 13,770 ft. (4,197 m)
Gannett Pk. 13,804 ft. (4,207 m)
Cerro Pinacate 1,390 m
YOSEMITE NP
KINGS CANYON NP
SEQUOIA NP
DEATH VALLEY NAT'L PARK
JOSHUA TREE NAT'L PARK
GRAND CANYON NP
ZION NAT'L PARK
BRYCE CANYON NAT'L PARK
CAPITOL REEF NP
CANYONLANDS NAT'L PARK
ARCHES NP
GREAT BASIN NAT'L PARK
PETRIFIED FOREST NAT'L PARK
YELLOWSTONE NAT'L PARK
GRAND TETON NP
CRATER LAKE NP
LASSEN VOLCANIC NP
REDWOOD NP
GLEN CANYON NRA
LAKE MEAD NRA
GRAND STAIRCASE-ESCALANTE NM
GRAND CANYON-PARASHANT NM
ORGAN PIPE CACTUS NM
SAGUARO NP

Southwestern United States

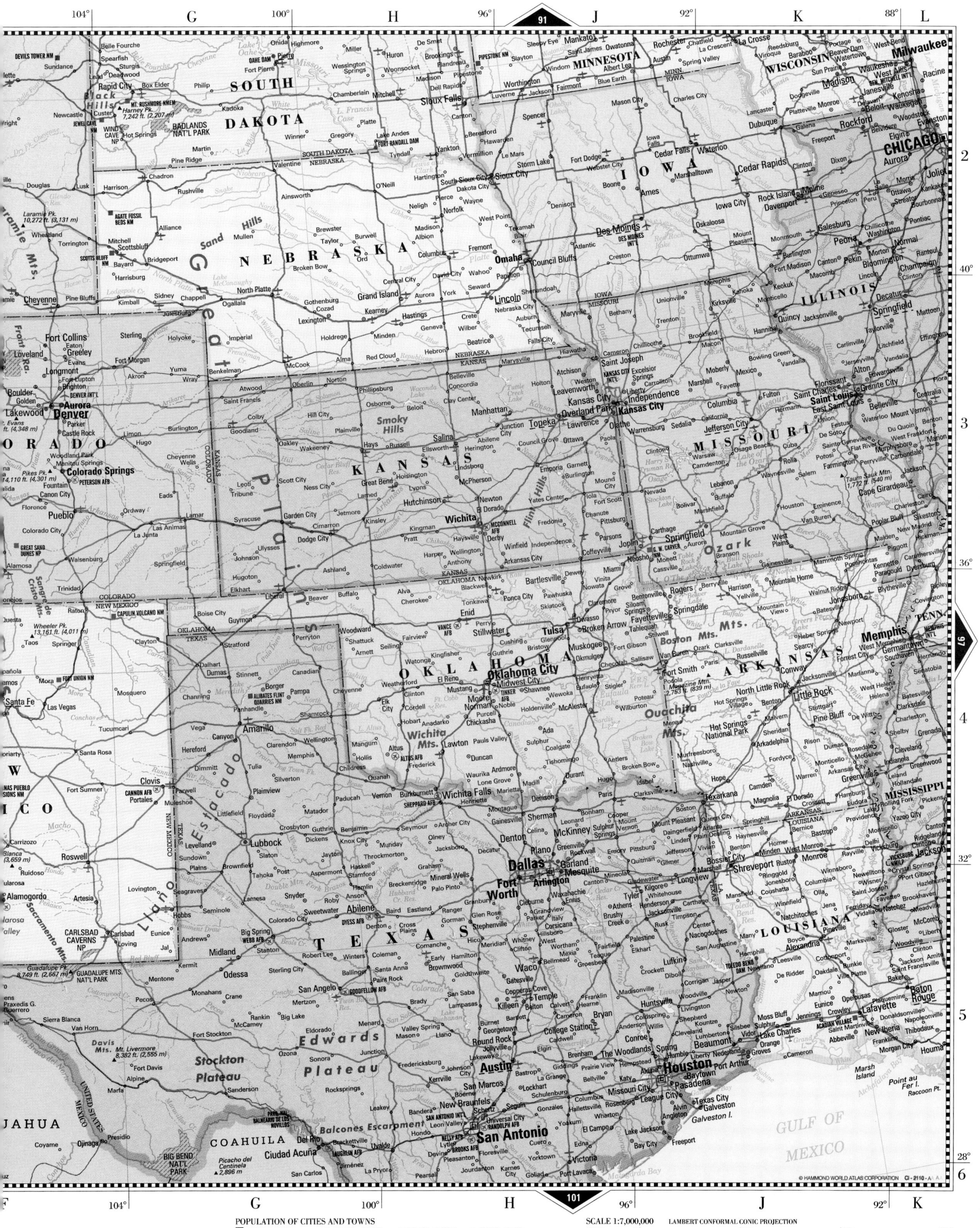

POPULATION OF CITIES AND TOWNS

- OVER 2,000,000
- 1,000,000 - 1,999,999
- 500,000 - 999,999
- 250,000 - 499,999
- 100,000 - 249,999
- 30,000 - 99,999
- 10,000 - 29,999
- UNDER 10,000

SCALE 1:7,000,000 LAMBERT CONFORMAL CONIC PROJECTION

MILES 0 100 200 300

KILOMETERS 0 100 200 300

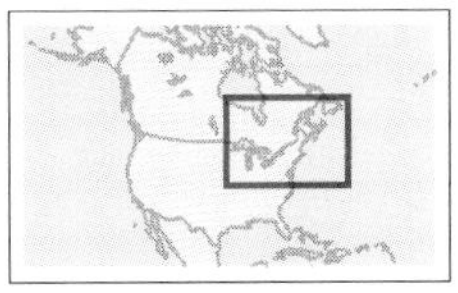

Southeastern Canada, Northeastern United States

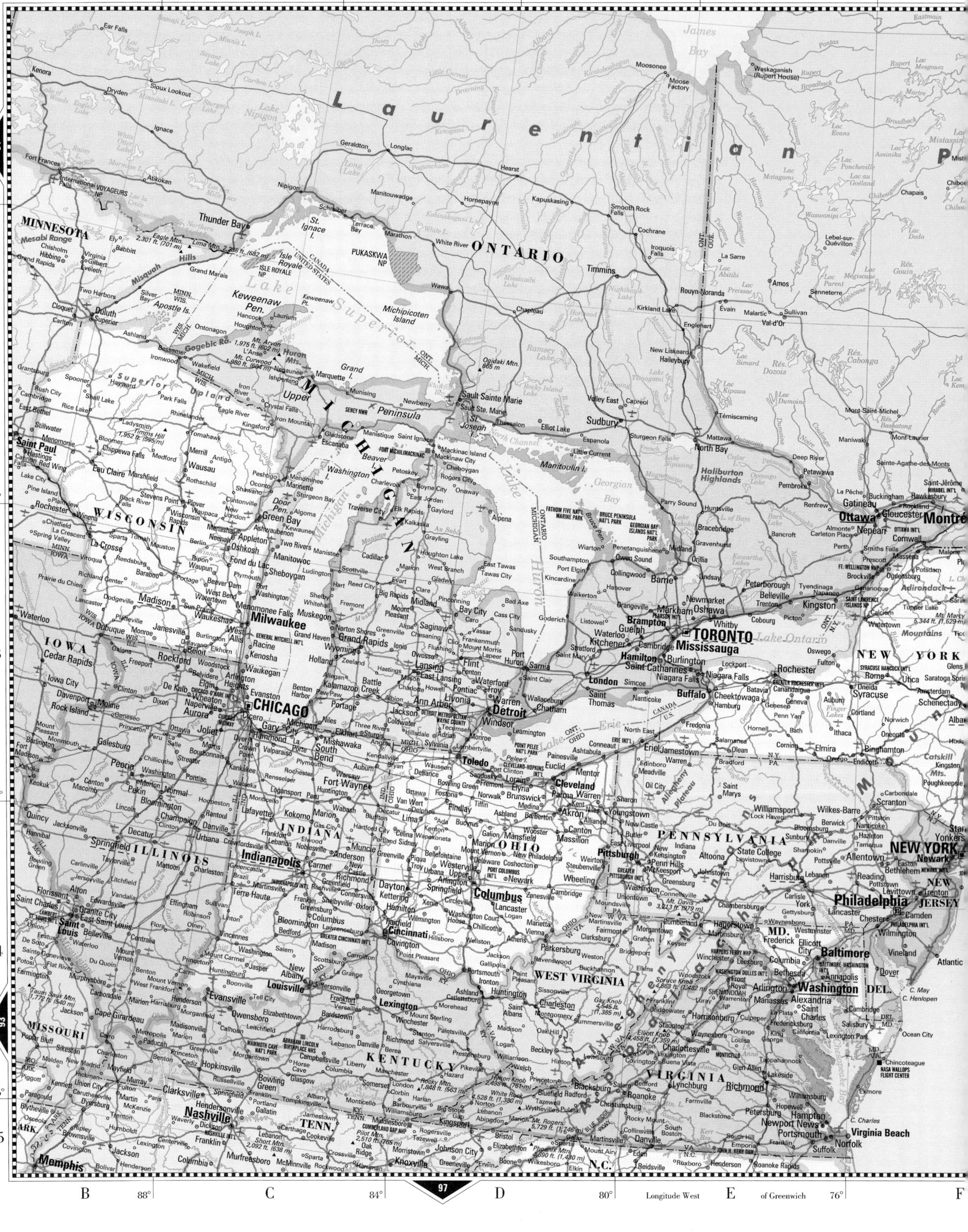

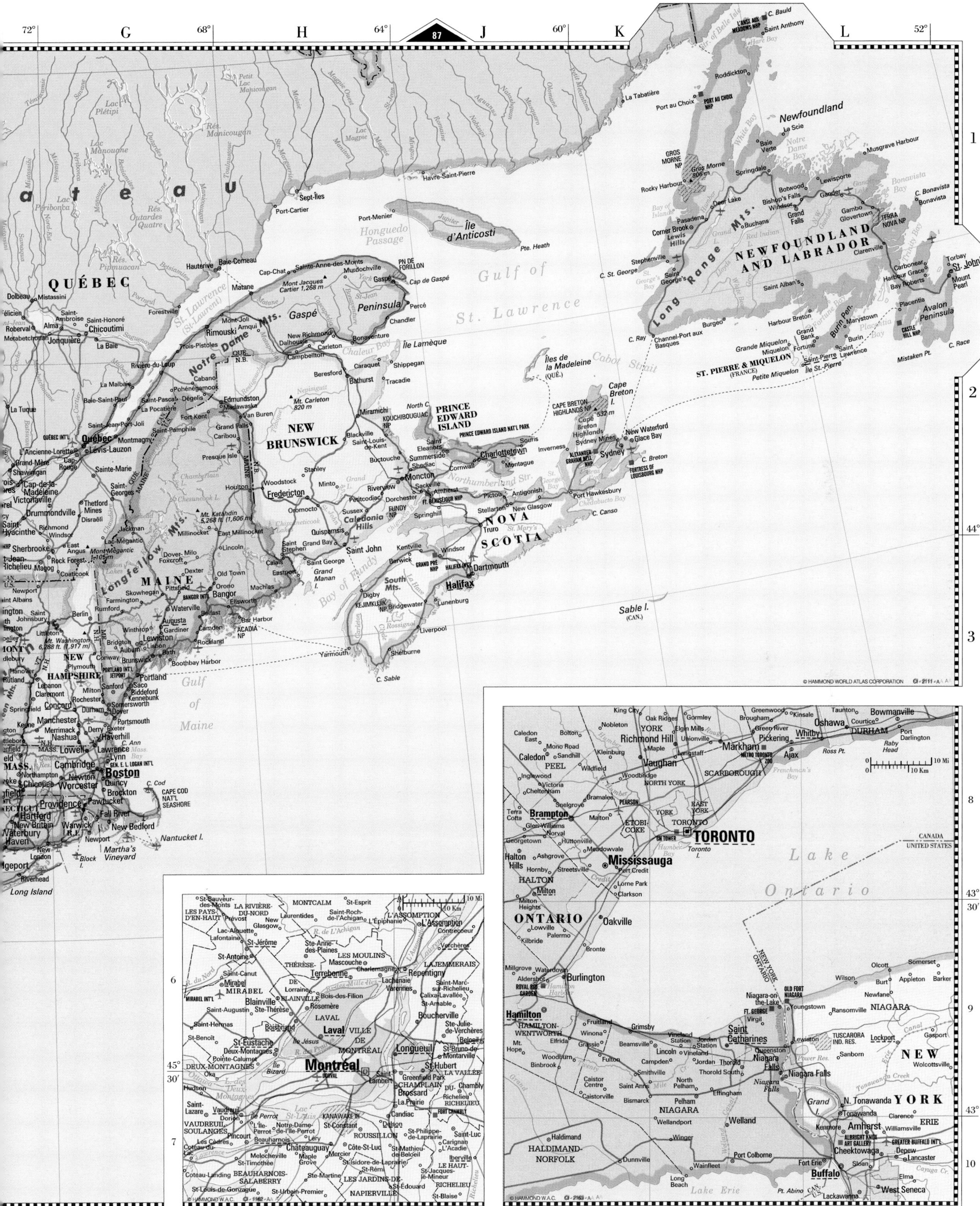

POPULATION OF CITIES AND TOWNS

■ OVER 2,000,000	◉ 500,000 - 999,999	⊕ 100,000 - 249,999	⊙ 10,000 - 29,999
◻ 1,000,000 - 1,999,999	◎ 250,000 - 499,999	⊖ 30,000 - 99,999	○ UNDER 10,000

SCALE 1:7,000,000 LAMBERT CONFORMAL CONIC PROJECTION

MILES 0 100 200 300

KILOMETERS 0 100 200 300

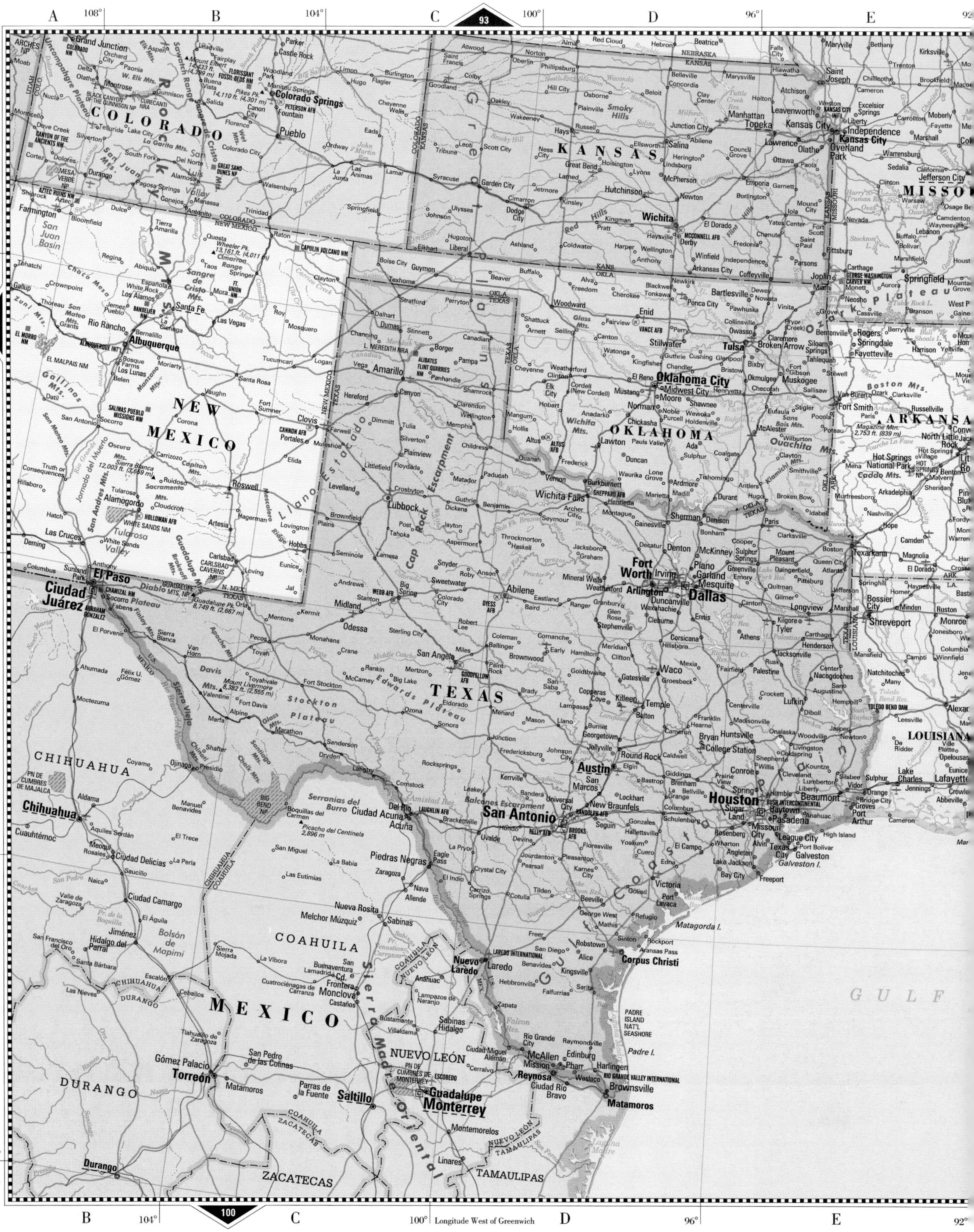
A
108°
B
104°
C
93
100°
D
96°
E
92
2
3
4
5
6
36°
32°
28°
24°
B
104°
100
C
100°
Longitude West of Greenwich
D
96°
E
92°
COLORADO
KANSAS
NEW MEXICO
OKLAHOMA
TEXAS
ARKANSAS
LOUISIANA
CHIHUAHUA
COAHUILA
NUEVO LEÓN
DURANGO
ZACATECAS
TAMAULIPAS
MEXICO
GULF
Grand Junction
Colorado Springs
Pueblo
Wichita
Topeka
Kansas City
Independence
Springfield
Tulsa
Oklahoma City
Albuquerque
Santa Fe
Rio Rancho
Amarillo
Lubbock
Wichita Falls
Fort Worth
Dallas
Arlington
Irving
El Paso
Ciudad Juárez
Chihuahua
Austin
San Antonio
Houston
Beaumont
Corpus Christi
Nuevo Laredo
Laredo
Monterrey
Guadalupe
Saltillo
Torreón
Durango
Matamoros
Brownsville
Reynosa
Shreveport
Texarkana
Fort Smith
Waco
Abilene
Midland
Odessa
San Angelo
Roswell
Las Cruces
Galveston
Victoria
Monclova
Ciudad Acuña
Piedras Negras
Edwards Plateau
Llano Estacado
Great Plains
Rocky Mts.
Ozark Plateau
Ouachita Mts.
Gulf Coastal Plain
Sierra Madre Oriental
Matagorda I.
Padre I.
PADRE ISLAND NAT'L SEASHORE
BIG BEND NP
Pikes Pk. 14,110 ft. (4,301 m)
Mount Elbert 14,433 ft. (4,399 m)
Wheeler Pk. 13,161 ft. (4,011 m)
Guadalupe Pk. 8,749 ft. (2,667 m)
Mount Livermore 8,382 ft. (2,555 m)
Magazine Mtn. 2,753 ft. (839 m)

Southeastern United States

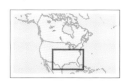

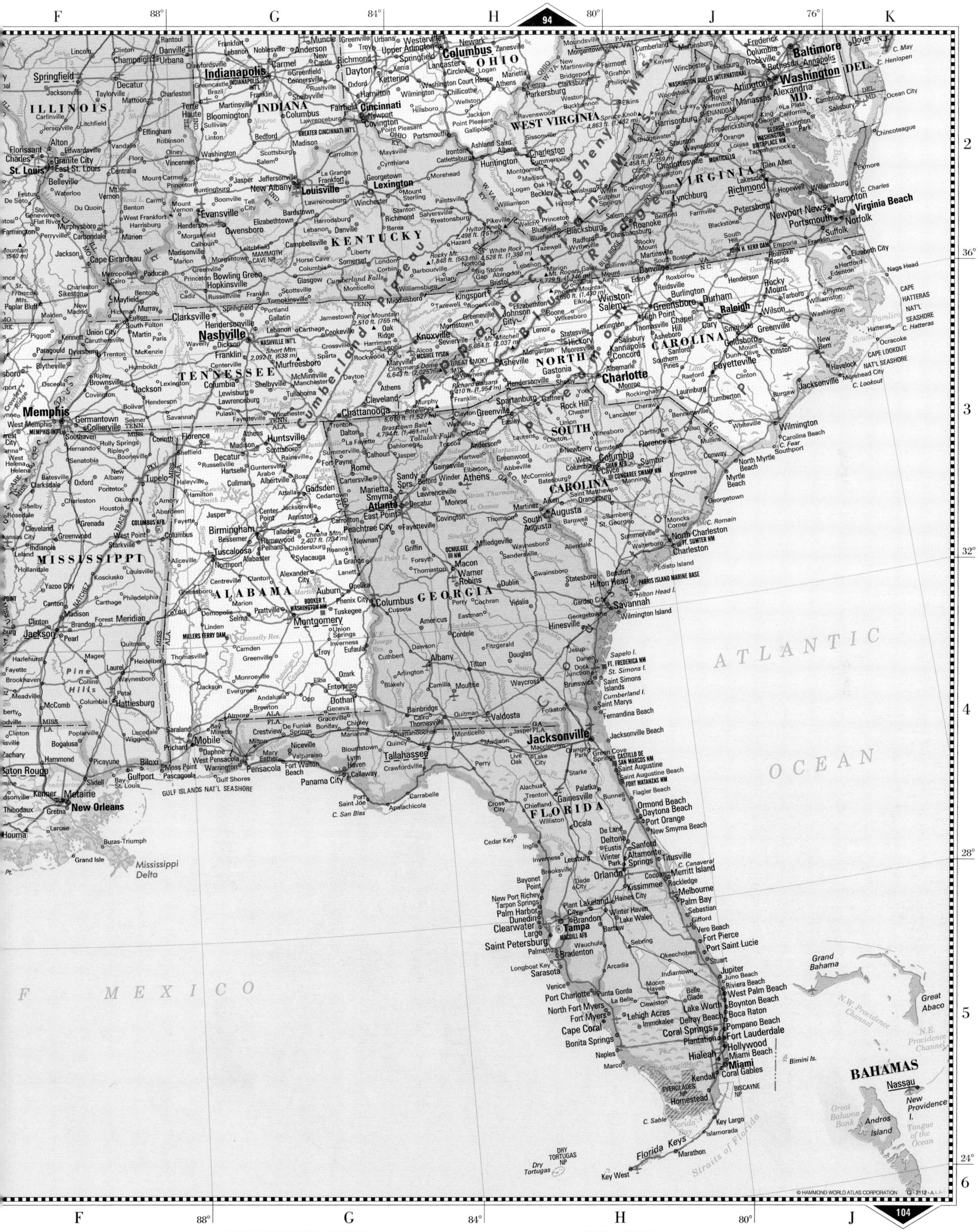

POPULATION OF CITIES AND TOWNS

- OVER 2,000,000
- 1,000,000 - 1,999,999
- 500,000 - 999,999
- 250,000 - 499,999
- 100,000 - 249,999
- 30,000 - 99,999
- 10,000 - 29,999
- UNDER 10,000

SCALE 1:7,000,000 LAMBERT CONFORMAL CONIC PROJECTION

MILES 0 100 200 300

KILOMETERS 0 100 200 300

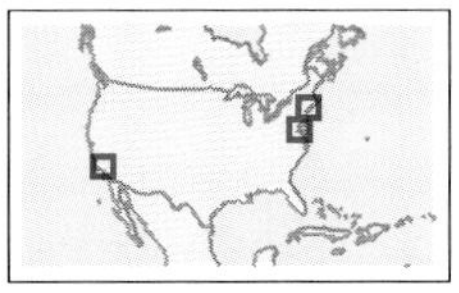

Los Angeles, New York, Philadelphia, Washington

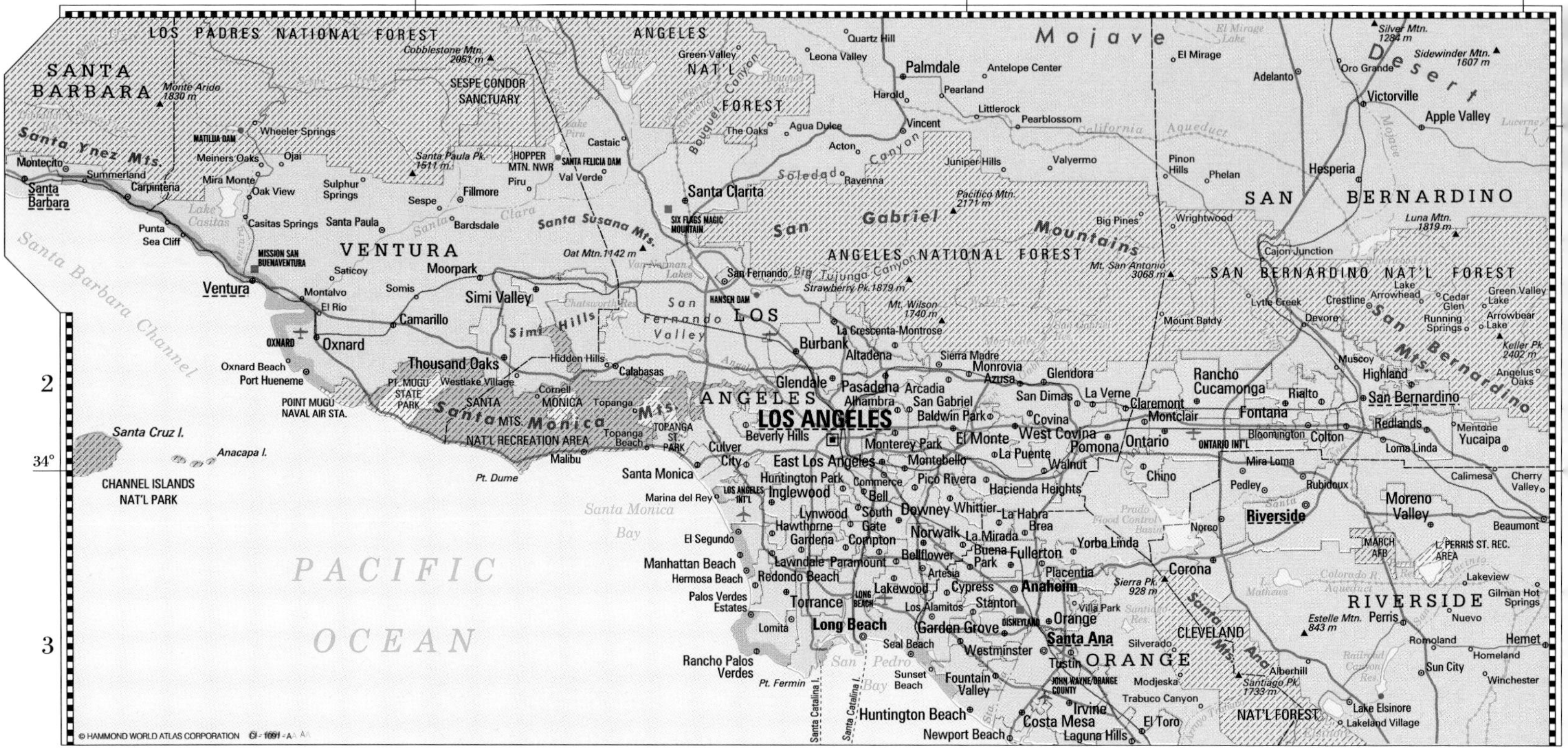

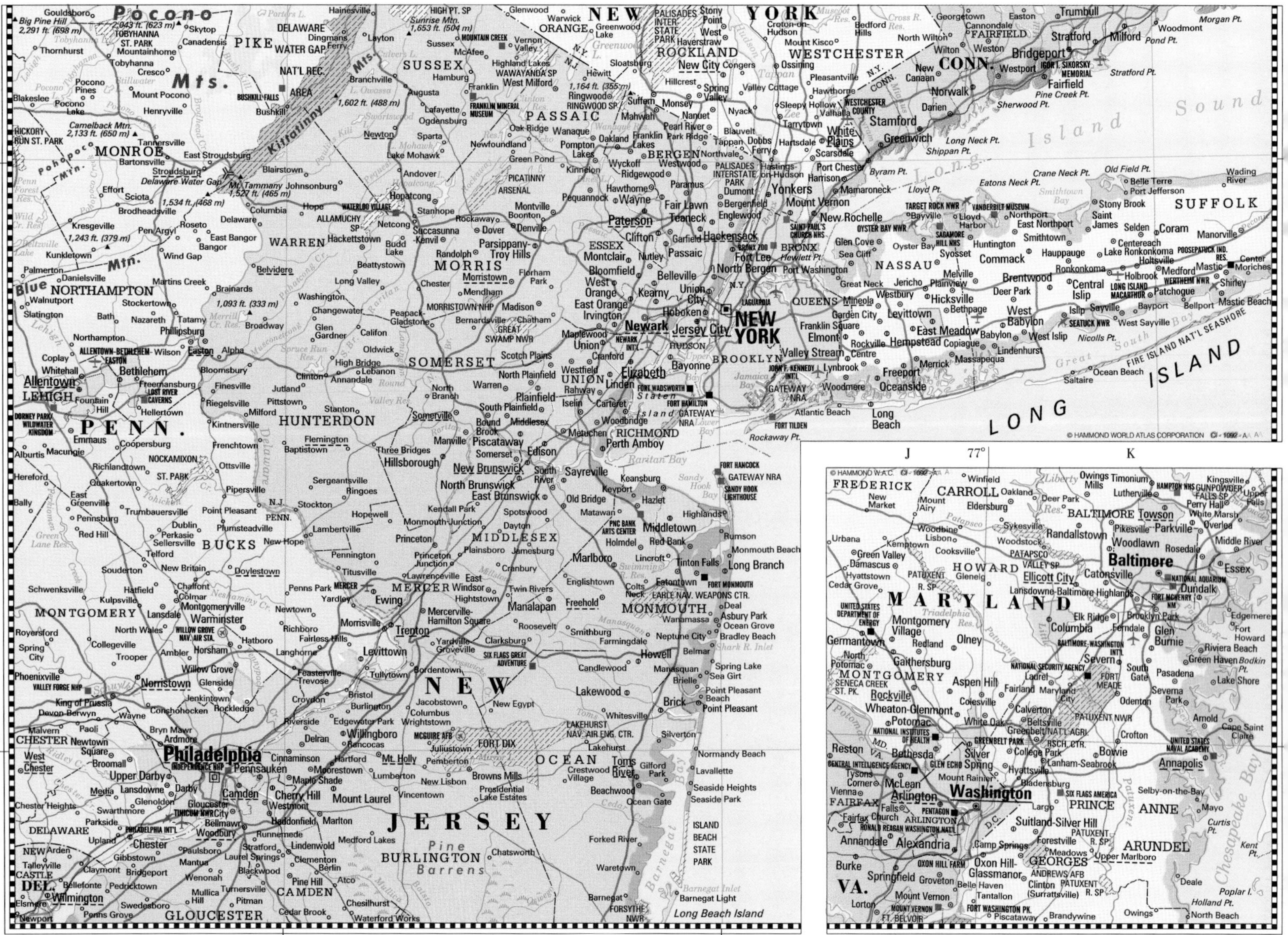

POPULATION OF CITIES AND TOWNS

- OVER 2,000,000
- 1,000,000 - 1,999,999
- 500,000 - 999,999
- 250,000 - 499,999
- 100,000 - 249,999
- 30,000 - 99,999
- 10,000 - 29,999
- UNDER 10,000

SCALE 1:1,170,000 LAMBERT CONFORMAL CONIC PROJECTION

MILES 0 10 20 30 40 50

KILOMETERS 0 10 20 30 40 50

Seattle, San Francisco, Detroit, Chicago

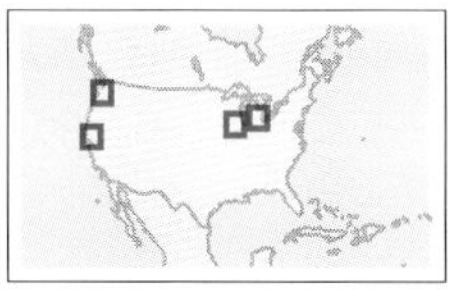

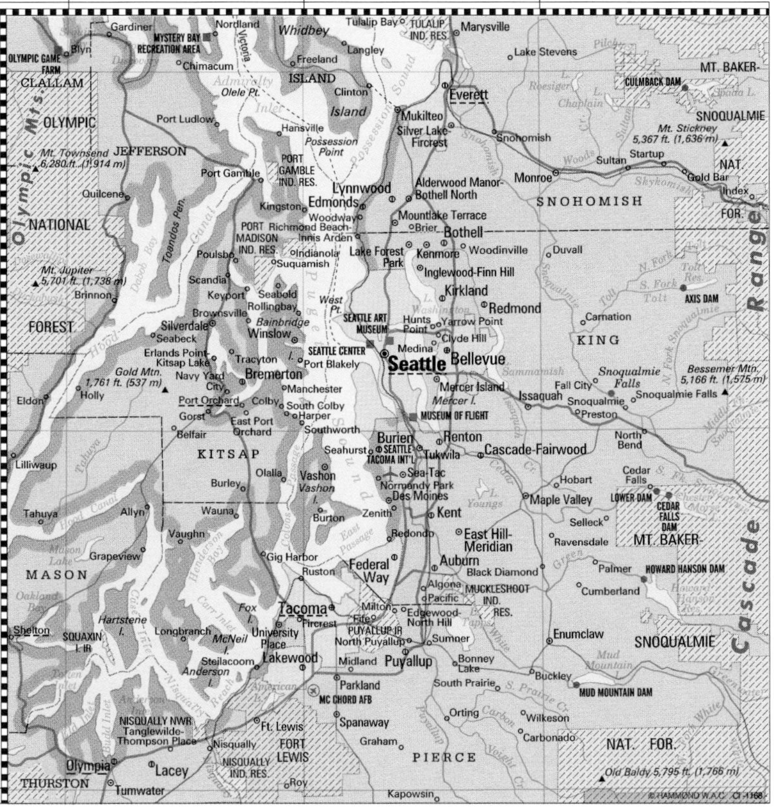

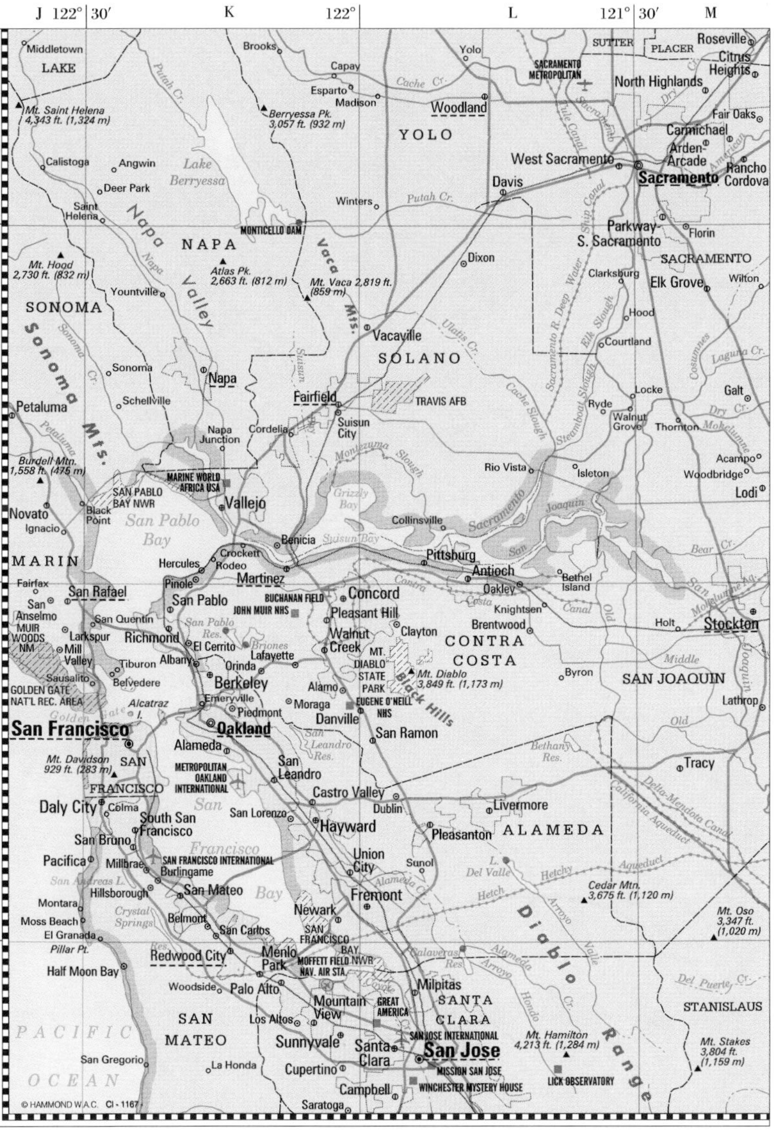

SCALE 1:1,170,000 LAMBERT CONFORMAL CONIC PROJECTION

MILES 0 10 20 30 40 50

KILOMETERS 0 10 20 30 40 50

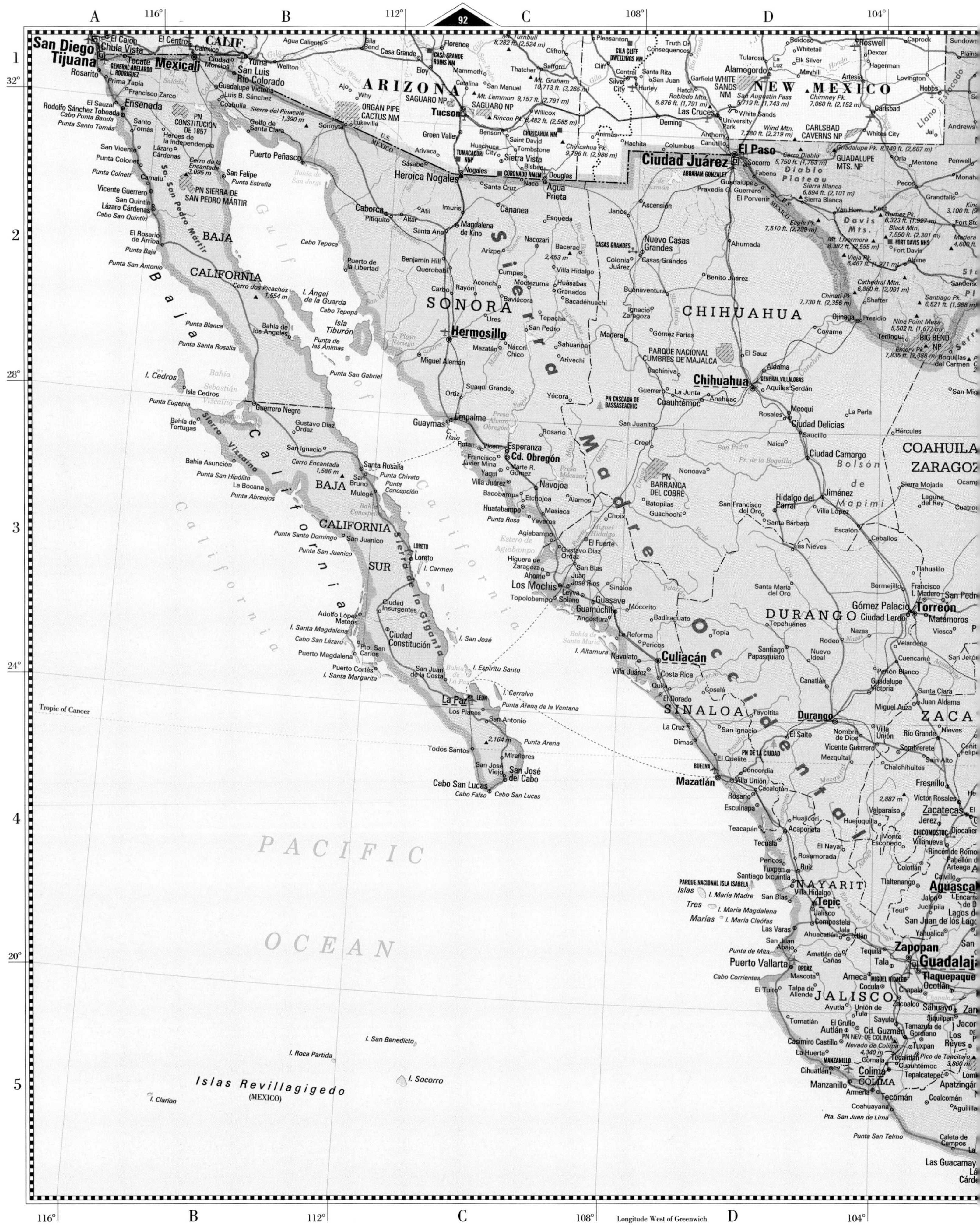

A
B
C
D
116°
112°
108°
104°
32°
28°
24°
20°
1
2
3
4
5
San Diego
Tijuana
Chula Vista
El Cajon
Tecate
Rosarito
Mexicali
Calexico
El Centro
CALIF.
Yuma
San Luis
Río Colorado
Ensenada
San Felipe
Puerto Peñasco
Sonoyta
Lukeville
ARIZONA
Tucson
Green Valley
Nogales
Heroica Nogales
Agua Prieta
Douglas
Bisbee
Sierra Vista
Tombstone
ORGAN PIPE CACTUS NM
SAGUARO NP
NEW MEXICO
Las Cruces
Alamogordo
Roswell
Carlsbad
El Paso
Ciudad Juárez
Deming
Silver City
WHITE SANDS NM
CARLSBAD CAVERNS NP
GUADALUPE MTS. NP
Caborca
Cananea
Magdalena de Kino
SONORA
Hermosillo
Guaymas
Empalme
Cd. Obregón
Navojoa
Huatabampo
Álamos
Sierra Madre Occidental
CHIHUAHUA
Chihuahua
Nuevo Casas Grandes
Casas Grandes
Cuauhtémoc
Ciudad Delicias
Ojinaga
Hidalgo del Parral
Ciudad Camargo
Jiménez
Bolsón de Mapimí
COAHUILA ZARAGOZA
Torreón
Gómez Palacio
Ciudad Lerdo
DURANGO
Durango
SINALOA
Culiacán
Los Mochis
Guasave
Guamúchil
El Fuerte
Mazatlán
Escuinapa
Zacatecas
Fresnillo
NAYARIT
Tepic
Puerto Vallarta
JALISCO
Zapopan
Guadalajara
Tlaquepaque
COLIMA
Colima
Manzanillo
Tecomán
Aguascalientes
BAJA CALIFORNIA
Isla Cedros
Guerrero Negro
Santa Rosalía
Mulegé
Loreto
BAJA CALIFORNIA SUR
Ciudad Constitución
La Paz
Todos Santos
Cabo San Lucas
San José del Cabo
Gulf of California
Isla Tiburón
Bahía Sebastián Vizcaíno
Tropic of Cancer
PACIFIC OCEAN
Islas Revillagigedo
(MEXICO)
I. Clarion
I. Roca Partida
I. San Benedicto
I. Socorro
Islas Tres Marías
Longitude West of Greenwich

Northern and Central Mexico

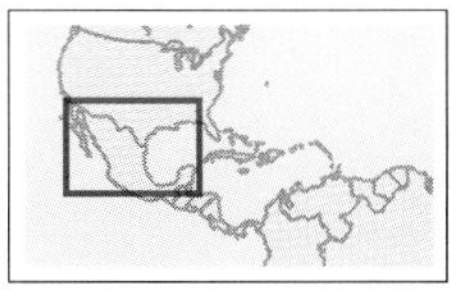

102

POPULATION OF CITIES AND TOWNS
- ■ OVER 2,000,000
- □ 1,000,000 - 1,999,999
- ◉ 500,000 - 999,999
- ◎ 250,000 - 499,999
- ● 100,000 - 249,999
- ● 30,000 - 99,999
- ● 10,000 - 29,999
- ○ UNDER 10,000

SCALE 1:7,000,000 LAMBERT CONFORMAL CONIC PROJECTION

MILES 0 100 200 300

KILOMETERS 0 100 200 300

Longitude West of Greenwich

SCALE 1:7,000,000 LAMBERT CONFORMAL CONIC PROJECTION

MILES 0 100 200 300

KILOMETERS 0 100 200 300

POPULATION OF CITIES AND TOWNS

- OVER 2,000,000
- 1,000,000 - 1,999,999
- 500,000 - 999,999
- 250,000 - 499,999
- 100,000 - 249,999
- 30,000 - 99,999
- 10,000 - 29,999
- UNDER 10,000

Southern Mexico, Central America, Western Caribbean

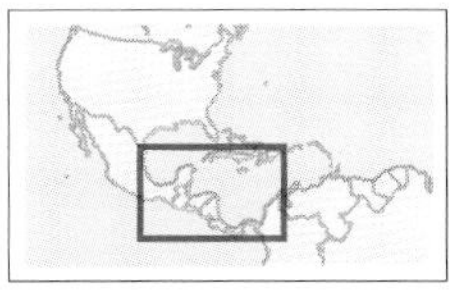

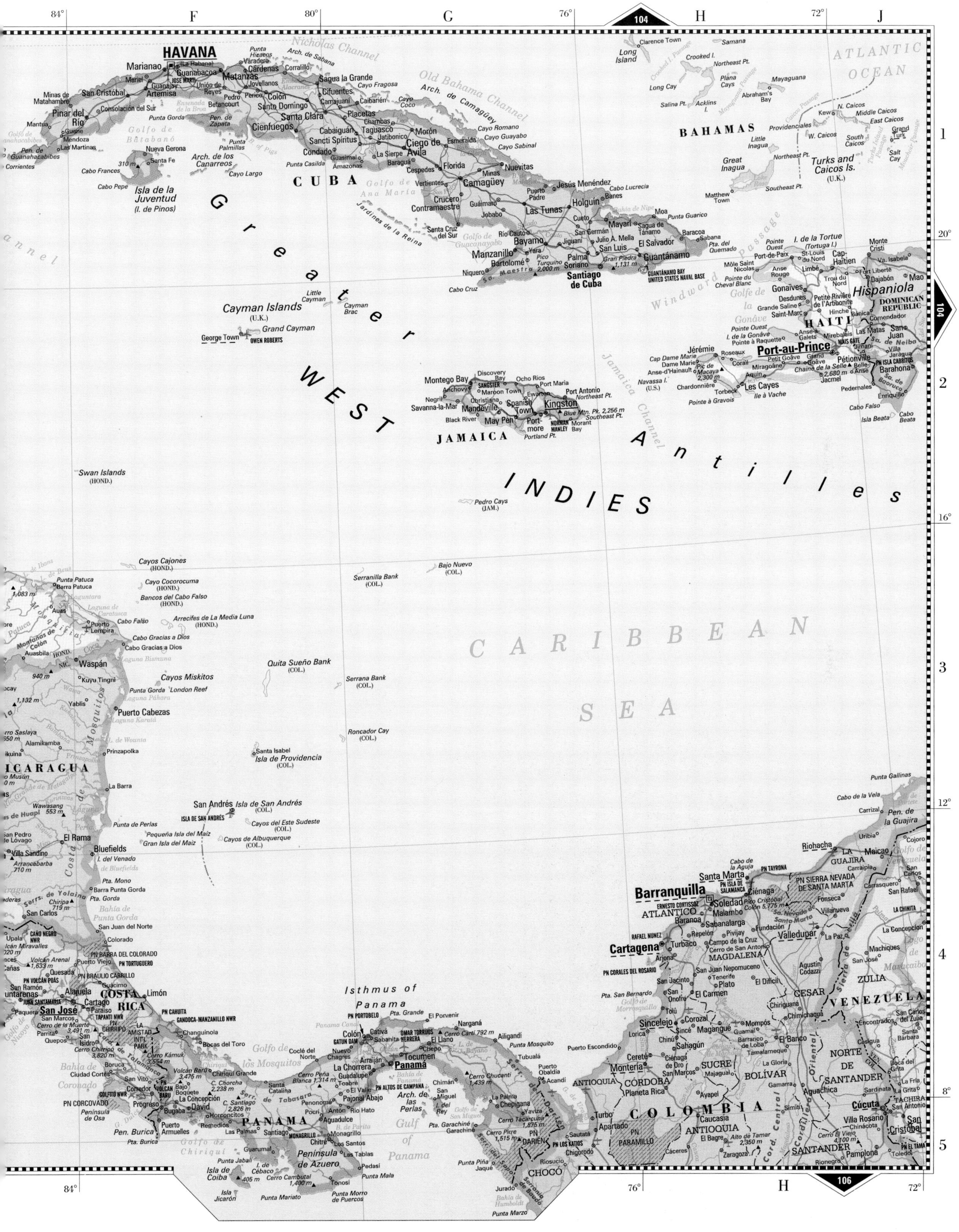

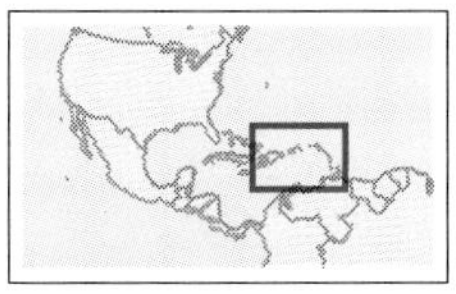

Eastern Caribbean, Bahamas

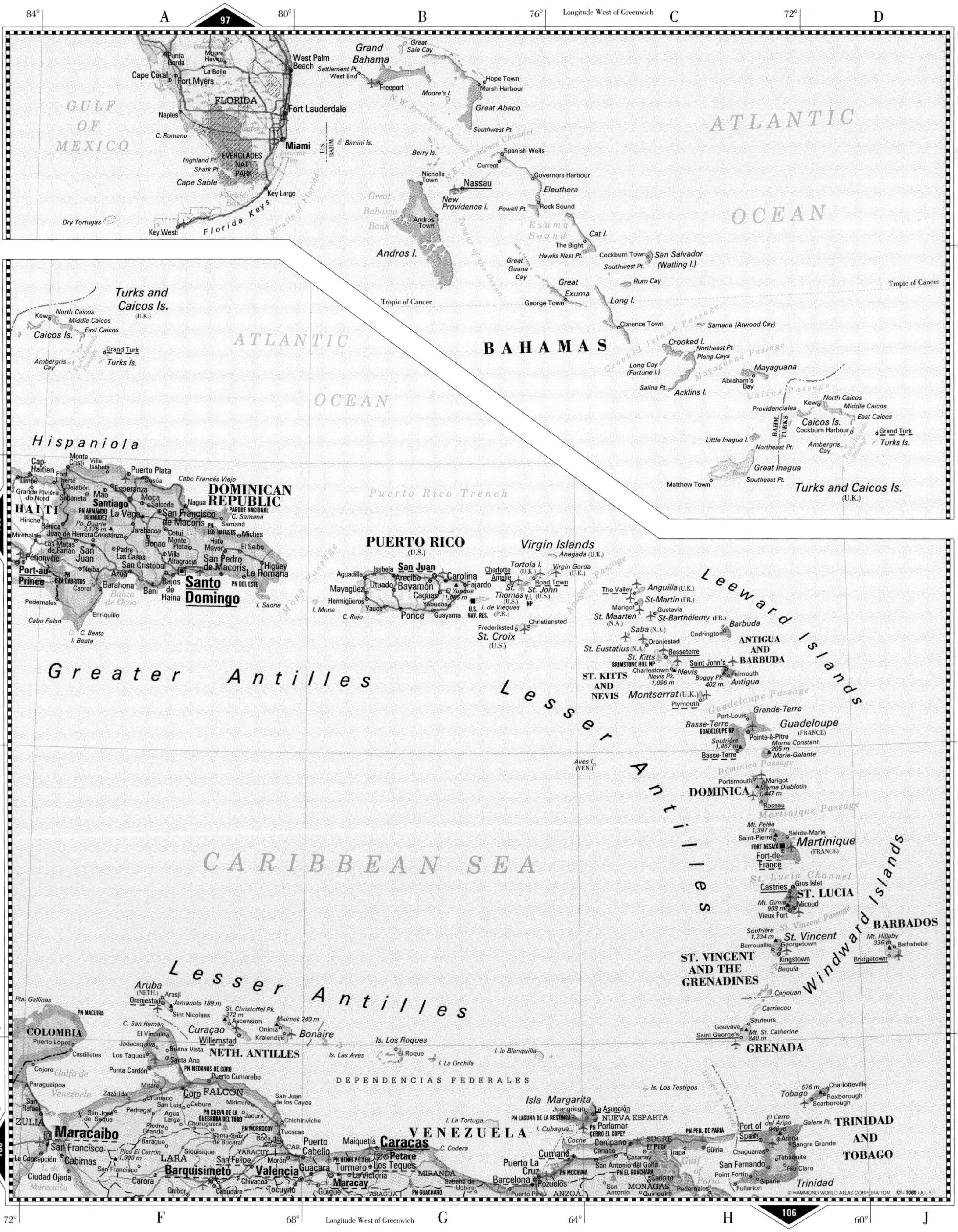

SCALE 1:7,000,000 LAMBERT CONFORMAL CONIC PROJECTION

MILES 0 100 200 300

KILOMETERS 0 100 200 300

POPULATION OF CITIES AND TOWNS

■ OVER 2,000,000	◉ 500,000 - 999,999	● 100,000 - 249,999	⊙ 10,000 - 29,999
◻ 1,000,000 - 1,999,999	◎ 250,000 - 499,999	◍ 30,000 - 99,999	○ UNDER 10,000

South America

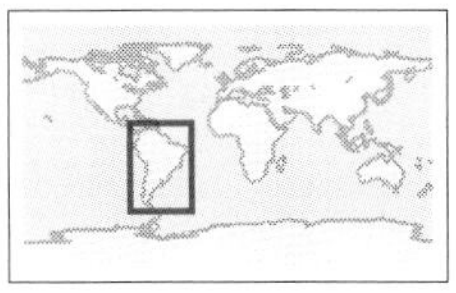

AREA OF OPTIMIZATION

The red band which surrounds this map defines the "Area of Optimization." Within this bounding curve is the most accurate conformal map that can be made of the region. Outside the optimized area, distortion increases rapidly, and tears or other irregularities in the grid may occur.

POPULATION OF CITIES AND TOWNS
- OVER 3,000,000
- 1,000,000 - 2,999,999
- 500,000 - 999,999
- 100,000 - 499,999
- UNDER 100,000

SCALE 1:28,000,000 OPTIMAL CONFORMAL PROJECTION
MILES 0 400 800 1200
KILOMETERS 0 400 800 1200

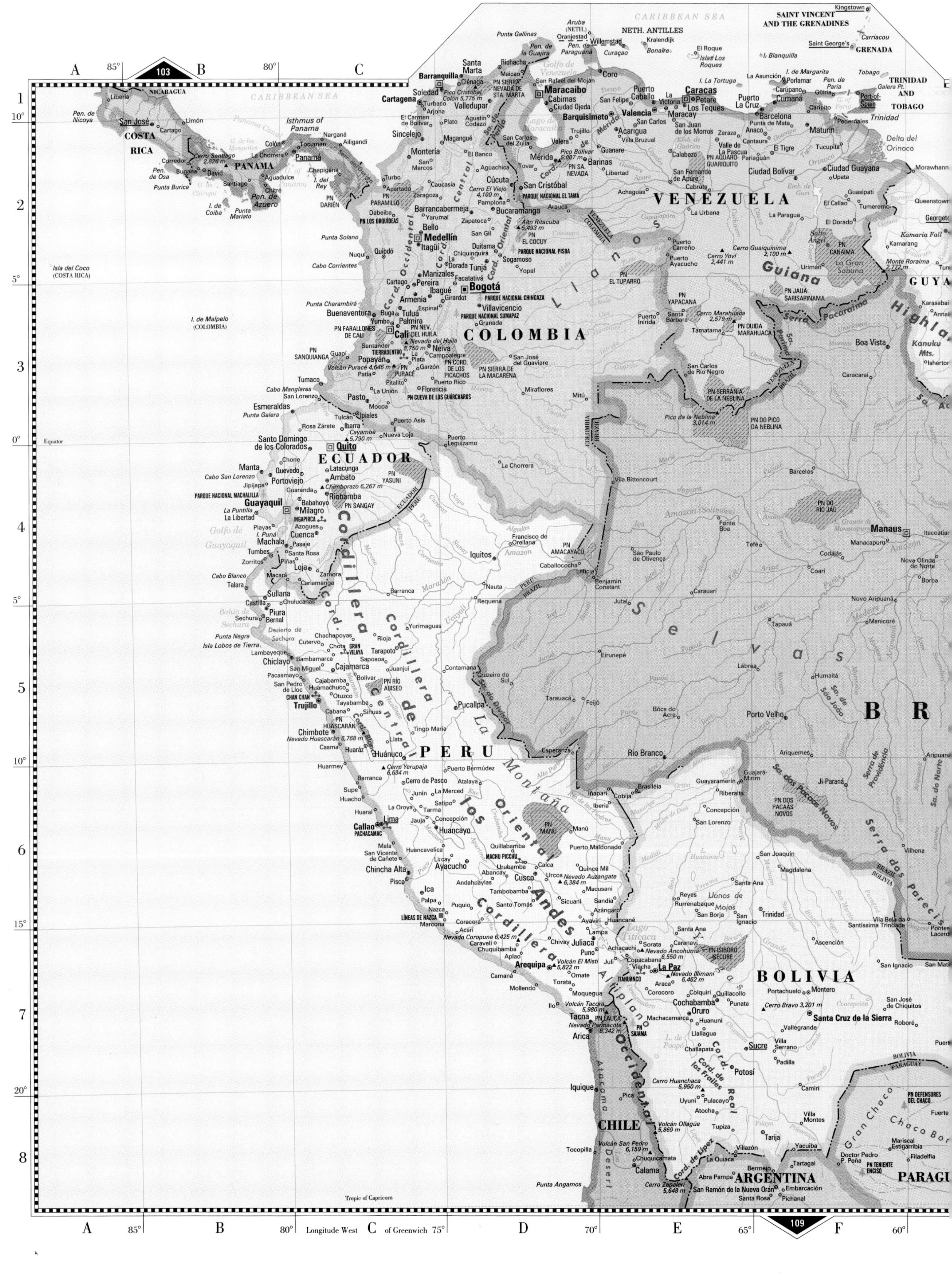

A
B
C
D
E
F
85°
80°
75°
70°
65°
60°
10°
5°
0°
15°
20°
1
2
3
4
5
6
7
8
103
109
Longitude West of Greenwich
Equator
Tropic of Capricorn
CARIBBEAN SEA
NETH. ANTILLES
Aruba (NETH.)
Oranjestad
Willemstad
Kralendijk
Bonaire
Curaçao
El Roque
Islas Los Roques
SAINT VINCENT AND THE GRENADINES
Kingstown
Carriacou
Saint George's
GRENADA
I. Blanquilla
I. La Tortuga
I. de Margarita
Tobago
Galera Pt.
TRINIDAD AND TOBAGO
Port-of-Spain
Trinidad
Punta Gallinas
Pen. de la Guajira
Pen. de Paraguaná
Golfo de Venezuela
Riohacha
Santa Marta
Barranquilla
Ciénaga
Maicao
PN SIERRA NEVADA DE STA. MARTA
Pico Cristóbal Colón 5,775 m
Cartagena
Soledad
Turbaco
Arjona
Valledupar
Maracaibo
Cabimas
Ciudad Ojeda
San Rafael del Mojan
Lago de Maracaibo
Coro
Punto Fijo
Puerto Cabello
San Felipe
Barquisimeto
Valencia
Maracay
Caracas
Petare
Los Teques
La Victoria
Puerto La Cruz
Barcelona
Cumaná
Carúpano
Porlamar
La Asunción
Maturín
Tucupita
Delta del Orinoco
NICARAGUA
CARIBBEAN SEA
Liberia
Pen. de Nicoya
San José
COSTA RICA
Limón
Cartago
Panama Canal
Isthmus of Panama
Colón
Panamá
PANAMA
David
Cerro Santiago 2,826 m
Pen. de Osa
Punta Burica
Golfo de Chiriquí
Santiago
Chitré
Pen. de Azuero
I. de Coiba
Punta Mariato
Golfo de Panamá
I. del Rey
PN DARIÉN
Isla del Coco (COSTA RICA)
I. de Malpelo (COLOMBIA)
Sincelejo
Montería
Magangué
El Banco
Turbo
Apartadó
PN PARAMILLO
PN LOS ORQUÍDEAS
Barrancabermeja
Bucaramanga
Cúcuta
San Cristóbal
PARQUE NACIONAL EL TAMA
Mérida
Pico Bolívar 5,007 m
Barinas
Medellín
Itagüí
Bello
Quibdó
Punta Solano
Cabo Corrientes
Manizales
Pereira
Armenia
Ibagué
Bogotá
Girardot
Tunja
Sogamoso
Duitama
Yopal
PARQUE NACIONAL PISBA
PN EL COCUY
Alto Ritacuba 5,493 m
Villavicencio
PARQUE NACIONAL CHINGAZA
PARQUE NACIONAL SUMAPAZ
Buenaventura
Tuluá
Palmira
Cali
Neiva
Nevado del Huila 5,750 m
Popayán
Volcán Puracé 4,646 m
Pasto
Tumaco
Ipiales
Punta Charambirá
PN FARALLONES DE CALI
PN SANQUIANGA
PN CUEVA DE LOS GUÁCHAROS
PN SIERRA DE LA MACARENA
PN CORD. DE LOS PICACHOS
Florencia
Puerto Asís
Mocoa
San José del Guaviare
Mitú
Miraflores
COLOMBIA
Llanos
Cord. Occidental
Cord. Central
Cord. Oriental
Puerto Carreño
Puerto Ayacucho
Puerto Inírida
PN EL TUPARRO
VENEZUELA
Ciudad Bolívar
Ciudad Guayana
San Fernando de Apure
Calabozo
El Tigre
Upata
Guasipati
El Callao
Tumeremo
El Dorado
La Paragua
Salto Ángel
PN CANAIMA
La Gran Sabana
Cerro Guaiquinima 2,100 m
Cerro Yaví 2,441 m
Guiana Highlands
Monte Roraima 2,772 m
Kamarang
Kamaria Fall
PN JAUA SARISARIÑAMA
Santa Bárbara
PN YAPACANA
Cerro Marahuaca 2,579 m
PN DUIDA MARAHUACA
Tamatama
San Carlos de Río Negro
PN SERRANÍA DE LA NEBLINA
Pico da Neblina 3,014 m
PN DO PICO DA NEBLINA
Serra Pacaraima
Boa Vista
Caracaraí
Kanuku Mts.
Santo Domingo de los Colorados
Quito
Esmeraldas
ECUADOR
Manta
Portoviejo
Latacunga
Ambato
Chimborazo 6,267 m
Riobamba
PN YASUNÍ
PN SANGAY
Guayaquil
Milagro
Golfo de Guayaquil
Cuenca
Machala
Loja
Cayambe 5,790 m
Nueva Loja
Puerto Leguízamo
La Chorrera
Iquitos
Nauta
Requena
Pucallpa
Tumbes
Talara
Sullana
Piura
Chiclayo
Lambayeque
Cajamarca
Trujillo
Chimbote
Nevado Huascarán 6,768 m
PN HUASCARÁN
Huánuco
Tingo María
Cerro de Pasco
Cerro Yerupaja 6,634 m
Huacho
Lima
Callao
Huancayo
Ayacucho
Cusco
Machu Picchu
PN MANÚ
Puerto Maldonado
Nevado Ausangate 6,384 m
Ica
Pisco
Chincha Alta
Nazca
Nevado Coropuna 6,425 m
Arequipa
Volcán El Misti 5,822 m
Juliaca
Puno
Lago Titicaca
Mollendo
Moquegua
Ilo
Tacna
Volcán Tacora 5,980 m
Nevado Parinacota 6,342 m
PN LAUCA
Arica
Iquique
Tocopilla
Calama
Chuquicamata
Volcán San Pedro 6,159 m
Cerro Zapaleri 5,648 m
Volcán Ollagüe 5,869 m
Atacama Desert
CHILE
Punta Angamos
PERU
Cordillera Occidental
Cordillera Central
Cordillera Oriental
La Montaña
Los Andes
Altiplano
LÍNEAS DE NAZCA
CHAN CHAN
Manaus
Amazon
Amazon (Solimões)
Tefé
Coari
Leticia
Benjamin Constant
Tabatinga
PN AMAZONAYACU
São Paulo de Olivença
Fonte Boa
Japurá
Barcelos
PN DO JAÚ
Manacapuru
Codajás
Carauari
Eirunepé
Cruzeiro do Sul
Tarauacá
Feijó
Rio Branco
Porto Velho
Lábrea
Humaitá
Ariquemes
Ji-Paraná
Guajará-Mirim
Selvas
BRAZIL
Serra dos Parecis
Sa. dos Pacaás Novos
PN DOS PACAÁS NOVOS
Vilhena
Vila Bela da Santíssima Trindade
Brasiléia
Cobija
Riberalta
Guayaramerín
BOLIVIA
La Paz
Nevado Illimani 6,462 m
Nevado Ancohuma 6,550 m
Cochabamba
Oruro
Sucre
Potosí
Tarija
Santa Cruz de la Sierra
Trinidad
Llanos de Mojos
San Borja
Montero
Cerro Bravo 3,201 m
Camiri
Villa Montes
Uyuni
Cerro Huanchaca 5,950 m
Cord. de Lípez
Cord. de los Frailes
Cord. Real
PN ISIBORO SÉCURE
Yacuiba
Villazón
La Quiaca
ARGENTINA
San Ramón de la Nueva Orán
Tartagal
Embarcación
PARAGUAY
Gran Chaco
Chaco Boreal
Mariscal Estigarribia
Filadelfia
Doctor Pedro P. Peña
PN DEFENSORES DEL CHACO
PN TENIENTE ENCISO
Fuerte Olimpo
San José de Chiquitos
Roboré

Northern South America

POPULATION OF CITIES AND TOWNS

■ OVER 2,000,000	◉ 500,000 - 999,999	⊙ 50,000 - 99,999
▣ 1,000,000 - 1,999,999	⊕ 100,000 - 499,999	○ UNDER 50,000

SCALE 1:15,000,000 LAMBERT CONFORMAL CONIC PROJECTION

MILES 0 200 400 600

KILOMETERS 0 200 400 600

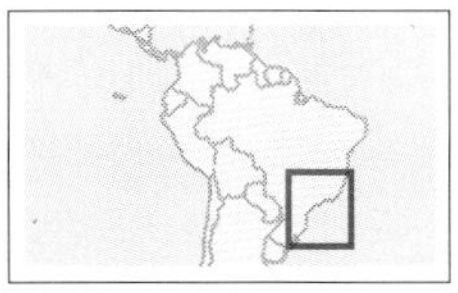

Southeastern Brazil

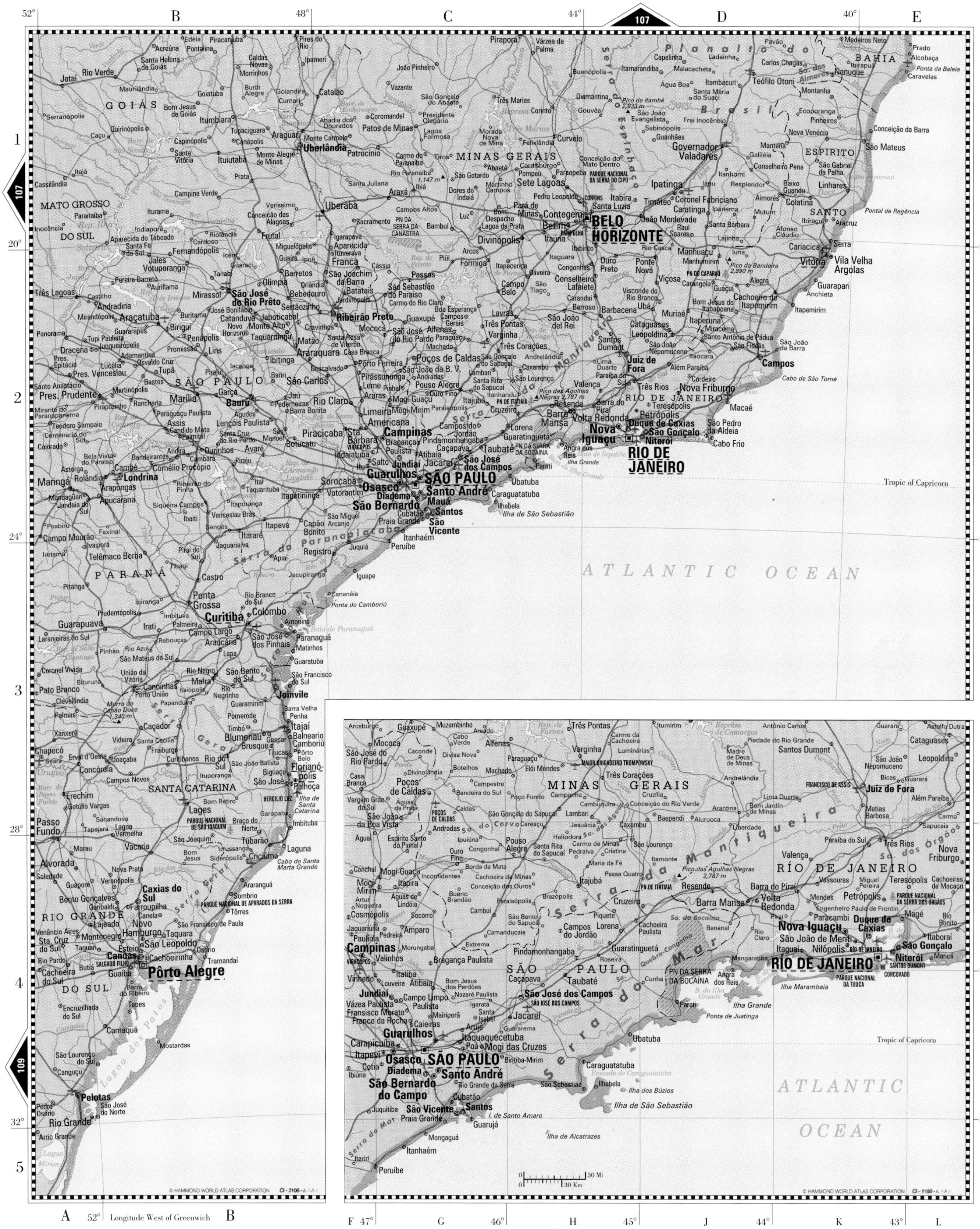

SCALE 1:7,000,000 LAMBERT CONFORMAL CONIC PROJECTION
MILES 0 100 200 300
KILOMETERS 0 100 200 300

POPULATION OF CITIES AND TOWNS

- OVER 2,000,000
- 1,000,000 - 1,999,999
- 500,000 - 999,999
- 250,000 - 499,999
- 100,000 - 249,999
- 30,000 - 99,999
- 10,000 - 29,999
- UNDER 10,000

Southern South America

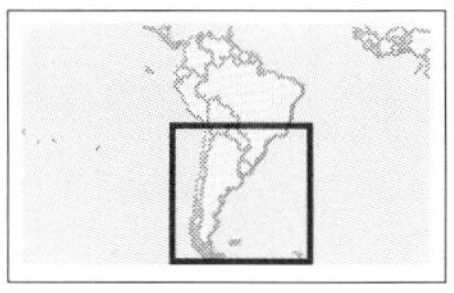

POPULATION OF CITIES AND TOWNS

- ■ OVER 2,000,000
- ◉ 500,000 - 999,999
- ⊙ 50,000 - 99,999
- ▣ 1,000,000 - 1,999,999
- ● 100,000 - 499,999
- ○ UNDER 50,000

SCALE 1:15,000,000 LAMBERT CONFORMAL CONIC PROJECTION

MILES 0 200 400 600

KILOMETERS 0 200 400 600

Index of the World

This index lists places and geographic features found in the atlas. Every name is followed by the country or area to which it belongs. Except for cities, towns, countries and cultural areas, all entries include a reference to feature type, such as province, river, island, peak, and so on. The page number and alpha-numeric code appear in blue to the right of each listing. The page number directs you to the largest scale map on which the name can be found. The code refers to the grid squares formed by the horizontal and vertical lines of latitude and longitude on each map. Following the letters from left to right, and the numbers from top to bottom, helps you to locate quickly the square containing the place or feature. Inset maps have their own alpha-numeric codes. Names that are accompanied by a point symbol are indexed to the symbol's location on the map. Other names are indexed to the initial letter of the name. The primary abbreviations used in this index are listed below.

Index Abbreviations

A	**Ab,Can**	Alberta
	Afg.	Afghanistan
	Afr.	Africa
	Ak,US	Alaska
	Al,US	Alabama
	Alb.	Albania
	Alg.	Algeria
	And.	Andorra
	Ang.	Angola
	Angu.	Anguilla
	Ant.	Antarctica
	Anti.	Antigua and Barbuda
	Ar,US	Arkansas
	Arch.	Archipelago
	Arg.	Argentina
	Arm.	Armenia
	Aru.	Aruba
	ASam.	American Samoa
	Ash.	Ashmore and Cartier Islands
	Aus.	Austria
	Austl.	Australia
	Az,US	Arizona
	Azer.	Azerbaijan
	Azor.	Azores
B	**Bahm.**	Bahamas, The
	Bahr.	Bahrain
	Bang.	Bangladesh
	Bar.	Barbados
	BC,Can	British Columbia
	Bela.	Belarus
	Belg.	Belgium
	Belz.	Belize
	Ben.	Benin
	Berm.	Bermuda
	Bhu.	Bhutan
	Bol.	Bolivia
	Bosn.	Bosnia and Herzegovina
	Bots.	Botswana
	Braz.	Brazil
	Bru.	Brunei
	Bul.	Bulgaria
	Burk.	Burkina Faso
	Buru.	Burundi
	BVI	British Virgin Islands
C	**Ca,US**	California
	CAfr.	Central African Republic
	Camb.	Cambodia
	Camr.	Cameroon
	Can.	Canada
	Can.	Canal
	Canl.	Canary Islands
	Cap.	Capital
	Cap. Terr.	Capital Territory
	Cay.	Cayman Islands
	C.d'Iv.	Côte d'Ivoire
	Chan.	Channel
	Chl.	Channel Islands
	Co,US	Colorado
	Col.	Colombia
	Com.	Comoros
	Cont.	Continent
	CpV.	Cape Verde Islands
	CR	Costa Rica
	Cr.	Creek
	Cro.	Croatia
	Ct,US	Connecticut
	Cyp.	Cyprus
	Czh.	Czech Republic
D	**DC,US**	District of Columbia
	De,US	Delaware
	Den.	Denmark
	Depr.	Depression
	Des.	Desert
	Dist.	District
	Djib.	Djibouti
	Dom.	Dominica
	Dpcy.	Dependency
	D.R.Congo	Democratic Republic of the Congo
	DRep.	Dominican Republic
E	**Ecu.**	Ecuador
	Eng,UK	England
	EqG.	Equatorial Guinea
	Erit.	Eritrea
	ESal.	El Salvador
	Est.	Estonia
	Eth.	Ethiopia
	Eur.	Europe
F	**Falk.**	Falkland Islands
	Far.	Faroe Islands
	Fed. Dist.	Federal District
	Fin.	Finland
	Fl,US	Florida
	Fr.	France
	FrG.	French Guiana
	FrPol.	French Polynesia
	FYROM	Former Yugoslav Rep. of Macedonia
G	**Ga,US**	Georgia
	Gam.	Gambia, The
	Gaza	Gaza Strip
	GBis.	Guinea-Bissau
	Geo.	Georgia
	Ger.	Germany
	Gha.	Ghana
	Gib.	Gibraltar
	Gre.	Greece
	Grld.	Greenland
	Gren.	Grenada
	Grsld.	Grassland
	Guad.	Guadeloupe
	Guat.	Guatemala
	Gui.	Guinea
	Guy.	Guyana
H	**Har.**	Harbor
	Hi,US	Hawaii
	Hon.	Honduras
	Hts.	Heights
	Hun.	Hungary
I	**Ia,US**	Iowa
	Ice.	Iceland
	Id,US	Idaho
	Il,US	Illinois
	IM	Isle of Man
	In,US	Indiana
	Indo.	Indonesia
	Int'l	International
	Ire.	Ireland
	Isl., Isls.	Island, Islands
	Isr.	Israel
	Isth.	Isthmus
	It.	Italy
J	**Jam.**	Jamaica
	Jor.	Jordan
K	**Kaz.**	Kazakhstan
	Kiri.	Kiribati
	Ks,US	Kansas
	Kuw.	Kuwait
	Ky,US	Kentucky
	Kyr.	Kyrgyzstan
L	**La,US**	Louisiana
	Lat.	Latvia
	Lcht.	Liechtenstein
	Leb.	Lebanon
	Les.	Lesotho
	Libr.	Liberia
	Lith.	Lithuania
	Lux.	Luxembourg
M	**Ma,US**	Massachusetts
	Madg.	Madagascar
	Madr.	Madeira
	Malay.	Malaysia
	Mald.	Maldives
	Malw.	Malawi
	Mart.	Martinique
	May.	Mayotte
	Mb,Can	Manitoba
	Md,US	Maryland
	Me,US	Maine
	Mex.	Mexico
	Mi,US	Michigan
	Micr.	Micronesia, Federated States of
	Mn,US	Minnesota
	Mo,US	Missouri
	Mol.	Moldova
	Mon.	Monument
	Mona.	Monaco
	Mong.	Mongolia
	Monts.	Montserrat
	Mor.	Morocco
	Moz.	Mozambique
	Mrsh.	Marshall Islands
	Mrta.	Mauritania
	Mrts.	Mauritius
	Ms,US	Mississippi
	Mt.	Mount
	Mt,US	Montana
	Mtn., Mts.	Mountain, Mountains
N	**NAm.**	North America
	Namb.	Namibia
	NAnt.	Netherlands Antilles
	Nat'l	National
	NB,Can	New Brunswick
	NC,US	North Carolina
	NCal.	New Caledonia
	ND,US	North Dakota
	Ne,US	Nebraska
	Neth.	Netherlands
	Nf,Can	Newfoundland and Labrador
	Nga.	Nigeria
	NH,US	New Hampshire
	NI,UK	Northern Ireland
	Nic.	Nicaragua
	NJ,US	New Jersey
	NKor.	North Korea
	NM,US	New Mexico
	NMar.	Northern Mariana Islands
	Nor.	Norway
	NP	National Park
	NS,Can	Nova Scotia
	Nv,US	Nevada
	NW,Can	Northwest Territories
	NY,US	New York
	NZ	New Zealand
O	**Oh,US**	Ohio
	Ok,US	Oklahoma
	On,Can	Ontario
	Or,US	Oregon
P	**Pa,US**	Pennsylvania
	PacUS	Pacific Islands, U.S.
	Pak.	Pakistan
	Pan.	Panama
	Par.	Paraguay
	PE,Can	Prince Edward Island
	Pen.	Peninsula
	Phil.	Philippines
	Phys. Reg.	Physical Region
	Pitc.	Pitcairn Islands
	Plat.	Plateau
	PNG	Papua New Guinea
	Pol.	Poland
	Port.	Portugal
	PR	Puerto Rico
	Prov.	Province
	Pt.	Point
Q	**Qu,Can**	Quebec
R	**Rec.**	Recreation(al)
	Reg.	Region
	Rep.	Republic
	Res.	Reservoir, Reservation
	Reun.	Réunion
	RI,US	Rhode Island
	Riv.	River
	Rom.	Romania
	Rsv.	Reserve
	Rus.	Russia
	Rwa.	Rwanda
S	**SAfr.**	South Africa
	Sam.	Samoa
	SAm.	South America
	SaoT.	São Tomé and Príncipe
	SAr.	Saudi Arabia
	Sc,UK	Scotland
	SC,US	South Carolina
	SD,US	South Dakota
	Sen.	Senegal
	Serb.	Serbia and Montenegro
	Sey.	Seychelles
	Sing.	Singapore
	Sk,Can	Saskatchewan
	SKor.	South Korea
	SLeo.	Sierra Leone
	Slov.	Slovenia
	Slvk.	Slovakia
	SMar.	San Marino
	Sol.	Solomon Islands
	Som.	Somalia
	Sp.	Spain
	Spr., Sprs.	Spring, Springs
	SrL.	Sri Lanka
	StH.	Saint Helena
	Str.	Strait
	StK.	Saint Kitts and Nevis
	StL.	Saint Lucia
	StV.	Saint Vincent and the Grenadines
	Sur.	Suriname
	Sval.	Svalbard
	Swaz.	Swaziland
	Swe.	Sweden
	Swi.	Switzerland
T	**Tah.**	Tahiti
	Tai.	Taiwan
	Taj.	Tajikistan
	Tanz.	Tanzania
	Terr.	Territory
	Thai.	Thailand
	Tn,US	Tennessee
	Tok.	Tokelau
	Trin.	Trinidad and Tobago
	Trkm.	Turkmenistan
	Trks.	Turks and Caicos Islands
	Turk.	Turkey
	Tuv.	Tuvalu
	Tx,US	Texas
U	**UAE**	United Arab Emirates
	Ugan.	Uganda
	UK	United Kingdom
	Ukr.	Ukraine
	Uru.	Uruguay
	US	United States
	USVI	U.S. Virgin Islands
	Ut,US	Utah
	Uzb.	Uzbekistan
V	**Va,US**	Virginia
	Val.	Valley
	Van.	Vanuatu
	VatC.	Vatican City
	Ven.	Venezuela
	Viet.	Vietnam
	Vol.	Volcano
	Vt,US	Vermont
W	**Wa,US**	Washington
	Wal,UK	Wales
	Wall.	Wallis and Futuna
	WBnk.	West Bank
	Wi,US	Wisconsin
	WSah.	Western Sahara
	WV,US	West Virginia
	Wy,US	Wyoming
Y	**Yem.**	Yemen
	Yk,Can	Yukon Territory
Z	**Zam.**	Zambia
	Zim.	Zimbabwe

A

Aachen, Ger. 31/F2
Aalen, Ger. 33/J2
Aalsmeer, Neth. 28/B4
Aalst, Belg. 30/D2
Aalten, Neth. 28/D5
Aalter, Belg. 28/A6
Aarau, Swi. 36/E3
Aarschot, Belg. 28/B7
Aba, Nga. 79/G5
Abā as Su'ūd, SAr. 52/D5
Ābādān, Iran 51/G4
Ābādeh, Iran 51/H4
Abaeté, Braz. 108/C1
Abaetetuba, Braz. 107/J4
Abakan, Rus. 46/K4
Abancay, Peru 106/D6
Abashiri, Japan 55/N3
Abasolo, Mex. 101/E4
Abay, Kaz. 46/H5
Abaza, Rus. 46/K4
Abbeville, La, US 93/J5
Abbeville, Fr. 30/A3
Abbottābād, Pak. 53/K2
Abdulino, Rus. 45/K1
Abéché, Chad 77/K5
Abengourou, C.d'Iv. 78/E5
Åbenrå, Den. 26/E1
Abeokuta, Nga. 79/F5
Aberdare, Wal, UK 24/C3
Abhá, SAr. 52/D5
Abhar, Iran 51/G2
Abidjan, C.d'Iv. 78/D5
Abilene, Tx, US 93/H4
Abingdon, Eng, UK 25/E3
Abnūb, Egypt 50/B5
Åbo (Turku), Fin. 42/D3
Abomey, Ben. 79/F5
Abony, Hun. 40/D2
Abu Dhabi (cap.), UAE 53/F4
Abū Ḩammād, Egypt 49/B4
Abū Ḩummuş, Egypt 49/B4
Abū Kabīr, Egypt 49/B4
Abū Kamāl, Syria 50/E3
Abuja (cap.), Nga. 79/G4
Abulog, Phil. 61/J5
Acadia National Park, Me, US 95/G2
Acámbaro, Mex. 101/E4
Acaponeta, Mex. 100/D4
Acapulco de Juárez, Mex. 102/B2
Acarigua, Ven. 106/E2
Acatzingo, Mex. 101/M7
Acayucan, Mex. 102/C2
Accra (cap.), Gha. 79/E5
Accrington, Eng, UK 23/F4
Acheng, China 55/K2
Achern, Ger. 31/H6
Achinsk, Rus. 46/K4
Acireale, It. 38/D4
Aconcagua (peak), Arg.,Chile 109/B3
Acopiara, Braz. 107/L5
Acqui Terme, It. 33/H4
Actopan, Mex. 101/L6
Açu, Braz. 107/L5
Ad Damīr, Sudan 52/B5
Ad Dammām, SAr. 52/F3
Ad Dilinjāt, Egypt 49/B4
Ad Dīwānīyah, Iraq 51/F4
Ad Duwaym, Sudan 77/M5
Ad-Dakhla, Mor. 76/B3
Ada, Ok, US 93/H4
Adamantina, Braz. 108/B2
Adams (mt.), Wa, US 90/C4
Adamstown (cap.), Pitc. 69/M7
'Adan, Yem. 52/D6
Adana, Turk. 49/D1
Adapazarı, Turk. 41/K5
Addis Ababa (cap.), Eth. 77/N6
Addison, Il, US 99/P16
Adekeieh (Ādī K'eyih), Erit. 52/C6
Adelaide, Austl. 73/A2
Aden (gulf) 52/E6
Adilābād, India 62/C4
Adirondack (mts.), NY, US 94/F2
Adıyaman, Turk. 50/D2
Adjud, Rom. 41/H2
Adliswil, Swi. 37/E3
Ado Ekiti, Nga. 79/G5
Ado Odo, Nga. 79/F5
Ādoni, India 62/C4
Adra, Sp. 34/D4
Adrano, It. 38/D4
Adrar, Alg. 76/E2
Adrian, Mi, US 94/C3
Adriatic (sea), It. 40/B4
Ādwa, Eth. 52/C6
Aegean (sea), Gre.,Turk. 39/J3
'Afak, Iraq 51/F3
Afghanistan (ctry.) 53/H2
Afragola, It. 38/D2
Africa (cont.) 74/*
'Afula, Isr. 49/G6
Afyon, Turk. 44/D5
Agadez, Niger 79/G2
Agadir, Mor. 76/D1
Agartala, India 63/F3
Agboville, C.d'Iv. 78/D5
Ağdam, Azer. 45/H5
Agde, Fr. 32/E5
Agen, Fr. 32/D4
Āghā Jārī, Iran 51/G4
Agoo, Phil. 61/J5
Āgra, India 62/C2
Agrigento, It. 38/C4
Agrínion, Gre. 39/G3
Agryz, Rus. 43/M4
Agua Dulce, Mex. 102/C2
Agua Fria Nat'l Mon. Az, US 92/E4
Agua Prieta, Mex. 92/E5
Aguachica, Col. 103/H4
Aguadilla, PR 104/E3
Aguaí, Braz. 108/G7
Agualva-Cacém, Port. 35/P10
Aguascalientes, Mex. 100/E4
Agudos, Braz. 108/B2
Aguilares, Arg. 109/C2
Aguilas, Sp. 34/E4
Agüimes, Canl. 35/X17
Agustín Codazzi, Col. 103/H4
Ahar, Iran 45/H5
Ahaus, Ger. 28/E4
Ahlat, Turk. 50/E2
Ahlen, Ger. 29/E5
Ahmadābād, India 62/B3
Ahmadnagar, India 62/B4
Ahmadpur East, Pak. 62/B2
Ahrensburg, Ger. 29/H1
Ahuachapán, ESal. 102/D3
Ahvāz, Iran 51/G4
Aichach, Ger. 37/H1
Aiken, SC, US 97/H3
'Aïn Beïda, Alg. 76/G1
'Aïn Sefra, Alg. 76/E1
Aina Haina, Hi, US 88/W13
Airdrie, Ab, Can. 90/E3
Aiud, Rom. 41/F2
Aix-en-Provence, Fr. 32/F5
Aíyion, Gre. 39/H3
Āīzawl, India 60/B4
Aizu-Wakamatsu, Japan 57/F2
Ajaccio, Fr. 38/A2
Ajalpan, Mex. 101/M8
Ajax, On, Can. 95/U8
Ajdābiyā, Libya 77/K1
Ajka, Hun. 40/C2
Ajmer, India 62/B2
Akashi, Japan 56/D3
Akçaabat, Turk. 44/F4
Akçakale, Turk. 50/D2
Akhalts'ikhe, Geo. 45/G4
Akharnaí, Gre. 39/N8
Akhisar, Turk. 44/C5
Akhmīm, Egypt 50/B5
Akhtubinsk, Rus. 45/H2
Aki, Japan 56/C4
Akita, Japan 55/N4
Akjoujt, Mrta. 78/B2
Akkaraipattu, SrL. 62/D6
'Akko, Isr. 49/D3
Akō, Japan 56/D3
Akola, India 62/C3
Åkrehamn, Nor. 20/C4
Akron, Oh, US 94/D3
Aksaray, Turk. 50/C2
Akşehir, Turk. 50/B2
Aksu, China 46/J5
Akune, Japan 56/B4
Akure, Nga. 79/G5
Akyazı, Turk. 41/K5
Al Aḩmadī, Kuw. 51/G4
Al 'Amārah, Iraq 51/F4
Al 'Aqabah, Jor. 49/D5
Al 'Ayn, UAE 53/G4
Al Azīzīyah, Libya 76/H1
Al Bāb, Syria 50/D2
Al Badrashayn, Egypt 49/B5
Al Bājūr, Egypt 49/B4
Al Başrah, Iraq 51/F4
Al Baydā, Libya 77/K1
Al Fāsher, Sudan 77/L5
Al Fashn, Egypt 50/B4
Al Fatḩah, Iraq 51/E3
Al Fāw, Iraq 51/G4
Al Fayyum, Egypt 49/B5
Al Hammām, Egypt 50/B4
Al Ḩammāmāt, Tun. 38/B4
Al Ḩasakah, Syria 50/E2
Al Ḩawāmidīyah, Egypt 49/B5
Al Ḩayy, Iraq 51/F3
Al Ḩillah, Iraq 51/F3
Al Hindīyah, Iraq 51/F3
Al Hoceima, Mor. 76/E1
Al Ḩudaydah, Yem. 52/D6
Al Hufūf, SAr. 52/E3
Al Iskandarīyah, Egypt 49/A4
Al Ismā'īlīyah, Egypt 49/C4
Al Jamm, Tun. 38/B5
Al Jīzah, Egypt 49/B4
Al Junaynah, Sudan 77/K5
Al Kāf, Tun. 76/G1
Al Karak, Jor. 49/D4
Al Khābūrah, Oman 53/G4
Al Khalīl (Hebron), WBnk. 49/D4
Al Khānkah, Egypt 49/B4
Al Khārijah, Egypt 77/M2
Al Kharţūm Baḩrī (Khartoum North), Sudan 77/M4
Al Khubar, SAr. 52/F3
Al Khums, Libya 76/H1
Al Kiswah, Syria 49/E3
Al Kūfah, Iraq 51/F3
Al Kūt, Iraq 51/F3
Al Lādhiqīyah (Latakia), Syria 49/D2
Al Madīnah, SAr. 52/C4
Al Madīnah al Fikrīyah, Egypt 50/B5
Al Maḩallah al Kubrá, Egypt 49/B4
Al Mahdīyah, Tun. 38/B5
Al Maḩmūdīyah, Egypt 49/B4
Al Manşūrah, Egypt 49/B4
Al Manzilah, Egypt 49/B4
Al Marāghah, Egypt 50/B5
Al Marj, Libya 77/K1
Al Marsá, Tun. 38/B4
Al Maţarīyah, Egypt 49/C4
Al Mawşil (Mosul), Iraq 51/E2
Al Mayādīn, Syria 50/E3
Al Minyā, Egypt 50/B4
Al Mubarraz, SAr. 52/E4
Al Mukallā, Yem. 52/E6
Al Muknīn, Tun. 38/B5
Al Munastīr, Tun. 38/B5
Al Musayyib, Iraq 51/F3
Al Qaḑārif, Sudan 52/C6
Al Qāmishlī, Syria 50/E2
Al Qanāţir al Khayrīyah, Egypt 49/B4
Al Qayrawān, Tun. 38/B5
Al Quşayr, Syria 49/E2
Al Ubayyiḑ, Sudan 77/M5
Al Wāsiţah, Egypt 49/B5
Alabama (state), US 97/G3
Alabaster, Al, US 97/G3
Alaca, Turk. 44/E4
Alagir, Rus. 45/H4
Alagoinhas, Braz. 107/L6
Alajuela, CR 103/E4
Alameda, Ca, US 99/K11
Alamo, Mex. 102/B1
Alamo, Ca, US 99/K11
Alamogordo, NM, US 93/F4
Alamosa, Co, US 93/F3
Åland (isl.), Fin. 20/G3
Alanya, Turk. 49/C1
Alaşehir, Turk. 50/B2
Alaska (pen.), US 85/F4
Alaska (gulf), US 85/J4
Alaska (state), US 85/G2
Alaska (range), Ak, US 85/H3
Alatyr', Rus. 45/H1
Alaverdi, Arm. 45/H4
Alba, It. 33/H4
Alba Iulia, Rom. 41/F2
Albacete, Sp. 34/E3
Albania (ctry.), Alb. 39/F2
Albany, Or, US 90/C4
Albany, Ga, US 97/G4
Albany (cap.), NY, US 94/F3
Albany, Ca, US 99/K11
Albemarle, NC, US 97/H3
Albenga, It. 33/H4
Albert (lake), D.R. Congo 77/M7
Albert Lea, Mn, US 91/K5
Alberta (prov.), Can. 86/E3
Alberton, SAfr. 80/Q13
Albertville, Al, US 97/G3
Albertville, Fr. 33/G4
Albi, Fr. 32/E5
Albina, Sur. 107/H2
Albion, Mi, US 94/C3
Alblasserdam, Neth. 28/B5
Ålborg, Den. 20/D4
Albufeira, Port. 34/A4
Albuquerque, NM, US 92/F4
Albury, Austl. 73/C3
Alcabideche, Port. 35/P10
Alcalá de Guadaira, Sp. 34/C4
Alcalá de Henares, Sp. 35/N9
Alcalá la Real, Sp. 34/D4
Alcamo, It. 38/C4
Alcantarilla, Sp. 34/E4
Alcázar de San Juan, Sp. 34/D3
Alcira, Sp. 35/E3
Alcobendas, Sp. 35/N8
Alcora, Sp. 35/E2
Alcorcón, Sp. 35/N9
Alcoy, Sp. 35/E3
Aldan, Rus. 47/N4
Aldershot, Eng, UK 25/F4
Alderwood Manor-Bothell North, Wa, US 99/C2
Aldine, Tx, US 93/J5
Aldridge, Eng, UK 25/E1
Aleg, Mrta. 78/B2
Alegrete, Braz. 109/E2
Aleksandrov, Rus. 42/H4
Aleksandrovsk, Rus. 43/N4
Aleksandrovsk-Sakhalinskiy, Rus. 55/N1
Aleksandrów Łódzki, Pol. 27/K3
Alekseyevka, Rus. 44/F2
Aleksin, Rus. 44/F1
Aleksinac, Serb. 40/E4
Além Paraíba, Braz. 108/L6
Alençon, Fr. 32/D2
Alenquer, Braz. 107/H4
Alessandria, It. 33/H4
Ålesund, Nor. 20/C3
Aleutian (isls.), Ak, US 85/B5
Alexander (isl.), Ant. 83/V
Alexander (arch.), US 85/L4
Alexander City, Al, US 97/G3
Alexandria, La, US 93/J5
Alexandria, MN, US 91/K4
Alexandria, Rom. 41/G4
Alexandroúpolis, Gre. 41/G5
Aleysk, Rus. 46/J4
Alfeld, Ger. 29/G5
Alfenas, Braz. 108/H6
Alfreton, Eng, UK 23/G5
Alfter, Ger. 31/G2
Algeciras, Sp. 34/C4
Algemesí, Sp. 35/E3
Algeria (ctry.) 76/F2
Alghero, It. 38/A2
Algiers (cap.), Alg. 76/F1
Algonquin, Il, US 99/P14
Algueirão, Port. 35/P10
Algund (Lagundo), It. 37/H4
Alhama de Murcia, Sp. 34/E4
Alhaurín el Grande, Sp. 34/C4
'Alī al Gharbī, Iraq 51/F3
Äli Bayramlı, Azer. 51/G2
Aliağa, Turk. 44/C5
Alibeyköy, Turk. 41/J5
Alicante, Sp. 35/E3
Alice, Tx, US 96/D5
Alice Springs, Austl. 68/C7
Alīgarh, India 62/C2
Alingsås, Swe. 20/E4
Alīpur, Pak. 62/B2
Alīpur Duār, India 62/E2
Alīrājpur, India 53/K4
Alkmaar, Neth. 28/B3
Allada, Ben. 79/F5
Allahābād, India 62/D2
Allanmyo, Myan. 60/B5
Allegheny (mts.), US 94/D4
Allen Park, Mi, US 99/F7
Allende, Mex. 101/E3
Allende, Mex. 96/C4
Allentown, Pa, US 94/F3
Alleppey, India 62/C6
Alliance, Ne, US 91/H5
Alliance, Oh, US 94/D3
Allschwil, Swi. 36/D2
Alma, Qu, Can. 95/G1
Alma, Mi, US 94/C3
Almada, Port. 35/P10
Almansa, Sp. 35/E3
Almaty, Kaz. 46/H5
Almazora, Sp. 35/E3
Almelo, Neth. 28/D4
Almenara, Braz. 107/K7
Almendralejo, Sp. 34/B3
Almere, Neth. 28/C4
Almería, Sp. 34/D4
Al'met'yevsk, Rus. 43/M5
Ålmhult, Swe. 20/E4
Almonte, Sp. 34/B4
Almuñécar, Sp. 34/D4
Alofi, NZ 69/J6
Alor Setar, Malay. 65/C5
Alotau, PNG 68/E6
Alphen aan de Rijn, Neth. 28/B4
Alps (mts.), It. 33/G4
Alsdorf, Ger. 31/F2
Alsfeld, Ger. 33/H1
Alsip, Il, US 99/Q16
Alta, Nor. 20/G1
Alta Floresta, Braz. 107/G5
Alta Gracia, Arg. 109/D3
Altagracia, Nic. 102/E4
Altamira, Braz. 107/H4
Altamira, Mex. 102/B1
Altamonte Springs, Fl, US 97/H4
Altamura, It. 40/C5
Altay, Mong. 54/D2
Altay, China 54/B2
Altdorf, Swi. 37/E4
Altena, Ger. 29/E6
Altenburg, Ger. 26/G3
Alton, Il, US 93/K3
Alton, Eng, UK 25/F4
Altoona, Pa, US 94/E3
Altos, Braz. 107/K5
Altrincham, Eng, UK 23/F5
Altus, Ok, US 93/H4
Alushta, Ukr. 44/E3
Alvarado, Mex. 101/P8
Alverca, Port. 35/P10
Alvesta, Swe. 20/E4
Alvin, Tx, US 93/J5
Alvorada, Braz. 108/A4
Alytus, Lith. 27/N1
Alzey, Ger. 31/H4
Am Timan, Chad 77/K5
Amadora, Port. 35/P10
Amagasaki, Japan 55/M5
Amagi, Japan 56/B4
Amaliás, Gre. 39/G4
Amalner, India 62/C3
Amambaí, Braz. 109/E1
Amanzimtoti, SAfr. 81/E3
Amarillo, Tx, US 93/G4
Amasya, Turk. 44/E4
Amazon (riv.), Braz. 106/G4
Ambahikily, Madg. 81/G8
Ambajogai, India 53/L5
Ambāla, India 53/L2
Ambalavao, Madg. 81/H8
Ambanja, Madg. 81/J6
Ambato, Ecu. 106/C4
Ambato Boeny, Madg. 81/H7
Ambatofinandrahana, Madg. 81/H8
Ambatolampy, Madg. 81/H7
Ambatondrazaka, Madg. 81/J7
Amberg, Ger. 33/J2
Ambikāpur, India 62/D3
Ambinanindrano, Madg. 81/J8
Ambinanitelo, Madg. 81/J6
Amboasary, Madg. 81/H9
Amboavory, Madg. 81/J7
Ambodiharina, Madg. 81/J8
Ambohimandroso, Madg. 81/H7
Ambon, Indo. 67/G4
Ambositra, Madg. 81/H8
Ambovombe, Madg. 81/H9
Ameca, Mex. 100/D4
Amecameca de Juárez, Mex. 101/R10
American Fork, Ut, US 92/E2
Americana, Braz. 108/C2
Americus, Ga, US 97/G3
Amersfoort, Neth. 28/C4
Amersham, Eng, UK 25/F3
Amet, India 62/B2
Amherst, NY, US 95/V10
Amiens, Fr. 30/B4
Amla, India 62/C3
Amman (cap.), Jor. 49/D4
Āmol, Iran 51/H2
Amozoc, Mex. 101/L7
Ampanefena, Madg. 81/J6
Ampanihy, Madg. 81/H9
Amparafaravola, Madg. 81/J7
Amparai, SrL. 62/D6
Amparo, Braz. 108/G7
Ampitatafika, Madg. 81/H7
Amposta, Sp. 35/F2
Amravati, India 62/C3
Amreli, India 62/B3
Amritsar, India 53/K2
Amstelveen, Neth. 28/B4
Amsterdam, NY, US 94/F3
Amsterdam (cap.), Neth. 28/B4
Amstetten, Aus. 40/B1
Amu Darya (riv.), Trkm. 46/G5
Amursk, Rus. 55/M1
An Nabk, Syria 49/E2
An Nahūd, Sudan 77/L5
An Najaf, Iraq 51/F4
An Nāşirīyah, Iraq 51/F4
Anaco, Ven. 106/F2
Anaheim, Ca, US 92/C4
Anakāpalle, India 62/D4
Analalava, Madg. 81/H6
Analavory, Madg. 81/H7
Anamur, Turk. 49/C1
Anan, Japan 56/D4
Anand, India 62/B3
Anantapur, India 62/C5
Anantnag, India 53/L2
Anapa, Rus. 44/F3
Anápolis, Braz. 107/J7
Añatuya, Arg. 109/D2
Ancaster, On, Can. 95/T9
Anchorage, Ak, US 85/J3
Ancona, It. 40/A4
Ancud, Chile 109/B5
Anda, China 55/K2
Andalusia, Al, US 97/G4
Andaman (sea), Asia 63/F5
Andaman (isls.), India 63/F5
Andenne, Belg. 31/E3
Andernach, Ger. 31/G3
Anderson, In, US 97/G1
Anderson, SC, US 97/H3
Andes, Cordillera de los (mts.), SAm. 106/C4
Andijon, Uzb. 46/H5
Andilamena, Madg. 81/J7
Andilanatoby, Madg. 81/J7
Andīmeshk, Iran 51/G3
Andira, Braz. 108/B2
Andong, SKor. 56/A2
Andorra (ctry.) 35/F1
Andorra la Vella (cap.), And. 35/F1
Andover, Eng, UK 25/E4
Andradas, Braz. 108/G7
Andradina, Braz. 108/B2
Andria, It. 40/C5
Andriba, Madg. 81/H7
Androka, Madg. 81/H9
Andros (isl.), Bah. 97/J5
Andújar, Sp. 34/C3
Anegada Passage (chan.), NAm. 104/E3
Anécho, Togo 79/F5
Angarsk, Rus. 54/E1
Angel, Salto (falls), Ven. 106/F2
Ängelholm, Swe. 20/E4
Angers, Fr. 32/C3
Angkor (ruin), Camb. 65/C3
Anglesey (isl.), Wal, UK 22/D5
Anglet, Fr. 34/E1
Angleton, Tx, US 93/J5
Angol, Chile 109/B4
Angola, Afr. 82/B2
Angola (ctry.) 82/C3
Angoulême, Fr. 32/D4
Angra dos Reis, Braz. 108/J7
Angren, Uzb. 46/H5
Anjār, India 62/B3
Anjou, Qu, Can. 95/N6
Ankang, China 59/B4
Ankara (cap.), Turk. 44/E5
Ankazoabo, Madg. 81/H8
Anklam, Ger. 27/G2
Anlong, China 63/J2
Anlu, China 61/G2
Ann Arbor, Mi, US 99/E7
Annaba, Alg. 76/G1
Annaberg-Buchholz, Ger. 33/K1
Annapolis (cap.), Md, US 94/E4
Annecy, Fr. 36/C6
Annecy-le-Vieux, Fr. 36/C6
Annemasse, Fr. 36/C5
Anniston, Al, US 97/G3
Annonay, Fr. 32/F4
Anosibe an' Ala, Madg. 81/J7
Ans, Belg. 31/E2
Ansan, SKor. 58/F7
Ansbach, Ger. 33/J2
Ansfelden, Aus. 40/B1
Anshan, China 58/B2
Anshun, China 60/E3
Ansŏng, SKor. 58/D4
Antakya, Turk. 49/E1
Antalaha, Madg. 81/J6
Antalya, Turk. 49/B1
Antananarivo (cap.), Madg. 81/H7
Antanifotsy, Madg. 81/H7
Antarctic (pen.), Ant. 83/W
Antarctic Circle 83/Z
Antarctica (cont.) 83/*
Antequera, Sp. 34/C4
Antibes, Fr. 33/G5
Anticosti, Île d' (isl.), Qu, Can. 95/J1
Antigua and Barbuda (ctry.), Anti. 104/F3
Antigua Guatemala, Guat. 102/D3
Antioch, Ca, US 99/L11
Antofagasta, Chile 109/B1
Antony, Fr. 30/B6
Antrim, NI, UK 22/B2
Antsalova, Madg. 81/H7
Antsirabe, Madg. 81/H7
Antsirañana, Madg. 81/J6
Antwerpen, Belg. 28/B6
Anūpgarh, India 62/B2
Anuradhapura, SrL. 62/D6
Anyang, SKor. 58/F7
Anzhero-Sudzhensk, Rus. 46/J4
Anzio, It. 38/C2
Aomori, Japan 55/N3
Aosta, It. 33/G4
Apan, Mex. 101/L7
Aparecida, Braz. 108/C2
Aparri, Phil. 61/J5
Apartadó, Col. 103/G5
Apatin, Serb. 40/D3
Apatity, Rus. 42/G2
Apatzingán de la Constitución, Mex. 100/E5
Apeldoorn, Neth. 28/C4
Apennines (mts.), It. 38/C1
Apia (cap.), Sam. 69/S9
Apizaco, Mex. 101/L7
Apóstoles, Arg. 109/E2
Appalachian (mts.), US 94/D4
Appenzell, Swi. 37/F3
Aprilia, It. 38/C2
Apsheronsk, Rus. 44/F3
Apucarana, Braz. 108/B2
Aqtaū, Kaz. 45/J4
Aqtöbe, Kaz. 45/L2
Aquidauana, Braz. 107/G8
Ar Ramādī, Iraq 51/E3
Ar Ramthā, Jor. 49/D3
Ar Rayyān, Qatar 52/F3
Ar Ruşayfah, Jor. 49/E3
Arabian (des.), Egypt 77/M2
Arabian (pen.), SAr. 52/D3
Arabian (sea), Asia 53/H5
Aracaju, Braz. 107/L6

Beatrice, Ne, US 93/H2
Beau Bassin, Mrts. 81/T15
Beaufort, SC, US 97/H3
Beaufort West, SAfr. 80/C4
Beaume, Fr. 32/F3
Beaumont, Tx, US 93/J5
Beauvais, Fr. 30/B5
Beāwar, India 62/B2
Bebedouro, Braz. 108/B2
Bebington, Eng, UK 23/E5
Bebra, Ger. 29/G7
Bečej, Serb. 40/E3
Béchar, Alg. 76/E1
Beckingen, Ger. 31/F5
Beckley, WV, US 97/H2
Beckum, Ger. 29/F5
Bedburg, Ger. 28/D6
Bedford, In, US 97/G2
Bedford, Eng, UK 25/F2
Bedlington, Eng, UK 23/G1
Bedworth, Eng, UK 25/E2
Beek, Neth. 31/E2
Beenleigh, Austl. 72/D4
Be'er Sheva', Isr. 49/D4
Beerzel, Belg. 28/B6
Beeville, Tx, US 96/D4
Begusarai, India 62/E2
Behbahān, Iran 51/G4
Behshahr, Iran 51/H2
Bei'an, China 55/K2
Beihai, China 65/E1
Beijing (cap.), China 59/H7
Beipiao, China 59/E2
Beira, Moz. 82/F4
Beirut (cap.), Leb. 49/D3
Beja, Port. 34/B3
Bejaïa, Alg. 76/G1
Béjar, Sp. 34/C2
Bekasi, Indo. 66/C5
Békés, Hun. 40/E2
Békéscsaba, Hun. 40/E2
Bekily, Madg. 81/H9
Belā, India 62/D2
Bela Crkva, Serb. 40/E3
Bela Vista, Braz. 107/G8
Belarus (ctry.) 18/F3
Belas, Port. 35/P10
Bełchatów, Pol. 27/K3
Belebey, Rus. 43/M5
Belém, Braz. 107/J4
Belen, Turk. 49/E1
Belev, Rus. 44/F1
Belfast (cap.), NI, UK 22/C2
Belfort, Fr. 36/C2
Belgaum, India 62/B4
Belgium (ctry.) 26/C3
Belgorod, Rus. 44/F2
Belgrade (cap.), Serb. 40/E4
Beli Manastir, Cro. 40/D3
Belize (ctry.), Belz. 102/D2
Belize City, Belz. 102/D2
Bell Ville, Arg. 109/D3
Bella Vista, Arg. 109/E2
Bellary, India 62/C4
Belle Glade, Fl, US 97/H5
Bellefontaine, Oh, US 94/D3
Belleville, On, Can. 94/E2
Bellevue, Wa, US 99/C2
Bellingham, Wa, US 90/C3
Bellinzona, Swi. 37/F5
Bello, Col. 106/C2
Belluno, It. 33/K3
Bellville, SAfr. 80/L10
Belmont, Ca, US 99/K11
Belmopan (cap.), Belz. 102/D2
Belo Horizonte, Braz. 108/D1
Belo Jardim, Braz. 107/L5
Belo-Tsiribihina, Madg. 81/H7
Beloeil, Qu, Can. 95/P6
Belogorsk, Rus. 55/K1
Beloha, Madg. 81/H9
Beloit, Wi, US 91/L5
Belomorsk, Rus. 42/G2
Belorechensk, Rus. 44/F3
Beloretsk, Rus. 43/N5
Belovo, Rus. 46/J4
Belper, Eng, UK 23/G5
Belton, Tx, US 93/H5
Belvidere, Il, US 91/L5
Bembéréké, Ben. 79/F4
Bemetāra, India 62/D3
Bemmel, Neth. 28/C5
Ben Tre, Viet. 65/D4
Benalmádena, Sp. 34/C4
Benavente, Sp. 34/C1
Bend, Or, US 90/C4
Bendigo, Austl. 73/C3
Bene Beraq, Isr. 49/F7
Benešov, Czh. 33/L2
Benevento, It. 40/B5
Bengal, Bay of (gulf), Asia 62/E4
Benghāzī, Libya 76/K1
Bengkayang, Indo. 66/C3
Bengkulu, Indo. 66/B4
Benguela, Ang. 82/B3
Beni, D.R. Congo 77/L7
Beni Mellal, Mor. 76/D1
Benicarló, Sp. 35/F2
Benicia, Ca, US 99/K10
Benidorm, Sp. 35/E3
Benin (ctry.) 79/F4
Benin City, Nga. 79/G5
Benin, Bight of (bay), Afr. 76/F6
Bennettsville, SC, US 97/J3
Bennington, Vt, US 94/F3
Bensenville, Il, US 99/Q16
Bensheim, Ger. 33/H2
Bentley, Eng, UK 23/G4
Bento Gonçalves, Braz. 108/B4
Benton, Ar, US 93/J4
Benton Harbor, Mi, US 94/C3
Bentong, Malay. 66/B3
Benxi, China 58/B2
Beppu, Japan 56/B4
Beraketa, Madg. 81/H8
Berat, Alb. 40/D5
Berbera, Som. 77/Q5
Berbérati, CAfr. 76/J7
Berchem, Belg. 28/B6
Berck, Fr. 25/H6
Berdsk, Rus. 46/J4
Berdyans'k, Ukr. 44/F3
Berdychiv, Ukr. 44/D2
Berea, Ky, US 97/G2
Berehove, Ukr. 40/F1
Berekum, Gha. 79/E5
Berettyóújfalu, Hun. 40/E2
Berezniki, Rus. 43/N4
Bergama, Turk. 44/C5
Bergamo, It. 33/H4
Bergara, Sp. 34/D1
Bergen, Nor. 20/C3
Bergen, Ger. 27/G1
Bergen op Zoom, Neth. 28/B5
Bergerac, Fr. 32/D4
Bergheim, Ger. 31/F2
Bergisch Gladbach, Ger. 31/G2
Bergkamen, Ger. 29/E5
Bergneustadt, Ger. 29/E6
Bergum, Neth. 28/D2
Berhampore, India 62/E3
Berhampur, India 62/D4
Bering (sea), Asia, NAm. 47/U4
Bering (str.), Rus., US 85/E3
Beringen, Belg. 28/C6
Berkel, Neth. 28/B5
Berkeley, Ca, US 99/K11
Berkhamsted, Eng, UK 25/F3
Berkley, Mi, US 99/F6
Berkovitsa, Bul. 41/F4
Berleburg, Ger. 29/F6
Berlin, NH, US 95/G2
Berlin (cap.), Ger. 27/G2
Bermejo, Bol. 109/D1
Bermeo, Sp. 34/D1
Bern (cap.), Swi. 36/D4
Bernal, Peru 106/B5
Bernburg, Ger. 26/F3
Beroun, Czh. 33/L2
Berovo, FYROM 40/F5
Bertoua, Camr. 76/H7
Berwick, Pa, US 94/E3
Berwyn, Il, US 99/Q16
Besançon, Fr. 36/C3
Beslan, Rus. 45/H4
Bessacarr, Eng, UK 23/G5
Bessemer, Al, US 97/G3
Best, Neth. 28/C5
Bet She'an, Isr. 49/D3
Bet Shemesh, Isr. 49/F8
Bethesda, Md, US 97/J2
Bethlehem, Pa, US 94/F3
Béthune, Fr. 30/B2
Betim, Braz. 108/C1
Betioky, Madg. 81/H8
Bettiah, India 62/D2
Betūl, India 62/C3
Beuningen, Neth. 28/C5
Beveren, Belg. 28/B6
Beverley, Eng, UK 23/H4
Beverly Hills, Mi, US 99/F6
Beverungen, Ger. 29/G5
Beverwijk, Neth. 28/B4
Bexbach, Ger. 31/G5
Bexhill, Eng, UK 25/G5
Beypazarı, Turk. 41/K5
Beyşehir, Turk. 50/B2
Bezhetsk, Rus. 42/H4
Béziers, Fr. 32/E5
Bhabua, India 62/D2
Bhadrak, India 62/E3
Bhadreswar, India 62/A3
Bhāgalpur, India 62/E2
Bhakkar, Pak. 53/K2
Bhaktapur, Nepal 62/E2
Bhānwad, India 62/A3
Bhārātpur, India 62/C2
Bharuch, India 62/B3
Bhātāpāra, India 62/D3
Bhatinda, India 53/K2
Bhatkal, India 62/B5
Bhātpāra, India 62/E3
Bhavāni, India 62/C5
Bhavnagar, India 62/B3
Bhawāni Mandi, India 62/C3
Bhawānipatna, India 62/D4
Bhilai, India 62/D3
Bhīlwāra, India 62/B2
Bhīmavaram, India 62/D4
Bhimunipatnam, India 62/D4
Bhind, India 62/C2
Bhiwandi, India 62/B4
Bhopāl, India 62/C3
Bhor, India 62/B4
Bhuban, India 62/E3
Bhubaneswar, India 62/E3
Bhusawal, India 62/C3
Bhutan (ctry.) 62/E2
Biafra, Bight of (bay), Camr. 76/G7
Biała Podlaska, Pol. 27/M2
Białogard, Pol. 27/J2
Białystok, Pol. 27/M2
Biancavilla, It. 38/D4
Biarritz, Fr. 34/E1
Bibā, Egypt 50/B4
Biberach an der Riss, Ger. 37/F1
Bicester, Eng, UK 25/E3
Bida, Nga. 79/G4
Bīdar, India 62/C4
Biddeford, Me, US 95/G3
Biddulph, Eng, UK 23/F5
Biel, Swi. 36/D3
Bielawa, Pol. 27/J3
Bielefeld, Ger. 29/F4
Biella, It. 33/H4
Bielsk Podlaski, Pol. 27/M2
Bielsko-Biała, Pol. 27/K4
Bien Hoa, Viet. 65/D4
Big Rapids, Mi, US 94/C3
Big Spring, Tx, US 93/G4
Biga, Turk. 41/H5
Bignona, Sen. 78/A3
Biguaçu, Braz. 108/B3
Bihać, Bosn. 40/B3
Bīhar, India 62/E2
Bijeljina, Bosn. 40/D3
Bijelo Polje, Serb. 40/D4
Bijnor, India 62/C2
Bīkaner, India 62/B2
Bikin, Rus. 55/L2
Bila Tserkva, Ukr. 44/D2
Bilāra, India 62/B2
Bilāspur, India 62/D3
Bilbao, Sp. 34/D1
Bilbays, Egypt 49/B4
Bilecik, Turk. 44/D4
Biłgoraj, Pol. 27/M3
Bilhorod-Dnistrovs'kyy, Ukr. 41/K2
Billingham, Eng, UK 23/G2
Billings, Mt, US 90/F4
Biloxi, Ms, US 97/F4
Bilqas Qism Awwal, Egypt 49/B4
Bilsi, India 62/C2
Bilzen, Belg. 31/E2
Bima, Indo. 67/E5
Bimbo, CAfr. 77/J7
Bin 'Arūs, Tun. 38/B4
Bina-Etāwa, India 62/C3
Binche, Belg. 31/D3
Bindki, India 62/D2
Bindura, Zim. 82/F4
Bingen, Ger. 31/G4
Bingerville, C.d'Iv. 78/E5
Binghamton, NY, US 94/F3
Bingley, Eng, UK 23/G4
Bingöl, Turk. 50/E2
Binh Son, Viet. 65/E3
Binjai, Indo. 66/A3
Biograd, Cro. 40/B4
Bīr, India 53/L5
Birāk, Libya 76/H2
Birao, CAfr. 77/K5
Birātnagar, Nepal 62/E2
Birecik, Turk. 50/D2
Birigui, Braz. 108/B2
Biritiba-Mirim, Braz. 108/G8
Bīrjand, Iran 53/G2
Birkenhead, Eng, UK 23/E5
Bîrlad, Rom. 41/H2
Birmingham, Al, US 97/G3
Birmingham, Eng, UK 25/E2
Birmingham, Mi, US 99/F6
Birni Nkonni, Niger 79/G3
Birobjian, Rus. 55/L2
Birsk, Rus. 43/M5
Biscay (bay), Fr.,Sp. 34/C1
Bisceglie, It. 40/C5
Bischheim, Fr. 31/G6
Bishkek (cap.), Kyr. 46/H5
Bishop Auckland, Eng, UK 23/G2
Bishop's Stortford, Eng, UK 25/G3
Biskra, Alg. 76/G1
Bislig, Phil. 67/G2
Bismarck (arch.), PNG 68/D5
Bismarck (cap.), ND, US 91/H4
Bismil, Turk. 50/E2
Bissau (cap.), GBis. 78/B4
Bistriţa, Rom. 41/G2
Bitlis, Turk. 50/E2
Bitola, FYROM 40/E5
Bitonto, It. 40/C5
Bitung, Indo. 67/G3
Bixby, Ok, US 96/E3
Biyalā, Egypt 49/B4
Biysk, Rus. 46/J4
Bjelovar, Cro. 40/C3
Black (sea), Eur.,Asia 41/J4
Blackburn, Eng, UK 23/F4
Blackfoot, Id, US 90/E5
Blackpool, Eng, UK 23/E4
Blagnac, Fr. 32/D5
Blagoevgrad, Bul. 41/F4
Blagoveshchensk, Rus. 55/K1
Blainville, Qu, Can. 95/N6
Blaj, Rom. 41/F2
Blanc (peak), Fr. 36/C6
Blanca, Costa (coast), Sp. 35/E4
Blanes, Sp. 35/G2
Blankenberge, Belg. 30/C1
Blansko, Czh. 33/M2
Blantyre, Malw. 82/G4
Blenheim, NZ 71/R11
Blida, Alg. 76/F1
Blieskastel, Ger. 31/G5
Bloemendaal, Neth. 28/B4
Bloemfontein (cap.), SAfr. 80/D3
Blois, Fr. 32/D3
Blomberg, Ger. 29/G5
Bloomingdale, Il, US 99/P16
Bloomington, Il, US 91/L5
Bloomington, In, US 97/G2
Bloomsburg, Pa, US 94/E3
Blora, Indo. 66/D5
Blue Island, Il, US 99/Q16
Blue Mountains, Austl. 73/D2
Blue Ridge (mts.), US 97/H3
Bluefield, WV, US 97/H2
Bluefields, Nic. 103/F4
Bluffton, In, US 94/C3
Blumenau, Braz. 108/B3
Blyth, Eng, UK 23/G1
Blytheville, Ar, US 93/K4
Bo, SLeo. 78/C5
Boa Esperança, Braz. 108/C2
Boa Vista, Braz. 106/F3
Boaco, Nic. 102/E3
Boadilla del Monte, Sp. 35/N9
Bobbili, India 62/D4
Bobigny, Fr. 30/B6
Bobingen, Ger. 37/G1
Böblingen, Ger. 33/H2
Bobo Dioulasso, Burk. 78/D4
Bobrov, Rus. 44/G2
Boca Raton, Fl, US 97/H5
Bocaiúva, Braz. 107/K7
Bocas del Toro, Pan. 103/F4
Bochnia, Pol. 27/L4
Bocholt, Ger. 28/D5
Bochum, Ger. 29/E6
Bodaybo, Rus. 47/M4
Bodegraven, Neth. 28/B4
Boden, Swe. 42/D2
Bodensee (Constance) (lake), Swi 37/F2
Bodhan, India 62/C4
Bodināyakkanūr, India 62/C5
Bodø, Nor. 20/E2
Bodrum, Turk. 50/A2
Bogalusa, La, US 97/F4
Bogandé, Burk. 79/E3
Bogatynia, Pol. 27/H3
Boğazlıyan, Turk. 44/E5
Bognor Regis, Eng, UK 25/F5
Bogor, Indo. 66/C5
Bogotá (cap.), Col. 106/D3
Bohicon, Ben. 79/F5
Boiro, Sp. 34/A1
Boisbriand, Qu, Can. 95/N6
Boise (cap.), Id, US 90/D5
Bojnūrd, Iran 51/J2
Boksburg, SAfr. 80/Q13
Bol, Chad 76/H5
Bolesławiec, Pol. 27/H3
Bolgatanga, Gha. 79/E4
Bolinao, Phil. 61/H5
Bolingbrook, Il, US 99/P16
Bolívar, Arg. 109/D4
Bolívar (peak), Ven. 106/D2
Bolivia (ctry.), Bol. 106/F7
Bologna, It. 33/J4
Bologoye, Rus. 42/G4
Bolton, Eng, UK 23/F4
Bolu, Turk. 41/K5
Bolvadin, Turk. 50/B2
Bolzano, It. 37/H5
Bom Despacho, Braz. 108/C1
Bom Jesus da Lapa, Braz. 107/K6
Bom Jesus do Itabapoana, Braz. 108/D2
Boma, D.R. Congo 82/B2
Bomaderry, Austl. 73/D2
Bon (cape), Tun. 38/B4
Bondoukou, C.d'Iv. 78/E4
Bondowoso, Indo. 66/D5
Bönen, Ger. 29/E5
Bongabong, Phil. 67/F1
Bongao, Phil. 67/E3
Bongor, Chad 76/J5
Bonita Springs, Fl, US 97/H5
Bonn, Ger. 31/G2
Bonthain, Indo. 67/E5
Bontoc, Phil. 61/J5
Bonyhád, Hun. 40/D2
Boone, Ia, US 91/K5
Boosaaso (Bender Cassim), Som. 77/Q5
Bootle, Eng, UK 23/E5
Boppard, Ger. 31/G3
Bor, Rus. 43/K4
Bor, Turk. 50/C2
Bor, Serb. 40/F3
Borås, Swe. 20/E4
Borāzjān, Iran 51/G4
Borča, Serb. 40/E3
Bordeaux, Fr. 32/C4
Borehamwood, Eng, UK 25/F3
Borger, Tx, US 93/G4
Borgerhout, Belg. 28/B6
Borghorst, Ger. 29/E4
Borisoglebsk, Rus. 45/G2
Borken, Ger. 28/D5
Borlänge, Swe. 20/E3
Borna, Ger. 26/G3
Borne, Neth. 28/D4
Bornem, Belg. 28/B6
Borneo (isl.), Asia 67/E3
Bornheim, Ger. 31/G2
Borovichi, Rus. 42/G4
Borşa, Rom. 41/F2
Borssele, Neth. 28/A6
Borūjerd, Iran 51/G3
Boryslav, Ukr. 27/M4
Borzya, Rus. 54/H1
Bosanska Dubica, Bosn. 40/C3
Bosanska Gradiška, Bosn. 40/C3
Bosanska Krupa, Bosn. 40/C3
Bosanski Brod, Bosn. 40/D3
Bosanski Petrovac, Bosn. 40/C3
Bosanski Šamac, Bosn. 40/D3
Bose, China 61/E4
Boskoop, Neth. 28/B4
Bosnia and Herzegovina (ctry.) 40/C3
Bosporus (str.), Turk. 44/D4
Bosporus (riv.), Turk. 51/N6
Bossangoa, CAfr. 76/J6
Bossier City, La, US 93/J4
Boston, Eng, UK 23/H6
Boston (cap.), Ma, US 95/G3
Botād, India 53/K4
Botevgrad, Bul. 41/F4
Bothell, Wa, US 99/C2
Bothnia (gulf), Swe., Fin 20/F3
Botoşani, Rom. 41/H2
Botou, China 59/D3
Botswana (ctry.) 82/D5
Bottrop, Ger. 28/D5
Botucatu, Braz. 108/B2
Bouaflé, C.d'Iv. 78/D5
Bouaké, C.d'Iv. 78/D5
Bouar, CAfr. 76/J6
Boucherville, Qu, Can. 95/P6
Bouguenais, Fr. 32/C3
Bouira, Alg. 76/F1
Boukoumbé, Ben. 79/F4
Boulder, Co, US 93/F2
Boulder City, Nv, US 92/D4
Boulogne-Billancourt, Fr. 30/B6
Boulogne-sur-Mer, Fr. 25/H5
Bourg-en-Bresse, Fr. 36/B5
Bourg-lès-Valence, Fr. 32/F4
Bourges, Fr. 32/E3
Bourgoin-Jallieu, Fr. 32/F4
Bournemouth, Eng, UK 25/E5
Bowling Green, Ky, US 97/G2
Bowling Green, Oh, US 94/D3
Boxmeer, Neth. 28/C5
Boxtel, Neth. 28/C5
Boyabat, Turk. 44/E4
Boynton Beach, Fl, US 97/H5
Bozoum, CAfr. 76/J6
Bozova, Turk. 50/D2
Bozüyük, Turk. 44/D5
Bozyazı, Turk. 49/C1
Bra, It. 33/G4
Bracknell, Eng, UK 25/F4
Brad, Rom. 41/F2
Bradenton, Fl, US 97/H5
Bradford, Pa, US 94/E3
Bradford, Eng, UK 23/G4
Braga, Port. 34/A2
Bragado, Arg. 109/D4
Bragança, Braz. 107/J4
Bragança, Port. 34/B2
Bragança Paulista, Braz. 108/G7
Brahmaputra (riv.), India 63/F2
Brăila, Rom. 41/H3
Braine-l'Alleud, Belg. 31/D2
Braine-le-Comte, Belg. 31/D2
Braintree, Eng, UK 25/G3
Brake, Ger. 29/F2
Brakel, Ger. 29/G5
Brampton, On, Can. 95/T8
Bramsche, Ger. 29/F4
Brandenburg, Ger. 26/G2
Brandon, Fl, US 97/H5
Brandon, Ms, US 97/F3
Braniewo, Pol. 27/K1
Brantford, On, Can. 95/S9
Branzoll (Bronzolo), It. 37/H4
Brasília (cap.), Braz. 107/J7
Braşov, Rom. 41/G3
Brasschaat, Belg. 28/B6
Bratislava (cap.), Slvk. 40/C1
Bratsk, Rus. 47/L4
Brattleboro, Vt, US 95/F3
Braulio Carrillo, CR 103/F4
Braunau am Inn, Aus. 33/K2
Braunschweig, Ger. 29/H4
Brava, Costa (coast), Sp. 35/G2
Brawley, Ca, US 92/D4
Bray, Ire. 22/B5
Brazil (ctry.), Braz. 105/D3
Brazzaville (cap.), Congo 82/C1
Brčko, Bosn. 40/D3
Breaza, Rom. 41/G3
Brecht, Belg. 28/B6
Břeclav, Czh. 33/M2
Breda, Neth. 28/B5
Bregenz, Aus. 37/F3
Bremen, Ger. 29/F2
Bremerhaven, Ger. 29/F1
Bremerton, Wa, US 99/B2
Bremervörde, Ger. 29/G2
Brenham, Tx, US 93/H5
Brentwood, Eng, UK 25/G3
Brescia, It. 33/J4
Bressuire, Fr. 32/C3
Brest, Bela. 27/M2
Brest, Fr. 32/A2
Breves, Braz. 107/H4
Brewer, Me, US 95/G2
Brežice, Slov. 40/B3
Bria, CAfr. 77/K6
Bridgend, Wal, UK 24/C3
Bridgeport, Ct, US 94/F3
Bridgetown (cap.), Bar. 104/G4
Bridgwater, Eng, UK 24/D4
Bridlington, Eng, UK 23/H3
Brieg Brzeg, Pol. 27/J3
Brielle, Neth. 28/B5
Brigham City, Ut, US 90/E5
Brighouse, Eng, UK 23/G4
Brighton, Co, US 93/F3
Brighton, Eng, UK 25/F5
Brikama, Gam. 78/A3
Brilon, Ger. 29/F6
Brindisi, It. 40/C5
Brisbane, Austl. 72/F6
Bristol, Tn, US 97/H2
Bristol, Eng, UK 24/D4
Bristol (chan.), Eng,Wal, UK 24/B4
British Columbia (prov.), Can. 86/D3
Brive-la-Gaillarde, Fr. 32/D4
Brno, Czh. 33/M2
Broadstairs, Eng, UK 25/H4
Brockton, Ma, US 95/G3
Brodnica, Pol. 27/K2
Broken Arrow, Ok, US 93/J3
Broken Hill, Austl. 73/B1
Bromsgrove, Eng, UK 24/D2
Bron, Fr. 36/A6
Bronte, It. 38/D4
Brooke's Point, Phil. 67/E2
Brookfield, Il, US 99/Q16
Brookfield, Wi, US 99/P13
Brookhaven, Ms, US 93/K5
Brooks (range), US 85/F2
Brossard, Qu, Can. 95/P7
Brownfield, Tx, US 93/G4
Brownhills, Eng, UK 25/E1
Brownsville, Tn, US 97/F3
Brownsville, Tx, US 96/D5
Bruay-la-Buissière, Fr. 30/B3
Bruchsal, Ger. 33/H2
Brugge, Belg. 30/C1
Brühl, Ger. 31/F2
Brumado, Braz. 107/K6
Brummen, Neth. 28/D4
Brumunddal, Nor. 20/D3
Brunei (ctry.) 66/D2
Brunssum, Neth. 31/E2
Brunswick, Oh, US 94/D3
Brunswick, Me, US 95/G3
Brunswick, Ga, US 97/H4
Brusque, Braz. 108/B3
Brussels (cap.), Belg. 31/D2

Bryan, Tx, US 93/H5
Bryansk, Rus. 44/E1
Bryce Canyon National Park, Ut, US 92/D3
Brynmawr, Wal, UK 24/C3
Brzesko, Pol. 27/L4
Buala, Sol. 68/E5
Bucak, Turk. 50/B2
Bucaramanga, Col. 106/D2
Buchanan, Libr. 78/C5
Bucharest (cap.), Rom. 41/H4
Buchholz in der Nordheide, Ger. 29/G2
Bückeburg, Ger. 29/G4
Buckley, Wal, UK 23/E5
Bucyrus, Oh, US 94/D3
Budaörs, Hun. 40/D2
Budapest (cap.), Hun. 40/D2
Budaun, India 62/C2
Büdingen, Ger. 33/H1
Buea, Camr. 76/G7
Buenaventura, Col. 106/C3
Buenavista, Mex. 101/Q9
Buenos Aires (cap.), Arg. 109/E3
Buffalo, NY, US 95/V10
Buffalo Grove, Il, US 99/Q15
Buftea, Rom. 41/G3
Buga, Col. 106/C3
Bugaba, Pan. 103/F4
Bugojno, Bosn. 40/C3
Bugul'ma, Rus. 43/M5
Buguruslan, Rus. 45/K1
Bühl, Ger. 37/E2
Buhuşi, Rom. 41/H2
Bujumbura (cap.), Buru. 82/E1
Bukavu, D.R. Congo 82/E1
Bukhoro, Uzb. 46/G6
Bukittinggi, Indo. 66/B4
Bukoba, Tanz. 82/F1
Bulan, Phil. 67/F1
Bulancak, Turk. 44/F4
Bulandshahr, India 62/C2
Bulawayo, Zim. 82/E5
Bulgaria (ctry.) 41/G4
Bullhead City, Az, US 92/D4
Bulukumba, Indo. 67/F5
Bumba, D.R. Congo 77/K7
Bundaberg, Austl. 72/D4
Bünde, Ger. 29/F4
Būndi, India 62/C2
Bunia, D.R. Congo 77/M7
Bunschoten, Neth. 28/C4
Bunya Park, Austl. 72/E6
Buon Me Thuot, Viet. 65/E3
Būr Sa'īd (Port Said), Egypt 49/C4
Būr Sūdān, Sudan 52/C5
Buraydah, SAr. 52/D3
Burbank, Ca, US 92/C4
Burbank, Il, US 99/Q16
Burdur, Turk. 50/B2
Burdwān, India 62/E3
Büren, Ger. 29/F5
Būrewāla, Pak. 53/K2
Burg, Ger. 26/F2
Burgdorf, Ger. 29/H4
Burgess Hill, Eng, UK 25/F5
Burghausen, Ger. 40/A1
Burgos, Sp. 34/D1
Burgstall (Postal), It. 37/H4
Burgsteinfurt, Ger. 29/E4
Burgwedel, Ger. 29/G3
Burhaniye, Turk. 44/C5
Burhānpur, India 62/C3
Burien, Wa, US 99/C3
Buriram, Thai. 65/C3
Burjasot, Sp. 35/E3
Burkburnett, Tx, US 93/H4
Burkina Faso (ctry.) 79/E3
Burlingame, Ca, US 99/K11
Burlington, Ia, US 91/L5
Burlington, NC, US 97/J2
Burlington, On, Can. 95/T9
Burnham-on-Sea, Eng, UK 24/D4
Burnie-Somerset, Austl. 73/C4
Burnley, Eng, UK 23/F4
Burntwood, Eng, UK 25/E1
Burrel, Alb. 40/D5
Burriana, Sp. 35/E3
Bursa, Turk. 44/D4
Burscheid, Ger. 29/E6
Burton, Mi, US 99/E6
Burton upon Trent, Eng, UK 23/G6
Burundi (ctry.) 82/E1
Bury, Eng, UK 23/F4
Bury Saint Edmunds, Eng, UK 25/G2
Bushey, Eng, UK 25/F3
Busko-Zdrój, Pol. 27/L3
Bussum, Neth. 28/C4
Busto Arsizio, It. 33/H4
Butare, Rwa. 82/E1
Butembo, D.R. Congo 77/L7
Butiá, Braz. 108/B4
Butler, Pa, US 94/E3
Butte-Silver Bow County, Mt, US 90/E4
Butterworth, Malay. 66/B2
Butuan, Phil. 67/G2
Buturlinovka, Rus. 45/G2
Butzbach, Ger. 33/H1
Buxtehude, Ger. 29/G2
Buxton, Eng, UK 23/G5
Buy, Rus. 42/J4
Buyant-Uhaa, Mong. 54/G3
Buynaksk, Rus. 45/H4
Büyükçekmece, Turk. 51/M6
Buzău, Rom. 41/H3
Buzuluk, Rus. 45/K1
Bydgoszcz, Pol. 27/J2
Bykhov, Bela. 44/D1
Bytom, Pol. 27/K3
Bytów, Pol. 27/J1

C

Ca Mau, Viet. 65/D4
Caazapá, Par. 109/E2
Cabaiguán, Cuba 103/G1
Cabañaquinta, Sp. 34/C1
Cabanatuan, Phil. 68/B3
Cabimas, Ven. 106/D1
Cabinda, Ang. 82/B2
Cabo Frio, Braz. 108/D2
Cabo San Lucas, Mex. 100/C4
Cabo San Lucas (cape), Mex. 100/C4
Cabot (str.), NS,NF, Can. 87/K4
Cabra, Sp. 34/C4
Cabugao, Phil. 61/J5
Caçador, Braz. 108/B3
Čačak, Serb. 40/E4
Caçapava, Braz. 108/H8
Cáceres, Braz. 106/G7
Cáceres, Sp. 34/B3
Cacheu, GBis. 78/A3
Cachoeira do Sul, Braz. 108/A4
Cachoeira Paulista, Braz. 108/H7
Cachoeirinha, Braz. 108/B4
Cachoeiro de Itapemirim, Braz. 108/D2
Čadca, Slvk. 27/K4
Cadillac, Mi, US 94/C2
Cadiz, Phil. 67/F1
Cádiz, Sp. 34/B4
Cádiz, Golfo de (gulf), Port.,Sp. 34/B4
Caen, Fr. 32/C2
Caerphilly, Wal, UK 24/C3
Cagliari, It. 38/A3
Cagnes-sur-Mer, Fr. 33/G5
Caguas, PR 104/E3
Cahors, Fr. 32/D4
Cahul, Mol. 41/J3
Caibarién, Cuba 103/G1
Caicó, Braz. 107/L5
Caieiras, Braz. 108/G8
Cairns, Austl. 72/B2
Cairo, Ga, US 97/G4
Cairo (cap.), Egypt 49/B5
Cajamarca, Peru 106/C5
Calabar, Nga. 79/H5
Calabozo, Ven. 106/E2
Calafat, Rom. 40/F4
Calahorra, Sp. 34/E1
Calais, Fr. 30/A2
Calama, Chile 109/C1
Călăraşi, Rom. 41/H3
Calatayud, Sp. 34/E2
Calbayog, Phil. 67/F1
Caldas da Rainha, Port. 34/A3
Caldas Novas, Braz. 108/B1
Caledon, On, Can. 95/T8
Caleta Olivia, Arg. 109/C6
Calexico, Ca, US 92/D4
Calgary, Ab, Can. 90/E3
Cali, Col. 106/C3
Calicut (Kozhikode), India 62/C5
California (state), US 92/B3
California (gulf), Mex. 92/D5
Callao, Peru 106/C6
Callaway, Fl, US 97/G4
Callosa de Segura, Sp. 35/E3
Caloundra, Austl. 72/D4
Calpulálpan, Mex. 101/L7
Caltagirone, It. 38/D4
Caltanissetta, It. 38/D4
Caluire-et-Cuire, Fr. 36/A6
Calumet City, Il, US 99/Q16
Calviá, Sp. 35/G3
Calvillo, Mex. 100/E4
Cam Pha, Viet. 65/D1
Cam Ranh, Viet. 65/E4
Camaçari, Braz. 107/L6
Camagüey, Cuba 103/G1
Camaiore, It. 33/J5
Camajuaní, Cuba 103/G1
Camaquã, Braz. 108/B4
Camargo, Sp. 34/D1
Camas, Sp. 34/B4
Cambará, Braz. 108/B2
Cambé, Braz. 108/B2
Cambodia (ctry.) 65/D3
Cambrai, Fr. 30/C3
Cambridge, Oh, US 94/D3
Cambridge, Md, US 97/J2
Cambridge, Ma, US 95/G3
Cambridge, On, Can. 95/S9
Cambridge, Eng, UK 25/G2
Cambrils, Sp. 35/F2
Camden, NJ, US 94/F4
Cameroon (ctry.), Camr. 76/H7
Cametá, Braz. 107/J4
Camiri, Bol. 106/F8
Camoapa, Nic. 102/E3
Camocim, Braz. 107/K4
Campbell, Ca, US 99/L12
Campbell River, BC, Can. 90/B3
Campbellsville, Ky, US 97/G2
Campeche, Mex. 102/D2
Campeche (bay), Mex. 101/G5
Campina Grande, Braz. 107/L5
Campinas, Braz. 108/F7
Campo Belo, Braz. 108/C2
Campo de la Cruz, Col. 103/H4
Campo Formoso, Braz. 107/K6
Campo Grande, Braz. 107/H8
Campo Largo, Braz. 108/B3
Campo Limpo Paulista, Braz. 108/G8
Campo Maior, Braz. 107/K4
Campo Mourão, Braz. 108/A3
Campoalegre, Col. 106/C3
Campobasso, It. 40/B5
Campos do Jordão, Braz. 108/H7
Campos dos Goytacazes, Braz. 108/D2
Campos Novos, Braz. 108/B3
Çan, Turk. 41/H5
Can Tho, Viet. 65/D4
Canada (ctry.) 86/*
Cañada de Gómez, Arg. 109/D3
Çanakkale, Turk. 41/H5
Canandaigua, NY, US 94/E3
Cananea, Mex. 92/E5
Canary (isls.) 76/B2
Cañas, CR 102/E4
Canaveral (cape), Fl, US 97/H4
Canavieiras, Braz. 107/L7
Canberra (cap.), Austr. 73/D2
Cancún, Mex. 102/E1
Candeias, Braz. 107/L6
Cândido Mota, Braz. 108/B2
Candon, Phil. 61/J5
Canela, Braz. 108/B4
Cangas, Sp. 34/A1
Cangas de Narcea, Sp. 34/B1
Cangzhou, China 59/D3
Canicatti, It. 38/C4
Canindé, Braz. 107/L4
Çankırı, Turk. 44/E4
Cannanore, India 62/C5
Cannes, Fr. 33/G5
Cannock, Eng, UK 24/D1
Canoas, Braz. 108/B4
Canoinhas, Braz. 108/B3
Canosa di Puglia, It. 40/C5
Cantaura, Ven. 106/F2
Canterbury, Eng, UK 25/H4
Canton, Il, US 91/L5
Canton, Ms, US 93/K4
Canton, Oh, US 94/D3
Canton, Mi, US 99/E7
Cantù, It. 33/H4
Canvey Island, Eng, UK 25/G3
Canyon, Tx, US 93/G4
Canyonlands National Park, Ut, US 92/E3
Cao Bang, Viet. 65/D1
Cao Lanh, Viet. 65/D4
Cap-de-la-Madeleine, Qu, Can. 95/F2
Cap-Haïtien, Haiti 103/H2
Capanema, Braz. 107/J4
Capannori, It. 33/J5
Capão Bonito, Braz. 108/B3
Caparica, Port. 35/P10
Cape Breton (isl.), Can. 95/J2
Cape Coast, Gha. 79/E5
Cape Cod Nat'l Seashore, Ma, US 95/G3
Cape Coral, Fl, US 97/H5
Cape Girardeau, Mo, US 93/K3
Cape Hatteras Nat'l Seashore, NC, US 97/K3
Cape Town (cap.), SAfr. 80/L10
Cape Verde (ctry.) 74/J9
Cape York (pen.), Austl. 70/G2
Capelinha, Braz. 108/D1
Capitão Poço, Braz. 107/J4
Čapljina, Bosn. 40/C4
Capua, It. 40/B5
Caracal, Rom. 41/G3
Caracas (cap.), Ven. 106/E1
Caraguatatuba, Braz. 108/H8
Carangola, Braz. 108/D2
Caransebeş, Rom. 40/F3
Carapicuíba, Braz. 108/G8
Caratinga, Braz. 108/D1
Caravaca de la Cruz, Sp. 34/E3
Carazinho, Braz. 109/F2
Carballo, Sp. 34/A1
Carbondale, Pa, US 94/F3
Carbonia, It. 38/A3
Carcagente, Sp. 35/E3
Carcassonne, Fr. 32/E5
Cárdenas, Mex. 102/C2
Cárdenas, Mex. 102/B1
Cárdenas, Cuba 103/F1
Cardiff (cap.), Wal, UK 24/C4
Carei, Rom. 40/F2
Cariacica, Braz. 108/D2
Cariaco, Ven. 104/F5
Cariamanga, Ecu. 106/C4
Caribbean (sea) 84/J8
Caribou, Me, US 95/G2
Caripito, Ven. 104/F5
Carletonville, SAfr. 80/P13
Carlisle, Pa, US 94/E3
Carlisle, Eng, UK 23/F2
Carlos M. De Cespedes, Cuba 103/G1
Carlsbad, NM, US 93/F4
Carlton, Eng, UK 23/G6
Carmagnola, It. 33/G4
Carmichael, Ca, US 99/M9
Carmo do Paranaíba, Braz. 108/C1
Carmona, Sp. 34/C4
Carnaxide, Port. 35/P10
Carnot, CAfr. 76/J7
Carol Stream, Il, US 99/P16
Carolina, PR 104/E3
Caroline (isls), Micr. 68/D4
Carouge, Swi. 36/C5
Carpathian (mts.), Eur. 27/J4
Carpentaria (gulf), Austl. 70/F2
Carpentersville, Il, US 99/P15
Carpentras, Fr. 32/F4
Carpi, It. 33/J4
Carrara, It. 33/J4
Carrickfergus, NI, UK 22/C2
Carrollton, Ga, US 97/G3
Çarşamba, Turk. 44/F4
Carson City (cap.), Nv, US 92/C3
Cartagena, Col. 103/H4
Cartagena, Sp. 35/E4
Cartago, Col. 106/C3
Cartago, CR 103/F4
Cartersville, Ga, US 97/G3
Carthage, Mo, US 93/J3
Carthage (Qarţājannah) (ruin), Tun. 38/B4
Caruaru, Braz. 107/L5
Carúpano, Ven. 106/F1
Carvin, Fr. 30/B3
Cary, NC, US 97/J3
Cary, Il, US 99/P15
Casa Branca, Braz. 108/F6
Casa Grande, Az, US 92/E4
Casablanca, Mor. 76/D1
Casal di Principe, It. 38/D2
Casale Monferrato, It. 33/H4
Casarano, It. 39/F2
Cascade (range), Wa, US 90/C5
Cascade-Fairwood, Or, US 99/C3
Cascais, Port. 35/P10
Cascavel, Braz. 107/L4
Cascavel, Braz. 109/F1
Cascina, It. 33/J5
Caserta, It. 40/B5
Casilda, Arg. 109/D3
Casper, Wy, US 91/G5
Caspian (sea), Asia 46/E5
Cassilândia, Braz. 108/B1
Cassino, It. 40/A5
Castanhal, Braz. 107/J4
Castaños, Mex. 96/C5
Castel del Piano, It. 38/C1
Castellammare di Stabia, It. 40/B5
Castellar del Vallès, Sp. 35/G2
Castelldefels, Sp. 35/K7
Castellón de la Plana, Sp. 35/E3
Castelo Branco, Port. 34/B3
Castelvetrano, It. 38/C4
Castilla, Peru 106/B5
Castleford, Eng, UK 23/G4
Castres, Fr. 32/E5
Castricum, Neth. 28/B3
Castries (cap.), StL. 104/F4
Castro, Chile 109/B5
Castro, Braz. 108/B3
Castro Valley, Ca, US 99/K11
Castrop-Rauxel, Ger. 29/E5
Castrovillari, It. 38/E3
Catacamas, Hon. 102/E3
Cataguases, Braz. 108/L6
Cataiñgan, Phil. 67/F1
Catalão, Braz. 108/C1
Catamarca, Arg. 109/C2
Catanduva, Braz. 108/B2
Catania, It. 38/D4
Catanzaro, It. 38/E3
Catarman, Phil. 67/F1
Catemaco, Mex. 102/C2
Caterham and Warlingham, Eng, UK 25/F4
Cativá, Pan. 103/G4
Caucaia, Braz. 107/L4
Caucasia, Col. 103/H5
Caucasus (mts.), Geo. 45/G4
Cauquenes, Chile 109/B4
Cavaillon, Fr. 32/F5
Caxambu, Braz. 108/J6
Caxias, Braz. 107/K4
Caxias do Sul, Braz. 108/B4
Cayce, SC, US 97/H3
Çayeli, Turk. 45/G4
Cayenne (cap.), FrG. 107/H3
Cayman (isls.), UK 103/F2
Cazin, Bosn. 40/B3
Ceará-Mirim, Braz. 107/L5
Cebu, Phil. 67/F1
Ceccano, It. 38/C2
Cecina, It. 33/J5
Cedar City, Ut, US 92/D3
Cegléd, Hun. 40/D2
Celaya, Mex. 101/E4
Celebes (isl.), Indo. 67/E4
Celebes (sea), Asia 67/F3
Celina, Oh, US 94/C3
Celle, Ger. 29/H3
Centenario, Arg. 109/C4
Center Point, Al, US 97/G3
Cento, It. 33/J4
Central African Republic (ctry.) 77/J6
Central Siberian (plat.), Rus. 47/L3
Centralia, Il, US 93/K3
Centralia, Wa, US 90/C4
Cerdanyola del Vallès, Sp. 35/L7
Ceres, Braz. 107/J7
Ceres, SAfr. 80/L10
Cereté, Col. 103/H4
Cergy, Fr. 30/B5
Cerignola, It. 40/B5
Çerkezköy, Turk. 41/J5
Çermik, Turk. 50/D2
Černavodă, Rom. 41/J3
Cerro Azul, Mex. 102/B1
Cerro de Pasco, Peru 106/C6
Cervia, It. 33/K4
Cesena, It. 33/K4
Cesenatico, It. 33/K4
Cēsis, Lat. 42/E4
České Budějovice, Czh. 33/L2
Çeşme, Turk. 39/K3
Cetinje, Serb. 40/D4
Ceuta, Sp. 34/C5
Ceyhan, Turk. 49/D1
Ceylânpınar, Turk. 50/E2
Ceylon (isl.), SrL. 62/D6
Chachapoyas, Peru 106/C5
Chachoengsao, Thai. 65/C3
Chad (lake), Afr. 76/H5
Chad (ctry.) 77/J4
Chālakudi, India 62/C5
Chalatenango, ESal. 102/D3
Chalco, Mex. 101/R10
Chalfont Saint Peter, Eng, UK 25/F3
Challans, Fr. 32/C3
Chalon-sur-Saône, Fr. 36/A4
Châlons-sur-Marne, Fr. 31/D6
Chālūs, Iran 51/G2
Cham, Ger. 33/K2
Chaman, Pak. 53/J2
Chamba, India 53/L2
Chambas, Cuba 103/G1
Chambersburg, Pa, US 94/E4
Chambéry, Fr. 32/F4
Chambly, Qu, Can. 95/P7
Champaign, Il, US 91/L5
Champlain (lake), Can.,US 94/F2
Champotón, Mex. 102/D2
Champs-sur-Marne, Fr. 30/B6
Chandausi, India 62/C2
Chanderi, India 62/C3
Chandīgarh, India 53/L2
Chandrapur, India 62/C4
Changchun, China 59/F2
Changde, China 61/F2
Changhua, Tai. 61/J3
Changhŭng, SKor. 58/D5
Changsha, China 61/G2
Changshu, China 59/L8
Changshun, China 61/E3
Changsŏng, SKor. 58/D5
Changsŭngp'o, SKor. 58/E5
Ch'angwŏn, SKor. 56/A3
Changzhi, China 59/C3
Changzhou, China 59/K8
Chanthaburi, Thai. 65/C3
Chanute, Ks, US 93/J3
Chapala, Mex. 100/E4
Chapayevsk, Rus. 45/J1
Chapecó, Braz. 108/A3
Chapel Hill, NC, US 97/J3
Chapeltown, Eng, UK 23/G5
Charata, Arg. 109/D2
Chārīkār, Afg. 53/J1
Chärjew, Trkm. 46/G6
Charleroi, Belg. 31/D3
Charleston, Il, US 97/F2
Charleston, SC, US 97/J3
Charleston (cap.), WV, US 94/D4
Charleville-Mézières, Fr. 31/D4
Charlotte, NC, US 97/H3
Charlotte Amalie, USVI 104/E3
Charlottetown (cap.), PE, Can. 95/J2
Chartres, Fr. 32/D2
Chascomús, Arg. 109/E4
Château-Thierry, Fr. 30/C5
Châteaudun, Fr. 32/D2
Châteauguay, Qu, Can. 95/N7
Châteauroux, Fr. 32/D3
Châtelet, Belg. 31/D3
Châtellerault, Fr. 32/D3
Chatham, NB, Can. 95/H2
Chatham, On, Can. 94/D3
Chatham, Eng, UK 25/G4
Chatrapur, India 62/E4
Chattanooga, Tn, US 97/G3
Chau Doc, Viet. 65/D4
Chaudfontaine, Belg. 31/E2
Chauk, Myan. 60/B4
Chaumont, Fr. 36/B1
Chaykovskiy, Rus. 43/M4
Cheb, Czh. 33/K1
Cheboksary, Rus. 43/K4
Chech'ŏn, SKor. 56/A2
Cheektowaga, NY, US 95/V10
Chegdomyn, Rus. 55/L1
Chegutu, Zim. 82/F4
Cheju, SKor. 55/K5
Chełm, Pol. 27/M3
Chełmno, Pol. 27/K2
Chelmsford, Eng, UK 25/G3
Chełmża, Pol. 27/K2
Cheltenham, Eng, UK 24/D3
Chelyabinsk, Rus. 43/P5
Chemnitz, Ger. 26/G3
Chennai (Madras), India 62/D5
Chenôve, Fr. 36/A3
Chenzhou, China 61/G3
Cherbourg, Fr. 32/C2
Cherchell, Alg. 76/F1
Cheremkhovo, Rus. 54/E1
Cherepovets, Rus. 42/H4
Cherkasy, Ukr. 44/E2
Cherkessk, Rus. 45/G3
Chernihiv, Ukr. 44/D2
Chernivtsi, Ukr. 41/G1
Chernushka, Rus. 43/N4
Cherven Bryag, Bul. 41/G4
Chervonohrad, Ukr. 27/N3
Chesapeake (bay), US 89/L4
Chesham, Eng, UK 25/F3
Cheshunt, Eng, UK 25/F3
Chester, Pa, US 94/F4
Chester, Eng, UK 23/F5
Chester-le-Street, Eng, UK 23/G2
Chesterfield, Eng, UK 23/G5
Chetumal, Mex. 102/D2
Cheyenne (cap.), Wy, US 91/G5
Chhatarpur, India 62/C3
Chhindwāra, India 62/C3
Chiai, Tai. 61/J4
Chiang Mai, Thai. 65/B2
Chiapa de Corzo, Mex. 102/C2
Chiat'ura, Geo. 45/G4
Chiautempan, Mex. 101/L7
Chiavari, It. 33/H4
Chiba, Japan 57/G3
Chibuto, Moz. 81/F2
Chicago, Il, US 99/Q16
Chicago Heights, Il, US 99/Q16
Chicago Ridge, Il, US 99/Q16
Chīchāwatni, Pak. 53/K2
Chichester, Eng, UK 25/F5
Chichibu, Japan 57/F3
Chichicastenango, Guat. 102/D3
Chichigalpa, Nic. 102/E3
Chickasha, Ok, US 93/H4
Chiclana de la Frontera, Sp. 34/B4

Chiclayo, Peru 106/C5
Chico, Ca, US 92/B3
Chicoloapan, Mex. 101/R10
Chicopee, Ma, US 95/F3
Chieti, It. 40/B4
Chigasaki, Japan 57/F3
Chigorodó, Col. 103/G5
Chihuahua, Mex. 96/B4
Chikballāpur, India 62/C5
Chikhli, India 62/C3
Chikmagalūr, India 62/C5
Chilapa de Álvarez, Mex. 102/B2
Chilaw, SrL. 62/C6
Chile (ctry.), Chile 105/B6
Chilecito, Arg. 109/C2
Chililabombwe, Zam. 82/E3
Chillán, Chile 109/B4
Chilliwack, BC, Can. 90/C3
Chilpancingo de los Bravos, Mex. 102/B2
Chimalhuacán, Mex. 101/R10
Chimaltenango, Guat. 102/D3
Chimbay, Uzb. 46/F5
Chimbote, Peru 106/C5
Chimichagua, Col. 103/H4
Chimoio, Moz. 82/F4
China (ctry.) 48/J6
Chinandega, Nic. 102/E3
Chincha Alta, Peru 106/C6
Chingleput, India 62/C5
Chingola, Zam. 82/E3
Chinhae, SKor. 56/A3
Chinhoyi, Zim. 82/F4
Chiniot, Pak. 53/K2
Chinju, SKor. 58/E5
Chino, Japan 57/F3
Chioggia, It. 33/K4
Chipata, Zam. 82/F3
Chipiona, Sp. 34/B4
Chiplūn, India 62/B4
Chippenham, Eng, UK 24/D4
Chiquimula, Guat. 102/D3
Chiquimulilla, Guat. 102/D3
Chiquinquirá, Col. 106/D2
Chīrāla, India 62/D4
Chirchiq, Uzb. 46/G5
Chirripó, CR 103/F4
Chishtiān Mandi, Pak. 53/K3
Chişinău (cap.), Mol. 41/J2
Chistopol', Rus. 43/L5
Chita, Rus. 54/G1
Chitose, Japan 55/N3
Chitradurga, India 62/C5
Chitrakut, India 62/D2
Chitré, Pan. 103/F5
Chittagong, Bang. 60/A4
Chittoor, India 62/C5
Chitungwiza, Zim. 82/F4
Chivasso, It. 33/G4
Chivilcoy, Arg. 109/D3
Chlef, Alg. 76/F1
Choch'iwŏn, SKor. 58/D4
Chodavaram, India 62/D4
Chodov, Czh. 33/K1
Chodzież, Pol. 27/J2
Chōfu, Japan 57/F3
Choisy-le-Roi, Fr. 30/B6
Chojnice, Pol. 27/J2
Cholet, Fr. 32/C3
Cholula de Rivadabia, Mex. 101/L7
Choluteca, Hon. 102/E3
Choma, Zam. 82/E4
Chŏmch'on, SKor. 56/A2
Chomutov, Czh. 33/K1
Chon Buri, Thai. 65/C3
Ch'ŏnan, SKor. 58/D4
Chone, Ecu. 106/B4
Ch'ŏngjin, NKor. 58/E2
Chŏngju, SKor. 58/D5
Ch'ŏngju, SKor. 58/D4
Chongqing, China 61/E2
Ch'ŏngsong, SKor. 56/A2
Chŏnju, SKor. 58/D5
Chorley, Eng, UK 23/F4
Chortkiv, Ukr. 44/C2
Chorzów, Pol. 27/K3
Chōshi, Japan 57/G3
Choszczno, Pol. 27/H2
Chota Nagpur (plat.), India 62/D3
Choybalsan, Mong. 54/G2
Christchurch, Eng, UK 25/E5
Christchurch, NZ 71/R11
Chrudim, Czh. 33/L2
Chrzanów, Pol. 27/K3
Chukchi (pen.), Rus. 47/T3
Chula Vista, Ca, US 92/C4
Chulucanas, Peru 106/B5
Ch'unch'ŏn, SKor. 58/D4
Ch'ungju, SKor. 58/D4
Ch'ungmu, SKor. 56/A3
Chuquicamata, Chile 109/C1
Chur, Swi. 37/F4
Churachandpur, India 60/B3
Churu, India 62/B2
Chusovoy, Rus. 43/N4
Chuxiong, China 60/D3
Chuzhou, China 61/H1
Ciadîr-Lunga, Mol. 41/J2
Ciamis, Indo. 66/C5
Ciampino, It. 38/C2
Cianjur, Indo. 66/C5
Cicero, Il, US 99/Q16
Ciechanów, Pol. 27/L2
Ciego de Ávila, Cuba 103/G1
Ciénaga, Col. 103/H4
Ciénaga de Oro, Col. 103/H4
Cienfuegos, Cuba 103/F1
Cieplice Śląskie Zdrój, Pol. 27/H3
Cieszyn, Pol. 27/K4
Cieza, Sp. 34/E3
Cifuentes, Cuba 103/F1
Cihanbeyli, Turk. 50/C2
Cijulang, Indo. 66/C5
Cilacap, Indo. 66/C5
Cîmpia Turzii, Rom. 41/F2
Cîmpina, Rom. 41/G3
Cîmpulung, Rom. 41/G3
Cîmpulung Moldovenesc, Rom. 41/G2
Cincinnati, Oh, US 97/G2
Çine, Turk. 50/B2
Cintalapa de Figueroa, Mex. 102/C2
Cipolletti, Arg. 109/C4
Cirebon, Indo. 66/C5
Cirencester, Eng, UK 24/E3
Cisnădie, Rom. 41/G3
Cisterna di Latina, It. 38/C2
Citlaltépetl (vol.), Mex. 101/M7
Citrus Heights, Ca, US 99/M9
Città di Castello, It. 33/K5
Ciudad Acuña, Mex. 93/G5
Ciudad Altamirano, Mex. 101/E5
Ciudad Bolívar, Ven. 106/F2
Ciudad Camargo, Mex. 96/B5
Ciudad Constitución, Mex. 100/C3
Ciudad de Dolores Hidalgo, Mex. 101/E4
Ciudad de Río Grande, Mex. 100/E4
Ciudad del Carmen, Mex. 102/D2
Ciudad Delicias, Mex. 96/B4
Ciudad Fernández, Mex. 102/B1
Ciudad Frontera, Mex. 96/C5
Ciudad Guayana, Ven. 106/F2
Ciudad Guzmán, Mex. 100/E5
Ciudad Hidalgo, Mex. 101/E5
Ciudad Ixtepec, Mex. 102/C2
Ciudad Juárez, Mex. 92/F5
Ciudad Lerdo, Mex. 100/E3
Ciudad Madero, Mex. 102/B1
Ciudad Mante, Mex. 102/B1
Ciudad Mendoza, Mex. 101/M8
Ciudad Miguel Alemán, Mex. 96/D5
Ciudad Obregón, Mex. 100/C3
Ciudad Ojeda, Ven. 106/D1
Ciudad Real, Sp. 34/D3
Ciudad Rodrigo, Sp. 34/B2
Ciudad Serdán, Mex. 101/M8
Ciudad Valles, Mex. 102/B1
Ciudad Victoria, Mex. 101/F4
Ciutadella de Menorca, Sp. 35/G3
Civitavecchia, It. 38/B1
Cixi, China 59/L9
Cizre, Turk. 50/E2
Claremont, NH, US 95/F3
Claremore, Ok, US 93/J3
Clarksburg, WV, US 97/H2
Clarksdale, Ms, US 93/K4
Clarksville, Tn, US 97/G2
Clausthal-Zellerfeld, Ger. 29/H5
Claveria, Phil. 61/J5
Clawson, Mi, US 99/F6
Clay Cross-North Wingfield, Eng, UK 23/G5
Clearwater, Fl, US 97/H5
Cleburne, Tx, US 93/H4
Cleethorpes, Eng, UK 23/H4
Clemson, SC, US 97/H3
Clermont-Ferrand, Fr. 32/E4
Clevedon, Eng, UK 24/D4
Cleveland, Ms, US 93/K4
Cleveland, Oh, US 94/D3
Cleveland, Tn, US 97/G3
Clichy, Fr. 30/B6
Clinton, Ms, US 93/K4
Clinton, Ok, US 93/H4
Clinton, Ia, US 91/L5
Clinton, Mi, US 99/G6
Clonmel, Ire. 21/B10
Cloppenburg, Ger. 29/F3
Clorinda, Arg. 109/E2
Clovis, Ca, US 92/C3
Clovis, NM, US 93/G4
Cluj-Napoca, Rom. 41/F2
Cluses, Fr. 36/C5
Clyde, Firth of (inlet), Sc, UK 22/C1
Coacalco, Mex. 101/Q9
Coachella, Ca, US 92/C4
Coalville, Eng, UK 23/G6
Coari, Braz. 106/F4
Coast (mts.), Can.,US 90/A2
Coast Ranges (range), Ca, US 88/B4
Coatepec, Mex. 101/N7
Coatzacoalcos, Mex. 102/C2
Cobán, Guat. 102/D3
Cobija, Bol. 106/E6
Cobourg, On, Can. 94/E3
Coburg, Ger. 33/J1
Cochabamba, Bol. 106/E7
Cochin, India 62/C6
Cocoa, Fl, US 97/H4
Codlea, Rom. 41/G3
Codó, Braz. 107/K4
Coelho Neto, Braz. 107/K4
Coesfeld, Ger. 29/E5
Coffeyville, Ks, US 93/J3
Coffs Harbour, Austl. 73/E1
Cognac, Fr. 32/C4
Coihaique, Chile 109/B6
Coimbatore, India 62/C5
Coimbra, Port. 34/A2
Coín, Sp. 34/C4
Cojutepeque, ESal. 102/D3
Colatina, Braz. 108/D1
Colchester, Eng, UK 25/G3
Coldwater, Mi, US 94/C3
Çölemerik, Turk. 51/E2
Coleraine, NI, UK 22/B1
Colima, Mex. 100/E5
Collado-Villalba, Sp. 35/N8
College, Ak, US 85/J3
College Station, Tx, US 93/H5
Collegno, It. 33/G4
Collierville, Tn, US 93/K4
Collingwood, On, Can. 94/D2
Colmar, Fr. 36/D1
Colmenar Viejo, Sp. 35/N8
Colne, Eng, UK 23/F4
Cologne (Köln), Ger. 31/F2
Colombia (ctry.), Col. 106/D3
Colombo, Braz. 108/B3
Colombo (cap.), SrL. 62/C6
Colomiers, Fr. 32/D5
Colón, Cuba 103/F1
Colón, Pan. 103/G4
Colorado (riv.), Tx, US 96/C3
Colorado (riv.), Arg. 109/C4
Colorado (state), US 92/F3
Colorado (riv.), US 88/D5
Colorado Springs, Co, US 93/F3
Colquiri, Bol. 106/E7
Columbia, Mo, US 93/J3
Columbia, Md, US 97/J2
Columbia, Tn, US 97/G3
Columbia (plat.), US 90/C2
Columbia (cap.), SC, US 97/H3
Columbia (riv.), Or,Wa, US 90/C4
Columbus, Ne, US 91/J5
Columbus, Ga, US 97/G3
Columbus, Ms, US 97/F3
Columbus, In, US 97/G2
Columbus (cap.), Oh, US 94/D4
Colwyn Bay, Wal, UK 22/E5
Comalcalco, Mex. 102/C2
Comănești, Rom. 41/H2
Comayagua, Hon. 102/E3
Combs-la-Ville, Fr. 30/B6
Comé, Ben. 79/F5
Comendador, DRep. 103/J2
Comilla, Bang. 63/F3
Comines, Belg. 30/B2
Comitán de Domínguez, Mex. 102/C2
Como, It. 37/F6
Comodoro Rivadavia, Arg. 109/C6
Comoros (ctry.) 81/G5
Compiègne, Fr. 30/B5
Compostela, Mex. 100/D4
Comrat, Mol. 41/J2
Conakry (cap.), Gui. 78/B4
Concarneau, Fr. 32/B3
Conceição do Araguaia, Braz. 107/J5
Concepción, Chile 109/B4
Concepción, Arg. 109/C2
Concepción, Par. 109/E1
Concepción del Uruguay, Arg. 109/E3
Conchal, Braz. 108/F7
Concord, NC, US 97/H3
Concord, Ca, US 99/K11
Concord (cap.), NH, US 95/G3
Concordia, Arg. 109/E3
Concórdia, Braz. 108/A3
Condado, Cuba 103/G1
Conegliano, It. 33/K4
Congleton, Eng, UK 23/F5
Congo (basin), D.R. Congo 77/K7
Congo (riv.), D.R. Congo 82/C1
Congo, Democratic Republic of the (ctry.) 74/E5
Congo, Republic of (ctry.) 74/D5
Congonhas, Braz. 108/D2
Conisbrough, Eng, UK 23/G5
Conneaut, Oh, US 94/D3
Connecticut (state), US 95/F3
Connellsville, Pa, US 94/E3
Connersville, In, US 97/G2
Conroe, Tx, US 93/J5
Conselheiro Lafaiete, Braz. 108/D2
Consett, Eng, UK 23/G2
Consolación del Sur, Cuba 103/F1
Constance (Bodensee) (lake), Ger.,Swi. 37/F2
Constanța, Rom. 41/J3
Constantine, Alg. 76/G1
Constitución, Chile 109/B4
Contai, India 62/E3
Contegem, Braz. 108/C1
Contramaestre, Cuba 103/G1
Conversano, It. 40/C5
Conway, Ar, US 93/J4
Conway, SC, US 97/J3
Conway, NH, US 95/G3
Cooch Behār, India 62/E2
Cook (mt.), NZ 71/R11
Cookeville, Tn, US 97/G2
Coonoor, India 62/C5
Coos Bay, Or, US 90/B5
Copenhagen (cap.), Den. 26/G1
Copertino, It. 39/F2
Copiapó, Chile 109/B2
Copperas Cove, Tx, US 93/H5
Coquimbo, Chile 109/B2
Coquitlam, BC, Can. 90/C3
Corabia, Rom. 41/G4
Coral (sea) 68/E6
Coral Gables, Fl, US 97/H5
Coral Sea Islands Territory (dpcy.), Austl. 72/B1
Coral Springs, Fl, US 97/H5
Corato, It. 40/C5
Corbeil-Essonnes, Fr. 32/E2
Corby, Eng, UK 25/F2
Corcovado, CR 103/F4
Cordeiro, Braz. 108/D2
Cordele, Ga, US 97/H4
Córdoba, Arg. 109/D3
Córdoba, Mex. 101/N8
Córdoba, Sp. 34/C4
Coria del Río, Sp. 34/B4
Corinth, Ms, US 97/F3
Corinth (Kórinthos) (ruin), Gre. 39/H4
Corinto, Nic. 102/E3
Corinto, Braz. 108/C1
Cork, Ire. 21/A11
Çorlu, Turk. 41/H5
Cornélio Procópio, Braz. 108/B2
Cornella, Sp. 35/L7
Corner Brook, Nf, Can. 95/K1
Corning, NY, US 94/E3
Cornwall, On, Can. 94/F2
Coro, Ven. 106/E1
Coroatá, Braz. 107/K4
Coromandel, Braz. 108/C1
Coromandel (coast), India 62/D5
Coron, Phil. 67/F1
Coronel, Chile 109/B4
Coronel Fabriciano, Braz. 108/D1
Coronel Oviedo, Par. 109/E2
Coronel Pringles, Arg. 109/D4
Coronel Suárez, Arg. 109/D4
Corozal, Col. 103/H4
Corozal, Belz. 102/D2
Corpus Christi, Tx, US 96/D5
Corralillo, Cuba 103/F1
Corrientes, Arg. 109/E2
Corsica (isl.), Fr. 38/A1
Corsicana, Tx, US 93/H4
Cortez, Co, US 92/E3
Cortland, NY, US 94/E3
Çorum, Turk. 44/E4
Corumbá, Braz. 106/G7
Corvallis, Or, US 90/C4
Cosamaloapan, Mex. 101/P8
Cosenza, It. 38/E3
Coshocton, Oh, US 94/D3
Coslada, Sp. 35/N9
Cosmópolis, Braz. 108/F7
Cosquín, Arg. 109/D3
Cossato, It. 33/H4
Costa Rica (ctry.), CR 103/F4
Cotabato, Phil. 67/F2
Côte D'Ivoire (ctry.) 78/D5
Côte-Saint-Luc, Qu, Can. 95/N7
Cotia, Braz. 108/G8
Cotonou, Ben. 79/F5
Cottbus, Ger. 27/H3
Coudekerque-Branche, Fr. 30/B1
Courcelles, Belg. 31/D3
Cournon-D'Auvergne, Fr. 32/E4
Courtenay, BC, Can. 86/D4
Coventry, Eng, UK 25/E2
Covilhã, Port. 34/B2
Covington, Ga, US 97/H3
Covington, Ky, US 97/G2
Cowes, Eng, UK 25/E5
Coxim, Braz. 107/H7
Coyotepec, Mex. 101/K7
Cozumel, Mex. 102/E1
Crailsheim, Ger. 33/J2
Craiova, Rom. 41/F3
Cramlington, Eng, UK 23/G1
Cran-Gevrier, Fr. 36/C6
Cranbourne, Austl. 73/G6
Cranbrook, BC, Can. 90/E3
Crater (lake), Or, US 92/B2
Crater Lake National Park, Or, US 92/B2
Crateús, Braz. 107/K5
Crato, Braz. 107/L5
Cravinhos, Braz. 108/C2
Crawfordsville, In, US 97/G1
Crawley, Eng, UK 25/F4
Creil, Fr. 30/B5
Crema, It. 33/H4
Cremona, It. 33/J4
Crest Hill, Il, US 99/P16
Crestview, Fl, US 97/G4
Crete (isl.), Gre. 39/J5
Créteil, Fr. 30/B6
Creutzwald-la-Croix, Fr. 31/F5
Crevillente, Sp. 35/E3
Crewe, Eng, UK 23/F5
Criciúma, Braz. 108/B4
Crimean (pen.), Ukr. 44/E3
Cristalina, Braz. 107/J7
Croatia (ctry.) 40/C3
Crosby, Eng, UK 23/E5
Crotone, It. 39/E3
Crowborough, Eng, UK 25/G4
Crowley, La, US 93/J5
Crown Point, In, US 94/C3
Crowthorne, Eng, UK 25/F4
Cruz Alta, Braz. 109/F2
Cruz das Almas, Braz. 107/L6
Cruz del Eje, Arg. 109/D3
Cruzeiro, Braz. 108/J7
Cruzeiro do Sul, Braz. 106/D5
Crystal Lake, Il, US 99/P15
Csongrád, Hun. 40/E2
Cuart de Poblet, Sp. 35/E3
Cuauhtémoc, Mex. 96/B4
Cuautitlán, Mex. 101/Q9
Cuautitlán Izcalli, Mex. 101/Q9
Cuautla, Mex. 101/L8
Cuba (ctry.), Cuba 103/F1
Cubatão, Braz. 108/G8
Çubuk, Turk. 44/E4
Cúcuta, Col. 103/H5
Cudahy, Wi, US 99/Q14
Cuddapah, India 62/C5
Cuenca, Ecu. 106/C4
Cuenca, Sp. 34/D2
Cuernavaca, Mex. 101/K8
Cueto, Cuba 103/H1
Cugir, Rom. 41/F3
Cuiabá, Braz. 107/G7
Cuijk, Neth. 28/C5
Cuilapa, Guat. 102/D3
Culemborg, Neth. 28/C5
Culiacán Rosales, Mex. 100/D3
Cullera, Sp. 35/E3
Culleredo, Sp. 34/A1
Cullman, Al, US 97/G3
Cumaná, Ven. 106/F1
Cumberland, Md, US 97/J2
Çumra, Turk. 50/C2
Cuneo, It. 33/G4
Cupertino, Ca, US 99/K12
Ćuprija, Serb. 40/E4
Curanilahue, Chile 109/B4
Curepipe, Mrts. 81/T15
Curicó, Chile 109/B3
Curitiba, Braz. 108/B3
Curitibanos, Braz. 108/B3
Currais Novos, Braz. 107/L5
Curtea de Argeș, Rom. 41/G3
Curup, Indo. 66/B4
Cururupu, Braz. 107/K4
Curuzú Cuatiá, Arg. 109/E2
Curvelo, Braz. 108/D1
Cusco, Peru 106/D6
Cutral-Có, Arg. 109/C4
Cuttack, India 62/E3
Cuxhaven, Ger. 29/F1
Cuyo, Phil. 67/F1
Cwmbran, Wal, UK 24/C3
Cyprus (ctry.) 49/C2
Czech Republic (ctry.) 27/H4
Częstochowa, Pol. 27/K3
Człuchów, Pol. 27/J2

D

Da Hinggan (mts.), China 55/J2
Da Lat, Viet. 65/E4
Da Nang, Viet. 65/E2
Da Xian, China 61/E2
Da'an, China 55/J2
Dabas, Hun. 40/D2
Dabou, C.d'Iv. 78/D5
Dabra, India 62/C2
Dąbrowa Górnicza, Pol. 27/K3
Dachau, Ger. 37/H1
Dādu, Pak. 62/A2
Dafang, China 60/E3
Dagana, Sen. 78/B2
Dagupan, Phil. 68/B3
Daharki, Pak. 62/A2
Dahūk, Iraq 51/E2
Daigo, Japan 57/G2
Daimiel, Sp. 34/D3
Dajabón, DRep. 103/J2
Dakar (cap.), Sen. 78/A3
Dakoro, Niger 79/G3
Dakovica, Serb. 40/E4
Dakovo, Cro. 40/D3
Dalaman, Turk. 50/B2
Dalandzadgad, Mong. 54/E3
Dalfsen, Neth. 28/D3
Dali, China 60/D3
Dalian, China 58/A3
Dallas, Tx, US 93/H4
Dal'negorsk, Rus. 55/M3
Dal'nerechensk, Rus. 55/L2
Daloa, C.d'Iv. 78/D5
Dalton, Ga, US 97/G3
Daltonganj, India 62/D3
Daly City, Ca, US 99/J11
Damān, India 62/B3
Damanhūr, Egypt 49/B4
Damascus (cap.), Syria 49/E3
Damietta (Dumyāṭ), Egypt 49/B4
Damoh, India 62/C3
Danané, C.d'Iv. 78/C5
Dandong, China 58/C2
Dangriga, Belz. 102/D2
Dangyang, China 61/F2
Danilov, Rus. 42/J4
Dankov, Rus. 44/F1
Danlí, Hon. 102/E3
Danube (riv.), Eur. 18/F4
Danube (delta), Rom. 41/J3
Danube, Mouths of the (delta), Rom.,Ukr. 41/J3
Danville, Ky, US 97/G2
Danville, Il, US 97/G1
Danville, Ca, US 99/K11
Dapaong, Togo 79/F4
Daphne, Al, US 97/G4
Daqing, China 55/K2
Dar es Salaam (cap.), Tanz. 82/G2
Dar'ā, Syria 49/E3
Daraga, Phil. 67/F1
Dārayyā, Syria 49/E3
Darbhanga, India 62/E2
Dardanelles (str.), Turk. 44/C4
Darhan, Mong. 54/F2
Darien, Il, US 99/P16
Darjiling, India 62/E2
Darling (riv.), Austl. 71/G6
Darlington, Eng, UK 23/G2
Darłowo, Pol. 27/J1
Darmstadt, Ger. 33/H2
Darnah, Libya 77/K1
Dartford, Eng, UK 25/G4
Dartmouth, NS, Can. 95/J2
Daru, PNG 68/D5
Daruvar, Cro. 40/C3
Darwen, Eng, UK 23/F4
Darwin, Austl. 68/C6
Dashhowuz, Trkm. 46/F5
Dassa-Zoumé, Ben. 79/F5
Datia, India 62/C2
Datong, China 59/C2
Datteln, Ger. 29/E5
Daugavpils, Lat. 42/E5
Daund, India 62/B4
Dāvangere, India 62/C5
Davao, Phil. 67/G2
Davenport, Ia, US 91/L5
Daventry, Eng, UK 25/E2
Daveyton, SAfr. 80/Q13
David, Pan. 103/F4
Davis, Ca, US 99/L9
Davlekanovo, Rus. 43/M5
Dawei (Tavoy), Myan. 65/B3
Dax, Fr. 32/C5
Dayong, China 61/F2
Dayrūt, Egypt 50/B5

F

G

Gracias, Hon. 102/D3
Gradačac, Bosn. 40/D3
Grafton, Austl. 73/E1
Grahamstown, SAfr. 80/D4
Grajaú, Braz. 107/J5
Grajewo, Pol. 27/M2
Gran Chaco (plain), Arg.,Par. 109/D2
Granada, Col. 106/D3
Granada, Nic. 102/E4
Granada, Sp. 34/D4
Granadilla de Abona, Canl. 35/X16
Grand Canyon National Park, Az, US 92/D3
Grand Canyon-Parashant Nat'l Mon., Az, US 92/D3
Grand Cayman (isl.), Cay. 103/F2
Grand Forks, ND, US 91/J4
Grand Haven, Mi, US 94/C3
Grand Portage Nat'l Mon., Mn, US 91/L4
Grand Rapids, Mi, US 94/C3
Grand Rapids, Mn, US 91/K4
Grand Staircase-Escalante Nat'l Mon., Ut, US 92/E3
Grand Teton National Park, Wy, US 92/E2
Grand Turk (cap.), UK 103/J1
Grand-Bassam, C.d'Iv. 78/E5
Grande Prairie, Ab, Can. 90/D2
Grande-Synthe, Fr. 30/B1
Granite City, Il, US 93/K3
Granollers, Sp. 35/L6
Grantham, Eng, UK 23/H6
Grants Pass, Or, US 90/C5
Grasse, Fr. 33/G5
Grassy Park, SAfr. 80/L11
Gravesend, Eng, UK 25/G4
Gravina di Puglia, It. 40/C5
Grays, Eng, UK 25/G4
Graz, Aus. 40/B2
Great (basin), Nv, US 88/C4
Great Bear (lake), NW, Can. 86/D2
Great Bend, Ks, US 93/H3
Great Divide (basin), Wy, US 90/F5
Great Dividing (range), Austl. 73/B3
Great Himalaya (range), China 62/D2
Great Plains (plain), Can.,US 86/F3
Great Salt (lake), Ut, US 92/D2
Great Sand Dunes National Park, Co, US 93/F3
Great Sandy (des.), Austl. 70/C4
Great Slave (lake), NW, Can. 86/E2
Great Smoky Mountains National Park, US 97/H3
Great Victoria (des.), Austl. 70/D5
Great Wall, China 54/F4
Great Yarmouth, Eng, UK 25/H1
Greater Antilles (isls.), Jam. 103/F1
Greece (ctry.), Gre. 39/G3
Greeley, Co, US 93/F2
Green River, Wy, US 90/F5
Green Valley, Az, US 92/E5
Greendale, Wi, US 99/Q14
Greeneville, Tn, US 97/H2
Greenfield, Ma, US 95/F3
Greenfield, In, US 97/G2
Greenfield, Wi, US 99/P14
Greenfield Park, Qu, Can. 95/P7
Greenland (dpcy.), Den. 87/L1
Greensboro, NC, US 97/J2
Greensburg, In, US 94/C4
Greensburg, Pa, US 94/E3
Greenville, Tx, US 93/H4
Greenville, Ms, US 93/K4
Greenville, Libr. 78/C5
Greenville, NC, US 97/J3
Greenville, SC, US 97/H3
Greenville, Oh, US 97/G1
Greenwood, Ms, US 93/K4
Greenwood, SC, US 97/H3
Greifswald, Ger. 27/G1
Greiz, Ger. 33/K1
Gremyachinsk, Rus. 43/N4
Grenada, Ms, US 93/K4
Grenada (ctry.), Gren. 104/F5
Grenchen, Swi. 36/D3
Grenoble, Fr. 32/F4
Gretna, La, US 97/F4
Greven, Ger. 29/E4
Grevenbroich, Ger. 28/D6
Grevenmacher, Lux. 31/F4
Greymouth, NZ 71/R11
Griffin, Ga, US 97/G3
Griffith, In, US 99/R16
Grigny, Fr. 30/B6
Grimbergen, Belg. 31/D2
Grimsby, Eng, UK 23/H4
Grimsby, On, Can. 95/T9
Grimstad, Nor. 20/D4
Gröbenzell, Ger. 37/H1
Groesbeek, Neth. 28/C5
Gronau, Ger. 28/E4
Groningen, Neth. 28/D2
Grosse Ile, Mi, US 99/F7
Grosse Pointe Farms, Mi, US 99/G7
Grosse Pointe Park, Mi, US 99/G7
Grosse Pointe Woods, Mi, US 99/G7
Grosseto, It. 38/B1
Grossgerau, Ger. 33/H2
Grottaglie, It. 40/C5
Grovdageaidnu-Kautokeino, Nor. 42/D1
Grover City, Ca, US 92/B4
Groves, Tx, US 93/J5
Groznyy, Rus. 45/H4
Grudziądz, Pol. 27/K2
Gryazi, Rus. 44/F1
Gryfice, Pol. 27/H2
Gryfino, Pol. 27/H2
Guaçuí, Braz. 108/D2
Guadalajara, Mex. 100/E4
Guadalajara, Sp. 34/D2
Guadalupe, Pan. 103/G4
Guadalupe, Mex. 100/E4
Guadalupe, Mex. 96/C5
Guadeloupe (dpcy.), Fr. 104/F3
Guadeloupe Passage (chan.), NAm. 104/F3
Guadix, Sp. 34/D4
Guaíba, Braz. 108/B4
Guáimaro, Cuba 103/G1
Guaira, Braz. 109/F1
Guaíra, Braz. 108/B2
Guajará-Mirim, Braz. 106/E6
Gualán, Guat. 102/D3
Gualeguaychú, Arg. 109/E3
Guam (isl.), Pac.,US 68/D3
Guamúchil, Mex. 100/C3
Guanabacoa, Cuba 103/F1
Guanajay, Cuba 103/F1
Guanajuato, Mex. 101/E4
Guanambi, Braz. 107/K6
Guanare, Ven. 106/E2
Guangyuan, China 60/E1
Guangzhou, China 61/G4
Guanhães, Braz. 108/D1
Guantánamo, Cuba 103/H1
Guarabira, Braz. 107/L5
Guaranda, Ecu. 106/C4
Guarapari, Braz. 108/D2
Guarapuava, Braz. 108/B3
Guararapes, Braz. 108/B2
Guaratinguetá, Braz. 108/H7
Guarda, Port. 34/B2
Guarujá, Braz. 108/G9
Guarulhos, Braz. 108/G8
Guasave, Mex. 100/C3
Guatemala (cap.), Guat. 102/D3
Guatemala (ctry.), Guat. 102/D3
Guaxupé, Braz. 108/G6
Guayama, PR 104/E3
Guayaquil, Ecu. 106/C4
Guayaramerín, Bol. 106/E6
Guaymas, Mex. 100/C3
Gubakha, Rus. 43/N4
Guben, Ger. 27/H3
Gubin, Pol. 27/H3
Gubkin, Rus. 44/F2
Gudermes, Rus. 45/H4
Gudivāda, India 62/D4
Güdür, India 62/C5
Guecho, Sp. 34/D1
Guelph, On, Can. 95/S8
Guéret, Fr. 32/D3
Guguletu, SAfr. 80/L11
Guidder, Camr. 76/H6
Guihulngan, Phil. 67/F1
Guildford, Eng, UK 25/F4
Guilin, China 61/F3
Guinea (ctry.) 78/C4
Guinea (gulf), Gui. 76/G7
Guinea-Bissau (ctry.) 78/B3
Guisborough, Eng, UK 23/G2
Gūjar Khān, Pak. 53/K2
Gujrānwāla, Pak. 53/K2
Gujrāt, Pak. 53/K2
Gukovo, Rus. 44/F2
Gulbarga, India 62/C4
Gulf Coastal (plain), Tx, US 96/D5
Gulfport, Ms, US 97/F4
Guliston, Uzb. 46/G5
Gulu, Ugan. 77/M7
Gummersbach, Ger. 29/E6
Gümüşhane, Turk. 44/F4
Guntūr, India 62/D4
Günzburg, Ger. 37/G1
Gunzenhausen, Ger. 33/J2
Gura Humorului, Rom. 41/G2
Gurdāspur, India 53/L2
Gürgentepe, Turk. 44/F4
Gurnee, Il, US 99/Q15
Gurupi, Braz. 107/J6
Gus'-Khrustal'nyy, Rus. 42/J5
Gusau, Nga. 79/G3
Güstrow, Ger. 26/G2
Gütersloh, Ger. 29/F5
Guthrie, Ok, US 93/H4
Guyana (ctry.), Guy. 106/G2
Guyancourt, Fr. 30/B6
Guymon, Ok, US 93/G3
Gwādar, Pak. 53/H3
Gwalior, India 62/C2
Gwanda, Zim. 82/E5
Gweru, Zim. 82/E4
Győr, Hun. 40/C2
Gyumri, Arm. 45/G4
Gyzylarbat, Trkm. 45/L5

H

Haaksbergen, Neth. 28/D4
Haaltert, Belg. 30/D2
Haan, Ger. 28/E6
Haar, Ger. 33/J2
Haarlem, Neth. 28/B4
Habiganj, Bang. 60/A3
Hachinohe, Japan 47/Q5
Hachiōji, Japan 57/F3
Hacılar, Turk. 50/C2
Hadano, Japan 57/F3
Ḥadera, Isr. 49/F7
Haderslev, Den. 26/E1
Haeju, NKor. 58/C3
Hāfizābād, Pak. 53/K2
Hagåtña (cap.), Guam 68/D3
Hagen, Ger. 29/E6
Hagerstown, Md, US 94/E4
Hagi, Japan 56/B3
Hague, The (cap.), Neth. 28/B4
Haguenau, Fr. 31/G6
Hai Duong, Viet. 65/D1
Hai Phong, Viet. 65/D1
Haicheng, China 58/B2
Haiger, Ger. 31/H2
Haikou, China 61/F4
Ḥā'il, SAr. 50/E5
Hailākāndi, India 60/B3
Hailar, China 55/H2
Hailsham, Eng, UK 25/G5
Hailun, China 55/K2
Haines City, Fl, US 97/H4
Haining, China 59/L9
Haiti (ctry.), Haiti 102/H3
Hajdúböszormény, Hun. 40/E2
Hajdúdorog, Hun. 40/E2
Hajdúnánás, Hun. 40/E2
Hajdúszoboszló, Hun. 40/E2
Hajnówka, Pol. 27/M2
Hakodate, Japan 55/N3
Hakui, Japan 57/E2
Hāla, Pak. 53/J3
Ḥalab (Aleppo), Syria 49/E1
Halawa, Hi, US 88/T10
Halden, Nor. 20/D4
Haldensleben, Ger. 26/F2
Haldimand, On, Can. 95/T10
Hale, Eng, UK 23/F5
Halesowen, Eng, UK 24/D2
Halifax, Eng, UK 23/G4
Halifax (cap.), NS, Can. 95/J2
Halle, Ger. 29/F4
Halle, Ger. 26/F3
Halle, Belg. 31/D2
Halle-Neustadt, Ger. 26/F3
Hallein, Aus. 40/A2
Hallsberg, Swe. 20/E4
Halluin, Fr. 30/C2
Halmstad, Swe. 20/E4
Ḥalq al Wādī, Tun. 38/B4
Ḣelsingborg, Swe. 20/E4
Haltern, Ger. 29/E5
Halton Hills, On, Can. 95/T8
Halver, Ger. 29/E6
Hamada, Japan 56/C3
Hamadān, Iran 51/G3
Hamakita, Japan 57/E3
Hamamatsu, Japan 57/E3
Hamar, Nor. 20/D3
Hamburg, NY, US 94/E3
Hamburg, Ger. 29/G1
Hämeenlinna, Fin. 42/E3
Hameln, Ger. 29/G4
Hamhŭng, NKor. 58/D3
Hamilton, On, Can. 95/T9
Hamilton, NZ 71/S10
Hamīrpur, India 62/D2
Hamm, Ger. 29/E5
Ḥammām Al Anf, Tun. 38/B4
Hamme, Belg. 28/B6
Hamminkeln, Ger. 28/D5
Hammond, La, US 97/F4
Hammond, In, US 99/R16
Hampton, Va, US 97/J2
Hamtramck, Mi, US 99/F7
Hanamaki, Japan 55/N4
Hanau, Ger. 26/E3
Hanford, Ca, US 92/C3
Haninge, Swe. 42/C4
Hannibal, Mo, US 93/K3
Hannover, Ger. 29/G4
Hanoi (cap.), Viet. 65/D1
Hanover, NH, US 95/F3
Hanover Park, Il, US 99/P16
Hānsi, India 53/L3
Hanumāngarh, India 62/B2
Hanzhong, China 54/F5
Haramachi, Japan 57/G2
Harare (cap.), Zim. 82/F4
Harbiye, Turk. 49/E1
Hardā, India 62/C3
Hardenberg, Neth. 28/D3
Harderwijk, Neth. 28/C4
Hardwār, India 53/L3
Harelbeke, Belg. 30/C2
Haren, Neth. 28/D2
Haren, Ger. 29/E3
Hārer, Eth. 77/P6
Hargeysa, Som. 77/P6
Harihar, India 62/C5
Harlingen, Tx, US 96/D5
Harlingen, Neth. 28/C2
Harlow, Eng, UK 25/G3
Härnösand, Swe. 42/C3
Harpenden, Eng, UK 25/F3
Harper, Libr. 78/D5
Harper Woods, Mi, US 99/F7
Harrisburg, Il, US 97/F2
Harrisburg (cap.), Pa, US 94/E3
Harrison, Ar, US 93/J3
Harrisonburg, Va, US 97/J2
Harrogate, Eng, UK 23/G4
Harsewinkel, Ger. 29/F5
Harson's Island, Mi, US 99/G6
Harstad, Nor. 20/F1
Hartford (cap.), Ct, US 95/F3
Hartlepool, Eng, UK 23/G2
Hartselle, Al, US 97/G3
Hārūnābād, Pak. 53/K3
Harvey, Il, US 99/Q16
Harwich, Eng, UK 25/H3
Hashimoto, Japan 56/D3
Hāsilpur, Pak. 53/K3
Haslingden, Eng, UK 23/F4
Hassan, India 62/C5
Hasselt, Belg. 31/E2
Hässleholm, Swe. 20/E4
Hastings, Ne, US 93/H2
Hastings, NZ 71/S10
Hastings, Eng, UK 25/G5
Hat Yai, Thai. 65/C5
Hatfield, Eng, UK 25/F3
Hāthras, India 62/C2
Hatta, India 62/C3
Hattiesburg, Ms, US 97/F4
Hattingen, Ger. 29/E6
Hatvan, Hun. 40/D2
Haugesund, Nor. 20/C4
Hautmont, Fr. 30/C3
Havana (cap.), Cuba 103/F1
Havant, Eng, UK 25/F5
Havelock, NC, US 97/J3
Haverhill, Ma, US 95/G3
Haverhill, Eng, UK 25/G2
Havířov, Czh. 27/K4
Havlíčkův Brod, Czh. 33/L2
Havza, Turk. 44/E4
Hawaii (isl.), US 88/U11
Hawaii (state), US 88/S10
Hawaii Kai, Hi, US 88/W13
Hawaiian (isls.), US 69/H2
Ḥawallī, Kuw. 51/G4
Hawarden, Wal, UK 23/E5
Ḥawsh 'Īsá, Egypt 49/B4
Ḣayange, Fr. 31/F5
Haydock, Eng, UK 23/F5
Haylaastay, Mong. 47/M5
Hayrabolu, Turk. 41/H5
Hays, Ks, US 93/H3
Haysyn, Ukr. 44/D2
Hayward, Ca, US 99/K11
Hazāribag, India 62/E3
Hazebrouck, Fr. 30/B2
Hazel Park, Mi, US 99/F7
Hazleton, Pa, US 94/F3
Healdsburg, Ca, US 92/B3
Heanor, Eng, UK 23/G6
Hechi, China 61/F3
Hechingen, Ger. 37/E1
Hedemora, Swe. 20/E3
Heemskerk, Neth. 28/B3
Heemstede, Neth. 28/B4
Heerde, Neth. 28/D4
Heerenveen, Neth. 28/C3
Heerhugowaard, Neth. 28/B3
Heerlen, Neth. 31/E2
Ḥefa (Haifa), Isr. 49/F6
Hefei, China 61/H2
Hegang, China 55/L2
Heide, Ger. 26/E1
Heidelberg, Ger. 33/H2
Heidenheim, Ger. 33/J2
Heilbronn, Ger. 33/H2
Heiligenhaus, Ger. 28/D6
Heiligenstadt, Ger. 29/H6
Heiloo, Neth. 28/B3
Heinola, Fin. 42/E3
Heinsberg, Ger. 28/D6
Heist-op-den-Berg, Belg. 31/D1
Helden, Neth. 28/D6
Helena (cap.), Mt, US 90/E4
Hellendoorn, Neth. 28/D4
Hellevoetsluis, Neth. 28/B5
Hellín, Sp. 34/E3
Helmond, Neth. 28/C6
Helmstedt, Ger. 26/F2
Helsingfors (Helsinki), Fin. 42/E3
Helsingør, Den. 20/E4
Hemel Hempstead, Eng, UK 25/F3
Hemer, Ger. 29/E6
Hemmingen, Ger. 29/G4
Hendek, Turk. 41/K5
Henderson, Nv, US 92/D3
Henderson, Tx, US 93/J4
Henderson, Ky, US 97/G2
Henderson, NC, US 97/J2
Hendersonville, Tn, US 97/G2
Hendrik-Ido-Ambacht, Neth. 28/B5
Hengelo, Neth. 28/D4
Hengshui, China 59/C3
Hengyang, China 61/G3
Heniches'k, Ukr. 44/E3
Hénin-Beaumont, Fr. 30/B3
Hennef, Ger. 31/G2
Henzada, Myan. 60/B5
Herāt, Afg. 53/H2
Herblay, Fr. 30/B6
Hercegnovi, Serb. 40/D4
Hercules, Ca, US 99/K10
Herdecke, Ger. 29/E6
Heredia, CR 103/E4
Hereford, Tx, US 93/G4
Hereford, Eng, UK 24/D2
Herentals, Belg. 28/B6
Herford, Ger. 29/F4
Herisau, Swi. 37/F3
Hermansverk, Nor. 20/C3
Hermiston, Or, US 90/D4
Hermosillo, Mex. 92/E5
Hernani, Sp. 34/E1
Herne, Ger. 29/E5
Herne Bay, Eng, UK 25/H4
Herning, Den. 20/D4
Heroica Caborca, Mex. 92/D5
Heroica Matamoros, Mex. 96/D5
Heroica Nogales, Mex. 92/E5
Hérouville-Saint-Clair, Fr. 32/C2
Herstal, Belg. 31/E2
Herten, Ger. 29/E5
Hertford, Eng, UK 25/F3
Herve, Belg. 31/E2
Hervey Bay, Austl. 72/D4
Herzberg am Harz, Ger. 29/H5
Herzele, Belg. 30/C2
Herzliyya, Isr. 49/F7
Herzogenaurach, Ger. 33/J2
Herzogenrath, Ger. 31/F2
Heshan, China 61/F4
Hessisch Oldendorf, Ger. 29/G4
Heusden-Zolder, Belg. 28/C6
Heusweiler, Ger. 31/F5
Heywood, Eng, UK 23/F4
Heze, China 59/C4
Hialeah, Fl, US 97/H5
Hibbing, Mn, US 91/K4
Hickory, NC, US 97/H3
Hidalgo del Parral, Mex. 96/B5
Hiddenhausen, Ger. 29/F4
Higashine, Japan 57/G1
High Point, NC, US 97/H3
High Wycombe, Eng, UK 25/F3
Highland, In, US 99/R16
Highland Park, Il, US 99/Q15
Highland Park, Mi, US 99/F7
Hihyā, Egypt 49/B4
Hiji, Japan 56/B4
Hikone, Japan 56/E3
Hilchenbach, Ger. 31/H2
Hilden, Ger. 28/D6
Hildesheim, Ger. 29/G4
Hille, Ger. 29/F4
Hillegom, Neth. 28/B4
Hillerød, Den. 20/E5
Hillsboro, Or, US 90/C4
Hillsborough, Ca, US 99/K11
Hilo, Hi, US 88/U11
Hilton Head Island, SC, US 97/H3
Hilversum, Neth. 28/C4
Himeji, Japan 56/D3
Himi, Japan 57/E2
Ḥimṣ, Syria 49/E3
Hinche, Haiti 103/H2
Hinckley, Eng, UK 25/E1
Hindley, Eng, UK 23/F4
Hindupur, India 62/C5
Hinesville, Ga, US 97/H4
Hinganghāt, India 62/C3
Hingoli, India 62/C4
Hingorja, Pak. 62/A2
Hınıs, Turk. 45/G5
Hinsdale, Il, US 99/Q16
Hirado, Japan 56/A4
Hirakata, Japan 56/D3
Hirata, Japan 56/C3
Hirosaki, Japan 55/N3
Hiroshima, Japan 56/C3
Hisai, Japan 56/E3
Hisār, India 62/C2
Hispaniola (isl.), Haiti 103/H1
Hitachi, Japan 57/G2
Hitachi-ōta, Japan 57/G2
Hitchin, Eng, UK 25/F3
Hitoyoshi, Japan 56/B4
Hjørring, Den. 20/D4
Hlohovec, Slvk. 40/C1
Hlukhiv, Ukr. 44/E2
Hmawbi, Myan. 60/C5
Ho, Gha. 79/F5
Hoa Binh, Viet. 65/D1
Hobara, Japan 57/G2
Hobart, Austl. 73/C4
Hobbs, NM, US 93/G4
Hoboken, Belg. 28/B6
Hod Hasharon, Isr. 49/F7
Hoddesdon, Eng, UK 25/F3
Hódmezővásárhely, Hun. 40/E2
Hodonín, Czh. 27/J4
Hoensbroek, Neth. 31/E2
Hof, Ger. 33/J1
Hoffman Estates, Il, US 99/P15
Hofgeismar, Ger. 29/G6
Hōfu, Japan 56/B3
Hohhot, China 54/G3
Hoi An, Viet. 65/E3
Hōjō, Japan 56/C4
Hokkaidō (isl.), Japan 55/N3
Hokota, Japan 57/G2
Holguín, Cuba 103/G1
Holland, Mi, US 94/C3
Hollister, Ca, US 92/B3
Hollogne-aux-Pierres, Belg. 31/E2
Hollola, Fin. 42/E3
Hollywood, Fl, US 97/H5
Holmfirth, Eng, UK 23/G4
Ḥolon, Isr. 49/F7
Holstebro, Den. 20/D4
Holyoke, Ma, US 95/F3
Holzminden, Ger. 29/G5
Holzwickede, Ger. 29/E5
Homberg, Ger. 28/D6
Hombourg-Haut, Fr. 31/F5
Homburg, Ger. 31/G5
Homestead, Fl, US 97/H5
Homewood, Al, US 97/G3
Homewood, Il, US 99/Q16
Homyel', Bela. 44/D1
Hon Quan, Viet. 65/D4
Honāvar, India 62/B5
Hondo, Japan 56/B4
Honduras (ctry.), Hon. 102/D3
Hong Gai, Viet. 65/D1
Hong Kong (reg.), China 61/G4
Hongch'ŏn, SKor. 56/A2
Honghu, China 61/G2
Hongjiang, China 61/F3
Hongsŏng, SKor. 58/D4
Honiara (cap.), Sol. 68/E5
Honolulu (cap.), Hi, US 88/T10
Hood (mt.), Or, US 90/C4
Hoofddorp, Neth. 28/B4
Hoogeveen, Neth. 28/D3
Hoogezand, Neth. 28/D2
Hoogstraten, Belg. 28/B6
Hoorn, Neth. 28/C3
Hopewell, Va, US 97/J2
Hopkinsville, Ky, US 97/G2
Horb am Neckar, Ger. 37/E1
Horgen, Swi. 37/E3
Horley, Eng, UK 25/F4
Horlivka, Ukr. 44/F2
Horn (cape), Chile 109/C8
Horn-Bad Meinberg, Ger. 29/F5
Hornell, NY, US 94/E3
Horsens, Den. 20/D5
Horsforth, Eng, UK 23/G4
Horsham, Eng, UK 25/F4
Horst, Neth. 28/D6
Hörstel, Ger. 29/E4
Horwich, Eng, UK 23/F4
Hoshangābād, India 62/C3
Hotaka, Japan 57/E2
Hot'Kovo, Rus. 43/X9
Houghton-le-Spring, Eng, UK 23/G2
Houma, China 59/B4
Houston, Tx, US 93/J5
Houten, Neth. 28/C4
Hove, Eng, UK 25/F5
Howrah, India 62/E3
Höxter, Ger. 29/G5
Hoyerswerda, Ger. 27/H3
Hoylake, Eng, UK 23/E5
Hoyland Nether, Eng, UK 23/G4
Hradec Králové, Czh. 33/L1
Hrazdan, Arm. 45/H4
Hrodna, Bela. 27/M2

Hrubieszów, Pol. 27/M3
Hsinchu, Tai. 61/J3
Hua Hin, Thai. 65/B3
Huacho, Peru 106/C6
Huadian, China 55/K3
Huai'an, China 59/D4
Huaibei, China 54/H5
Huaihua, China 61/F3
Huainan, China 59/D4
Huaiyin, China 59/D4
Huajuapan de León, Mex. 102/B2
Hualien, Tai. 61/J4
Huamantla, Mex. 101/M7
Huambo, Ang. 82/C3
Huancavelica, Peru 106/C6
Huancayo, Peru 106/C6
Huanchaca (peak), Bol. 106/E8
Huang (Yellow) (riv.), China 55/H4
Huangshan, China 61/H2
Huangshi, China 61/G2
Huánuco, Peru 106/C5
Huaral, Peru 106/C6
Huaraz, Peru 106/C5
Huascarán (peak), Peru 106/C5
Huatabampo, Mex. 100/C3
Huatuxco, Mex. 101/N7
Huauchinango, Mex. 101/L6
Huaying, China 61/E2
Hubli-Dhārwār, India 62/C4
Hückelhoven, Ger. 28/D6
Hückeswagen, Ger. 29/E6
Hucknall, Eng, UK 23/G5
Huddersfield, Eng, UK 23/G4
Huddinge, Swe. 42/C4
Hudiksvall, Swe. 42/C3
Hudson (bay), Can. 87/H2
Hue, Viet. 65/D2
Huehuetenango, Guat. 102/D3
Huejotzingo, Mex. 101/L7
Huejutla de Reyes, Mex. 102/B1
Huelva, Sp. 34/B4
Huesca, Sp. 35/E1
Huetamo de Nuñez, Mex. 101/E5
Hui Xian, China 59/C4
Huimanguillo, Mex. 102/C2
Huissen, Neth. 28/C5
Huixtla, Mex. 102/C3
Huizen, Neth. 28/C4
Huizhou, China 61/G4
Hull, Qu, Can. 94/F2
Hulst, Neth. 28/B6
Hultsfred, Swe. 20/E4
Humaitá, Braz. 106/F5
Humble, Tx, US 93/J5
Humboldt, Tn, US 97/F3
Humenné, Slvk. 27/L4
Hunchun, China 55/L3
Hunedoara, Rom. 40/F3
Hungary (ctry.) 40/D2
Hunjiang, China 58/D2
Huntingdon, Eng, UK 25/F2
Huntington, WV, US 97/H2
Huntington, In, US 94/C3
Huntington Beach, Ca, US 92/C4
Huntsville, Tx, US 93/J5
Huntsville, On, Can. 94/E2
Huntsville, Al, US 97/G3
Hunucmá, Mex. 102/D1
Huolin Gol, China 55/H2
Huozhou, China 59/B3
Huron (lake), Can.,US 94/D2
Hürth, Ger. 31/F2
Huşi, Rom. 41/J2
Husum, Ger. 26/E1
Hutchinson, Mn, US 91/K4
Hutchinson, Ks, US 93/H3
Huy, Belg. 31/E2
Huyton-with-Roby, Eng, UK 23/F5
Huzhou, China 59/L9
Hwange, Zim. 82/E4
Hyde, Eng, UK 23/F5
Hyderābād, India 62/C4
Hyderābād, Pak. 62/A2
Hyères, Fr. 33/G5
Hythe, Eng, UK 25/H4
Hyūga, Japan 56/B4
Hyvinkää, Fin. 42/E3

I

I-n-Guezzâm, Alg. 79/G2
I-n-Salah, Alg. 76/F2
Iaşi, Rom. 41/H2
Ibadan, Nga. 79/F5
Ibagué, Col. 106/C3
Ibara, Japan 56/C3
Ibarra, Ecu. 106/C3
Ibb, Yem. 52/D6
Ibbenbüren, Ger. 29/E4
Ibi, Sp. 35/E3
Ibicaraí, Braz. 107/L6
Ibitinga, Braz. 108/B2
Ibiúna, Braz. 108/F8
Ibiza, Sp. 35/F3
Ibotirama, Braz. 107/K6
Ibshawāy, Egypt 49/B5
Ica, Peru 106/C6
Iceland (ctry.) 20/N6
Ichalkaranji, India 62/B4
Ichchāpuram, India 62/D4
Ichinomiya, Japan 57/E3
Ichinoseki, Japan 55/N4
Icó, Braz. 107/L5
Icod de los Vinos, Canl. 35/X16
Idaho (state), US 90/E3
Idar, India 62/B3
Idar-Oberstein, Ger. 31/G4
Idfū, Egypt 52/B4
Idlib, Syria 49/E2
Idstein, Ger. 31/H3
Ieper, Belg. 30/B2
Ifanadiana, Madg. 81/H8
Ife, Nga. 79/G5
Igarapava, Braz. 108/C2
Igarapé-Miri, Braz. 107/J4
Igarka, Rus. 46/J3
Igatpuri, India 62/B4
Iğdır, Turk. 45/H5
Iglesias, It. 38/A3
Ignacio, Ca, US 99/J10
Igra, Rus. 43/M4
Iguala, Mex. 101/K8
Igualada, Sp. 35/F2
Iguape, Braz. 108/C3
Iguatu, Braz. 107/L5
Iida, Japan 57/E3
Iisalmi, Fin. 42/E3
Iiyama, Japan 57/F2
Iizuka, Japan 56/B4
Ijebu Ode, Nga. 79/F5
IJsselstein, Neth. 28/C4
Ijuí, Braz. 109/F2
Ijūin, Japan 56/B5
Ikare, Nga. 79/G5
Ikeda, Japan 56/C3
Ikeja, Nga. 79/F5
Ikerre, Nga. 79/G5
Ikire, Nga. 79/G5
Ikirun, Nga. 79/G5
Ikorodu, Nga. 79/F5
Ila Orangun, Nga. 79/G4
Ilam, Nepal 62/E2
Ilan, Tai. 61/J3
Ilaro, Nga. 79/F5
Iława, Pol. 27/K2
Ilawe-Ekiti, Nga. 79/G5
Ilebo, D.R. Congo 82/D1
Ilesha, Nga. 79/G5
Ilgın, Turk. 50/B2
Ílhavo, Port. 34/A2
Ilhéus, Braz. 107/L6
Iligan, Phil. 67/F2
Ilium (Troy) (ruin), Turk. 39/K3
Ilkeston, Eng, UK 23/G6
Illapel, Chile 109/B3
Illingen, Ger. 31/G5
Illinois (state), US 94/B4
Illizi, Alg. 76/G2
Illkirch-Graffenstaden, Fr. 31/G6
Illzach, Fr. 36/D2
Ilmenau, Ger. 33/J1
Ilo, Peru 106/D7
Ilobu, Nga. 79/G5
Iloilo, Phil. 67/F1
Ilorin, Nga. 79/G4
Imabari, Japan 56/C3
Imaichi, Japan 57/F2
İmamoğlu, Turk. 50/C2
Imari, Japan 56/A4
Imatra, Fin. 42/F3
Imerimandroso, Madg. 81/J7
İmişli, Azer. 51/G2
Immokalee, Fl, US 97/H5
Imola, It. 33/J4
Imperatriz, Braz. 107/J5
Imperia, It. 33/H5
Imphāl, India 60/B3
Ina, Japan 57/E3
Inca, Sp. 35/G3
Inch'ŏn, SKor. 58/F7
İncirliova, Turk. 50/A2
Indaiatuba, Braz. 108/C2
Indanan, Phil. 67/F2
Independence, Mo, US 93/J3
Independence, Ks, US 93/J3
India (ctry.) 62/C3
Indian (ocean) 17/N6
Indiana, Pa, US 94/E3
Indiana (state), US 94/C3
Indianapolis (cap.), In, US 94/C4
Indianola, Ms, US 93/K4
Indija, Serb. 40/E3
Indio, Ca, US 92/C4
Indochina (reg.), Laos 65/C1
Indonesia (ctry.) 67/E4
Indore, India 62/C3
İnegöl, Turk. 44/D4
Inezgane, Mor. 76/D1
Ingenio, Canl. 35/X17
Inglewood-Finn Hill, Wa, US 99/C2
Ingolstadt, Ger. 33/J2
Inhambane, Moz. 82/G5
Inhumas, Braz. 107/J7
Inkster, Mi, US 99/F7
Innichen (San Candito), It. 33/K3
Ino, Japan 56/C4
Inowrocław, Pol. 27/K2
Insein, Myan. 60/C5
Inta, Rus. 43/N2
Inuyama, Japan 57/E3
Invercargill, NZ 71/Q12
Inza, Rus. 45/H1
Ioánnina, Gre. 39/G3
Iowa (state), US 93/J2
Ipameri, Braz. 108/B1
Ipatinga, Braz. 108/D1
Ipiales, Col. 106/C3
Ipiaú, Braz. 107/L6
Ipoh, Malay. 66/B3
Iporá, Braz. 107/H7
Ipswich, Eng, UK 25/H2
Ipu, Braz. 107/K4
Iquique, Chile 106/D8
Iquitos, Peru 106/D4
Iráklion, Gre. 39/J5
Iran (ctry.) 48/E6
Irapuato, Mex. 101/E4
Iraq (ctry.) 50/E3
Irati, Braz. 108/B3
Irbid, Jor. 49/D3
Irbīl, Iraq 51/F2
Irecê, Braz. 107/K6
Ireland (ctry.), Ire. 21/A4
Iri, SKor. 58/D5
Iringa, Tanz. 82/G2
Irish (sea), Ire.,UK 22/C4
Irkutsk, Rus. 54/E1
Irlam, Eng, UK 23/F5
Ironton, Oh, US 97/H2
Irún, Sp. 34/E1
Irvine, Ca, US 92/C4
Irving, Tx, US 96/D3
Isahaya, Japan 56/B4
Ischia, It. 40/A5
Ise, Japan 57/E3
Isehara, Japan 57/F3
Iserlohn, Ger. 29/E6
Isernia, It. 40/B5
Isesaki, Japan 57/F2
Iseyin, Nga. 79/F5
Ishibashi, Japan 57/F2
Ishigaki, Japan 68/B2
Ishige, Japan 57/F2
Ishikawa, Japan 57/G2
Ishim, Rus. 43/R4
Ishimbay, Rus. 45/L1
Ishinomaki, Japan 57/G1
Ishioka, Japan 57/G2
Isil'kul', Rus. 46/H4
Isiro, D.R. Congo 77/L7
İskenderun, Turk. 49/E1
İskilip, Turk. 44/E4
Isla, Mex. 102/C2
Isla Cristina, Sp. 34/B4
İslâhiye, Turk. 49/E1
Islāmābād (cap.), Pak. 53/K2
Islāmpur, India 62/E2
Isle Royale National Park, Mi, US 94/B2
Ismail Samani (peak), Taj. 46/H6
Isnā, Egypt 52/B3
Isoanala, Madg. 81/H8
Ísparta, Turk. 50/B2
Israel (ctry.) 49/C3
Issoire, Fr. 32/E4
Issy-les-Moulineaux, Fr. 30/B6
İstanbul, Turk. 51/M6
Istres, Fr. 32/F5
Isulan, Phil. 67/F2
Itabaiana, Braz. 107/L6
Itaberaba, Braz. 107/K6
Itabira, Braz. 108/D1
Itabirito, Braz. 108/D2
Itaboraí, Braz. 108/L7
Itabuna, Braz. 107/L6
Itacoatiara, Braz. 106/G4
Itaguaí, Braz. 108/K7
Itagüí, Col. 106/C2
Itaituba, Braz. 107/G4
Itajaí, Braz. 108/B3
Itajubá, Braz. 108/H7
Itako, Japan 57/G3
Italy (ctry.) 18/E4
Itamaraju, Braz. 107/L7
Itampolo, Madg. 81/G9
Itanhaém, Braz. 108/G9
Itaobim, Braz. 107/K7
Itapagé, Braz. 107/L4
Itapecuru-Mirim, Braz. 107/K4
Itapemirim, Braz. 108/D2
Itaperuna, Braz. 108/D2
Itapetinga, Braz. 107/K7
Itapetininga, Braz. 108/B2
Itapeva, Braz. 108/B2
Itapevi, Braz. 108/G8
Itapipoca, Braz. 107/L4
Itapira, Braz. 108/G7
Itaquaquecetuba, Braz. 108/G8
Itararé, Braz. 108/B3
Itārsi, India 62/C3
Itatiba, Braz. 108/G7
Itaúna, Braz. 108/C2
Itayanagi, Japan 55/N3
Ithaca, NY, US 94/E3
Itō, Japan 57/F3
Itoigawa, Japan 57/E2
Itu, Braz. 108/C2
Ituiutaba, Braz. 108/B1
Itumbiara, Braz. 108/B1
Iturama, Braz. 108/B1
Ituverava, Braz. 108/C2
Ityāy al Bārūd, Egypt 49/B4
Itzehoe, Ger. 26/E2
Ivaiporã, Braz. 108/B3
Ivangrad, Serb. 40/D4
Ivanjica, Serb. 40/E4
Ivano-Frankivs'k, Ukr. 44/C2
Ivanovo, Rus. 42/J4
Ivdel, Rus. 46/G3
Ivohibe, Madg. 81/H8
Ivory (coast), C.d'Iv. 78/D5
Ivrea, It. 33/G4
Iwai, Japan 57/F2
Iwaki, Japan 57/G2
Iwakuni, Japan 56/C3
Iwami, Japan 56/D3
Iwamizawa, Japan 55/N3
Iwanuma, Japan 57/G1
Iwata, Japan 57/E3
Iwo, Nga. 79/G5
Ixelles, Belg. 31/D2
Ixmiquilpan, Mex. 101/K6
Ixtapaluca, Mex. 101/L7
Ixtlán del Río, Mex. 100/D4
Iyo, Japan 56/C4
Izberbash, Rus. 45/H4
Izegem, Belg. 30/C2
Izhevsk, Rus. 43/M4
Izkī, Oman 53/G4
Izmayil, Ukr. 41/J3
İzmir, Turk. 44/C5
İzmit, Turk. 41/J5
İznik, Turk. 41/J5
Izúcar de Matamoros, Mex. 101/L8
Izuhara, Japan 56/A3
Izumi, Japan 56/D3
Izumi, Japan 56/B4
Izumi-Sano, Japan 56/D3
Izumo, Japan 56/C3
Izyum, Ukr. 44/F2

J

Jabalpur, India 62/C3
Jablah, Syria 49/D2
Jablonec nad Nisou, Czh. 27/H3
Jaboatão dos Guararapes, Braz. 107/L5
Jaboticabal, Braz. 108/B2
Jacareí, Braz. 108/H8
Jackson, Mo, US 93/K3
Jackson, Mi, US 94/C3
Jackson, Tn, US 97/F3
Jackson (cap.), Ms, US 93/K4
Jacksonville, Il, US 93/K3
Jacksonville, Ar, US 93/J4
Jacksonville, NC, US 97/J3
Jacksonville, Al, US 97/G3
Jacksonville, Fl, US 97/H4
Jacksonville Beach, Fl, US 97/H4
Jacmel, Haiti 103/H2
Jacobābād, Pak. 62/A2
Jacobina, Braz. 107/K6
Jacona de Plancarte, Mex. 100/E5
Jaén, Sp. 34/D4
Jaffna, SrL. 62/C6
Jagdalpur, India 62/D4
Jagtiāl, India 62/C4
Jaguaquara, Braz. 107/L6
Jaguarão, Braz. 109/F3
Jaguariaíva, Braz. 108/B3
Jaguariúna, Braz. 108/G7
Jahrom, Iran 51/H4
Jailolo, Indo. 67/G3
Jaisalmer, India 62/B2
Jājapur, India 62/E3
Jajce, Bosn. 40/C3
Jakarta (cap.), Indo. 66/C5
Jakobstad (Pietarsaari), Fin. 42/D3
Jalal-Abad, Kyr. 46/H5
Jalālābād, Afg. 53/K2
Jalapa, Guat. 102/D3
Jalapa, Mex. 101/N7
Jales, Braz. 108/B2
Jalīb ash Shuyūkh, Kuw. 51/F4
Jalisco, Mex. 100/D4
Jalostotitlán, Mex. 100/E4
Jalpaiguri, India 62/E2
Jáltipan de Morelos, Mex. 102/C2
Jamaica (chan.), NAm. 103/H2
Jamaica (ctry.), Jam. 103/G2
Jamālpur, India 62/E2
Jamālpur, Bang. 62/E3
Jambi, Indo. 66/B4
Jamestown, NY, US 94/E3
Jammāl, Tun. 38/B5
Jammu, India 53/K2
Jāmpur, Pak. 53/K3
Jamshedpur, India 62/E3
Jamūi, India 62/E3
Janakkala, Fin. 42/E3
Janaúba, Braz. 107/K7
Jandaia do Sul, Braz. 108/B2
Jangaon, India 62/C4
Jangipur, India 62/E3
Januária, Braz. 107/K7
Japan (sea), Asia 55/L3
Japan (ctry.) 55/M4
Jaramānah, Syria 49/E3
Jardín América, Arg. 109/E2
Jardinópolis, Braz. 108/C2
Jaridih, India 62/E3
Jarjīs, Tun. 76/H1
Jarocin, Pol. 27/J3
Jarosław, Pol. 27/M3
Jarrow, Eng, UK 23/G2
Järvenpää, Fin. 20/H3
Jasło, Pol. 27/L4
Jasper, In, US 97/G2
Jasper, Al, US 97/G3
Jaspur, India 62/C2
Jastrzębie Zdroj, Pol. 27/K4
Jászberény, Hun. 40/D2
Jataí, Braz. 108/B1
Jatibonico, Cuba 103/G1
Játiva, Sp. 35/E3
Jaú, Braz. 108/B2
Java (isl.), Indo. 66/C5
Java (sea), Indo. 66/D5
Jávea, Sp. 35/F3
Jawor, Pol. 27/J3
Jayapura, Indo. 67/K4
Jędrzejów, Pol. 27/L3
Jefferson City (cap.), Mo, US 93/J3
Jeffersonville, In, US 97/G2
Jēkabpils, Lat. 42/E4
Jelenia Góra, Pol. 27/H3
Jelgava, Lat. 42/D4
Jemappes, Belg. 30/C3
Jember, Indo. 66/D5
Jena, Ger. 26/F3
Jennings, La, US 93/J5
Jequié, Braz. 107/K6
Jequitinhonha, Braz. 107/K7
Jérémie, Haiti 103/H2
Jerez de García Salinas, Mex. 100/E4
Jerez de la Frontera, Sp. 34/B4
Jerusalem (cap.), Isr. 49/G8
Jesenice, Slov. 40/B2
Jesi, It. 33/K5
Jessheim, Nor. 20/D3
Jessore, Bang. 62/E3
Jesús María, Arg. 109/D3
Jesús Menéndez, Cuba 103/G1
Jetpur, India 62/B3
Jeypore, India 62/D4
Jhā Jhā, India 62/E3
Jhālawār, India 62/C3
Jhang Sadar, Pak. 53/K2
Jhanjhārpur, India 62/E2
Jhānsi, India 62/C2
Jhārsuguda, India 62/D3
Jhelum, Pak. 53/K2
Ji-Paraná, Braz. 106/F6
Jiamusi, China 55/L2
Ji'an, China 61/G3
Jiangmen, China 61/G4
Jiangyin, China 61/J2
Jiaohe, China 55/K3
Jiaojiang, China 61/J2
Jiaozuo, China 59/C4
Jiaxing, China 59/L9
Jiayuguan, China 54/D4
Jičín, Czh. 33/L1
Jiddah, SAr. 52/C4
Jieshou, China 59/C4
Jiguaní, Cuba 103/G1
Jihlava, Czh. 33/L2
Jijel, Alg. 76/G1
Jijiga, Eth. 77/P6
Jilin, China 55/K3
Jīma, Eth. 77/N6
Jimaní, DRep. 103/J2
Jiménez, Mex. 96/B5
Jimo, China 59/E3
Jinan, China 59/D3
Jinchang, China 54/E4
Jincheng, China 59/C4
Jīnd, India 62/C2
Jindřichuv Hradec, Czh. 33/L2
Jingdezhen, China 61/H2
Jingmen, China 61/G2
Jinhua, China 61/H2
Jining, China 59/D4
Jining, China 59/C2
Jinja, Ugan. 77/M7
Jinotega, Nic. 102/E3
Jinotepe, Nic. 102/E4
Jinshi, China 61/F2
Jintūr, India 62/C4
Jinxi, China 59/E2
Jinzhou, China 59/E2
Jipijapa, Ecu. 106/B4
Jiquilpan de Juárez, Mex. 100/E5
Jishou, China 61/F2
Jisr ash Shughūr, Syria 49/E2
Jitra, Malay. 65/C5
Jiujiang, China 61/G2
Jiutai, China 55/K3
Jiutepec, Mex. 101/K8
Jixi, China 55/L2
Jiyuan, China 59/C4
Jīzān, SAr. 52/D5
Jizzakh, Uzb. 46/G5
Joaçaba, Braz. 108/B3
João Monlevade, Braz. 108/D1
João Pessoa, Braz. 107/M5
João Pinheiro, Braz. 108/C1
Jobabo, Cuba 103/G1
Jodhpur, India 62/B2
Joensuu, Fin. 42/F3
Jōetsu, Japan 57/F2
Jogbani, India 62/E2
Johannesburg, SAfr. 80/Q13
Johnson City, Tn, US 97/H2
Johnstown, Pa, US 94/E3
Johor Baharu, Malay. 66/B3
Joinvile, Braz. 108/B3
Jojutla, Mex. 101/K8
Joliet, Il, US 99/P16
Joliette, Qu, Can. 94/F2
Jollyville, Tx, US 93/H5
Jolo, Phil. 67/F2
Jombang, Indo. 66/D5
Jona, Swi. 37/E3
Jönköping, Swe. 20/E4
Jonquière, Qu, Can. 95/G1
Joplin, Mo, US 93/J3
Jordan (ctry.) 49/D4
Jorhāt, India 60/B3
Jos, Nga. 79/H4
Jose Abad Santos, Phil. 67/G2
José Bonifácio, Braz. 108/B2
José Cardel, Mex. 101/N7
Joshua Tree National Park, Ca, US 92/D4
Joué-lès-Tours, Fr. 32/D3
Jovellanos, Cuba 103/F1
Jowai, India 60/B3
Juan de Fuca (str.), US,Can. 90/B3
Juazeiro, Braz. 107/K5
Juazeiro do Norte, Braz. 107/L5
Juba, Sudan 77/M7
Jüchen, Ger. 28/D6
Juchitán de Zaragoza, Mex. 102/C2
Juigalpa, Nic. 102/E3
Juiz de Fora, Braz. 108/K6
Juliaca, Peru 106/D7
Jülich, Ger. 31/F2
Julio A. Mella, Cuba 103/H1
Jullundur, India 53/L2
Jumilla, Sp. 34/E3
Jumla, Nepal 62/D2
Junāgadh, India 62/B3
Junction City, Ks, US 93/H3
Jundiaí, Braz. 108/G8
Juneau (cap.), Ak, US 85/M4
Junín, Arg. 109/D3
Jupiter, Fl, US 97/H5
Juquitiba, Braz. 108/F8
Jūrmala, Lat. 42/D4
Jutiapa, Guat. 102/D3
Juticalpa, Hon. 102/E3
Jyväskylä, Fin. 42/E3

K

Kaalualu, Hi, US 88/U11
Kaarina, Fin. 42/D3
Kaarst, Ger. 28/D6
Kabale, Ugan. 82/E1
Kabankalan, Phil. 67/F2
Kabul (cap.), Afg. 53/J2
Kabwe, Zam. 82/E3
Kadaianallur, India 62/C6
Kadaň, Czh. 33/K1
Kadınhanı, Turk. 50/C2
Kadiri, India 62/C5
Kadirli, Turk. 50/D2
Kadoma, Zim. 82/E4
Kaduna, Nga. 79/G4
Kāduqli, Sudan 77/L5
Kaédi, Mrta. 78/B2
Kaélé, Camr. 76/H5
Kaesŏng, NKor. 58/D3
Kaffrine, Sen. 78/B3
Kafr ash Shaykh, Egypt 49/B4
Kafr az Zayyāt, Egypt 49/B4
Kafue, Zam. 82/E4
Kaga, Japan 56/E2
Kaga Bandoro, CAfr. 77/J6
Kagan, Uzb. 46/G6
Kağıthane, Turk. 51/M6
Kağızman, Turk. 45/G4
Kagoshima, Japan 56/B5
Kahramanmaraş, Turk. 50/D2
Kahror Pakka, Pak. 53/K3
Kâhta, Turk. 50/D2
Kahului, Hi, US 88/T10
Kaifeng, China 59/C4
Kaili, China 61/E3
Kailua, Hi, US 88/U11
Kailua, Hi, US 88/W13
Kainan, Japan 56/D3
Kaiserslautern, Ger. 31/G5
Kaiyuan, China 59/F2
Kaiyuan, China 60/D4
Kajaani, Fin. 20/H2
Kakamega, Kenya 77/M7
Kakamigahara, Japan 57/E3

Kakhovka, Ukr. 41/L2
Kākināda, India 62/D4
Kakuda, Japan 57/G2
Kalaa Kebira, Tun. 38/B5
Kalach, Rus. 45/G2
Kalach-na-Donu, Rus. 45/G2
Kalachinsk, Rus. 46/H4
Kalahari (des.), Afr. 80/B2
Kalamákion, Gre. 39/N8
Kalamariá, Gre. 40/F5
Kalamáta, Gre. 39/H4
Kalamazoo, Mi, US 94/C3
Kalasin, Thai. 65/C2
Kalemie, D.R. Congo 82/E2
Kaltern (Caldaro), It. 37/H4
Kalgoorlie-Boulder, Austl. 68/B8
Kalianda, Indo. 66/C5
Kalibo, Phil. 67/F1
Kaliningrad, Rus. 43/W9
Kaliningrad, Rus. 27/L1
Kalininsk, Rus. 45/H2
Kalinkavichy, Bela. 44/D1
Kalisz, Pol. 27/K3
Kalix, Swe. 42/D2
Kāliyāganj, India 62/E2
Kallithéa, Gre. 39/N9
Kalmar, Swe. 20/F4
Kalmthout, Belg. 28/B6
Kalocsa, Hun. 40/D2
Kālol, India 62/B3
Kālpi, India 62/C2
Kaluga, Rus. 44/F1
Kalundborg, Den. 26/F1
Kalush, Ukr. 44/C2
Kalutara, SrL. 62/C6
Kalyān, India 62/B4
Kamaishi, Japan 55/N4
Kaman, Turk. 44/E5
Kāmāreddi, India 62/C4
Kāmārhāti, India 62/E3
Kambar, Pak. 62/A2
Kamchatka (pen.), Rus. 47/R4
Kamen, Ger. 29/E5
Kamen'-na-Obi, Rus. 46/J4
Kamenka, Rus. 45/H1
Kamensk-Shakhtinskiy, Rus. 44/G2
Kamensk-Ural'skiy, Rus. 43/P4
Kameoka, Japan 56/D3
Kamiisco, Japan 55/N3
Kamina, D.R. Congo 82/E2
Kaminoyama, Japan 57/G1
Kamloops, BC, Can. 90/C3
Kamo, Japan 57/F2
Kamogawa, Japan 57/G3
Kamojima, Japan 56/D3
Kamp-Lintfort, Ger. 28/D5
Kampala (cap.), Ugan. 77/M7
Kampar, Malay. 66/B3
Kampen, Neth. 28/C3
Kampóng Saom, Camb. 65/C4
Kam'yanets'-Podil's'kyy, Ukr. 44/C2
Kamyshin, Rus. 45/H2
Kananga, D.R. Congo 82/D2
Kanash, Rus. 43/K5
Kanasin, Mex. 102/D1
Kanazawa, Japan 57/E2
Kanchanaburi, Thai. 65/B3
Kānchīpuram, India 62/C5
Kandalaksha, Rus. 42/G2
Kandhkot, Pak. 62/A2
Kāndi, India 62/E3
Kandi, Ben. 79/F4
Kandukūr, India 62/C4
Kandy, SrL. 62/D6
Kaneohe, Hi, US 88/W13
Kangar, Malay. 65/C5
Kangasala, Fin. 20/H3
Kangnŭng, SKor. 56/A2
Kanjiža, Serb. 40/E2
Kankan, Gui. 78/C4
Kannapolis, NC, US 97/H3
Kannauj, India 62/C2
Kano, Nga. 79/H4
Kan'onji, Japan 56/C3
Kanoya, Japan 56/B5
Kānpur, India 62/D2
Kansas (state), US 93/H3
Kansas City, Ks, US 93/J3
Kansas City, Mo, US 93/J3
Kansk, Rus. 46/K4
Kantābānji, India 62/D3
Kanuma, Japan 57/F2
Kanye, Bots. 80/D2
Kaohsiung, Tai. 61/J4
Kaolack, Sen. 78/A3
Kapan, Arm. 45/H5
Kapellen, Belg. 28/B6
Kapfenberg, Aus. 40/B2
Kaposvár, Hun. 40/C2
Kara, Togo 79/F4
Karabük, Turk. 44/E4
Karacabey, Turk. 44/D4
Karachev, Rus. 44/E1
Karāchi, Pak. 62/A3
Karād, India 62/B4
Karaj, Iran 51/G3
Karakol, Kyr. 46/H5
Karaköse, Turk. 45/G5
Karaman, Turk. 50/C2
Karamay, China 46/J5
Karamürsel, Turk. 41/J5
Karangasem, Indo. 67/E5
Kāranja, India 62/C3
Karapınar, Turk. 50/C2
Karasu, Turk. 41/K5
Karasuk, Rus. 46/H4
Karatsu, Japan 56/A4
Karawang, Indo. 66/C5
Karazhal, Kaz. 46/H5
Karbalā', Iraq 51/F3
Karcag, Hun. 27/L5
Kardhitsa, Gre. 39/G3
Karhula, Fin. 20/H3
Karīmnagar, India 62/C4
Kārkāl, India 62/B5
Karleby (Kokkola), Fin. 42/D3
Karlovac, Cro. 40/B3
Karlovo, Bul. 41/G4
Karlovy Vary, Czh. 33/K1
Karlsfeld, Ger. 37/H1
Karlshamn, Swe. 20/E4
Karlskoga, Swe. 20/E4
Karlskrona, Swe. 20/E4
Karlsruhe, Ger. 33/H2
Karlstad, Swe. 20/E4
Karmāla, India 62/C4
Karnāl, India 62/C2
Karnobat, Bul. 41/H4
Karonga, Malw. 82/F2
Kars, Turk. 45/G4
Kartaly, Rus. 45/M1
Kartuzy, Pol. 27/K1
Karviná, Czh. 27/K4
Karwar, India 62/B5
Kasai, Japan 56/D3
Kasama, Japan 57/G2
Kasama, Zam. 82/F3
Kasane, Bots. 82/E4
Kasaoka, Japan 56/C3
Kāsaragod, India 62/C5
Kaseda, Japan 56/B5
Kāsganj, India 62/C2
Kāshān, Iran 51/G3
Kashi, China 46/H6
Kashihara, Japan 56/D3
Kashima, Japan 57/G3
Kashima, Japan 56/B4
Kashin, Rus. 42/H4
Kashiwazaki, Japan 57/F2
Kāshmar, Iran 51/J3
Kasimov, Rus. 45/G1
Kaspiysk, Rus. 45/H4
Kassala, Sudan 52/C5
Kassel, Ger. 29/G6
Kastamonu, Turk. 44/E4
Kasterlee, Belg. 28/B6
Kastoría, Gre. 40/E5
Kasukabe, Japan 57/F3
Kasūr, Pak. 53/K2
Katahdin (mt.), Me, US 95/G2
Kateríni, Gre. 39/H2
Kāthgodām, India 62/C2
Kāthmāndu (cap.), Nepal 62/E2
Kathua, India 53/L2
Kati, Mali 78/C3
Katiola, C.d'Iv. 78/D4
Katlehong, SAfr. 80/Q13
Katowice, Pol. 27/K3
Katsina, Nga. 79/G3
Katsuragi, Japan 56/D3
Katsuta, Japan 57/G2
Katsuura, Japan 57/G3
Katsuyama, Japan 56/E2
Katwijk aan Zee, Neth. 28/B4
Kauai (isl.), US 88/S9
Kaufbeuren, Ger. 37/G2
Kauhajoki, Fin. 42/D3
Kaumalapau, Hi, US 88/T10
Kaunas, Lith. 27/M1
Kavadarci, FYROM 40/F5
Kavajë, Alb. 40/D5
Kavála, Gre. 41/G5
Kavalerovo, Rus. 55/M3
Kāvali, India 62/C5
Kavaratti, India 62/B5
Kavieng, PNG 68/E5
Kawagoe, Japan 57/F3
Kawaguchi, Japan 57/F3
Kawamata, Japan 57/G2
Kawardha, India 62/D3
Kawasaki, Japan 57/F3
Kayes, Mali 78/C3
Kayseri, Turk. 50/C2
Kayuagung, Indo. 66/B4
Kazakhstan (ctry.) 46/G5
Kazan', Rus. 43/L5
Kazanlŭk, Bul. 41/G4
Kāzerūn, Iran 51/G4
Kazincbarcika, Hun. 27/L4
Kazuno, Japan 55/N3
Kearney, Ne, US 93/H2
Keawakapu, Hi, US 88/T10
Kebumen, Indo. 66/C5
Kecskemét, Hun. 40/D2
Kėdainiai, Lith. 27/M1
Kediri, Indo. 66/D5
Kędzierzyn-Koźle, Pol. 27/K3
Keelung (Chilung), Tai. 61/J3
Keene, NH, US 95/F3
Kefar Sava, Isr. 49/F7
Kehl, Ger. 31/G6
Keighley, Eng, UK 23/G4
Kelang, Malay. 66/B3
Kelheim, Ger. 33/J2
Kélo, Chad 76/J6
Kelowna, BC, Can. 90/D3
Kelso, Wa, US 90/C4
Keluang, Malay. 66/B3
Kem', Rus. 42/G2
Kemerovo, Rus. 46/J4
Kemi, Fin. 20/H2
Kempen, Ger. 28/D6
Kempston, Eng, UK 25/F2
Kempten, Ger. 37/G2
Kempton Park, SAfr. 80/Q13
Kendal, Eng, UK 23/F3
Kendall, Fl, US 97/H5
Kendari, Indo. 67/F4
Kendrāpāra, India 62/E3
Kenema, SLeo. 78/C5
Kenilworth, Eng, UK 25/E2
Kénitra, Mor. 76/D1
Kenmore, NY, US 95/V10
Kenner, La, US 97/F4
Kennett, Mo, US 93/K3
Kennewick, Wa, US 90/D4
Kenosha, Wi, US 99/Q14
Kent, Oh, US 94/D3
Kent, Wa, US 99/C3
Kentaū, Kaz. 46/G5
Kentucky (state), US 94/C4
Kenya (peak), Kenya 77/N8
Kenya (ctry.) 74/F4
Keonjhar, India 62/E3
Kerava, Fin. 20/H3
Kerch, Ukr. 44/F3
Keren, Erit. 52/C5
Kérkira, Gre. 39/F3
Kerkrade, Neth. 31/F2
Kermān, Iran 51/J4
Kérou, Ben. 79/F4
Kerrville, Tx, US 93/H5
Keşan, Turk. 41/H5
Kesen'numa, Japan 55/N4
Keshod, India 62/B3
Keskin, Turk. 44/E5
Kestel, Turk. 44/D4
Keszthely, Hun. 40/C2
Ketchikan, Ak, US 85/M4
Kétou, Ben. 79/F5
Kętrzyn, Pol. 27/L1
Kettering, Eng, UK 25/F2
Kevelaer, Ger. 28/D5
Key Largo, Fl, US 97/H5
Key West, Fl, US 97/H5
Kežmarok, Slvk. 27/L4
Khabarovsk, Rus. 55/M2
Khabarovsk Kray, Rus. 47/P4
Khairpur, Pak. 62/A2
Khalándrion, Gre. 39/N8
Khalkís, Gre. 39/H3
Khambhāliya, India 53/J4
Khambhat, India 62/B3
Khāmgaon, India 62/C3
Khamīs Mushayţ, SAr. 52/D5
Khammam, India 62/D4
Khān Yūnus, Gaza 49/D4
Khānābād, Afg. 53/J1
Khānaqīn, Iraq 51/F3
Khandwa, India 53/L4
Khānewāl, Pak. 53/K2
Khaniá, Gre. 39/J5
Khānpur, Pak. 62/B2
Khanty-Mansiysk, Rus. 46/G3
Kharagpur, India 62/E3
Kharkiv, Ukr. 44/F2
Kharmanli, Bul. 41/G5
Khartoum (cap.), Sudan 52/B5
Khasavyurt, Rus. 45/H4
Khashuri, Geo. 45/G4
Khemis Miliana, Alg. 76/F1
Khénifra, Mor. 76/D1
Kherson, Ukr. 41/L2
Khilok, Rus. 54/G1
Khimki, Rus. 43/W9
Khíos, Gre. 39/K3
Khiva, Uzb. 46/G5
Khmel'nytskyy, Ukr. 44/C2
Kholm, Afg. 53/J1
Kholmsk, Rus. 55/N2
Khomeynīshahr, Iran 51/G3
Khon Kaen, Thai. 65/C2
Khorramābād, Iran 51/G3
Khorramshahr, Iran 51/G4
Khouribga, Mor. 76/D1
Khujand, Taj. 46/G5
Khulna, Bang. 62/E3
Khurda, India 62/E3
Khust, Ukr. 27/M4
Khuzdār, Pak. 53/J3
Khvalynka, Rus. 55/L3
Khvoy, Iran 45/H5
Kičevo, FYROM 40/E5
Kidal, Mali 79/F2
Kidapawan, Phil. 67/G2
Kidderminster, Eng, UK 24/D2
Kidsgrove, Eng, UK 23/F5
Kiel, Ger. 26/F1
Kielce, Pol. 27/L3
Kien An, Viet. 65/D1
Kierspe, Ger. 29/E6
Kiev (cap.), Ukr. 44/D2
Kiffa, Mrta. 78/C2
Kifisiá, Gre. 39/N8
Kigali (cap.), Rwa. 77/M8
Kihei, Hi, US 88/T10
Kikinda, Serb. 40/E3
Kikwit, D.R. Congo 82/C2
Kilgore, Tx, US 93/J4
Kilimanjaro (peak), Tanz. 82/G1
Kilimli, Turk. 41/K5
Kilis, Turk. 49/E1
Kiliya, Ukr. 41/J3
Killeen, Tx, US 93/H5
Kimbe, PNG 68/E5
Kimberley, SAfr. 80/D3
Kimch'aek, NKor. 58/E2
Kimch'ŏn, SKor. 56/A2
Kimhae, SKor. 56/A3
Kimitsu, Japan 57/F3
Kimje, SKor. 58/D5
Kimovsk, Rus. 44/F1
Kimry, Rus. 42/H4
Kindia, Gui. 78/B4
Kindu, D.R. Congo 82/E1
Kinel', Rus. 45/J1
Kineshma, Rus. 42/J4
King William's Town, SAfr. 80/D4
Kingman, Az, US 92/D4
Kings Canyon National Park, Ca, US 92/C3
King's Lynn, Eng, UK 25/G1
Kingsport, Tn, US 97/H2
Kingston, On, Can. 94/E2
Kingston, NY, US 94/F3
Kingston (cap.), Jam. 103/G2
Kingston upon Hull, Eng, UK 23/H4
Kingston upon Thames, Eng, UK 25/F4
Kingstown (cap.), StV. 104/F4
Kingsville, Tx, US 96/D5
Kingswood, Eng, UK 24/D4
Kınık, Turk. 44/C5
Kinshasa (cap.), D.R. Congo 82/C1
Kinston, NC, US 97/J3
Kipushi, D.R. Congo 82/E3
Kiranomena, Madg. 81/H7
Kirchheim unter Teck, Ger. 26/E4
Kirchlengern, Ger. 29/F4
Kiribati (ctry.) 68/H5
Kırıkhan, Turk. 49/E1
Kırıkkale, Turk. 44/E5
Kirishi, Rus. 42/G4
Kırkağaç, Turk. 44/C5
Kirkby, Eng, UK 23/F5
Kirkby in Ashfield, Eng, UK 23/G5
Kirkee, India 62/B4
Kirkland, Qu, Can. 95/N7
Kirkland, Wa, US 99/C2
Kırklareli, Turk. 41/H5
Kirksville, Mo, US 91/K5
Kirkūk, Iraq 51/F3
Kirov, Rus. 43/L4
Kirov, Rus. 44/E1
Kirovo-Chepetsk, Rus. 43/L4
Kirovohrad, Ukr. 44/E2
Kirovsk, Rus. 42/G2
Kirsanov, Rus. 45/G1
Kırşehir, Turk. 44/E5
Kiruna, Swe. 42/D2
Kiryū, Japan 57/F2
Kisangani, D.R. Congo 77/L7
Kisarazu, Japan 57/F3
Kiselevsk, Rus. 46/J4
Kishanganj, India 62/E2
Kishangarh, India 62/B2
Kishiwada, Japan 56/D3
Kishorganj, Bang. 62/F3
Kiskőrös, Hun. 40/D2
Kiskunfélegyháza, Hun. 40/D2
Kiskunhalas, Hun. 40/D2
Kislovodsk, Rus. 45/G4
Kismaayo (Chisimayu), Som. 77/P8
Kissimmee, Fl, US 97/H4
Kisumu, Kenya 77/M8
Kisvárda, Hun. 27/M4
Kita, Mali 78/C3
Kita-Ibaraki, Japan 57/G2
Kitakata, Japan 57/F2
Kitakyūshū, Japan 56/B4
Kitami, Japan 55/N3
Kitchener, On, Can. 94/D3
Kittery, Me, US 95/G3
Kitwe, Zam. 82/E3
Kitzingen, Ger. 33/J2
Kizel, Rus. 43/N4
Kızılhisar, Turk. 50/B2
Kızıltepe, Turk. 50/E2
Kizlyar, Rus. 45/H4
Kladanj, Bosn. 40/D3
Kladno, Czh. 33/L1
Klagenfurt, Aus. 40/B2
Klaipėda, Lith. 42/D5
Klamath Falls, Or, US 90/C5
Klangenan, Indo. 66/C5
Klatovy, Czh. 33/K2
Klausen (Chiusa), It. 37/H4
Kleppestø, Nor. 20/C3
Klerksdorp, SAfr. 80/P13
Kleve, Ger. 28/D5
Klintsy, Rus. 44/E1
Ključ, Bosn. 40/C3
Kłodzko, Pol. 27/J3
Klosterneuburg, Aus. 40/C1
Kloten, Swi. 37/E3
Kluczbork, Pol. 27/K3
Knin, Cro. 40/C3
Knjaževac, Serb. 40/F4
Knottingley, Eng, UK 23/G4
Knysna, SAfr. 80/C4
Koani, Tanz. 82/G2
Kobayashi, Japan 56/B5
Kōbe, Japan 56/D3
Koblenz, Ger. 31/G3
Kobrin, Bela. 27/N2
Kočani, FYROM 40/F5
Kočevje, Slov. 40/B3
Koch'ang, SKor. 58/D5
Kōchi, Japan 56/C4
Kodiak, Ak, US 85/H4
Kodiak (isl.), US 85/H4
Kodinār, India 62/B3
Koforidua, Gha. 79/E5
Kōfu, Japan 57/F3
Koga, Japan 57/F2
Køge, Den. 26/G1
Kogi, Nga. 79/G4
Kohāt, Pak. 53/K2
Kohīma, India 60/B3
Kohtla-Järve, Est. 42/E4
Kohŭng, SKor. 58/D5
Kokkola (Karleby), Fin. 42/D3
Kokomo, In, US 94/C3
Kokrajhar, India 62/F2
Kökshetaū, Kaz. 46/G4
Koksijde, Belg. 30/B1
Kokubu, Japan 56/B5
Kolār, India 62/C5
Kolbermoor, Ger. 33/K3
Kolda, Sen. 78/B3
Kolding, Den. 26/E1
Kolhāpur, India 62/B4
Kolīn, Czh. 33/L1
Kolkata (Calcutta), India 62/E3
Koło, Pol. 44/A1
Kołobrzeg, Pol. 27/H1
Kolomna, Rus. 44/F1
Kolomyya, Ukr. 41/G1
Kolpashevo, Rus. 46/J4
Kolpino, Rus. 43/T7
Kolwezi, D.R. Congo 82/E3
Komagane, Japan 57/E3
Komárno, Slvk. 27/K5
Komárom, Hun. 27/K5
Komatsu, Japan 56/E2
Komatsushima, Japan 56/D3
Komló, Hun. 40/D2
Komono, Japan 56/E3
Komotiní, Gre. 41/G5
Komsomol'sk-na-Amure, Rus. 55/M1
Komsomol'skiy, Rus. 43/P2
Kon Tum, Viet. 65/D3
Konakovo, Rus. 42/H4
Kondopoga, Rus. 42/G3
Kondūz, Afg. 46/G6
Kongju, SKor. 58/D4
Kongsberg, Nor. 20/D4
Kongsvinger, Nor. 20/E3
Königs Wusterhausen, Ger. 27/G2
Königsbrunn, Ger. 37/G1
Königslutter am Elm, Ger. 29/H4
Königswinter, Ger. 31/G2
Konin, Pol. 27/K2
Köniz, Swi. 36/D4
Konjic, Bosn. 40/C4
Konotop, Ukr. 44/E2
Końskie, Pol. 27/L3
Konstancin-Jeziorna, Pol. 27/L2
Konstantynów Łódzki, Pol. 27/K3
Konstanz, Ger. 37/F2
Kontich, Belg. 28/B6
Konya, Turk. 50/C2
Konz, Ger. 31/F4
Kopargaon, India 62/B4
Kópavogur, Ice. 20/N7
Köpenick, Ger. 27/G2
Koper, Slov. 40/A3
Kopeysk, Rus. 43/P5
Köping, Swe. 42/C4
Koprivnica, Cro. 40/C2
Koraput, India 62/D4
Korba, India 62/D3
Korbach, Ger. 29/F6
Korçë, Alb. 40/E5
Korea (bay), China, N. 55/J4
Korenovsk, Rus. 44/F3
Korhogo, C.d'Iv. 78/D4
Kórinthos (Corinth), Gre. 39/H4
Kōriyama, Japan 57/G2
Koronadal, Phil. 67/F2
Koror (cap.), Palau 68/C4
Korosten', Ukr. 44/D2
Korostyshiv, Ukr. 44/D2
Korsakov, Rus. 55/N2
Korschenbroich, Ger. 28/D6
Korsør, Den. 26/F1
Kortenberg, Belg. 31/D2
Kortrijk, Belg. 30/C2
Koryazhma, Rus. 43/K3
Kosai, Japan 57/E3
Kościan, Pol. 27/J2
Kościerzyna, Pol. 27/J1
Kosciusko (mt.), Austl. 73/D3
Koshigaya, Japan 57/F3
Košice, Slvk. 27/L4
Kosovo (reg.), Serb. 39/G1
Kosovska Mitrovica, Serb. 40/E4
Kostopil', Ukr. 44/C2
Kostroma, Rus. 42/J4
Kostrzyn, Pol. 27/H2
Kostyantynivka, Ukr. 44/F2
Koszalin, Pol. 27/J1
Kot Addu, Pak. 53/K2
Kot Kapūra, India 53/K2
Kota, India 62/C2
Kota Baharu, Malay. 65/C5
Kota Kinabalu, Malay. 67/E2
Kotaagung, Indo. 66/B5
Kotabaru, Indo. 67/E4
Kotabumi, Indo. 66/B4
Kotel'nich, Rus. 43/L4
Kotel'nikovo, Rus. 45/G3
Kothagūdem, India 62/D4
Köthen, Ger. 26/F3
Kotka, Fin. 42/E3
Kotlas, Rus. 43/K3
Kotor, Serb. 40/D4
Kotovo, Rus. 45/H2
Kotovsk, Rus. 45/G1
Kotri, Pak. 62/A2
Kottayam, India 62/C6
Koudougou, Burk. 79/E3
Koulikoro, Mali 78/D3
Koumra, Chad 76/J6
Koupela, Burk. 79/E3
Koutiala, Mali 78/D3
Kouvola, Fin. 42/E3
Kovel', Ukr. 44/C2
Kovilpatti, India 62/C6
Kovrov, Rus. 42/J4
Kovūr, India 62/C5
Kovylkino, Rus. 45/G1
Kowloon, China 61/G4
Kōyama, Japan 56/B5
Kozan, Turk. 50/C2
Kozáni, Gre. 39/G2
Kozhikode (Calicut), India 62/C5
Kozienice, Pol. 27/L3
Kozlu, Turk. 41/K5
Kozluk, Turk. 50/E2
Kozyatyn, Ukr. 44/D2
Kpalimé, Togo 79/F5
Kpandu, Gha. 79/F5
Kraaifontein, SAfr. 80/L10
Kragujevac, Serb. 40/E3
Kraków, Pol. 27/K3
Kraljevo, Serb. 40/E4
Kralupy nad Vltavou, Czh. 33/L1
Kramators'k, Ukr. 44/F2
Kramfors, Swe. 42/C3
Kranj, Slov. 40/B2
Krapkowice, Pol. 27/J3
Kraśnik, Pol. 27/M3
Kraśnik Fabryczny, Pol. 27/M3
Krasnoarmeysk, Rus. 45/H2
Krasnodar, Rus. 44/F3
Krasnodar Kray, Rus. 46/D5
Krasnogorsk, Rus. 43/W9
Krasnohrad, Ukr. 44/E2
Krasnokamensk, Rus. 55/H1
Krasnokamsk, Rus. 43/M4
Krasnoslobodsk, Rus. 45/H2
Krasnotur'insk, Rus. 46/G4
Krasnoural'sk, Rus. 43/P4
Krasnoyarsk, Rus. 46/K4
Krasnystaw, Pol. 27/M3
Krasnyy Kut, Rus. 45/H2
Krasnyy Luch, Ukr. 44/F2
Krasnyy Sulin, Rus. 44/G3
Krefeld, Ger. 28/D6
Kremenchuk, Ukr. 44/E2
Krems an der Donau, Aus. 33/L2
Kreuzau, Ger. 31/F2
Kreuzlingen, Swi. 37/F2
Kreuztal, Ger. 31/G2
Kribi, Camr. 76/G7
Krichev, Bela. 44/D1
Kriens, Swi. 37/E3
Krimpen aan de IJssel, Neth. 28/B5
Krishnagiri, India 62/C5
Kristiansand, Nor. 20/C4
Kristianstad, Swe. 20/E4
Kristiansund, Nor. 20/C3
Kristinehamn, Swe. 20/E4
Kriva Palanka, FYROM 40/F4
Krnov, Czh. 27/J3
Krolevets', Ukr. 44/E2
Kroměříž, Czh. 27/J4
Kronach, Ger. 33/J1
Kronshtadt, Rus. 43/S6
Kroonstad, SAfr. 80/D2
Kropotkin, Rus. 45/G3
Krosno, Pol. 27/L4
Krotoszyn, Pol. 27/J3
Krško, Slov. 40/B3
Krugersdorp, SAfr. 80/P13
Krujë, Alb. 40/D5
Kruševac, Serb. 40/E4
Krymsk, Rus. 44/F3
Kryvyy Rih, Ukr. 41/L2

L

Merano, It. 37/H4
Merauke, Indo. 67/K5
Merced, Ca, US 92/B3
Mercedes, Arg. 109/C3
Mercedes, Uru. 109/E3
Mercedes, Arg. 109/E2
Mercer Island, Wa, US 99/C2
Merefa, Ukr. 44/F2
Merelbeke, Belg. 28/A6
Mergui (Myeik), Myan. 65/B3
Mérida, Ven. 106/D2
Mérida, Mex. 102/D1
Mérida, Sp. 34/B3
Meridian, Ms, US 97/F3
Mérignac, Fr. 32/C4
Merksem, Belg. 28/B6
Merlo, Arg. 109/E3
Merrimack, NH, US 95/G3
Merritt Island, Fl, US 97/H4
Mersin, Turk. 49/D1
Merthyr Tydfil, Wal, UK 24/C3
Meru, Kenya 77/N7
Merzifon, Turk. 44/E4
Merzig, Ger. 31/F5
Mesa, Az, US 92/E4
Mesa Verde National Park, Co, US 92/E3
Mesagne, It. 40/C5
Meschede, Ger. 29/F6
Mesomeloka, Madg. 81/J8
Mesquite, Tx, US 93/H4
Messaad, Alg. 76/F1
Messina, It. 38/D3
Mestre, It. 33/K4
Metairie, La, US 97/F4
Metán, Arg. 109/D2
Metepec, Mex. 101/Q10
Mettmann, Ger. 28/D6
Metz, Fr. 31/F5
Metzingen, Ger. 37/F1
Mevasseret Ẕiyyon, Isr. 49/G8
Mexborough, Eng, UK 23/G5
Mexicali, Mex. 92/D4
Mexico, Mo, US 93/K3
Mexico (gulf), NAm. 89/H6
Mexico (ctry.), Mex. 84/G7
Mexico (cap.), Mex. 101/Q10
Meybod, Iran 51/H3
Meyerton, SAfr. 80/Q13
Meyrin, Swi. 36/C5
Meyzieu, Fr. 36/A6
Mezhdurechensk, Rus. 46/J4
Mezőkövesd, Hun. 27/L5
Mezőtúr, Hun. 40/E2
Mhamdia Fūshānah, Tun. 38/B4
Mhow, India 62/C3
Miami, Ok, US 93/J3
Miami, Fl, US 97/H5
Miami Beach, Fl, US 97/H5
Mīāndoāb, Iran 51/F2
Miandrivazo, Madg. 81/H7
Mīāneh, Iran 51/F2
Miānwāli, Pak. 53/K2
Mianyang, China 60/E2
Miass, Rus. 43/P5
Michalovce, Slvk. 27/L4
Michigan (lake), US 94/C2
Michigan (state), US 94/C2
Michigan City, In, US 94/C3
Michurinsk, Rus. 45/G1
Micronesia, Federated States of (ctry.) 68/D4
Middelburg, SAfr. 80/Q12
Middelburg, Neth. 28/A5
Middelharnis, Neth. 28/B5
Middelkerke, Belg. 30/B1
Middlesboro, Ky, US 97/H2
Middlesbrough, Eng, UK 23/G2
Middleton, Eng, UK 23/F4
Midland, On, Can. 94/E2
Midland, Mi, US 94/C3
Midland, Tx, US 93/G5
Midlothian, Il, US 99/Q16
Midyat, Turk. 50/E2
Mie, Japan 56/B4
Międzyrzec Podlaski, Pol. 27/M3
Międzyrzecz, Pol. 27/H2
Mielec, Pol. 27/L3
Miercurea Ciuc, Rom. 41/G2
Mieres, Sp. 34/C1
Migdal Ha'emeq, Isr. 49/G6
Miguelópolis, Braz. 108/B2
Mihara, Japan 56/C3
Miharu, Japan 57/G2
Mihrābpur, Pak. 53/J3
Mijas, Sp. 34/C4
Mikhaylovka, Rus. 45/G2
Mikkeli, Fin. 42/E3
Mikuni, Japan 56/E2
Milagro, Ecu. 106/C4
Milan (Milano), It. 33/H4
Milano (Milan), It. 33/H4
Milas, Turk. 50/A2
Milazzo, It. 38/D3
Mildura, Austl. 73/B2
Mililani Town, Hi, US 88/V13
Mill Valley, Ca, US 99/J11
Millau, Fr. 32/E4
Millbrae, Ca, US 99/K11
Milledgeville, Ga, US 97/H3
Millerovo, Rus. 45/G2
Milpitas, Ca, US 99/L12
Milton, On, Can. 95/T8
Milton Keynes, Eng, UK 25/F2
Milwaukee, Wi, US 99/Q13
Mīnā' Su'ūd, Kuw. 51/G4
Minamata, Japan 56/B4
Minas, Cuba 103/G1
Minas, Uru. 109/E3
Minas de Matahambre, Cuba 103/F1
Minatitlán, Mex. 102/C2
Minden, La, US 93/J4
Minden, Ger. 29/F4
Mineiros, Braz. 107/H7
Mineral Wells, Tx, US 93/H4
Mineral'nye Vody, Rus. 45/G3
Mingäçevir, Azer. 45/H4
Mingāora, Pak. 53/K2
Minna, Nga. 79/G4
Minnesota (state), US 91/K4
Mino, Japan 57/E3
Minorca (isl.), Sp. 35/H2
Minsk (cap.), Bela. 42/E5
Mińsk Mazowiecki, Pol. 27/L2
Minturno, It. 40/A5
Minūf, Egypt 49/B4
Minusinsk, Rus. 46/K4
Minyā al Qamḩ, Egypt 49/B4
Mirabel, Qu, Can. 95/M6
Miracema, Braz. 108/D2
Miracema do Norte, Braz. 107/J5
Miraj, India 62/B4
Miramar, Arg. 109/E4
Miranda de Ebro, Sp. 34/D1
Mirandola, It. 33/J4
Mirandópolis, Braz. 108/B2
Mirassol, Braz. 108/B2
Mirfield, Eng, UK 23/G4
Miri, Malay. 66/D3
Mirnyy, Rus. 47/M3
Miryang, SKor. 56/A3
Misaki, Japan 56/D3
Misantla, Mex. 101/N7
Mishawaka, In, US 94/C3
Mishima, Japan 57/F3
Misilmeri, It. 38/C3
Miskolc, Hun. 27/L4
Mişrātah, Libya 76/J1
Mission, Tx, US 96/D5
Mission Viejo, Ca, US 92/C4
Mississauga, On, Can. 95/T8
Mississippi (riv.), US 89/H5
Mississippi (state), US 97/F3
Missouri (state), US 93/J3
Missouri (riv.), US 88/G3
Missouri City, Tx, US 93/J5
Mitchell, SD, US 93/H2
Mitilíni, Gre. 39/K3
Mito, Japan 57/G2
Mitry-Mory, Fr. 30/B6
Mitsinjo, Madg. 81/H7
Mits'iwa, Erit. 77/N4
Mitsukaidō, Japan 57/F2
Mitsuke, Japan 57/F2
Mittweida, Ger. 26/G3
Mitú, Col. 106/D3
Mixquiahuala, Mex. 101/K6
Miyako, Japan 55/N4
Miyakonojō, Japan 56/B5
Miyanojō, Japan 56/B5
Miyazaki, Japan 56/B5
Miyazu, Japan 56/D3
Miyoshi, Japan 56/C3
Mizunami, Japan 57/E3
Mjölby, Swe. 20/E4
Mkokotoni, Tanz. 82/G2
Mladá Boleslav, Czh. 33/L1
Mladenovac, Serb. 40/E3
Mława, Pol. 27/L2
Moa, Cuba 103/H1
Moaña, Sp. 34/A1
Moanda, Gabon 82/B1
Mobaye, CAfr. 77/K7
Moberly, Mo, US 93/J3
Mobile, Al, US 97/F4
Mochudi, Bots. 80/D2
Mocoa, Col. 106/C3
Mococa, Braz. 108/F6
Modāsa, India 62/B3
Modena, It. 33/J4
Modesto, Ca, US 92/B3
Modica, It. 38/D4
Mödling, Aus. 40/C1
Modriča, Bosn. 40/D3
Modugno, It. 40/C5
Moe, Austl. 73/C3
Moers, Ger. 28/D6
Moga, India 53/L2
Mogadishu (cap.), Som. 77/Q7
Mogi das Cruzes, Braz. 108/G8
Mogi-Guaçu, Braz. 108/G7
Mogi-Mirim, Braz. 108/G7
Mogocha, Rus. 55/H1
Mohács, Hun. 40/D3
Mohammedia, Mor. 76/D1
Mohyliv-Podil's'kyy, Ukr. 41/H1
Moineşti, Rom. 41/H2
Moita, Port. 35/Q10
Mojave (des.), Ca, US 88/C5
Mōka, Japan 57/F2
Mokokchūng, India 60/B3
Mokp'o, SKor. 58/D5
Mol, Belg. 28/C6
Mola di Bari, It. 40/C5
Molde, Nor. 20/C3
Moldova (ctry.) 41/H2
Moldova Nouă, Rom. 40/E3
Molepolole, Bots. 80/D2
Molfetta, It. 40/C5
Molina de Segura, Sp. 34/E3
Moline, Il, US 93/K2
Molins de Rei, Sp. 35/L7
Mollendo, Peru 106/D7
Mollet del Vallès, Sp. 35/L6
Mölln, Ger. 26/F2
Moluccas (arch.), Indo. 67/G3
Mombasa, Kenya 82/G1
Mombetsu, Japan 55/N3
Mona Passage (chan.), NAm. 104/D3
Monaco (cap.), Mona. 33/G5
Monaco (ctry.) 33/G5
Moncada, Sp. 35/E3
Moncalieri, It. 33/G4
Monchegorsk, Rus. 42/G2
Mönchengladbach, Ger. 28/D6
Monclova, Mex. 96/C5
Moncton, NB, Can. 95/H2
Mondovì, It. 33/G4
Mondragón, Sp. 34/D1
Mondragone, It. 40/A5
Monfalcone, It. 40/A3
Monforte, Sp. 34/B1
Mongaguá, Braz. 108/G9
Mongo, Chad 77/J5
Mongolia (ctry.) 54/D2
Mongu, Zam. 82/D4
Monheim, Ger. 28/D6
Monmouth, Il, US 93/K2
Monopoli, It. 40/C5
Monor, Hun. 40/D2
Monreale, It. 38/C3
Monroe, Ga, US 97/H3
Monroe, La, US 93/J4
Monroe, NC, US 97/H3
Monroe, Wi, US 93/K2
Monroe, Mi, US 94/D3
Monrovia (cap.), Libr. 78/C5
Mons, Belg. 30/C3
Monster, Neth. 28/B4
Mont-de-Marsan, Fr. 32/C5
Mont-Royal, Qu, Can. 95/N6
Montana (state), US 90/F4
Montana, Bul. 41/F4
Montargis, Fr. 32/E2
Montauban, Fr. 32/D4
Montbéliard, Fr. 36/C2
Montcada i Reixac, Sp. 35/L7
Montceau-les-Mines, Fr. 32/F3
Monte Alegre, Braz. 107/H4
Monte Alto, Braz. 108/B2
Monte Carmelo, Braz. 108/C1
Monte Caseros, Arg. 109/E3
Monte Sant'Angelo, It. 41/B5
Montego Bay, Jam. 103/G2
Montélimar, Fr. 32/F4
Montemorelos, Mex. 96/D5
Montenegro, Braz. 108/B4
Montereau-Faut-Yonne, Fr. 32/E2
Monterey, Ca, US 92/B3
Montería, Col. 103/H4
Montero, Bol. 106/F7
Monteros, Arg. 109/C2
Monterotondo, It. 38/C1
Monterrey, Mex. 96/C5
Montes Claros, Braz. 107/K7
Montesilvano Marina, It. 40/B4
Montevideo (cap.), Uru. 109/E3
Montgeron, Fr. 30/B6
Montgomery (cap.), Al, US 97/G3
Montigny-le-Bretonneux, Fr. 30/B6
Montigny-lès-Metz, Fr. 31/F5
Montijo, Port. 35/Q10
Montijo, Sp. 34/B3
Montilla, Sp. 34/C4
Montivilliers, Fr. 32/D2
Montluçon, Fr. 32/E3
Montpelier (cap.), Vt, US 95/F2
Montpellier, Fr. 32/E5
Montréal, Qu, Can. 95/N6
Montréal-Nord, Qu, Can. 95/N6
Montreux, Swi. 36/C5
Montserrat (dpcy.), Fr. 104/F3
Monywa, Myan. 60/B4
Monza, It. 33/H4
Monzón, Sp. 35/F2
Moore, Ok, US 93/H4
Mooresville, NC, US 97/H3
Moosburg, Ger. 33/J2
Moose Jaw, Sk, Can. 91/G3
Mopti, Mali 78/D3
Moquegua, Peru 106/D7
Mór, Hun. 40/D2
Mora, NM, US 93/F4
Mora, Swe. 20/E3
Morada Nova, Braz. 107/L5
Morādābād, India 62/C2
Morafenobe, Madg. 81/H7
Moraga, Ca, US 99/K11
Morales, Guat. 102/D3
Moramanga, Madg. 81/J7
Morarano Chrome, Madg. 81/J7
Moratuwa, SrL. 62/C6
Morelia, Mex. 101/E5
Morena, India 62/C2
Moreni, Rom. 41/G3
Moreno Valley, Ca, US 92/C4
Morgan City, La, US 93/K5
Morganton, NC, US 97/H3
Morioka, Japan 55/N4
Moriyama, Japan 56/D3
Morlaix, Fr. 32/B2
Morlanwelz, Belg. 31/D3
Morley, Eng, UK 23/G4
Moro, Pak. 62/A2
Morocco (ctry.) 76/C1
Morogoro, Tanz. 82/G2
Morombe, Madg. 81/G8
Morón, Cuba 103/G1
Morón, Arg. 109/E3
Mörön, Mong. 54/E2
Morón de la Frontera, Sp. 34/C4
Morondava, Madg. 81/H8
Moroni (cap.), Com. 81/G5
Moroto, Ugan. 77/M7
Morrinhos, Braz. 108/B1
Morris, Il, US 93/K2
Morristown, Tn, US 97/H2
Morro Bay, Ca, US 92/B4
Morshansk, Rus. 45/G1
Morton, Il, US 93/K2
Morton Grove, Il, US 99/Q15
Mortsel, Belg. 28/B6
Morvi, India 62/B3
Morwell, Austl. 73/C3
Mosbach, Ger. 33/H2
Moscow (cap.), Rus. 43/W9
Moscow Univ. Ice Shelf, Ant. 83/J
Moses Lake, Wa, US 90/D4
Moshi, Tanz. 82/G1
Mosonmagyaróvár, Hun. 40/C2
Moss, Nor. 20/D4
Moss Point, Ms, US 97/F4
Mosselbaai, SAfr. 80/C4
Mössingen, Ger. 37/F1
Mossoró, Braz. 107/L5
Most, Czh. 33/K1
Mostaganem, Alg. 76/F1
Mostar, Bosn. 40/C4
Móstoles, Sp. 35/N9
Mosul (Al Mawşil), Syria 51/E2
Motala, Swe. 20/E4
Motīhāri, India 62/D2
Motomiya, Japan 57/G2
Motril, Sp. 34/D4
Motul de Carrillo Puerto, Mex. 102/D1
Mouila, Gabon 82/B1
Moulins, Fr. 32/E3
Moultrie, Ga, US 97/H4
Moundou, Chad 76/J6
Moundsville, WV, US 97/H2
Mount Abu, India 62/B3
Mount Baker-Snoqualmie, Wa, US 99/D1
Mount Clemens, Mi, US 99/G6
Mount Gambier, Austl. 73/B3
Mount Hagen, PNG 68/D5
Mount Pearl, Nf, Can. 95/L2
Mount Pleasant, Tx, US 93/J4
Mount Pleasant, Mi, US 94/C3
Mount Prospect, Il, US 99/P15
Mount Rainier National Park, Wa, US 90/C4
Mount Vernon, Wa, US 90/C3
Mount Vernon, Il, US 93/K3
Mount Vernon, Oh, US 94/D3
Mountain Ash, Wal, UK 24/C3
Mountain View, Ca, US 99/K12
Mountlake Terrace, Wa, US 99/C2
Mouscron, Belg. 30/C2
Mouths of the Niger, Nga. 76/G6
Moyuta, Guat. 102/D3
Mozambique (ctry.) 82/G4
Mozambique (chan.), Afr. 82/J10
Mozhaysk, Rus. 42/H5
Mozhga, Rus. 43/M4
Mpika, Zam. 82/F3
Mrągowo, Pol. 27/L2
Mtsensk, Rus. 44/F1
Mualama, Moz. 82/G4
Muar, Malay. 66/B3
Muarabungo, Indo. 66/B4
Mucojo, Moz. 82/H3
Mudanjiang, China 55/K3
Mudanya, Turk. 41/J5
Mudon, Myan. 65/B2
Mufulira, Zam. 82/E3
Muğla, Turk. 50/B2
Mühldorf, Ger. 33/K2
Muju, SKor. 58/D4
Mukacheve, Ukr. 27/M4
Mukhayyam al Yarmūk, Syria 49/E3
Muktsar, India 53/K2
Mülhausen, Ger. 29/H6
Mülheim an der Ruhr, Ger. 28/D6
Mulhouse, Fr. 36/D2
Müllheim, Ger. 36/D2
Multān, Pak. 53/K2
Mumbai (Bombay), India 62/B4
Muncar, Indo. 66/D5
München, Ger. 37/H1
Muncie, In, US 97/G1
Mundelein, Il, US 99/Q15
Münden, Ger. 29/G6
Mundo Novo, Braz. 109/F1
Mungaolī, India 62/C3
Munger, India 62/E2
Münster, Ger. 29/E5
Munster, Ger. 29/H3
Munster, In, US 99/R16
Münstereifel, Ger. 31/F2
Muntok, Indo. 66/C4
Murakami, Japan 57/F1
Murcia, Sp. 35/E4
Muret, Fr. 32/D5
Murfreesboro, Tn, US 97/G3
Muriaé, Braz. 108/D2
Murmansk, Rus. 42/G1
Murom, Rus. 42/J5
Muroran, Japan 55/N3
Muroto, Japan 56/D4
Murphysboro, Il, US 93/K3
Murray, Ky, US 97/F2
Murray (riv.), Austl. 73/A2
Murwāra, India 62/D3
Muş, Turk. 50/E2
Muscat (cap.), Oman 53/G4
Mushābani, India 62/E3
Mushin, Nga. 79/F5
Muskego, Wi, US 99/P14
Musoma, Tanz. 82/F1
Mustafakemalpaşa, Turk. 44/D4
Mustang, Ok, US 93/H4
Mut, Turk. 49/C1
Mutare, Zim. 82/F4
Mutsamudu, Com. 81/H6
Mutsu, Japan 55/N3
Muttenz, Swi. 36/D2
Muzaffargarh, Pak. 53/K2
Muzaffarnagar, India 62/C2
Muzaffarpur, India 62/E2
Mwanza, Tanz. 82/F1
Mwene-Ditu, D.R. Congo 82/D2
My Tho, Viet. 65/D4
Myanmar (Burma) (ctry.) 63/G3
Myaungmya, Myan. 60/B5
Myingyan, Myan. 60/B4
Myitkyinā, Myan. 60/C3
Mykolayiv, Ukr. 41/L2
Myrhorod, Ukr. 44/E2
Myrtle Beach, SC, US 97/J3
Myślenice, Pol. 27/K4
Mysore, India 62/C5
Myszków, Pol. 27/K3
Mytishchi, Rus. 43/W9
Mzuzu, Malw. 82/F3

N

N'Djamena (cap.), Chad 76/J5
Naaldwijk, Neth. 28/B4
Naarden, Neth. 28/C4
Nabadwīp, India 62/E3
Nabari, Japan 56/E3
Naberezhnye Chelny, Rus. 43/M5
Nābul, Tun. 38/B4
Nacaome, Hon. 102/E3
Nachi-Katsuura, Japan 56/D4
Náchod, Czh. 33/M1
Nacogdoches, Tx, US 93/J5
Nadiād, India 62/B3
Nador, Mor. 76/E1
Naga, Phil. 68/B3
Nagahama, Japan 56/E3
Nagai, Japan 57/G1
Nagano, Japan 57/F2
Nagaoka, Japan 57/F2
Nagaokakyō, Japan 56/D3
Nagaon (Nowgong), India 60/B3
Nagasaki, Japan 56/A4
Nagato, Japan 56/B3
Nāgaur, India 62/B2
Nāgda, India 62/C3
Nāgercoil, India 62/C6
Nagold, Ger. 37/E1
Nagoya, Japan 57/E3
Nāgpur, India 62/C3
Nagykanizsa, Hun. 40/C2
Nagykőrös, Hun. 40/D2
Naha, Japan 68/B2
Nahariyya, Isr. 49/D3
Nahāvand, Iran 51/G3
Nainpur, India 62/D3
Nairobi (cap.), Kenya 77/N8
Najafābād, Iran 51/G3
Najībābād, India 62/C2
Naju, SKor. 58/D5
Nakajō, Japan 57/F1
Nakaminato, Japan 57/G2
Nakamura, Japan 56/C4
Nakano, Japan 57/F2
Nakatsu, Japan 56/B4
Nakatsugawa, Japan 57/E3
Nakhodka, Rus. 55/L3
Nakhon Pathom, Thai. 65/C3
Nakhon Phanom, Thai. 65/D2
Nakhon Ratchasima, Thai. 65/C3
Nakhon Sawan, Thai. 65/C3
Nakhon Si Thammarat, Thai. 65/B4
Nakło nad Notecią, Pol. 27/J2
Nakskov, Den. 26/F1
Nakuru, Kenya 82/G1
Nal'chik, Rus. 45/G4
Nalgonda, India 62/C4
Nālūt, Libya 76/H1
Nam Dinh, Viet. 65/D1
Namangan, Uzb. 46/H5
Namerikawa, Japan 57/E2
Namibe, Ang. 82/B4
Namibia (ctry.) 82/C5
Namie, Japan 57/G2
Namp'o, NKor. 58/C3
Nampula, Moz. 82/G4
Nāmrup, India 60/B3
Namur, Belg. 31/D3
Namwŏn, SKor. 58/D5
Namysłów, Pol. 27/J3
Nan, Thai. 65/C2
Nanaimo, BC, Can. 90/C3
Nanakuli, Hi, US 88/V13
Nanao, Japan 57/E2
Nanchang, China 61/G2
Nanchong, China 60/E2
Nancy, Fr. 31/F6
Nānded, India 62/C4
Nandurbār, India 62/B3
Nandyāl, India 62/C4
Nangapinoh, Indo. 66/D4
Nangong, China 59/C3
Nanjing, China 61/H1
Nankoku, Japan 56/C4
Nanning, China 65/E1
Nānpāra, India 62/D2
Nanping, China 61/H3
Nanterre, Fr. 30/B6
Nantes, Fr. 32/C3
Nanticoke, Pa, US 94/E3
Nanticoke, On, Can. 95/R10
Nantong, China 61/J1
Nanuque, Braz. 108/D1
Nanyang, China 59/C4
Náousa, Gre. 40/F5
Napa, Ca, US 99/K10
Naperville, Il, US 99/P16
Napier, NZ 71/S10
Naples, Fl, US 97/H5
Napoli, It. 40/B5
Nara, Japan 56/D3
Naranjos, Mex. 102/B1
Narasannapeta, India 62/D4
Narathiwat, Thai. 65/C5
Nārāyanganj, Bang. 62/F3
Nārāyanpet, India 62/C4
Narbonne, Fr. 32/E5
Nardò, It. 39/F2
Narkatiāganj, India 62/D2
Narón, Sp. 34/A1
Nārowāl, Pak. 53/K2
Närpiö (Närpes), Fin. 42/D3
Narra, Phil. 67/E2

Narsimhapur, India 62/C3
Narsingarh, India 62/C3
Naruto, Japan 56/D3
Narva, Est. 42/F4
Narvacan, Phil. 61/J5
Narvik, Nor. 42/C1
Nar'yan-Mar, Rus. 43/M2
Naryn, Kyr. 46/H5
Nashua, NH, US 87/J4
Nashua, NH, US 95/G3
Nashville (cap.), Tn, US 94/C4
Našice, Cro. 40/D3
Nāsik, India 62/B4
Nasīrābād, India 62/B2
Nassau (cap.), Bahm. 97/J5
Nasser (lake), Egypt 77/M3
Nässjö, Swe. 20/E4
Næstved, Den. 26/F1
Natal, Braz. 107/L5
Natchez, Ms, US 93/K5
Natchitoches, La, US 93/J5
Nāthdwāra, India 62/B3
Naturns (Naturno), It. 37/G4
Naucalpan, Mex. 101/Q10
Naumburg, Ger. 26/F3
Nauru (ctry.) 68/F5
Navalmoral de la Mata, Sp. 34/C3
Navapolatsk, Bela. 42/F5
Naviraí, Braz. 109/F1
Năvodari, Rom. 41/J3
Navojoa, Mex. 100/C3
Navolato, Mex. 100/D3
Navsāri, India 62/B3
Nawābganj, India 62/D2
Nawābshāh, Pak. 62/A2
Nawoiy, Uzb. 46/G5
Naxçıvan, Azer. 45/H5
Nazaré, Braz. 107/L6
Nazca, Peru 106/D6
Naze, Japan 68/B2
Nazerat (Nazareth), Isr. 49/G6
Nazilli, Turk. 50/B2
Nazrēt, Eth. 77/N6
Nazyvayevsk, Rus. 46/H4
Ndalatando, Ang. 82/B2
Ndele, CAfr. 77/K6
Ndola, Zam. 82/E3
Néa Ionía, Gre. 39/N8
Néa Ionía, Gre. 39/H3
Neath, Wal, UK 24/C3
Nebitdag, Trkm. 51/H2
Nebraska (state), US 93/G2
Neckarsulm, Ger. 33/H2
Necochea, Arg. 109/E4
Nederland, Tx, US 93/J5
Nederweert, Neth. 28/C6
Neftekamsk, Rus. 43/M4
Negombo, SrL. 62/C6
Negotin, Serb. 40/F3
Negotino, FYROM 40/F5
Negro (riv.), Arg. 109/D5
Negro (riv.), Uru. 109/E3
Neijiang, China 60/E2
Neiva, Col. 106/C3
Nek'emtē, Eth. 77/N6
Nelidovo, Rus. 42/G4
Nellore, India 62/C5
Nelson, Eng, UK 23/F4
Nelson, NZ 71/R11
Nelson (riv.), Mb, Can. 86/G3
Nelspruit, SAfr. 81/E2
Néma, Mrta. 78/D2
Nemuro, Japan 55/P3
Neosho, Mo, US 93/J3
Nepal (ctry.) 62/D2
Nepālganj, Nepal 62/D2
Nepanagar, India 62/C3
Nepean, On, Can. 94/F2
Nerekhta, Rus. 42/J4
Nerja, Sp. 34/D4
Nes Ziyyona, Isr. 49/F8
Nesher, Isr. 49/G6
Neston, Eng, UK 23/E5
Netanya, Isr. 49/F7
Netherlands (ctry.) 28/B5
Netherlands Antilles (dpcy.), Neth. 106/E1
Netphen, Ger. 31/H2
Nettetal, Ger. 28/D6
Nettuno, It. 38/C2
Neu-Ulm, Ger. 37/G1
Neubrandenburg, Ger. 27/G2
Neuburg an der Donau, Ger. 26/F4
Neuchâtel, Swi. 36/C4
Neufahrn bei Freising, Ger. 37/H1
Neuilly-sur-Seine, Fr. 30/B6
Neumarkt (Enga), It. 37/H5
Neumarkt in der Oberpfalz, Ger. 33/J2
Neumünster, Ger. 26/E1
Neunkirchen, Ger. 31/G5
Neunkirchen-Seelscheid, Ger. 31/G2
Neuquén, Arg. 109/C4
Neuruppin, Ger. 26/G2
Neusäss, Ger. 37/G1
Neuss, Ger. 28/D6
Neustadt am Rübenberge, Ger. 29/G3
Neustadt an der Weinstrasse, Ger. 31/H5
Neustadt bei Coburg, Ger. 33/J1
Neustadt in Holstein, Ger. 26/F1
Neustrelitz, Ger. 26/G2
Neuwied, Ger. 31/G3
Nevada (state), US 92/C3
Nevel', Rus. 42/F4
Nevel'sk, Rus. 55/N2
Nevers, Fr. 32/E3
Nevesinje, Bosn. 40/D4
Nevinnomyssk, Rus. 45/G3
Nevşehir, Turk. 50/C2
New Albany, In, US 97/G2
New Amsterdam, Guy. 106/G2
New Bedford, Ma, US 95/G3
New Berlin, Wi, US 99/P14
New Bern, NC, US 97/J3
New Braunfels, Tx, US 93/H5
New Britain, Ct, US 95/F3
New Brunswick (prov.), Can. 95/H2
New Caledonia (isl.), NCal. 69/U12
New Caledonia (dpcy.), Fr. 69/U11
New Castle, Pa, US 94/D3
New Castle, In, US 97/G2
New Delhi (cap.), India 62/C2
New Guinea (isl.), Indo.,PNG 68/C5
New Hampshire (state), US 95/G3
New Haven, Ct, US 95/F3
New Iberia, La, US 93/K5
New Jersey (state), US 94/F3
New Kensington, Pa, US 94/E3
New Lenox, Il, US 99/Q16
New London, Ct, US 95/F3
New Mexico (state), US 92/F4
New Orleans, La, US 97/F4
New Philadelphia, Oh, US 94/D3
New Plymouth, NZ 71/R10
New Port Richey, Fl, US 97/H4
New Smyrna Beach, Fl, US 97/H4
New South Wales, Austl. 73/D1
New Westminster, BC, Can. 90/C3
New York, NY, US 94/F3
New York (state), US 94/F3
New Zealand (ctry.) 71/Q10
Newark, Oh, US 97/H1
Newark, NJ, US 94/F3
Newark, Ca, US 99/K11
Newark-on-Trent, Eng, UK 23/H5
Newberry, SC, US 97/H3
Newburn, Eng, UK 23/G2
Newbury, Eng, UK 25/E4
Newcastle, SAfr. 81/E2
Newcastle, Austl. 73/D2
Newcastle upon Tyne, Eng, UK 23/G2
Newcastle-under-Lyme, Eng, UK 23/F6
Newfoundland (prov.), Can. 95/K1
Newfoundland (isl.), Can. 95/L1
Newmarket, On, Can. 94/E2
Newmarket, Eng, UK 25/G2
Newnan, Ga, US 97/G3
Newport, Ky, US 97/G2
Newport, RI, US 95/G3
Newport, Eng, UK 25/E5
Newport, Wal, UK 24/D3
Newquay, Eng, UK 24/A6
Newry, NI, UK 22/B3
Newton, Ks, US 93/H3
Newton, Ma, US 95/G3
Newton Abbot, Eng, UK 24/C5
Newton-le-Willows, Eng, UK 23/F5
Newtownabbey, NI, UK 22/C2
Newtownards, NI, UK 22/C2
Neyrīz, Iran 51/H4
Neyshābūr, Iran 51/J2
Neyveli, India 62/C5
Neyyāttinkara, India 62/C6
Nezahualcóyotl, Mex. 101/Q10
Ngabang, Indo. 66/C3
Ngaoundéré, Camr. 76/H6
Nha Trang, Viet. 65/E3
Niagara (falls), Can., US 95/U9
Niagara Falls, On, Can. 95/U9
Niagara Falls, NY, US 95/U9
Niamey (cap.), Niger 79/F3
Nicaragua (ctry.), Nic. 103/E3
Nicaragua (lake), Nic. 103/E4
Nicastro-Sambiase, It. 38/E3
Nice, Fr. 33/G5
Niceville, Fl, US 97/G4
Nichinan, Japan 56/B5
Nicolás Romero, Mex. 101/Q9
Nicosia (cap.), Cyp. 49/C2
Nidda, Ger. 33/H1
Nienburg, Ger. 29/G3
Nieuw-Amsterdam, Sur. 107/G2
Nieuw-Nickerie, Sur. 107/G2
Nieuwegein, Neth. 28/C4
Nieuwerkerk aan de IJssel, Neth. 28/B5
Niğde, Turk. 50/C2
Nigel, SAfr. 80/Q13
Niger (ctry.) 76/G4
Niger (riv.) 76/F5
Nigeria (ctry.) 76/G6
Nigrán, Sp. 34/A1
Nihonmatsu, Japan 57/G2
Niigata, Japan 57/F2
Niihama, Japan 56/C4
Niimi, Japan 56/C3
Niitsu, Japan 57/F2
Nijkerk, Neth. 28/C4
Nijlen, Belg. 28/B6
Nijmegen, Neth. 28/C5
Nikel', Rus. 42/F1
Nikki, Ben. 79/F4
Nikkō, Japan 57/F2
Nikolayevsk-na-Amure, Rus. 47/Q4
Nikol'sk, Rus. 45/H1
Nikopol', Ukr. 44/E3
Niksar, Turk. 44/F4
Nikšić, Serb. 40/D4
Nile (delta), Egypt 49/B4
Nile (riv.), Afr. 77/M3
Niles, Oh, US 94/D3
Niles, Mi, US 94/C3
Niles, Il, US 99/Q15
Nilópolis, Braz. 108/K7
Nīmāj, India 62/B2
Nîmes, Fr. 32/F5
Ningbo, China 61/J2
Ninh Binh, Viet. 65/D1
Ninove, Belg. 30/D2
Niort, Fr. 32/C3
Nipigon (lake), Can. 94/B1
Nirasaki, Japan 57/F3
Nirmal, India 62/C4
Niš, Serb. 40/E4
Niscemi, It. 38/D4
Nishino'omote, Japan 56/B5
Nishio, Japan 57/E3
Nishiwaki, Japan 56/D3
Niterói, Braz. 108/K7
Nitra, Slvk. 40/D1
Nivelles, Belg. 31/D2
Nizāmābād, India 62/C4
Nizhnekamsk, Rus. 43/L5
Nizhneudinsk, Rus. 47/K4
Nizhnevartovsk, Rus. 46/H3
Nizhniy Lomov, Rus. 45/G1
Nizhniy Novgorod, Rus. 43/K4
Nizhniy Tagil, Rus. 43/N4
Nizhyn, Ukr. 44/D2
Nizip, Turk. 50/D2
Nkayi, Congo 82/B1
N'kongsamba, Camr. 79/H5
Noākhāli, Bang. 62/F3
Noāmundi, India 62/E3
Nobeoka, Japan 56/B4
Noboribetsu, Japan 55/N3
Nogales, Az, US 92/E5
Nogales, Mex. 101/M8
Nogata, Japan 56/B4
Nogent-sur-Oise, Fr. 30/B5
Noginsk, Rus. 43/X9
Nogoyá, Arg. 109/E3
Nohar, India 62/B2
Noisiel, Fr. 30/B6
Nokia, Fin. 42/D3
Nola, CAfr. 76/J7
Nome, Ak, US 85/E3
Nong Khai, Thai. 65/C2
Nonsan, SKor. 58/D4
Noordwijk aan Zee, Neth. 28/B4
Noordwijkerhout, Neth. 28/B4
Norala, Phil. 67/F2
Norden, Ger. 29/E1
Nordenham, Ger. 29/F1
Norderstedt, Ger. 29/G1
Nordhausen, Ger. 26/F3
Nordhorn, Ger. 29/E4
Nordkapp (cape), Nor. 20/H1
Nördlingen, Ger. 26/F4
Norfolk, Va, US 97/J2
Norfolk, Ne, US 93/H2
Noril'sk, Rus. 46/J3
Normal, Il, US 93/K2
Norman, Ok, US 93/H4
Norridge, Il, US 99/Q16
Norristown, Pa, US 94/F3
Norrköping, Swe. 42/C4
Norrtälje, Swe. 42/C4
North (sea), Eur. 18/D3
North (chan.), UK 22/C1
North (cape), NZ 71/R9
North (isl.), NZ 71/R10
North America (cont.) 84/*
North Bay, On, Can. 94/E2
North Bend, Or, US 92/A2
North Carolina (state), US 97/H3
North Cascades National Park, Wa, US 90/C3
North Charleston, SC, US 97/J3
North Chicago, Il, US 99/Q15
North Cowichan, BC, Can. 90/C3
North Dakota (state), US 91/H4
North Fort Myers, Fl, US 97/H5
North Highlands, Ca, US 99/L9
North Korea (ctry.) 58/D2
North Lakhimpur, India 60/B3
North Las Vegas, Nv, US 92/D3
North Little Rock, Ar, US 93/J4
North Magnetic Pole 83/N
North Platte, Ne, US 93/G2
North Saskatchewan (riv.), Ab,Sk, Can. 86/E3
North Shields, Eng, UK 23/G2
North Tonawanda, NY, US 95/V9
North Vancouver, BC, Can. 86/D4
Northampton, Ma, US 95/F3
Northampton, Eng, UK 25/F2
Northbrook, Il, US 99/Q15
Northeim, Ger. 29/G5
Northern Dvina (riv.), Rus. 43/J3
Northern Ireland, NI, UK 22/B2
Northern Marianas (dpcy.), Pac.,US 68/D3
Northfield, Mn, US 91/K4
Northfleet, Eng, UK 25/G4
Northport, Al, US 97/G3
Northwest Territories (terr.), Can. 86/E2
Northwich, Eng, UK 23/F5
Norton Shores, Mi, US 94/C3
Norwalk, Oh, US 94/D3
Norwalk, Ct, US 94/F3
Norway (ctry.) 20/C3
Norwich, Eng, UK 25/H1
Noshiro, Japan 55/N3
Nosivka, Ukr. 44/D2
Noşratābād, Iran 53/G3
Nosy-Varika, Madg. 81/J8
Noto, It. 38/D4
Nøtterøy, Nor. 20/D4
Nottingham, Eng, UK 23/G6
Nottuln, Ger. 29/E5
Nouâdhibou, Mrta. 76/B3
Nouakchott (cap.), Mrta. 78/B2
Nouméa (cap.), NCal. 69/V13
Nova Andradina, Braz. 107/H8
Nova Cruz, Braz. 107/L5
Nova Friburgo, Braz. 108/L7
Nova Gorica, Slov. 40/A3
Nova Gradiška, Cro. 40/C3
Nova Iguaçu, Braz. 108/K7
Nova Kakhovka, Ukr. 41/L2
Nova Pazova, Serb. 40/E3
Nova Scotia (prov.), Can. 95/J2
Nova Venécia, Braz. 108/D1
Nova Zagora, Bul. 41/H4
Novara, It. 33/H4
Novato, Ca, US 99/J10
Nové Město nad Váhom, Slvk. 27/J4
Nové Zámky, Slvk. 27/K5
Novelda, Sp. 35/E3
Novgorod, Rus. 42/F4
Novi, Mi, US 99/E7
Novi Bečej, Serb. 40/E3
Novi Ligure, It. 33/H4
Novi Pazar, Bul. 41/H4
Novi Pazar, Serb. 40/E4
Novi Sad, Serb. 40/D3
Novo Hamburgo, Braz. 108/B4
Novo Horizonte, Braz. 108/B2
Novoanninskiy, Rus. 45/G2
Novocheboksarsk, Rus. 43/K4
Novocherkassk, Rus. 44/G3
Novogrudok, Bela. 42/E5
Novohrad-Volyns'kyy, Ukr. 44/C2
Novokuybyshevsk, Rus. 45/J1
Novokuznetsk, Rus. 46/J4
Novomoskovsk, Rus. 44/F1
Novorossiysk, Rus. 44/F3
Novoshakhtinsk, Rus. 44/F3
Novosibirsk, Rus. 46/J4
Novotroitsk, Rus. 45/L2
Novoukrayinka, Ukr. 44/D2
Novovolyns'k, Ukr. 27/N3
Novovyatsk, Rus. 43/L4
Novozybkov, Rus. 44/D1
Novska, Cro. 40/C3
Nový Jičín, Czh. 27/K4
Nowa Ruda, Pol. 27/J3
Nowa Sól, Pol. 27/H3
Nowgong, India 62/C2
Nowogard, Pol. 27/H2
Nowshera, Pak. 53/K2
Nowy Sącz, Pol. 27/L4
Nowy Targ, Pol. 27/L4
Noya, Sp. 34/A1
Noyon, Fr. 30/C4
Nsawam, Gha. 79/E5
Nuenen, Neth. 28/C6
Nueva Concepción, Guat. 102/D3
Nueva Gerona, Cuba 103/F1
Nueva Italia de Ruiz, Mex. 100/E5
Nueva Loja, Ecu. 106/C3
Nueva Ocotepéque, Hon. 102/D3
Nueva Rosita, Mex. 96/C5
Nueve de Julio, Arg. 109/D4
Nuevitas, Cuba 103/G1
Nuevo Casas Grandes, Mex. 92/F5
Nuevo Laredo, Mex. 96/D5
Nuku'alofa (cap.), Tonga 69/H7
Nukus, Uzb. 46/F5
Numata, Japan 57/F2
Numazu, Japan 57/F3
Nunavut (terr.), Can. 87/G2
Nuneaton, Eng, UK 25/E1
Nunspeet, Neth. 28/C4
Nuoro, It. 38/A2
Nurmijärvi, Fin. 20/H3
Nürnberg, Ger. 33/J2
Nürtingen, Ger. 33/H2
Nuth, Neth. 31/E2
Nyala, Sudan 77/K5
Nyandoma, Rus. 42/J3
Nyasa (lake), Afr. 82/F3
Nyborg, Den. 26/F1
Nybro, Swe. 20/E4
Nyeri, Kenya 82/G1
Nyíregyháza, Hun. 27/L5
Nykøbing, Den. 26/F1
Nyköping, Swe. 42/C4
Nynäshamn, Swe. 42/C4
Nyon, Swi. 36/C5
Nysa, Pol. 27/J3
Nyūzen, Japan 57/E2
Nzérékoré, Gui. 78/C5

O

Oahu (isl.), US 88/S10
Oak Creek, Wi, US 99/Q14
Oak Forest, Il, US 99/Q16
Oak Lawn, Il, US 99/Q16
Oak Park, Mi, US 99/F7
Oak Park, Il, US 99/Q16
Oak Ridge, Tn, US 97/G2
Oakland, Ca, US 99/K11
Oakley, Ca, US 99/L10
Oaxaca de Juárez, Mex. 102/B2
Ob' (riv.), Rus. 46/G3
Obama, Japan 56/D3
Oberá, Arg. 109/E2
Oberhausen, Ger. 28/D6
Oberkirch, Ger. 31/H6
Oberursel, Ger. 33/H1
Óbidos, Braz. 107/G4
Obihiro, Japan 55/N3
Obluch'ye, Rus. 55/L2
Obninsk, Rus. 44/F1
Obo, CAfr. 77/L6
Oborniki, Pol. 27/J2
Obrenovac, Serb. 40/E3
Obuasi, Gha. 79/E5
Ocala, Fl, US 97/H4
Occidental, Cordillera (mts.), Ecu. 106/C3
Oceanside, Ca, US 92/C4
Och'amch'ire, Geo. 45/G4
Ochtrup, Ger. 29/E4
Ocna Mureş, Rom. 41/F2
Ocotal, Nic. 102/E3
Ocotlán, Mex. 100/E4
Ocoyoacac, Mex. 101/Q10
Ocozocoautla de Espinosa, Mex. 102/C2
Octeville, Fr. 32/C2
Oda, Gha. 79/E5
Ōda, Japan 56/C3
Ōdate, Japan 55/N3
Odawara, Japan 57/F3
Ödemiş, Turk. 50/A2
Odense, Den. 26/F1
Odesa, Ukr. 41/K2
Odessa, Tx, US 93/G5
Odintsovo, Rus. 43/W9
Odivelas, Port. 35/P10
Oegstgeest, Neth. 28/B4
Oeiras, Braz. 107/K5
Oelde, Ger. 29/F5
Oelsnitz, Ger. 33/K1
Oer-Erkenschwick, Ger. 29/E5
Of, Turk. 44/G4
Ofaqim, Isr. 49/D4
Offa, Nga. 79/G4
Offenbach, Ger. 33/H1
Offenburg, Ger. 36/D1
Oga, Japan 55/M4
Ōgaki, Japan 56/E3
Ogbomosho, Nga. 79/G4
Ogden, Ut, US 92/E2
Ogre, Lat. 42/E4
Ogulin, Cro. 40/B3
Ohio (state), US 94/D3
Ohrid, FYROM 40/E5
Oieras, Port. 35/P10
Oil City, Pa, US 94/E3
Oisterwijk, Neth. 28/C5
Ōita, Japan 56/B4
Ojinaga, Mex. 93/F5
Ojiya, Japan 57/F2
Ojo de Agua, Mex. 101/Q9
Oka, Nga. 79/G5
Okāra, Pak. 53/K2
Ōkawa, Japan 56/B4
Okaya, Japan 57/F2
Okayama, Japan 56/C3
Okazaki, Japan 57/E3
Okeechobee (lake), Fl, US 97/H5
Okha, Rus. 47/Q4
Okhtyrka, Ukr. 44/E2
Oklahoma (state), US 93/H4
Oklahoma City (cap.), Ok, US 93/H4
Okmulgee, Ok, US 93/J4
Oktyabr'sk, Rus. 45/J1
Oktyabr'skiy, Rus. 43/M5
Ōkuchi, Japan 56/B4
Okulovka, Rus. 42/G4
Olathe, Ks, US 93/J3
Olavarría, Arg. 109/D4
Oława, Pol. 27/J3
Olbia, It. 38/A2
Olching, Ger. 37/H1
Oldebroek, Neth. 28/C4
Oldenburg, Ger. 29/F2
Oldenzaal, Neth. 28/D4
Oldham, Eng, UK 23/F4
Olean, NY, US 94/E3
Oleiros, Sp. 34/A1
Oleksandriya, Ukr. 44/E2
Olenegorsk, Rus. 42/G1
Olesa de Montserrat, Sp. 35/K6
Oleśnica, Pol. 27/J3
Ölgiy, Mong. 54/B2
Olhão, Port. 34/B4
Olímpia, Braz. 108/B2
Olinda, Braz. 107/M5
Oliva, Sp. 35/E3
Olivais, Port. 34/A3
Oliveira, Braz. 108/C2
Olivet, Fr. 32/D3
Ollūr, India 62/C5
Olmaliq, Uzb. 46/G5
Olofström, Swe. 20/E4
Olomouc, Czh. 27/J4
Olot, Sp. 35/G1
Olpe, Ger. 29/E6
Olsberg, Ger. 29/F6
Olsztyn, Pol. 27/L2
Olten, Swi. 36/D3
Oltu, Turk. 45/G4
Olympia (cap.), Wa, US 99/B3
Olympic National Park, Wa, US 90/B4
Olympos (Mount Olympus) (peak), Gre. 39/H2
Ōmachi, Japan 57/E2
Omagh, NI, UK 22/A2
Omaha, Ne, US 93/J2
Oman (ctry.) 53/G4
Oman (gulf), Oman 52/G4
Omegna, It. 33/H4
Omiš, Cro. 40/C4
Ōmiya, Japan 57/G2
Ōmiya, Japan 55/M4
Ommen, Neth. 28/D3
Omsk, Rus. 46/H4
Ōmura, Japan 56/A4
Ōmuta, Japan 56/B4
Omutninsk, Rus. 43/M4
Onagawa, Japan 57/G1
Onda, Sp. 35/E3
Ondo, Nga. 79/G5
Ondörhaan, Mong. 54/G2
Onega, Rus. 42/H3
Oneida, NY, US 94/F3
Oneonta, NY, US 94/F3
Onex, Swi. 36/C5
Ongole, India 62/D4
Ongtüstik Qazaqstan, Kaz. 46/G5
Onitsha, Nga. 79/G5
Ono, Japan 56/D3
Ōno, Japan 56/E3
Onoda, Japan 56/B4
Onomichi, Japan 56/C3
Ontario, Or, US 92/C1
Ontario (prov.), Can. 86/H3
Ontario (lake), Can.,US 94/E3
Onteniente, Sp. 35/E3
Onyang, SKor. 58/D4
Oostburg, Neth. 28/A6
Oosterhout, Neth. 28/B5
Oostkamp, Belg. 30/C1
Opatija, Cro. 40/B3
Opava, Czh. 27/J4
Opelika, Al, US 97/G3
Opelousas, La, US 93/J5
Ophir, Ak, US 85/G3

Opoczno, Pol. 27/L3
Opole, Pol. 27/J3
Opportunity, Wa, US 90/D4
Or 'Aqiva, Isr. 49/F6
Or Yehuda, Isr. 49/F7
Orai, India 62/C2
Oral, Kaz. 45/J2
Oran, Alg. 76/E1
Orange, Austl. 73/D2
Orange, Tx, US 93/J5
Orange (riv.), Nam,SAfr. 80/B3
Orange, Fr. 32/F4
Orange Park, Fl, US 97/H4
Orange Walk, Belz. 102/D2
Orangeburg, SC, US 97/H3
Orangeville, On, Can. 95/S8
Oranienburg, Ger. 27/G2
Oranjestad, Aru.. 106/D1
Orăştie, Rom. 41/F3
Oraviţa, Rom. 40/E3
Orchard Homes, Mt, US 90/E4
Ordu, Turk. 44/F4
Örebro, Swe. 20/E4
Oregon (state), US 90/C4
Oregon City, Or, US 90/C4
Orekhovo-Zuyevo, Rus. 42/H5
Orël, Rus. 44/F1
Orenburg, Rus. 45/K2
Orense, Sp. 34/B1
Orhangazi, Turk. 41/J5
Orhei, Mol. 41/J2
Oria, Sp. 34/D4
Oriental, Cordillera (mts.), Col.,Ecu. 106/C5
Orihuela, Sp. 35/E3
Orillia, On, Can. 94/E2
Orinda, Ca, US 99/J11
Oristano, It. 38/A3
Oriximiná, Braz. 107/G4
Orizaba, Mex. 101/M8
Orkney, SAfr. 80/P13
Orland Park, Il, US 99/Q16
Orlândia, Braz. 108/C2
Orlando, Fl, US 97/H4
Orléans, Fr. 32/D3
Orlová, Czh. 27/K4
Ormoc, Phil. 67/F1
Ormond Beach, Fl, US 97/H4
Ormskirk, Eng, UK 23/F4
Örnsköldsvik, Swe. 42/C3
Orodara, Burk. 78/D4
Orono, Me, US 95/G2
Oroquieta, Phil. 67/F2
Orosháza, Hun. 40/E2
Oroszlány, Hun. 40/D2
Oroville, Ca, US 92/B3
Orsay, Fr. 30/B6
Orsha, Bela. 42/F5
Orsk, Rus. 45/L2
Orşova, Rom. 40/F3
Ortaköy, Turk. 50/C2
Ortaköy, Turk. 44/E4
Orūmīyeh, Iran 51/F2
Oruro, Bol. 106/E7
Osa, Rus. 43/M4
Ōsaka, Japan 56/D3
Osan, SKor. 58/D4
Osasco, Braz. 108/G8
Oschersleben, Ger. 26/F2
Osh, Kyr. 46/H5
Oshawa, On, Can. 95/V8
Oshogbo, Nga. 79/G5
Osijek, Cro. 40/D3
Osipovichi, Bela. 44/D1
Oskarshamn, Swe. 20/F4
Öskemen, Kaz. 46/J5
Oslo (cap.), Nor. 20/D4
Osmānābād, India 62/C4
Osmancık, Turk. 44/E4
Osmaniye, Turk. 49/E1
Osnabrück, Ger. 29/F4
Osório, Braz. 108/B4
Osorno, Chile 109/B5
Oss, Neth. 28/C5
Ossett, Eng, UK 23/G4
Ostashkov, Rus. 42/G4
Osten (Oostende), Belg. 30/B1
Osterholz-Scharmbeck, Ger. 29/F2
Osterode am Harz, Ger. 29/H5
Östersund, Swe. 20/E3
Östhammar, Swe. 42/C3
Ostrava, Czh. 27/K4
Ostróda, Pol. 27/K2
Ostrogozhsk, Rus. 44/F2
Ostrołęka, Pol. 27/L2
Ostrov, Rus. 42/F4
Ostrov, Czh. 33/K1
Ostrów Mazowiecka, Pol. 27/L2
Ostrów Wielkopolski, Pol. 27/J3
Ostrowiec Świętokrzyski, Pol. 27/L3
Ostuni, It. 40/C5
Osuna, Sp. 34/C4
Osvaldo Cruz, Braz. 108/B2
Oswego, NY, US 94/E3
Oswestry, Eng, UK 23/E6
Oświęcim (Auschwitz), Pol. 27/K3
Ōta, Japan 57/F2
Ōtake, Japan 56/C3
Otaru, Japan 47/Q5
Ōtawara, Japan 57/G2
Otradnyy, Rus. 45/J1
Otrokovice, Czh. 27/J4
Ōtsu, Japan 56/D3
Ottawa, Ks, US 93/J3
Ottawa (riv.), Can. 94/E2
Ottawa (cap.), On, Can. 94/F2
Ottignies-Louvain-la-Neuve, Belg. 31/D2
Ottobrunn, Ger. 33/J2
Ottumwa, Ia, US 93/J2
Ottweiler, Ger. 31/G5
Otwock, Pol. 27/L2
Ouagadougou (cap.), Burk. 79/E3
Ouargla, Alg. 76/G1
Ouarzazate, Mor. 76/D1
Oud-Beijerland, Neth. 28/B5
Oudenaarde, Belg. 30/C2
Oudtshoorn, SAfr. 80/C4
Oued Zem, Mor. 76/D1
Ouesso, Congo 76/J7
Ouezzane, Mor. 76/D1
Ouidah, Ben. 79/F5
Oujda, Mor. 76/E1
Oullins, Fr. 36/A6
Oulu, Fin. 42/E2
Oupeye, Belg. 31/E2
Ouricuri, Braz. 107/K5
Ourinhos, Braz. 108/B2
Ouro Fino, Braz. 108/G7
Ouro Preto, Braz. 108/D2
Outreau, Fr. 25/H5
Outremont, Qu, Can. 95/N6
Ovalle, Chile 109/B3
Overath, Ger. 31/G2
Overijse, Belg. 31/D2
Overland Park, Ks, US 93/J3
Oviedo, Sp. 34/C1
Owase, Japan 56/E3
Owasso, Ok, US 93/J3
Owen Sound, On, Can. 94/D2
Owensboro, Ky, US 97/G2
Owo, Nga. 79/G5
Owosso, Mi, US 94/C3
Oxford, Ms, US 97/F3
Oxford, Eng, UK 25/E3
Oxkutzcab, Mex. 102/D1
Oxnard, Ca, US 92/C4
Oyabe, Japan 57/E2
Oyama, Japan 57/F2
Oyem, Gabon 76/H7
Oyo, Nga. 79/F5
Oyonnax, Fr. 36/B5
Ozark, Al, US 97/G4
Ozark (mts.), Ar,Mo, US 96/E3
Ózd, Hun. 40/E1
Ozoir-la-Ferrière, Fr. 30/B6
Ozorków, Pol. 27/K3
Ōzu, Japan 56/C4

P

P'yŏngyang (cap.), NKor. 58/C3
Pa-an, Myan. 65/B2
Paarl, SAfr. 80/L10
Pabellón de Arteaga, Mex. 100/E4
Pabianice, Pol. 27/K3
Pābna, Bang. 62/E3
Pacasmayo, Peru 106/C5
Pachino, It. 38/D4
Pachuca, Mex. 101/L6
Pacific (ocean) 16/B4
Pacific Palisades, Hi, US 88/W13
Pacifica, Ca, US 99/K11
Pacitan, Indo. 66/D5
Paço de Arcos, Port. 35/P10
Padang, Indo. 66/B4
Padangpanjang, Indo. 66/B4
Padangsidempuan, Indo. 66/A3
Paderborn, Ger. 29/F5
Padova, It. 33/J4
Paducah, Ky, US 97/F2
Pagadian, Phil. 67/F2
Pago Pago (cap.), ASam. 69/T10
Paignton, Eng, UK 24/C6
Painesville, Oh, US 94/D3
Paithan, India 62/C4
Pakanbaru, Indo. 66/B3
Pakistan (ctry.) 53/H3
Pakokku, Myan. 60/B4
Pākpattan, Pak. 53/K2
Paks, Hun. 40/D2
Pakxe, Laos 65/D3
Palafrugell, Sp. 35/G2
Palagonia, It. 38/D4
Pālakollu, India 62/D4
Palangkaraya, Indo. 66/D4
Pālanpur, India 62/B3
Palapye, Bots. 82/E5
Palatine, Il, US 99/P15
Palatka, Fl, US 97/H4
Palau, Mex. 101/E3
Palau (ctry.) 68/C4
Pālayankottai, India 62/C6
Palembang, Indo. 66/B4
Palencia, Sp. 34/C1
Palenque, Mex. 102/D2
Palermo, It. 38/C3
Pālghar, India 53/K5
Palhoça, Braz. 108/B3
Pāli, India 62/B2
Pālitāna, India 62/B3
Palm Bay, Fl, US 97/H4
Palm Harbor, Fl, US 97/H4
Palm Springs, Ca, US 92/C4
Palma, Sp. 35/G3
Palma del Río, Sp. 34/C4
Palma di Montechiaro, It. 38/C4
Palma Soriano, Cuba 103/H1
Palmares, Braz. 107/L5
Palmas, Braz. 108/A3
Palmdale, Ca, US 92/C4
Palmeira, Braz. 108/B3
Palmeira dos Índios, Braz. 107/L5
Palmerston North, NZ 71/S11
Palmetto, Fl, US 97/H5
Palmi, It. 38/D3
Palmira, Col. 106/C3
Palni, India 62/C5
Palo Alto, Ca, US 99/K12
Palo Verde, CR 102/E4
Palos Hills, Il, US 99/Q16
Palpalá, Arg. 109/C1
Palu, Indo. 67/E4
Pamangkat, Indo. 66/C3
Pamiers, Fr. 32/D5
Pampa, Tx, US 93/G4
Pampas (plain), Arg. 109/D4
Pamplona, Col. 103/H5
Pamplona, Sp. 34/E1
Panagyurishte, Bul. 41/G4
Panaji, India 62/B4
Panama (canal), Pan. 106/B2
Panamá (cap.), Pan. 103/G4
Panama (ctry.), Pan. 103/F2
Panama City, Fl, US 97/G4
Panama, Golfo de (gulf), Pan. 103/G4
Panama, Isthmus of (isth.), Pan. 103/F4
Pančevo, Serb. 40/E3
Pandharpur, India 62/C4
Panevėžys, Lith. 42/E5
Panfilov, Kaz. 46/J5
Pangkalanberandan, Indo. 66/A3
Pangkalpinang, Indo. 66/C4
Pangutaran, Phil. 67/F2
Pānīpat, India 62/C2
Panna, India 62/D3
Pánuco, Mex. 102/B1
Panzhihua, China 60/D3
Panzós, Guat. 102/D3
Pápa, Hun. 40/C2
Papantla, Mex. 101/M6
Papeete (cap.), FrPol. 69/X15
Papeete, FrPol. 69/X15
Papenburg, Ger. 29/E2
Papendrecht, Neth. 28/B5
Papillion, Ne, US 93/H2
Papua New Guinea (ctry.) 68/D5
Pará de Minas, Braz. 108/C1
Paracambi, Braz. 108/K7
Paracatu, Braz. 107/J7
Paraćin, Serb. 40/E4
Paradip, India 62/E3
Paragominas, Braz. 107/J4
Paraguaçu Paulista, Braz. 108/B2
Paraguarí, Par. 109/E2
Paraguay (riv.), Par. 109/E1
Paraguay (ctry.) 105/C5
Paraíba do Sul, Braz. 108/K7
Paraíso, Mex. 102/C2
Paraíso do Norte de Goiás, Braz. 107/J6
Parakou, Ben. 79/F4
Paramaribo (cap.), Sur. 107/G2
Paraná, Arg. 109/D3
Paraná (riv.), Arg.,Braz. 109/E3
Paranaguá, Braz. 108/B3
Paranaíba, Braz. 108/B1
Paranavaí, Braz. 109/F1
Parang, Phil. 67/F2
Parbhani, India 62/C4
Parchim, Ger. 26/F2
Pardes Ḩanna-Karkur, Isr. 49/F7
Pardubice, Czh. 33/L1
Pare, Indo. 66/D5
Parede, Port. 35/P10
Parepare, Indo. 67/E4
Pariaman, Indo. 66/B4
Parintins, Braz. 107/G4
Paris, Tx, US 93/J4
Paris (cap.), Fr. 30/B6
Park Ridge, Il, US 99/Q16
Parkersburg, WV, US 97/H2
Parkland, Wa, US 99/C3
Parkway-Sacramento, Ca, US 99/L9
Parla, Sp. 35/N9
Parlakhemundi, India 62/D4
Parli, India 62/C4
Parma, Oh, US 94/D3
Parma, It. 33/J4
Parnaíba, Braz. 107/K4
Parnamirim, Braz. 107/L5
Pärnu, Est. 42/E4
Parow, SAfr. 80/L10
Parral, Chile 109/B4
Parras de la Fuente, Mex. 96/C5
Parsons, Ks, US 93/J3
Partinico, It. 38/C3
Partizansk, Rus. 55/L3
Partizánske, Slvk. 27/K4
Partūr, India 62/C4
Pārvathīpuram, India 62/D4
Pasadena, Ca, US 92/C4
Pasadena, Tx, US 93/J5
Pasaje, Ecu. 106/C4
Pasān, India 62/D3
Pascagoula, Ms, US 97/F4
Paşcani, Rom. 41/H2
Pasco, Wa, US 90/D4
Pāsighāt, India 60/B2
Pasinler, Turk. 45/G5
Pasni, Pak. 53/H3
Paso de los Libres, Arg. 109/E2
Paso Robles (El Paso de Robles), Ca, US 92/B4
Passau, Ger. 33/K2
Passo Fundo, Braz. 108/A4
Passos, Braz. 108/C2
Pastavy, Bela. 42/E5
Pasto, Col. 106/C3
Pasuruan, Indo. 66/D5
Patagonia (phys. reg.), Arg. 109/B6
Pātan, India 62/B3
Paterna, Sp. 35/E3
Paternò, It. 38/D4
Paterson, NJ, US 94/F3
Pathānkot, India 53/L2
Pathein (Bassein), Myan. 60/B5
Pati, Indo. 66/D5
Patía, Col. 106/C3
Patiāla, India 53/L2
Patikul, Phil. 67/F2
Patna, India 62/E2
Patnongon, Phil. 67/F1
Patnos, Turk. 51/E2
Pato Branco, Braz. 108/A3
Patos, Braz. 107/L5
Patos de Minas, Braz. 108/C1
Pátrai, Gre. 39/G3
Patrocínio, Braz. 108/C1
Pattani, Thai. 65/C5
Pattukkottai, India 62/C5
Patuākhāli, Bang. 62/F3
Pátzcuaro, Mex. 101/E5
Pau, Fr. 32/C5
Paulínia, Braz. 108/F7
Paulo Afonso, Braz. 107/L5
Paungde, Myan. 60/B5
Pavia, It. 33/H4
Pavlodar, Kaz. 46/H4
Pavlohrad, Ukr. 44/E2
Pavlovo, Rus. 42/J5
Pawtucket, RI, US 95/G3
Payakumbuh, Indo. 66/B4
Paysandú, Uru. 109/E3
Payson, Ut, US 92/E2
Pazarcık, Turk. 50/D2
Pazardzhik, Bul. 41/G4
Peace (riv.), BC, Can. 86/D3
Peachtree City, Ga, US 97/G3
Pearl, Ms, US 97/F3
Pearl (har.), US 88/W13
Pearl City, Hi, US 88/W13
Pechora, Rus. 43/N2
Pecos, Tx, US 96/C4
Pecos (riv.), NM,Tx, US 93/G5
Pécs, Hun. 40/D2
Pedernales, DRep. 103/J2
Pederneiras, Braz. 108/B2
Pedra Azul, Braz. 107/K7
Pedreira, Braz. 108/G7
Pedreiras, Braz. 107/K4
Pedro Betancourt, Cuba 103/F1
Pedro Juan Caballero, Par. 109/E1
Pedro Leopoldo, Braz. 108/C1
Pehuajó, Arg. 109/D4
Peine, Ger. 29/H4
Pekalongan, Indo. 66/C5
Pekin, Il, US 93/K2
Pelham, Al, US 97/G3
Pelhřimov, Czh. 33/L2
Pelotas, Braz. 108/A4
Pematangsiantar, Indo. 66/A3
Pemba, Moz. 82/H3
Penápolis, Braz. 108/B2
Penarth, Wal, UK 24/C4
Pendleton, Or, US 90/D4
Penedo, Braz. 107/L6
Peniche, Port. 34/A3
Penn Hills, Pa, US 94/E3
Pennsylvania (state), US 94/E3
Penonomé, Pan. 103/F4
Pensacola, Fl, US 97/G4
Penticton, BC, Can. 90/D3
Penza, Rus. 45/H1
Penzance, Eng, UK 24/A6
Perabumulih, Indo. 66/B4
Pérama, Gre. 39/N9
Pereira, Col. 106/C3
Pereira Barreto, Braz. 108/B2
Pergamino, Arg. 109/D3
Perico, Cuba 103/F1
Périgueux, Fr. 32/D4
Peringat, Malay. 65/C5
Peristéri, Gre. 39/N8
Perm', Rus. 43/N4
Pernik, Bul. 40/F4
Perote, Mex. 101/M7
Perpignan, Fr. 32/E5
Perry, Ga, US 97/H3
Persian (gulf), Asia 52/E3
Perth, Austl. 68/A8
Pertuis, Fr. 32/F5
Peru, In, US 94/C3
Peru, Il, US 93/K2
Peru (ctry.), Peru 106/C5
Perugia, It. 38/C1
Peruíbe, Braz. 108/G9
Péruwelz, Belg. 30/C2
Pervomaysk, Rus. 45/G1
Pervomays'k, Ukr. 41/K1
Pervoural'sk, Rus. 43/N4
Pesaro, It. 33/K5
Pescara, It. 40/B4
Peshāwar, Pak. 53/K2
Peshtera, Bul. 41/G4
Pessac, Fr. 32/C4
Pestovo, Rus. 42/G4
Petaḩ Tiqwa, Isr. 49/F7
Petaluma, Ca, US 99/J10
Petare, Ven. 106/E1
Petatlán, Mex. 101/E5
Peterborough, On, Can. 94/E2
Peterborough, Eng, UK 25/F1
Peterlee, Eng, UK 23/G2
Petersburg, Va, US 97/J2
Petershagen, Ger. 29/F4
Pétionville, Haiti 103/H2
Petlād, India 62/B3
Petrel, Sp. 35/E3
Petrich, Bul. 41/F5
Petrila, Rom. 41/F3
Petrodvorets, Rus. 43/S7
Petrolina, Braz. 107/K5
Petropavl, Kaz. 46/G4
Petropavlovsk-Kamchatskiy, Rus. 47/R4
Petrópolis, Braz. 108/K7
Petrovsk, Rus. 45/H1
Petrovsk-Zabaykal'skiy, Rus. 54/F1
Petrozavodsk, Rus. 42/G3
Pfaffenhofen an der Ilm, Ger. 33/J2
Pforzheim, Ger. 33/H2
Pfungstadt, Ger. 33/H2
Phalodi, India 62/B2
Phan Rang-Thap Cham, Viet. 65/E4
Phan Thiet, Viet. 65/E4
Pharr, Tx, US 96/D5
Phayao, Thai. 65/B2
Phenix City, Al, US 97/G3
Phet Buri, Thai. 65/B3
Philadelphia, Pa, US 94/F4
Philippine (sea), Asia 68/B3
Philippines (ctry.) 68/B3
Phitsanulok, Thai. 65/C2
Phnom Penh (cap.), Camb. 65/D4
Phoenix (cap.), Az, US 92/D4
Phra Nakhon Si Ayutthaya, Thai. 65/C3
Phrae, Thai. 65/C2
Phu Tho, Viet. 65/D1
Phuket, Thai. 65/B5
Piacenza, It. 33/H4
Piaseczno, Pol. 27/L2
Piazza Armerina, It. 38/D4
Picayune, Ms, US 97/F4
Pickering, On, Can. 95/U8
Picos, Braz. 107/K5
Piedade, Port. 35/P10
Piedmont, Ca, US 99/K11
Piedras Negras, Mex. 96/C4
Piekary Śląskie, Pol. 27/K3
Pierre (cap.), SD, US 91/H4
Pierrefonds, Qu, Can. 95/N7
Piešťany, Slvk. 27/J4
Pietarsdart (Jakobstad), Fin. 42/D3
Pietermaritzburg, SAfr. 81/E3
Pietersburg, SAfr. 82/E5
Pijnacker, Neth. 28/B4
Piła, Pol. 27/J2
Pilar, Par. 109/E2
Pilar, Phil. 67/F1
Pilcomayo (riv.), SAm. 109/D1
Pilkhua, India 62/C2
Pimpri-Chinchwad, India 53/K5
Pinamalayan, Phil. 67/F1
Pinar del Río, Cuba 103/F1
Pinatubo (mt.), Phil. 68/B3
Pindamonhangaba, Braz. 108/H7
Pindaré-Mirim, Braz. 107/J4
Pindi Gheb, Pak. 53/K2
Pindwāra, India 62/B3
Pine Bluff, Ar, US 93/J4
Pinerolo, It. 33/G4
Pinetown, SAfr. 81/E3
Pineville, La, US 93/J5
Pingdingshan, China 59/C4
Pingdu, China 59/D3
P'ingtung, Tai. 61/J4
Pingxiang, China 61/G3
Pingxiang, China 65/D1
Pinhal, Braz. 108/G7
Pinhal Novo, Port. 35/Q10
Pinheiro, Braz. 107/J4
Pinneberg, Ger. 29/G1
Pinole, Ca, US 99/K10
Pinsk, Bela. 44/C1
Pinto, Sp. 35/N9
Piombino, It. 38/B1
Pionki, Pol. 27/L3
Piotrków Trybunalski, Pol. 27/K3
Piplān, Pak. 53/K2
Piqua, Oh, US 94/C3
Piracicaba, Braz. 108/C2
Piraiévs, Gre. 39/N9
Piraju, Braz. 108/B2
Pirapora, Braz. 108/C1
Pirapòzinho, Braz. 108/B2
Pirássununga, Braz. 108/C2
Pires do Rio, Braz. 108/B1
Pirgos, Gre. 39/G4
Piripiri, Braz. 107/K4
Pirmasens, Ger. 31/G5
Pirna, Ger. 27/G3
Pirot, Serb. 40/F4
Pisa, It. 33/J5
Pisco, Peru 106/C6
Písek, Czh. 33/L2
Pishīn, Pak. 53/J2
Pistoia, It. 33/J5
Pisz, Pol. 27/L2
Pitalito, Col. 106/C3
Pitcairn Islands (dpcy.), UK 69/N7
Piteå, Swe. 42/D2
Piteşti, Rom. 41/G3
Pittsburg, Ks, US 93/J3
Pittsburg, Ca, US 99/L10
Pittsburgh, Pa, US 94/E3
Pittsfield, Ma, US 94/F3
Pittston, Pa, US 94/F3
Piuí, Braz. 108/C2
Piura, Peru 106/B5
Pivdennyy Buh (riv.), Ukr. 44/D2
Pivijay, Col. 103/H4
Placetas, Cuba 103/G1
Plainview, Tx, US 93/G4
Plaisir, Fr. 30/A6
Planeta Rica, Col. 103/H4
Plant City, Fl, US 97/H4
Plantation, Fl, US 97/H5
Plasencia, Sp. 34/B2
Plata, Río de la (estu.), SAm. 109/E4
Plato, Col. 103/H4
Platte (riv.), Ne, US 93/H2
Plattsburgh, NY, US 94/F2
Plauen, Ger. 33/K1
Plav, Serb. 40/D4
Playas, Ecu. 106/B4
Pleasant Hill, Ca, US 99/K11
Pleasant Prairie, Wi, US 99/Q14
Pleasanton, Ca, US 99/L11
Pleiku, Viet. 65/D3
Pleszew, Pol. 27/J3
Plettenberg, Ger. 29/E6
Pljevlja, Serb. 40/D4
Płock, Pol. 27/K2
Ploemeur, Fr. 32/B3
Ploieşti, Rom. 41/H3
Płońsk, Pol. 27/L2
Plymouth, Eng, UK 24/B6
Plymouth (cap.), Monts. 104/F3
Plzeň, Czh. 33/K2
Pô, Burk. 79/E4
Po (riv.), It. 33/G4
Poá, Braz. 108/G8
Pobé, Ben. 79/F5
Pocatello, Id, US 92/D2
Pochep, Rus. 44/E1
Poconé, Braz. 107/G7
Poços de Caldas, Braz. 108/G6
Podgorica, Serb. 40/D4
Podol'sk, Rus. 43/W9
Podporozh'ye, Rus. 42/G3
Podujevo, Serb. 40/E4
Poggibonsi, It. 33/J5
Pogradec, Alb. 40/E5
P'ohang, SKor. 56/A2
Pohoiki, Hi, US 88/U11
Pointe-à-Pitre, Fr. 104/F3
Pointe-Claire, Qu, Can. 95/N7
Pointe-Noire, Congo 82/B1
Poitiers, Fr. 32/D3
Pokaran, India 53/K3
Pokhara, Nepal 62/D2
Pokhvistnevo, Rus. 45/K1
Pol-e Khomrī, Afg. 53/J1
Pola de Laviana, Sp. 34/C1
Pola de Lena, Sp. 34/C1
Pola de Siero, Sp. 34/C1

Rio do Sul, Braz. 108/B3
Río Gallegos, Arg. 109/C7
Río Grande, Arg. 109/C7
Rio Grande, Braz. 108/A5
Rio Grande (riv.), Mex.,US 96/C4
Rio Grande City, Tx, US 96/D5
Rio Grande da Serra, Braz. 108/G8
Rio Largo, Braz. 107/L5
Rio Negrinho, Braz. 108/B3
Rio Negro, Braz. 108/B3
Rio Pardo, Braz. 108/A4
Rio Rancho, NM, US 92/F4
Río Tercero, Arg. 109/D3
Rio Verde, Braz. 108/B1
Río Verde, Mex. 102/B1
Riobamba, Ecu. 106/C4
Ríohacha, Col. 103/H4
Riom, Fr. 32/E4
Ripley, Eng, UK 23/G5
Ripollet, Sp. 35/L6
Rishon Leẕiyyon, Isr. 49/F8
Rîşnov, Rom. 41/G3
Rivadavia, Arg. 109/C3
Rivas, Nic. 102/E4
Rive-de-Gier, Fr. 32/F4
River Rouge, Mi, US 99/F7
Rivera, Uru. 109/E3
Riverside, Ca, US 92/C4
Riverton, Wy, US 92/E2
Riverview, NB, Can. 95/H2
Riverview, Mi, US 99/F7
Riviera Beach, Fl, US 97/H5
Rivière-du-Loup, Qu, Can. 95/G2
Rivne, Ukr. 44/C2
Rivoli, It. 33/G4
Rixensart, Belg. 31/D2
Riyadh (cap.), SAr. 52/E4
Rize, Turk. 45/G4
Road Town (cap.), BVI, UK 104/E3
Roanne, Fr. 32/F3
Robertsganj, India 62/D3
Robertsport, Libr. 78/C5
Robstown, Tx, US 96/D5
Rocha, Uru. 109/F3
Rochdale, Eng, UK 23/F4
Rochefort, Fr. 32/C4
Rochester, Mn, US 93/J1
Rochester, NY, US 94/E3
Rochester, NH, US 95/G3
Rochester, Eng, UK 25/G4
Rochester Hills, Mi, US 99/F6
Rock Forest, Qu, Can. 95/G2
Rock Hill, SC, US 97/H3
Rock Island, Il, US 93/K2
Rock Springs, Wy, US 92/E2
Rockford, Il, US 93/K2
Rockhampton, Austl. 72/C3
Rockingham, NC, US 97/J3
Rockledge, Fl, US 97/H4
Rockville, Md, US 97/J2
Rockwall, Tx, US 93/H4
Rocky (mts.), Can.,US 88/C1
Rocky Mount, NC, US 97/J3
Rocky Mountain National Park, Co, US 92/F2
Rodez, Fr. 32/E4
Ródhos (Rhodes), Gre. 50/B2
Roermond, Neth. 28/C6
Roeselare, Belg. 30/C2
Rogachev, Bela. 44/D1
Rogatica, Bosn. 40/D4
Rogers, Ar, US 93/J3
Rohri, Pak. 62/A2
Roi Et, Thai. 65/C2
Rolândia, Braz. 108/B2
Rolla, Mo, US 93/K3
Rolling Meadows, Il, US 99/P15
Roman, Rom. 41/H2
Romania (ctry.) 41/F3
Romans-sur-Isère, Fr. 32/F4
Romblon, Phil. 67/F1
Rome, NY, US 94/F3
Rome, Ga, US 97/G3
Rome (cap.), It. 38/C2
Romeoville, Il, US 99/P16
Romilly-sur-Seine, Fr. 32/E2
Romny, Ukr. 44/E2
Romorantin-Lanthenay, Fr. 32/D3
Romsey, Eng, UK 25/E5
Romulus, Mi, US 99/F7
Ronda, Sp. 34/C4
Rondonópolis, Braz. 107/H7
Rongcheng, China 58/B4
Rønne, Den. 27/H1
Ronne Ice Shelf, Ant. 83/W
Ronneby, Swe. 20/E4
Ronnenberg, Ger. 29/G4
Ronse, Belg. 30/C2
Roodeport, SAfr. 80/P13
Roorkee, India 62/C2
Roosendaal, Neth. 28/B5
Roquetas de Mar, Sp. 34/D4
Rosa Zárate, Ecu. 106/C3
Rosario, Arg. 109/D3
Rosário, Braz. 107/K4
Rosario de la Frontera, Arg. 109/D2
Rosário do Sul, Braz. 109/F3
Rosarito, Mex. 92/C4
Roseau (cap.), Dom. 104/F4
Roseburg, Or, US 92/B2
Roselle, Il, US 99/P16
Rosenberg, Tx, US 93/J5
Rosenheim, Ger. 33/K3
Roseville, Ca, US 99/M9
Roseville, Mi, US 99/G6
Rosh Ha'ayin, Isr. 49/F7
Roşiori de Vede, Rom. 41/G3
Roskilde, Den. 26/G1
Roslavl', Rus. 44/E1
Rosmalen, Neth. 28/C5
Rosolini, It. 38/D4
Rösrath, Ger. 31/G2
Ross Ice Shelf, Ant. 83/N
Rossano Stazione, It. 38/E3
Rosso, Mrta. 78/B2
Rossosh', Rus. 44/F2
Rostock, Ger. 26/G1
Rostov, Rus. 42/H4
Rostov, Rus. 44/F3
Roswell, NM, US 93/F4
Rota, Sp. 34/B4
Rotenburg, Ger. 29/G2
Rotherham, Eng, UK 23/G5
Rothwell, Eng, UK 23/G4
Rothwell, Eng, UK 25/F2
Rotorua, NZ 71/S10
Rottenburg am Neckar, Ger. 37/E1
Rotterdam, Neth. 28/B5
Rottweil, Ger. 37/E1
Roubaix, Fr. 30/C2
Rouen, Fr. 32/D2
Round Lake Beach, Il, US 99/P15
Round Rock, Tx, US 93/H5
Rouyn-Noranda, Qu, Can. 94/E1
Rovaniemi, Fin. 42/E2
Rovereto, It. 37/H6
Rovigo, It. 33/J4
Rovinj, Cro. 40/A3
Roxas, Phil. 67/E1
Roxas, Phil. 67/F1
Roxas, Phil. 61/J5
Roy, Ut, US 92/D2
Royal Oak, Mi, US 99/F7
Royal Tunbridge Wells, Eng, UK 25/G4
Royan, Fr. 32/C4
Royston, Eng, UK 25/F2
Royton, Eng, UK 23/F4
Rožňava, Slvk. 27/L4
Rtishchevo, Rus. 45/G1
Rubí, Sp. 35/L7
Rubizhne, Ukr. 44/F2
Rubtsovsk, Rus. 46/J4
Rucphen, Neth. 28/B5
Rūdnyy, Kaz. 43/P5
Rudolstadt, Ger. 33/J1
Rufino, Arg. 109/D3
Rufisque, Sen. 78/A3
Rugby, Eng, UK 25/E2
Rugeley, Eng, UK 23/G6
Ruma, Serb. 40/D3
Rumbek, Sudan 77/L6
Rumia, Pol. 27/K1
Rumoi, Japan 55/N3
Runcorn, Eng, UK 23/F5
Rundu, Namb. 82/C4
Ruse, Bul. 41/G4
Rushden, Eng, UK 25/F2
Russas, Braz. 107/L4
Russellville, Ar, US 93/J4
Russellville, Al, US 97/G3
Rüsselsheim, Ger. 26/E4
Russia (ctry.) 46/H3
Rust'avi, Geo. 45/H4
Rustenburg, SAfr. 80/P12
Ruston, La, US 93/J4
Ruvo di Puglia, It. 38/E2
Ruzayevka, Rus. 45/H1
Ružomberok, Slvk. 27/K4
Rwanda (ctry.) 82/E1
Ryazan', Rus. 44/F1
Ryazhsk, Rus. 44/G1
Rybinsk, Rus. 42/H4
Rybnik, Pol. 27/K3
Ryde, Eng, UK 25/E5
Ryōtsu, Japan 57/F1
Rypin, Pol. 27/K2
Ryton, Eng, UK 23/G2
Ryūgasaki, Japan 57/G3
Ryukyu (isls.), Japan 68/B2
Rzeszów, Pol. 27/M3
Rzhev, Rus. 42/G4

S

's Heerenberg, Neth. 28/D5
's Hertogenbosch, Neth. 28/C5
Sa Dec, Viet. 65/D4
Saalfeld, Ger. 33/J1
Saarbrücken, Ger. 31/F5
Saarlouis, Ger. 31/F5
Šabac, Serb. 40/D3
Sabadell, Sp. 35/L6
Sabae, Japan 56/E3
Sabanalarga, Col. 103/H4
Sabhā, Libya 76/H2
Sabinas, Mex. 96/C5
Sabinas Hidalgo, Mex. 96/C5
Sablayan, Phil. 67/F1
Sabzevār, Iran 51/J2
Sacavém, Port. 35/P10
Săcele, Rom. 41/G3
Saco, Me, US 95/G3
Sacramento (cap.), Ca, US 99/M9
Sādiqābād, Pak. 62/B2
Sadowara, Japan 56/B4
Sādri, India 62/B2
Safāqis, Tun. 76/H1
Säffle, Swe. 20/E4
Safford, Az, US 92/E4
Safi, Mor. 76/D1
Safonovo, Rus. 42/G5
Safranbolu, Turk. 44/E4
Saga, Japan 56/B4
Sagae, Japan 57/G1
Sagaing, Myan. 60/B4
Sagamihara, Japan 57/F3
Sāgar, India 62/C3
Sagay, Phil. 67/F1
Sagua de Tánamo, Cuba 103/H1
Sagua la Grande, Cuba 103/F1
Sagunto, Sp. 35/E3
Sahagún, Col. 103/H4
Sahagún, Mex. 101/L7
Sahara (des.), Afr. 76/G3
Sahāranpur, India 53/L3
Saharsa, India 62/E2
Sahavato, Madg. 81/J8
Sāhibganj, India 62/E2
Sāhīwāl, Pak. 53/K2
Sahuayo de Morelos, Mex. 100/E4
Saïda, Alg. 76/F1
Saidpur, India 62/D2
Saigō, Japan 56/D2
Saigon, Viet. 65/D4
Saijō, Japan 56/C4
Saiki, Japan 56/B4
Sailu, India 62/C4
Saint Albans, WV, US 97/H2
Saint Albans, Eng, UK 25/F3
Saint Albert, Ab, Can. 90/E2
Saint Augustine, Fl, US 97/H4
Saint Austell, Eng, UK 24/B6
Saint Catharines, On, Can. 95/U9
Saint Charles, Md, US 97/J2
Saint Charles, Mo, US 93/K3
Saint Charles, Il, US 99/P16
Saint Clair Shores, Mi, US 99/G6
Saint Francis, Wi, US 99/Q14
Saint George, Ut, US 92/D3
Saint George's (cap.), Gren. 104/F4
Saint Helens (mt.), Wa, US 90/C4
Saint Helens, Eng, UK 23/F5
Saint Helier (cap.), Chl, UK 32/B2
Saint Ives, Eng, UK 25/F2
Saint John, NB, Can. 95/H2
Saint John's (cap.), Anti. 104/F3
Saint John's (cap.), Nf, Can. 95/L2
Saint Johnsbury, Vt, US 95/F2
Saint Joseph, Mo, US 93/J3
Saint Kitts and Nevis (ctry.), StK. 104/F3
Saint Lawrence (gulf), Can. 95/J1
Saint Lawrence (riv.), Can.,US 94/F2
Saint Louis, Mo, US 93/K3
Saint Lucia (ctry.), StL. 104/F4
Saint Paul (cap.), Mn, US 94/A2
Saint Peter, Mn, US 91/K4
Saint Peter Port (cap.), Chl, UK 32/B2
Saint Petersburg, Fl, US 97/H5
Saint Petersburg, Rus. 43/T7
Saint Pierre and Miquelon (dpcy.), Can. 95/K2
Saint Simons Island, Ga, US 97/H4
Saint Thomas, On, Can. 94/D3
Saint Vincent and the Grenadines (ctry.), StV. 104/F4
Saint-Amand-les-Eaux, Fr. 30/C3
Saint-André, Reun. 81/S15
Saint-Avold, Fr. 31/F5
Saint-Benoît, Reun. 81/S15
Saint-Brieuc, Fr. 32/B2
Saint-Bruno-de-Montarville, Qu, Can. 95/P6
Saint-Chamond, Fr. 32/F4
Saint-Constant, Qu, Can. 95/N7
Saint-Cyr-l'École, Fr. 30/B6
Saint-Denis, Fr. 30/B6
Saint-Denis, Reun. 81/S15
Saint-Dié, Fr. 36/C1
Saint-Dizier, Fr. 31/D6
Saint-Étienne, Fr. 32/F4
Saint-Étienne-du-Rouvray, Fr. 32/D2
Saint-Eustache, Qu, Can. 95/N6
Saint-Georges, Qu, Can. 95/G2
Saint-Germain-en-Laye, Fr. 30/B6
Saint-Ghislain, Belg. 30/C3
Saint-Herblain, Fr. 32/C3
Saint-Hubert, Qu, Can. 95/P6
Saint-Hyacinthe, Qu, Can. 94/F2
Saint-Jean-de-la-Ruelle, Fr. 32/D3
Saint-Jean-sur-Richelieu, Qu, Can. 94/F2
Saint-Jérôme, Qu, Can. 95/N6
Saint-Joseph, Reun. 81/S15
Saint-Lambert, Qu, Can. 95/P6
Saint-Laurent, Qu, Can. 95/N6
Saint-Léonard, Qu, Can. 95/N6
Saint-Leu, Reun. 81/S15
Saint-Lô, Fr. 32/C2
Saint-Louis, Sen. 78/A2
Saint-Louis, Reun. 81/S15
Saint-Louis, Fr. 36/D2
Saint-Luc, Qu, Can. 95/P7
Saint-Malo, Fr. 32/B2
Saint-Marc, Haiti 103/H2
Saint-Martin-d'Hères, Fr. 32/F4
Saint-Maur-des-Fossés, Fr. 30/B6
Saint-Michel-sur-Orge, Fr. 30/B6
Saint-Nazaire, Fr. 32/B3
Saint-Nicolas, Belg. 31/E2
Saint-Omer, Fr. 30/B2
Saint-Paul, Reun. 81/S15
Saint-Pierre, Reun. 81/S15
Saint-Pierre-des-Corps, Fr. 32/D3
Saint-Pol-sur-Mer, Fr. 30/B1
Saint-Quentin, Fr. 30/C4
Saint-Raphaël, Fr. 33/G5
Sainte-Foy, Qu, Can. 95/G2
Sainte-Foy-lès-Lyon, Fr. 36/A6
Sainte-Geneviève-des-Bois, Fr. 30/B6
Sainte-Julie, Qu, Can. 95/P6
Sainte-Marie, Fr. 104/F4
Sainte-Thérèse, Qu, Can. 95/N6
Saintes, Fr. 32/C4
Sainthia, India 62/E3
Saito, Japan 56/B4
Sakai, Japan 57/F2
Sakaide, Japan 56/C3
Sakaiminato, Japan 56/C3
Sakata, Japan 55/M4
Sakawa, Japan 56/C4
Sakété, Ben. 79/F5
Sakhalin (isl.), Rus. 47/Q4
Sakhnīn, Isr. 49/G6
Şäki, Azer. 45/H4
Sakon Nakhon, Thai. 65/D2
Sakrand, Pak. 53/J3
Saku, Japan 57/F2
Saky, Ukr. 44/E3
Sala, Swe. 42/C4
Šal'a, Slvk. 40/C1
Salado (riv.), Arg. 109/E4
Salamá, Guat. 102/D3
Salamanca, Mex. 101/E4
Salamanca, Sp. 34/C2
Salamís, Gre. 39/N9
Salamīyah, Syria 49/E2
Salavat, Rus. 45/K1
Salé, Mor. 76/D1
Sale, Eng, UK 23/F5
Salekhard, Rus. 46/G3
Salem, India 62/C5
Salem, NH, US 95/G3
Salem (cap.), Or, US 90/C4
Salerno, It. 40/B5
Salford, Eng, UK 23/F5
Salgótarján, Hun. 40/D1
Salgueiro, Braz. 107/L5
Salihli, Turk. 50/B2
Salina, Ks, US 93/H3
Salina Cruz, Mex. 102/C2
Salinas, Braz. 107/K7
Salinas, Ca, US 92/B3
Salinópolis, Braz. 107/J4
Salisbury, Md, US 97/K2
Salisbury, NC, US 97/H3
Salisbury, Eng, UK 25/E4
Salmās, Iran 51/F2
Salmon Arm, BC, Can. 90/D3
Salo, Fin. 42/D3
Salon-de-Provence, Fr. 32/F5
Salonta, Rom. 40/E2
Sal'sk, Rus. 45/G3
Salt Lake City (cap.), Ut, US 90/F5
Salta, Arg. 109/C1
Saltillo, Mex. 96/C5
Salto, Braz. 108/C2
Salto, Uru. 109/E3
Salto del Guairá, Par. 109/F1
Sālūr, India 62/D4
Salurn (Salorno), It. 37/H5
Salvador, Braz. 107/L6
Salvatierra, Mex. 101/E4
Salyan, Azer. 51/G2
Salzburg, Aus. 40/A2
Salzgitter, Ger. 29/H4
Salzkotten, Ger. 29/F5
Salzwedel, Ger. 26/F2
Sam Son, Viet. 65/D2
Sama, Sp. 34/C1
Sāmalkot, India 62/D4
Samālūt, Egypt 50/B4
Samandağı, Turk. 49/D1
Samandira, Turk. 51/N7
Samannūd, Egypt 49/B4
Samara, Rus. 45/J1
Samarinda, Indo. 67/E4
Samarqand, Uzb. 46/G6
Sāmarrā', Iraq 51/E3
Samasata, Pak. 53/K3
Şamaxı, Azer. 45/J4
Sambalpur, India 62/D3
Sambas, Indo. 66/C3
Sambava, Madg. 81/J6
Sambir, Ukr. 27/M4
Samch'ŏk, SKor. 56/A2
Samch'ŏnp'o, SKor. 58/E5
Samnangjin, SKor. 56/A3
Samoa (ctry.) 69/R9
Samobor, Cro. 40/B3
Samokov, Bul. 41/F4
Samsun, Turk. 44/F4
Samut Prakan, Thai. 65/C3
Samut Sakhon, Thai. 65/C3
Samut Songkhram, Thai. 65/B3
San, Mali 78/D3
San Andrés, Col. 103/F3
San Andrés del Rabanedo, Sp. 34/C1
San Andrés Tuxtla, Mex. 102/C2
San Angelo, Tx, US 96/C4
San Anselmo, Ca, US 99/J11
San Antonio, Chile 109/B3
San Antonio Abad, Sp. 35/F3
San Antonio del Táchira, Ven. 103/H5
San Benedetto del Tronto, It. 40/A4
San Bernardino, Ca, US 92/C4
San Bernardo, Chile 109/B3
San Bruno, Ca, US 99/K11
San Buenaventura, Mex. 96/C5
San Carlos, Nic. 103/E4
San Carlos, Ven. 106/E2
San Carlos, Chile 109/B4
San Carlos, Uru. 109/F3
San Carlos, Ca, US 99/K11
San Carlos de Bariloche, Arg. 109/B5
San Carlos del Zulia, Ven. 103/J4
San Cataldo, It. 40/D5
San Cristóbal, Ven. 103/H5
San Cristóbal, Cuba 103/F1
San Cristóbal de las Casas, Mex. 102/C2
San Diego, Ca, US 92/C4
San Felipe, Ven. 106/E1
San Felipe, Chile 109/B3
San Felipe Torres Mochas, Mex. 101/E4
San Fernando, Chile 109/B3
San Fernando, Trin. 104/F5
San Fernando, Phil. 61/J5
San Fernando, Sp. 34/B4
San Fernando de Apure, Ven. 106/E2
San Fernando de Henares, Sp. 35/N9
San Fernando de Monte Cristi, DRep. 103/J2
San Fernando de Presas, Mex. 101/F3
San Francisco, Arg. 109/D3
San Francisco, ESal. 102/D3
San Francisco, Ca, US 99/J11
San Francisco del Rincón, Mex. 101/E4
San Gil, Col. 106/D2
San Giovanni in Fiore, It. 38/E3
San Giovanni Rotondo, It. 40/B5
San Ignacio, Belz. 102/D2
San Isidro, CR 103/F4
San Jacinto, Col. 103/H4
San Javier, Sp. 35/E4
San Jose, Phil. 67/F1
San Jose, Ca, US 99/L12
San José (cap.), CR 103/E4
San José de los Remates, Nic. 102/E3
San José de Mayo, Uru. 109/E3
San José del Cabo, Mex. 100/C4
San José del Guaviare, Col. 106/D3
San Juan, Arg. 109/C3
San Juan, PR 104/E3
San Juan Bautista, Par. 109/E2
San Juan Bautista Tuxtepec, Mex. 102/B2
San Juan de Alicante, Sp. 35/E3
San Juan de Aznalfarache, Sp. 34/B4
San Juan de La Maguana, DRep. 103/J2
San Juan de los Lagos, Mex. 100/E4
San Juan de los Morros, Ven. 106/E2
San Juan del Río, Mex. 102/B1
San Juan Nepomuceno, Col. 103/H4
San Justo, Arg. 109/D3
San Leandro, Ca, US 99/K11
San Lorenzo, Hon. 102/E3
San Lorenzo, Nic. 102/E3
San Lorenzo, Ca, US 99/K11
San Luis, Cuba 103/H1
San Luis, Arg. 109/C3
San Luis, Guat. 102/D2
San Luis de la Paz, Mex. 102/A1
San Luis Obispo, Ca, US 92/B4
San Luis Potosí, Mex. 101/E4
San Luis Río Colorado, Mex. 92/D4
San Marcos, Col. 103/H4
San Marcos, Guat. 102/D3
San Marcos, Tx, US 93/H5
San Marino (cap.), SMar. 33/K5
San Marino (ctry.) 33/K5
San Martín, Arg. 109/C3
San Martín de los Andes, Arg. 109/B5
San Mateo, Ca, US 99/K11
San Miguel, ESal. 102/D3
San Miguel de Allende, Mex. 101/E4
San Miguel de Tucumán, Arg. 109/C2
San Nicolás de los Arroyos, Arg. 109/D3
San Nicolás de los Garza, Mex. 101/E3
San Onofre, Col. 103/H4
San Pablo, Ca, US 99/K11
San Pablo de las Salinas, Mex. 101/Q9
San Pédro, C.d'Iv. 78/D5
San Pedro, Arg. 109/E3
San Pedro, Arg. 109/D1
San Pedro, Par. 109/E1
San Pedro Carchá, Guat. 102/D3
San Pedro de las Colonias, Mex. 96/C5
San Pedro Sula, Hon. 102/D3
San Rafael, Arg. 109/C3
San Rafael, Ca, US 99/J11
San Ramon, Ca, US 99/L11
San Ramón de la Nueva Orán, Arg. 109/D1
San Remo, It. 33/G5
San Roque, Sp. 34/C4
San Salvador (cap.), ESal. 102/D3
San Salvador de Jujuy, Arg. 109/C1
San Sebastián, Sp. 34/E1
San Sebastián de los Reyes, Sp. 35/N8
San Sebastián de Yalí, Nic. 102/E3
San Sebastiano, It. 33/J4
San Severo, It. 40/B5
San Vicente, ESal. 102/D3
San Vicente de Cañete, Peru 106/C6
San Vicente del Raspeig, Sp. 35/E3
Sanaa (cap.), Yem. 52/D5
Sanandaj, Iran 51/F3
Sānāwad, India 62/C3
Sancti Spíritus, Cuba 103/G1
Sanda, Japan 56/D3
Sandakan, Malay. 67/E2
Sandanski, Bul. 41/F5
Sandbach, Eng, UK 23/F5
Sandefjord, Nor. 20/D4
Sandhurst, Eng, UK 25/F4
Sandıklı, Turk. 50/B2

Sandnes, Nor. 20/C4
Sandomierz, Pol. 27/L3
Sandusky, Oh, US 94/D3
Sandvika, Nor. 20/D4
Sandviken, Swe. 42/C3
Sandy, Ut, US 92/E2
Sandy Springs, Ga, US 97/G3
Sanford, NC, US 97/J3
Sanford, Fl, US 97/H4
Sanford, Me, US 95/G3
Sangamner, India 62/B4
Sangenjo, Sp. 34/A1
Sangju, SKor. 56/A2
Sāngli, India 62/B4
Sangmélima, Camr. 76/H7
Sanjō, Japan 57/F2
Sankt Augustin, Ger. 31/G2
Sankt Gallen, Swi. 37/F3
Sankt Ingbert, Ger. 31/G5
Sankt Jakob (San Giacomo), It. 37/H4
Sankt Leonhard in Passeier (San Leonardo in Passiria), It. 37/H4
Sankt Martin in Passeier (San Martino in Passiria), It. 37/H4
Sankt Pölten, Aus. 40/B1
Sankt Wendel, Ger. 31/G5
Sanlúcar de Barrameda, Sp. 34/B4
Sanmenxia, China 59/B4
Sanming, China 61/H3
Sannicandro Garganico, It. 40/B5
Sano, Japan 57/F2
Sanok, Pol. 27/M4
Sant Adrià de Besòs, Sp. 35/L7
Sant Boi de Llobregat, Sp. 35/L7
Sant Cugat del Vallès, Sp. 35/L7
Sant Feliu de Guíxols, Sp. 35/G2
Sant Feliu de Llobregat, Sp. 35/L7
Sant Pere de Ribes, Sp. 35/K7
Sant Vicenç dels Horts, Sp. 35/L7
Santa Ana, Bol. 106/E6
Santa Ana, Hon. 102/E3
Santa Ana, ESal. 102/D3
Santa Ana, Ca, US 92/C4
Santa Bárbara, Hon. 102/D3
Santa Bárbara, Braz. 108/D1
Santa Barbara, Ca, US 92/C4
Santa Bárbara d'oeste, Braz. 108/C2
Santa Catarina, Mex. 101/E3
Santa Clara, Cuba 103/G1
Santa Clara, Ca, US 99/L12
Santa Coloma de Gramanet, Sp. 35/L7
Santa Cruz, Phil. 61/J5
Santa Cruz, Ca, US 92/B3
Santa Cruz de Barahona, DRep. 103/J2
Santa Cruz de la Palma, Canl. 35/X16
Santa Cruz de la Sierra, Bol. 106/F7
Santa Cruz de Tenerife, Canl. 35/X16
Santa Cruz del Quiché, Guat. 102/D3
Santa Cruz do Rio Pardo, Braz. 108/B2
Santa Cruz do Sul, Braz. 108/A4
Santa Eugenia de Ribeira, Sp. 34/A1
Santa Eulalia del Río, Sp. 35/F3
Santa Fe, Arg. 109/D3
Santa Fe (cap.), NM, US 93/F4
Santa Fé do Sul, Braz. 108/B2
Santa Helena de Goiás, Braz. 108/B1
Santa Inês, Braz. 107/J4
Santa Isabel, Braz. 108/G8
Santa Luzia, Braz. 107/J4
Santa Luzia, Braz. 108/D1
Santa Maria, Braz. 109/F2
Santa Maria, Ca, US 92/B4
Santa Maria Capua Vetere, It. 40/B5
Santa Maria da Vitória, Braz. 107/K6
Santa Marta, Col. 103/H4
Santa Pola, Sp. 35/E3
Santa Rita, Braz. 107/M5
Santa Rita do Sapucaí, Braz. 108/H7
Santa Rosa, Arg. 109/D4
Santa Rosa, Braz. 109/F2
Santa Rosa, Ca, US 92/B3
Santa Rosa, CR 102/E4
Santa Rosa, Ecu. 106/C4
Santa Rosa de Copán, Hon. 102/D3
Santa Rosa de Viterbo, Braz. 108/C2
Santa Vitória do Palmar, Braz. 109/F3
Santana do Livramento, Braz. 109/E3
Santander, Sp. 34/D1
Santander de Quilichao, Col. 106/C3
Santarém, Braz. 107/H4
Santarém, Port. 34/A3
Santiago, Pan. 103/F4
Santiago, Phil. 61/J5
Santiago, Braz. 109/F2
Santiago (cap.), Chile 109/B3
Santiago de Compostela, Sp. 34/A1
Santiago de Cuba, Cuba 103/H1
Santiago del Estero, Arg. 109/D2
Santiago Ixcuintla, Mex. 100/D4
Santiago Papasquiaro, Mex. 100/D3
Santiago Pinotepa Nacional, Mex. 102/B2
Santo Anastácio, Braz. 108/B2
Santo André, Braz. 108/G8
Santo Ângelo, Braz. 109/F2
Santo Antônio, SaoT. 76/G7
Santo Antônio de Pádua, Braz. 108/D2
Santo Domingo, Cuba 103/F1
Santo Domingo (cap.), DRep. 104/D3
Santo Domingo de los Colorados, Ecu. 106/C4
Santo Domingo Tehuantepec, Mex. 102/C2
Santo Tomé, Arg. 109/E2
Santo Tomé, Arg. 109/D3
Santos, Braz. 108/G8
Santos Dumont, Braz. 108/K6
Sanya, China 65/E2
São Bento do Sul, Braz. 108/B3
São Bernardo do Campo, Braz. 108/G8
São Borja, Braz. 109/E2
São Carlos, Braz. 108/C2
São Fidélis, Braz. 108/D2
São Francisco do Sul, Braz. 108/B3
São Gabriel, Braz. 109/F3
São Gonçalo, Braz. 108/K7
São Gonçalo do Sapuçaí, Braz. 108/H6
São Gotardo, Braz. 108/C1
São Joachim da Barra, Braz. 108/C2
São João da Boa Vista, Braz. 108/G6
São João da Madeira, Port. 34/A2
São João de Meriti, Braz. 108/K7
São João del Rei, Braz. 108/C2
São João Nepomuceno, Braz. 108/K6
São José, Braz. 108/B3
São José do Rio Pardo, Braz. 108/G6
São José do Rio Prêto, Braz. 108/B2
São José dos Campos, Braz. 108/H8
São José dos Pinhais, Braz. 108/B3
São Leopoldo, Braz. 108/B4
São Lourenço, Braz. 108/H7
São Lourenço do Sul, Braz. 108/B4
São Luís, Braz. 107/K4
São Manoel, Braz. 108/B2
São Mateus, Braz. 108/E1
São Mateus do Sul, Braz. 108/B3
São Paulo, Braz. 108/G8
São Pedro da Aldeia, Braz. 108/D2
São Sebastião, Braz. 108/H8
São Sebastião do Paraíso, Braz. 108/C2
São Tomé (cap.), SaoT. 76/G7
São Tomé And Príncipe (ctry.) 76/F7
São Vicente, Braz. 108/G8
São Vicente (cape), Port. 34/A4
Sapele, Nga. 79/G5
Sappemeer, Neth. 28/D2
Sapporo, Japan 55/N3
Saqqez, Iran 51/F2
Sara Buri, Thai. 65/C3
Sarāb, Iran 51/F2
Sarajevo (cap.), Bosn. 40/D4
Saraland, Al, US 97/F4
Saran', Kaz. 46/H5
Sarandë, Alb. 39/G3
Sārangpur, India 62/C3
Saransk, Rus. 45/H1
Sarapul, Rus. 43/M4
Sarasota, Fl, US 97/H5
Saratoga, Ca, US 99/K12
Saratoga Springs, NY, US 94/F3
Saratov, Rus. 45/H2
Sarayköy, Turk. 50/B2
Sarcelles, Fr. 30/B6
Sardārshahar, India 62/B2
Sardinia (isl.) 38/A2
Sargodha, Pak. 53/K2
Sarh, Chad 76/J6
Sārī, Iran 51/H2
Sarıkamış, Turk. 45/G4
Sarikei, Malay. 66/D3
Sariwŏn, NKor. 58/C3
Sarkant, Kaz. 46/H5
Şarkışla, Turk. 44/F5
Sarnen, Swi. 37/E4
Sarnia, On, Can. 99/H6
Sarny, Ukr. 44/C2
Sárospatak, Hun. 27/L4
Sarrebourg, Fr. 31/G6
Sarreguemines, Fr. 31/G5
Sarstedt, Ger. 29/G4
Sartrouville, Fr. 30/B6
Sárvár, Hun. 40/C2
Sarzana, It. 33/H4
Sasarām, India 62/D3
Sasebo, Japan 56/A4
Saskatchewan (riv.), Sk, Can. 86/F3
Saskatchewan (prov.), Can. 86/F3
Saskatoon, Sk, Can. 90/G2
Sasolburg, SAfr. 80/P13
Sasovo, Rus. 45/G1
Sassari, It. 38/A2
Sassenheim, Neth. 28/B4
Sātāra, India 62/B4
Satna, India 62/D3
Sátoraljaújhely, Hun. 27/L4
Satpayev, Kaz. 46/G5
Satu Mare, Rom. 27/M5
Saudi Arabia (ctry.) 52/D4
Sauk Rapids, MN, US 91/K4
Saulgau, Ger. 37/F1
Sault Sainte Marie, On, Can. 94/C2
Saumur, Fr. 32/C3
Saurimo, Ang. 82/D2
Sava, It. 40/C5
Savalou, Ben. 79/F5
Savanna-la-Mar, Jam. 103/G2
Savannah, Ga, US 97/H3
Savannakhet, Laos 65/D2
Sāvantvādi, India 62/B4
Sāveh, Iran 51/G3
Savigny-sur-Orge, Fr. 30/B6
Savona, It. 33/H4
Savonlinna, Fin. 42/F3
Sawahlunto, Indo. 66/B4
Sawara, Japan 57/G3
Sayama, Japan 57/F3
Şaydā, Leb. 49/D3
Sayula, Mex. 100/E5
Saywūn, Yem. 52/E5
Scarborough, Eng, UK 23/H3
Schaerbeek, Belg. 31/D2
Schaffhausen, Swi. 37/E2
Schagen, Neth. 28/B3
Schaumburg, Il, US 99/P15
Schenefeld, Ger. 29/G1
Schererville, In, US 99/R17
Schertz, Tx, US 93/H5
Schiedam, Neth. 28/B5
Schiffweiler, Ger. 31/G5
Schijndel, Neth. 28/C5
Schilde, Belg. 28/B6
Schiltigheim, Fr. 31/G6
Schlanders (Silandro), It. 37/G4
Schleswig, Ger. 26/E1
Schloss Holte-Stukenbrock, Ger. 29/F5
Schlüchtern, Ger. 33/H1
Schluderns (Sluderno), It. 37/G4
Schmalkalden, Ger. 33/J1
Schmallenberg, Ger. 29/F6
Schmelz, Ger. 31/F5
Schneverdingen, Ger. 29/G2
Schofield Barracks, Hi, US 88/V12
Schönebeck, Ger. 26/F2
Schöningen, Ger. 26/F2
Schopfheim, Ger. 31/G4
Schortens, Ger. 29/E1
Schoten, Belg. 28/B6
Schramberg, Ger. 37/E1
Schrobenhausen, Ger. 26/F4
Schwabach, Ger. 33/J2
Schwäbisch Gmünd, Ger. 26/E4
Schwäbisch Hall, Ger. 33/H2
Schwalbach, Ger. 31/F5
Schwalmtal, Ger. 28/D6
Schwandorf im Bayern, Ger. 33/K2
Schwanewede, Ger. 29/F2
Schwechat, Aus. 40/C1
Schwedt, Ger. 27/H2
Schweinfurt, Ger. 33/J1
Schwelm, Ger. 29/E6
Schwerin, Ger. 26/F2
Schwerte, Ger. 29/E6
Schwyz, Swi. 37/E3
Sciacca, It. 38/C4
Scicli, It. 38/D4
Scordia, It. 38/D4
Scotland, UK 21/C2
Scottsbluff, Ne, US 93/G2
Scottsboro, Al, US 97/G3
Scottsdale, Az, US 92/E4
Scranton, Pa, US 94/F3
Scunthorpe, Eng, UK 23/H4
Sea-Tac, Wa, US 99/C3
Seaford, Eng, UK 25/G5
Seaham, Eng, UK 23/G2
Seahurst, Wa, US 99/C3
Searcy, Ar, US 93/K4
Seattle, Wa, US 99/C2
Sébaco, Nic. 102/E3
Sebastian, Fl, US 97/H5
Sebeş, Rom. 41/F3
Şebinkarahisar, Turk. 44/F4
Secunda, SAfr. 80/Q13
Secunderābād, India 62/C4
Sedalia, Mo, US 93/J3
Sedan, Fr. 31/D4
Sederot, Isr. 49/D4
Sedona, Az, US 92/E4
Seesen, Ger. 29/H5
Segamat, Malay. 66/B3
Segezha, Rus. 42/G3
Ségou, Mali 78/D3
Segovia, Sp. 34/C2
Seguin, Tx, US 93/H5
Sehnde, Ger. 29/G4
Sehore, India 62/C3
Seinäjoki, Fin. 42/D3
Seine (riv.), Fr. 32/F3
Seki, Japan 57/E3
Sekondi, Gha. 79/E5
Selb, Ger. 33/K1
Selby, Eng, UK 23/G4
Selçuk, Turk. 50/A2
Selebi-Phikwe, Bots. 82/E5
Sélestat, Fr. 36/D1
Sélibabi, Mrta. 78/B3
Selm, Ger. 29/E5
Selma, Al, US 97/G3
Semarang, Indo. 66/D5
Semenov, Rus. 43/K4
Semey, Kaz. 46/J4
Semiluki, Rus. 44/F2
Semnān, Iran 51/H3
Semporna, Malay. 67/E3
Sena, Thai. 65/C3
Sendai, Japan 55/N4
Sendai, Japan 56/B5
Senden, Ger. 29/E5
Senden, Ger. 37/G1
Senegal (ctry.) 78/B3
Senftenberg, Ger. 27/H3
Senhor do Bonfim, Braz. 107/K6
Senica, Slvk. 27/J4
Senigallia, It. 33/K5
Senlis, Fr. 30/B5
Sens, Fr. 32/E2
Sensuntepeque, ESal. 102/D3
Senta, Serb. 40/E3
Seoni, India 62/C3
Seonī Mālwā, India 62/C3
Seoul (cap.), SKor. 58/F6
Seoul (cap.), SKor. 58/F6
Sept-Îles, Qu, Can. 95/H1
Sequoia National Park, Ca, US 92/C3
Seraing, Belg. 31/E2
Serang, Indo. 66/C5
Serbia and Montenegro (ctry.) 40/E3
Serdobsk, Rus. 45/H1
Seremban, Malay. 66/B3
Sergach, Rus. 43/K5
Sergiyev Posad, Rus. 42/H4
Seria, Bru. 66/D3
Seriate, It. 33/H4
Serik, Turk. 49/B1
Serov, Rus. 46/G4
Serowe, Bots. 82/E5
Serpukhov, Rus. 44/F1
Serra, Braz. 108/D2
Serra Talhada, Braz. 107/L5
Sérrai, Gre. 41/F5
Serrinha, Braz. 107/L6
Sertãozinho, Braz. 108/C2
Sesimbra, Port. 34/A3
Sestroretsk, Rus. 43/S6
Sesvete, Cro. 40/C3
Sète, Fr. 32/E5
Sete Lagoas, Braz. 108/C1
Sethārja, Pak. 62/A2
Sétif, Alg. 76/G1
Seto, Japan 57/E3
Settimo Torinese, It. 33/G4
Setúbal, Port. 35/Q10
Setúbal (bay), Port. 34/A3
Sevastopol', Ukr. 44/E3
Sevenoaks, Eng, UK 25/G4
Severnyy, Rus. 43/P2
Severodvinsk, Rus. 42/H2
Severomorsk, Rus. 42/G1
Severoural'sk, Rus. 43/N3
Seville, Sp. 34/C4
Sevlievo, Bul. 41/G4
Seward (pen.), US 85/E2
Seychelles (ctry.) 75/H5
Seydişehir, Turk. 50/B2
Seynod, Fr. 36/C6
Sfîntu Gheorghe, Rom. 41/G3
Shadrinsk, Rus. 43/P4
Shagamu, Nga. 79/F5
Shah Alam, Malay. 66/B3
Shāhdādkot, Pak. 62/A2
Shahdol, India 62/D3
Shaḩḩāt, Libya 77/K1
Shāhjahānpur, India 62/C2
Shahr-e Kord, Iran 51/G3
Shājāpur, India 62/C3
Shakargarh, Pak. 53/L2
Shakhtinsk, Kaz. 46/H5
Shakhty, Rus. 44/G3
Shakhun'ya, Rus. 43/K4
Shaki, Nga. 79/F4
Shalqar, Kaz. 45/L3
Shāmgarh, India 62/C3
Shāmli, India 53/L3
Shamokin, Pa, US 94/E3
Shanghai, China 59/L8
Shangqiu, China 59/C4
Shangrao, China 61/H2
Shantou, China 61/H4
Shaoguan, China 61/G3
Shaoxing, China 61/J2
Shaoyang, China 61/F3
Sharon, Pa, US 94/D3
Shar'ya, Rus. 43/K4
Shashi, China 61/G2
Shaw, Eng, UK 25/E4
Shawinigan, Qu, Can. 95/F2
Shawnee, Ok, US 93/H4
Shchekino, Rus. 44/F1
Shchelkovo, Rus. 43/W9
Shchigry, Rus. 44/F2
Shchūchīnsk, Kaz. 46/H4
Sheberghān, Afg. 53/J1
Sheboygan, Wi, US 91/M5
Shefar'am, Isr. 49/G6
Sheffield, Al, US 97/G3
Sheffield, Eng, UK 23/G5
Shekhūpura, Pak. 53/K2
Shelby, NC, US 97/H3
Shelbyville, Tn, US 97/G3
Shelbyville, In, US 97/G2
Shenandoah National Park, Va, US 97/J2
Shenyang, China 58/B2
Shenzhen, China 61/G4
Shepetivka, Ukr. 44/C2
Sherbrooke, Qu, Can. 95/G2
Sherghāti, India 62/D3
Sheridan, Wy, US 92/F1
Sherman, Tx, US 93/H4
Shetland (isls.), UK 18/C2
Shibata, Japan 57/F2
Shibīn al Kaum, Egypt 49/B4
Shibīn al Qanāṭir, Egypt 49/B4
Shido, Japan 56/D3
Shijiazhuang, China 59/C3
Shikārpur, Pak. 62/A2
Shilka, Rus. 54/H1
Shillong, India 60/A3
Shimabara, Japan 56/B4
Shimamoto, Japan 56/D3
Shimanovsk, Rus. 55/K1
Shimizu, Japan 57/F3
Shimoda, Japan 57/F3
Shimodate, Japan 57/F2
Shimonoseki, Japan 56/B4
Shingū, Japan 56/D4
Shinjō, Japan 55/N4
Shinminato, Japan 57/E2
Shinyanga, Tanz. 82/F1
Shiogama, Japan 57/G1
Shipley, Eng, UK 23/G4
Shirakawa, Japan 57/G2
Shīrāz, Iran 51/H4
Shirbīn, Egypt 49/B4
Shiroishi, Japan 57/G1
Shirone, Japan 57/F2
Shīrvān, Iran 51/J2
Shishou, China 61/G2
Shivpurī, India 62/C2
Shiyan, China 61/F1
Shizuishan, China 54/F4
Shizunai, Japan 55/N3
Shizuoka, Japan 57/F3
Shkodër, Alb. 40/D4
Shōbara, Japan 56/C3
Sholāpur, India 62/C4
Shorāpur, India 62/C4
Shoreham-by-Sea, Eng, UK 25/F5
Shorewood, Wi, US 99/Q13
Shorkot, Pak. 53/K2
Shostka, Ukr. 44/E2
Shpola, Ukr. 44/D2
Shreveport, La, US 93/J4
Shrewsbury, Eng, UK 24/D1
Shuangcheng, China 47/N5
Shuangyashan, China 55/L2
Shubrā al Khaymah, Egypt 49/B4
Shubrā Khīt, Egypt 49/B4
Shujāābād, Pak. 53/K3
Shumen, Bul. 41/H4
Shumerlya, Rus. 43/K5
Shurugwi, Zim. 82/E4
Shūshtar, Iran 51/G3
Shuya, Rus. 42/J4
Shwebo, Myan. 65/A1
Shymkent, Kaz. 46/G5
Siālkot, Pak. 53/K2
Siasi, Phil. 67/F2
Šiauliai, Lith. 42/D5
Sibay, Rus. 45/L1
Šibenik, Cro. 40/B4
Siberia (reg.), Rus. 46/K3
Sibi, Pak. 53/J3
Sibiu, Rom. 41/G3
Sibolga, Indo. 66/A3
Sibsāgar, India 60/B3
Sibu, Malay. 66/D3
Sibuco, Phil. 67/F2
Sibut, CAfr. 77/J6
Sicily (isl.), It. 38/C3
Sicuani, Peru 106/D6
Šid, Serb. 40/D3
Siddipet, India 62/C4
Sidhi, India 62/D3
Sidhpur, India 62/B3
Sidi Bel-Abbes, Alg. 76/E1
Sīdī Bū Zayd, Tun. 76/G1
Sidi Ifni, Mor. 76/C2
Sīdī Sālim, Egypt 49/B4
Sidney, Oh, US 94/C3
Siedlce, Pol. 27/M2
Siegburg, Ger. 31/G2
Siegen, Ger. 31/H2
Siemreab, Camb. 65/C3
Siena, It. 33/J5
Sieradz, Pol. 27/K3
Sierpc, Pol. 27/K2
Sierra Leone (ctry.) 78/B4
Sierra Madre Occidental (mts.), Mex. 100/C2
Sierra Madre Oriental (mts.), Mex. 100/E3
Sierra Nevada (mts.), Ca, US 92/B3
Sierra Vista, Az, US 100/C2
Sighetu Marmaţiei, Rom. 41/F2
Sighişoara, Rom. 41/G2
Sigmaringen, Ger. 37/F1
Sigtuna, Swe. 42/C4
Siguatepeque, Hon. 102/E3
Sihorā, India 62/D3
Siilinjärvi, Fin. 42/E3
Siirt, Turk. 50/E2
Sīkar, India 62/C2
Sikasso, Mali 78/D4
Sikeston, Mo, US 93/K3
Silao, Mex. 101/E4
Silay, Phil. 67/F1
Silchar, India 60/B3
Silifke, Turk. 49/C1
Silīguri, India 62/E2
Silistra, Bul. 41/H3
Silivri, Turk. 41/J5
Silkeborg, Den. 20/D4
Silla, Sp. 35/E3
Silopi, Turk. 50/E2
Silvassa, India 62/B3
Silver City, NM, US 92/E4
Silver Lake-Fircrest, Wa, US 99/C2
Silyānah, Tun. 38/A4
Simav, Turk. 50/B2
Simcoe, On, Can. 95/S10
Simeria, Rom. 40/F3
Simferopol', Ukr. 44/E3
Şimleu Silvaniei, Rom. 40/F2
Simrishamn, Swe. 27/H1
Simunul, Phil. 67/E3
Sin-le-Noble, Fr. 30/C3
Sinai (pen.), Egypt 50/C4
Sinaia, Rom. 41/G3
Sincé, Col. 103/H4
Sincelejo, Col. 103/H4
Sindangbarang, Indo. 66/C5
Sindelfingen, Ger. 33/H2
Sinendé, Ben. 79/F4
Sinfra, C.d'Iv. 78/D5
Singapore (ctry.) 66/B3
Singapore (cap.), Sing. 66/B3
Singen, Ger. 37/E2
Singida, Tanz. 82/F1
Singkawang, Indo. 66/C3
Sinop, Braz. 107/G6
Sinop, Turk. 44/E4
Sint-Genesius-Rode, Belg. 31/D2
Sint-Gillis-Waas, Belg. 28/B6
Sint-Katelijne-Waver, Belg. 28/B6
Sint-Niklaas, Belg. 28/B6
Sint-Oedenrode, Neth. 28/C5
Sint-Pieters-Leeuw, Belg. 31/D2
Sint-Truiden, Belg. 31/E2
Sintang, Indo. 66/D3
Sintra, Port. 35/P10
Sinŭiju, NKor. 58/C2
Sinzig, Ger. 31/G2
Siocon, Phil. 67/F2
Siófok, Hun. 40/D2

T

Tandil, Arg. 109/E4
Tando Ādam, Pak. 62/A2
Tando Allāhyār, Pak. 53/J3
Tando Muhammad Khān, Pak. 62/A2
Tanga, Tanz. 82/G2
Tanganyika (lake), Afr. 82/E2
Tangará da Serra, Braz. 106/G6
Tanger (Tangier), Mor. 34/C5
Tangshan, China 59/J7
Tanjungbalai, Indo. 66/A3
Tanjungkarang-Telukbetung, Indo. 66/C5
Tanjungpandan, Indo. 66/C4
Tanjungpinang, Indo. 66/B3
Tanjungpura, Indo. 66/A3
Tānk, Pak. 53/K2
Ţanţā, Egypt 49/B4
Tantoyuca, Mex. 102/B1
Tanuku, India 62/D4
Tanzania (ctry.) 82/F2
Taolañaro, Madg. 81/H9
Taourirt, Mor. 76/E1
T'aoyüan, Tai. 61/J3
Tapachula, Mex. 102/C3
Tapolca, Hun. 40/C2
Taquara, Braz. 108/B4
Taquari, Braz. 108/B4
Taquaritinga, Braz. 108/B2
Tara, Rus. 46/H4
Ţarābulus, Leb. 49/D2
Tarakan, Indo. 67/E3
Taranto, It. 40/C5
Tarapoto, Peru 106/C5
Tarawa (cap.), Kiri. 68/G4
Tarbes, Fr. 32/D5
Tarboro, NC, US 97/J3
Taree, Austl. 73/E1
Tarhūnah, Libya 76/H1
Tarifa, Sp. 34/C4
Tarija, Bol. 106/F8
Tarin (Torino), It. 33/G4
Tarkwa, Gha. 79/E5
Tarma, Peru 106/C6
Tarnobrzeg, Pol. 27/L3
Tarnów, Pol. 27/L3
Taroudannt, Mor. 76/D1
Tarpon Springs, Fl, US 97/H4
Tarragona, Sp. 35/F2
Tarsus, Turk. 49/D1
Tartagal, Arg. 109/D1
Tartu, Est. 42/E4
Ţarţūs, Syria 49/D2
Tarumizu, Japan 56/B5
Tashkent (cap.), Uzb. 46/G5
Tasikmalaya, Indo. 66/C5
Tasman (sea) 68/E8
Tasmania, Austl. 73/C3
Tata, Hun. 40/D2
Tatabánya, Hun. 27/K5
Tatarsk, Rus. 46/H4
Tatāwīn, Tun. 76/H1
Tateyama, Japan 57/F3
Tatsuno, Japan 57/E3
Tatvan, Turk. 50/E2
Tauá, Braz. 107/K5
Taubaté, Braz. 108/H8
Taufkirchen, Ger. 37/H1
Taungdwingyi, Myan. 60/B4
Taunggyi, Myan. 65/B1
Taunsa, Pak. 53/K2
Taunton, Ma, US 95/G3
Taunton, Eng, UK 24/C4
Taunusstein, Ger. 31/H3
Taupo, NZ 71/S10
Tauragė, Lith. 27/M1
Tauranga, NZ 71/S10
Taverny, Fr. 30/B5
Tavşanlı, Turk. 50/B2
Tawau, Malay. 67/E3
Tawzar, Tun. 76/G1
Taxco, Mex. 101/K8
Tay Ninh, Viet. 65/D4
Taylor, Mi, US 99/F7
Taylorville, Il, US 93/K3
Tayshet, Rus. 47/K4
Taytay, Phil. 67/E1
Taza, Mor. 76/E1
Tchaourou, Ben. 79/F4
Tczew, Pol. 27/K1
Teapa, Mex. 102/C2
Tébessa, Alg. 76/G1
Tebingtinggi, Indo. 66/A3
Tecamachalco, Mex. 101/M8
Tecate, Mex. 92/C4
Tecomán, Mex. 100/E5
Tecpan de Galeana, Mex. 101/E5
Tecuala, Mex. 100/D4
Tecuci, Rom. 41/H3
Tefé, Braz. 106/F4
Tegal, Indo. 66/C5
Tegelen, Neth. 28/D6
Tegucigalpa (cap.), Hon. 102/E3
Tehrān (cap.), Iran 51/G3
Tehuacán, Mex. 101/M8
Tehuantepec (gulf), Mex. 102/C3
Tejen, Trkm. 53/H1
Tejupilco de Hidalgo, Mex. 101/E5
Tekax de Álvaro Obregón, Mex. 102/D1
Tekeli, Kaz. 46/H5
Tekirdağ, Turk. 41/H5
Tekkali, India 62/D4
Tel Aviv-Yafo, Isr. 49/F7
Tela, Hon. 102/E3
T'elavi, Geo. 45/H4
Telde, Canl. 35/X16
Telêmaco Borba, Braz. 108/B3
Telford Dawley, Eng, UK 24/D1
Telgte, Ger. 29/E5
Telica, Nic. 102/E3
Tellicherry, India 62/C5
Telok Anson, Malay. 66/B3
Teloloapan, Mex. 101/K8
Telšiai, Lith. 42/D5
Tema, Gha. 79/E5
Tembilahan, Indo. 66/B4
Tembisa, SAfr. 80/Q13
Temerin, Serb. 40/D3
Temirtaū, Kaz. 46/H4
Tempe, Az, US 92/E4
Temryuk, Rus. 44/F3
Temse, Belg. 28/B6
Temuco, Chile 109/B4
Tenancingo, Mex. 101/K8
Tendō, Japan 57/G1
Tenggarong, Indo. 67/E4
Tenkodogo, Burk. 79/E4
Tennessee (riv.), US 97/F3
Tennessee (state), US 97/G3
Tenosique de Pino Suárez, Mex. 102/D2
Tenryū, Japan 57/E3
Teófilo Otoni, Braz. 108/D1
Tepalcatepec, Mex. 100/E5
Tepeji del Río de Ocampo, Mex. 101/K7
Tepexpan, Mex. 101/R9
Tepic, Mex. 100/D4
Teplice, Czh. 27/G3
Tepotzotlán, Mex. 101/Q9
Tequila, Mex. 100/E4
Tequisquiapan, Mex. 101/K6
Teramo, It. 40/A4
Teresina, Braz. 107/K5
Teresópolis, Braz. 108/L7
Terlan (Terlano), It. 37/H4
Termas de Río Hondo, Arg. 109/D2
Termini Imerese, It. 38/C4
Termiz, Uzb. 53/J1
Termoli, It. 40/B4
Ternate, Indo. 67/G3
Terneuzen, Neth. 28/A6
Terni, It. 38/C1
Ternopil', Ukr. 44/C2
Terracina, It. 38/C2
Terrassa, Sp. 35/L6
Terrebonne, Qu, Can. 95/N6
Teruel, Sp. 35/E2
Teslić, Bosn. 40/C3
Tessaoua, Niger 79/G3
Tessenie (Teseney), Erit. 52/C5
Tete, Moz. 82/F4
Tétouan, Mor. 34/C5
Tetovo, FYROM 40/E4
Tettnang, Ger. 37/F2
Teverya, Isr. 49/D3
Tewantin-Noosa, Austl. 72/D4
Texarkana, Tx, US 93/J4
Texas (state), US 96/C4
Texas City, Tx, US 93/J5
Texcoco, Mex. 101/R9
Texmelucan, Mex. 101/L7
Teykovo, Rus. 42/J4
Teziutlán, Mex. 101/M7
Tezontepec de Aldama, Mex. 101/K6
Tezpur, India 60/B3
Tezu, India 60/C3
Thai Binh, Viet. 65/D1
Thai Nguyen, Viet. 65/D1
Thailand (ctry.) 65/C3
Thailand (gulf) 65/C4
Thal, Pak. 53/K2
Thalwil, Swi. 37/E3
Thames, NZ 71/S10
Thames (riv.), Eng, UK 25/G3
Thāna, India 62/B4
Thanh Hoa, Viet. 65/D2
Thanjavur, India 62/C5
Tharād, India 62/B3
Thatcham, Eng, UK 25/E4
Thaton, Myan. 65/B2
The Dalles, Or, US 90/C4
The Woodlands, Tx, US 93/J5
Thebes (ruin), Egypt 52/B3
Theodore Roosevelt National Park, US 91/G4
Thessaloníki, Gre. 40/F5
Thetford, Eng, UK 25/G2
Thetford Mines, Qu, Can. 95/G2
Thibodaux, La, US 93/K5
Thiers, Fr. 32/E4
Thiès, Sen. 78/A3
Thika, Kenya 82/G1
Thimphu (cap.), Bhu. 62/E2
Thionville, Fr. 31/F5
Thiruvananthapuram (Trivandrum), India 62/C6
Thívai, Gre. 39/H3
Tholen, Neth. 28/B5
Thomaston, Ga, US 97/G3
Thomasville, Ga, US 97/H4
Thomasville, NC, US 97/H3
Thonon-les-Bains, Fr. 36/C5
Thornaby-on-Tees, Eng, UK 23/G2
Thorne, Eng, UK 23/H4
Thornton Cleveleys, Eng, UK 23/E4
Thorold, On, Can. 95/U9
Thoubāl, India 60/B3
Thu Dau Mot, Viet. 65/D4
Thun, Swi. 36/D4
Thunder Bay, On, Can. 91/L3
Tianguá, Braz. 107/K4
Tianjin, China 59/H7
Tianmen, China 61/G2
Tianshui, China 54/F5
Tiaret, Alg. 76/F1
Ticul, Mex. 102/D1
Tidjikdja, Mrta. 78/C2
Tiel, Neth. 28/C5
Tieling, China 58/B1
Tielt, Belg. 30/C2
Tienen, Belg. 31/D2
Tierp, Swe. 42/C3
Tierra Blanca, Mex. 101/N8
Tiffin, Oh, US 94/D3
Tifton, Ga, US 97/H4
Tighina (Bendery), Mol. 41/J2
Tigris (riv.), Iraq 51/F4
Tijuana, Mex. 92/C4
Tīkamgarh, India 62/C3
Tikhoretsk, Rus. 44/G3
Tikhvin, Rus. 42/G4
Tilburg, Neth. 28/C5
Ţimā, Egypt 50/B5
Timaru, NZ 71/R11
Timashevsk, Rus. 44/F3
Timbaúba, Braz. 107/L5
Timbó, Braz. 108/B3
Timimoun, Alg. 76/F2
Timişoara, Rom. 40/E3
Timmins, On, Can. 94/D1
Timon, Braz. 107/K5
Timor (isl.), Indo. 68/B5
Timóteo, Braz. 108/D1
Timrå, Swe. 42/C3
Tindivanam, India 62/C5
Tindouf, Alg. 76/D2
Tineo, Sp. 34/B1
Tingo María, Peru 106/C5
Tinley Park, Il, US 99/Q16
Tinrhir, Mor. 76/D1
Tiptūr, India 62/C5
Tiranë (cap.), Alb. 40/D5
Tiraspol, Mol. 41/J2
Tirat Karmel, Isr. 49/F6
Tire, Turk. 50/A2
Tîrgovişte, Rom. 41/G3
Tîrgu Jiu, Rom. 41/F3
Tîrgu Mureş, Rom. 41/G2
Tîrgu Neamţ, Rom. 41/H2
Tîrgu Secuiesc, Rom. 41/H2
Tîrnăveni, Rom. 41/G2
Tiruchchirāppalli, India 62/C5
Tiruchendūr, India 62/C6
Tiruchengodu, India 62/C5
Tirunelveli, India 62/C6
Tirupati, India 62/C5
Tiruppattūr, India 62/C5
Tiruppūr, India 62/C5
Tiruvannāmalai, India 62/C5
Titicaca (lake), Peru 106/E7
Titlagarh, India 62/D3
Titov Veles, FYROM 40/E5
Titusville, Fl, US 97/H4
Tivaouane, Sen. 78/A3
Tiverton, Eng, UK 24/C5
Tixtla de Guerrero, Mex. 102/B2
Tizayuca, Mex. 101/L7
Tizimín, Mex. 102/D1
Tiznit, Mor. 76/D2
Tlalnepantla, Mex. 101/Q9
Tlapa de Comonfort, Mex. 102/B2
Tlapacoyan, Mex. 101/M7
Tlaquepaque, Mex. 100/E4
Tlaquiltenango, Mex. 101/K8
Tlaxcala, Mex. 101/L7
Tlemcen, Alg. 76/E1
Toamasina, Madg. 81/J7
Toba, Japan 57/E3
Tobias Barreto, Braz. 107/L6
Tocantins (riv.), Braz. 107/J4
Tochigi, Japan 57/F2
Tochio, Japan 57/F2
Tocopilla, Chile 109/B1
Tocumen, Pan. 103/G4
Toda Bhīm, India 62/C2
Togo (ctry.) 79/F4
Tōkai, Japan 57/E3
Tōkamachi, Japan 57/F2
Tokat, Turk. 44/F4
Tokoroa, NZ 71/S10
Tokorozawa, Japan 57/F3
Tokushima, Japan 56/D3
Tokuyama, Japan 56/B3
Tōkyō (cap.), Japan 57/F3
Tola, Nic. 102/E4
Toledo, Braz. 109/F1
Toledo, Sp. 34/C3
Toliara, Madg. 81/G8
Tolosa, Sp. 34/D1
Tolú, Col. 103/H4
Toluca, Mex. 101/Q10
Tol'yatti, Rus. 45/J1
Tomakomai, Japan 55/N3
Tomar, Port. 34/A3
Tomaszów Lubelski, Pol. 27/M3
Tomaszów Mazowiecki, Pol. 27/L3
Tombouctou, Mali 78/E2
Tomelloso, Sp. 34/D3
Tomsk, Rus. 46/J4
Tonalá, Mex. 102/C2
Tonawanda, NY, US 95/V9
Tonbridge, Eng, UK 25/G4
Tondano, Indo. 67/F3
Tonga (ctry.) 69/H7
Tongaat, SAfr. 81/E3
Tongchuan, China 59/B4
Tongduch'on, SKor. 58/G6
Tongeren, Belg. 31/E2
Tonghae, SKor. 58/E4
Tonghua, China 58/C2
Tongliao, China 59/E2
Tongling, China 61/H2
Tongren, China 61/F3
Tönisvorst, Ger. 28/D6
Tonk, India 62/C2
Tonkin (gulf), Asia 65/D1
Tonoshō, Japan 56/D3
Tønsberg, Nor. 20/D4
Tooele, Ut, US 92/D2
Toowoomba, Austl. 72/C4
Topeka (cap.), Ks, US 93/J3
Toplița, Rom. 41/G2
Topol'čany, Slvk. 27/K4
Torbalı, Turk. 50/A2
Torbat-e Ḩeydarīyeh, Iran 51/J3
Torghay, Kaz. 46/G4
Torhout, Belg. 30/C1
Torino (Turin), It. 33/G4
Tornio, Fin. 20/H2
Törökszentmiklós, Hun. 40/E2
Toronto (cap.), On, Can. 95/U8
Toropets, Rus. 42/F4
Tororo, Ugan. 77/M7
Torquay, Eng, UK 24/C6
Torrance, Ca, US 92/C4
Torre del Greco, It. 40/B5
Torre-Pacheco, Sp. 35/E4
Torrejón de Ardoz, Sp. 35/N9
Torrelavega, Sp. 34/C1
Torremaggiore, It. 40/B5
Torremolinos, Sp. 34/C4
Torrente, Sp. 35/E3
Torreón, Mex. 96/C5
Tôrres, Braz. 108/B4
Torres Novas, Port. 34/A3
Torres Vedras, Port. 34/A3
Torrevieja, Sp. 35/E4
Tortona, It. 33/H4
Tortosa, Sp. 35/F2
Toruń, Pol. 27/K2
Torzhok, Rus. 42/G4
Tosa, Japan 56/C4
Tosashimizu, Japan 56/C4
Tosno, Rus. 42/F4
Tosu, Japan 56/B4
Tosya, Turk. 44/E4
Totana, Sp. 34/E4
Totness, Sur. 107/G2
Tottori, Japan 56/D3
T'oufen, Tai. 61/J3
Tougan, Burk. 78/E3
Touggourt, Alg. 76/G1
Toul, Fr. 31/E6
Toulon, Fr. 32/F5
Toulouse, Fr. 32/D5
Toungoo, Myan. 65/B2
Tourcoing, Fr. 30/C2
Tourlaville, Fr. 32/C2
Tournai, Belg. 30/C2
Tours, Fr. 32/D3
Towada, Japan 57/G2
Townsville, Austl. 72/B2
Toyama, Japan 57/E2
Toyohashi, Japan 57/E3
Toyokawa, Japan 57/E3
Toyo'oka, Japan 56/D3
Toyoshina, Japan 57/E2
Toyota, Japan 57/E3
Tra Vinh, Viet. 65/D4
Trabzon, Turk. 44/F4
Tracy, Ca, US 99/M11
Tralee, Ire. 21/A10
Tramandaí, Braz. 108/B4
Tramin (Termeno), It. 37/H5
Tranås, Swe. 20/E4
Trang, Thai. 65/B5
Trani, It. 40/C5
Trapani, It. 38/C3
Trappes, Fr. 30/B6
Traralgon, Austl. 73/C3
Traun, Aus. 33/L2
Traunreut, Ger. 40/A2
Traunstein, Ger. 33/K3
Travnik, Bosn. 40/C3
Trbovlje, Slov. 40/B2
Třebíč, Czh. 33/L2
Trebinje, Bosn. 40/D4
Treinta y Tres, Uru. 109/F3
Trelew, Arg. 109/C5
Trelleborg, Swe. 26/G1
Trenčín, Slvk. 27/K4
Trenque Lauquen, Arg. 109/D4
Trento, It. 37/H5
Trenton, On, Can. 94/E2
Trenton (cap.), NJ, US 94/F3
Trenton, Mi, US 99/F7
Tres Arroyos, Arg. 109/D4
Três Corações, Braz. 108/H6
Três Lagoas, Braz. 108/B2
Três Marias, Braz. 108/C1
Três Pontas, Braz. 108/H6
Três Rios, Braz. 108/K7
Tres Valles, Mex. 102/B2
Treviglio, It. 33/H4
Treviso, It. 33/K4
Trichūr, India 62/C5
Trier, Ger. 31/F4
Trieste, It. 40/A3
Triggiano, It. 40/C5
Tríkala, Gre. 39/G3
Trincomalee, SrL. 62/D6
Trindade, Braz. 107/J7
Třinec, Czh. 27/K4
Trinidad, Bol. 106/F6
Trinidad, Uru. 109/E3
Trinidad and Tobago (ctry.), Trin. 104/F5
Triolet, Mrts. 81/T15
Tripoli (cap.), Libya 76/H1
Trípolis, Gre. 39/H4
Tripunittura, India 62/C6
Trnava, Slvk. 40/C1
Trois-Rivières, Qu, Can. 95/F2
Troisdorf, Ger. 31/G2
Troitsk, Rus. 43/P5
Trollhättan, Swe. 20/E4
Tromsø, Nor. 20/F1
Trondheim, Nor. 20/D3
Tropic of Capricorn 72/A3
Trowbridge, Eng, UK 24/D4
Troy, NY, US 94/F3
Troy, Oh, US 97/G1
Troy, Al, US 97/G4
Troy, Mi, US 99/F6
Troyan, Bul. 41/G4
Troyes, Fr. 32/F2
Trstenik, Serb. 40/E4
Trujillo, Ven. 106/D2
Trujillo, Peru 106/C5
Trujillo, Hon. 102/E3
Truro, Eng, UK 24/A6
Truth or Consequences, NM, US 96/B3
Trutnov, Czh. 27/H3
Trzcianka, Pol. 27/J2
Tsabong, Bots. 80/C2
Tsakane, SAfr. 80/Q13
Tsetserleg, Mong. 54/E2
Tsévié, Togo 79/F5
Tshikapa, D.R. Congo 82/D2
Tsiroanomandidy, Madg. 81/H7
Ts'khinvali, Geo. 45/G4
Tsu, Japan 56/E3
Tsubame, Japan 57/F2
Tsubata, Japan 57/E2
Tsuchiura, Japan 57/G2
Tsukumi, Japan 56/B4
Tsuru, Japan 57/F3
Tsuruga, Japan 56/E3
Tsurugi, Japan 56/E2
Tsuyama, Japan 56/D3
Tuamotu (arch.), FrPol. 69/L6
Tuao, Phil. 61/J5
Tuapse, Rus. 44/F3
Tuba, Phil. 61/J5
Tuban, Indo. 66/D5
Tubarão, Braz. 108/B4
Tubbergen, Neth. 28/D4
Tübingen, Ger. 37/F1
Tubize, Belg. 31/D2
Tubou, Fiji 68/H6
Ţubruq (Tobruk), Libya 77/K1
Tucson, Az, US 92/E4
Tucupita, Ven. 106/F2
Tucuruí, Braz. 107/J4
Tudela, Sp. 34/E1
Ţūkh, Egypt 49/B4
Tukums, Lat. 42/D4
Tukwila, Wa, US 99/C3
Tula, Mex. 101/K6
Tula, Rus. 44/F1
Tulancingo, Mex. 101/L6
Tulare, Ca, US 92/C3
Tulcán, Ecu. 106/C3
Tulcea, Rom. 41/J3
Ţūlkarm, WBnk. 49/G7
Tullahoma, Tn, US 97/G3
Tulle, Fr. 32/D4
Tulsa, Ok, US 93/J3
Tultitlán, Mex. 101/Q9
Tuluá, Col. 106/C3
Tulun, Rus. 47/L4
Tumaco, Col. 106/C3
Tumbes, Peru 106/B4
Tumen, China 55/K3
Tumkūr, India 62/C5
Tumwater, Wa, US 99/B4
Tunceli, Turk. 50/D2
Tūnis (cap.), Tun. 38/B4
Tunisia (ctry.) 76/H1
Tunjá, Col. 106/D2
Tunuyán, Arg. 109/C3
Tupã, Braz. 108/B2
Tupaciguara, Braz. 108/B1
Tupelo, Ms, US 97/F3
Tupiza, Bol. 106/E8
Tura, India 62/F2
Turbaco, Col. 103/H4
Turbat, Pak. 53/H3
Turbo, Col. 103/G4
Turčiansky Svätý Martin, Slvk. 27/K4
Turda, Rom. 41/F2
Turek, Pol. 27/K2
Tŭrgovishte, Bul. 41/H4
Turgutlu, Turk. 44/C5
Turhal, Turk. 44/F4
Turkey (ctry.) 50/C2
Türkistan, Kaz. 46/G5
Türkmenbashi (Krasnowodsk), Trkm. 51/H2
Turkmenistan (ctry.) 46/F6
Türkoğlu, Turk. 50/D2
Turks and Caicos (isls.), UK 104/C2
Turlock, Ca, US 92/B3
Turnhout, Belg. 28/B6
Turnu Măgurele, Rom. 41/G4
Turpan, China 54/B3
Tuscaloosa, Al, US 97/G3
Tuskegee, Al, US 97/G3
Tutayev, Rus. 42/H4
Tuticorin, India 62/C6
Tuttlingen, Ger. 37/E2
Tuusula, Fin. 42/E3
Tuvalu (ctry.) 68/G5
Tuxpan, Mex. 100/D4
Tuxpan, Mex. 100/E5
Tuxpan de Rodríguez Cano, Mex. 102/B1
Tuxtla Gutiérrez, Mex. 102/C2
Túy, Sp. 34/A1
Tuy Hoa, Viet. 65/E3
Tuyen Quang, Viet. 65/D1
Tuymazy, Rus. 43/M5
Tuzla, Bosn. 40/D3
Tver', Rus. 42/G4
Tweed Heads, Austl. 73/E1
Twello, Neth. 28/D4
Twin Falls, Id, US 92/D2
Two Rivers, Wi, US 91/M4
Tychy, Pol. 27/K3
Tyldesley, Eng, UK 23/F4
Tyler, Tx, US 93/J4
Tynemouth, Eng, UK 23/G1
Tyrnyauz, Rus. 45/G4
Tyumen', Rus. 43/Q4

U

Ub, Serb. 40/E3
Ubá, Braz. 108/D2
Übach-Palenberg, Ger. 31/F2
Ubatã, Braz. 107/L6
Ubatuba, Braz. 108/H8
Ube, Japan 56/B4
Úbeda, Sp. 34/D3
Uberaba, Braz. 108/C1
Uberlândia, Braz. 108/B1
Überlingen, Ger. 37/F2
Ubon Ratchathani, Thai. 65/D3
Ubrique, Sp. 34/C4
Ucayali (riv.), Peru 106/D5
Uccle, Belg. 31/D2
Uchaly, Rus. 43/N5
Udagamandalam, India 62/C5
Udaipur, India 62/B3
Uddevalla, Swe. 20/D4
Uden, Neth. 28/C5
Udgīr, India 62/C4
Udhampur, India 53/L2
Udine, It. 40/A2
Udipi, India 62/B5
Udon Thani, Thai. 65/C2
Ueda, Japan 57/F2
Uelzen, Ger. 29/H3
Ueno, Japan 56/E3
Uenohara, Japan 57/F3
Uetersen, Ger. 29/G1
Uetze, Ger. 29/H4
Ufa, Rus. 43/M5
Uganda (ctry.) 77/M7
Uglegorsk, Rus. 55/N2
Uglich, Rus. 42/H4
Uherské Hradiště, Czh. 27/J4

W

Weesp – Żywie

Weesp, Neth. 28/C4
Wegberg, Ger. 28/D6
Weiden, Ger. 33/K2
Weifang, China 59/D3
Weihai, China 58/B4
Weilheim, Ger. 37/H2
Weimar, Ger. 26/F3
Weinan, China 59/B4
Weingarten, Ger. 37/F2
Weinheim, Ger. 26/E4
Weirton, WV, US 94/D3
Weissenburg im Bayern, Ger. 33/J2
Weissenfels, Ger. 26/F3
Weisswasser, Ger. 27/H3
Wejherowo, Pol. 27/K1
Weligama, SrL. 62/D6
Welkom, SAfr. 80/D2
Welland, On, Can. 95/U10
Wellingborough, Eng, UK 25/F2
Wellington, SAfr. 80/L10
Wellington (cap.), NZ 71/R11
Wels, Aus. 40/B1
Welshnafen (Nova Levante), It. 37/H5
Wenatchee, Wa, US 90/C4
Wenchi, Gha. 79/E5
Wenden, Ger. 31/G2
Wendeng, China 58/B4
Wenzhou, China 61/J3
Werdau, Ger. 33/K1
Werdohl, Ger. 29/E6
Werkendam, Neth. 28/B5
Werl, Ger. 29/E5
Wermelskirchen, Ger. 29/E6
Werne an der Lippe, Ger. 29/E5
Wernigerode, Ger. 29/H5
Wertheim, Ger. 33/H2
Wervik, Belg. 30/C2
Wesel, Ger. 28/D5
Weslaco, Tx, US 96/D5
West Allis, Wi, US 99/P13
West Bank 49/G7
West Bank (ctry.) 49/D3
West Bank 50/C3
West Bend, Wi, US 93/K2
West Bridgford, Eng, UK 23/G6
West Bromwich, Eng, UK 24/E1
West Chicago, Il, US 99/P16
West Columbia, SC, US 97/H3
West Fargo, ND, US 91/J4
West Helena, Ar, US 93/K4
West Ice Shelf, Ant. 83/F
West Indies (isls.) 103/F2
West Jordan, Ut, US 92/E2
West Lincoln, Ne, US 93/H2
West Memphis, Ar, US 93/K4
West Monroe, La, US 93/J4
West Palm Beach, Fl, US 97/H5
West Pensacola, Fl, US 97/G4
West Sacramento, Ca, US 99/L9
West Seneca, NY, US 95/V10
West Valley City, Ut, US 92/E2
West Vancouver, BC, Can. 90/C3
West Virginia (state), US 94/D4
Westerlo, Belg. 28/B6
Western Ghats (mts.), India 62/B4
Western Sahara 76/C3
Westerstede, Ger. 29/E2
Westerville, Oh, US 97/H1
Westervoort, Neth. 28/C5
Westhoughton, Eng, UK 23/F4
Westland, Mi, US 99/F7
Westminster, Md, US 94/E4
Westmont, Il, US 99/P16
Westmount, Qu, Can. 95/N7
Weston-Super-Mare, Eng, UK 24/D4
Westonaria, SAfr. 80/P13
Wete, Tanz. 82/G2
Wetter, Ger. 29/E6
Wetteren, Belg. 28/A6
Wettingen, Swi. 37/E3
Wetzikon, Swi. 37/E3
Wetzlar, Ger. 33/H1
Wevelgem, Belg. 30/C2
Wewak, PNG 68/D5
Weymouth, Eng, UK 24/D5
Whangarei, NZ 71/R10
Wharton, Tx, US 93/H5
Wheaton, Il, US 99/P16
Wheeling, WV, US 94/D3
Wheeling, Il, US 99/Q15
Whickham, Eng, UK 23/G2
Whitby, On, Can. 95/V8
Whitefield, Eng, UK 23/F4
Whitehaven, Eng, UK 22/E2
Whitehorse (cap.), Yk, Can. 85/L3
Whitetail, NM, US 100/D1
Whitley Bay, Eng, UK 23/G1
Whitstable, Eng, UK 25/H4
Whyalla, Austl. 68/C8
Wichita, Ks, US 93/H3
Wichita Falls, Tx, US 93/H4
Widnes, Eng, UK 23/F5
Wiehl, Ger. 31/G2
Wieliczka, Pol. 27/L4
Wieluń, Pol. 27/K3
Wiener Neustadt, Aus. 40/C2
Wierden, Neth. 28/D4
Wiesbaden, Ger. 31/H3
Wigan, Eng, UK 23/F4
Wigston, Eng, UK 25/E1
Wijchen, Neth. 28/C5
Wijk bij Duurstede, Neth. 28/C5
Wil, Swi. 37/F3
Wilhelmshaven, Ger. 29/F1
Wilkes-Barre, Pa, US 94/F3
Willebroek, Belg. 28/B6
Willemstad, NAnt. 106/E1
Williamsburg, Va, US 97/J2
Williamsport, Pa, US 94/E3
Willich, Ger. 28/D6
Willmar, Mn, US 91/K4
Wilmette, Il, US 99/Q15
Wilmington, NC, US 97/J3
Wilmington, De, US 94/F4
Wilmington Island, Ga, US 97/H4
Wilmslow, Eng, UK 23/F5
Wilnsdorf, Ger. 31/H2
Wilrijk, Belg. 28/B6
Wilson, NC, US 97/J3
Wimborne Minster, Eng, UK 24/E5
Winchester, Ky, US 97/G2
Winchester, Va, US 97/J2
Winchester, Eng, UK 25/E4
Windhoek (cap.), Namb. 82/C5
Windsor, Nf, Can. 95/L1
Windsor, Eng, UK 25/F4
Windsor, On, Can. 99/F7
Windward Passage (chan.), Cuba,Haiti 103/H2
Winfield, Ks, US 93/H3
Winneba, Gha. 79/E5
Winnetka, Il, US 99/Q15
Winnipeg (cap.), Mb, Can. 91/J3
Winnipeg (lake), Can. 91/J2
Winnipegosis (lake), Mb, Can. 91/H2
Winschoten, Neth. 28/E2
Winsford, Eng, UK 23/F5
Winston-Salem, NC, US 97/H2
Winter Haven, Fl, US 97/H4
Winter Park, Fl, US 97/H4
Winterswijk, Neth. 28/D5
Winterthur, Swi. 37/E3
Wipperfürth, Ger. 29/E6
Wisbech, Eng, UK 25/G1
Wisch, Neth. 28/D5
Wisconsin (state), US 91/L4
Wismar, Ger. 26/F2
Witbank, SAfr. 80/Q12
Witham, Eng, UK 25/G3
Witney, Eng, UK 25/E3
Witten, Ger. 29/E6
Wittenberg, Ger. 26/G3
Wittenberge, Ger. 26/F2
Wittlich, Ger. 31/F4
Wittmund, Ger. 29/E1
Witzenhausen, Ger. 29/G6
Włocławek, Pol. 27/K2
Włodawa, Pol. 27/M3
Wodonga, Austl. 73/C3
Wodzisław Śląski, Pol. 27/K4
Woerden, Neth. 28/B4
Woking, Eng, UK 25/F4
Wokingham, Eng, UK 25/F4
Wolfen, Ger. 26/G3
Wolfenbüttel, Ger. 29/H4
Wolfsburg, Ger. 29/H4
Wolgast, Ger. 27/G1
Wollongong, Austl. 73/D2
Wołomin, Pol. 27/L2
Woluwé-Saint-Lambert, Belg. 31/D2
Wolvega, Neth. 28/D3
Wolverhampton, Eng, UK 24/D1
Wombwell, Eng, UK 23/G4
Wŏnju, SKor. 56/A2
Wŏnsan, NKor. 58/D3
Wood Dale, Il, US 99/P16
Woodburn, Or, US 90/C4
Woodhaven, Mi, US 99/F7
Woodinville, Wa, US 99/C2
Woodland, Ca, US 99/L9
Woodridge, Il, US 99/P16
Woodstock, Il, US 99/N15
Wooster, Oh, US 94/D3
Worcester, Ma, US 95/G3
Worcester, Eng, UK 24/D2
Worcester, SAfr. 80/L10
Workington, Eng, UK 22/E2
Worksop, Eng, UK 23/G5
Worms, Ger. 33/H2
Worth, Il, US 99/Q16
Wörth am Rhein, Ger. 31/H5
Worthing, Eng, UK 25/F5
Wrexham, Wal, UK 23/F5
Wrocław, Pol. 27/J3
Września, Pol. 27/J2
Wuhan, China 61/G2
Wuhu, China 61/H2
Wülfrath, Ger. 28/E6
Wum, Camr. 79/H5
Wūn, India 62/C3
Wunstorf, Ger. 29/G4
Wuppertal, Ger. 29/E6
Würselen, Ger. 31/F2
Würzburg, Ger. 33/H2
Wuustwezel, Belg. 28/B6
Wuwei, China 54/E4
Wuxi, China 59/L8
Wuxue, China 61/G2
Wuzhou, China 61/F4
Wyandotte, Mi, US 99/F7
Wyoming, Mi, US 94/C3
Wyoming (state), US 90/G4
Wyszków, Pol. 27/L2

X

Xa Binh Long, Viet. 65/D4
Xaçmaz, Azer. 45/J4
Xai-Xai, Moz. 81/F2
Xankändi, Azer. 45/H5
Xanten, Ger. 28/D5
Xánthi, Gre. 41/G5
Xanxerê, Braz. 108/A3
Xenia, Oh, US 97/H2
Xiamen, China 61/H3
Xi'an, China 59/B4
Xiangfan, China 61/G1
Xiangtan, China 61/G3
Xianning, China 61/G2
Xiantao, China 61/G2
Xianyang, China 59/B4
Xiaogan, China 61/G2
Xiaoshan, China 59/L9
Xichang, China 60/D3
Xicotepec, Mex. 101/M6
Xifeng, China 54/F4
Xigazê, China 62/E2
Xingcheng, China 59/E2
Xinghua, China 59/D4
Xingtai, China 59/C3
Xingyi, China 60/E3
Xining, China 54/E4
Xinji, China 59/C3
Xintai, China 59/D4
Xinxiang, China 59/C4
Xinyang, China 61/G1
Xinyi, China 59/D4
Xinyu, China 61/G3
Xinzhou, China 61/G2
Xique-Xique, Braz. 107/K6
Xuchang, China 59/C4

Y

Ya'an, China 60/D2
Yabuki, Japan 57/G2
Yacuiba, Bol. 106/F8
Yādgīr, India 62/C4
Yagoua, Camr. 76/J5
Yahyalı, Turk. 50/C2
Yaita, Japan 57/F2
Yaizu, Japan 57/F3
Yakacık, Turk. 49/E1
Yakeshi, China 55/J2
Yakima, Wa, US 90/C4
Yako, Burk. 79/E3
Yakutsk, Rus. 47/N3
Yala, Thai. 65/C5
Yalova, Turk. 41/J5
Yalta, Ukr. 44/E3
Yalvaç, Turk. 50/B2
Yamaga, Japan 56/B4
Yamagata, Japan 57/G1
Yamaguchi, Japan 56/B3
Yamatotakada, Japan 56/D3
Yambol, Bul. 41/H4
Yamoto, Japan 57/G1
Yamoussoukro (cap.), C.d'Iv. 78/D5
Yamunānagar, India 53/L2
Yanagawa, Japan 56/B4
Yanai, Japan 56/C4
Yan'an, China 59/B3
Yanaul, Rus. 43/M4
Yancheng, China 59/E4
Yandoon, Myan. 60/B5
Yangjiang, China 61/F4
Yangmei, Tai. 61/J3
Yangon (cap.), Myan. 65/B2
Yangquan, China 59/C3
Yangtze (Chang) (riv.), China 55/J5
Yangzhou, China 61/H1
Yanji, China 55/K3
Yantai, China 59/E3
Yao, Japan 56/D3
Yaoundé (cap.), Camr. 76/H7
Yara, Cuba 103/G1
Yaransk, Rus. 43/K4
Yarımca, Turk. 41/J5
Yaroslavl', Rus. 42/H4
Yartsevo, Rus. 46/K3
Yarumal, Col. 106/C2
Yasnyy, Rus. 45/L2
Yasugi, Japan 56/C3
Yāsūj, Iran 51/G4
Yatabe, Japan 57/G2
Yateley, Eng, UK 25/F4
Yatsuo, Japan 57/E2
Yatsushiro, Japan 56/B4
Yauco, PR 104/E3
Yavne, Isr. 49/F8
Yawatahama, Japan 56/C4
Yazd, Iran 51/H4
Yazoo City, Ms, US 93/K4
Yecla, Sp. 35/E3
Yefremov, Rus. 44/F1
Yehud, Isr. 49/F7
Yejmiadzin, Arm. 45/H4
Yelabuga, Rus. 43/M5
Yelan', Rus. 45/G2
Yelets, Rus. 44/F1
Yellow (Huang) (riv.), China 54/G4
Yellowknife (cap.), NW, Can. 86/E2
Yellowstone (lake), Wy, US 90/F4
Yellowstone (riv.), Mt,Wy, US 91/G4
Yellowstone National Park, US 92/E1
Yen Bai, Viet. 65/D1
Yenakiyeve, Ukr. 44/F2
Yenangyaung, Myan. 60/B4
Yendi, Gha. 79/E4
Yenişehir, Turk. 41/J5
Yeniseysk, Rus. 46/K4
Yeovil, Eng, UK 24/D5
Yerevan (cap.), Arm. 45/H4
Yerköy, Turk. 44/E5
Yermak, Kaz. 46/H4
Yerres, Fr. 30/B6
Yeşilkent, Turk. 49/E1
Yessentuki, Rus. 45/G3
Yevla, India 62/B3
Yevlax, Azer. 45/H4
Yevpatoriya, Ukr. 44/E3
Yeysk, Rus. 44/F3
Yiannitsá, Gre. 40/F5
Yibin, China 60/E2
Yichang, China 61/F2
Yichun, China 61/G3
Yıldızeli, Turk. 44/F5
Yima, China 59/B4
Yinchuan, China 54/F4
Yingcheng, China 61/G2
Yingkou, China 58/B2
Yingtan, China 61/H2
Yining, China 46/J5
Yixing, China 59/K8
Yiyang, China 61/G2
Yizheng, China 61/H1
Ylöjärvi, Fin. 42/D3
Yŏch'ŏn, SKor. 58/D5
Yogyakarta, Indo. 66/D5
Yōkaichi, Japan 56/E3
Yokkaichi, Japan 56/E3
Yokohama, Japan 57/F3
Yokosuka, Japan 57/F3
Yonezawa, Japan 57/G2
Yong'an, China 61/H3
Yŏngch'ŏn, SKor. 56/A3
Yŏngdŏk, SKor. 56/A2
Yŏngju, SKor. 56/A2
Yongzhou, China 61/F3
Yonkers, NY, US 94/F3
Yopal, Col. 106/D2
York, Pa, US 94/E4
York, Eng, UK 23/G4
York, NE, US 93/H2
Yorkton, Sk, Can. 91/H3
Yoro, Hon. 102/E3
Yosemite National Park, Ca, US 92/C3
Yoshida, Japan 56/C4
Yoshkar-Ola, Rus. 43/L4
Yŏsu, SKor. 58/D5
Youngstown, Oh, US 94/D3
Yozgat, Turk. 44/E5
Ypsilanti, Mi, US 99/E7
Ystad, Swe. 27/G1
Yuba City, Ca, US 92/B3
Yūbari, Japan 55/N3
Yucatan (pen.), Mex. 101/H5
Yucatan Channel (chan.), NAm. 102/E1
Yuci, China 59/C3
Yueyang, China 61/G2
Yūki, Japan 57/F2
Yukon (riv.), Can.,US 85/G3
Yukon Territory (terr.), Can. 86/D2
Yüksekova, Turk. 51/F2
Yukuhashi, Japan 56/B4
Yulin, China 65/E2
Yulin, China 65/E1
Yuma, Az, US 92/D4
Yumbo, Col. 106/C3
Yumen, China 54/D4
Yurga, Rus. 46/J4
Yurimaguas, Peru 106/C5
Yur'yevets, Rus. 42/J4
Yuscarán, Hon. 102/E3
Yuzhno-Sakhalinsk, Rus. 55/N2
Yverdon, Swi. 36/C4

Z

Zaandam, Neth. 26/C2
Zaanstad, Neth. 28/B4
Ząbki, Pol. 27/L2
Ząbkowice Śląskie, Pol. 27/J3
Zábřeh, Czh. 33/M2
Zabrze, Pol. 27/K3
Zacapa, Guat. 102/D3
Zacapu, Mex. 101/E5
Zacatecas, Mex. 100/E4
Zacatecoluca, ESal. 102/D3
Zacatelco, Mex. 101/L7
Zacatepec, Mex. 101/K8
Zacatlán, Mex. 101/M7
Zachary, La, US 97/F4
Zadar, Cro. 40/B3
Zafra, Sp. 34/B3
Żagań, Pol. 27/H3
Zaghwān, Tun. 38/B4
Zagreb (cap.), Cro. 40/B3
Zāhedān, Iran 53/H3
Zahirābād, India 62/C4
Zaḩlah, Leb. 49/D3
Zākhū, Iraq 51/E2
Zakopane, Pol. 27/K4
Zalaegerszeg, Hun. 40/C2
Zalău, Rom. 27/M5
Zambia (ctry.) 82/E3
Zamboanga, Phil. 67/F2
Zambrów, Pol. 27/M2
Zamora, Ecu. 106/C4
Zamora, Sp. 34/C2
Zamora de Hidalgo, Mex. 100/E5
Zamość, Pol. 27/M3
Zandvoort, Neth. 28/B4
Zanjān, Iran 51/G2
Zanzibar, Tanz. 82/G2
Zaoyang, China 61/G1
Zaozhuang, China 59/D4
Zapala, Arg. 109/B4
Zapolyarnyy, Rus. 42/F1
Zapopan, Mex. 100/E4
Zaporizhzhya, Ukr. 44/E3
Zara, Turk. 44/F5
Zaragoza (Saragossa), Sp. 35/E2
Zárate, Arg. 109/E3
Zarauz, Sp. 34/D1
Zaraza, Ven. 106/E2
Zaria, Nga. 79/G4
Zărneşti, Rom. 41/G3
Żary, Pol. 27/H3
Žatec, Czh. 33/K1
Zaventem, Belg. 31/D2
Zavitinsk, Rus. 55/K1
Zawiercie, Pol. 27/K3
Žďár nad Sázavou, Czh. 33/L2
Zduńska Wola, Pol. 27/K3
Zedelgem, Belg. 30/C1
Zefat, Isr. 49/D3
Zeist, Neth. 28/C4
Zeitz, Ger. 26/G3
Zele, Belg. 28/B6
Zelenodol'sk, Rus. 43/L5
Zelenogorsk, Rus. 43/S6
Zelenograd, Rus. 43/W8
Zelenokumsk, Rus. 45/G3
Zemst, Belg. 28/B7
Zenica, Bosn. 40/C3
Zentsūji, Japan 56/C3
Žepče, Bosn. 40/D3
Zernograd, Rus. 44/G3
Zevenaar, Neth. 28/D5
Zevenbergen, Neth. 28/B5
Zeya, Rus. 55/K1
Zghartā, Leb. 49/D2
Zgierz, Pol. 27/K3
Zgorzelec, Pol. 27/H3
Zhambyl, Kaz. 46/H5
Zhanatas, Kaz. 46/G5
Zhangaözen, Kaz. 45/K4
Zhangaqazaly, Kaz. 46/G5
Zhangjiakou, China 59/C2
Zhangshu, China 61/G2
Zhangye, China 54/E4
Zhangzhou, China 61/H3
Zhanjiang, China 61/F4
Zhaodong, China 55/K2
Zhaoqing, China 61/G4
Zhaotong, China 60/D3
Zhayyq (Ural) (riv.), Kaz. 46/F5
Zheleznodorozhnyy, Rus. 43/L3
Zheleznogorsk, Rus. 44/E1
Zheleznogorsk-Ilimskiy, Rus. 47/L4
Zhengzhou, China 59/C4
Zhenjiang, China 61/H1
Zhetiqara, Kaz. 45/M1
Zhezqazghan, Kaz. 46/G5
Zhicheng, China 61/F2
Zhigulevsk, Rus. 45/J1
Zhlobin, Bela. 44/D1
Zhmerynka, Ukr. 44/D2
Zhob, Pak. 53/J2
Zhodino, Bela. 42/F5
Zhongshan, China 61/G4
Zhoukou, China 59/C4
Zhouzhou, China 59/G7
Zhovtneve, Ukr. 41/L2
Zhucheng, China 59/D4
Zhuhai, China 61/G4
Zhukovka, Rus. 44/E1
Zhukovskiy, Rus. 43/X9
Zhumadian, China 59/C4
Zhuzhou, China 61/G3
Zhytomyr, Ukr. 44/D2
Zibo, China 59/D3
Zielona Góra, Pol. 27/H3
Ziftá, Egypt 49/B4
Zigong, China 60/E2
Ziguinchor, Sen. 78/A3
Zihuatanejo, Mex. 101/E5
Zile, Turk. 44/E4
Žilina, Slvk. 27/K4
Zima, Rus. 54/E1
Zimbabwe (ctry.) 82/E4
Zimnicea, Rom. 41/G4
Zinder, Niger 79/H3
Zion, Il, US 99/Q15
Zion National Park, Ut, US 92/D3
Zitácuaro, Mex. 101/E5
Zittau, Ger. 27/H3
Zixing, China 61/G3
Ziyyon, Isr. 49/G8
Zlatoust, Rus. 43/N5
Zlín, Czh. 27/J4
Złotoryja, Pol. 27/H3
Złotów, Pol. 27/J2
Znam'yanka, Ukr. 44/E2
Znojmo, Czh. 33/M2
Zoersel, Belg. 28/B6
Zoetermeer, Neth. 28/B4
Zográfos, Gre. 39/N9
Zolotonosha, Ukr. 44/E2
Zomba, Malw. 82/G4
Zonguldak, Turk. 41/K5
Zonhoven, Belg. 28/C7
Zottegem, Belg. 30/C2
Zouérat, Mrta. 76/C3
Zrenjanin, Serb. 40/E3
Zug, Swi. 37/E3
Zugdidi, Geo. 45/G4
Zuidhorn, Neth. 28/D2
Zülpich, Ger. 31/F2
Zumpango de Ocampo, Mex. 101/K7
Zumpango del Río, Mex. 102/B2
Zunyi, China 61/E3
Zürich, Swi. 37/E3
Zutphen, Neth. 28/D4
Zuwārah, Libya 76/H1
Zuyevka, Rus. 43/L4
Zvishavane, Zim. 82/F5
Zvolen, Slvk. 27/K4
Zvornik, Bosn. 40/D3
Zweibrücken, Ger. 31/G5
Zwevelgem, Belg. 30/C2
Zwickau, Ger. 33/K1
Zwijndrecht, Neth. 28/B5
Zwijndrecht, Belg. 31/D1
Zwolle, Neth. 28/D3
Żyrardów, Pol. 27/L2
Zyryan, Kaz. 54/A2
Żywiec, Pol. 27/K4